www.wadsworth.com

wadsworth.com is the World Wide Web site for Wadsworth and is your direct source to dozens of online resources.

At *wadsworth.com* you can find out about supplements, demonstration software, and student resources. You can also send email to many of our authors and preview new publications and exciting new technologies.

wadsworth.com
Changing the way the world learns®

The Police
in the Community

Strategies for the 21st Century

Third Edition

Linda S. Miller
Executive Director of the
Upper Midwest Community
Policing Institute

Kären M. Hess
Normandale Community College
Bloomington, Minnesota

WADSWORTH
THOMSON LEARNING

Australia • Canada • Mexico • Singapore • Spain • United Kingdom • United States

WADSWORTH
TM
THOMSON LEARNING

Executive Editor, Criminal Justice: Sabra Horne
Criminal Justice Editor: Shelley Murphy
Development Editor: Terri Edwards
Assistant Editor: Dawn Mesa
Editorial Assistant: Lee McCracken
Marketing Manager: Jennifer Somerville
Marketing Assistant: Neena Shandra
Project Editor: Jennie Redwitz
Print/Media Buyer: Tandra Jorgensen
Permissions Editor: Stephanie Keough-Hedges
Production Service Coordinator: Peggy Francomb,
      Shepherd, Incorporated

Technology Project Manager: Susan DeVanna
Text Designer: Andrew Ogus
Photo Researcher: Terri Wright
Copy Editor: Carol Hoke
Cover Designer: Bill Stantou
Cover Image: Kevin R. Morris/Corbis
Compositor: Shepherd, Incorporated
Printer: Phoenix Color Corp
Index: Christine M. H. Orthmann

Printed in the United States of America
3 4 5 6 7 04 03
ISBN 0-534-53946-7

Wadsworth/Thomson Learning
10 Davis Drive
Belmont, CA 94002-3098
USA

For more information about our products, contact us:
Thomson Learning Academic Resource Center
1-800-423-0563
http://www.wadsworth.com

International Headquarters
Thomson Learning
International Division
290 Harbor Drive, 2nd Floor
Stamford, CT 06902-7477
USA

UK/Europe/Middle East/South Africa
Thomson Learning
Berkshire House
168-173 High Holborn
London WC1V 7AA
United Kingdom

Asia
Thomson Learning
60 Albert Street, #15-01
Albert Complex
Singapore 189969

Canada
Nelson Thomson Learning
1120 Birchmount Road
Toronto, Ontario M1K 5G4
Canada

CONTENTS IN BRIEF

CONTENTS

Chapter 10   Interacting with Victims and Witnesses   261

PREFACE

Community policing offers one avenue for making neighborhoods safer. Community policing is not a program or a series of programs. It is a philosophy, a belief that working together, the police and the community can accomplish what neither can accomplish alone. The *synergy* that results from community policing can be powerful. It is like the power of a finely tuned athletic team, with each member contributing to the total effort. Occasionally heroes may emerge, but victory depends on a team effort.

Community policing differs from earlier efforts such as team policing, community relations, crime prevention programs or neighborhood watch programs. Community policing involves a rethinking of the role of the police and a restructuring of the police organization. Its two core concepts are community/police collaboration and partnerships and a problem-solving approach to policing. These dual themes are present throughout the text. This text discusses in Section One the evolution of community policing and the changes in our communities and our law enforcement agencies which have occurred. The section then examines the problem-solving approach to policing and how community policing might be implemented.

The text emphasizes developing the interpersonal skills needed to build good relationships with all those the police have sworn "to serve and protect." This includes those who are culturally, racially or socioeconomically different from the mainstream, those who are physically or mentally disabled and those who are elderly. It also includes youths, both as victims and as offenders, gangs and gang members, and victims of crime. In addition, interacting effectively with members of the media is vital to the success of community policing. Developing these relationships is the focus of Section Two.

Section Three describes community policing in the field. It begins with a look at early experiments in crime prevention and the evolution of community policing strategies. The remainder of the section is entirely new material dealing with understanding and preventing violence, programs aimed at youths including gangs, and community efforts to deal with crime and drugs. The final chapter explains what research has found and explores what the future might hold for community policing.

HOW TO USE THIS TEXT

The text is structured to enhance understanding and remembering the main concepts. To get the most from this text, first look through the listing of Contents to give yourself a framework. Think about the specific subjects included in the topic of community policing as a whole. Then read the section openers for a closer look at the three broad divisions of the text. Finally, complete the following steps for each chapter:

1. Read the "Do You Know" questions at the beginning of the chapter. These present the chapter objectives in a way that should make you think about your current level of knowledge. For example:

Do You Know . . . When modern policing began?

2. Read the chapter, highlighting, underlining or taking notes. Watch for answers to the "Do You Know" questions in bold italics. For example:

Modern policing began with the formation of the London Metropolitan Police.

Also pay attention to words in bold type. These are key terms which you should be able to define. The definitions should be clear from the text.

3. Read the chapter summary. You will find that you have now read key points three times. This triple-strength approach should take the information from your short-term memory into your long-term memory.

4. To solidify the information, return to the "Do You Know" questions at the beginning of the chapter and answer each question. Write down any questions you have about the information in the chapter. Look at the list of key terms and make certain you understand and can define each term. If you do not remember what a specific term means, look it up in the glossary to refresh your memory.

5. Read the discussion questions at the end of the chapter and think about what you can contribute to a class discussion.

If you follow these steps, and if you periodically review the "Do You Know" questions, you should master the content of this text.

ACKNOWLEDGMENTS

We would like to thank the following individuals for their careful review of previous editions of this text and for their numerous suggestions for improvement: James S. Albritton, Marquette University; Michael B. Blankenship, Memphis State University; W.D. Braddock, Boise State University; William Castleberry, The University of Tennessee at Martin; Vincent Del Castillo, John Jay College of Criminal Justice; Burt C. Hagerman, Oakland Community College; Robert Ives, Rock Valley College; Deborah Wilkins Newman, Middle Tennessee State University; James E. Newman, Rio Hondo Community College; Willard M. Oliver, Glenville State College; Carroll S. Price, Penn Valley Community College; Charles L. Quarles, University of Mississippi; Mittie D. Southerland, Murray State University; B. Grant Stitt, University of Nevada-Reno; Gregory B. Talley, Broome Community College; and Gary T. Tucker, Sinclair Community College.

A sincere thank you, also, to the reviewers of the this edition for their invaluable suggestions for improving the text: John Evans, Walters State Community College; David Kessler, Kent State University; Lynette Lee-Sammons, California State University, Sacramento; Richard Martin, Elgin Community College; Robert Wadman, Weber State University.

An additional thank you goes to Christine Orthmann for her comprehensive indexes and for her review of and data entry for the Instructor's Manual that accompanies this text. Finally, a sincere thank you to our editors at Wadsworth, Sabra Horne and Shelley Murphy as well as Peggy Francomb, Production Services Coordinator at Shepherd, Inc. Any errors in content or expression are the sole responsibility of the authors.

FOREWORD

A democratic society has to be the most difficult environment within which to police. Police in many countries operate for the benefit of the government. The police of America operate for the benefit of the people policed. Because of that environment, we are compelled to pursue ways to advance our policing approach, involve people who are part of our environment and enhance our effectiveness. Our policing methodology is changed or molded by trial and error, the daring of some policing leaders, the research and writing of academicians and the response of our communities to the way we do business.

Over the past 30 years, we have tried a variety of approaches to doing our job better. Some have remained. Many have been abandoned, thought to be failures. They may, however, have been building blocks to our current policing practices and for what is yet to come. For instance, the community relations and crime prevention programs of the 1960s and the experiments with team policing in the 1970s are quite visible in the business of community policing. So should be the knowledge gained from research such as that conducted in the 1970s and 1980s associated with random patrol, directed patrol, foot patrol, one-officer/two officer cars and the effectiveness (or lack thereof) of rapid response to all calls for service.

If we look at our past, we should not be surprised at the development and support of community policing as the desired policing philosophy in our country today. It merely responds to the customers' needs and their demand for our policing agencies to be more effective. And therein lies the most important outcome of community policing—effectiveness. Yes, we have responded to millions of calls for service, made millions of arrests and added thousands to our policing ranks. If we're honest about it, however, we may be hard-pressed to see the imprint of our efforts in our communities. Community policing, involving problem solving, community engagement and organizational transformation, can contribute significantly to the satisfaction of the community policed and to those policing.

This text provides insight into the meaning of community policing and presents many dimensions necessary to consider when developing a community policing strategy. Its content should help readers to understand the practical side of community policing, recognize the community considerations that need to exist and develop methods applicable to their unique environments.

Donald J. Burnett
General Partner
Law Enforcement Assistance Network

ABOUT THE AUTHORS

This text is based on the practical experience of Linda S. Miller, who has spent 23 years in law enforcement and the expertise of Kären M. Hess, who has been developing instructional programs for 25 years. The text has been reviewed by numerous experts in the various areas of criminal investigation as well.

Linda S. Miller is executive director of the Upper Midwest Community Policing Institute (UMCPI) and a former sergeant with the Bloomington (Minnesota) Police Department. She was with the department 20 years, serving as a patrol supervisor, a crime prevention officer, a patrol officer and a police dispatcher. Ms. Miller has been a member of the Minnesota Peace and Police Officers Association, the International Police Association, the Midwest Gang Investigator's Association, the International Association of Women Police and the Minnesota Association of Women in Police. She was a member of the People-to-People's Women in Law Enforcement delegation to the Soviet Union in 1990. Sgt. Miller is a frequent presenter to community groups and is also an instructor.

Kären M. Hess holds a PhD in English and in instructional design from the University of Minnesota and a PhD in criminal justice from Pacific Western University. Other West/Wadsworth Thomson Learning texts Dr. Hess has coauthored are *Criminal Investigation* (Sixth Edition), *Criminal Procedure, Corrections in the 21st Century: A Practical Approach, Introduction to Law Enforcement and Criminal Justice* (Sixth Edition), *Introduction to Private Security* (Fifth Edition), *Juvenile Justice* (Third Edition), *Management and Supervision in Law Enforcement* (Third Edition), *Police Operations* and *Seeking Employment in Criminal Justice and Related Fields* (Third Edition).

She is a member of the Academy of Criminal Justice Sciences, the American Association of University Women, the American Correctional Association, the American Society for Industrial Security, the American Society for Law Enforcement Trainers, the American Society of Criminologists, the Association for Supervision and Curriculum Development, the International Association of Chiefs of Police, the Minnesota Association of Chiefs of Police, the National Institute of Justice, the Police Executive Research Forum and the Text and Academic Authors Association, which has just named Dr. Hess to their Council of Fellows.

SECTION ONE

An Overview

The community and the police depend on each other. The common police motto—"To serve and protect"—suggests a target population of individuals who require service and protection. Most police departments stress the importance of community relations, and many have taken community relations beyond image enhancement and crime prevention programs and have started involving the community in policing itself. Paruch (1998, p. 81) notes:

> Law enforcement has gone through an evolutionary change where community policing has become the norm rather than the exception for many departments. . . .
>
> The true purpose of community policing is to have the police and the community agree upon problems and mutually solve them. It is also to get citizens involved, to empower them to take control of their neighborhoods and be active participants in improving the quality of life in their communities. With this proactive approach, police and citizens working together to improve the quality of life can result in a reduction of crime and fear of crime.

The section looks first at the evolution of police-community relations. Since people first came together in groups, they have had some responsibility for ensuring that those within the group did as was expected. The United States' method of "preserving the peace," modeled after that used in England, has evolved through several stages. The relationship between the community and its police has been severely strained at times, and attempts to improve it have taken several forms. Recently, emphasis on improved public relations and crime prevention has expanded to a more encompassing philosophy of community policing, including problem-solving policing in many jurisdictions (Chapter 1).

Next an in-depth look at the police is presented (Chapter 2). Who are the people behind the badges? How have they changed over the years? How might they change in the future? How does the public generally view the police? What aspects of the police role contribute to this view?

The focus in Chapter 3 is on the people and agencies involved in community-police relations. Who are the members of a community? How do communities differ? How have they changed over the years? What future changes might be anticipated? What aspects of a community must be understood by those working within it? What is expected of community members? What do community members expect?

This is followed by an examination of problem-solving policing, a key component of the community policing philosophy (Chapter 4). The section concludes with a discussion on implementing community policing—guidelines and cautions (Chapter 5).

Reference: Paruch, George. "Making Sure Community Policing Initiatives Work." *Law and Order*, Vol. 46, No. 10, October 1998, pp. 81–84.

CHAPTER 1

The Evolution of Community Policing

The police are the public and the public are the police.

   Sir Robert Peel

Do you know

When "modern" policing began?

What Sir Robert Peel's principles emphasize?

What the three eras of policing are?

What the police relationship with the community was in each era?

What the professional model of policing emphasizes?

What some common types of crime prevention programs are?

What community policing is?

What two themes are apparent in the various definitions of community policing?

Can you define these terms:

community policing

community relations

frankpledge system

hue and cry

human relations

paradigm

paradigm shift

patronage system

proactive

professional model

progressive era

public relations

reactive

reform era

spoils system

"thin blue line"

tithing

tithing system

INTRODUCTION

Community policing did not just magically appear as a panacea for society's ills. It has been centuries in its evolution and may indeed be merely a stepping stone to yet another form of policing in the future. As society's needs change, so do the methods it uses to "keep the peace."

This chapter begins with a brief history of policing and its evolution in the United States. This is followed by an examination of three strategic eras of policing and the paradigm shifts that occurred. Next the influence of public relations, community relations and crime prevention programs is explored. The chapter concludes with an in-depth look at community policing, including definitions, major features, potential problems and the incorporation of a problem-solving approach.

◉ A BRIEF HISTORY OF POLICING

Throughout history societies have established rules to govern the conduct of individuals and have devised punishments for those who break the rules. The earliest record of an ancient society's need for rules to control human behavior dates back to approximately 2300 B.C., when Sumerian rulers codified their concept of offenses against society. Since then such rules have been modified and adapted. According to Wrobleski and Hess (2000, p. 4):

> The beginnings of just laws and social control were destroyed during the Dark Ages as the Roman Empire disintegrated. Hordes of Germanic invaders swept into the old Roman territory of Britain, bringing their own laws and customs. These German invaders intermarried with the conquered English, the result being the hardy Anglo-Saxon.

The Anglo-Saxons grouped their farms around small, self-governing villages that policed themselves. This informal arrangement became more structured under King Alfred the Great (A.D. 849–899), who required every male to enroll for police purposes in a group of 10 families, known as a **tithing**. The **tithing system** established the principle of collective responsibility for maintaining local law and order.

The tithing system worked well until 1066, when William the Conqueror, a Norman, invaded and conquered England. William, concerned about national security, replaced the tithing system of "home rule" with 55 military districts called shires,* each headed by a Norman officer called a reeve, hence the title shire-reeve (the origin of the word *sheriff*). William also established the **frankpledge system,** which required all free men to swear loyalty to the king's law and to take responsibility for maintaining the local peace.

By the 17th century, law enforcement duties were divided into two separate units, a day watch and a night watch. The day watch consisted of constables who served as jailers and fulfilled other government duties. Citizens worked on the night watch. Each citizen was expected to take a turn watching for fires, bad weather and disorderly individuals. Some towns also expected the night watchman to call out the time.

---

* a shire is equivalent to U.S. counties.

If a watchman or any other citizen saw a crime in progress, they were expected to give the **hue and cry,** summoning all citizens within earshot to join in pursuing and capturing the wrongdoer. Preserving the peace was the duty of *all* citizens.

By the end of the 18th century, most people with sufficient means paid others to stand their assigned watch for them, marking the beginning of a paid police force and, in effect, the original neighborhood watch.

The system of day and night watchmen was very ineffective. Because wealthy citizens could avoid the watch duty by hiring someone to take their place, those they hired were hesitant to invoke their authority against the well-to-do. According to Richardson (1970, p. 10), by the mid-1700s New York City's night watch was "a parcel of idle, drinking, vigilant snorers, who never quelled any nocturnal tumult in their lives . . . but would, perhaps, be as ready to join in a burglary as any thief in Christendom."

London, suffering from the impact of the Industrial Revolution, was experiencing massive unemployment and poverty. It had become a disorderly city with enormous, crime-ridden slums and a significant juvenile delinquency problem. Some citizens had even begun to carry weapons for self-protection. In an attempt to address the problems, Parliament convened five parliamentary commissions of inquiry between 1780 and 1820. When Sir Robert Peel was appointed Home Secretary, he proposed that London appoint civilians, paid by the community, to serve as police officers. The Metropolitan Police Act was passed in 1829 and modern policing began.

◈ THE BEGINNINGS OF "MODERN" POLICE FORCES

"Modern" policing began with the formation of the London Metropolitan Police, founded by Sir Robert Peel in 1829.

Peel set forth the following principles on which the police force was to be based:

- The duty of the police is to prevent crime and disorder.
- The power of the police to fulfill their duties is dependent on public approval and on their ability to secure and maintain public respect.
- Public respect and approval also mean the willing cooperation of the public in the task of securing observance of the law.
- The police must seek and preserve public favor not by pandering to public opinion but by constantly demonstrating absolutely impartial service to law.
- The police should strive to maintain a relationship with the public that gives reality to the tradition that *the police are the public and the public are the police.*
- The test of police efficiency is the absence of crime and disorder, not the visible evidence of police action in dealing with these problems.

Peel's principles emphasized the interdependency of the police and the public as well as the prevention of crime and disorder.

As Gehrand notes (2000, p. 111): "Peel also recognized that the police were only successful at their jobs when they elicited public approval and assistance in their actions

London Metropolitan Police uniforms have a distinctive look that sets them apart from police departments in other parts of the world.

without resorting to force or the severity of law. These beliefs hold true today. No police department can control crime and disorder without the consent and voluntary compliance by the public."

Peel envisioned a close police-citizen relationship that helped the police maintain order in London.

As originally envisioned by the architects of London's Metropolitan Police—acknowledged to be the first modern police department—a police officer's job was primarily crime prevention and social maintenance, not crime detection. Police were to serve as local marshals who actively maintained order by interacting with the neighborhoods they served.

POLICING IN THE UNITED STATES

Those who came to America in 1620 and their descendants, through the American Revolution, rejected the British Crown's rule that permitted British soldiers to take over homes and to have complete authority over the colonists. Our founders wanted to ensure that no such power would exist in the newly created nation. As former Chief Justice of the U.S. Supreme Court Warren E. Burger (1991, p. 26) stated: "The Founders, conscious of the risks of abuse of power, created a system of liberty with order and placed the Bill of Rights as a harness on government to protect people from misuse of the powers." Nonetheless, the system of policing and maintaining order in the northern part of the United States was modeled on the police system developed in England.

At the time the Metropolitan Police Force was established in London, the United States was still operating under a day-and-night-watch system similar to the one that had been used in England. In the 1830s several large cities established separate paid day watches. In 1833 Philadelphia became the first city to pay both the day and night watches. Boston followed in 1838 with a six-officer police force. In 1844 New York City took the first step toward organizing a big-city police department similar to the one that exists today across the country when it consolidated its day and night watches under the control of a police chief. The police department was modeled on the London Metropolitan Police and Peel's principles. Other cities followed the example set by New York. By 1857 Boston, Chicago, New Orleans, Newark, Cincinnati, Philadelphia and Baltimore had consolidated police departments that were modeled on London's Metropolitan Police. The new police chiefs of these departments faced the beginning of tremendous personnel problems among their officers. Early professionals found security services in disarray.

> What those first chiefs of police found in their newly consolidated forces was a motley, undisciplined crew composed, as one commentator on the era described it, principally of "the shiftless, the incompetent, and the ignorant." Tales abounded of police officers in the 1850s who assaulted their superior officers, who released prisoners from the custody of other officers, who were found sleeping or drunk on duty, or who could be bribed for almost anything (Garmire, 1989, p. 17).

Despite these problems, and because there were also many honest, dedicated police officers, the citizens considered the police a source of assistance. Early police officers' duties included more community assistance and service than often imagined. Even at the beginning of this century, law enforcement was one of the only government-sanctioned services to help citizens 24 hours a day, 7 days a week. Welfare, parole, probation and unemployment offices did not exist. Police in New York, for example, distributed coal to the poor, monitored the well-being of vulnerable citizens, served as probation and parole officers and helped establish playgrounds in the city.

It was more than a decade after the formation of the first police forces in the United States that attempts were made to require police officers to wear uniforms. Police officers' well-known resistance to change was apparent even then. The rank-and-file reaction against uniforms was immediate. Police officers claimed that uniforms were "un-American" and "a badge of degradation and servitude." In Philadelphia, police officers even objected to wearing badges on their coats. It was a bitter four-year struggle before they were finally persuaded to wear a complete uniform.

In 1856 New York City required its officers to be uniformed, but each local ward[1] could determine the style of dress. As a result, in some sections of the city police officers wore straw hats, whereas in others they wore felt. In some wards summer uniforms were white "duck" suits; in other wards they were multicolored outfits.

Policing in the South had different origins—the slave patrols found in the Southern colonies and states. By 1700 most Southern colonies, concerned about the dangers the oppressed slaves could create, had established a code of laws to regulate slaves. These codes prohibited slaves from having weapons, gathering in groups, leaving the plantation without a pass or resisting punishment.

---

[1]A ward is an administrative division of a city or town.

Predictably, many slaves resisted their bondage. According to Foner (1975) the resistance usually consisted of running away, criminal acts and conspiracies or revolts. Compounding the problem, in some Southern states slaves came to outnumber the colonists. For example, in 1720 South Carolina's population was 30% white and 70% black (Simmons, 1976, p. 125). As Reichel (1999, p. 82) notes, the white colonists' fear of the slaves as a dangerous threat led to the development of special enforcement officers with general enforcement powers as a transition to modern police. Dulaney (1996) contends that these slave patrols were the first truly American police system. He notes that by 1750 every Southern colony had a slave patrol that formally required all white men to serve as patrollers. In actuality, however, the patrollers were generally poor white men.

In most colonies and states, patrols could enter any plantation and break into slaves' dwellings, punish slaves found outside their plantation, search, beat and even kill any slaves found to be violating the slave code. Asirvatham (2000, p. 2) suggests:

> Twentieth-century Southern law enforcement was essentially a direct outgrowth of the 19th-century slave patrols employed to enforce curfews, catch runaways, and suppress rebellions. Even later on, in Northern and Southern cities alike, "free men of color" were hired as cops only in order to keep other African-Americans in line [enforcing Jim Crow laws supporting segregation]. Until the 1960s black cops, by law or by custom, weren't given powers of arrest over white citizens, no matter how criminal.

The evolution of law enforcement in both the North and South is often divided into three distinct eras.

◆ THE THREE ERAS OF POLICING

Three major paradigm shifts have occurred in the evolution of policing in the United States. A **paradigm** is a model or a way of viewing a specific aspect of life such as politics, medicine, education and even the criminal justice system. A **paradigm shift** is simply a new way of thinking about a specific subject. Kelling and Moore (1991, p. 6) describe these paradigm shifts as specific "eras" of policing in the United States.

The three eras of policing are political, reform and community.

The Political Era

The political era extended into the first quarter of the 20th century and witnessed the formation of police departments. During this era police were closely tied to politics. This was very dissimilar to the situation in England, where the police were centralized under the king, and the police chief had the authority to fire officers. In the United States the police were decentralized under the authority of the municipality in which they worked. The chief had no authority to fire officers; therefore, the police were often undisciplined. "The image of 'Keystone Cops'—police as clumsy bunglers—was widespread and often descriptive of realities in U.S. policing" (Kelling and Moore, p. 9).

Police officers usually lived in their community and were members of the majority group. Since foot patrol was the most common policing strategy used, officers became close to the public.

During the political era the police sought an intimate relationship with the community.

During this era chiefs of police were politically appointed and had a vested interest in keeping those who appointed them in power. Politicians rewarded those who voted for them with jobs or special privileges. This was referred to as the **patronage system,** or the **spoils system,** from the adage "To the victor go the spoils."

In 1929 President Herbert Hoover appointed the National Commission on Law Observance and Enforcement to study the criminal justice system. Hoover named George W. Wickersham, former U.S. Attorney General, as its chairman. When the report was published in 1931, it became one of the "most important events in the history of American Policing" (Walker, 1997, p. 154). The Wickersham Commission focused two reports on the police. Report 11, *Lawlessness in Law Enforcement,* described the problem of police brutality, concluding that "the third degree—the inflicting of pain, physical or mental, to extract confessions or statements—is extensively practiced." Specific tactics included protracted questioning, threats and intimidation, physical brutality, illegal detention and refusal to allow access of counsel to suspects (National Commission on Law Observance and Enforcement, 1931, p. 4). Report 14, *The Police,* examined police administration and called for expert leadership, centralized administrative control and higher standards for personnel—in effect, for police professionalism (Wrobleski and Hess, p. 7).

The inefficiency and corruption of the police led to the second era of policing, the reform era.

The Reform Era

August Vollmer and O. W. Wilson are usually attributed with spearheading the reform movement that called for a drastic change in the organization and function of police departments. This **reform era** is often referred to as the **progressive era.**

One basic change during this era was to disassociate policing from politics, which was accomplished in a variety of ways. In Los Angeles, for example, the chief of police position became a civil-service job that required applicants to pass a civil-service test. In Milwaukee the chief of police was appointed for life by a citizen commission.

With the disassociation of policing from politics came a change in emphasis in the role of the police in that citizens began to equate policing with fighting crime. The police considered social-service-type functions less desirable and avoided them whenever possible.

The relationship between the police and the public also changed during the reform era. As Kelling and Moore (p. 12) note: "Police leaders in the reform era redefined the nature of a proper relationship between police officers and both politicians and citizens. Police would be impartial law enforcers who related to citizens in professionally neutral and distant terms." *Dragnet,* one of the first and most popular police shows ever televised, depicted this era perfectly. The main character, Sgt. Joe Friday, typified the impartial and distant reform-era officer with his often-repeated line, "Just the facts, ma'am."

The public viewed the police as professionals who remained detached from the citizens they served.

During the reform era the police relationship with the community they served was professionally remote.

During this era the concept of the **"thin blue line"** developed. This phrase refers to the line that separates law-abiding, peaceful citizens from the murderous, plundering villains who prey upon them. The phrase also suggests a distance between the police and the public they serve. The "thin blue line" describes the dangerous threats to communities, with police standing between that danger and law-abiding citizens. It suggests both police heroism and isolation.

Adding to the distancing of police from the public during the reform era was the replacement of foot patrols with motorized patrols. O. W. Wilson's preventive patrol by squad car coupled with an emphasis on rapid response to calls for service became the dual focus of policing during this era. The police image became one of officers roaring through city streets in high-powered squad cars, lights flashing and sirens wailing. The police were viewed as professional crime fighters. Consequently, policing during the reform era is often referred to as the *professional model.*

The professional model *emphasized crime control by preventive automobile patrol coupled with rapid response to calls.*

The problems the first police administrators faced did not change much, but under the professional model their answers did. Many police methods were challenged during the 1960s, when social change exploded in the United States as the result of several significant events that occurred almost simultaneously.

The civil rights movement began in the late 1950s as a grassroots movement to change the blatantly unequal social, political and economic systems in the United States. Confrontations between blacks and the police, who were almost completely male and white, increased during this time. Representing the status quo and defending it, the manner in which the police handled protest marches and civil disobedience often aggravated these situations.

Punctuated by the assassinations of President Kennedy, Malcolm X, Martin Luther King, Jr., Medgar Evers and Robert Kennedy, the events of the decade were, for the first time in history, documented in detail and viewed by millions of Americans on television. The antiwar movement, based on college campuses, was also televised. When demonstrators at the 1968 Democratic convention in Chicago were beaten by the Chicago police, the demonstrators chanted: "The whole world is watching." Watching what was later termed a police riot, Americans were shocked.

Plagued by lack of training and confronted by a confusing array of social movements as well as an emerging drug culture, the police became the "enemy." Officers heard themselves referred to as "pigs" by everyone from students to well-known entertainers. They represented the status quo, the establishment and everything that stood in the way of peace, equality and justice. Police in the 1960s were at war with the society they served. Never had the relationship between the law enforcement community and the people it served been so strained.

In addition to the questionable way police handled race riots and antiwar demonstrations in the sixties, several big-city police departments were charged with corruption at

Antiwar riots and flag burnings in the 1960s pitted police against protesters.

that time. The 1960s changed the face of the United States, and law enforcement was no exception. Studies in the 1970s on corruption and criminal behavior among police agencies brought great pressure on the entire criminal justice system to change its methods, attitudes and image. Media coverage of law enforcement practices educated the public, who ultimately demanded change.

Understanding Community Policing (1994, pp. 6–7) describes the social and professional "awakening" that occurred during the 1960s and 1970s:

> Antiwar protestors, civil rights activists, and other groups began to demonstrate in order to be heard. Overburdened and poorly prepared police came to symbolize what these groups sought to change in their government and society. Focusing attention on police policies and practices became an effective way to draw attention to the need for wider change. Police became the targets of hostility, which ultimately led police leaders to concerned reflection and analysis. . . .
>
> Between 1968 and 1973 three Presidential Commissions made numerous recommendations for changes in policing. . . .
>
> A number of organizations within the policing field also became committed to improving policing methods in the 1970s. Among those on the forefront of this movement for constructive change were the Police Foundation, the Police Executive Research Forum, the National Organization of Black Law Enforcement Executives, the Urban Sheriffs' Group of the National Sheriffs' Association and the International Association of Chiefs of Police. These organizations conducted much of the basic research that led police to reevaluate traditional policing methods.

In response to the negative police image that emerged during the 1960s, several departments across the country established programs to enhance their relationships with the communities they served. These programs included public-relations programs, community-relations programs and crime prevention programs.

Efforts to Enhance Relations between the Police and the Community. To avoid confusion, it is helpful to distinguish among *public relations, community relations* and *human relations* because these terms are used frequently throughout this text and in other literature on policing.

- **Public relations:** Efforts to enhance the police image—"We'll tell you what we're doing, but leave us alone to fight crime."
- **Community relations:** Efforts to interact and communicate with the community— team policing, community resource officers and school liaison officers.
- **Human relations:** Efforts to relate to and understand other people or groups of people—the focus of Section Two.

Public relations efforts are usually one-way efforts to raise the image of the police. These efforts by police departments include hosting departmental open houses and providing speakers for school and community events. Many police departments have established a public-relations office or division and have assigned specific officers to the public-relations effort. Such efforts reflect the growing recognition by police administrators that they need public support.

In the past several decades, especially in the late 1970s and also as a result of the widening gap between the police and the public, many police departments began community-relations programs. Unlike public-relations efforts, which were primarily one-to-one communications, often media generated, community-relations programs sought to bring the police and community closer through isolated police tactics such as team policing and community resource officers. Efforts to enhance community relations also frequently involved citizens through crime prevention programs.

Crime Prevention Programs

Crime prevention programs that enlist citizens' aid include Operation Identification programs, neighborhood- or block-watch programs and home- and automobile-security programs.

Such programs, which continue to be strategies used in many community policing efforts, are discussed in detail in Section Three.

The Law Enforcement Assistance Administration (LEAA). Another response to the negative image of the police was the establishment of the Law Enforcement Assistance Administration in 1968. Over the next several years LEAA provided billions of dollars to the "war on crime," funding studies and programs for law enforcement.

LEAA awarded more than $9 billion to state and local governments to improve police, courts and correctional systems, to combat juvenile delinquency and to finance innovative crime-fighting projects. Tens of thousands of programs and projects were supported with LEAA funds, and millions of hours were applied to identify effective, efficient, economical ways to reduce crime and improve criminal justice (Wrobleski and Hess, p. 29).

Although the consensus among law enforcement officials today is that LEAA was mostly mismanaged, there was also a very positive aspect of LEAA. This was the Law Enforcement Education Program (LEEP), which provided thousands of officers with funding for higher education.

The Courts. The courts also had a major impact on criminal justice during the 1960s. Several legal decisions limited police powers and clarified the rights of the accused.

In 1961 *Mapp v Ohio* extended the exclusionary rule to every court and law enforcement officer in the country. The exclusionary rule, established in 1914 in *Weeks v United States*, mandated that federal courts must refuse to consider evidence obtained by unreasonable and therefore unconstitutional search and seizure, no matter how relevant the evidence was to the case:

In 1963 in *Gideon v Wainwright* the Court ruled 9-0 that the due process clause of the Fourteenth Amendment requires states to provide free counsel to indigent (impoverished) defendants in all felony cases:

The next landmark case came the following year in *Escobedo v Illinois* (1964), when the Supreme Court ruled that if individuals confess without being told of their right to have a lawyer present and are then allowed to have a lawyer present during questioning, the confessions are not legal.

In 1966 this right to have a lawyer present, and at public expense if necessary, was reaffirmed along with other Fifth Amendment rights that ensue to a person who is being held and questioned by the police in what is probably the best-known Supreme Court case—*Miranda v Arizona*. The Court held that evidence obtained by police during custodial interrogation of a suspect cannot be used in court unless the suspect is informed of the following four basic rights before questioning:

• The suspect's right to remain silent
• The right of the police to use in a court of law any statement made by the suspect
• The suspect's right to have an attorney present during questioning
• The suspect's right to have a court-appointed attorney before questioning if the suspect cannot afford one

Another landmark decision was handed down in 1968 in *Terry v Ohio*. This case established the right of police officers to stop and question a person to investigate suspicious behavior and to frisk that person if the officer has reason to believe the person is armed:

> The police have the authority to detain a person for questioning even without probable cause to believe that the person has committed a crime. Such an investigatory stop does not constitute an arrest and is permissible when prompted by both the observation of unusual conduct leading to a reasonable suspicion that criminal activity may be afoot and the ability to point to specific and articulable facts to justify the suspicion. Subsequently, an officer may frisk a person if the officer reasonably suspects that he or she is in danger.

Other Problems and Challenges during the Progressive Era. Despite these efforts, reported crime increased and the public's fear of crime intensified. An influx of immigrants added to the problems of major cities. The deinstitutionalizing of mental patients in the 1970s caused thousands of mentally disabled individuals to enter the mainstream of the United States, often without means to support themselves. This, coupled with the return of many Vietnam veterans who found it difficult to reenter society, resulted in a large homeless population.

Another challenge to the effectiveness of the professional model was the Kansas City Preventive Patrol Study. This classic study found that increasing or decreasing preventive patrol efforts had no significant effect on crime, citizen fear of crime, community attitudes toward the police, police response time or traffic accidents. As Klockars (1983, p. 130) notes: "It makes about as much sense to have police patrol routinely in cars to fight crime as it does to have firemen patrol routinely in fire trucks to fight fire."

Many law enforcement officials view the Kansas City Preventive Patrol Study as the beginning of a new era in policing. It was considered by police as the first experimental design used in policing and, as such, was a landmark. It set the stage for further research in policing and is viewed as the first true movement in the *professionalization* of policing. Its findings are also controversial. There were real problems with the research design and implementation of this study; however, it caused us to question the assumptions we had made in policing. It concluded what many police officials already knew but did not want publicized for fear of the impact on police budgets. Other research conducted in the 1970s also questioned police effectiveness:

> Research about preventive patrol, rapid response to calls for service, and investigative work—the three mainstays of police tactics—was uniformly discouraging.
>
> Research demonstrated that preventive patrol in automobiles had little effect on crime, citizen levels of fear, or citizen satisfaction with police. Rapid response to calls for service likewise had little impact on arrests, citizen satisfaction with police, or levels of citizen fear. Also, research into criminal investigation effectiveness suggested that detective units were so poorly administered that they had little chance of being effective (Kelling, 1988, p. 4).

By the mid-1970s the general period of reform in policing in the United States slowed. Many promising reforms, such as team policing, had not caused any major changes. (Chapter 5 discusses team policing and its demise.) The reform movement was jump-started by two articles: Herman Goldstein's "Problem-Oriented Policing" article in 1979 and James Q. Wilson and George L. Kelling's "Broken Windows" article in 1982.

Other reasons for reevaluating police methods were the changing nature of the people who became police and their frustration with the traditional role of the patrol officer. Although patrol was given lip service as the backbone of policing, it was seen as the least desirable assignment. A change was needed at the patrol level to attract more highly educated and less militaristic recruits. The patrol officer had to become important to the department in accomplishing its mission.

Finally, many businesses and individuals began to hire private security officers to ensure their safety. The public assumed that the police alone were unable to "preserve the peace." While some called for greater cooperation between public and private policing, others argued that the public should collaborate with all policing efforts.

A combination of the dissatisfaction with criminal justice and the role of patrol officers, research results, the trend toward private policing and the writings of Goldstein and Wilson and Kelling led to the third era of policing—the community era.

The Community Era

In the 1980s many police departments began experimenting with more community involvement in the "war on crime." Also during this decade several cities tested Herman Goldstein's problem-oriented approach to policing. The emphasis in many departments began to shift from crime fighting to crime prevention.

According to some historians, the Community Era had its roots in the Kerner Commission Report, which was released in February 1968 by the President's National Advisory Committee on Civil Disorder. The report condemned racism in the United States and called for aid to black communities to avert further racial polarization and violence.

Gradually law enforcement has become more responsive to the public's desire for a different kind of policing. Today there is considerable citizen-police interaction and problem solving. Although still resistant to change, police agencies are now more likely to respond to the needs and wishes of the communities they serve. The significant changes in the way police address sexual assault, domestic violence, sexual abuse of children, drunk driving and missing children attest to this new responsiveness. The public wants the police to be proactive; citizens want police to try to prevent crime in addition to apprehending criminals after they have committed a crime.

During the community era the police sought to reestablish a close relationship with the community.

Highlights of the three eras of policing are summarized in Table 1.1.

Table 1.1 The Three Eras of Policing

	Political Era 1840s to 1930s	Reform Era 1930s to 1980s	Community Era 1980s to Present
Authorization	politics and law	law and professionalism	community support (political), law and professionalism
Function	broad social services	crime control	broad provision of services
Organizational design	decentralized	centralized, classical	decentralized, task forces, matrices
Relationship to community	intimate	professional, remote	intimate
Tactics and technology	foot patrol	preventive patrol and rapid response to calls	foot patrol, problem solving, public relations
Outcome	citizen, political satisfaction	crime control	quality of life and citizen satisfaction

SOURCE: Summarized from George L. Kelling and Mark H. Moore. "From Political to Reform to Community: The Evolving Strategy of Police." In *Community Policing: Rhetoric or Reality,* edited by Jack R. Greene and Stephen D. Mastrofski. New York: Praeger Publishers, 1991, pp. 6, 14–15, 22–23.

The community era is referred to by many names: community policing, community-oriented policing (COP), neighborhood policing and the like. Currently the term *community policing* is most commonly used.

At the heart of most "new" approaches to policing is a return to the ancient idea of community responsibility for the welfare of society—police officers become *a part* of the community, not *apart* from it. A comparison of traditional policing and community policing is made in Table 1.2.

While community policing is considered innovative, one of its central tenets of involvement with and responsiveness to the community is similar to the principles set forth by Sir Robert Peel in 1829 when he established the London Metropolitan Police and stated: "The police are the public and the public are the police." Policing has strayed so far from these principles in the past century that the concepts central to community policing seem fresh and sensible today.

◉ COMMUNITY POLICING DEFINED

Where traditionally policing has been **reactive**, responding to calls for service, community policing is **proactive**, anticipating problems and seeking solutions to them. The term *proactive* is beginning to take on an expanded definition. Not only is it taking on the meaning of anticipating problems, but it is also taking on the Steven Covey slant, that of accountability and choosing a response rather than reacting the same way each time a similar situation occurs. Police are learning that you do not obtain different results by applying the same methods. In other words, to get different results you need to apply different tactics. This is the focus of Chapter 4.

According to Frazier (2000, p. 1): "Community-oriented policing is proactive, solution-based, and community driven. It occurs when a law enforcement agency and law-abiding citizens work together to do four things:

• Arrest offenders

• Prevent crime

• Solve ongoing problems and

• Improve the overall quality of life

O'Connor (1999, p. 1) defines community policing as "a department-wide philosophy of full-service, personalized and decentralized policing, where citizens feel empowered to work in proactive partnerships with the police at solving the problems of crime, fear of crime, disorder, decay, and quality of life." This philosophy gives officers the necessary time to connect with the communities they serve and to work with them to actually solve problems instead of just offering quick and momentary fixes (Miller, 1996, p. 6).

The Upper Midwest Community Policing Institute (UMCPI) provides this definition: "Community policing is an organization-wide philosophy and management approach that promotes community, government and police partnerships; proactive problem solving; and community engagement to address the causes of crime, fear of crime and other community issues."

Table 1.2 Comparison of Traditional Policing and Community Policing

Question	Traditional Policing	Community Policing
Who are the police?	A government agency principally responsible for law enforcement.	Police are the public and the public are the police: the police officers are those who are paid to give full-time attention to the duties of every citizen.
What is the relationship of the police force to other public service departments?	Priorities often conflict.	The police are one department among many responsible for improving the quality of life.
What is the role of the police?	Focusing on solving crimes.	A broader problem-solving approach.
How is police efficiency measured?	By detection and arrest rates.	By the absence of crime and disorder.
What are the highest priorities?	Crimes that are high value (e.g., bank robberies) and those involving violence.	Whatever problems disturb the community most.
What, specifically, do police deal with?	Incidents.	Citizens' problems and concerns.
What determines the effectiveness of police?	Response times.	Public cooperation.
What view do police take of service calls?	Deal with them only if there is no real police work to do.	Vital function and great opportunity.
What is police professionalism?	Swift effective response to serious crime.	Keeping close to the community.
What kind of intelligence is most important?	Crime intelligence (study of particular crimes or series of crimes).	Criminal intelligence (information about the activities of individuals or groups).
What is the essential nature of police accountability?	Highly centralized; governed by rules, regulations and policy directives; accountable to the law.	Emphasis on local accountability to community needs.
What is the role of headquarters?	To provide the necessary rules and policy directives.	To preach organizational values.
What is the role of the press liaison department?	To keep the "heat" off operational officers so they can get on with the job.	To coordinate an essential channel of communication with the community.
How do the police regard prosecutions?	As an important goal.	As one tool among many.

SOURCE: Malcolm K. Sparrow. *Implementing Community Policing.* U.S. Department of Justice, National Institute of Justice. November 1988, pp. 8–9.

Community policing *is a philosophy that emphasizes working proactively with citizens to reduce fear, solve crime-related problems and prevent crime.*

McCarthy (n.d., p. 1), a community policing officer for the Braintree Police Department, says: "Community policing is a collaborative effort between the police and the community that identifies problems of crime and disorder and involves the community in the search for solutions. It is founded on close, mutually beneficial ties between police and community members."

The City-Borough of Juneau (1999, p. 1) has both a formal and an informal definition of community policing. Formally: "Community Policing is a philosophy that promotes strategies to address the causes and reduce the fear of crime and social disorder through problem-solving tactics and community-police partnerships." Informally:

> Community Policing means police become part of the neighborhood, with the emphasis on stopping crime before it happens. It gives citizens more control over the quality of life in their community. It helps police better understand the needs of residents while helping residents develop greater trust in police. In essence the community joins the police department. Together they work to create a better, safer place to live and raise a family.

New Orleans police officers keep the peace during a second-line funeral procession through the Florida and Desire public-housing projects. The parade was in honor of the last man to die in the projects before the police department opened police substations in both Florida and Desire. The officers are part of a special volunteer unit to work out of the substations. Since the substations opened, the murder rate in these projects has gone from almost 10% of the record 1994 total of 421 to almost nothing.

Running through these definitions are two basic themes: police/community collaboration and a proactive, problem-solving approach to the police function.

These two themes are also incorporated throughout this text.

Some criminologists go beyond defining community policing to describe its key features as well as its essential elements.

◈ FEATURES OF COMMUNITY POLICING

Trojanowicz and Bucqueroux (1994, pp. 131–132) state what they perceive to be the goal of community policing as solving problems—improved relations with citizens is a welcome by-product. Several major features associated with it are regular contact between officers and citizens; a department-wide philosophy and department-wide acceptance; internal and external influence and respect for officers; well-defined role—does both proactive and reactive policing—a full-service officer; direct service—the same officer takes complaints and gives crime prevention tips; citizens identify problems and cooperate in setting up the police agenda; police accountability is ensured by the citizens receiving the service in addition to administrative mechanisms; the officer is the leader and catalyst for change in the neighborhood to reduce fear, disorder, decay and crime.

The chief of police is an advocate and sets the tone for the delivery of both law enforcement and social services in the jurisdictions. Officers educate the public about issues (like response time or preventive patrol) and the need to prioritize services. Increased trust between the police officer and citizens because of long-term, regular contact results in an enhanced flow of information to the police. The officer is continually accessible in person, by telephone or in a decentralized office with regular visibility in the neighborhood.

Officers are viewed as having a "stake in the community." They are role models because of regular contact with citizens (especially youth role model). Influence is from "the bottom up"—citizens receiving service help set priorities and influence police policy; meaningful organizational change and departmental restructuring—ranging from officer selection to training, evaluation and promotion. When intervention is necessary, informal social control is the first choice. Officers encourage citizens to solve many of their own problems and volunteer to assist neighbors. Officers encourage other service providers like animal control, firefighters and mail carriers to become involved in community problem solving. Officers mobilize all community resources, including citizens, private and public agencies and private businesses. Success is determined by a reduction in citizen fear, neighborhood disorder and crime.

Identification and awareness of these features has allowed law enforcement departments nationwide to implement the principles and philosophy of community policing. In fact, community policing has come a long way since publication of the first edition of this text in 1994. Frazier (p. 2) notes that currently 87% of the country is served by a department that practices community policing. In addition, a national network of 28 regional community policing institutes and the Community Policing Consortium (comprised of IACP, NOBLE, PERF, NSA and the Police Foundation) has trained over 100,000 law enforcement personnel and community members in the principles of community policing.

◈ THE ESSENTIAL ELEMENTS
OF COMMUNITY POLICING

Cordner (1999, p. 137) suggests: "It [community policing] started out as a fuzzy notion about increasing police-citizen contact and reducing fear of crime, then settled into a period during which it was seen as having two primary components—problem solving and community engagement." He provides a framework consisting of four dimensions for viewing community policing and determining whether the essential elements are in place.

The Philosophical Dimension

Many advocates of community policing stress that it is a philosophy rather than a program. And it does have that important dimension. The three important elements within this dimension are citizen input, a broadened function and personalized service. Cordner (p. 138) contends that citizen input meshes well with an agency that "is part of a government 'of the people, for the people, and by the people.'" A broadened police function means expanding responsibility into areas such as order maintenance and social services, as well as protecting and enhancing the lives of our most vulnerable citizens: juveniles, the elderly, minorities, the disabled, the poor and the homeless. The personal service element supports tailored policing based on local norms and values as well as on individual needs.

The Strategic Dimension

A philosophy without means of putting it into practice is viewed by many as an empty shell. This is where the strategic dimension comes in. This dimension "includes the key operational concepts that translate philosophy into action" (p. 139). The three strategic elements of community policing, according to Cordner, are reoriented operations, a geographic focus and a prevention emphasis.

The reorientation in operations shifts reliance on the squad car to emphasis on face-to-face interactions. It may also include differential calls for service. The geographic focus changes patrol officers' basic unit of accountability from time of day to location. Officers are given permanent assignments so they can get to know the citizens within their area. Finally, the prevention emphasis is proactive, seeking to raise the status of prevention/patrol officers to the level traditionally enjoyed by detectives.

The Tactical Dimension

The tactical dimension translates the philosophical and strategic dimensions into concrete programs and practices. The most important tactical elements, according to Cordner, are positive interactions, partnerships and problem solving. Officers are encouraged to get out of their vehicles and initiate positive interactions with the citizens within their beat. They are also encouraged to seek out opportunities to partner with organizations and agencies and to mediate between those with conflicting interests, for example, landlords and tenants, adults and juveniles. The third essential element, problem solving rather than responding to isolated incidents, is the focus of Chapter 4.

Cordner's fourth dimension, the organizational dimension, is discussed in Chapter 5.

◈ POTENTIAL PITFALLS ASSOCIATED WITH COMMUNITY POLICING

Bayley (1991, pp. 226–236) cites several potential problems associated with community policing. First, public safety might decline because the public is not very interested in participating in crime prevention efforts. Second, he suggests that the police may become too soft on crime and lose the ability to control violence in the community. "Can the police put on a velvet glove and keep their iron hand in shape?" he asks (p. 228).

Another potential problem with community policing is that the rationale for having police is diminished. As crime fighters they were extremely important to communities. If, however, the police prove to be ineffective crime fighters, there is no reason to believe they will be effective crime preventers. Further, the public may become a special-interest group for the police. According to Bayley (p. 229): "Community policing seeks to transform the police from what has been described as 'an army of occupation' into an accepted, unremarkable, and individually responsive part of the community."

Community policing may also adversely increase the power of the police in comparison to that of other governmental agencies. Community policing seeks to build strong ties between the police and the community. Such ties may cause problems, however, when other government officials realize and resent the power police departments and individual officers may have to lobby citizens for financial resources and officer assignments or transfers. Police chiefs nationwide have found themselves in conflict with mayors and city councils as individual police officers lobby for needed resources. A closer relationship between the police and the public may also result in the citizens' increased ability to influence internal department matters.

Another potential problem with community policing is that its emphasis on crime prevention gives police the authority to keep careful watch on people in the community. Closely related to this problem is a fear that community policing will increase government surveillance of private citizens. To date, the problems Bayley cited have not come to pass. In addition, the old guard police, who have been very apprehensive about COP, are beginning to see that COP is not soft on crime.

In addition, community policing, because it promotes adapting policing to local circumstances, may lead to the unequal application of justice. "Local commanders may begin to think it is more important not to alienate loud voices than to protect quiet ones" (Bayley, p. 232). Closely related to this is the potential that community policing may lessen the protection given to unpopular people such as the homeless. It may even lead to vigilantism.

Finally, community policing may worsen a growing dualism in policing; affluent neighborhoods embrace the community-oriented mode whereas poorer urban areas and ghettos return to an emphasis on law enforcement and crime fighting.

Despite these potential problems, Bayley does not advocate abandoning community policing. Rather, he suggests that if a department adopts community policing as a philosophy, it should be aware of the potential hazards and avoid them. He (p. 236) cautions: "Community policing does not represent a small, technical shift in policing; it is a paradigmatic change in the way police operate. It is the most fundamental change in policing since the rise of police professionalism early in this century. Because community policing is serious and fateful, we must be open minded about its potential infirmities as well as its promise." In other words, community policing cannot be considered a cure-all for the problems of crime and fear of crime in our communities.

Perhaps the single biggest problem with community policing is gaining acceptance of the first-line supervisor, whose authority may appear to be weakened by allowing the patrol officer a great deal of discretion. In addition, patrol officers may not accept community policing as an effective method to reduce crime, and without their genuine support, it will not work. Another problem is the tremendous community support that patrol officers may garner, giving the officers tremendous power. A positive twist to this potential problem, however, is that some police agencies are finding there is no longer a need for police boards because the police are in such close and constant contact with the citizens of the community.

Although none of these potential pitfalls and problems have been documented to date, they remain a consideration.

SUMMARY

"Modern" policing began with the formation of the London Metropolitan Police, based on principles set forth by Sir Robert Peel. His principles emphasized the interdependence of the police and the public as well as the prevention of crime and disorder.

Policing in the United States has had three distinct paradigm shifts or eras: political, reform and community. During the political era the police sought an intimate relationship with the community. During the reform era the relationship was professionally remote. During the community era the relationship was again perceived to be intimate.

During the 1960s and 1970s relations between the police and the public were extremely strained. In an effort to improve relations, many police departments instituted public-relations programs whose goal was to improve the image of the police. Many departments also began crime prevention programs that enlisted the aid of citizens, including programs such as Operation Identification, neighborhood or block watches and home- and automobile-security programs.

Community policing is a philosophy that emphasizes working with citizens to reduce fear, solve crime-related problems and prevent crime. Two basic themes consistent in the various definitions of community policing are police/community collaboration and a problem-solving approach to the police function.

DISCUSSION QUESTIONS

1. From the perspective of law enforcement, what are the strengths and weaknesses of each of the three eras of policing? Answer this question from the perspective of a citizen.

2. What lessons should community policing advocates learn from history?

3. Are any community policing strategies being used in your community? If so, which ones?

4. What advantages does community policing offer? Disadvantages?

5. How is the relationship between the police and the public typically portrayed in popular television programs and movies? In the news media?

6. How might the historical role of the police in enforcing slavery in the South and later segregation contribute to present-day police-minority relations?

7. Can you see any evidence of the patronage or spoils system of policing in the 21st century?

8. What is the relationship of community policing and problem-solving policing?

9. Which form of policing do you believe has the most potential for your community? Why?

10. Have you witnessed any examples of the "thin blue line"?

INFOTRAC® COLLEGE EDITION ASSIGNMENTS

- Use Infotrac to help answer the discussion questions when appropriate.
- Find an article on community policing and outline it. Be prepared to discuss your reaction to the article with the class.
- Read and outline the encyclopedia selection on Sir Robert Peel OR read and outline the article on the "thin blue line."
- Search community relations and pick one selection that relates directly to community policing.

COMMUNITY PROJECT

Individually or in a self-formed group, visit your local police department to obtain any printed material they have on community policing.

REFERENCES

Asirvatham, Sandy. "Good Cop, Bad Cop." *Baltimore City Paper,* May 2000.

Bayley, David H. "Community Policing: A Report from the Devil's Advocate." In *Community Policing: Rhetoric or Reality,* edited by Jack R. Greene and Stephen D. Mastrofski. New York: Praeger Publishers, 1991, pp. 226–237.

Burger, Warren E. "Introduction." *The Bench & Bar of Minnesota,* May/June 1991, p. 26.

City-Borough of Juneau. "Community Policing Definitions." *Our City,* Vol. 5, Spring 1999.

Cordner, Gary W. "The Elements of Community Policing." In *Policing Perspectives: An Anthology,* edited by Larry K. Gaines and Gary W. Cordner. Los Angeles: Roxbury Publishing Company, 1999, pp. 137–149.

Dulaney, W. Marvin. *Black Police in America.* Bloomington, IN: Indiana University Press, 1996.

Foner, P. S. *History of Black Americans: From Africa to the Emergence of the Cotton Kingdom.* Westport, CT: Greenwood, 1975.

Frazier, Thomas C. "Director's Notes: A Definition of Community Policing." Washington, DC: Office of Community Oriented Policing Services, April 2000.

Garmire, Bernard L., ed. *Local Government Police Management.* Mimeographed. Published by the International City Management Association, *Law and Order,* August 1989.

Gehrand, Keith. "University Policing and the Community." *Law and Order,* Vol. 48, No. 12, December 2000, pp. 111–117.

Kelling, George L. "Police and Communities: The Quiet Revolution." *Perspectives on Policing,* June 1988.

Kelling, George L. and Moore, Mark H. "From Political to Reform to Community: The Evolving Strategy of Police." In *Community Policing: Rhetoric or Reality,* edited by Jack R. Greene and Stephen D. Mastrofski. New York: Praeger Publishers, 1991, pp. 3–25.

Klockars, Carl B. *Thinking about Police: Contemporary Readings.* New York: McGraw-Hill, 1983.

McCarthy, John. "Definition of Community Policing." Braintree Police Department Home Page, nd.

Miller, Linda. "Community Policing as a Viable Alternative to Traditional Crime Fighting Methods." *Minnesota Cities,* August 1996, pp. 6–9.

National Commission on Law Observance and Enforcement, *Report on Lawlessness in Law Enforcement.* Washington, DC: Government Printing Office, 1931.

O'Connor, Tom. "Definitions of Community Policing." November 1999. http://faculty.ncwc.edu/toconnor/205/205lec13.htm

Reichel, Philip L. "Southern Slave Patrols as a Transitional Police Type." In *Policing Perspectives: An Anthology,* edited by Larry K. Gaines and Gary W. Cordner. Los Angeles: Roxbury Publishing Company, 1999, pp. 79–92.

Richardson, J. F. *The New York Police.* New York: Oxford University Press, 1970.

Simmons, R. C. *The American Colonies.* New York: McKay, 1976.

Trojanowicz, Robert and Bucqueroux, Bonnie. *Community Policing.* Cincinnati: Anderson, 1994.

Understanding Community Policing: A Framework for Action. Washington, DC: Bureau of Justice Assistance, August 1994.

Walker, Samuel. *Popular Justice: A History of American Criminal Justice,* 2nd edition. New York: Oxford University Press, 1997.

Wrobleski, Henry M. and Hess, Kären M. *An Introduction to Law Enforcement and Criminal Justice,* 6th ed. Belmont, CA: Wadsworth Thomson Learning, 2000.

CHAPTER 2

The Role of the Police

*The strength of a democracy and the quality of
life enjoyed by its citizens are determined in large
measure by the ability of the police to discharge
their duties.*

    Herman Goldstein

Do you know

What a mission statement is?

What police spend the majority of their time
doing?

How law enforcement agencies have traditionally
been organized?

What participatory leadership is?

How the makeup of the police force has changed
in recent years?

What characteristics are attributed to the police
subculture?

Where the police image comes from?

What a negative contact is?

What the public expects of the police?

What dilemma faces law enforcement?

When agencies or officers exercise discretion?

How discretion fits into the community policing
philosophy?

What three ethics checks are?

Can you define these terms:

decentralization

discretion

empowered

flat organization

mission statement

negative contacts

911 policing

paradox

participatory leadership

police culture

selective enforcement

Total Quality Management

INTRODUCTION

Although "police officers" are the professionals discussed in this chapter, the concepts reviewed apply equally to those with different titles such as deputies or sheriffs. While this chapter focuses on police officers as professionals, always remember that police officers are first and foremost people. They are sons, daughters, mothers, fathers, brothers, sisters, aunts, uncles, neighbors and friends. They may belong to community organizations, attend local churches and be active in politics. Their individual attributes greatly influence who they are as police officers.

This chapter begins by discussing why we have police and how this is expressed through mission statements including the two sometimes conflicting roles of law enforcement and service to the public. This is followed by an examination of how police departments are typically organized and managed. Next the chapter describes who the police are and some characteristics of their culture. This is followed by a discussion of the police image and public expectations of the police. Then the role of police discretion and use of force are discussed. The chapter concludes with an examination of ethics and policing.

◈ THE POLICE MISSION

Why do most law enforcement agencies exist? What is their *mission?* The answer is obvious to those who say the purpose is to catch "bad guys." Others believe the purpose is to prevent crime, maintain order or protect the public. Articulating the reason for an agency's existence helps its members focus on the same goals and determine how to accomplish their purpose.

A mission statement *is a written declaration of purpose.*

A mission statement is a "road map" that delineates how an agency will arrive at a desired destination. Without it, a law enforcement agency can wander, appearing inconsistent, inefficient and purposeless.

The mission statement tells you what the agency's commitment is to the community it serves and how it views its relationship with the community. A mission statement can reveal rather accurately the state of police-community relations.

A mission statement can also focus a police department's energies and resources. Will the department continue to be reactive and focused on fighting crimes that have already occurred or proactive, focused on identifying problems and attacking them? As Wilson and Kelling (1989, p. 49) note, a community-oriented policing philosophy requires redefining the police mission: "To help the police become accustomed to fixing broken windows as well as arresting window-breakers requires doing things that are very hard for many administrators to do." Consider the following mission statement of the Aurora (Illinois) Police Department:

> We, the Aurora Police Department, exist to serve all people within our jurisdiction with respect, fairness and compassion. We are committed to the prevention of crime and the protection of life and property; the preservation of peace, order

and safety; the enforcement of laws and ordinances; and the safeguarding of constitutional guarantees.

With community service as our foundation, we are driven by goals to enhance the quality of life, investigating problems as well as incidents, seeking solutions and fostering a sense of security in communities and individuals. We nurture public trust by holding ourselves to the highest standards of performance and ethics.

To fulfill its mission, the Aurora Police Department is dedicated to providing a quality of work environment and the development of its members through effective training and leadership (Nila, 1990, p. 43).

How are mission statements developed? A committee, composed of members of the community and police officers, assesses various police functions. Why would a law-enforcement agency include input from the community when it develops its mission statement? Community input improves police-community relations and increases the likelihood of an agency accomplishing its missions.

The public identifies the services it expects from its police department. If those expectations go unmet, the department generally suffers loss of financing and political support as well as increased interference in day-to-day operations.

Developing a mission statement that reflects an agency's commitment to the community it serves can be the vehicle to positive, meaningful police-community relations as well as to a more effective police department. This mission statement in large part determines where the agency places its priorities.

Closely related to the mission statement are the goals and objectives set by a department. Rodgers (1995, p. 117) cautions: "History shows that programs emphasizing a 'kinder, gentler' philosophy or image don't sit well with police officers." He cites the Houston Police Department's Neighborhood-Oriented Policing (NOP) program. According to Rodgers, officers perceived the program as more social work than police work and referred to it as "Nobody on Patrol." To avoid such perceptions, top management should emphasize that their primary mission is detecting and apprehending law violators and that the community-policing program enhances their ability to do so. In fact, community policing is tougher on crime than traditional policing because it is able to rely on citizens helping the police and sharing responsibility for their neighborhood.

Fighting Crime vs. Service to the Public

Police departments are often divided on whether their emphasis should be proactive or reactive. Every department will have officers who are incident oriented (reactive) and believe their mission is to do **911 policing.** That is, they are incident driven—reactive—and may speak disparagingly of the community-policing officers as social workers.

Is the best police officer the one who catches the most "bad guys"? Certainly police departments will continue to apprehend the "bad guys." The crimes they target may, however, contribute to negative police-community relations. The police usually focus on certain kinds of crime, particularly common crimes such as burglary, robbery, assault and auto theft. The police expect that offenders who commit these crimes might flee or try to avoid arrest in some other way. Police may need to use force to bring offenders to justice.

Police officers generally do *not* enforce white-collar crimes. They would not, for example, investigate or arrest a businessperson for insider trading, price fixing or cheating on income taxes. White-collar crime involves those who are in business, the professions or public life—those who tend to be relatively well-to-do, powerful people.

Common crimes can conceivably be committed by anyone, rich or poor. The vast majority of these crimes, however, are committed by those from society's lowest socio-economic level. Those at or near the poverty level include the majority of our minority populations.

As Klockars (1985, p. 57) notes, since the police officers' domain is the streets: "Those people who spend their time on the street will receive a disproportionate amount of police attention . . . particularly people who are too poor to have backyards, country clubs, summer homes, automobiles, air conditioning, or other advantages that are likely to take them out of the patrolman's sight."

These facts contribute to the *impression* that the police are focused solely on the kind of crime poor people and minorities commit, hence, the *impression* that they are hostile to those who are poor or members of minority groups. This negative impression does little to foster good community relations.

Police work involves much more than catching criminals. It is a complex, demanding job requiring a wide range of abilities. Studies suggest that 80 percent of police officers' time is spent on non-enforcement activities. The vast majority of the problems police attend to are in response to citizen requests for service.

The majority of police actions have nothing to do with criminal law enforcement but involve service *to the community.*

A NYC officer taking childrens' fingerprints at a rural hospital "health fair" (Northern Dutchess).

Service to the community includes peacekeeping; preventing suicides; looking for lost or runaway children or vulnerable adults; protecting children and other vulnerable people; maintaining public safety; assisting motorists with disabled vehicles; dealing with emergencies and crisis situations, such as accidents and natural disasters; delivering death notifications; resolving conflicts; preventing crime; and educating the public.

Rowell (2000, p. 1) suggests that community-policing officers view citizens as clients because these officers have both protector and servant roles. In a similar vein, Mastrofski (1999a, p. 4) has coined the phrase "policing for people." Such policing has six criteria: attentiveness, reliability, responsiveness, competence, manners and fairness.

Mastrofski et al. (1998) studied the way patrol officers spent their time and found that about 25 percent of officer time was spent in public encounters. General patrol accounted for slightly more time, travel to a specific destination 15 percent, problem-directed activities 10 percent, administration 10 percent, and personal time the balance.

Reporting on the same study, Parks et al. (1999, p. 500) found, as anticipated, that community-policing specialists spent less time on undirected general patrol: roughly 20 to 30 minutes less than their patrol-generalist colleagues in an average eight-hour shift. Not anticipated, however, was the finding that community policing specialists in both sites spent less time in encounters with citizens than did patrol generalists.

Another unanticipated finding was that foot patrols tended to gravitate toward citizens who were more receptive to police and whose problems were more easily solved (p. 515). It seems that traditional, reactive policing may provide "more egalitarian service, or at least may bring the police to the scene of those situations which seem most likely to require immediate intervention" (p. 515).

Defining exactly what police work entails is almost impossible. Most would agree, however, that people have always called the police for help. They call not only about criminal matters but also about a variety of situations where they perceive a need for government intervention. The police respond to such calls and usually take whatever action is needed. It has been said that the police are the only social-service agency available 24 hours a day, 7 days a week, and they make house calls.

Neighborhood Cops or Special Ops?

The reactive or proactive controversy can be seen in the parallel development of two contradictory models in policing in the last decade: community-oriented policing (COP) and special weapons and tactics (SWAT) teams.

Robinson (2000, p. 14) notes that COP grew out of the public's dissatisfaction with police forces seen as "occupying armies" rather than public servants. In contrast, SWAT teams were established in Los Angeles to control the riots of the 1960s. Such teams are by nature reactive. The rapid growth of SWAT teams is apparent from a 1997 survey reporting that nearly 90 percent of departments surveyed in cities with populations over 50,000 had paramilitary units, as did 70 percent of agencies in areas with populations under 50,000 ("Study Sees Cause for Alarm . . .," 1999, p. 9). This same report notes that state and local departments are being supplied with intelligence, equipment and training spawning a "culture of paramilitarism" (p. 1). As Cassidy (1997, p. 2) observes: "This transformation [the militarization of local law enforcement] is largely a consequence of a drug war that has incrementally evolved into a real domestic offensive with all the accouterments and ordnance of war." The result of this militarization has led to complaints that "an occupying army is marching through America's streets—that they are too aggressive, too heavily armed, too scary—and that they erode the public's perception of police as public servants."

Unfortunately, as Cassidy (p. 7) suggests: "After a decades long national addiction to waging war on drugs framed largely as a war against 'unruly minority ethnics' the deployment of cops dressed like extras in a Stallone movie waving automatic weapons around poor neighborhoods seems almost inevitable."

However, as Glick (2000, p. 42) contends: "Despite critics' complaints that tactical teams are a threat to the nation itself, SWAT callouts are usually for defensive purposes and the majority end without a gun battle." SWAT teams should be viewed as a line of defense, not offense, suggests Glick. He (p. 44) concludes: "They are peace officers—husbands and fathers, wives and mothers, and they are preparing for the unthinkable. One day they may be asked to rescue their own children, in addition to the lives of others, including suspects."

A balance is certainly needed for fighting the war on drugs and crime and for serving and collaborating with citizens to resolve crime problems and make neighborhoods safe through community policing. For departments moving toward community policing, a change is needed in organizational structure.

⟨◇⟩ ORGANIZATION OF THE POLICE DEPARTMENT

The traditional law enforcement organization design has been that of a pyramid-shaped hierarchy based on a military model, as Figure 2.1 depicts.

Command officers and supervisors had complete authority over subordinates, and they had little tolerance for ideas originating at the bottom of the pyramid. Communication flowed downward through the bureaucratic chain of command. According to Goodbody (1995, p. 12):

> A bureaucracy takes on a life of its own, and will, along with the people who have a vested interest in it, resist and undermine all attempts at reform. This is especially true if the reform entails a complete reorganization of existing practices and procedures. . . .
>
> Police bureaucracies differ in two essential ways from more conventional bureaucracies. First, supervision is based on a military system of rank that vests police supervisors with significantly more authority than their counterparts in the civilian sector. The quasi-military organization of policing, with uniforms and ranks as a visible component of every interaction, tends to make the police among the more rigid and authoritarian of bureaucracies. Second, police bureaucracies rely heavily on punishment to enforce rules.

This bureaucratic organizational structure worked well for decades. Recently, however, it has been called into question, with many looking to corporate America as a more appropriate organizational model.

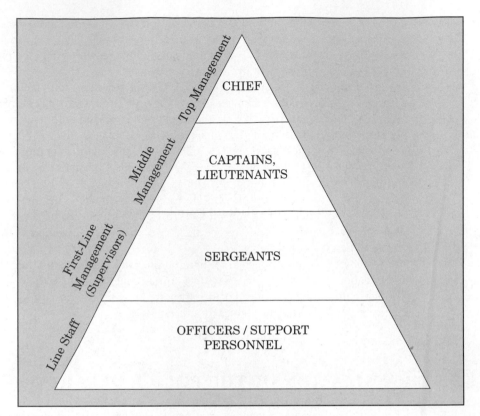

Figure 2.1 Typical Police Department Management Structure

To remain competitive, business and industry are undergoing extensive changes in organization and management styles. Law enforcement agencies also face the need for change to meet the competition of private policing. According to Harr and Hess (2000, p. 71): "Private security is the nation's primary protective resource today, outspending public law enforcement by more than 73 percent and employing nearly three times the workforce."

Law enforcement agencies must compete not only with private police but also for the college graduates now entering the workforce. In addition, like business, many departments are turning to a **flat organization:** fewer lieutenants and captains, fewer staff departments, fewer staff assistants, more sergeants and more patrol officers. Typical pyramid-organization charts will have the top pushed down and the sides expanded at the base. Some police departments are experimenting with alternative organization designs, for example placing the patrol officers at the top with everyone under them having a supporting role (Figure 2.2).

Byrne (1997, p. 43) reports on the results of a reorganization effort by the Green Bay (Wisconsin) Police Department that included:

Figure 2.2   The Inverted Flattened Pyramid of Authority—Organizational Hierarchy

. . . elimination of the ranks of assistant chief, deputy chief, inspector and sergeant, reduction of administrative and supervisory staff by 21%, reinvestment of department resources in field police services, and decentralization of field police services.

The reorganization increased the number of officers on the street from 135 to 151—and it was all accomplished without any increase in the department's budget.

Progressive businesses are restructuring top-heavy organizations, pushing authority and decision making as low as possible. Successful businesses concentrate on soliciting ideas from everyone in their organization about every aspect of their operation. This approach can be applied to policing, especially in small departments. If officer retention is to be maintained and loyalty and morale preserved and heightened, officers must be **empowered,** that is given authority, enabled to make decisions. Maguire (1997, p. 547) notes:

The organizational structures of large municipal police departments in the United States have changed substantially. . . . Precinct-based police organizations employing only sworn police officers have been transformed into highly centralized, specialized, formal organizations with tall hierarchies and large administrative units. Community policing reformers have attempted to reverse this progression toward more "bureaucratic" organizational forms. They argue that police should thin out their administrative components to cut red tape and to focus more resources on the goals of the organization; deformalize, eliminating unnecessary rules and policies; despecialize, to encourage departmentwide problem solving; "delayerize," to enhance communications and decision making by flattening the organizational hierarchy.

Mastrofski (1999b, p. 8) adds: "National surveys of departments of over 100 sworn [officers] . . . found that between 1987 and 1993 there was very little change in the structure of police organizations." However, from 1993 to 1999, decision making became more decentralized, geographic command and authority became more popular and organizational hierarchies flattened (p. 8). **Decentralization,** Turner (2000, p. 50) notes, generally refers to a department's organizational structure and operations: "It is an operating principle that encourages flattening of the organization and places decision-making authority and autonomy at the level where information is plentiful. In police organizations, this is usually at the level of the patrol officer, where officers interacting with the public need the freedom to exercise discretion within predetermined parameters."

According to Reiter (1999, p. 8): "By inverting the organizational pyramid, law enforcement agencies take a bold and symbolic step toward becoming empowered." Blanchard (1996, p. 85) explains that inverting the organizational pyramid (see Figure 2.2) symbolizes that the chief serves the organization and is responsible for its leadership. Reiter (p. 10) concludes that: "Trust is the essence of leadership in an empowered organization. Empowered leaders push decision making down to the officer level because they have confidence in their officers' abilities and believe that many decisions are best made at that level." Furthermore, a study by Russell and MacLachlan (1999, p. 31) found that decentralization and collaborative decision making improved employee satisfaction.

◉ MANAGEMENT STYLES

Yet another change is that community policing usually requires a different management style. The traditional autocratic style effective during the industrial age will not have the same effect in the 21st century. One viable alternative to the autocratic style of management is participatory leadership.

In **participatory leadership** *each individual has a voice in decisions, but top management still has the ultimate decision-making authority.*

What is important is that everyone has an opportunity to express their views on a given issue or problem. Bennett and Hess (2001, p. 63) stress:

Democratic or participative leadership has been evolving since the 1930s and 1940s. Democratic leadership does not mean that every decision is made only after discussion and a vote. It means rather that management welcomes employees' ideas and input. Employees are encouraged to be innovative. Management development of a strong sense of individual achievement and responsibility is a necessary ingredient of participative or consultative leadership.

Democratic or participative managers are interested in their subordinates and their problems and welfare. Management still makes the final decision but takes into account the input from employees.

Table 2.1 summarizes the key concepts of and compares the authoritarian and participatory styles of management.

Total Quality Management

The pioneer in **Total Quality Management (TQM)** was W. Edwards Deming, a management guru who helped Japanese businesses to recover and prosper. TQM is basically a management system that tries to ensure that an organization consistently meets and

Table 2.1   Old and New Style Leadership Compared

Authoritarian Style	Participatory Style
Response to incidents	Problem solving
Individual effort and competitiveness	Teamwork
Professional expertise	Community orientation; ask customers what they want
Go by the "book"; decisions by emotion	Use data-based decision making
Tell subordinates	Ask and listen to employees
Boss as patriarch and order giver	Boss as coach and teacher
Maintain status quo	Create, innovate, experiment
Control and watch employees	Trust employees
Reliance on scientific investigation and technology rather than people	Reliance on skilled employees—a better resource than machines
When things go wrong, blame employees	Errors mean failed systems/processes—improve them
Organization is closed to outsiders	Organization is open

SOURCE: Wayne W. Bennett and Kären M. Hess. *Management and Supervision in Law Enforcement*, 3ʳᵈ edition. Belmont, CA: Wadsworth Thomson Learning, 2001, p. 65. Reprinted by permission.

exceeds customer requirements. Although his 14 points were originally aimed at businesses, several apply to law enforcement, particularly to the community policing philosophy, including instituting modern methods of training on the job and modern methods of supervision, breaking down barriers between staff areas, eliminating numerical goals for the work force, and instituting a vigorous program of education and training (Deming, 1982, p. 17).

Although an in-depth discussion of TQM is beyond the scope of this text, it is worthy of consideration as Stevens (2000, p. 204) suggests:

There are four reasons police management should adapt Total Quality Management (TQM) as a managerial style:

1. The police have their critics, some of whom suggest that the authority of police managers at all levels is affected by a host of regulations and obstructions advanced by politicians, community leaders, and organizational leaders in both public and private sectors.

2. The American public has a litigious nature and brings civil suits against police departments and management at all levels in record numbers often influencing day-to-day, serve and protect decisions.

3. Community policing type strategies are at the core of future police services.

4. Community policing strategies and TQM have similar ideals that seem to promote each other.

◈ WHO ARE THE POLICE?

Traditionally, police officers were a fairly homogeneous group: white, male, with a high-school education and a military background. This has changed; police officers have become a more heterogeneous group.

Today police departments have more minority and female officers. The educational level of the officers is much higher, and fewer have military experience. Police are also as interested in helping people as they are in fighting crime.

Such changes in the makeup of the police force are fundamental to the community policing philosophy. As police departments become more representative of the communities they serve, they will be better able to understand the problems they must address. As officers become better educated, they will be better equipped to devise solutions to community problems. However, one impediment might be the existing police culture.

◈ THE POLICE CULTURE

Law enforcement agencies, not unlike most other organizations, develop a unique organizational **police culture** consisting of informal values, beliefs and expectations that is passed on to newcomers in the department. Adcox (2000, p. 20) suggests that: "This informal police culture exercises power influence over the conduct of employees separate from and sometimes at odds with the formal rules, regulations, procedures and role authority of managers." Haught (1998, p. 1) contends that: "An agency's true culture is its default setting." In other words, it is the behavior that occurs when supervisors or visitors are not present.

The police have tremendous power over the citizens they serve and protect. Police may face a life-threatening situation at any time. Their lives may depend on each other. They experience situations others would not be likely to understand. As a result, they have developed their own culture or value system. According to Goldstein (1990, pp. 29–30):

> The strength of the subculture grows out of the peculiar characteristics and conflicting pressures of the job: the ever-present physical danger; the hostility directed at the police because of their controlling role; the vulnerability of police officers to allegations of wrongdoing; unreasonable demands and conflicting expectations; uncertainty as to the function and authority of officers; a prevalent feeling that the public does not really understand what the police have to "put up with" in dealing with citizens; a stifling working environment; the dependence that officers place on each other to get the job done and to provide for their personal safety; and the shared sense of awareness, within a police department, that it is not always possible to act in ways in which the public would expect one to act.

The police culture has been characterized as clannish, secretive and isolated. As McErlain (2001, p. 87) suggests: "A 'Code of Silence' exists today in the law enforcement profession. Those who would suggest that some law enforcement officers today no longer hide behind the banner of loyalty are either naïve or concealing reality, contributing to the problem and enabling others to do the same." He notes that: "Some progress has been made in tearing down this age-old problem, but in many ways a police culture that exalts loyalty over integrity still exists."

Trautman (2001, p. 68) reports on a study conducted by the National Institute of Ethics (NIE) which asked 3,714 officers and recruits from throughout the country to provide insight about the "most secret element of any profession: direct participation in the code of silence." Of the 1,116 officers who participated (42 percent), 532 or 46 percent said they had witnessed misconduct by another employee but had not taken action. Of these officers, 47 percent said they had felt pressure to take part in the code of silence from the officers who committed the misconduct.

Personality traits often attributed to this culture include authoritarianism and cynicism. According to Flynn (1998, p. 12): "Much police cynicism arises from the fact that very young officers with little frame of reference experience too soon the apparent irrelevancy of both law and department policy to the reality of their working lives."

A culture also involves core beliefs held in common. Such beliefs in the police culture may include the following:

- Police are the only real crime fighters.
- No one understands them or what police work is all about.
- They owe 100 percent loyalty to other officers.
- They must often bend the rules to win the war against criminals because the courts have given criminals too many civil rights.
- The public is unappreciative and quick to criticize.
- Patrol is the worst assignment.

Flynn (p. 12) suggests that a good illustration of the organizational culture within many departments is the contrast in behaviors officers expect from the public compared to the behaviors they value in themselves:

- Officers expect the public to respect and defer to their authority, yet they resist, with all the powers their collective-bargaining units can muster, the authority of their own supervisors.
- Officers expect witnesses to tell them what happened at the scene of a crime but refuse to provide information vital to their department's internal investigations.
- Officers decry the peer pressure exerted by gang members who insist on silence and a refusal to cooperate with authorities, then fall victims themselves to that very same peer pressure when they refuse to assist in internal investigations of wrongdoing by their peers, out of a fear of ostracism.

In addition, police work is often unpleasant. Police often have to deal with ugly situations and antisocial behavior. Police are lied to, spit upon and sworn at. They see unspeakable atrocities. Because of their shared experiences and unique exposure to their community, many police officers develop negative characteristics as coping mechanisms.

Two dominant characteristics of the police culture are isolation and a "them-versus-us" world view.

Such isolation and "them-versus-us" world view conflicts with a community-oriented philosophy of policing. As communities move toward a return to foot patrol and an emphasis on improving police-community relations, police isolation and their world view are likely to change. Having looked at how the police often see themselves, now focus on how the public often views the police.

◈ THE POLICE IMAGE

How does the public view the police?

- The handsome, relatively realistic cops of *NYPD Blue* and *Homicide?*
- The laid-back, bumbling police department of Mayberry and its two officers, Andy Griffith and Don Knotts?
- Unselfish, fearless heroes who protect the weak and innocent? Dirty Harrys?
- Hard-hearted, brutal oppressors of the underclass?
- Corrupt abusers of power, who become part of the criminal world?

Our society has varied images of law enforcement professionals. As noted in Chapter 1, that image is greatly affected by how the public perceives the criminal justice system within which the police function. Many Americans believe in an ideal justice system in which fairness and equality are guiding principles, truth and justice prevail, and the accused is innocent until proven guilty. Law enforcement professionals are part of this idealized vision; many view police officers and sheriff's deputies as unselfish, fearless, compassionate protectors of the weak and defenseless, who can uncover the truth, bring the guilty to justice and make things "right."

In contrast, others in our society see a criminal justice system that is neither fair nor just. Some individuals point out that the system employs officers who are overwhelmingly white, middle-class males. They also believe that some officers abuse their power and, in some cases, also abuse those with whom they come in contact in the line of duty.

The most recent *Gallup Poll* (2000), which rated the honesty and ethical standards of 45 occupations, ranked police officers eighth, tied with dentists, college teachers and engineers—very respectable company. The top seven rankings, in order, went to nurses, druggists/pharmacists, veterinarians, medical doctors, grade-school and high-school teachers, clergy and judges. As some might suspect, the lowest ranking went to car salesmen, preceded by telemarketers.

Jones (1999, p. 191) notes that police officers have consistently received higher public-approval ratings than the other components of the criminal-justice system. He also notes, however, that they usually receive lower approval ratings from racial minorities than from Caucasians.

Sources of the Police Image

An individual's opinion of the police is based on many factors. Among the factors that contribute to the police image are television programs, movies, newspapers, magazines, books, the opinions of friends and family, your education, where you live, your economic status, whether you are handicapped, your gender, whether you are a member of a minority group and, most important, your contact with the criminal justice system.

The police image is affected by individual backgrounds, the media and citizens' personal experiences with the criminal justice system.

The media have an enormous impact on public opinion. The police image is affected by the manner in which television and newspaper stories present crime and law enforcement activities. Improving police-media relations is the focus of Chapter 9.

An additional source of the police image is the folklore surrounding citizen interaction with police. People tend to embellish their contacts with the police. In addition, many stories people tell about contacts with the police are actually not theirs but a contact that a friend of a friend had. Unfortunately, few, if any, of these stories can be traced to their origin, but in the meantime, police end up with a negative image. Further, police seldom run in the same social circles where the stories are recounted and therefore have no means of defending themselves, their co-workers, their departments or their actions.

Yet another contributor is police work itself. Police officers are charged with some of society's most distasteful and dangerous tasks and are allowed to use reasonable force to affect arrests. They are even permitted, under very strict circumstances, to use deadly force. This ability, however, creates a paradox for the police image—using force to achieve peace. Nonetheless, the nature of police work and the power they are legally permitted to use make the police extremely powerful and contribute to their image.

The police image is also shaped by appearance and police actions.

The police image is further affected by the police uniform and equipment. The uniform most police officers wear is a very visible reminder of the authority and power bestowed upon police. In fact, officers know that the uniform plays a major part in their ability to gain cooperation and compliance from the public. Much of their authority comes simply from what they are wearing. People recognize and react to visible symbols of authority.

The uniform and its trappings—patches, badges, medals, mace, nightsticks, handcuffs and guns—can be overwhelmingly intimidating and can evoke negative public responses. Reflective sunglasses and handcuff or gun tie tacks can add to this negative image.

Officers' behavior also has a direct impact on their image. One behavior that may negatively affect the police image is accepting gratuities, no matter how small, such as free coffee. In a study of religion, race and public opinion about police officers accepting gratuities, Jones (p. 203) reports: "One of the pitfalls of police officer gratuities is the creation of public resentment toward law enforcement officials, particularly from segments of the public that have often clashed with police in the past. One such segment is certain religious groups in African-American communities." He suggests that: "If relations between police and racial minorities are to improve, then certain time-worn police practices that offend a large number in those communities should be reexamined."

The manner in which police exercise their authority also has an impact on the police image. The attitude of law enforcement officers, their education, their personal image of policing, discipline, professionalism and interaction with the community have enormous impact on the public's perception of the police.

The police uniform with its badge, patches and gunbelt conveys authority.

© Bob Daemmrich/The Image Works

Seemingly innocent and humorous police novelty items have caused major confrontations between police and the communities they serve. Some police product companies produce calendars, posters, T-shirts and mugs that support, encourage and make light of police brutality. Almost always meant to be humorous, the public may not share the same sense of humor. Such items can be immensely destructive to police-community relations. Particularly offensive examples include slogans such as "Brutality, the fun part of police work" and takeoffs on the Dirty Harry line, "Go ahead, make my day."

A few years ago a black suspect died in police custody as the result of a carotid hold applied by police officers during a struggle. In response to the black community's anger and concern, the chief of police issued an order prohibiting the carotid hold. Already in severe conflict with their chief over several other issues, two officers produced and sold T-shirts within the department that said, "Don't choke 'em, smoke 'em." The T-shirts went on sale the day of the suspect's funeral. It is not difficult to understand how destructive this was to the police image and community relations in that city as well as in other cities where the media reported these events.

In contrast with this unfortunate incident is the Hug-a-Bear Program that many departments now use. Plush teddy bears are used to calm traumatized children officers encounter in the course of fulfilling their duties. The bears, sometimes donated to the department by community organizations, are often carried in patrol cars and have been invaluable at accident scenes, in child-abuse situations and at the scene of fires. Programs such as this can reduce the effect of *negative contacts* people may have with the police.

Personal Contacts

Individual encounters with citizens most often determine the quality of police work. One factor that contributes to a negative police image and difficulty in maintaining good community relations is what police commonly refer to as negative contacts.

Negative contacts *are unpleasant interactions between the police and the public. They may or may not relate to criminal activity.*

Although officers have many opportunities to assist citizens, much of what they must do causes people unhappiness. Many people have police contact only when something goes wrong in their lives. Citizens commonly interact with the police when they receive a traffic citation, have an illegally parked vehicle towed, have a loud party terminated, have been victimized, discuss a child who is in trouble with the law, have a domestic "disagreement" broken up, are arrested for driving while intoxicated (DWI) or some other offense, or receive a death notification.

Many more possible scenarios in which citizens become angry or disillusioned occur daily because of the actions police officers must take to perform their duties.

For the most part, the police have no way to eliminate negative contacts and still perform their duties. A major challenge of law enforcement is to build good community relations despite the often-adversarial nature of the job. The fact that many negative contacts take place between police and noncriminal individuals, the so-called "average citizen," makes the task especially difficult.

More positive contacts are needed. For example, the Fremont (Nebraska) Police Department has put a new spin on the phrase "gotcha." In Fremont, officers observing young people doing something good, (for example, wearing a bike helmet or picking up litter) give out tickets for soda pop and French fries at local fast-food restaurants. This works best for bike patrol officers. As one such officer said, "Young people have a totally different perception of police officers on bikes with their black shorts and yellow shirts" ("Rewarding Good Deeds . . .," 2000, p. 9).

PUBLIC EXPECTATIONS

Otherwise law-abiding citizens who receive traffic tickets or who are arrested for DWI often believe they should be excused and that the police should concentrate on "real" criminals. Most police officers feel that citizens want the law enforced to the letter *except* when it comes to themselves.

The public often demands that the police crack down on crime, on drunk drivers and even on traffic violations. For many police departments, the majority of their complaints involve traffic problems. Citizens often demand that police enforce speed laws near their homes. Inevitably, when the police respond by issuing citations to violators, some of those who want the laws to be strictly enforced are ticketed; they often feel betrayed and angry. Somehow they see their own violation of the speed law as different from that of teenagers or "outsiders," and they feel they deserve "a break." Most police officers have been asked, "Why don't you spend your time catching real criminals instead of picking on citizens?"

People expect the law to be enforced except when enforcement limits their own behavior.

Citizens become incensed when crime flourishes and hold the police responsible for combating crime. They hear it constantly referred to as a "war on crime" or "war on drugs," which demands an all-out attack by police upon criminals. But like American soldiers in Vietnam, the police are fighting a war they can't win because it requires assuming social responsibilities that belong to politicians rather than to police.

The police are placed in the dilemma of being expected to win the wars on crime and drugs but are given no control over the causes of these problems. The police cannot win these wars.

Klockars (1991, p. 244) also holds this view:

The fact is that the "war on crime" is a war police not only cannot win, but cannot in any real sense fight. They cannot win it because it is simply not within their power to change those things—such as unemployment, the age distribution of the population, moral education, freedom, civil liberties, ambitions, and the social and economic opportunities to realize them—that influence the amount of crime in any society. Moreover, any kind of real war on crime is something no democratic society would be prepared to let its police fight. We would simply be unwilling to tolerate the kind of abuses to the civil liberties of innocent citizens—to us—that fighting any kind of a real war on crime would inevitably involve.

In addition, when citizens have a problem, they expect the police to help resolve it. In fact, police sociologist Egon Bittner (1974) states that we have police for just that reason—because *"something-ought-not-to-be-happening-about-which-something-ought-to-be-done-NOW!"* The *NOW* portion of Bittner's explanation refers to the police's unique ability to use force to correct a situation. Klockars (1985, p. 16) notes that Bittner purposely did not refer to the situation as *illegal* because the police are called upon in many situations that do not involve an illegality. Bittner left the purpose of police involvement wide open: *Something ought to be done.*

People also expect the police to help them when they have a problem or when someone else is causing a problem.

What actions, if any, the police take in response to citizens' requests is usually up to the individual officer's discretion.

◈ POLICE DISCRETION

The police have awesome power—to use force, to lock people up and even to take someone's life. Police have broad discretionary powers. According to Adcox (p. 16):

Discretion is making a decision based on individual choice or judgment and is influenced by a number of factors. These factors include not only the law and established organizational guidelines, but also individual personal values and beliefs, as well as the values, beliefs and norms of one's peers and work groups [emphasis added].

Each agency exercises discretion when it establishes its mission, policies and procedures. Each officer exercises discretion when deciding whether to issue citations or make arrests when laws are violated.

Officers make those choices based on a variety of reasons such as these:

• Is there evidence to prove a violation in court?
• Will a good purpose be served by arrest or citation, or is police contact sufficient to end the violation?
• What type of crime and suspect are involved?
• What circumstances exist at the time?

Officers would probably not arrest a stranded motorist in a blizzard who, in danger of freezing to death, breaks into an alarmed commercial building. Nor would they be likely to arrest a driver who develops chest pain and breathing difficulty and drives through a stop sign in an attempt to maneuver off the road. In these cases the value of police discretion, or **selective enforcement,** is clear. It makes sense to most people not to enforce the letter of the law.

Police discretion also poses a problem for police, however, because citizens know that the officer can act subjectively. The person an officer tickets or arrests may feel discriminated against. The public is also concerned that discretion gives the police too much freedom to pick and choose when and against whom they will enforce the law. Citizens worry that discretion allows the police too much room to discriminate against some and overlook the violations of the wealthy and powerful.

Police agencies and officers have broad discretion in deciding which laws to enforce, under which circumstances and against whom. Some people believe the law should be enforced consistently and in every instance. Most officers, however, believe that such police action would soon be unacceptable, far too harsh and virtually impossible.

The police are not the only players in the criminal justice system to exercise discretion. Prosecutors exercise discretion when determining priorities for prosecution and in plea negotiations. Judges exercise discretion in preliminary hearings, exclusionary rulings and sentencing. Parole boards, parole officers, probation officers, corrections officials and prison guards also exercise discretion.

Reasons for Police Discretion

Police departments are bureaucracies subject to rules and regulations that may contribute to irrational and inappropriate behavior. Such regulations limit an officer's ability to use common sense or act in a humane way in certain situations. Such limitations subject the officer to critical media coverage and adverse public opinion. For example, the police strictly upheld the law and towed a car containing a crying and screaming paraplegic girl because the vehicle was parked 15 minutes too long in a restricted zone. Millions of Americans and Canadians viewed this episode on national television.

Discretion is necessary for a number of reasons. The statute books are filled with archaic or ambiguous laws. Some laws are almost never enforced, and no one expects them to be. There are not enough police to act on every violation. They must select which laws they will enforce. Police prioritize the offenses they act upon. Crime is of more concern than a violation of a regulation, and serious crime is a greater threat than minor crime. The police act accordingly. Discretion is important to maintaining good community relations. If the police were to enforce the letter of the law, community resentment would soon follow. The police need community support if they are to succeed. Community standards influence how the police enforce laws. In most urban areas, significant changes have occurred in the past several years in the enforcement of drunk-driving laws. Now violators are routinely arrested and charged; the police rarely overlook this kind of violation.

Changes in Police Discretion

Law enforcement has responded to an increased public awareness of the dangers of tolerating drunk driving. Agencies, as well as individual officers, have a mandate from the public to strictly enforce DWI laws. Police discretion in this area is limited.

Similar changes have occurred in other areas as well. The public has ceased tolerating crimes that occur among family members. Once among the laws that the public knew the police would not enforce, many police strictly uphold laws against spouse beating and the physical and sexual abuse of children. Again, a significant change in police discretion has occurred in this area. Community policing has also had a great impact on police discretion. Officers are trusted to use good judgment in everyday activities with fewer limits and restricting rules.

Community policing emphasizes wider use of officer discretion.

In *Terry v Ohio* (1968), the Supreme Court recognized the role that discretion plays in policing. It granted police authority to stop and question people in *field interrogations*. Research has found this tactic to significantly reduce crime.

The Downside of Police Discretion

Officers usually work independently without direct supervision and have tremendous power to decide what action they will take, who they will arrest and which laws they will enforce. Unfortunately, some police officers may use their discretion illegally to obtain bribes or payoffs.

Discretion and the Police Image

Unless the police exercise their discretion with care, the community may complain about an actual or perceived abuse of power or discrimination in the way police enforce the law. If the community believes that the police overlook violations committed by a certain segment of society or strictly enforce laws against another, severe community-relations problems will develop. For example, officer discretion in the Jeffrey Dahmer murder case in Milwaukee led to an outpouring of criticism for both police and probation officers.

A police agency's policies, procedures and priorities and the manner in which it equips and assigns its officers indicate how that agency will exercise discretion. Individual officers have the greatest amount of discretion. Police officers often work alone, exercising wide discretion in matters of life and death, honor and dishonor in an environment that is tension filled and often hostile. In addition, within the police bureaucracy, discretion increases as one moves down the organizational hierarchy. Thus, patrol officers—the most numerous, lowest-ranking and newest to police work—have the greatest amount of discretion. All officers should be acutely aware of the power they wield and the immense impact the exercise of discretion has on the community and the police-community relationship.

While officers often operate independently, without direct supervision, it is important to remember that the community watches how officers perform their duties. The public notes how and when officers enforce the law. Citizens may form opinions about their police department and about all officers in that department based on an individual officer's actions. Perhaps the most critical discretionary decision an officer can make is when and how much force to use.

◉ USE OF FORCE

Police officers are trained and equipped to overcome the resistance they can expect to encounter as they perform their duties. Certain types of criminals, usually those who commit common crimes, are likely to evade arrest and require the police to find and forcibly take them into custody. Police deal with noncriminal situations that can also require overcoming resistance. Suicidal individuals may require forceful intervention. So might out-of-control mental patients. Henriquez (1999, p. 155) notes that: "During 1997, the last year for which complete data are available, police used force at a rate of 3.41 times per 10,000 calls for service. This translates to a rate of use of force of 0.0341. Expressed another way, police did not use force 99.966 percent of the time."

The use of force by the police encompasses a wide range of possible actions, from the officer's mere presence to the use of deadly force. The police presence affects a majority of citizens. The police uniform and squad cars are symbols of the officer's power to enforce the law and bring violators to justice—by the use of force if necessary. The visual image of power and authority created by the uniform and equipment facilitates the officer's ability to gain public compliance. The police image is also affected, either positively or negatively, by whether a department develops an authority-heavy image. Care must be taken not to develop such an intimidating image that it alienates the community.

Controversy on the use of force by police is almost always discussed in terms of police brutality, which is considered a problem by a large segment of the public. The extent of the problem is perceived differently among urban and suburban, rich and poor, and minority and majority populations. Valid reasons exist for why different people have different perceptions of the problem. One reason is that the job the police are required to do differs from community to community.

First recall that because the police must intervene in crimes where apprehension is likely to be resisted, most of their enforcement efforts are directed toward "common" criminals. In contrast, white-collar criminals are unlikely to flee or resist. They tend to see their situation as a legal dilemma to be won or lost in court. White-collar criminals are relatively wealthy and have a career and a place in the community; they have too much to lose to simply flee. Because police-enforcement efforts focus on common criminals, who are frequently poor, the most use of force by the police will be directed against this part of the population.

Citizens in white suburban areas are more likely to see the police in more positive circumstances when they report a crime and have been victimized; when they need assistance after an automobile accident, in a medical emergency, when their child is lost or when their car has run out of gas; and when they have locked themselves out of a car or home—or want their home watched.

In each scenario the police are there to lend assistance. Citizens in suburban areas may never see a police officer use force. The most negative experience they are likely to have with a police officer is receiving a traffic ticket.

When people from these widely separated communities talk about the police, it seems as though they are speaking of entirely different entities. On the one hand, police may be referred to as brutal, racist aggressors whereas others describe them as professional, helpful, efficient protectors. Which is the true picture of the police?

While the public has many stereotypes of the police, those stereotypes are shattered or reinforced each time a citizen has personal contact with a police officer. Each individual police contact can have a positive or negative impact on police-community relations.

Most citizens understand and support law enforcement officers' obligation to enforce the law and to use appropriate force when necessary. All officers have a duty to the profession to encourage public support by professional behavior respectful of each citizen's rights. Sometimes, however, public support of the police does not exist in a community. Lack of support may be the result of the unique characteristics of coercion.

The Paradoxes of Coercive Power

A **paradox** is a seemingly contradictory statement that may nonetheless be true. Muir (1977) has described four paradoxes of coercive power that affect policing.

The Paradox of Dispossession. This paradox suggests that the less one has, the less one has to lose. Those in the middle and upper class usually care about their material possessions, careers and reputations, making them more likely to obey the law (and the police). In contrast, those with little or nothing to lose cannot be easily coerced. Therefore, officers may need to resort to threaten the only thing such people have—their bodies and their freedom.

The Paradox of Detachment. This paradox, frequently evident in domestic disputes, suggests that the less the victim cares about preserving something, the less the victimizer cares about taking it hostage. Things once important are no longer important. A person's possessions, career or reputation are of no importance if they cannot be used to coerce a violent spouse. What police officers must do is try to identify something that once had meaning for the individual and get that person to value it again.

The Paradox of Irrationality. This paradox suggests that the more delirious the threatener, the more serious the threat; the more delirious the victim, the less serious the threat. Police encounter many people who are so drunk, mentally ill, terrorized or traumatized that they are irrational. In such instances officers seek to make the person more rational.

The paradox of irrationality requires people to become aware of the consequences of their actions, restoring rationality. How? Officers use an edge of fear initially invoked upon their approach. Fear makes people stop and think. It gets their attention. Then officers can teach people, being patient as they become more rational.

The Paradox of Face. This paradox suggests that the nastier one's reputation, the less nasty one has to be. As one officer put it: "I was very aggressive and by-the-book and got the reputation for being an asshole. I knew it, and it didn't bother me. It's easier to be known as an asshole than to have to be one."

The paradox of face suggests that officers must do what they want to avoid. The lesson is not for officers to have a nasty reputation but to understand how the need for it affects the people they encounter. Usually officers should treat people with respect and make them feel safe. People tend to develop nasty reputations when they feel threatened. An unruly crowd requires officers to do whatever earns their respect and to then try to educate them as to how they might protest in respectable, legal ways.

Muir's paradoxes of power illustrate that officers can behave ethically and still survive.

◉ ETHICAL POLICING

The tremendous power that policing has over people's lives requires that police officers represent good over evil. To maintain the public trust, police must be men and women of good character who hold foremost the ideals of fairness and justice. The manner in which police use their discretion to enforce the law and solve problems determines whether the public views the police as ethical.

The ethical way to act is not always clear in many situations. Officers frequently have their decisions reviewed and questioned after a crisis has passed. Unfortunately, the police have often not been given appropriate guidance in ethical decision making. Given the complexities of enforcing the law in a diverse population, it is inadequate to teach rookie officers the technical skills of policing and then send them into the community under the assumption they will do the "right thing."

A move toward higher ethical standards is perhaps reflected by the decision of many police departments to require their police officers to have a college education. There is an increasing need to begin a dialog within the police community on ethics—what ethical behavior is and how to achieve it in the profession. Incredibly, a discussion of ethics is not a standard part of the training and education of officers. If a prospective officer has a good record, the department assumes the candidate meets ethical standards.

One simple adage, set forth by Blanchard and Peale (1988, p. 9), might serve as a starting point for a discussion on ethics: "There is no right way to do a wrong thing." They (p. 20) suggest three questions that can be used as personal "ethics checks."

Three ethics-check questions are:

• *Is it legal?*

• *Is it balanced?*

• *How will it make me feel about myself?*

The first question should pose little problem for most officers. Much time is spent on criminal and constitutional law in most law enforcement programs. The focus of the second question is whether the decision is fair to everyone involved, in the short term and long term. Does the decision create a win-win situation? The third question is perhaps the most crucial. Would you mind seeing your decision published in the paper? Would you feel good if your friends and family knew about your decision?

Blanchard and Peale (p. 79) suggest the following five principles of ethical power for individuals:

Purpose. I see myself as being an ethically sound person. I let my conscience be my guide. No matter what happens, I am always able to face the mirror, look myself straight in the eye, and feel good about myself.

Pride. I feel good about myself. I don't need the acceptance of other people to feel important. A balanced self-esteem keeps my ego and my desire to be accepted from influencing my decisions.

Patience. I believe that things will eventually work out well. I don't need everything to happen right now. I am at peace with what comes my way.

Persistence. I stick to my purpose, especially when it seems inconvenient to do so. My behavior is consistent with my intentions. As Churchill said, "Never! Never! Never! Never give up!"

Perspective. I take time to enter each day quietly in a mood of reflection. This helps me to get myself focused and allows me to listen to my inner self and to see things more clearly.

Ethical behavior by individual officers and by the department as a whole is indispensable to effective police-community partnerships. Yet as Peak et al. (1998, p. 20) note: "Many academics and practitioners are concerned that the potential for ethical dilemmas is increased with the shift to COPPS, given the nature of ethics training, decentralization, expanded discretionary authority and officers' greater proximity to citizens."

Ethical Dilemmas

Ethical dilemmas are often rooted in the ends-versus-means controversy. This is aptly illustrated in the policing methods of Andy Sipowicz of *NYPD Blue,* who firmly believes that when he has the bad guy dead to rights but lacks evidence, he can use whatever means are necessary to obtain that evidence, including strong-arm tactics. Adcox (p. 19) explains that the tendency of police to place ends over means is not new: "There is ample historical evidence to suggest that similar police values, beliefs and practices have existed since the inauguration of modern policing in the United States." Historically, some officers have valued results over duty and principle with "the standard measurement of good police work [becoming] goal achievement, with all else being secondary" (Adcox, p. 19).

As Thompson (2001, p. 77) notes: "The American public readily understands and recognizes that the police are entitled to special privileges and exceptions relative to obeying the laws." They can exceed speed limits and violate traffic laws to enforce the law. They can carry concealed weapons and own or have access to weapons that are restricted to citizens. Sometimes this leads new recruits to receive a message that says they are above the law. As Thompson (p. 79) suggests: "Officers need to know the limitations on their behavior. . . . Equality under the law is the foundation of American criminal justice. If law enforcement officers believe they are above the law, then this subverts the very essence of law enforcement and criminal justice in our society."

A belief that officers are above the law, coupled with the code of silence previously discussed can leave officers in ethical dilemmas. A study by the National Institute of Justice, The Measurement of Police Integrity, surveyed 3,235 officers from 30 departments and found that the majority of respondents said they would not report a fellow officer for accepting free gifts, meals or discounts, or for having a minor traffic accident while under the influence of alcohol ("How Do You Rate?" 2000, p. 1). These behaviors were not considered major transgressions by the respondents. Three behaviors they did find serious were accepting a cash bribe, stealing money from a found wallet and stealing property from a crime scene.

Closely related to unethical behavior as a result of believing that the ends justify the means is actually corrupt behavior.

Police Corruption

Since policing began, corruption in law enforcement has been a problem. Strandberg (2000, p. 100) notes that: "Corruption takes on many forms, and something seemingly insignificant can put an officer on a slippery slope, leading to major crimes." This sentiment is echoed by Trautman (2000, p. 65): "Research repeatedly confirms that most scandals start with one employee doing relatively small unethical acts and *grow to whatever level the leadership allows*" [emphasis added].

This parallels the Broken Window theory of crime. According to Adams (2000, p. 2): "If the toleration of minor law violations leads to more serious crime on the street, it would also follow that the toleration of minor law violations by the police will lead to more serious crime on the force." He suggests that if we free police from limits on their behavior: "We create a culture within police departments that the end justifies the means. This culture, in turn, increases antagonism between the police and the communities they serve, escalating the violence that is perceived to be necessary to keep the peace." It can also lead to corruption.

When discussing police corruption, some believe that it is just a few "rotten apples" that give a department a bad name. Trautman suggests: "The 'rotten apple' theory that some administrators propose as the cause of their demise is usually nothing more than a self-serving, superficial façade, intended to draw attention away from their own failures."

Byers (2000, p. 4) describes the "venerable 'rotten barrel theory' of police corruption" which suggests that unethical, illegal behavior is pervasive throughout a department and can be traced to top management. A "few bad apples can spoil the whole bunch." He notes that in addition to the "rotten apple" and the "rotten barrel" theories, a middle ground has been identified. The "rotten group" theory of police corruption is based on a 1998 report by the General Accounting Office on police corruption in the United States:

> The most commonly identified pattern of drug-related police corruption involved small groups of officers who protected and assisted each other in criminal activities, rather than the traditional patterns of non-drug-related police corruption that involved just a few isolated individuals or systemic corruption pervading an entire police department or precinct (Government Accounting Office, 1998, p. 3).

Swope (2001, p. 80) suggests that perhaps the problem is not in "bad apples" but in bad barrels: "It is the barrel, the culture of the police organization, that can cause the root shaking scandals that periodically face some police organizations."

The importance of management and of ethical officers within the department in curbing corruption cannot be underestimated. Among the most important forms of corruption, according to Strandberg, is adherence to the code of silence. It might be viewed as the No. 1 barrier to lasting improvements in police-community relations, especially in communities of color where such misconduct has been more prevalent (p. 100).

The scandals rocking the Los Angeles Police Department illustrate the emphasis on ends over means and on the code of silence. Hundreds of criminal convictions may be questioned due to a police-corruption scandal involving allegations of officers framing innocent people, lying in court and shooting unarmed suspects ("LAPD Corruption Scandal . . . ," 1999, p. 3). The *Washington Post* reports that at the latest count, 32 criminal convictions had been overturned and 20 officers fired, suspended or quit ("Police Corruption Scandal . . .," 2000, p. A20).

Cortrite (2000, p. 8), a police officer for over 30 years in a department bordering the LAPD, suggests that the underlying problem is the LAPD culture. He contends that the LAPD has touted itself as the greatest department in the world. This has led to a feeling that officers can do whatever they want without having to answer to the public, politicians or even the courts. Such an attitude has created not only arrogance but also complacency. Their second cultural mistake, says Cortrite, "is their command and control management style." He feels officers who don't meet supervisors' expectations have been given suspensions of draconian proportions, such as six months off without pay. In addition, their policies-and-procedures manual encompasses several thick volumes. Cortrite sees the culture as one "based on fear and lack of trust."

Cortrite concludes that: "The huge majority of cops are highly ethical people. Trusting them more with the responsibility to maintain the ethical standards of the organization will empower them to eliminate any unethical conduct from their midst."

Investigative Commissions

Monahan (2000, p. 79) reports that many police chiefs or politicians convene an investigative commission or board of inquiry following a scandal. For example, the Knapp Commission was convened in 1972 by Mayor John Lindsay who ordered an investigation in the New York City Police Department. This commission uncovered widespread corruption in the NYPD. But 20 years later, many of the corruption issues identified by the Knapp Commission resurfaced and were identified by the Mollen Commission.

The scandal involving the videotaped beating of Rodney King resulted in the Christopher Commission. This commission found that a significantly large number of officers posed a much higher risk for use of excessive force. A new chief was appointed who implemented many reforms, but they were not institutionalized. Monahan (p. 83) notes: "That the reforms did not become a permanent part of the organization is made clear by the Rampart scandal." This scandal led to formation of the Rampart Board of Inquiry. This board concluded that "the vast majority of LAPD Officers were hard working, honest, and responsible individuals" (Los Angeles Police Department Board of Inquiry into the Rampart Corruption Incident).

The lesson to be learned from the investigative commissions, says Monahan (p. 84) is that too often the implemented reforms are only temporary: "Changes were temporary because too much was dependent on the appointment and characteristics of the incoming police administrator. Departments did not internalize the reforms so that with the passage of time, or once the chief left, the officers reverted to their corrupt behavior."

Police corruption is an issue to be faced and dealt with. In a department where corruption is tolerated, the public trust will fade. And, as Fulton (2000, p. 250) asserts: "The public trust is a most valuable commodity. You can't touch it or see it, but when you walk into a community, you can feel when it's there and when it's not. Without the public trust, a police department is hollow and ineffective."

SUMMARY

Community policing will require a change in mission statement, departmental organization and leadership style. A mission statement is a written declaration of purpose. Departments must find in their mission a balance between fighting crime and service to the public. The majority of police actions do not involve criminal law enforcement, but rather are community-service oriented.

The traditional law enforcement organization design has been that of a pyramid-shaped hierarchy based on a military model. However, to implement community policing, the pyramid might be inverted. Another change might occur in leadership style, with a preference for participatory leadership, where each individual has a voice in decisions, but top management still has the ultimate decision-making authority.

Today's police departments have more minority and female officers. The educational level of the officers is much higher, and fewer have military experience than in years past. Most officers are also as interested in helping people as they are in fighting crime. A dominant characteristic of the police subculture is isolation and a "them-versus-us" world view.

The police image is affected by individual backgrounds, the media and personal experiences with the criminal justice system. It is also shaped by how police look—their uniform and equipment—and by what they do. Negative contacts are unpleasant interactions between the police and the public. They may or may not involve criminal activity.

People expect the police to enforce the law unless it adversely affects them. People also expect the police to help them when they have a problem. The police face the dilemma of being expected to win the wars on crime and drugs without having control over the causes of these problems. The police cannot win these wars.

Police use of discretion and force will profoundly affect police-community relations. Each agency exercises discretion when it establishes its mission, policies and procedures. Each officer exercises discretion when deciding whether to issue citations or make arrests when laws are violated. Community policing emphasizes wider use of officer discretion. Police discretion and authority to use power are balanced by the responsibility to act ethically. Three questions to check police ethical standards are: (1) Is it legal? (2) Is it balanced? and (3) How will it make me feel about myself?

DISCUSSION QUESTIONS

1. What is the image of the police in your community? What factors are responsible for this image? Could the police image be made more positive?
2. What expectations do you have of law enforcement agencies?
3. Does police discretion frequently lead to abuse of alleged perpetrators?
4. Are police officers now more violent and less ethical than their predecessors?
5. Does the image of law enforcement affect officers' ability to get the job done?
6. How do you explain the development of the two contradictory models in policing: community-oriented policing (COP) and special weapons and tactics (SWAT) teams? Can they coexist?
7. What should be a department's ideal balance between fighting crime and service to the community?
8. Have you witnessed police exercise their discretion? How did it impress you?
9. Can you give examples of each of the four paradoxes of coercive power as they operate in police work?
10. What decisions commonly made by police officers involve ethical considerations?

INFOTRAC COLLEGE EDITION ASSIGNMENTS

- Use Infotrac to help answer the discussion questions when appropriate.
- Outline two articles on leadership, one from a law enforcement journal, one from a business journal. Give the complete cite for each. Compare the contents of the two articles, and be prepared to discuss your outlines in class.
- Research and outline at least one of the following: police discretion, police culture, police ethics or police corruption.

COMMUNITY PROJECT

Visit a police department and obtain a copy of their mission statement and, if possible, their organizational chart. Be prepared to discuss how these fit with the discussion in this chapter.

REFERENCES

Adams, Noah. "Broken Windows Theory of Policing." *All Things Considered.* National Public Radio, March 7, 2000.

Adcox, Ken. "Doing Bad Things for Good Reasons." *The Police Chief,* Vol. LXVII, No. 1, January 2000, pp. 16–28.

Bennett, Wayne W. and Hess, Kären M. *Management and Supervision in Law Enforcement,* 3rd ed. Belmont, CA: Wadsworth Thomson Learning, 2001.

Bittner, Egon. "Florence Nightingale in Pursuit of Willie Sutton: A Theory of Police." In *The Potential for Reform of Criminal Justice,* edited by H. Jacob. Beverly Hills: Sage, 1974, pp. 17–44.

Blanchard, Kenneth. "Turning the Organizational Pyramid Upside Down." In *Leader of the Future,* edited by F. Hesselbein, M. Goldsmith and R. Beckard. San Francisco: Jossey-Bass, 1996, p. 85.

Blanchard, Kenneth and Peale, Norman Vincent. *The Power of Ethical Management.* New York: Fawcett Crest, 1988.

Byers, Bryan. "Ethics and Criminal Justice: Some Observations on Police Misconduct." *ACJS Today,* Vol. XXI, Issue 3, September/October 2000, pp. 1, 4–8.

Byrne, Edward C. "Putting Police Work Back on the Street." *Law and Order,* Vol. 45, No. 5, May 1997, pp. 43–45.

Cassidy, Peter. "US: The Rise in Paramilitary Policing." *Covert Action Quarterly,* Fall 1997.

Cortrite, Mike. "What's the LAPD's Problem? It's the Culture!" *Law Enforcement News,* Vol. XXVI, No. 535, June 15, 2000, p. 8.

Deming, W. Edwards. *Quality, Productivity, and Competitive Position.* Cambridge, MA: Institute of Technology, Center for Advanced Engineering Study, 1982.

Flynn, Edward A. "Toward a New Mind-Set in Policing." *Law Enforcement News,* January 1998, p. 12.

Fulton, Roger. "Preventing Corruption." *Law Enforcement Technology,* Vol. 27, No. 12, December 2000, p. 250.

Gallup Poll, 2000. "Honesty and Ethics in Professions." http://www.gallup.com/poll/indicators/indhnstyethcs.asp

Glick, Larry. "The Paramilitary: A Product of 'Parareportage.' " *Police,* Vol. 24, No. 4, April 2000, pp. 42–44.

Goldstein, Herman. *Problem-Oriented Policing.* New York: McGraw-Hill Publishing Company, 1990.

Goodbody, William L. "A Square Peg in Bureaucracy's Round Hole." *Law Enforcement News,* June 30, 1995, pp. 12, 14.

Government Accounting Office. "Report to the Honorable Charles B. Rangel, House of Representatives, Law Enforcement: Information on Drug-Related Police Corruption." Washington, DC: USGPO, May 1998, p. 3.

Harr, J. Scott and Hess, Kären M. *Seeking Employment in Criminal Justice and Related Fields,* 3rd ed. Belmont, CA: Wadsworth Publishing Company, 2000.

Haught, Lunell. "Meaning, Resistance and Sabotage—Elements of a Police Culture." *Community Policing Exchange,* Phase VI, # 20 May/June 1998, p. 1.

Henriquez, Mark. "The IACP National Police Use-of-Force Database Project." *The Police Chief,* Vol. LXVI, No. 10, October 1999, pp. 154–159.

"How Do You Rate? The Secret to Measuring a Department's 'Culture of Integrity.' " *Law Enforcement News,* Vol. XXVI, No. 541, October 15, 2000, pp. 1, 6.

Jones, Mark. "Religion, Race, and Public Opinion about Police Officer Gratuities." *Journal of Contemporary Criminal Justice,* Vol. 15, No. 2, May 1999, pp. 191–204.

Klockars, Carl B. *The Idea of Police.* Newbury Park: Sage Publishing Company, 1985.

Klockars, Carl B. "The Rhetoric of Community Policing." In *Community Policing: Rhetoric or Reality,* edited by Jack R. Greene and Stephen D. Mastrofski. New York: Praeger Publishing, 1991, pp. 239–258.

"LAPD Corruption Scandal Forces Review of Many Convictions." *Criminal Justice Newsletter,* Vol. 30, No. 9, May 3, 1999, pp. 2–4.

Los Angeles Police Department Board of Inquiry into the Rampart Corruption Incident, *Final Report* (Executive Summary), March 28, 2000. Available at *www.LAPDOnline.org*

Maguire, Edward R. "Structural Change in Large Municipal Police Organizations during the Community Policing Era." *Justice Quarterly,* Vol. 14, No. 3, September 1997, pp. 547–576.

Mastrofski, Stephen D. *Ideas in American Policing: Policing for People.* Washington, DC: Police Foundation, March 1999a.

Mastrofski, Stephen D. "Thinking Out Loud: How Far Has CJ Research Come in 10 Years?" *Law Enforcement News,* June 15, 1999b, pp. 8–10.

Mastrofski, Stephen D.; Parks, Roger B.; Reiss, Albert J., Jr.; and Worden, Robert E. "Policing Neighborhoods: A Report from Indianapolis." Washington, DC: National Institute of Justice Research Preview, July 1998.

McErlain, Ed. "Acknowledging the Code of Silence." *Law and Order,* Vol. 49, No. 1, January 2001, p. 47.

Monahan, Francis J. "Investigative Commissions Implemented Reforms Prove Ephemeral." *The Police Chief,* Vol. LXVII, No. 10, October 2000, pp. 79–84.

Muir, William Ker. *Police: Streetcorner Politicians.* Chicago: University of Chicago Press, 1977.

Nila, Michael J. "Defining the Police Mission: A Community/Police Perspective." *The Police Chief,* October 1990, pp. 43–47.

Parks, Roger B.; Mastrofski, Stephen D.; Dejong, Christina; and Gray, M. Kevin. "How Officers Spend Their Time with the Community." *Justice Quarterly,* Vol. 15, No. 3, September 1999, pp. 484–518.

Peak, Kenneth J; Stitt, B. Grant; and Glensor, Ronald W. "Ethical Considerations in Community Policing and Problem Solving." *Police Quarterly,* Vol. 1, No. 3, 1998, pp. 19–34.

"Police Corruption Scandal in L.A. Is Growing Bigger by the Week." (Minneapolis/St. Paul) *Star Tribune,* February 13, 2000, p. A20.

Reiter, Michael S. "Empowered Policing." *FBI Law Enforcement Bulletin,* Vol. 68, No. 2, February 1999, pp. 7–11.

"Rewarding Good Deeds Is Just the Ticket." *Law Enforcement News,* Vol. XXVI, No. 535, June 15, 2000, p. 9.

Robinson, Patricia A. "Neighborhood Cops or Special Ops? Policing in the New Millennium." *The Law Enforcement Trainer,* Vol. 15, No. 2, March/April 2000, pp. 14–16, 45.

Rodgers, Todd. "A Blueprint for Community Policing." *Law and Order,* March 1995, pp. 116–121.

Rowell, James D. "The Pro-Active Approach to Crime Fighting." *The Law Enforcement Trainer,* Vol. 15, No. 2, March/April 2000, pp. 8–10.

Russell, Gregory D. and MacLachlan, Susan. "Community Policing, Decentralized Decision Making and Employee Satisfaction." *Journal of Crime and Justice,* Vol. 22, No. 2, 1999, pp. 31–54.

Stevens, Dennis J. "Improving Community Policing Using Managerial Style and Total Quality Management." *Law and Order,* Vol. 48, No. 10, October 2000, pp. 197–204.

Strandburg, Keith W. "Light Dawns on the Dark Side." *Law Enforcement Technology,* Vol. 27, No. 7, July 2000, pp. 96–104.

"Study Sees Cause for Alarm as Police Adopt a More Paramilitary Posture." *Law Enforcement News,* Vol. XXV, No. 519, October 15, 1999, pp. 1, 9.

Swope, Ross. "Bad Apples or Bad Barrel?" *Law and Order,* Vol. 49, No. 1, January 2001, pp. 80–85.

Thompson, David. "Above the Law?" *Law and Order,* Vol. 49, No. 1, January 2001, pp. 77–79.

Trautman, Neal. "How Organizations Become Corrupt: The Corruption Continuum." *Law and Order,* Vol. 48, No. 5, May 2000, pp. 65–68.

Trautman, Neal. "Truth about Police Code of Silence Revealed." *Law and Order,* Vol. 49, No. 1, January 2001, pp. 68–76.

Turner, Yvonne C. "'Decentralizing' the Specialized Unit Function in Small Police Agencies." *The Police Chief,* Vol. LXVII, No. 2, February 2000, pp. 50–51.

Wilson, James Q. and Kelling, George L. "Making Neighborhoods Safe." *The Atlantic Monthly,* February 1989, pp. 46–52.

CHAPTER 3

The Community

I believe in the United States of America as a government of the people, by the people, for the people.
 American Creed

Do you know

How U.S. citizens established the "public peace"?

What a social contract is?

How to define community?

What the broken window phenomenon refers to?

What demographics includes?

What role organizations and institutions play within a community?

What power structures exist within a community?

What issues in the criminal justice system affect police-community relations?

How the medical model and the justice model view criminals?

What restorative justice is?

How citizens/communities have been involved in community policing?

Can you define these terms:

bifurcated society

broken window phenomenon

community

demographics

diversion

formal power structure

ghetto

heterogeneous

homogeneous

incivilities

informal power structure

justice model

medical model

NIMBY syndrome

plea bargaining

privatization

recidivism

restorative justice

social capital

social contract

syndrome of crime

tipping point

INTRODUCTION

The opening sentence of the American Creed, adopted by the House of Representatives on April 3, 1918, uses language attributed to Abraham Lincoln in his *Address at Gettysburg,* November 19, 1863: "We here highly resolve that these dead shall not have died in vain; that this nation, under God, shall have a new birth of freedom; and that government of the people, by the people, and for the people, shall not perish from the earth." The philosophy implicit in the American Creed is central to the concept of "community" in the United States. Each community is part of a larger social order.

The U.S. Constitution and Bill of Rights, as well as federal and state statutes and local ordinances, establish the "public peace" in the United States.

In the United States individual freedom and rights are balanced with the need to establish and maintain order. The United States was born out of desire for freedom. In fact, former President Jimmy Carter noted: "America did not invent human rights. In a very real sense, it is the other way around. Human rights invented America."

The importance of individual rights to all citizens is a central theme to the following discussion of community. Citizens have established a criminal justice system in an effort to live in "peace," free from crime and violence. As the gatekeepers to the criminal justice system, the police have an inherent link with the public, as Sir Robert Peel expressed in 1829: "Police, at all times, should maintain a relationship with the public that gives reality to the historic tradition that the police are the public and the public are the police; the police being the only members of the public who are paid to give full-time attention to duties which are incumbent on every citizen in the interests of community welfare and existence."

To ensure the peace, citizens of the United States have also entered into an unwritten *social contract.*

The social contract *provides that for everyone to receive justice, each person must relinquish some freedom.*

In civilized society, people cannot simply do as they please. They are expected to conform to federal and state laws, as well as local rules and regulations established by and for the community in which they live. Increased mobility and economic factors have weakened the informal social contract that once helped to keep the peace in our society. As a result the police, as agents of social control, have had to fill the breach, increasing the need for law-abiding citizens to join with the police in making their communities free from drugs and crime.

Correia (2000, p. 5) suggests that the traditional law enforcement model of policing strongly reflected a classical liberal theory of democratic governance, emphasizing the rights and responsibilities of the individual. In contrast, community policing is driven by "*communitarian* values and philosophical principles, in which *community* values and needs are paramount in political and civic activities." He notes: "This philosophical shift to communitarian principles requires fundamental changes in citizen-to-citizen and citizen-to-government relations in law enforcement."

This chapter begins with definitions of *community* and *social capital* as well as lack of community. This is followed by a look at crime and violence in our communities and an explanation of community demographics. Next the organizations and institutions within a community, the public-private policing interaction and the power structure within a community are described. Then the role of the criminal justice system in community policing is discussed. The chapter concludes with an explanation of citizen/community involvement in community policing.

COMMUNITY DEFINED

What does the word *community* bring to mind? To many people it conjures up images of their hometown. To others it may bring images of a specific block, a neighborhood or an idyllic small town where everyone knows everyone and they all get along.

Community has also been defined as a group of people living in an area under the same government. In addition, community can refer to a social group or class having common interests. Community may even refer to society as a whole—the public. This text uses a specific meaning for *community*.

Community *refers to the specific geographic area served by a police department or law enforcement agency and the individuals, organizations and agencies within that area.*

Police officers must understand and be a part of this defined community if they are to fulfill their mission. The community may cover a very small area and have a very limited number of individuals, organizations and agencies; it may perhaps be policed by a single officer. Or the community may cover a vast area and have thousands of individuals and hundreds of organizations and agencies and be policed by several hundred officers. And while police jurisdiction and delivery of services is based on geographic boundaries, a community is much more than a group of neighborhoods administered by a local government. The schools, businesses, public and private agencies, churches and social groups are vital elements of the community. Also of importance are the individual values, concerns and cultural principles of the people living and working in the community and the common interests they share with neighbors. Where integrated communities exist, people share a sense of ownership and pride in their environment. They also have a sense of what is acceptable behavior, which makes policing in such a community much easier.

Community *also refers to a feeling of belonging—a sense of integration, a sense of shared values and a sense of "we-ness."*

Research strongly suggests that a sense of community is the "glue" that binds communities to maintain order and provides the foundation for effective community action. It also suggests that shared values, participation in voluntary associations, spiritual or church-based connectedness and positive interaction with neighbors indicate a strong sense of community and correlate with participation in civic and government activities (Correia, p. 9).

Harpold (2000, pp. 23–24) describes six types of neighborhoods that exhibit different levels of "well-being" of which community policing officers should be aware. The *integral neighborhood* has well-manicured lawns and well-maintained buildings and shows a high level of pride. Citizens interact and support one another and also link to outside organizations. The *parochial neighborhood* residents share similar values and cultures, insulating themselves and taking care of their own, usually without involving the police. The *diffuse neighborhood* residents have much in common but seldom interact, limiting their ability to problem-solve.

The *stepping-stone neighborhood* consists of small single-family residences, townhouses and apartments whose residents tend to move out quickly. Nonetheless, they tend to get involved in community organizations and to assume leadership positions. The *transitory neighborhood* residents either move often or have little in common and, hence, the neighborhood lacks cohesion. Finally, the *anomic neighborhood* is characterized by isolation and alienation. Residents have resigned themselves to accept criminal victimization as a way of life. Recognizing what type of neighborhood a community policing officer is involved in will help determine what strategies might be most appropriate, as discussed in Section Three of this text.

◈ SOCIAL CAPITAL

Communities might also be looked at in terms of their **social capital.** Coleman (1990, p. 302) developed this concept, which he defined as: "A variety of different entities having two characteristics in common: They all consist of some aspect of a social structure, and they facilitate certain actions of individuals who are within the structure." Coleman saw the two most important elements in social capital as being *trustworthiness*, that is, citizens' trust of each other and their public institutions, and *obligations*, that is, expectation that service to each other will be reciprocated.

Putnam (1995) refined the definition of social capital as the reserves of *trust* and *engagement* in a community. He also identified two levels of social capital: local and public. Local social capital is that found among family members and citizens and their immediate, informal groups. Public social capital is that found in networks tying individuals to broader community institutions such as schools, civic organizations, churches and the like as well as to networks linking individuals to various levels of government—including the police. According to Correia (p. 53): "Taken together, the concepts of sense of community and social capital go a long way toward describing the strength of a community's social fabric."

Community Factors Affecting Social Capital

Correia reports on a study using Community Action Support Teams (CAST) and the community factors affecting social capital in six cities: Hayward, California; Davenport, Iowa; Ann Arbor, Michigan; Sioux City, Iowa; Pocatello, Idaho; and Ontario, California. Data came from self-administered mail surveys, direct observations and interviews. Of the 22 hypotheses tested, seven were supported by the data (pp. 34–35):

1. Trust in others depends on the level of safety an individual feels in his or her environment. Therefore, the higher the levels of perceived safety, the higher levels of local social capital will be.
2. The lower the levels of physical disorder, the higher the levels of perceived sense of safety will be.
3. Females will hold lower levels of perceived safety than males.
4. The higher levels of public social capital, the higher levels of collective action will be.
5. The more that individuals trust one another, the more likely they will be to engage in collective activities. Consequently, the higher the level of local social capital, the higher the level of engagement in collective action will be.
6. The more individuals trust one another, the more likely they will be to interact. Therefore, the higher the levels of local social capital, the higher the levels of neighboring activity will be.
7. The higher the levels of civic activity, the higher the levels of public social capital will be.

Correia concludes (p. 41):

> Effective community policing may be limited to those areas with high levels of social cohesion; most likely, these areas do not need community policing as badly as others. This suggest that communities lacking high levels of Putnam's social capital, yet with high levels of community policing activity, are possibly beyond repair; their stocks of social capital cannot be replenished without extraordinary effort, nor can their strained social cohesion be repaired exclusively by police efforts. Consequently, this method of law enforcement may in fact raise more expectations than it is able to satisfy.

In effect: "Social capital is a prerequisite to citizen engagement in community efforts" (Correia, p. 48). The implications of this significant finding are discussed in Chapter 5.

Sociologists have been describing for decades either the loss or the breakdown of "community" in modern, technological, industrial, urban societies such as ours. Proponents of community policing in some areas may be missing a major sociological reality—the absence of "community"—in the midst of all the optimism about police playing a greater role in encouraging it.

◈ LACK OF COMMUNITY

Community implies a group of people with a common history and understandings and a sense of themselves as "us" and outsiders as "them." Unfortunately, many communities lack this "we-ness." In such areas, the police and public have a "them-versus-us" relationship. Areas requiring the most police attention are usually those with the least shared values and limited sense of community. Skogan (1996, p. 31) cautions: "Above all, police and citizens may have a history of not getting along with each other. Especially in disadvantaged neighborhoods, there too often is a record of antagonistic relationships between residents and the police, who may be perceived as arrogant, brutal, and uncaring—not as potential partners."

> Beginning in the 1960s, police were portrayed by television as "cruising" through neighborhoods and descending from their cars to dispense rough (and sometimes unfair) physical justice. Police were portrayed as no longer for the neighborhood but against it. As the perception of the police changed, so did the image of the relatively peaceful, culturally homogeneous neighborhood. Instead, in some areas, ethnicity took on the image of poverty. . . .
>
> Many urban communities, particularly those inhabited by minorities, began to experience great economic and social upheaval. . . . Disorder, substance abuse, and violence were expected parts of these communities. . . . Rules of social behavior and acceptable levels of law enforcement were imposed by outside agencies rather than the citizens (*Community Police Partnerships for COP*, 1996, p. 2).

When citizens are unable to maintain social control, the result is social disorganization. According to Greene (1998, p. 46): "The social disorganization perspective argues that neighborhood decay not only reduces the horizontal bonds between neighbors within communities but also reduces the vertical linkages between communities and larger political, social, and economic institutions." All entities within a community—individuals as well as organizations and agencies—must work together to keep that community healthy. Such partnerships are vital, for a community cannot be healthy if unemployment and poverty are widespread; people are hungry; health care is inadequate; prejudice separates people; preschool children lack proper care and nutrition; senior citizens are allowed to atrophy; schools remain isolated and remote; social services are fragmented and disproportionate; and government lacks responsibility and accountability.

Broken Windows

In such unhealthy communities, disorder and crime may flourish. In a classic article, "Broken Windows," Wilson and Kelling (1982, p. 31) contend:

> Social psychologists and police officers tend to agree that if a window in a building is broken *and is left unrepaired*, all the rest of the windows will soon be broken. This is as true in nice neighborhoods as in run-down ones. Window-breaking does not necessarily occur on a large scale because some areas are inhabited by determined window-breakers whereas others are populated by window-lovers; rather, one unrepaired broken window is a signal that no one cares, and so breaking more windows costs nothing. (It has always been fun.)

The broken window phenomenon *suggests that if it appears "no one cares," disorder and crime will thrive.*

Wilson and Kelling based their *broken window* theory, in part, on research done in 1969 by a Stanford psychologist, Philip Zimbardo. Zimbardo arranged to have a car

The broken window that remains unfixed gives the impression that no one cares. Crime is likely to flourish in such an environment.

© Hazel Hankin/Stock, Boston

without license plates parked with its hood up on a street in the Bronx and a comparable car on a street in Palo Alto, California. The car in the Bronx was attacked by vandals within 10 minutes, and within 24 hours it had been totally destroyed and stripped of anything of value. The car in Palo Alto sat untouched. After a week Zimbardo took a sledgehammer to it. People passing by soon joined in, and within a few hours that car was also totally destroyed. According to Wilson and Kelling (p. 31): "Untended property becomes fair game for people out for fun or plunder, and even for people who ordinarily would not dream of doing such things and who probably consider themselves as law-abiding."

Broken windows and smashed cars are very visible signs of people not caring about their community. Other less subtle signs include unmowed lawns, piles of accumulated trash and graffiti, often referred to as **incivilities.** A U.S. Department of Justice, National Institute of Justice study, *Crime, Grime, Fear and Decline* ("Incivilities Play. . . ," 1999, p. 12) described incivilities as rowdiness, drunkenness, fighting, prostitution, abandoned buildings, litter, broken windows and graffiti. The study found that incivilities did not have independent impacts on changes in house value, home ownership or education levels but that incivilities did shape later changes in poverty and vacancy rates. A key finding of the study was that incivilities play less of a role in crime than social fabric (social capital).

Incivilities and social disorder occur when social control mechanisms have eroded. Increases in incivilities may increase the fear of crime and reduce citizens' sense of safety. They may physically or psychologically withdraw, isolating themselves from their neighbors. Or increased incivilities and disorder may bring people together to "take back the neighborhood."

It is extremely difficult to maintain community policing when the values of groups within a given area clash. For example, controversy may exist between gay communities and orthodox Christian or Jewish communities in the same area. Do each of these communities deserve a different style of policing based on the "community value system"? Do "community" police officers ignore behavior in a community where the majority of residents approve of that behavior but enforce sanctions against the same behavior in enclaves where that behavior causes tension? These are difficult ethical questions.

Another factor that negates a sense of community is the prevalence of violence. We live in a violent society. The United States was born through a violent revolution. The media emphasizes violence, constantly carrying news of murder, rape and assault. It seems that if a movie or television program is to succeed, at least three or four people must meet a violent death or suffer some physical injury. The average cartoon that children watch contains more violence than most adults realize. Children learn that violence is acceptable and justified under some circumstances. Citizens expect the police to prevent violence, but the police cannot do it alone. Individuals must come together to help stop violence and in so doing can build a sense of community.

◉ COMMUNITIES AND CRIME

As Greene (p. 45) suggests: "The relationship between crime and disorder in community settings is complicated by many factors including land use (e.g., residential, commercial, industrial), population and residential density, housing stock age and infrastructure, the local economy, and local social ethos." He further suggests a linkage between crime and disorder and poverty, inequality, community mobility, the ethnic and racial composition of communities, family structure, and the density and types of housing. Greene notes that the police have little opportunity to directly affect these community crime factors but that other government agencies such as those associated with education, housing, job training, family support and health care can affect the crime factors.

Saville (1996, p. 1) describes a theory called the "ecology of crime," which explains how criminal opportunities are created in neighborhoods. He suggests that every neighborhood has a crime "threshold" (p. 7): "The basic idea is that just like a natural ecosystem, a neighborhood has the capacity to hold only a certain number of things. Add too many and the system will collapse because it exceeds its carrying capacity."

This is close in concept to the "tipping point" described by Gladwell (1996). The **tipping point** is the point at which an ordinary, stable phenomenon can turn into a crisis. He uses the analogy of a health epidemic, which he stresses is a nonlinear situation, that is, small changes can have huge effects and large changes can have small effects—in contrast to linear situations where every extra increment of effort will produce a corresponding improvement in result. He uses as another example the experience of pouring ketchup:

> Like all children encountering this problem for the first time [pouring ketchup], I assumed that the solution was linear; that steadily increasing hits on the base of the bottle would yield increasing amounts of ketchup on the other end. Not so, my father said, and he recited a ditty that, for me, remains the most concise statement of the fundamental nonlinearity of everyday life: "Tomato ketchup in a bottle—None will come and then the lot'll."

How does this relate to neighborhoods? Gladwell (p. 5) explains that this principle of nonlinearity can be applied to the phenomenon of "white flight": "A racist white neighborhood, for example, might empty out when blacks reach 5 percent of the population. A liberal white neighborhood, on the other hand, might not tip until blacks make up 40 or 50 percent." Communities need to recognize when they are approaching the "tipping point" or the "threshold" in a given situation. In addition to understanding the complex concept of community, it is also important to assess the demographics of the area.

◆ COMMUNITY DEMOGRAPHICS

Demographics refers to the characteristics of the individuals who live in a community.

Demographics include a population's size, distribution, growth, density, employment rate, ethnic makeup and vital statistics such as average age, education and income.

Although people generally assume that the smaller the population of a community, the easier policing becomes, this is not necessarily true. Small communities generally have fewer resources. It is also difficult to be the sole law enforcement person being, in effect, on call 24 hours a day. A major advantage of a smaller community is that people know each other. A sense of community is likely to be greater in such communities than in large cities such as Chicago or New York.

When assessing law enforcement's ability to police an area, density of population is an important variable. Studies have shown that as population becomes denser, people become more aggressive. In densely populated areas, people become more territorial and argue more frequently about "turf."

Rapid population growth can invigorate a community, or it can drain its limited resources. Without effective planning and foresight, rapid population growth can result in serious problems for a community, especially if the population growth results from an influx of immigrants or members of an ethnic group different from the majority in that area.

The community's *vital statistics* are extremely important from a police-community partnership perspective. What is the average age of individuals within the community? Are there more young or elderly individuals? How many single-parent families are there? What is the divorce rate? What is the common level of education? What is the dropout rate? What is the ratio of blue-collar to professional workers in the community? How does the education of those in law enforcement compare? What is the percentage of latchkey children? Such children may pose a significant challenge for police.

Income and income distribution are also important. Do great disparities exist? Would the community be described as affluent, moderately well-off or poor? How does the income of those in law enforcement compare? Closely related to income is the level of employment. How much unemployment exists? How do those who are unemployed exist? Are they on welfare? Do they commit crimes to survive? Are they homeless?

The ethnic makeup of the community is another consideration. Is the community basically homogeneous? A **homogeneous** community is one in which people are all quite similar. A **heterogeneous** community, in contrast, is one in which individuals are quite different from each other. Most communities are heterogeneous. Establishing and maintaining good relations among the various subgroups making up the community is a challenge. Usually one ethnic subgroup will have the most power and control. Consider the consequences if a majority of police officers are also members of this ethnic subgroup.

The existence of *ghettos* in many of our major cities poses extreme challenges for law enforcement. A **ghetto** is an area of a city usually inhabited by individuals of the same race or ethnic background who live in poverty and, to outsiders, apparent social disorganization. Consequently, ghettos, minorities and crime are frequently equated. Because ghettos are the focus of many anticrime efforts, this is often perceived as a clear bias by law enforcement against members of racial or ethnic minorities.

Poverty, unemployment, substandard housing and inadequate education have all figured into theories on the causes of crime. They are often part of the underlying problems manifested in crime.

Hungry ghetto-dwellers search through trash bags for food on West Houston Street in New York City.

◑ A RAPIDLY CHANGING POPULATION

Communities have been undergoing tremendous changes in the past half century. As Table 3.1 shows, the white population has declined from consisting of 87 percent in 1950 to a projected 67 percent in 2010 and a slim majority of 51 percent by 2050. These distinctions may be blurred, however, as noted in "The Face of the U.S. Population in 2050" (1997, p. 113): "The growing rate of intermarriage among whites, blacks, Hispanics, and Asians (although most intermarriages are of whites with other groups) ensures that the future of the United States will not be a set of distinct cultures and languages, let alone a unique ethnic identification."

In addition to a change in ethnic makeup, the United States is also experiencing a widening of the gap between those with wealth and those living in poverty. The middle class is shrinking, and the gap between the "haves" and the "have nots" is widening, resulting in a **bifurcated society.** According to the *New York Times* ("Gap between Rich, Poor. . . ," 1999, p. A11): "The gap between rich and poor has grown into an economic chasm so wide that this year the richest 2.7 million Americans, the top 1 percent, will have as much after-tax money to spend as the bottom 100 million. . . . The data show that income disparity has grown so much that four out of five households, or about 217 million people, are taking home a thinner slice of the economic pie today than in 1977."

The following trends in the United States are likely to continue: The minority population will increase, and white dominance will end; the number of legal and illegal immigrants will increase, and the elderly population will increase. Wilson (1998, pp. 10–13) cites seven population trends in the 21st century:

- Trend One: For dropouts and unskilled workers, finding family wage jobs with benefits will become more difficult.

- Trend Two: The number of youths failing school will continue to escalate without changes in school policies, tutorial support systems, and parental involvement.

- Trend Three: The high incarceration rates of the 1990s will result in a flood of unemployed releases from prisons and jails in the next two decades.

Table 3.1   U.S. Population by Race and Hispanic Origin: Observed Population, 1950–1995; Projected Population, 2000–2050 (percentage of total population)

	1950	1970	1990	1995	2010	2030	2050
Total[a]	100	100	100	100	100	100	100
White	87	83	76	74	67	59	51
Black	10	11	12	12	13	13	14
Asian	1	1	3	3	5	7	8
Hispanic	3	5	9	10	14	20	26

[a]The total U.S. population includes American Indians, Eskimos, and Aleuts.
SOURCE: *The New Americans: Economic, Demographic, and Fiscal Effects of Immigration.* Washington, DC: National Academy Press, 1997, p. 121.

- Trend Four: There is an increase in the number of fatherless children, who are more prone to delinquency and other social pathologies.
- Trend Five: There is an increase in the number of high-poverty areas.
- Trend Six: Community abandonment. (Frustrated criminal justice, housing, and economic development officials often view communities with very high rates of crime, housing abandonment, substance abuse, and gangs as beyond help.)
- Trend Seven: Without policies to correct asset deficiencies, an increasing percentage of families will not achieve self-sufficiency and efforts to revitalize poor communities will continue to have limited success.

Wilson (p. 14) concludes: "Our real crime reduction and community revitalization challenges involve finding ways to reduce poverty, the number of high-poverty communities, family disintegration, and the number of young people entering criminal careers."

◆ ORGANIZATIONS AND INSTITUTIONS

In addition to understanding the demographics of the community and being able to relate to a great variety of individuals, police officers must also be knowledgeable of the various organizations and institutions within the community and establish effective relationships with them. Effective policing requires involving social services, schools, health services, businesses, employment offices and government agencies.

A strong network of community organizations and institutions fosters a cohesiveness and shared intolerance of criminal behavior and encourages citizens to cooperate in controlling crime, thereby increasing the likelihood that illegal acts will be detected and reported. These networks and partnerships are essential, for no single organization or group is able to address all the problems and concerns of a community. And all the organizations and groups working *beyond* their individual capacity are unable to do more than apply localized, specific band-aid solutions to the total community problems.

Organizations and institutions can play a key role in enhancing community safety and quality of life.

Sulton (1990, p. 3) stresses that: "Community institutions are the basic fabric from which our complex society is woven." Thus, it is society itself that encourages or discourages conditions related to crime. According to Sulton (p. 1):

All theories of causes of crime share common threads. They assume that crime is a socially defined phenomenon caused by the failure of community institutions to constrain behavior so that it conforms to the law and does not threaten the rights, safety, and lives of others. According to this perspective, crime reduction depends on eradication of the social conditions that produce crime.

A good relationship between the schools in the community and the police is vital to maintaining order. Other organizations and institutions that police officers should interact effectively with include the Department of Human Services, health care providers, emergency services providers and any agencies working with youths. Communities may also have libraries, museums and zoos that would welcome a good relationship with the police. Such cooperation often poses problems, however, as Wilson and Kelling (1989, p. 52) note:

> The problem of interagency cooperation may, in the long run, be the most difficult of all. The police can bring problems to the attention of other city agencies, but the system is not always organized to respond. In his book *Neighborhood Services*, John Mudd calls it the "rat problem": "If a rat is found in an apartment, it is a housing inspection responsibility; if it runs into a restaurant, the health department has jurisdiction; if it goes outside and dies in an alley, public works takes over." A police officer who takes public complaints about rats seriously will go crazy trying to figure out what agency in the city has responsibility for rat control and then inducing it to kill the rats.

In other words, if responsibility is fragmented, little gets accomplished.

THE PUBLIC-PRIVATE POLICING INTERACTION

A good relationship between the private security industry and the police is also becoming more important. Many communities and even police departments are using **privatization,** contracting with private security agencies or officers to provide services typically considered to be law enforcement functions. Examples of privatization include prisoner transport and prisoner housing.

Many police departments are also relinquishing responsibility for responding to home security alarms to private security firms. The number of false alarms generated by private alarm systems is staggering and severely depletes the resources of many police departments. As one municipality, population approximately 45,000, reports ("To Be or Not to Be . . . ," 2000, p. 1):

> When properly installed, used and maintained, alarms can be a real asset to a community. When misused or neglected, they become a liability. In 1999, the [Apple Valley (Minnesota) Police Department] responded to over 1200 false alarms and billed $14,000 for this service. . . .
>
> Responding to false alarms wastes time and money for officers who are sworn to protect. . . . Repeat false alarms also create a level of complacency for the officers responding.

The need for public and private police forces to establish good working relationships was recognized by the National Institute of Justice in the early 1980s when it began urging cooperation between the agencies and established the Joint Council of Law Enforcement and Private Security Association.

The International Association of Chiefs of Police (IACP) has also recognized this need for cooperation by establishing a Private Sector Liaison Committee (PSLC). According to Reader and Martin (1999, p. 28): "The PSLC's mission is to tackle issues that can best be solved by having the public and private sector jointly address concerns and work together towards solutions."

Foote (1999, p. 61) also suggests the importance of public and private partnerships: "By pairing the knowledge and expertise of police departments with the technological capacity of private sector security companies, all parties win with more effective and efficient systems that reduce crime and increase public safety in the community." Seamon (1999, p. 17) further suggests: "The past two decades have seen a dramatic expansion of private security worldwide, greatly outpacing the growth of public law enforcement. There are compelling reasons to promote the collaboration of private security and public law enforcement for the advancement of public safety." In fact, as Slahor (1997, p. 31) concludes: "The future safety and security of people and property will depend on a partnership between the police and private security."

Unfortunately, police often view private security employees as poorly trained, poorly paid individuals who could not land a police job. Names such as "rent-a-cop" and "cop-in-a-box" add to this negative perception. Despite this image, private security plays a major role in safeguarding Americans and their property.

◈ THE POWER STRUCTURE

Most communities have both a formal and an informal power structure.

The formal power structure *includes divisions of society with wealth and political influence such as federal, state and local agencies and governments, commissions and regulatory agencies.*

The public can usually readily identify the formal power structure. Often policy decisions made at the federal and state level directly affect local decisions. In addition, federal and state funding can directly influence local programs.

The informal power structure *includes religious groups, wealthy subgroups, ethnic groups, political groups and public interest groups.*

The public cannot as readily identify the informal power structure, which includes banks, real estate companies and other large and influential businesses in a community. The informal power structure is not merely a few people controlling the masses; rather, the control groups are entire subcultures that influence other subcultures. It has been alleged that four hundred families control the wealth of the United States, affecting every other subculture. Awareness of the way informal groups, especially wealthy and political groups, exercise their ideologies is important. How informal group pressure is forced into an organization's formal structure is key to understanding why the community at large often conflicts with the criminal justice system.

Wilson and Kelling (1982, p. 34) suggest: "The essence of the police role in maintaining order is to reinforce the informal control mechanisms of the community itself. The police cannot, without committing extraordinary resources, provide a substitute for that informal control."

Law enforcement personnel must understand the different subgroups within their jurisdiction and the power struggles that occur among them. They must also be aware of this reality: Democracy does not always ensure equality. Although most cultures do not readily adapt to the white, middle-class style of living, in most communities that is where the power lies.

Each community is a distinct social system and, as such, has certain elements that cause and influence needs and affect ways in which needs are served and problems are solved. The elements of a community social system include: *Goals, ends and objectives*— what members of the community social system expect to accomplish or gain from being a part of the system. Norms—the written and unwritten rules that describe what is socially acceptable and what is not. Status roles—the expectations for the various positions in the system, including perceptions of employment and family roles of men and women. Power—control over people or resources. In a community social system different types and levels of authority and influence affect the way the system operates. Social rank—the subtle and not-so-subtle rankings of worth attached to individuals in the system, often based on wealth, education, church affiliation and group membership. Facilities and resources—the means available to a system to attain its ends.

◈ THE CRIMINAL JUSTICE SYSTEM

Many people equate policing or law enforcement with the criminal justice system when, in fact, it is only one part of this system. The other two components, courts and corrections, are much less visible in most communities. But because the police are the most visible component of the system, they often become *the* criminal justice system in the eyes of the community.

In the criminal justice process, the role of law enforcement is to detect or act on reports of law violations, to apprehend suspects reasonably believed responsible for such violations and to bring those suspects/defendants before a court of law. The court then assesses the charge and the evidence as presented by both the prosecution, for which the police officer may be a witness, and the defense to determine the defendant's guilt or innocence. If found guilty of the charge the offender may be sentenced by the court to confinement in a correctional facility or be allowed to return to the community under supervision.

This three-part system provides a procedure of checks and balances intended to ensure that no person is accused of a crime and then deprived of freedom without every reasonable step being taken to guarantee fairness and equity throughout the process, guarantees consistent with the Fourteenth Amendment requirements of the "due process" and "equal protection" clauses. The courts are often criticized by the public as being the weak link in the criminal justice process, letting too many offenders off easy and allowing wealthy defendants to buy their way out of convictions. Those who criticize judges usually do so based on whether they agree with a judge's procedures and sentencing practices. But critics must remember that the system is designed to work the way it does. After all, if we assumed that everyone arrested by the police is guilty of a crime, there would be no need for prosecutors, judges, juries or courtrooms. The accused could be taken directly to prison.

Many people have a limited understanding of the role the courts and corrections play in crime control. Indeed, at times various components of the criminal justice system seem to work against each other. When the perception or the reality is that criminals are not being convicted or are being released early from prison, some people demand more police and ask why they are not doing their job.

Members of the law enforcement community often become frustrated by such attitudes and incidents. Decisions made in court can discourage officers, who may become cynical and wonder why they work so hard to make arrests when they see cases dismissed or plea bargained. Officers may also become frustrated when those who are convicted are given a light sentence or probation. Officers may be further aggravated by what they view as inadequacies of the corrections system, aware of the many career criminals whose behavior has not improved even after they have been through prison, probation, parole, halfway houses and rehabilitation programs. But officers are not alone in their disappointment. The public, too, can be frustrated by the performance of the courts and corrections.

The public has a negative opinion of the courts because of their failure to process cases promptly, their inconsistency in plea bargaining and the long tenure accorded to judges. Many believe that the courts provide "assembly-line" justice, and the legal process is filled with delays. Aspects of the correctional system that have impeded good public relations include failures to reform offenders, the early release of recidivists and the growing prison population.

To help overcome negative opinions and improve public relations, agencies within the criminal justice system are now actively seeking partnerships with others in the community. Jurik et al. (2000, pp. 293–294) note that community partnerships have become increasingly popular and that: "Crime prevention partnerships that join criminal justice agencies to work with business, university, or other community members have been a prominent part of this trend." They studied a community-criminal justice partnership between a western university (WU) and a juvenile corrections agency (JCA) over four years. They (p. 313) concluded:

> Partnerships offer the promise of an organizational niche to work partially inside, partially outside, and partially across large bureaucracies. From this niche, change agents may circumvent obstacles faced by others working entirely in or outside of existing organizations. In a partnership model, change agents may more easily develop a nexus of support for transforming organizations and communities.
>
> With regard to the inculcation of a community research-service ethos at WU, the WU-JCA partnership was highly successful. Faculty members and students became involved in the community, a service learning curricula was adopted, and spin-off community service and research opportunities prospered at WU. The commitment of resources by several top WU administrators greatly encouraged this community-oriented ethos.

What constitutes good criminal justice administration is open to debate. Numerous controversial issues related to the effectiveness of the criminal justice system affect police-community partnerships. Although many issues are outside police officers' appropriate sphere of action, they affect the system as a whole. Therefore, police officers need to be aware of these issues and their potential impact.

Controversial issues in the criminal justice system that affect police-community partnerships include plea bargaining, diversion, sentencing, rehabilitation, community alternatives to prisons, victims' rights and capital punishment.

Plea Bargaining. Plea bargaining is a practice by which prosecutors charge a defendant with a less serious crime in exchange for a guilty plea, thus eliminating the time and expense of a trial.

Diversion. Diversion is a system operating in most states that "diverts" juvenile status offenders and delinquents from the jurisdiction of the courts, whenever possible. This practice evolved because, once juvenile delinquents are labeled, they tend to act out and perpetuate that negative role.

Sentencing. Judges often have considerable discretion in sentencing. When the community perceives sentences as too lenient, it sparks controversy. Police officers often believe that sentences are too light for serious crimes.

Rehabilitation. One objective of the correction process is rehabilitation, an objective that many have come to believe is an unattainable goal. The **recidivism,** or repeat offense rate of criminal behavior, is very high.

Community Alternatives to Prison. Among the alternatives to prison are community supervision programs, including probation or parole, halfway houses and house arrest with electronic monitoring. Community supervision seeks to help offenders become productive, law-abiding members of the community while alleviating the burden of correctional overcrowding and the expense of incarceration. These alternatives become especially controversial when a community must determine the location of the facilities. Citizens often have the **NIMBY syndrome,** that is, "not in my backyard."

Victims' Rights. As violent crime increases, a growing number of people are protesting the treatment of victims by the criminal justice system. The law enforcement community has responded to this protest in a number of ways, as discussed in Chapter 7.

Capital Punishment. The debate continues on the merits and effectiveness of capital punishment as a deterrent to crime and a form of retribution.

Other Issues. Another controversial issue in the criminal justice system is that it has operated reactively, concentrating its efforts on fighting crime to keep the "public peace" and allowing police officers to function as armed social workers. Many believe the system has been short-sighted, focusing almost exclusively on detecting individual offenses and specific ways to eliminate each crime instead of concentrating on developing strategies to proactively attack the syndromes of crime. A **syndrome of crime** is a group of signs, causes and symptoms that occur together to foster specific crimes. The syndromes of crime are central to problem-oriented policing, discussed in detail in Chapter 4.

Another issue within the criminal justice system has been a shift in basic philosophy from a *medical model* to a *justice model.*

The medical model *sees those who break the law as victims of society; the* justice model *views lawbreakers as responsible for their own actions.*

No longer will society take the blame for individual criminals. Justice is served by having individuals be responsible for their own actions and suffer the consequences when they break the law. This change in philosophy is likely to enhance relations between those in the criminal justice system and law-abiding citizens.

In addition, a new meaning has been attached to the medical model, equating it with the way health maintenance organizations (HMOs) are approaching medicine from a preventive stance. As Harpold (p. 23) notes:

> Police departments would do well to take their cues from the medical profession. Physicians know a great deal about disease and the nature of injuries; they treat patients based on the collective knowledge and experience in the treatment of illness. They observe the symptoms present in the patient, diagnose the disease, prescribe the treatment, then monitor the patient's progress. At the same time, they practice preventive medicine and educate the public. To treat the causes of illness in the community, the police must do the same.

A relatively new approach being taken by some in the criminal justice system is that of *restorative justice.*

◈ RESTORATIVE JUSTICE

Restorative justice can be traced back to the Code of Hammurabi in 2000 B.C. This type of justice holds offenders accountable to the victim and the victim's community, rather than to the state. Rather than seeking retribution (punishment), it seeks restitution—to repair the damages as much as possible and to restore the victim, the community and the offender. Under common law, criminals were often required to reimburse victims for their losses. Beginning in the twelfth century, however, under William the Conqueror, crimes were considered offenses against the king's peace, with offenders ordered to pay fines to the state. This tradition was brought to the United States. In the 1970s, reformers began trying to change the emphasis of the criminal justice system from the offender back to the victim. The Victim Witness Protection Act of 1982 marked the reemergence of the victim in the criminal justice process.

Restorative justice *advocates a balanced approach to sentencing that involves offenders, victims, local communities and government to alleviate crime and violence and obtain peaceful communities.*

Table 3.2 summarizes the differences between the traditional retributive approach to justice and restorative justice.

According to Bilchik (1998, p. 5): "The community is responsible for the well-being of all its members, including both victim and offender." Figure 3.1 illustrates the restorative justice approach.

Levrant et al. (1999, p. 3) suggest: "Restorative justice has emerged as an increasingly popular correctional paradigm that is drawing support not only from conservatives but

Table 3.2 Paradigms of Justice—Old and New

Old Paradigm Retributive Justice	New Paradigm Restorative Justice
1. Crime defined as violation of the state	1. Crime defined as violation of one person by another
2. Focus on establishing blame, on guilt, on past (did he/she do it?)	2. Focus on problem solving, on liabilities and obligations, on future (what should be done?)
3. Adversarial relationships and process normative	3. Dialogue and negotiation normative
4. Imposition of pain to punish and deter/prevent	4. Restitution as a means of restoring both parties; reconciliation/restoration as goal
5. Justice defined by intent and by process: right rules	5. Justice defined as right relationships; judged by the outcome
6. Interpersonal, conflictual nature of crime obscured, repressed; conflict seen as individual vs. state	6. Crime recognized as interpersonal conflict; value of conflict recognized
7. One social injury replaced by another	7. Focus on repair of social injury
8. Community on sidelines, represented abstractly by state	8. Community as facilitator in restorative process
9. Encouragement of competitive, individualistic values	9. Encouragement of mutuality
10. Action directed from state to offender: • victim ignored • offender passive	10. Victim's and offender's roles recognized in both problem and solution: • victim rights/needs recognized • offender encouraged to take responsibility
11. Offender accountability defined as taking punishment	11. Offender accountability defined as understanding impact of action and helping decide how to make things right
12. Offense defined in purely legal terms, devoid of moral, social, economic, political dimensions	12. Offense understood in whole context—moral, social, economic, political
13. "Debt" owed to state and society in the abstract	13. Debt/liability to victim recognized
14. Response focused on offender's past behavior	14. Response focused on harmful consequences of offender's behavior
15. Stigma of crime unremovable	15. Stigma of crime removable through restorative action
16. No encouragement for repentance and forgiveness	16. Possibilities for repentance and forgiveness
17. Dependence upon proxy professionals	17. Direct involvement by participants

SOURCE: Howard Zehr. *IARCA Journal*, March 1991, p. 7. Used by permission of the International Association of Residential and Community Alternatives.

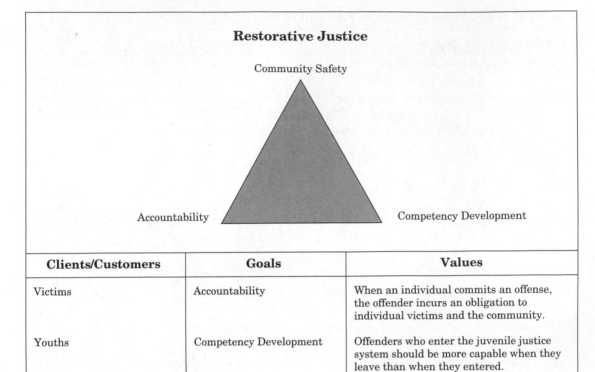

Figure 3.1 Restorative Justice Approach

Adapted from Maloney, D.; Romig D.; and Armstrong, T. 1998. *Juvenile Probation: The Balanced Approach.* Reno, NV: National Council of Juvenile and Family Court Judges.
SOURCE: Shay Bilchik. *Guide for Implementing the Balanced and Restorative Justice Model.* Washington, DC: Office of Juvenile Justice and Delinquency Prevention, December 1998, p. 6.

also from liberals." The most common forms of restorative sentences include restitution (payments to victims) and community service. Other restorative justice practices include victim impact statements, family group conferences, sentencing circles and citizen reparative boards.

Outlaw and Ruback (1999, p. 847) explored the factors related to the imposition of victim restitution, the factors related to the payment of victim restitution, and the effects of restitution on future arrests. Their results ($n = 481$) indicated that "judges ordered restitution most often when damages were easy to quantify and that offenders were most likely to make payment when they were able to pay and when the victim was a business. Restitution payment was related negatively to rearrest." Their research indicated that successful completion of a restitution order was one of the strongest predictors of lowered recidivism, especially for those who were more fully integrated into the community, that is, older, married and employed.

Helfgott et al. (2000, p. 5) conducted a pilot study of citizens, victims and offenders participating in a restorative justice program at the Washington State Reformatory. The results showed that the program was effective in meeting the four goals established: "The seminar provided a safe environment for inmates to begin making amends for their crimes and for victims to heal, facilitated constructive communication between polarized groups, and encouraged participants to develop creative ways of thinking about justice and strategies for dealing with crime."

Quinn (1998, p. 11) sees restorative justice as a form of community justice. He (p. 13) notes that in one study, 50 percent fewer victims who participated in mediation expressed fear of revictimization by the same offender when compared to victims who did not participate in mediation. In addition, offenders were more likely to understand the impact of their crime and to have a heightened sense of responsibility. Quinn also cited studies indicating that recidivism for offenders who participated in restorative justice activities was lower than for comparison groups of like offenders processed regularly.

CITIZEN/COMMUNITY INVOLVEMENT

Once upon a time, when food resources in a village were seemingly gone, a creative individual—knowing that each person always has a little something in reserve—proposed that the community make *stone soup.*

After a stone was set to boil, people in the community were asked if they had "just a little something" to improve the soup. One person found a carrot, another brought a few potatoes, another a bit of meat and so on. When the soup was finished, it was thick and nourishing. Such is the situation in our communities today. Because resources are stretched to the limit, we tend to hold on to our time, talent or money. These self-protective actions leave most groups without enough resources to effectively handle community problems. Perhaps it is time to adopt the "stone soup" stance of cooperation.

As noted in *Understanding Community Policing* (1994, p. 4): "Community policing is democracy in action. It requires the active participation of local government, civic and business leaders, public and private agencies, residents, churches, schools and hospitals. All who share a concern for the welfare of the neighborhood should bear responsibility for safeguarding that welfare."

Citizen/community involvement has taken the form of civilian review boards, citizen patrols and citizen police academies.

Civilian Review Boards

The movement for citizen review has been a major political struggle for over 40 years and remains one of the most controversial issues in police work today. Supporters of civilian review boards believe it is impossible for the police to objectively review actions of their colleagues and emphasize that the police culture demands police officers support each other, even if they know something illegal has occurred. Opponents of civilian review boards stress that civilians cannot possibly understand the complexities of the policing profession and that it is demeaning to be reviewed by an external source. And although police unions have bitterly opposed civilian review throughout the country, Bayley (1998, p. 3) notes: "Civilian review of police discipline, once considered anathema, has gradually become accepted by police."

Walker (2001, p. 2–1) outlines the history of civilian review as falling into three broad periods:

> Between the 1920s and the mid-1950s, oversight first emerged as a radical idea, and after World War II was eventually embodied in a few experimental agencies. In the second period, from the late 1950s through the 1960s, civilian review as it was called, became one of the major demands of civil rights leaders. Extremely bitter conflicts over this issue erupted in Philadelphia and New York City. The demise of review boards in those two cities by the end of the decade appeared to signal the death of citizen oversight. The third period began with the quiet revival of oversight in 1969 with the creation of the Kansas City Office of Citizen Complaints and continues to the present day.

Currently, most departments handle officer discipline internally, with department personnel investigating complaints against officers and determining whether misconduct occurred. Finn (2000), however, notes that the 1990s showed a "considerable increase" in citizen oversight of the police. He (p. 22) describes the four main types of oversight systems:

- Citizens investigate allegations of police misconduct and recommend a finding to the head of the agency.
- Officers investigate allegations and develop findings. Then, citizens review and recommend that the head of the agency approve or reject the findings.
- Complainants may appeal findings established by the agency to citizens who review them and make recommendations to the head of the agency.
- An auditor investigates the process the agency uses to accept and investigate complaints and reports to the agency and the community the thoroughness and fairness of the process.

In Favor of Civilian Oversight. Citizens who demand to be involved in the review process maintain that internal police discipline is tantamount to allowing the "fox to investigate thefts in the chicken coop." According to these citizens, police protect each other and cover up improper or illegal conduct. Citizens believe that this perpetuates abuses and sends a message to brutal officers that their behavior will be shielded from public scrutiny.

Law Enforcement News ("Who's Watching the Watchers? Everyone," 1999, p. 1) reported: "The belief that police departments are capable of policing themselves took a withering barrage of hits in 1999." On the East coast an unarmed street peddler, Amadou Diallo, was fatally shot by members of the New York PD plainclothes Street Crimes Unit; on the West coast the drug-corruption scandal in the Los Angeles PD broke.

In some larger cities, police have lost the power to investigate complaints against fellow officers. The trend is toward more openness and citizen involvement in these matters. Officers should assume that they will be required to be more accountable for their actions. Officers may be held to a higher standard and will need to be prepared to justify their use of force in certain situations.

Finn (p. 26) describes ways citizen oversight can benefit police agencies, including "bettering an agency's image with the community, enhancing an agency's ability to police itself, and, most important, improving an agency's policies and procedures." He (p. 27) concludes: "If both sides make a sincere and sustained effort to work together, citizen oversight can help law enforcement administrators perform their jobs more effectively and with increased public support."

Walker (p. 1–3) believes that the problem of police misconduct is *not a matter of a few rotten apples but of failed organizations.* He suggests citizen oversight is "a means . . . for changing police organizations in order to reduce officer misconduct." Walker (p. 1–4) defines citizen oversight as "a procedure for providing input into the complaint process by individuals who are not sworn officers." He (p. 1–15) suggests:

> It [citizen oversight] represents a form of political control by adding a new mechanism for direct citizen input into police matters. It resembles the judicial control of police behavior by creating a quasi-judicial process of investigating and adjudicating complaints. It incorporates aspects of professional police management by strengthening the disciplinary process. And it parallels community policing by emphasizing citizen input into policing.

Walker (p. 1–16) summarizes the arguments of advocates for citizen oversight:

- That police misconduct is a serious problem and that internal police complaint procedures fail to address this problem.
- That citizen oversight will provide more thorough and fair investigation of complaints than those conducted by the police themselves.
- That citizen oversight agencies will sustain more complaints.
- That oversight agencies will result in more discipline of guilty officers.
- That more disciplinary actions will deter police misconduct more effectively than internal police procedures.
- That complaint review by oversight agencies will be perceived as independent and will provide greater satisfaction for complainants and also improve public attitudes about the police.
- That citizen oversight will help professionalize police departments and improve the quality of policing.

Some have even suggested removing review from the local level and elevating it to state authorities: "Due to the common reluctance of local district or county attorneys to prosecute police officers accused of human rights violations, each state should create a special prosecutor's office to handle criminal prosecutions of officers accused of criminal acts, including cases of brutality and corruption" (Human Rights Watch, 1998, p. 1).

In Opposition to Civilian Oversight. Theoretically, citizen review boards offer an efficient and effective means of identifying officer misdeeds and reconciling them to the satisfaction of the community at large. However, although civilian review boards may be good in theory, they are often poor in reality. They frequently fail to operate objectively, lack impartial or specialized agents to conduct essential investigations, and are devoid of any enforcement power needed to carry out their recommendations. Furthermore, the people who volunteer to serve on the board are not necessarily representative of the community and, in many cases, are "vocal rabble rousers" who wish to impose their values upon the community. Opponents to civilian review boards cite such shortcomings as reasons to do without these ineffectual entities.

Police often maintain it would be unfair to allow those outside police work to judge their actions because only police officers understand the complexities of their job and, in particular, how and when they must use force. They stress that few citizens understand such concepts as "command presence" and "verbal force" so often necessary in high-risk encounters. As one police sergeant put it: "The public should walk a mile in our combat boots before they judge us."

Walker (p. 1–17) also summarizes the arguments of opponents of citizen oversight who believe that oversight achieves none of its goals and often makes matters worse:

- That police misconduct is not as serious a problem as people allege.
- That police officers are capable of and do in fact conduct fair and thorough investigations.
- That police internal affairs units sustain a higher rate of complaints than do citizen oversight agencies.
- That police departments mete out tougher discipline than oversight agencies.
- That internal police disciplinary procedures deter police misconduct more effectively than oversight agencies.
- That internal police disciplinary procedures provide greater satisfaction to complainants and the general public.
- That external citizen oversight agencies harm policing by deterring effective crime-fighting by police officers and also by undermining the managerial authority of police chief executives.

Opponents also argue that citizen oversight has resulted in corruption and inefficiency and that police should have full responsibility for managing their own conduct just as other professionals such as physicians and lawyers do.

Striking a Balance. Successful resolution of this issue requires that the concerns of both the community and the police be addressed. The desired outcome would be that the police maintain the ability to perform their duties without the fear that they will be second-guessed, disciplined or sued by those who do not understand the difficulties of their job *and* that citizens are not brutally or disrespectfully treated by officers.

The key, according to Walker (p. 1–21) is that successful oversight agencies do more than simply investigate complaints: "They take a proactive view of their role and actively seek out the underlying causes of police misconduct or problems with the complaint process." He (p. 7–12) concludes:

The effectiveness of an oversight agency depends on its formal structure and the power it possesses, the activities it engages in, the quality of its leadership, the support it receives from the public and the responsible elected officials, and the attitude of the law enforcement agency it is responsible for overseeing. But embracing all of these elements, and ultimately more important than any one of them, is the vision that guides an oversight agency. That vision must include a commitment to holding the police accountable for their actions and the administrative wisdom to create the policies and procedures to ensure that accountability will be enhanced.

As a final thought we should again warn that oversight is no panacea. Police misconduct will not disappear over night. Nor should we realistically expect that it will ever be completely ended. But we can realistically expect that it can be substantially reduced, to the point where ordinary citizens can expect to be treated with dignity and respect by the police, and not have to live in fear of physical abuse or rude and insulting treatment. And that, ultimately, is the goal of citizen oversight of the police: a civilized society served by a civil police.

Citizen Patrol

Community policing is rooted in law enforcement's dependence on the public's eyes, ears, information and influence to exert social control. Nonetheless, it is sometimes difficult for citizen volunteers to win the respect and support of the police, who often have strong opinions about civilian involvement in what they consider "police business."

The Elliot Lake Police Service in Ontario has a C.O.P. program, which trains members of the community to patrol their neighborhoods in cars and report suspicious activities to the police via cellular phones or radios. The cars and the cellular communication systems are supplied by the police.

Many of the citizen patrols established throughout the country focus on the drug problem. For example, the Fairlawn Coalition in Washington, DC, established nightly patrol groups to walk the streets of Fairlawn and act as a deterrent to drug trafficking. Wearing bright orange hats, the citizen patrols drove drug dealers from their positions simply by standing out on the streets with them and later by bringing in video cameras, still cameras and much publicity. The citizen group decided not to invite the Guardian Angels or Nation of Islam to help them, fearing their aggressive tactics could escalate into violence. They chose instead to include men and women aged 40 and older to create a presence on the street but to pose no threat to the physical well-being of dealers.

The Blockos in Manhattan, New York, used a similar approach. To combat street-level drug dealing in their middle-class neighborhood, residents held some meetings and decided to go out into the street as a group and stand near the dealers. They also had a graphic artist provide posters to announce their meetings, and a member persuaded the *New York Times* to publish a story on their efforts.

Another tactic was used in Manhattan by a group called 210 Stanton, referring to the address of a building that was headquarters of a major drug-selling operation. Community patrol officers guarded the entrances to the building, requiring all visitors to sign in. If the visitors were going to the apartment where the drug dealing was occurring, officers accompanied them. In addition, information provided by residents helped solidify the case against the apartment where most of the drug dealing was taking place. Search warrants were issued, charges filed and the resident convicted.

In Brooklyn, New York, five Muslims founded Umma, meaning "community" in Arabic and Swahili, to reduce crime and improve the quality of life in their neighborhood. This organization began two-person patrols to break up sidewalk dice shooting, reduce the volume on blaring radios, walk children to and from school, and report burglaries and drug sales to police. Umma worked closely with police to develop a neighborhood crime hotline as well as short- and long-term antidrug strategies. This relationship helped others become more accepting of the police, and the police, in turn, came to trust Umma members.

Some citizen groups have exchange programs to reduce the chance of retribution by local drug retailers. Such exchange programs provide nearby neighborhoods with additional patrols while reducing the danger. Local dealers were less likely to recognize a vigil-keeper who lived in another neighborhood.

Citizen Police Academies

Another type of community involvement is through citizens' police academies, a relatively recent innovation designed to familiarize citizens with law enforcement and to keep the department in touch with the community.

The first recorded U.S. citizen police academy (CPA) began in 1985 in Orlando, Florida. This program was modeled after a citizen police academy in England, which began in 1977. Maffe and Burke (1999, p. 77) suggest: "Police 'academies' for citizens are the latest hot item for law enforcement." In fact, Kanable (1999, p. 56) believes: "If citizen police academies were graded, there's no doubt they'd receive an A+ from law enforcement officers throughout the nation." Such academies help a community's residents become more familiar with the day-to-day operations of their police department and to understand the procedures, responsibilities and demands placed on their officers. Maffe and Burke contend: "The benefits of a citizen police academy are significant and foremost in the power of proactive policing within the community. . . . Proactive law enforcement, such as a police citizen academy, places officers in a positive light. Understanding and cooperating with citizens is vital for effective police-community relations."

Kanable (p. 57) contends: "Although the concept of what the citizen police academy is all about is consistent across the nation, the curricula are as different as the departments putting them together. The Toledo (Ohio) Citizen Police Academy introduces participants to community-oriented problem solving; the K-9 unit and a firearms safety demonstration. Other topics include police ethics, discipline policy and philosophy, communications, drug enforcement and education, and criminal and traffic law. It includes a ride-along as well ("The Citizen Academy").

The Sedgwick County Sheriff's Department Citizen Police Academy has won national recognition. Its 13-week program's purpose is: "To develop a harmonious working relationship between members of the community and law enforcement while at the same time opening a mutually supportive avenue for communication" ("Sedgwick County Sheriff's . . .").

Table 3.3 Typical Agenda of a 12- to 13-Week CPA

I. Administration and Professional Standards
  - Introduction and welcome from the chief
  - Administrative information and department overview
  - Officer selection
  - Ethics
  - Internal affairs
  - History of policing

II. Operations
  - Field training
  - Patrol procedures
  - Communications
  - Ride-alongs
  - Traffic law and radar operation
  - Accident investigations
  - Officer safety/use of force
  - Driving while intoxicated enforcement
  - K-9 operations
  - Firearms
  - Tactical demonstrations

III. Investigations
  - Child abuse/family violence
  - Narcotics
  - Criminal investigations

IV. Legal Issues
  - Criminal justice system
  - Juvenile law
  - Probation/parole
  - Corrections

V. Crime Prevention
  - Drug Awareness Resistance Education/Gang Resistance Education and Training Program
  - Neighborhood Crime Watch
  - Citizens on Patrol
  - Auto theft prevention
  - Target hardening/insurance reduction surveys

VI. Special Topics
  - Federal and state criminal justice system and agencies
  - Economics of crime
  - Criminology
  - Citizen police academy alumni association information
  - Forensic hypnosis
  - Emergency medical services
  - Special weapons and tactics

SOURCE: Giant Abutalebi Aryani et al. "The Citizen Police Academy: Success through Community Partnerships." *FBI Law Enforcement Bulletin,* Vol. 69, No. 5, May 2000, p. 19.

"Building the Trust" (1999, p. 60) describes the 12-week academy of the Fond du Lac County (Wisconsin) Sheriff's Department, which includes community services, civil process, the dive team, the boat patrol, the K-9 unit, drugs, patrol, domestics, SWAT, emergency communication, corrections, crime-scene processing, investigations/interrogations, arson, surveillance and the criminal justice system. Table 3.3 presents a typical agenda of a 12- to 13-week CPA.

The San Luis Obispo County Sheriff's Citizen Academy provides community members with an inside look at the sheriff's office, law enforcement ethics, criminal law, investigations, patrol procedures, communications, crime prevention, drug enforcement and drug education.

Maffe and Burke (p. 80) note that citizen police academies have limitations. First, although attendees may sign "hold-harmless" waivers, the agency may still find itself with a lawsuit if a participant is injured or killed while attending the academy. Second, officers and administrators may resist developing or participating in an academy, feeling law enforcement activities should not be open to the public. Third, an agency may lack resources needed to provide a citizen academy. Finally, a graduate might abuse the information gained through this program. To minimize this final limitation, any department establishing a citizen police academy should conduct thorough background checks on all applicants.

Typical requirements for admission to a citizen police academy include a minimum age of 21 years, living or working in the department's jurisdiction and no prior felony convictions or misdemeanor arrests within one year of application.

Aryani et al. (2000, p. 17) stress: "Like the police academy, success of the CPA depends on the administrative support, the strength of the curriculum and staff members, and the selection of students." They (p. 21) conclude: "Citizen police academies represent a vital part of community-oriented policing. CPAs keep the public involved by making them part of the police family."

Some departments, such as in Waco, Texas, and Hartford, Wisconsin, have Citizen Police Academy Alumni Associations to provide an opportunity for continued education in law enforcement and related fields. They also allow participants to have a more interactive association with the police department.

A twist on the citizens' academy is the Teen Citizen Academy of the Arroyo Grande Police Department. Designed for youths 13 to 18 years old, the academy provides an overview of topics such as gangs, drugs, weapons safety and personal safety.

Ride-Along Programs

Ride-along programs are a popular, yet controversial, means to improve police-community relations and get citizens involved in the efforts of the department and its officers. These programs are designed to give local citizens a close-up look at the realities of policing and what police work entails while giving officers a chance to connect with citizens in a positive way.

Many ride-along programs permit any responsible juvenile or adult to participate, but other programs have restrictions and may limit ridership. Participation by officers in a ride-along program is usually voluntary. Whether riders are allowed to use still or video cameras during a ride-along varies from department to department. Many departments also require their riders to dress appropriately.

Despite the numerous benefits of ride-along programs, some departments do not get involved for legitimate reasons such as insurance costs, liability and concerns about the public's safety. Some departments ask participants to sign a waiver exempting the officer, the department and the city from liability.

Sometimes a ride-along does more than foster police-community relations. In Denver, for example, officers who take clergy as riders have help with death notifications as well as a number of other situations, such as handling runaways, emotionally disturbed persons, victims of natural disasters, persons threatening suicide, substance abusers, child-abuse victims and victims of sexual assault. Boston's ride-along program with probation officers helps the police identify lawbreakers and gather information from those traveling in the same circles as offenders.

SUMMARY

Community policing must begin with an understanding of what communities are and how they function. Citizens of the United States have established the "public peace" through the U.S. Constitution and Bill of Rights, as well as through federal and state statutes and local ordinances. They also adhere to a social contract, which states that for everyone to receive justice, each person must give up some freedom.

Community refers to the specific geographic area served by a police department or law enforcement agency and the individuals, organizations and agencies within that area. Community also refers to a feeling of belonging—a sense of integration, a sense of shared values and a sense of "we-ness." The broken window phenomenon suggests that if it appears "no one cares," disorder and crime will thrive.

Understanding a community requires police to know about its demographics. Demographics include population or size, distribution, growth, density and vital statistics such as average age, average education and average income as well as employment rate and ethnic makeup. Three important changes that will alter the demographics of our communities are: (1) white dominance will end; minorities will increase, (2) the elderly population will increase, and (3) the number of legal and illegal immigrants will increase.

Organizations and institutions can play a key role in enhancing community safety and quality of life. The private security industry can also play an important role in improving a community's well-being.

Operating within each community is a power structure that can enhance or endanger police-community relations. The formal power structure includes those with wealth and political influence: federal, state and local agencies and governments, commissions, regulatory agencies and power groups. The informal power structure includes religious groups, wealthy subgroups, ethnic groups, political groups and public-interest groups.

Also operating within communities and affecting the police-community relationship tremendously is the criminal justice system, including the courts and corrections. Controversial issues in the criminal justice system that affect community policing include plea bargaining, diversion, sentencing, rehabilitation, community alternatives to prisons, victim's rights and capital punishment. The criminal justice system is moving away from a medical model of criminality to a justice model. The medical model sees those who break the law as victims of society; the justice model views lawbreakers as responsible for their own actions.

Restorative justice advocates a balanced approach to sentencing that involves offenders, victims, local communities and government to alleviate crime and violence and obtain peaceful communities. Other forms of citizen/community involvement include civilian review boards, citizen patrols and citizen police academies.

DISCUSSION QUESTIONS

1. How would you describe your community?
2. What instances of *broken windows* have you seen in your neighborhood? Other neighborhoods?
3. Can you give examples of the NIMBY syndrome?
4. What major changes have occurred in your community in the past 10 years? In your state?
5. Who is included in the power structure in your community?
6. Do you favor the medical model or the justice model for dealing with criminals? Why?

7. How extensively are the services of private security used in your community? Do they cooperate with or compete against the local police?

8. Do you favor use of civilian review boards? Why or why not?

9. Which seems more "just" to you: retributive justice or restorative justice?

10. What factors are most important in establishing a "sense of community"?

INFOTRAC COLLEGE EDITION ASSIGNMENTS

- Use InfoTrac to help answer the discussion questions as appropriate.
- Locate and outline two articles dealing with community leadership. Be prepared to share your outlines with the class.
- Research and outline your findings of at least one of the following subjects: broken windows, ghettos, restorative justice or social contract.

COMMUNITY PROJECT

Use your telephone directory to determine what city services/community resources are available locally. Select one to contact and determine what relationship (if any) exists between it and your local police department.

REFERENCES

Aryani, Giant Abutalebi; Garrett, Terry D.; and Alsabrook, Carl L. "The Citizen Police Academy: Success through Community Partnerships." *FBI Law Enforcement Bulletin,* Vol. 69, No. 5, May 2000, pp. 16–21.

Bayley, David H. "Policing in America: Assessment and Prospects." *Ideas in American Policing.* Washington, DC: Police Foundation, February 1998.

Bilchik, Shay. *Guide for Implementing the Balanced and Restorative Justice Model.* Washington, DC: Office of Juvenile Justice and Delinquency Prevention, December 1998.

"Building the Trust." *Law Enforcement Technology,* Vol. 26, No. 10, October 1999, p. 60.

"The Citizen Academy, Toledo, Ohio." www.tpd.toledo.oh.us/citz-acd.html

"Citizen Police Academy Alumni Association, Waco, Texas." www.accesswaco.com/ community/groups/Citizens PoliceAcademy/ index.html

Coleman, J. *Foundations of Social Theory.* Cambridge: Harvard University Press, 1990.

Community Police Partnerships for COP, Vol. II, June 1996. www.communitypolicing.org/ partners/index.html

Correia, Mark E. *Citizen Involvement: How Community Factors Affect Progressive Policing.* Washington, DC: Police Executive Research Forum, 2000.

Elliot Lake Police Service. C.O.P. (Citizens on Patrol). www.elliotlake.com/police/COP.htm. September 4, 2000.

"The Face of the U.S. Population in 2050." *The New Americans: Economic, Demographic, and Fiscal Effects of Immigration.* Washington, DC: National Academy Press, 1997, pp. 76–134.

Finn, Peter. "Getting Along with Citizen Oversight." *FBI Law Enforcement Bulletin,* Vol. 69, No. 8, August 2000, pp. 22–27.

Foote, Michael B. "Interactive Security: Police and Private Security Join Forces." *The Police Chief,* Vol. LXVI, No. 6, June 1999, pp. 57–61.

"Gap between Rich, Poor Has Become More Substantial." *New York Times.* Reprinted in (Minneapolis/St. Paul) *Star Tribune,* September 5, 1999, p. A11.

Gladwell, Malcolm. "The Tipping Point." *Subject to Debate,* October 1996, pp. 1, 4–6, 11.

Greene, Jack R. "Communities and Crime: Reflections on Strategies for Crime Control." *What Can the Federal Government Do to Decrease Crime and Revitalize Communities?* NIJ Research Forum, October 1998, pp. 45–51. (NCJ 172210)

Harpold, Joseph A. "A Medical Model for Community Policing." *FBI Law Enforcement Bulletin,* Vol. 69, No. 6, June 2000, pp. 23–27.

Helfgott, Jacqueline B.; Lovell, Madeline L.; Lawrence, Charles F.; and Parsonage, William H. "Results from the Pilot Study of the Citizens, Victims, and Offenders Restoring Justice Program at the Washington State Reformatory." *Journal of Contemporary Criminal Justice,* Vol. 16, No. 1, February 2000, pp. 5–31.

Human Rights Watch. "Shielded from Justice: Police Brutality and Accountability in the United States." *Reports 98,* 1998, pp. 1–3.

"Incivilities Play Less of a Role in Crime than 'Social Fabric,' According to Study." *NCJA Justice Bulletin,* Vol. 19, No. 11, November 1999, p. 12.

Jurik, Nancy C; Blumenthal, Joel; Smith, Brian; and Portillos, Edwardo L. "Organizational Cooptation or Social Change?" *Journal of Contemporary Criminal Justice,* Vol. 16, No. 3, August 2000, pp. 293–320.

Kanable, Rebecca. "An Apple for the Officer: Citizen Police Academies Keep Officers in Touch with the Community." *Law Enforcement Technology,* Vol. 26, No. 10, October 1999, pp. 56–57.

Levrant, Sharon; Cullen, Francis T.; Fulton, Betsy; and Wozniak, John F. "Reconsidering Restorative Justice: The Corruption of Benevolence Revisited?" *Crime and Delinquency,* Vol. 45, No. 1, January 1999, pp. 3–27.

Maffe, Steven R. and Burke, Tod W Police Academies." *Law and Or... No. 10, October 1999, pp. 77–80.

Outlaw, Maureen C. and Ruback, R. Barry. "Predators and Outcomes of Victim Restitution Orders." *Justice Quarterly,* Vol. 16, No. 4, December 1999, pp. 847–869.

Putnam, R. "Tuning In, Tuning Out: The Strange Disappearance of Social Capital in America." *PS: Political Science and Politics,* December 1995, pp. 664–683.

Quinn, Thomas. "Restorative Justice: An Interview with Visiting Fellow Thomas Quinn." *National Institute of Justice Journal,* March 1998, pp. 10–16.

Reader, Lockheed and Martin, Stan. "Public/Private Commitment = Significantly Fewer False Alarms." *The Police Chief,* Vol. LXVI, No. 6, June 1999, pp. 28–31.

Saville, Gregory. "Searching for a Neighborhood's Crime Threshold." *Subject to Debate,* October 1996, pp. 1, 7.

Seamon, Thomas. "Partners in Public Safety." *The Police Chief,* Vol. LXVI, No. 6, June 1999, pp. 17–21.

"Sedgwick County Sheriff's Department Citizen Police Academy." www.sedgwick.ks.us/sheriff/CPA/index.html

Skogan, Wesley G. "The Community's Role in Community Policing." *National Institute of Justice Journal,* August 1996, pp. 31–34.

Slahor, Stephenie. "Partners in Crimefighting: Police and Private Security." *Access Control,* July 1997, p. 31.

Sulton, Anne Thomas. *Inner-City Crime Control. Can Community Institutions Contribute?* Washington, DC: The Police Foundation, 1990.

"To Be or Not to Be . . . ALARMED!" *Apple Valley City News,* Summer 2000, p. 1.

"Tri-Community Citizen Police Academy, Hartford, Wisconsin." www.hartfordpolice.org/tri.htm

Understanding Community Policing. Washington, DC: Bureau of Justice Assistance, August 1994.

Walker, Samuel. *Police Accountability: The Role of Citizen Oversight.* Belmont, CA: Thomson/Wadsworth Publishing, 2001 (in press).

"Who's Watching the Watchers? Everyone." *Law Enforcement News,* Vol. XXV, Nos. 523–524, December 15/31, 1999, p. 1.

Wilson, Cicero. "Economic Shifts that Will Impact Crime Control and Community Revitalization." *What Can the Federal Government Do to Decrease Crime and Revitalize Communities?* NIJ Research Forum, October 1998, pp. 9–14. (NCJ 172210)

Wilson, James Q. and Kelling, George L. "The Police and Neighborhood Safety: Broken Windows." *The Atlantic Monthly,* March 1982, pp. 29–38.

Wilson, James Q. and Kelling, George L. "Making Neighborhoods Safe." *The Atlantic Monthly,* February 1989, pp. 46–52.

RESOURCE

National Citizen Police Academy Association, President Michael Koster, 630-801-6563.

CHAPTER 4

Problem-Oriented Policing and Problem Solving

A problem well stated is a problem half solved.
   Charles Kettering

Do you know

Who is credited with originating problem-oriented policing?

What problem solving requires police to do?

How efficiency and effectiveness differ? Which is emphasized by community policing?

What the first step in Goldstein's problem-oriented policing is?

What four stages of problem solving are used in the SARA model?

What three areas problem analysis considers?

What the magnet phenomenon is?

What the purpose and goal of the DOC model is?

What crime-specific planning is?

What the focus of crime mapping is?

What effect mental locks and killer phrases have on problem solving?

Can you define these terms:

community wellness
creativity
crime-specific planning
DOC model
effectiveness
efficiency
geographic profiling

hot spots
incident
innovation
killer phrases
magnet address
magnet phenomenon
magnet telephone

mediation
mental locks
problem-oriented policing
   (POP)
problem-solving approach

INTRODUCTION

A **problem-solving approach** involves identifying problems and making decisions about how best to deal with them. A basic characteristic of community policing is that it is proactive rather than reactive, meaning it involves recognizing problems and seeking their underlying causes.

To illustrate, a man and his buddy, who could not swim, were fishing on a riverbank when a young boy floated past, struggling to stay afloat. The fisherman jumped in and pulled the young boy from the water. He resumed his fishing, but within a few minutes another person came floating by, again struggling to stay afloat. Again, the fisherman reacted by jumping in and pulling the person to safety. He then resumed his fishing and again, within minutes, another person came floating by. The fisherman got up and started heading upstream. His buddy called after him, "Where are you going?" To which the fisherman replied, "I'm going to find out who's pushing all of these people into the river!"

It is usually more effective to get to the source of a problem rather than simply reacting to deal with it. This chapter focuses on a problem-solving approach to policing. It begins with a look at problem-oriented policing (POP) and the relationship between community-oriented policing and problem solving. Next efficiency and effectiveness are described, followed by an explanation of the importance of addressing substantive problems. Then the four-stage SARA model for problem solving is examined, including a look at problem analysis. This is followed by a discussion on making ethical decisions using the DOC model and using mediation as a problem-solving tool. Then problem solving and crime-specific planning are discussed as well as crime analysis. This is followed by a discussion of how technology is used for problem solving, including explanations of crime mapping, Geographic Information Systems and geographic profiling. Next common mistakes in problem solving are examined, as well as the role of creativity in problem-solving efforts. The chapter concludes with a look at problem solving at work, describing several promising practices from the field and highlighting key features of programs that have recently won the Herman Goldstein Award for Excellence in Problem-Oriented Policing.

◈ PROBLEM-ORIENTED POLICING (POP)

Herman Goldstein is credited with originating problem-oriented policing.

Goldstein (1990, p. 20), who coined the term **problem-oriented policing (POP)**, criticizes the professional model of policing as being incident driven: "In the vast majority of police departments, the telephone, more than any policy decision by the community or by management, continues to dictate how police resources will be used." The primary work unit in the professional model is the **incident,** that is, an isolated event that requires a police response. The institution of 911 has greatly increased the demand for police services and the public's expectation that the police will respond quickly.

Goldstein (p. 33) suggests: "Most policing is limited to ameliorating the overt, offensive symptoms of a problem." He suggests that police are more productive if they respond to incidents as symptoms of underlying community problems. He (p. 66) defines a problem as "a cluster of similar, related, or recurring incidents rather than a single incident, a substantive community concern, and a unit of police business." Once the problems in a community are identified, police efforts can focus on addressing the possible causes of such problems.

Problem-solving policing requires police to group incidents and, thereby, identify underlying causes of problems in the community.

Although problem solving may be ideal, law enforcement cannot ignore specific incidents. When calls come in, most police departments respond. Problem solving has a dual focus. First, it requires that incidents be linked to problems. Second, time devoted to "preventive" patrol must be spent proactively, determining community problems and their underlying causes. As Wilson and Kelling (1989, p. 46) note:

> The police know from experience what research by Glenn Pierce, in Boston, and Lawrence Sherman, in Minneapolis, has established: fewer than 10 percent of the addresses from which the police receive calls account for more than 60 percent of those calls. If each call is treated as a separate incident with neither a history nor a future, then each dispute will be handled by police officers anxious to pacify the complainants and get back on patrol as quickly as possible. . . .
>
> A study of domestic homicides in Kansas City showed that in eight out of ten cases the police had been called to the incident address at least once before; in half the cases they had been called *five times* or more.

A problem-solving approach relies heavily on citizen involvement. According to Goldstein (p. 21): "The police must do more than they have done in the past to engage the citizenry in the overall task of policing. . . . A community must police itself. The police can, at best, only assist in that task."

An illustrative analogy can be drawn between a physician and a patient. The physician can examine the patient, take the patient's history and prescribe a treatment based on the patient's symptoms. To recover, however, the patient must be honest and thorough in describing the symptoms and must follow the prescribed treatment. Further, in medicine as in policing, the best approach is to prevent the illness in the first place. As Wadman and Olson (1990, p. 37) note: "In order to understand current trends in policing, we should compare the problem of crime with the problem of disease. For centuries, scientists have searched for cures to the various ailments that afflict mankind. It wasn't until the twentieth century that medical science discovered that the best cure was not to have the disease at all." Just as physicians cannot be blamed for the existence of disease, police cannot be blamed for the existence of crime.

> The police can no longer accept total responsibility for our crime problems. Success will be achieved only when the police and the community join forces to develop solutions.
>
> Community wellness is the result of a sharing of responsibility and authority for the causes of crime and for crime itself. . . . Unless the community actively involves itself with its police department and the department's attempt to solve community problems, we will forever be mired in reactive, rather than proactive, policing (Nila, 1990, p. 47).

Wadman and Olson (p. 92) make this analogy: "Much like fighting a forest fire, the wellness concept demands that personnel and equipment be diverted to create the 'fire-breaks' that reduce the opportunities for crimes to be committed. This is where the real risks come in." The **community wellness** approach to policing also recognizes that police must fulfill their "crime fighter" role. In that role, too, however, the relationship between the police and community can be critical.

Regardless of whether police officers respond to incidents, seek symptoms of problems or both, the public can help or hinder their efforts. Police and community members must discuss and agree to any community involvement program before it is adopted. At times well-meaning individuals and community groups, acting unilaterally, can actually interfere with a police effort and cause unnecessary destruction, injury and even death.

The dual themes of this book are the manner in which police can engage the community in the issue of crime and disorder and the necessity of a problem-solving approach to such issues.

COMMUNITY-ORIENTED POLICING AND PROBLEM SOLVING (COPPS)

During the past quarter-century, law enforcement agencies around the country have combined the operational strategies of community-oriented policing and problem solving (COPPS) to address crime and quality-of-life issues. Frazier (2000, p. 11), director of the Office of Community Oriented Policing Services, asserts: "Police need to act as problem solvers and peacemakers in their communities. Police and citizens must work together if we are to develop long-term solutions to crime, and if we are to enhance trust between police and the communities they serve."

Just what is problem solving? Martinez (1998, p. 605) provides a working definition: "Problem solving is the process of moving toward a goal when the path to that goal is uncertain. We solve problems every time we achieve something without having known beforehand how to do so. . . . Errors are part of the process of problem solving. . . . If no mistakes are made, then almost certainly no problem solving is taking place."

Many practitioners equate community policing and problem solving. As Wilson and Kelling (p. 49) note: "Community-oriented policing means changing the daily work of the police to include investigating problems as well as incidents. It means defining as a problem whatever a significant body of public opinion regards as a threat to community order. It means working with the good guys, and not just against the bad guys." Wilson and Kelling suggest that community policing requires the police mission to be redefined "to help the police become accustomed to fixing broken windows as well as arresting window-breakers."

The differences between incident-driven, reactive policing and problem-driven, proactive policing is illustrated in Figure 4.1. The National Institute of Justice requires that problem-solving systems follow five basic principles: officers of all ranks and from all units should be able to use the system as part of their daily routine; the system must encourage the use of a broad range of information, including but not limited to conventional police data; the system should encourage a broad range of solutions, including but

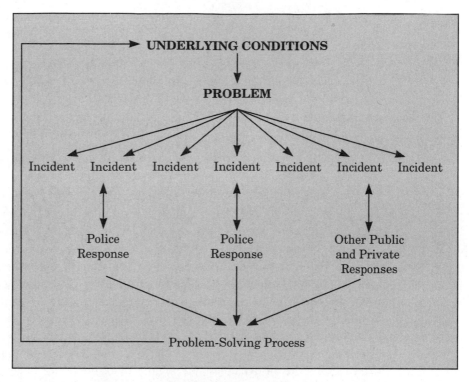

Figure 4.1 Problem-Solving Policing

SOURCE: John E. Eck and William Spelman. *Problem Solving: Problem-Oriented Policing in Newport News.* Washington, DC: Police Executive Research Forum, 1987, p. 4. © 1987 Police Executive Research Forum. Reprinted with permission by PERF.

not limited to the criminal justice process; the system should require no additional resources and no special units; and finally, any large police agency must be able to apply it (Eck and Spelman, 1987, p. xix).

Goldstein's problem-oriented policing model is a basic component of community policing. Throughout this chapter it will be referred to as a problem-solving approach. Community policing combines this problem-solving approach and police/community collaboration. Goldstein (Rosen, 1997, p. 8) draws a clear distinction between problem-oriented policing and community policing:

> I've always assumed that community policing, and the package of changes commonly conveyed by that term, is designed to place emphasis on one great need in policing, which is to engage the community, to emphasize the point that the job of social control essentially in our society depends upon networks other than the police, that the police can only facilitate those networks and support them. Problem-oriented policing, on the other hand, places the major emphasis on the need to reconceptualize what the police are doing more generally, to focus attention on the wide range of specific problems that police confront and to try to encourage a more analytical approach to those problems. Then, as a result of that

analysis, to think through different strategies, one of which is to engage more intensively with the community in the context of dealing with that particular problem. There's a big difference, but I think the difference is primarily in emphasis. We need more engagement in community; we also have a critical need for thinking differently about what the police are expected to do and investing heavily in systematic analysis of the various pieces of police business.

Goldstein (pp. 14–15) cites five concerns that have most strongly influenced the development of problem-oriented policing:

1. The police field is preoccupied with management, internal procedures and efficiency to the exclusion of appropriate concern for effectiveness in dealing with substantive problems.

2. The police devote most of their resources to responding to calls from citizens, reserving too small a percentage of their time and energy for acting on their own initiative to prevent or reduce community problems.

3. The community is a major resource with an enormous potential, largely untapped, for reducing the number and magnitude of problems that otherwise become the business of the police.

4. Within their agencies, police have readily available to them another huge resource: their rank-and-file officers, whose time and talent have not been used effectively.

5. Efforts to improve policing have often failed because they have not been adequately related to the overall dynamics and complexity of the police organization. Adjustments in policies and organizational structure are required to accommodate and support change.

A problem-solving approach to policing was developed in response to these concerns. The first concern that influenced the development of a problem-solving approach to policing was that of efficiency and effectiveness.

◈ EFFICIENCY AND EFFECTIVENESS

Efficiency involves minimizing waste, expense or unnecessary effort. Efficiency results in a high ratio of output to input. Efficiency is doing things right. **Effectiveness** has to do with producing the desired result or goal. Effectiveness is doing the right thing. Ideally, both efficiency and effectiveness are present in policing.

There can be effectiveness without efficiency, but there cannot be efficiency without effectiveness because any effort that does not achieve the desired goal is wasted. Police, along with other emergency services, face an inherent contradiction between effectiveness and efficiency. To have the capacity to respond to an emergency quickly, staffing levels must be sufficient to have personnel available to respond at all times. To have that capacity, however, requires a number of personnel with substantial slack time. Without slack time, all personnel may be busy when emergencies occur, reducing response effectiveness. Unfortunately, too often police departments have emphasized efficiency, for example, rapid response to calls, number of citations issued and the like, rather than what will produce the desired outcomes of the department.

The story is told of a bus driver who refused to stop to pick up passengers if he was behind schedule. Although efficient, this bus driver was totally ineffective in the view of the stranded would-be passengers. The bus driver had lost sight of his purpose.

Efficiency, doing things right, has been the traditional emphasis in law enforcement. Effectiveness, doing the right things, is the emphasis in community policing.

According to Goldstein (p. 32), a problem-solving approach to policing is "a comprehensive plan for improving policing in which the high priority attached to addressing substantive problems shapes the police agency, influencing all changes in personnel, organization, and procedures." This focus on substantive problems (effectiveness) rather than on the smooth functioning of the organization (efficiency) is a radical change and difficult for some departments to make. Those departments that have made the shift in focus have achieved excellent results. *T. A. P.*

Tactical Action Plan

◈ ADDRESSING SUBSTANTIVE PROBLEMS

Traditionally police have responded to incidents, handled them as effectively as possible and then moved on to the next call. This fragmented approach to policing conceals patterns of incidents that may be symptomatic of deeper problems. Goldstein (p. 33) contends: "The first step in problem-oriented policing is to move beyond just handling incidents. It calls for recognizing that incidents are often merely overt symptoms of problems."

The first step in problem solving is to group incidents as problems.

The basic elements in a problem-solving approach combine steps a police department can take and theoretical assumptions to make the steps work. They include the following (Goldstein, pp. 32–49):

- Grouping incidents as problems.
- Focusing on substantive problems as the heart of policing.
- Seeking effectiveness as the ultimate goal.
- Using systematic inquiry.
- Disaggregating and accurately labeling problems.
- Analyzing the multiple interests in problems.
- Capturing and critiquing the current response.
- Adopting a proactive stance.
- Strengthening the decision-making processes and increasing accountability.
- Evaluating results of newly implemented responses.

Many departments have developed problem-solving approaches that incorporate these basic elements.

�◆ **THE SARA MODEL: A FOUR-STAGE PROBLEM-SOLVING PROCESS**

Eck and Spelman (p. 42) describe the four-stage problem-solving process used in the Newport News Police Department and known as the SARA Model.

The four stages of the SARA problem-solving model are scanning, analysis, response and assessment.

Scanning refers to identifying the problem. Analysis is learning the problem's causes, scope and effects. Response is acting to alleviate the problem, that is, selecting the alternative solution or solutions to try. Assessment is determining whether the response worked. Beck (1996, p. 9) describes this model:

Scanning—Officers determine problems through personal experience, through communications with residents or through calls for service.

Analysis—Officers learn everything possible about the players, incidents and actions that may have been used to deal with the problem. If an officer understands all of the components of a problem, the officer can create a customized response to fit the problem.

Response—Officers develop a goal based on careful analysis. The goal is reached using a customized response to fit the problem. Solutions are designed to eliminate the problem, reduce the problem, reduce the harm created by the problem, deal with a problem more effectively, and remove the problem from police consideration. The officer locates an agency that can better handle the problem.

Assessment—Officers evaluate the effectiveness of their response. Did the officers achieve their goal? Did the response to the problem reduce calls for service, satisfy residents or businesses, create a more manageable problem or result in a noticed difference by policymakers in amount of complaints?

The SARA model of problem solving shows that there are no failures, only responses that do not provide the desired goal. When a response does not give the desired results, the officer can examine the results and try a different response. Wolfer et al. (1999, p. 11) suggest: "The SARA model helps police reduce the crime rate, as well as the fear of crime among citizens."

The SARA Model in Action

Bean (1999, pp. 4–5) provides an example of how the SARA model can be used to problem solve.

Problem Analysis

Table 4.1 illustrates potential sources of information for identifying problems. To assist in problem analysis, the Newport News Police Department developed a problem-analysis guide that lists topic headings police should consider in assessing problems.

Problem analysis considers the individuals involved, the incidents and the responses.

Armed Robberies at the Kimmerly Glen Apartment Complex

By Officer Phillip W. Bean
Charlotte-Mecklenburg (NC) Police Department

As a member of a bike patrol squad assigned to the northeast area of Charlotte, North Carolina, I regularly visited the 11 apartment complexes in my district. They seemed to be magnets for crimes such as auto theft, larcenies from autos and burglaries.

Scanning

Residents of the 13-building Kimmerly Glen apartment complex were reporting repeated auto larcenies at the complex. Then they began reporting more violent armed robberies. The middle-income residents of the 260 apartment units were being attacked and robbed as they walked to and from their cars.

The goal of this POP project was to reduce the incidence of robbery by making the environment surrounding the property less conducive to this type of activity and educating citizens on how to avoid becoming victims.

Analysis

A review of reports and interviews with victims helped me understand the problem and its potential harms. I looked at which days and at what times most crimes were occurring and also surveyed the property, noting its layout was particularly conducive to this type of problem. For example, the property was bordered by tall shrubbery, and the complex itself was poorly lit, features enabling perpetrators to conduct their ambush-style attacks on residents without anyone else in the complex witnessing them.

Response

I planted bait cars and tried all-night surveillance to locate the suspects and reduce the incidents on this property and in surrounding areas, which had also experienced increased crime. I contacted the complex's managers and a representative from the city's Department of Transportation and requested an upgrade on the streetlights around the complex. I also explained to complex management that the high shrubbery around the breezeways and doorways of the apartments were contributing to the incidence of robbery. The management staff made environmental changes to the property immediately.

I then initiated quarterly crime prevention meetings and suggested to residents ways to avoid victimization, since what they seemed to need most was basic education on how to protect themselves and secure their property. I also encouraged residents to call 911 if they observed any suspicious activity and was surprised to learn that many of them did not know how to use the 911 system. Other officers encouraged residents to be good witnesses and neighbors and to report suspicious activity. They also worked with citizens to help prevent future robberies. In addition, apartment management aided the police by distributing information in monthly newsletters.

Assessment

The armed robbery problem was completely eradicated during the 10 months following the project's implementation, and larcenies from autos were reduced 33 percent over the same time period. Results were measured through an analysis of crime statistics and calls for service.

Residents now call 911 if they witness criminal activity, rather than waiting until a crime has occurred, which has helped me identify robbery suspects and has contributed to the dramatic drop in crime at the complex.

I still hold quarterly meetings at the Kimmerly Glen and similar meetings at other complexes. Turnout at these meetings varies with the concerns residents have about activity in the community. Presently, I'm trying to start meetings at other area complexes where residents are experiencing problems, before they reach the level similar to Kimmerly Glen. I will continue to monitor the problem through feedback from citizens during community meetings, constant contact with apartment management and ongoing analysis of crime statistics.

Table 4.1   Potential Sources of Information for Identifying Problems

Crime Analysis Unit—Time trends and patterns (time of day, day of week, monthly, seasonal, and other cyclical events), and patterns of similar events (offender descriptions, victim characteristics, locations, physical settings and other circumstances).

Patrol—Recurring calls, bad areas, active offenders, victim types, complaints from citizens.

Investigations—Recurring crimes, active offenders, victim difficulties, complaints from citizens.

Crime Prevention—Physical conditions, potential victims, complaints from citizens.

Vice—Drug dealing, illegal alcohol sales, gambling, prostitution, organized crime.

Communications—Call types, repeat calls from same location, temporal peaks in calls for service.

Chief's Office—Letters and calls from citizens, concerns of elected officials, concerns from city manager's office.

Other Law Enforcement Agencies—Multi-jurisdictional concerns.

Elected Officials—Concerns and complaints.

Local Government Agencies—Plans that could influence crimes, common difficulties, complaints from citizens.

Schools—Juvenile concerns, vandalism, employee safety.

Community Leaders—Problems of constituents.

Business Groups—Problems of commerce and development.

Neighborhood Watch—Local problems regarding disorder, crime and other complaints.

Newspapers and Other News Media—Indications of problems not detected from other sources, problems in other jurisdictions that could occur in any city.

Community Surveys—Problems of citizens in general.

SOURCE: John E. Eck and William Spelman. *Problem Solving: Problem-Oriented Policing in Newport News.* Washington, DC: Police Executive Research Forum, 1987, p. 46. © 1987 Police Executive Research Forum. Reprinted with permission by PERF.

Their problem-analysis guide highlights the complex interaction of individuals, incidents and responses occurring within a social context and a physical setting.

The problems Newport News Police identified and how they approached them are discussed later in the chapter. Based on the Newport News experience, Eck and Spelman (p. 3) offer 12 suggestions as to what a problem-oriented policing agency should do:

1. Focus on problems of concern to the public.

2. Zero in on effectiveness as the primary concern.

3. Be proactive.

4. Be committed to systematic inquiry as the first step in solving substantive problems.

5. Encourage use of rigorous methods in making inquiries.

6. Make full use of the data in police files and the experience of police personnel.

7. Group like incidents together so that they can be addressed as a common problem.

8. Avoid using overly broad labels in grouping incidents so separate problems can be identified.

9. Encourage a broad and uninhibited search for solutions.

10. Acknowledge the limits of the criminal justice system as a response to problems.

11. Identify multiple interests in any one problem and weigh them when analyzing the value of different responses.

12. Be committed to taking some risks in responding to problems.

Note the similarities between these suggestions and the basic elements of problem-solving policing set forth by Goldstein on p. 91.

When identifying problems, it is important to be aware of the *magnet phenomenon.*

*The **magnet phenomenon** occurs when a phone number or address is associated with a crime simply because it was a convenient number or address to use.*

A **magnet telephone** is one that is available when no other telephones are, for example, a telephone in a convenience store that is open all night and on weekends. Victims of or witnesses to a crime in the area may use that telephone to report the crime, even though the store was not the scene of the crime. Similarly, a **magnet address** is one that is easy for people to give, for example, a high school or a theater.

When specific crimes are identified during the first stage of problem solving, crime-specific planning may be appropriate. Before looking at crime-specific planning, however, consider two other challenges a problem-solving approach presents to departments embracing community policing: making ethical decisions and using mediation as a problem-solving tool.

◈ MAKING ETHICAL DECISIONS

Romano et al. (2000, p. 98) suggest that SARA needs an additional component to address ethics and moral decision making. To this end, Facing History and Ourselves (FHAO), a national educational and training organization whose mission is to engage students in examining racism, prejudice and anti-Semitism, developed a framework for addressing ethical and moral issues: the DOC model.

*The **DOC** model—Dilemmas-Options-Consequences—challenges officers to carefully consider their decisions and the short- and long-term consequences of those decisions. The goal is to fuse problem solving and morality.*

Romano et al. (p. 99) suggest that if officers are facing a *dilemma* and a decision that "feels" wrong, they should ask themselves questions such as: What feels wrong? Is there a moral or ethical threat to me or someone else? Will I, or someone in the community, be affected or hurt physically or emotionally or be treated disrespectfully? Such questions prompt officers to think about how others feel and how they may or may not be affected by the actions officers take.

After the dilemma is identified, an action is needed, leading to the *options* phase and questions such as: What are my options? Am I considering all options? Am I being open-minded and creative? Do my options rely only on me, or could I use a resource or someone's help? Whose?

For each choice, officers must assess the *consequences* by asking: What happens because of my choice? What if I do nothing? Who is affected by what I do? How? Will I protect myself? Will I protect the quality of life and dignity of others? Will I preserve my moral and ethical integrity? What are the short-term effects? The long-term effects?

In addition to considering the ethics involved in problem solving, community policing officers often find that they must rely on their skills in mediation as well.

◈ MEDIATION AS A PROBLEM-SOLVING TOOL

Research shows that most calls for service involve landlord/tenant disputes, loud parties, rowdy teens, traffic complaints and even many domestic calls, not requiring law enforcement intervention. But police traditionally use enforcement strategies such as rapid response and random patrol to address these problems. As Dowling (1999, p. 5) suggests, community policing officers need to arrest the arresting response: "Law enforcement's traditional response to criminal activity has been limited only to arrest. This is a response that severely handicaps the ability of an agency to effectively problem solve. . . . What is needed is a multifaceted approach to crime, one that takes into account all reasons why the problem exists." Buerger et al. (1999, p. 125) discuss how officers with traditional law enforcement expectations must adjust when placed in community policing assignments: "Shifting from a control perspective to a partnership role often requires officers to abandon confrontation, command, and coercion in favor of participation, promotion, and persuasion."

Cooper (1999b, p. 1) defines **mediation** as "the intervention of a third party into an interpersonal dispute, where the third party assists the disputants in fashioning their (the disputants) own resolution." He notes that mediation is often termed "ADR" or Alternative Dispute Resolution. Police mediation typically occurs in five main arenas (Buerger et al., pp. 129–130): (1) conflicts between cohabiting persons or individuals with kinship ties, usually called *domestics*; (2) conflicts between landlords and tenants; (3) conflicts between acquaintances, including residential neighbors; (4) disputes between neighborhood residents and locations (commercial or residential) deemed to be attractive nuisances, such as crack houses, bars, porn shops, saunas, health spas, massage-parlor prostitution fronts, fraternity houses, etc.; and (5) disputes between guardians/owners and regulating bodies such as bars and liquor commissions, subsidized housing sites and their funding sources.

Mediation may provide a short-term solution, but this is often the result of the perceived coercive power of the mediating officer (resolve this, or else . . .). According to Buerger et al. (p. 132): "It is primarily within the context of problem- and community-oriented policing—where officers are designated responsibility for specific areas of the community and solving its problems—where long-term mediation can be accomplished." Cooper (1999a) outlines the following mediation basics:

- Explain mediation concepts to participants.
- Introduce parties who do not know one another.
- Deliver ground rules (e.g., one person speaks at a time; no profanity allowed).
- Advise of confidentiality (discussion remains confidential; officer may file confidential police report).
- Explain nature of agreement (parties remain bound; legal action may follow breach).
- Discuss alternatives (e.g., arbitration).
- Allow parties to convey their version of the incident.
- Give parties chance to rebut.
- Ask questions, clarify issues by restating, seek agreement on issues.
- Parties brainstorm possible solutions; officer encourages, makes suggestions.
- Officer clarifies agreement, seeks verification from parties, may put in writing.

As Cooper (2000, p. 10) notes: "When departments use mediation to resolve conflicts in their communities, they empower residents to take responsibility for their actions and to resolve their own problems, not just in arguments with their neighbors but in other areas of their lives, as well." Cooper (1999b, p. 1) suggests other benefits of patrol officer mediation: "Bolstering community policing initiatives, helping police not escalate scenes, reducing repeat calls-for-service, and improving police-citizen relations."

Mediation can take many forms, including the one the Santa Rosa Police Department uses to address community crime and disorder problems: Interest Based Negotiation (IBN). In Santa Rosa, the SARA and IBN models were used to address a dispute between Cambodian residents in an apartment complex and surrounding single-family homes with their property owner. As a result of the negotiating process, the residents and the property owner agreed that community members would select a property-management firm. The process also led to developing a community-based forum to address both police and community responses to neighborhood problems. In 1999 the success of the program was recognized when the Santa Rosa PD received the James Q. Wilson Award for Excellence in Community Policing (*COPPS*, 1999, pp. 70–71).

PROBLEM-ORIENTED POLICING AND CRIME-SPECIFIC PLANNING

To maintain effective police-community partnerships, police must also fulfill their crime-fighting role. Police can approach this role with many of the problem-solving skills just discussed, using crime-specific planning, a more specific strategy than problem-oriented policing in that it considers underlying problems categorized by type of offense. **Crime-specific planning** involves reviewing the following factors:

- The offense: Seriousness, frequency of occurrence, susceptibility to control, whether a crime of opportunity or calculation, the modus operandi and any violent characteristics present.

- The target: Property taken or damaged, when attacked, how attacked, where located, number of potential targets in area, accessibility, transportation patterns surrounding the target.
- Impact: On the community, public concern, drain on resources of the criminal justice system.
- Response: Of the victim, the community, the criminal justice system.

Crime-specific planning uses the principles of problem solving to focus on identified crime problems.

A careful analysis of these factors provides the basis for problem solving and deriving alternatives for approaching each specific crime problem.

Crime Analysis

According to Wideman (2000, p. 59): "Crime analysis is the systematic gathering, evaluation, and analysis of information on individuals and/or activities suspected of being, or known to be, criminal in nature." Woods (1999, p. 17) contends that crime analysis is a key tool in any crime reduction strategy. In fact, as Wernicke and Stallo (2000, p. 56) point out: "An increasing number of agencies, large and small, are establishing crime analysis units."

Assistance is available to agencies developing crime analysis units from the International Association of Crime Analysts (IACA), a group "dedicated to advocacy for professional standards, to providing practical educational opportunities and to the creation of an international network for the standardization of analytic techniques" (Wernicke and Stallo, p. 57). Their Web site is http://www.iaca.net.

Also of assistance to crime analysis is computer software that provides probability assessments. As Miles (2000, p. 102) notes, software is available that lets investigators quantify and combine judgments to assess the probability that evidence proves guilt or innocence, simplifying the task and eliminating the guesswork. By mathematically evaluating circumstantial evidence, investigators can come to more reliable conclusions that will lead to sounder verdicts.

Further assistance in crime analysis and problem solving is available from technological advances made in crime mapping and in geographic profiling.

USING TECHNOLOGY FOR PROBLEM SOLVING

Technology has become an indispensable tool for law enforcement. In fact: "Some say the computer is changing policing today the way the two-way radio changed policing in the 1940s" (Wartell and Greenhalgh, 2000, p. 1). Computers can greatly assist departments using the SARA model for problem solving. In the scanning phase, crime analysis can use information from the Records Management System (RMS) to identify problems. Computer Aided Dispatch (CAD) can identify locations getting repeat calls for police service. Likewise, databases, charts, graphs and spreadsheets can identify similarities in incidents indicating a need for problem solving. Basic analysis can also be done with computerized data, including crime mapping and Geographic Information Systems (GIS).

Crime Mapping—Geographic Information Systems

As Rogers (2000, p. 36) notes: "Crime analysis and crime mapping technology are changing the way law enforcement does business." "Cutting-edge systems," says Fortner (1998, p. 16), "go beyond merely identifying high-crime areas to offer more insights into 'hot-spots,' patterns, history and perhaps strategies against crime and its perpetrators."

Crime mapping changes the focus from the criminal to the location of crimes—the hot spots *where most crimes occur.*

Braiden (1998, p. 8) comments: "Structured as it is, the criminal justice system puts 95 percent of its resources into the hunt [trying to catch the bad guys] while the habitat [the hot spot] is left almost untouched. We can never win working that way, because the habitat never stops supplying new customers for the hunt. . . . I cannot think of two special-interest groups more philosophically opposed to each other than hunters and animal right activists, yet there are two things they totally agree upon: The species will survive the hunt; it will not survive loss of its habitat."

Aragon (2000, p. 8) presents several facts that support use of crime mapping and attention to hot spots:

- Two-thirds of all crime occurs indoors, not visible to the police.
- Most serious crimes are perpetrated within a short time frame; for example, the average armed robbery takes approximately 90 seconds.
- Patrol officers intercept less than 1 percent of street crimes.
- The same 10 percent of locations within a jurisdiction generate approximately 65 percent of that jurisdiction's total calls for service.

Aragon concludes:

Law enforcement is behind the power curve and must work on strategies for preventing incidents from occurring in the first place. The analogy I find highly applicable . . . is this: less successful agencies "shoot where the target was"; run-of-the-mill agencies "shoot where the target is"; successful agencies "shoot where the target is going."

Kanable (1999, p. 41) notes: "With crime mapping, officers can be directed to rub out trouble spots. They can patrol areas where crime is occurring in their district. Extra patrols can be brought in from officers working on budgeted overtime."

A National Institute of Justice Crime Mapping Research Center survey showed that police departments with 100 or more officers used computer crime mapping 35 percent of the time (Rogers, 1999, p. 76). The National Institute of Justice has released *Mapping Crime: Principle and Practice,* a research guide to help police understand crime data analysis through crime mapping and designed for agencies just starting to use geographic information systems (GIS). It is available on the Web at www.ncjrs.org/nij/mapping/for.html.

Warden and Shaw (2000, pp. 81–86) describe how mapping helped predict a residential break-in pattern in Edmonton, Alberta, Canada (Adapted and reprinted by permission).

Problem Identification. In November 1998, Constable Jerry Shaw (the Crime Analysis Section's Crime Mapping Specialist) observed break-and-enter crime clusters within a specific area of the North Division. Tactical Crime Hot Spot maps were created and forwarded to the Division's Criminal Investigation Section Staff Sergeant.

The geographic area in question was primarily an older residential area where the crime clusters were self-evident and had, compared to previous crime maps of the same area, revealed a marked increase in activity.

Problem Solving. Crime mapping showed where the suspects operated and the evolving pattern of their movement. Time/date sequencing of 240 break-ins in the hot-spot area revealed these were daytime break-and-enters. Also, the method of entry was similar in each case: either a window next to the door lock was broken, or the door itself was pried open. A comparison of method of entry for each incident tied the suspects to specific break-ins.

The above analyses were collected in a Microsoft Excel spreadsheet to show time/ date/location and method of entry.

Predictive Tool. Based on the cluster movement over time and space, Constable Shaw was able to predict the approximate area in which the suspects would next operate, providing investigators a geographic starting point for surveillance team placement.

Results. The combination of investigative work, crime maps, tactical analysis and pattern prediction enabled investigators to set up surveillance in the area of highest probability. Two suspects were soon apprehended while engaged in a residential break-in and were taken into custody.

The investigation, supported by the tactical analysis, conclusively linked the two suspects to more than 123 residential break-ins, of which 77 were cleared by victims identifying their stolen property; 27 were cleared by "recent possession," i.e., pawned property; and the remaining 43 were cleared on the basis of the similar fact analysis.

More than $500,000 worth of property was stolen in these break-ins. Property valued at $70,000 was recovered. . . . The two accused pled guilty; each was sentenced to nearly eight years in prison.

LaVigne and Wartell (1999, p. 298) suggest that geographic information systems allow law enforcement agencies to accomplish five important tasks: (1) Identify problems and reveal trends and patterns. (2) Analyze problems by using multiple data sources. (3) Assess efforts to evaluate responses. (4) Show and assess resource allocations. (5) Share information with the community and other agencies.

Some departments post on their Web sites information gathered from crime mapping, a practice that has sparked heated debate. As Wartell (2000, p. 52) notes, real-estate agents are concerned about the effects such data have on housing prices. Although most departments' maps are not detailed enough to show exact addresses, the concern for privacy is still an issue. However, as Wartell (p. 55) contends: "Making crime maps and data easily available can increase public awareness and participation in keeping their communities crime-free. This can help to reduce the workload on department personnel and increase community policing potential."

Crime mapping has evolved further into the relatively new science of geographic profiling.

Geographic Profiling

Geographic profiling, as Pilant (1999, p. 38) explains, "takes conventional crime mapping techniques and turns them inside out. Instead of predicting the date or the site of the next crime, it takes the locations of past crimes and using a complex mathematical algorithm [developed by Deputy Inspector Rossmo of the Vancouver, B.C., Police Department], calculates probabilities of the suspect's residence." Nislow (2000, p. 1) explains: "The computer calculates the probability of [a certain] point being the offender's home. . . . Those areas where it is least likely a suspect would live are colored a cool blue. Those areas where it is most likely are red." Nislow (p. 10) suggests: "Geographic profiling can't solve a crime, but it can provide a focus, especially where there are too many suspects or too many tips."

Geographic profiling has proven highly accurate in cases solved by the FBI, the Royal Canadian Mounted Police and several state police departments. According to MacKay (1999, pp. 56–57), an accurate geographic profile can help investigators prioritize suspect lists; direct patrol saturation and static stakeouts; conduct neighborhood canvasses; make better use of police information systems, major case management systems, task force computer systems and the like; take advantage of outside agency information systems; limit the sample size for forensic testing; and access sex offender registries.

MacKay (p. 58) suggests: "When used with powerful crime linkage systems such as the FBI's Violent Criminal Apprehension Program (VICAP) . . . and psychological profiling techniques, or even as a stand-alone system, geographic profiling can help law enforcement officers solve serial crimes more effectively and efficiently." He (p. 59) gives the following case study:

> Although the series of 14 rapes that started in 1984 ended in 1995, the investigator refused to close the file. In 1998, the Lafayette City, Louisiana, Police Department obtained a psychological profile from the FBI as well as a geographic profile that identified a neighborhood that they had not considered before. Through the use of both they were able to prioritize the more than 2,000 tips they had. A suspect was asked for a DNA sample and fingerprints because he lived in the top 2.2 percent (0.5 square mile) of the area. Matches were obtained from both; he confessed and has been charged with the rapes.

Despite advances in technology, human intelligence and creativity are also still extremely important in problem solving. Consider next some of the most common mistakes that occur in problem solving.

◉ COMMON MISTAKES IN PROBLEM SOLVING

As Bennett and Hess (2000, p. 130) note: "Common mistakes in problem solving and decision making include spending too much energy on unimportant details, failing to resolve important issues, being secretive about true feelings, having a closed mind and not expressing ideas. . . . Inability to decide, putting decisions off to the last minute, failing to set deadlines, making decisions under pressure and using unreliable sources of information are other common errors in problem solving and decision making." Other mistakes commonly made during problem solving and decision making include making multiple decisions about the same problem, finding the right decision for the wrong problem (that is, dealing with symptoms rather than causes), failing to consider the costs, delaying a decision and making decisions while angry or excited.

Bennett and Hess (p. 130) offer a checklist against which to evaluate decisions. Is the decision: consistent with the agency's mission, goals and objectives; a long-term solution; cost effective; legal; ethical; practical; and acceptable to those responsible for implementing it?

PROBLEM SOLVING AND CREATIVITY

Several structured approaches to problem solving have been discussed. These approaches will be more effective if creativity is incorporated into the approach. **Creativity** is a process of breaking old connections and discovering useful new connections. It is often synonymous with **innovation.** von Oech (1983, p. 7) states: "Discovery consists of looking at the same thing as everyone else and thinking something different." However, effective problem solving can be sabotaged if you fall prey to mental locks or killer phrases.

In problem solving, it is important to avoid **mental locks,** or ways of thinking that prevent creativity. Some examples of mental locks are:

- "That's Not Logical"—Sometimes logic limits creativity. Both creative and logical thinking are usually needed for the toughest problems.
- "Be Practical"—Practicality is important when seeking solutions. However, when problem solving, practicality can limit creative solutions. von Oech (p. 54) calls the realm of the possible a "germinal seedbed." He encourages people to ask "what if" questions to stimulate the imagination.
- "Avoid Ambiguity"—When thinking creatively, ambiguity can help. von Oech (pp. 76–78) presents this exercise:

  In the following line of letters, cross out six letters so that the remaining letters, without altering their sequence, will spell a familiar English word.

  BSAINXLEATNTEARS

  Many people approach this problem by noting there are 16 letters, and that if they cross out 6, they will have a 10-letter word. They ask themselves, "Which letters should I cross out?" This, however, will lead to the wrong answer because it is the wrong question. To solve the problem, ask yourself, "What else could 'cross out six letters' mean?" von Oech (p. 78) suggests you literally cross out the "S," the "I," the "X," the "L," the "E," and so on. If you try this approach, you will be left with the word *banana.*

- "To Err Is Wrong"—Risk taking is a necessary part of progress. To err is wrong only if you do not learn from the "mistake." Henry Ford once said, "Failure is the opportunity to begin again more intelligently."
- "That's Not My Area"—Our society has become so complex that specialization is often necessary. Sometimes, however, someone who is outside a specific field but who

is genuinely interested in and perhaps affected by a problem can suggest the most brilliant alternative. This is, in fact, often true of citizens. Alternatives to crime-related problems may be generated by nonlaw enforcement professionals if given an opportunity.

- "I'm Not Creative"—As the saying goes: "If you think you can or if you think you can't, you're right." Never demean yourself or your abilities, including your ability to be creative. You would not be this far into this text if you were not a capable individual. You have absorbed a great deal of information, and you have years of experience to relate to that information. If you wish, you can approach policing in creative ways.

While mental locks are self-imposed obstacles to creative problem solving, killer phrases are used by others on you, or by you on others, to deter creative solutions. **Killer phrases** are judgmental, critical statements; they are put-downs that stifle creativity. Some of the most common killer phrases are: "That's too radical. It's contrary to policy. That's not our area. We'll never get help. That's too much hassle. It just won't work. It's too impractical. It costs too much. We've never done it that way before. Get serious" (Buchholz and Roth, 1987, p. 136). Avoid such phrases when you are thinking and in your discussions with others if you want creative solutions to the numerous problems you will encounter in policing.

Two barriers to creative problem solving are mental locks and killer phrases.

◈ PROBLEM SOLVING AT WORK

The theoretical foundation of problem solving in Newport News was discussed earlier. During the problem-identification process, several problems became evident (Eck and Spelman, p. 44). Table 4.2 illustrates how police categorized the problems so they could be analyzed. The way the department addressed the problem of commercial burglaries illustrates the problem-solving approach. The patrol officers surveyed the area and found that some major streets had been barricaded due to a major highway-construction project. This resulted in limited vehicle traffic, limited police patrol at night and a large increase in nighttime burglaries. To alleviate these problems, patrol officers were instructed to leave their squads and patrol the area on foot at night. The officers also persuaded the merchants to clean up the piles of trash and debris that could easily conceal the burglars' activities.

Besides dealing with the environment, Sgt. Quail, the officer in charge, also analyzed the specific problem (p. 83):

He collected offense reports of burglaries committed in the area. To help identify geographic patterns, he plotted them on a detailed spot map. To identify M.O. and repeat offender patterns, Quail recorded a description of the suspects, time of commission, type of property taken, and similar information on a specially designed form. Finally, he suspected that some of the offenders were using vacant apartments located above some of the businesses to conceal stolen property; he began to investigate this possibility.

These efforts resulted in the apprehension of several burglars and a decrease in the burglary rate. When the construction was completed and the barriers

Table 4.2 Types of Problems

	Citywide	Neighborhood
Crime problems	Domestic homicides	Personal robberies (Central business district)
	Gas station driveoffs	Commercial burglaries (Jefferson Avenue business district)
	Assaults on police officers	
		Vacant buildings (Central business district)
		Residential burglaries (New Briarfield Apts)
		Residential burglaries (Glenn Gardens Apts)
		Larcenies (Beechmont Gardens Apts)
		Thefts from autos (Newport News Shipbuilding)
		Drug dealing (32d and Chestnut)
Disorder problems	Runaway youths	Rowdy youths (Peninsula Skating Rink)
	Driving under the influence	Shot houses (Aqua Vista Apts)
	Disturbances at convenience stores	Disturbances (Marshall Avenue 7-Eleven)
		Dirt bikes (Newmarket Creek)
		Disturbances (Village Square Shopping Center)

SOURCE: John E. Eck and William Spelman. *Problem Solving: Problem-Oriented Policing in Newport News.* Washington, DC: Police Executive Research Forum, 1987, p. 82. © 1987 Police Executive Research Forum. Reprinted with permission by PERF.

removed, the burglaries decreased further. Since construction is frequent, Sgt. Quail began to develop a policy and procedure statement so that police and city agencies could communicate better regarding construction projects, street closing and potential burglary problems.

Promising Practices from the Field

The COPS (Community Oriented Policing Services) office Web site—www.usdoj.gov/cops/cp_resources/promise_prac/success_stories/ss_sd.htm—contains numerous examples of promising practices in problem solving. Two examples follow.

San Diego, CA—Prostitution. A business strip was plagued with a prostitution problem. The initial police response was to attempt undercover arrests of "johns" and prostitutes. Although they were able to take hundreds of johns into custody, few prostitutes were arrested because they knew the undercover detectives on sight.

The police decided to take a problem-solving approach to improve results. In examining the problem, officers learned many of the prostitutes were transients who would stay in the area only while it was profitable. To diminish profitability, the police obtained a temporary restraining order (TRO) prohibiting the defendants (prostitutes) from flagging down motorists, loitering on corners or participating in other solicitation conduct within 100 yards of the plantiffs (local business owners). Violation of the TRO meant an immediate five days in jail and a $1,000 fine.

One month after the TRO was obtained, the problem had been solved. Prostitutes abandoned the area, customers no longer cruised the business strip, and businesses reported increased revenues. The area has remained free of prostitution for over three years.

Mankato, MN—Minnesota Police Reclaimed Park for Use by Law-Abiding Citizens. One area of a local park had become the gathering place for "Motorheads"— a group of car devotees—who would meet every day around noon to drink and socialize. Their parties would continue throughout the day and into the evening, so that by 10 P.M., the crowd had grown to between 300 and 400 people. Problems linked to the Motorhead parties included the harrassing of other park users, assaults, public urination, public and juvenile drinking, suspected drug dealing and thousands of dollars in criminal property damage to the park. The initial police response included police park patrols, installation of flood lights in the area where the parties were occurring and the scheduling of many nonparty events at the park. None of these approaches, however, were effective.

Taking a problem-solving approach, officers spent several weeks observing and interacting with the party-goers. During this time, they learned the Motorheads liked the spot because it was next to a large parking lot, had two exits and, while being out of sight, still allowed them to see the police coming from a distance. Interviews with former park users revealed they had stopped visiting the park because they were intimidated by the party group. A community meeting was then held to solicit more information about the problem.

The officers partnered with the city parks director to develop a long-term solution to the problem. Aiming to lessen the appeal of the park to the partiers, park officials reduced the size of the large parking lot and restricted the flow of traffic to one way. Meanwhile, the officers had found an alternative site for the party group—an empty, highly visible downtown parking lot near the police department where activity could be easily monitored.

Once the Motorheads relocated downtown, young families and other former park attendees resumed use of the park. Even though some Motorhead-related problems continued downtown (juvenile drinking, drug sales, reckless driving), immediate targeted enforcement efforts by the police convinced the Motorheads to "clean up their act" or risk losing access to the downtown lot.

The Herman Goldstein Award for Excellence in Problem-Oriented Policing. The Herman Goldstein Award for Excellence in Problem-Oriented Policing was established in 1993, honoring Professor Herman Goldstein for conceiving and developing the theory of problem-oriented policing. This award is given to innovative, effective problem-oriented policing projects that have demonstrated measurable success in reducing specific crime, disorder or public safety problems.

The 1998 Winner: Operation Cease Fire, Boston Police Department. (Adapted from Brito and Allan, 1999, pp. 328–339.)

Scanning—In 1987 Boston had 22 victims of youth homicide. In 1990 that figure had risen to 73 victims—a 230 percent increase. Responding to six or seven shootings every night, police were overwhelmed. For many of Boston's youths, the city had become a dangerous, even deadly, place. So a gun project working group was formed.

The working group's line-level personnel were convinced the gun violence problem was a gang problem because most victims and offenders were gang members and because the worst offenders in the cycle of fear, gun acquisition and gun use were gang members. Another part of the problem identified was that many of the youths involved were not "bad" or inherently dangerous but were participating because gang membership had become a means of self-protection.

Analysis—The Harvard team framed the relevant issues in gun market terms. Gun trafficking and other means of illegal firearm acquisition represented the supply side, whereas fear and other factors potentially driving illicit gun acquisition and use represented the demand side. Research techniques included geographic mapping of youth homicides, gun market analysis using BPD/ATF gun recovery and tracing data, gathering of criminal histories of youth homicide victims and offenders and collection of hospital emergency room data. Key findings of this research included:

- Most youth gun and knife homicides and woundings occurred in three specific neighborhoods.
- Of the 1,550 firearms recovered from youths, 52.1 percent were semiautomatic pistols.
- Trace analysis revealed that 34 percent of traceable firearms recovered from youths were first sold at retail establishments in Massachusetts.
- Of all traceable guns recovered from youths, 26 percent were less than two years old and, thus, almost certainly trafficked rather than stolen.
- Nearly 20 percent of all guns recovered from youths had obliterated serial numbers, suggesting they were relatively new "trafficked" guns.
- Of the 155 youth gun and knife homicide victims, 75 percent had been arraigned for at least one offense in Massachusetts courts.
- Boston had roughly 61 gangs with 1,300 members in the three high-risk neighborhoods previously identified. Although this represented less than 3 percent of the youths ages 14 to 24 in these neighborhoods, these gangs were responsible for at least 60 percent of Boston's youth homicides.

Response—The working group framed two main responses into a program called "Cease Fire." The first response was to mount a direct law enforcement attack on illicit gun trafficking by (1) using trace information to identify gun traffickers and (2) systematically debriefing gang offenders facing serious charges for violent, drug and other crimes.

The second, and perhaps more important, response involved creating a very powerful deterrent to gang-related violence by making clear to youths that future violence would most certainly result in overwhelming crackdowns and "costs" imposed on the gang. Such "costs" would extend to the whole gang, not just the shooter, and might include cash-flow problems caused by street-drug market disruption, arrests from outstanding warrants, the humiliation of strict probation enforcement and possibly severe sanctions brought by federal involvement. Because of their familiarity with local gangs, the working group was usually able to link a particular act of violence to a certain gang relatively quickly and dispense sanctions swiftly. Operation Cease Fire transformed the police response to violence, turning uncertain, slow and often mild responses into ones that were certain, rapid and of whatever severity the working group deemed appropriate.

Assessment—In the project's first two years, youth homicides dropped roughly 70 percent. Between 50 and 60 percent of the residents in the three identified high-risk neighborhoods felt satisfied the BPD was doing all it could to reduce area crime, with more than 33 percent of those residents reporting a great deal of confidence in the BPD's ability to prevent crime (up from an average 10 percent in 1995). Citywide, 76 percent of residents felt safe out alone in their neighborhoods at night (compared with 55 percent in 1995). Perhaps the most noteworthy result was that 88 percent of residents said they would be willing to work with each other and police to reduce and prevent crime.

The 1999 Winner: Street Sweeping Broadway Style, Green Bay, Wisconsin, Police Department. (Adapted from "Lights Shine a Little Brighter on Broadway," by permission, 1999, p. 1.)

Scanning—Green Bay's Broadway Business District was decaying, trashed by a population of alcoholic transients who panhandled from pedestrians, slept on park benches, stirred up fights in the local bars and urinated in the doorways of neighborhood businesses. Law-abiding citizens avoided the district, leaving legitimate businesses to suffer financially.

Analysis—A comprehensive analysis of the area revealed that numerous environmental factors contributed to the corrosion of the district and that most problems were alcohol-related. Furthermore, enforcement and regulation of liquor licenses were very lax, and many liquor retailers were found to be selling to customers who were already drunk.

Response—A five-step process was developed to reverse the decay and reclaim the neighborhood:

1. Implementation of a "no serve" list for habitual drunkards and individuals who were involved in many of the neighborhood's violent incidents.
2. Increased regulation of liquor licenses and the prompt closing of establishments found in violation.
3. Applying principles of Crime Prevention through Environment Design (CPTED), such as adding lights to the dark areas behind bars and installing iron bars down the middle of park benches to keep transients from sleeping on them.
4. Working with the local media to change public perceptions of the district.
5. Starting targeted police enforcement of a zero-tolerance policy called Operation Hot Seat.

Assessment—By the end of three years, the number of calls to the Broadway district had decreased 58 percent, and calls to the rescue squad had fallen 70 percent. The business district experienced a resurgence in investment, jobs and area improvements.

Summary descriptions of the runners-up for the 1999 Herman Goldstein Award for Excellence in Problem-Oriented Policing are contained in the Appendix.

© Roy Stevens, Helen Frost Associates

This alley in the Hill district of Pittsburgh might become a key target for a problem-solving police department.

SUMMARY

Herman Goldstein is credited with originating problem-oriented policing. One concern of such an orientation is differentiating between efficiency and effectiveness. Efficiency, doing things right, has been the traditional emphasis in law enforcement. Effectiveness, doing the right things, is the emphasis in community policing.

The first step in problem solving is to group incidents as problems. Four stages of problem solving are scanning, analysis, response and assessment. Problem analysis considers the individuals involved, the incidents and the responses. Such analysis should take into account the magnet phenomenon, which occurs when a phone number or address is associated with a crime simply because it was a convenient number or address to use.

The DOC model—Dilemmas-Options-Consequences—challenges officers to carefully consider their decisions and the short- and long-term consequences of those decisions. The goal is to fuse problem solving and morality.

Crime-specific planning uses the principles of problem-solving policing to focus on identified crime problems. Crime mapping shifts the focus from the criminal to the location of crimes—the hot spots where most crimes occur. Both crime-specific planning and problem solving can be more effective if those working on the problem approach it creatively. Two barriers to creative problem solving are mental locks and killer phrases.

DISCUSSION QUESTIONS

1. How do you approach problems? Do you use a systematic approach?
2. Do you think problem solving takes more time than the traditional approach to policing?
3. Does your department use problem solving?
4. Do you consider yourself creative? What helps you to be so? What hinders you?
5. What difficulties can you foresee for a department that uses problem-solving-techniques?
6. How do problem solving and crime-specific planning differ?
7. Considering the list of mental locks, do you find yourself thinking in any of these ways? If so, what can you do to unlock your creativity?
8. In what kinds of problems do you think a problem-solving approach would be most effective?
9. What is the relationship between community policing and a problem-solving approach to policing?
10. How might computers help police in their problem-solving efforts?

INFOTRAC COLLEGE EDITION ASSIGNMENTS

- Use InfoTrac to help answer the discussion questions when applicable.
- Find an example of a police-community partnership that successfully used problem solving to deal with community issues. (You might also see the Community Policing Consortium at www.communitypolicing.org; the Police Executive Research Forum at www.PoliceForum.org/; or other community policing sites.
- Research at least one of the following subjects: crime mapping, geographic profiling or problem-oriented policing. Take good notes and be prepared to share them in class.

COMMUNITY PROJECT

Select and research a chronic problem that exists in your community. Form a problem-solving team with classmates, assign appropriate roles (police, business owner, school official, residents, etc.) and, using the SARA problem-solving model, develop solutions. Be creative.

REFERENCES

Aragon, Randall. "Community Policing: It's What's Up Front that Counts." *Law Enforcement News,* Vol. XXVI, No. 528, February 29, 2000, p. 8.

Bean, Phillip W. "Armed Robberies at the Kimmerly Glen Apartment Complex." *Problem Solving Quarterly,* Vol. 12, Nos. 1/2, Winter/Spring, 1999, pp. 4–5.

Beck, Brian. "Problem Solving for Police Officers." *Minnesota Cities,* August 1996, pp. 8–9.

Bennett, Wayne W. and Hess, Kären M. *Management & Supervision in Law Enforcement,* 3rd ed. Belmont, CA: West/Wadsworth Publishing Company, 2000.

Braiden, Chris. "Policing—the Hunt and the Habitat." *Law Enforcement News,* Vol. XXIV, October 31, 1998, p. 8.

Brito, Corina Sole and Allan, Tracy, eds. *Problem-Oriented Policing,* Volume 2. Police Executive Research Forum, 1999.

Buchholz, Steve and Roth, Thomas. *Creating the High-Performance Team.* New York: John Wiley and Sons, 1987.

Buerger, Michael E.; Petrosino, Anthony J.; and Petrosino, Carolyn. "Extending the Police Role: Implications of Police Mediation as a Problem-Solving Tool." *Police Quarterly,* Vol. 2, No. 2, June 1999, pp. 125–149.

Cooper, Christopher. *Mediation & Arbitration by Patrol Police Officers.* Lanham, MD: University of America, Inc. 1999a.

Cooper, Christopher. "Mediation by Patrol Police Officers." *Police Forum,* April 1999b, pp. 1–6.

Cooper, Christopher. "Training Patrol Officers to Mediate Disputes." *FBI Law Enforcement Bulletin,* Vol. 69, No. 2, February 2000, pp. 7–10.

COPPS: Community Oriented Policing and Problem Solving—Now and Beyond. California Department of Justice, July 1999.

Dowling, Kevin W. "Arresting the Arresting Response: Training Community Police Officers to Be Problem Solvers." *Community Policing Exchange,* Phase VI, #25, March/April 1999, p. 5.

Eck, John E. and Spelman, William. *Problem-Solving: Problem-Oriented Policing in Newport News.* Washington, DC: The Police Executive Research Forum, 1987.

Fortner, Ronald E. "Computer Technology: Mapping the Future." *Police,* Vol. 22, No. 7, July 1998, pp. 16–21.

Frazier, Thomas C. "Community Policing Efforts Offer Hope for the Future." *The Police Chief,* Vol. LXVI, No. 8, August 2000, p. 11.

Goldstein, Herman. *Problem-Oriented Policing.* New York: McGraw-Hill Publishing Company, 1990.

Kanable, Rebecca. "Taking 'Murderapolis' off the Map: Minneapolis Uses Pin Mapping Software to Give Crime Stats a Serious Poke." *Law Enforcement Technology,* Vol. 26, No. 4, April 1999, pp. 40–43.

LaVigne, Nancy and Wartell, Julie. "Crime Mapping for Problem Solving." In *Problem-Oriented Policing: Crime-Specific Problems, Critical Issues, and Making POP Work,* Volume 2, edited by Corina Sole Brito and Tracy Allan. Police Executive Research Forum, 1999, pp. 297–322.

"Lights Shine a Little Brighter on Broadway." *Law Enforcement News,* Vol. XXV, No. 521, November 15, 1999, p. 1.

MacKay, Ron. "Geographic Profiling: A New Tool for Law Enforcement." *The Police Chief,* Vol. LXVI, No. 12, December 1999, pp. 51–59.

Martinez, Michael E. "What Is Problem Solving?" *Phi Delta Kappan,* April 1998, pp. 605–609.

Miles, Martin J. "Computer-Based Probability Assessments." *Law Enforcement Technology,* Vol. 27, No. 5, May 2000, pp. 102–105.

Nila, Michael J. "Defining the Police Mission: A Community/Police Perspective." *The Police Chief,* October 1990, pp. 43–47.

Nislow, Jennifer. "Location, Location, Location: Geographic Profiling Helps Police Close in on Serial Criminals." *Law Enforcement News,* Vol. XXVI, No. 535, June 15, 2000, pp. 1, 10.

Pilant, Lois. "Crime Mapping and Analysis." *The Police Chief,* Vol. LXVI, No. 12, December 1999, pp. 38–49.

Rogers, Donna. "Getting Crime Analysis on the Map." *Law Enforcement Technology,* Vol. 26, No. 11, November 1999, pp. 76–79.

Rogers, Donna. "Trends in Crime Analysis and Crime Mapping." *Law Enforcement Technology,* Vol. 27, No. 5, May 2000, pp. 36–42.

Romano, Linda J.; McDevitt, Jack; Jones, Jimmie; and Johnson, William. "Combined Problem-Solving Models Incorporate Ethics Analysis." *The Police Chief,* Vol. LXVII, No. 8, August 2000, pp. 98–102.

Rosen, Marie Simonetti. "A LEN Interview with Professor Herman Goldstein, the 'Father' of Problem-Oriented Policing." *Law Enforcement News,* February 14, 1997, pp. 8–10.

von Oech, Roger. *A Whack on the Side of the Head.* New York: Warner Books, 1983.

Wadman, Robert C. and Olson, Robert K. *Community Wellness: A New Theory of Policing.* Washington, DC: Police Executive Research Forum, 1990.

Warden, John and Shaw, Jerry. "Predicting a Residential Break-In Pattern." In *Crime Mapping Case Studies: Successes in the Field,* Volume 2, edited by Nancy LaVigne and Julie Wartell. Police Executive Research Forum, 2000, pp. 81–87.

Wartell, Julie. "Putting Crime on the Map." *Police,* Vol. 24, No. 6, June 2000, pp. 52–55.

Wartell, Julie and Greenhalgh, Fiona. "Using Technology for Problem Solving." *Problem Solving Quarterly,* Vol. 13, No. 1, Winter 2000, pp. 1, 6–7.

Wernicke, Susan C. and Stallo, Mark A. "Steps toward Integrating Crime Analysis into Local Law Enforcement." *The Police Chief,* Vol. LXVII, No. 7, July 2000, pp. 56–57.

Wideman, Dean A. "Multifunctional Aspects of Crime Analysis in the Investigation of Violent and Sexual Crimes." *The Police Chief,* Vol. LXVII, No. 7, July 2000, pp. 59–63.

Wilson, James Q. and Kelling, George L. "Making Neighborhoods Safe." *The Atlantic Monthly,* February 1989, pp. 46–52.

Wolfer, Loreen; Baker, Thomas E.; and Zezza, Ralph. "Problem-Solving Policing: Eliminating Hot Spots." *FBI Law Enforcement Bulletin,* Vol. 68, No. 11, November 1999, pp. 9–14.

Woods, Mike. "Crime Analysis: A Key Tool in Any Crime Reduction Strategy." *The Police Chief,* Vol. LXVI, No. 4, April 1999, pp. 17–30.

CHAPTER 5

Implementing Community Policing

There is nothing more difficult to plan, more uncertain of success, or more dangerous to manage than the establishment of a new order; because the innovator has for enemies all those who have derived advantage from the old order and finds but lukewarm defenders among those who stand to gain from the new one.

    Machiavelli

Do you know

What basic changes are required in making the transition to community policing?

What a department's vision should include?

Who should be included in a needs assessment?

Which may be more important, targeting a "critical mass" of individuals or mobilizing the community at large?

What a strategic plan includes?

What the most important consideration is in selecting strategies to implement community policing?

What "POST-21" is?

Whether training should be the spearhead of change?

What the most important areas are to cover in training?

What transition managers should anticipate and prepare for?

What common pitfalls there are in making the transition to a community policing philosophy?

What impediments to community policing may need to be overcome?

When conducting evaluations, how failures should be viewed?

Can you define these terms:

change management

critical mass

directed imbalance

experimental imbalance

strategic planning

systems thinking

transition management

vision

INTRODUCTION

You have looked at the theory of community policing as well as at the key players—the community and the police. You have also considered a basic component of community policing—problem solving. The challenge of community policing is to move from theories about using problem-solving techniques and partnerships to reduce crime and violence to actual implementation.

This chapter begins with a consideration of the basic nature of change, how it influences implementing community policing and the changes needed to successfully transition. This is followed by a discussion of how the community policing philosophy should be reflected in a vision and mission statement and the possible impact on the entire police organization. Next is a look at needs assessment for both the department and community, followed by an explanation of strategic planning and ways to develop strategies. Then the importance of hiring, promoting and training is presented. Next are examples of how community policing has been implemented, including a discussion of the benefits that might be achieved. Anticipating and preparing for resistance is covered next, followed by pitfalls to avoid and impediments to overcome. The chapter concludes with ways to evaluate progress and a look at a new advocacy group for community policing.

CHANGE

It has been said that nothing is constant except change. Nonetheless, police administrators, supervisors and even line personnel frequently resist change in any form and prefer the status quo. But change is occurring and will continue to occur. Police departments can resist, or they can accept the challenge and capitalize on the benefits that may result. Issues requiring departments to change include technological advances, demographic changes, fiscal constraints, shifting values, the need to do more with less, heightened media coverage of police misconduct and citizen fear of escalating gang violence.

Change takes time. Traditions die hard. Most police officers will find proposed changes to their culture extremely threatening. However, although the police culture is tremendously strong, remember that a huge ship can be turned by a small rudder. It just takes time and steadfast determination.

Abshire and Paynter (2000, p. 54) contend: "To do it well community policing should be viewed as a constant work in progress." They interviewed the chief of police of the San Diego Police Department who commented: "Success doesn't happen overnight. It's been 12 years and we're still identifying some areas where we can really improve and expand community policing through our department." Chief Bejarano also noted: "It [community policing] is not a project. It's not a program. It's a culture."

It is also helpful to be familiar with the five categories of "adopters" to expect within any organization, as Figure 5.1 shows. The innovators are risk takers. They embrace uncertainty and change. The early adopters are opinion leaders, the ones to whom others come for advice. The early majority accept new ideas slightly ahead of the majority. The late majority is more skeptical. They can be persuaded but usually require a great deal of peer pressure. The late adopters are the most difficult to convince. They tend to

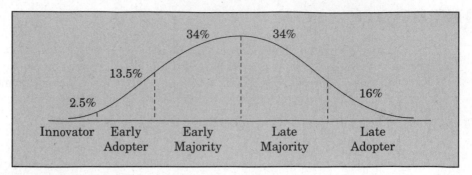

Figure 5.1   Change Takes Time

be suspicious of all innovations. Recognizing these individual characteristics may be helpful in developing strategies to "sell" community policing to the troops.

Finally, it is important to heed the comment of Goldstein (1993, p. 2): "Policing in the United States is much like a large, intricate, complex apparatus with many parts. Change of any one part requires changes in many others and in the way the parts fit and work together."

Some changes have already occurred within many departments that should make the transition to community policing easier, including better-educated police officers who are less inclined to accept orders unquestioningly and a shift in incentives with intrinsic, personal-worth-type rewards becoming as important as extrinsic, monetary rewards. Other changes are needed to move from the traditional, reactive, incident-driven mode of policing to the proactive, problem-solving, collaborative mode typical of community policing.

⬦ NEEDED CHANGES

Some changes basic to implementing the community policing philosophy have already been briefly described in Chapter 2.

Community policing will require a change in mission statement, departmental organization, leadership style and the general approach to "fighting crime."

How these changes fit into the transition from a philosophy to practice will become evident.

The Community Policing Consortium (CPC) (2000, p. 1) suggests two kinds of management required for the transition to community policing, change management and transition management: "**Change management** is the development of an overall strategy which will review the present state of the organization, envision the future state of the organization and devise the means of moving from one to the other. **Transition management** is overseeing, controlling and leading that move from present state to future state."

Although the consortium uses the term *management*, it also recognizes the importance of *leadership* in this transition: "To embark wholeheartedly on the transition process first requires a leader who is open, willing to make change and provides support for those decisions with commitment and energy." This leader must also have a vision for the department and the community. In fact, Moore (1998, p. 7) suggests that one word describes how a manager differs from a leader: *vision.*

CREATING A VISION AND MISSION STATEMENT

Vision might be thought of as intelligent foresight. According to Moore (p. 7): "Vision starts with a mental image that gradually evolves from abstract musings to a concrete series of mission statements, goals and objectives." Moore describes an exercise to use in creating a vision (pp. 7–8):

• Think about the most significant events or experiences in your department's history. Go back as far as you can remember.

• Draw a line on a piece of paper that traces these points on a timeline. Show positive events as peaks and negative events as valleys.

• Think about what made each event a peak or valley. What strengths and weaknesses become obvious?

• Next think ahead. Does the line you've drawn suggest other peaks ahead? What might lead to them? What positive traits within the department can help make them happen? Does the line also suggest potential valleys? How can you prevent them?

Examining the department's past for strengths and weaknesses, successes and failures is an important step in creating a vision for the future.

This vision should include the essential elements of the community policing philosophy: problem solving, empowering everyone, forming community partnerships and being proactive—making preventing crime as important as enforcing the law.

The vision for each department will be different. It must be tailored to reflect the personnel within the department and the community the department serves. Vision should be something everyone involved can buy into and feel a part of. This means involving leaders from within the department and the community from the beginning of the transition if possible. The Community Policing Consortium recommends that the entire work force be directly involved in the envisioning and planning processes—at least having a cross-section of the work force representing all ranks or grades and incorporating sworn, unsworn and civilian personnel and their respective union representations. It also recommends that those who have been identified as antagonistic to the change process be deliberately co-opted. They cannot be ignored because they will not go away. Actively seek ways to avert their antagonism.

Ramsey (2000, p. 16) draws an interesting analogy between a successful transition to community policing and winning a 4-by-100-meter relay race: "In the relay race, the outcome depends not only on how fast the individual contestants run, but also on the smooth handoff of the baton from one runner to the next. It is the same in policing. Smooth handoffs get the best results. We are more likely to solve problems of crime and disorder when we share information, coordinate activities and involve everyone, smoothly and enthusiastically."

He takes the analogy one step further by asking the reader to imagine what would happen in a relay race if the runners were told after they passed the baton that they must leave the stadium because the outcome was not their concern. Noting that this would be "preposterous," he suggests that is exactly what is done in policing: "We forget that everyone—police officers and citizens—needs to feel a sense of ownership and achievement." This sense of ownership and achievement should start with the vision statement.

Once the vision is articulated, it should be translated into a mission statement as discussed in Chapter 2. The development of a mission statement is important for any organization, but it is critical in developing and implementing community policing. Its importance cannot be overstated. Again, the mission statement must be something everyone can buy into and feel a part of. Once the vision and mission statement have been articulated, the next step is to conduct a needs assessment.

ASSESSING NEEDS

A needs assessment should include not only the department but also the community of which it is a part.

Analyzing the Department

Recall from Chapter 2 that departments who have successfully implemented community policing have made several organizational changes:

• The bureaucracy is flattened with fewer in management roles and more line personnel.

• It is also decentralized, pushing authority levels and decision making as far down the management line as possible.

• Those in management positions become leaders rather than managers, encouraging input from those they supervise on important decisions. They also let go of some traditional supervisory practices, serving more as models and mentors.

• Patrol officers are given new responsibilities, becoming more self-supervising and self-motivated. They are empowered to make decisions and problem solve with their community partners.

• Permanent shifts and areas are assigned, allowing officers and supervisors to develop in-depth knowledge of the individuals, businesses and organizations in the neighborhoods where they work.

In addition, Carter (1999, p. 105) suggests: "Successful implementation of community policing requires a complete philosophical change in organizational culture. This includes policy changes in a wide range of areas such as deployment, assignment, supervision, personnel evaluation, response alternatives to calls, call management, and a host of related changes to the infrastructure."

The department's organization should be carefully analyzed to identify barriers within the agency likely to impede the community policing initiative. This needs assessment should also consider external constraints controlled by others outside the department such as finance and budgeting, hiring rules and state-mandated training programs.

One of the most important implementation needs, Mittleman (2000, p. 51) stresses, is that "community policing must permeate the entire department from the top down. Line personnel must be given time away from calls for service to practice community policing."

Analyzing the Community

At the heart of the community policing philosophy is the recognition that the police can no longer "go it alone." Edwards (1998, p. 5) suggests: "They must tap the eyes, ears and voices of law-abiding citizens."

A starting point is to analyze the community's demographics. What is the average age? Educational level? Economic level? What is the racial composition? Recall the social capital discussed in Chapter 3. How much social capital is available for community policing efforts?

Correia (2000, p. 54) suggests: "In communities with low levels of Putnam's social capital and high levels of COP activities, police officers may be perceived as facilitators who take responsibility for engaging citizens in alleviating complex social problems. On the other hand, in areas with high levels of Putnam's social capital and high levels of community policing, COP may be characterized as a partnership—that is a collaborative effort featuring citizens and police working together to develop and implement effective problem-solving activities to enhance quality of life." Correia further suggests that COP activity may be driven more by community factors than by factors internal to police organizations.

Duffee et al. (1999, p. 9) also hold this belief: "We believe that economic, political, and demographic forces have far greater effects on neighborhood life than do neighborhood institutions or the police." Their research identified seven neighborhood processes that figure prominently in building and sustaining strong neighborhoods.

The first is *internal coordination*. This refers to the extent to which groups and organizations with separate functions but common location act together to achieve neighborhood goals. Examples of police influence in this area include increased planning and coordination among police and social services, among police and city agencies, and among resident groups and businesses. Community policing program components might include resident organization collaboration, empowering frontline officers to problem solve and crime prevention activities.

The second is *external linkages*. This refers to the extent to which a neighborhood has ties to nonlocal centers of resources and expertise. Police influence in this area might involve the full range of citizen involvement. A community policing program component might be coordination with government agencies in problem solving.

Third is *concerns for exchange value/improved collective consumption*. This refers to the extent to which use of space in a neighborhood is tested against a criterion of improving collective consumption rather than profit maximization or exchange value. Police influences might include pressure on renters and drug dealers. Community policing program components might include order maintenance, geomapping, city agency coordination, crime prevention activity and problem solving.

Fourth is the *quality of process concerns*. This refers to the extent to which neighborhood collective action is attentive to its processes as well as its outcomes. The neighborhood is self-evaluative and concerned with renewal. Police influences might include a concern for inclusion as well as concerns for group process. Community policing program components might include resident surveys and meetings, mobilization efforts and feedback from problem solving.

Fifth is *autonomy*—the extent to which a neighborhood can influence decisions about actions taken about it. The neighborhood keeps its identity while participating in nonlocal networks. Police influences might include legitimizing and funding neighborhood planning councils, asking citizens to be more than just the "eyes and ears" of the department. Community policing program components might include decentralized command, resident decisions in issues and tactics and place-specific data analysis.

Sixth is *shared culture*, that is, the extent to which a neighborhood is conscious of cultural uniqueness and shares symbols of common place. Police influences might include a shared concern for environment and physical beauty. Community policing program components might include block parties and ceremonies recognizing collective action.

And seventh, *dialogue*—the extent to which information about the neighborhood is shared and accurate. Conflicts are addressed when all participants are recognized as having legitimacy to speak. Police influences might range from limited dialogue to considerable two-way planning. Community policing program components might include resident partnerships, foot and bike patrols, decentralized command, empowering frontline officers, problem solving and crime prevention (pp. 11, 16).

Duffey et al. (p. 27) conclude: "If the ultimate goal of community policing is improving the quality of life in neighborhoods, then there must be a concern with the general processes of neighborhood building rather than police approaches to neighborhoods." To accomplish this, police must develop a comprehensive picture of their community. They can do this by surveys and direct interaction with citizens.

Benedict et al. (1999, p. 144) recommend: "Tailoring a community policing program to meet the needs of the community necessitates that the police first determine what the needs of the community are." How? Johnson and Bromley (1999, p. 133) suggest: "One of the most important steps a police agency must take as part of a comprehensive community oriented policing strategy is to solicit information from its community members." They conducted a survey at the University of South Florida to determine where this community thought university police should concentrate their investigative efforts in solving crime—an interesting approach to overcoming the resistance many citizens have about community policing being "soft on crime." Leading the list in this survey was sexual assault. The second portion of the survey asked respondents to rank the priority of police activities. Their ranking from most important to least important was: motor vehicle patrol, drug enforcement, foot patrol, crime prevention program, public assistance, drug and alcohol education, bike patrol, alcohol enforcement and traffic enforcement.

It would be enlightening to conduct a similar survey with police officers and their managers. Such shared information could go far in building trust among line officers, managers and citizens.

Benedict et al. (p. 148) used a mail survey of a random stratified sample consisting of 360 residents, of which 205 (57 percent) responded. The survey asked respondents how concerned they were about their personal safety during the day or at night and how concerned they were about their children's safety while playing in their neighborhood and at schools. In addition, it asked questions about concerns over city ordinance violations such as speeding vehicles, illegal parking and excessive noise. Finally, respondents were asked questions about tactics the police could use to better serve the community and ensure citizen safety.

The Bureau of Justice Statistics (BJS) and the Office of Community Oriented Policing Services (COPS) has available for local law enforcement agencies a computer software package designed to help conduct public opinion surveys about how well the police are doing their jobs. The program can be downloaded from www.ojp.usdoj.gov/bjs. The project used the standard National Crime Victimization Survey (NCVS) questionnaire as the core data-collection instrument. Smith and Hayeslip (1998, p. 35) suggest: "Using this software, localities can conduct their own telephone surveys of residents on crime victimization, attitudes toward policing and other community-related issues."

While conducting needs assessments, you should also pay attention to who might be community leaders to enlist in the community policing initiative. According to Correia (p. 56): "It appears that the number of participants actively engaged in a community policing program is not as important as the character of the individuals participating. A 'critical mass' of individuals with high levels of social engagement may be more effective in solving a community's problems than a large number of individuals with low levels of social cohesion." A critical mass in physics is the smallest amount of a fissionable material that will sustain a nuclear chain reaction. In the context of community policing efforts, a **critical mass** is the smallest number of citizens/organizations needed to support and sustain the community policing initiative. Correia (p. 57) concludes:

It may be more important for COP-oriented police agencies to target this "critical mass" of individuals than to try to mobilize the community at large.

Once the needs assessment has been conducted, the next step is to develop a blueprint, that is, to do some strategic planning. *P.C. -26 - did a child know it was wrong*

◆ STRATEGIC PLANNING

Strategic planning is long-term, large-scale, future-oriented planning. It begins with the vision and mission statement already discussed. It is grounded in those statements and guided by the findings of the needs assessment. From here, specific goals and objectives and an accompanying timeline are developed. Wittham (1998, p. 23) suggests several essential elements of strategic planning for law enforcement:

- A *manage-for-results orientation*—requires people to distance themselves somewhat from their daily duties and think about the big picture.

- *Environmental analysis*—primary activities here are data gathering and analysis of relevant trends.

- *Organizational assessment*—determines an organization's capabilities (strengths and weaknesses) in light of its mission. Resource assessment (e.g., human, facilities, budget and financial) is conducted. The product of this step should be a precise listing of all the organization's competencies and shortcomings.

Switzer (2000, p. 39) suggests: "To implement community-oriented policing success-fully, it is important to have a strategic plan that identifies where the department stands in the implementation process, where the department would like to be, and most impor-tantly, how the department intends to get there." Because each community is unique, no template can be suggested. However, the key elements outlined in the vision and mis-sion statement should be incorporated, as should a plan for addressing areas identified as weaknesses in the needs assessment.

As the plan is being developed it is important that those developing it engage in **sys-tems thinking.** DeParis (2000, p. 108) explains: "Systems thinking is a conceptual frame-work that recognizes the contribution of each component to the system; i.e., everything affects everything else." Planners must think in terms of the whole rather than the indi-vidual parts.

The strategic plan should include community partnerships and problem solving as well as any needed cultural and organizational changes in the department. It should also include a realistic timeline and a way to assess progress. It must also be tied to the department's budget.

Remember that the strategic plan is long range. Departments don't successfully implement community policing in a year or two. It takes time—years for most depart-ments to fully implement it. Again, all interested parties should be allowed input into the strategic plan, and it should be realistic.

At the end of each year, progress toward accomplishing the vision, mission state-ment, goals and objectives should be measured. This may require a change in how per-formance has typically been assessed. Historically police have measured their failures—the number of crimes committed and the number of arrests made. Such statistics are relatively easy to gather and to analyze. Assessing the effectiveness of crime prevention efforts, however, is much more difficult. How does a department measure reduced fear of crime or satisfaction with the police service? Nonetheless, as the Community Policing Consortium notes: "What gets measured gets done."

In addition to having a realistic timeline, the strategic plan must also be tied to the agency's budget. Without the resources to implement the activities outlined in the long-range plan, they are not likely to be accomplished. Again, the transition will take time and, in some instances, additional resources.

The Community Policing Consortium cautions: "Don't get lost in the process." The consortium explains:

> The plan can become an end in itself. The project manager, the planning group, draft papers, lengthy dialogue, revised drafts, additional papers, circulated memo-randa, further discussion, establishing working groups or sub-committees—this is the stuff that bureaucracies are made of. Some people actually enjoy it. The strategic plan and the planning process are only a means to an end—delivering the future organization built on core values, agreed goals and an effective imple-mentation process.

Strategic plans need not be elaborate. Small departments with limited resources might follow the example Kurz (2000, p. 28) describes. His department implemented strategic planning in the small town of Durham, New Hampshire: "The Durham strategic plan project consisted of three phases: a survey of citizen satisfaction with police services; a survey of police officer satisfaction with the department; and a one-day planning session attended by police officers and community leaders." The introduction to the 2000 strategic plan (p. 34) states:

> The Durham Police Department 2000 Strategic Plan is designed to be an evolving document, constantly reviewed, updated, and brought into line with the desires of the community. It is the culmination of a series of exercises, all designed to ensure that the vision, mission, and objectives of the agency are successfully achieved. . . . An outgrowth of this process is the enhanced ability to effectively manage resources, provide accountability through measured results and adjust to change. Successful planning requires the fortitude to change course when opportunities and community demands arise. Ultimately, it is the planning process itself that keeps the agency focused on what it wishes to accomplish and the best route to get there.

◉ DEVELOPING STRATEGIES

Hundreds of strategies have been developed to implement community policing. Among the most common are use of foot, bike and horse patrol; block watches; newsletters; community surveys; citizen volunteer programs; storefronts; special task units; and educational programs. Another common strategy is to assign officers to permanent beats and teach them community organizing and problem-solving skills. Some communities help train landlords in how to keep their properties crime free. Many communities encourage the development of neighborhood organizations, and some have formed teams (partnerships); for example, code and safety violations might be corrected by a team consisting of police, code enforcers, fire officials and building code officers.

Other communities have turned to the World Wide Web to connect with their citizens. In Los Angeles, for example: "Community leaders see the new Web site as a bridge to the public and an important repository for the latest news, facts and figures on the LAPD" (Malinowski et al., 2000, p. 62). LAPDOnline averages 100,000 hits per day, totaling over 23 million hits between August 1998 and February 2000. Naturally, smaller departments would not expect such impressive results, but even the smallest communities might find a computer expert to volunteer to set up and manage a Web site for the department.

One innovative strategy the Beaufort (South Carolina) Police Department used is the Process Action Team (PAT) as described by Nagy (2000, p. 34):

> A PAT can be used to address internal processes within the department as well as the community. Some examples of internal processes PAT has addressed include crisis incident response planning, administration of discipline, field training officer program development and a department forms manual.
>
> If a complaint or problem seems to exist, the management team officer assigns members to a PAT. The PAT conducts meetings using the total-quality-management facilitator method. A lower-ranking officer leads the PAT, maintains the project file, reports on progress, and ultimately must assist the team in reaching consensus on a solution to the problem.

"What works?" "Has somebody tried . . . ?" "What can we do about . . . ?" "Why can't we . . . ?" Nancy Gist, director of the Bureau of Justice Statistics notes these are questions communities nationwide are asking as they tackle the challenges of reducing violence, drugs and other crimes. Gist suggests:

In *350 Tested Strategies to Prevent Crime: A Resource for Municipal Agencies and Community Groups,* the National Crime Prevention Council has taken a major step toward helping us meet that challenge. By taking a novel approach— considering strategies rather than programs—this book helps communities focus on adapting and tailoring program ideas and crime prevention techniques to local needs and circumstances and to comprehensive plans (National Crime Prevention Council, 1995, foreword).

The most important consideration in selecting strategies to implement community policing is to ensure that the strategies fit the unique needs of the community.

Section Three describes numerous strategies that have been used throughout the country as departments move toward community policing.

◉ HIRING AND PROMOTING

DeLong (1999, p. 6) asserts: "The process of recruiting and selecting personnel is one of the most important considerations in the successful implementation of the community policing philosophy." Officers for the 21st century working in a department that has made the transition to community policing will need attitudes and skills that are different from those they used in the past.

One new assessment instrument has the support of community policing experts across the country: the "Police Officer Screening Test for the 21st Century" or "POST-21."

"POST-21" is an add-on to an agency's existing application examination and selection process that is designed to identify applicants with traits and attitudes compatible with a community policing environment.

Harris and Kolkman (2000, p. 64) explain that the text has three objectives: (1) to bring the hiring process to a more personal level by evaluating the applicants' "community" perspective, (2) to assist agencies in finding candidates who are "service-minded" as well as those with a traditional crime-fighting mindset and (3) to reduce costs by identifying candidates compatible with the community policing philosophy, reducing training costs after selection. The test consists of four parts (Harris and Kolkman, pp. 64–65):

1. Evaluation of the applicant's "policing orientation," or whether a person has the ability and inclination to utilize a variety of policing strategies in working with the community.
2. A series of questions to test flexibility in responses.
3. Evaluation of realistic expectations of police officer duties.
4. An essay section on problem-solving techniques.

Whether an agency uses this specific instrument or not, the content is what should be considered when selecting—and promoting—officers. Are they community oriented?

For example, do they volunteer in the community? Are they problem solvers? Good communicators?

The oral interview can be very helpful in selecting what Capsambelis (1999, p. 4) refers to as "the customer-oriented cop." He describes how situations can be designed to assess job skills, including judgment, problem sensitivity, problem solving and oral communication. He suggests asking a candidate how he or she would respond to a call from an elderly couple having a problem with juveniles cutting through their yard. Knowing the candidate lacks law enforcement experience, what is evaluated is whether the candidate uses a problem-solving approach.

Lord and Schoeps (2000) conducted a study that identified 22 attributes that one large metropolitan police department considered critical for effective community policing officers: remains rational and composed while conducting regular job obligations; is willing and able to take control of situations at work; is able to make decisions; alcohol use does not interfere with personal or job responsibilities; is free from illegal drug use; able to identify and solve problems; has ability to keep abreast of current laws, procedures, and technology necessary for job functions; is in good health; is physically competent to do the job; does not abuse medications—prescriptions or over-the-counter medications; without personal biases, can receive, evaluate, and act on information from people of different cultures, values, and standards; does not require constant supervision to complete tasks; possesses a work history that is unencumbered with firing, disciplinary problems, or excessive lateness or tardiness; and cares about finishing a task even if it means work and time.*

◉ TRAINING

Training is critical for a successful transition to community policing. The Community Policing Consortium recommends that departments embark on a training program for all personnel at all levels to explain the change process and reduce fear and resistance. Training should also explore the community policing philosophy and the planning process and encourage all stakeholders to participate. The consortium advises, however:

"DON'T *make training the spearhead of change."*

The consortium says that many efforts have been made to place training at the leading edge of change in both the public and private sector. Much time and energy are expended in such efforts, but, no matter how effective the training, they will be neutralized if what is learned is at variance with practices and procedures occurring in the department. The consortium stresses: "Unless the culture, structure and management of the organization are in harmony with the training, then the impact of the latter will be minimized. . . . What is needed is the agreed vision, values, goals, and objectives to drive the organization and affect every aspect of policing—not expecting a training program to be a short cut to acceptance."

As the community policing philosophy takes hold in a department, officers will be more receptive to the training they will need to be effective community policing officers.

---

*Although most of these attributes would be desirable in any police officer, Lord and Schoeps suggest that attributes emphasizing problem solving and decision making are especially critical.

Paoline et al. (2000, p. 582) describe several areas in which training would be essential: "Training that enhances officers' capacity to perform community-policing functions—analyzing problems, working with community groups, developing and implementing responses that do not rely on the criminal law—could shape officers' outlooks on the police role and their attitudes toward the public."

Among the most important areas to include in training are communication skills, problem-solving skills and leadership skills.

Communication skills are the focus of Section Two. Problem-solving skills were discussed in Chapter 4. Leadership skills that Mook and Dempsey (2000, p. 115) identified include:

- The ability to motivate people to achieve goals.
- Knowledge of job and community.
- Ability to set an example for positive behavior.
- Willingness to assume responsibility and to accept responsibility for mistakes.
- Skill in diplomacy.
- Skill in communicating with individuals and groups.
- Ability to adapt to and facilitate change.
- Skill in organizing and prioritizing time, resources and community meetings.
- Knowledge of diverse populations.
- Skill in conflict resolution.

Other areas Mook and Dempsey (p. 116) suggest should be included in training are time- and stress-management and ethics.

◈ EXAMPLES OF IMPLEMENTING COMMUNITY POLICING

Tempe, Arizona, has a comprehensive model for community policing that involves numerous elements. Chief of Police Brown notes: "We said community policing is going to be an evolution, not a revolution. We did not want to come in and say, 'Effective next Monday, we will be a community policing organization.' It's been a gradual change process for us, and it's growing every day" (Rosen, 1994).

Pratt (1995, pp. 57–58) describes a five-step approach to implementing community policing:

1. Problem Identification/Assessment. Consult civic, political, business, religious and media leaders, consult the public through town hall meetings or informally at educational, cultural and social activities within identifiable neighborhoods. Determine priorities, trying to place the public's needs ahead of the department's needs.

2. Plan Development. The overall objective of crime reduction must be kept in mind. Strategy obviously will depend upon the nature of the specific crime problem chosen

for attack. Any program must consider ethnic, social, economic and other cultural factors in the area and will differ from one area to another. The strategy must fit the problem and the tactics must fit the neighborhood.

3. Personnel Selection/Development/Training. Strong ties between officers and citizens can best be formed by considering ethnic, religious, national origin or economic factors, with assignment of officers who are either representative of such groups or are empathetic with them.

4. Community Preparation. Include full information to the community of intended police action, how the residents will benefit from those actions and what role citizens may be expected to play, along with the legal and safety limits placed upon citizen actions.

5. Ongoing Evaluation and, Where Appropriate, Modification. It is vital to monitor progress, evaluating each phase and tactic so that timely modifications can be made as appropriate.

A ten-step implementation plan used in the Pueblo County Sheriff's Department is described by Corsentino (1996, pp. 2, 8):

1. Developed a strategic plan.
2. Leadership planted community policing seeds with officers and support units so that they would take ownership.
3. The department incorporated team policing into all sectors and encouraged deputies to go beyond basic law enforcement decisions to problem solving.
4. The department decentralized decision making where and when possible and encouraged officers to work on critical issues as they determine a need.
5. The department changed its organizational culture to a customer orientation and used this approach to interact with citizens.
6. Designed a new approach to strategic planning that involves officers and citizens more closely in the organizational changes required to support community policing.
7. Designed and rebuilt the system for better operating efficiency.
8. Established community outreach programs such as DARE, GREAT, and DFSZ (Drug Free School Zone).
9. Personnel encouraged good relations with the media, and the media in turn were instrumental in improving the department's image.
10. Trained, trained, trained—taught, taught, taught—coached, coached, coached.

Understanding Community Policing (1994, p. 33) stresses: "Timing is an important factor in the implementation process. Implementation that moves too slowly may dampen enthusiasm and reduce momentum, while implementation that moves too quickly may create confusion and resentment and may threaten the success of the project through the use of hurried and ill conceived methods." This monograph (p. 42) also suggests: "Media involvement ensures a wide dissemination of the community policing message and encourages the media to stay involved in future community policing events."

Lessons Learned from Team Policing

Walker (1993, pp. 36–37) suggests that those implementing community policing should take some lessons from what was learned from the team policing programs instituted during the mid-1960s to mid-1970s. Both community policing and team policing had a neighborhood focus, decentralized decision making, community input and a new police role. But the basic goals of community policing differ radically from team policing, with community policing rejecting the crime-attack model in favor of an emphasis on order maintenance and quality-of-life problems. In addition, the team policing effort faced three major obstacles (pp. 41–44):

1. Opposition from middle management—captains and lieutenants resented their loss of authority as greater responsibility was placed on sergeants and police officers.

2. Trial by peers—where it was a success, or reputed to be a success, there was resentment on the part of other officers, often as the result of unequal workloads.

3. Problems with dispatching technology—dispatching technology remained centralized, with team members spending as much as half their time outside their team area.

The most important lesson to be learned from team policing, according to Walker (p. 44), was the problems associated with unclear definition of goals. He (p. 54) notes:

> The problem of unclear goals is probably greater in community policing than in team policing. . . . Community policing . . . represents a radical role redefinition, eschewing crime control in favor of attention to problems that have traditionally been defined as not part of the police role. . . .
>
> Redefining the police role in such a radical fashion introduces a number of problems. The most important is socializing the various actors and publics into the new role. Resocializing police officers is a major change. . . . Equally difficult is the task of resocializing the public.

Doing the Little Things—A Shift in Policy Focus

Hoffmann (2000, p. 54) offers a final piece of advice to those implementing community policing:

> The Broken-Windows theory contends that a broken window left unfixed is a sign that nobody cares and can lead to serious crime, abandonment of neighborhoods to criminals, and urban decay. "The policy corollary is that minor problems warrant serious attention, a premise that challenges reigning criminal justice practices," George L. Kelling said in a Department of Justice lecture series.

◈ BENEFITS THAT MIGHT BE ACHIEVED

The benefits of implementing community policing are numerous, both to the department and to the community at large. Community policing brings police closer to the people, building relationships between police and community and among community members themselves. As police interaction with the community becomes more positive, productive partnerships are formed, and community and officer leadership skills are developed. Citizens see that problems have solutions, giving them courage to tackle other community issues. As citizens feel more empowered to get involved, prevention and detection of crime increases, leading to reduced fear of crime in the community and improved quality of life. Reduced levels of crime allow more police resources to be allocated to services that have the greatest impact on the quality of community life. Making effective use of the talents and resources available within communities further extends severely strained police resources. Community policing also provides real challenges for officers, making them more than "order takers and report writers," which leads to increased job satisfaction among officers.

Research conducted by Sherwood (2000, p. 191) found that: "Officers from the department that was observed to be more advanced in implementing community policing reported significantly higher scores for skill variety, task identity, task significance and autonomy." Sherwood (p. 209) reports: "Allowing officers to work regularly with neighborhood residents creates a natural work unit that will increase skill variety and task identity. Furthermore, by granting police officers the increased responsibility and authority to engage in proactive problem solving, managers enhance the vertical loading of the job and increase autonomy. Combining tasks into a more identifiable and complete piece of work to be performed by the officer also strengthens skill variety and task identity." Community policing also makes the police department *effective*, instead of only *efficient*, which leads to greater community satisfaction with police services.

◉ ANTICIPATING AND PREPARING FOR RESISTANCE

As the chapter-opening quote by Machiavelli suggests, establishing a new order can be difficult, even dangerous to manage.

Managers should anticipate and prepare for resistance to the community policing philosophy and the changes that accompany the transition.

Consider the following analogy: A professional truck driver does not drive his 50-ton trailer-truck the same way he drives a sports car. In the truck, he corners more slowly and avoids braking sharply; otherwise the trailer's momentum can overturn or jackknife the truck.

Police organizations also have considerable momentum. Resistance to change can be reduced by two kinds of imbalance within an organizational structure that can render it susceptible to change: **directed imbalance** and **experimental imbalance.**

Directed Imbalance. A physical comparison to describe directed imbalance is that of riding a bicycle. Think of how, when riding a bicycle, your body unconsciously shifts in the opposite direction of a turn to be made. Without this shift in balance, you are likely to tip over. You are also likely to fall if you shift in preparation for a turn and then do *not* turn. Sparrow (1988, p. 3) suggests: "Directed imbalances within a police organization will be those imbalances that are created in anticipation of the proposed change in orientation. They will be the changes that make sense only under the assumption that the whole project will be implemented, and that it will radically alter organizational priorities." He gives the following examples of directed imbalance:

- Movement of the most talented and promising personnel into the newly defined jobs
- Making it clear that the route to promotion lies within such jobs
- Recategorizing the crime statistics according to their effect on the community
- Redesigning the staff evaluation system to account for contributions to the nature and quality of community life
- Providing inservice training in problem-solving skills for veteran officers and managers
- Altering training to include problem-solving skills
- Establishing new communication channels with other public services

Experimental Imbalance. Experimental imbalance, as the name implies, creates an atmosphere of trial and error and of risk taking. It encourages officers at all levels to be creative and seek innovative ways to approach community problems.

Misunderstandings and fears will need to be dealt with. Some officers will fear loss of turf or power and authority. Others will fear added responsibilities. Moving from the known to the unknown is difficult for many. The Community Policing Consortium suggests a communication strategy geared to overcoming resistance; increasing readiness for change; preparing and equipping people for the change; and helping reduce uncertainty and anxiety. Their list of do's and don'ts is not prioritized but contains items that should be considered to overcome resistance.

Do

- Pursue an open and consultative communication process.
- Adopt and role-model a participatory management style.
- Apply the KISS principle—Keep It Straight and Simple.
- Encourage the open expression of employee feelings and opinions.
- Help employees attain a new frame of reference for the organization and their expectations.
- Be alert to using every opportunity to respond positively to employees about the change process and help them embrace it.
- Explain where the needs of the individuals and of the organization converge and how divergence will be addressed.
- Reinforce any self-motivation identified in staff and use those drives effectively for the change process.

Don't

- Adopt an autocratic management style or communication pattern internally.
- Try to placate staff by making promises in order to win them over.
- Suggest that staff are to blame.

- Suggest that staff don't
- Argue with staff to win
- Directly attack emplo
- Deny employees their
- Excuse or compromis
- Take anger personall

�◈ PITFALLS TO A

Community policing
(1996) cautions:

> In the adoption (
> certain pitfalls th
> mentation of th
> simply equivale
> chance of gettir
> more important is what does the p
> specific officers are doing. Foot patrol without the elements of part-
> ships with the community will not amount to much.

Common pitfalls in making the transition to community policing include unrealistic expectations and focusing on short-term instead of long-term results; adopting a task force approach; resisting the move toward community empowerment; taking advantage of the position; and misrepresenting an inadequate program as legitimate in order to receive funding.

Reconciling Expectations and Results

One pitfall is the common expectation that implementing a new strategy such as community policing, highly touted as an effective method of crime reduction, will have immediate and measurable results. It may have immediate results—but not the ones citizens were expecting. Friedmann explains:

> It is entirely possible and even expected that if community policing is successful, attitudes towards police and crime, as well as crime itself, will initially go up rather than down. This is reasonable to expect because of at least two considerations. First, the sensitizing of citizens may make them more alarmed by crime. Second, with the building of trust and changing [of] the relationship between police and community, citizens may be willing to report crime and public order related behavior more than before.

Ironically, this increased citizen vigilance and reporting, although a desirable and positive outcome of successful community policing, may initially indicate an *increase* in

and widespread skepticism regarding the effectiveness
...isunderstandings, generated by ambiguous promises, can
...orts to build the relationships with citizens necessary for
...re making predictions and promises regarding the long-term
...policing, make sure everyone understands the possible short-term
...n warns: "Committing to an immediate reduction of crime may be
...e thing to make for police and/or civic leaders."
...1) cautions against another hazard of inflated expectations: "Community
...es a heavy burden of responsibility on rank-and-file officers to develop cre-
...ghborhood-specific programs. This is an enormous burden indeed and the
...sant truth may be that it is unrealistic to expect that much creativity among the
...e rank and file."

Task Force Approach

Another pitfall is the inability of a department's management to gain the commitment of
the entire organization. This often occurs when an agency adopts a specialized unit or
task force approach, isolating acceptance of the philosophy to those in the community
policing unit. Matthews (1995, p. 34) states: "When an organization divides itself into
'those who serve the public' and 'those who do real police work,' barriers of animosity are
created." In describing his department's implementation of community policing, Koenig
(1998, p. 8) says that responsibility for community policing is vested in about 190 members of their 12,000-member organization. He believes: "This is unacceptable and, if left
alone, will eventually destroy our opportunity for progress. Community policing simply
cannot be contained in a small room within each area from which the SLOs [Senior
Lead Officers] work each day. It has to move out into the patrol cars, into the detective
squad rooms and into our classrooms."

Matthews (p. 34) lists other possible pitfalls to a task force approach to community
policing implementation: employee resentment exists because of job description, "real
police" vs. "social worker" mentality; only selected officers are trained in concept;
community-based officers are segregated from others; officers are responsible for taking
action, but decision-making authority resides with management; specific problems are
targeted, and documentation is limited to isolated, special projects.

Community Empowerment

One agency reported their new community policing officer (CPO) was eager to conduct
his first community meeting, having compiled a full and detailed agenda. His training
had taught him the difficulty in developing viable community resource groups, and he
knew initial meetings were often unproductive because of the miscellaneous complaints
and bickering that occurred until the individuals learned to function as a group. Hoping
to get through his agenda without being sidetracked with complaints, he opened his
meeting with, "I have a lot to cover so I won't listen to any complaints. We are going to
stick to the topic. If I hear any complaints, I'm leaving."

While pleased with his command of the meeting, the CPO had taken a huge step
backward by creating the perception that the police are not interested in community

input. Not surprisingly, the community did not become active participants, and this community policing project failed. Police training and socialization teach officers to stabilize and control situations. However, CPOs must relax this tendency to allow community input and empowerment, without which community policing is not possible (*Community Policing Pages*, 2000).

Taking Advantage of Your Position

A COPS grants officer served as a school liaison officer at the local high school, working the day shift, Monday through Friday. A school administrator, concerned about a possible growing problem with gangs, asked the COPS officer to work some night shifts to determine which students were out roaming the streets at night. Instead of scheduling himself for the afternoon-to-evening shift, where his contact with roaming youths would be increased, he chose to work the midnight shift, selecting nights when that shift was at maximum staffing to minimize his chances of being assigned radio calls. He also scheduled himself to work the Thursday night/Friday morning shift to give himself a longer weekend, being able to get off duty early Friday morning. To make matters worse, he boasted of his scheme at the midnight shift roll call.

Unfortunately, this officer's "scheme" was very damaging because it created the perception that the community policing program was a way to get a soft assignment. Officers' work schedules must comply with their work requirements, and empowering officers to become creative problem solvers does not mean supervision is abandoned. Challenging officers to justify their actions can be a useful mechanism for helping them think through strategies and tactics, helping to revise faulty practices and end abuses of the position (*Community Policing Pages*).

Walker (p. 48) concludes: "If community policing has the potential for unleashing the untapped creativity of officers on the street, it also has the danger of allowing them to revert to the gross abuses of a previous era in policing."

Misrepresentation—Talking the Talk without Walking the Walk

Community Policing Pages reports:

> One department adopted community policing by forming a Neighborhood Patrol Unit. Their "community policing" tactics consist of serving warrants. An officer in the unit was candid enough to say ". . . we're just called a neighborhood unit so we could get the federal funding."

The strategy: If the title sounds like community policing, it will bring in new money. Unfortunately, according to *Community Policing Pages*, too many so-called community policing programs have no real community policing component, while others use only limited community policing techniques. This deception, however, undermines the chances for success of legitimate community policing efforts. *Community Policing Pages* urges: "True supporters of community policing need to expose this abuse. If they do not, these programs will be cited as evidence that community policing has failed when the funding cycle runs dry."

◈ IMPEDIMENTS TO OVERCOME

Sadd and Grinc (1996, pp. 1–2) report on a National Institute of Justice survey of eight cities implementing innovative neighborhood-oriented policing (INOP). This study revealed the following:

- The major implementation challenges were resistance by police officers to community policing and the difficulty of involving other public agencies and organizing the community.

- With the exception of one site, the involvement of other public agencies was limited.

- Police officers generally did not understand community policing. They saw INOP assignment as conferring an elite status; perceived INOP as less productive, more time consuming, and more resource-intensive than traditional policing; and felt their powers, particularly to enforce the law, were restrained.

- Average citizens had less knowledge than community leaders about INOP and were reluctant to participate.

This survey (p. 13) also looked at the "untested assumptions of community policing that residents really want closer contact with the police and want to work with them to reduce crime." The survey found that many citizens didn't want to become involved in community policing efforts because of "outright hostility—the historically negative relationship between the police and residents of economically disadvantaged communities." Hoffmann (pp. 53–54) notes the impact of one agency's "redirection" of police services to no longer answer non-life-threatening calls:

> If your $30,000 car were stolen from your driveway, you would have to wait for a civilian telephone report writer to call you back sometime between 8 and 10 A.M. . . . Victims became hostile at the idea that their car theft was considered such an insignificant event that the police didn't bother to come to their house. . . .
>
> Advocates of COP emphasize that citizens need to make a partnership with the police—but in reality the average Joe wants to have dinner, help his kids with their homework, watch some TV and leave crime fighting to the police. How are the police to form a partnership when they don't respond to an auto theft, something that most people regard as a major event in their life?

Another implementation problem the survey identified (p. 14) was the nature of the target neighborhoods:

> The economically disadvantaged urban areas that generally serve as testing grounds for community policing tend to be highly disorganized, characterized by poverty, unemployment, inadequate educational services, and high crime rates. In areas encumbered by such an array of problems it is often difficult to find well-organized community groups that are attempting to address quality-of-life issues.

The survey also identified conflict among community leaders and residents regarding what issues they should address (p. 14): "In reality the community is often an aggregate of competing groups."

Zhao et al. (1995, p. 19) cite several factors impeding implementation of community policing.

Impediments to COP implementation include:

- *Organizational impediments—resistance from middle management, line officers and unions; confusion about what COP is; problems in line-level accountability; officers' concern that COP is "soft" on crime; and lack of COP training*

- *Community impediments—community resistance, community's concern that COP is "soft" on crime, civil service rules, pressure to demonstrate COP reduces crime and lack of support from local government*

- *Transition impediments—balancing increased foot patrol activities while maintaining emergency response time*

◈ EVALUATING PROGRESS

As the Community Policing Consortium warns, without specifying desired outcomes as part of the strategic plan, the community policing initiative could be reduced to another series of community relations exercises rather than the anticipated cultural, organizational and structural change achieved through community policing in partnership and problem solving. Recall from Chapter 4 that the SARA model of problem solving shows that there are no failures, only responses that do not provide the desired goal. Remember also from Chapter 4 the mental lock: "To Err Is Wrong." Avoid this thinking trap by understanding risk taking is a necessary part of progress, and erring is wrong only if you fail to learn from your "mistake." Edison is quoted as saying he did not fail 25,000 times to make a storage battery. He simply knew 25,000 ways *not* to make one.

Evaluating progress can take many forms. It should have been built into the strategic plan in concrete form. Which goals and objectives have been met? Which have not? Why not? The evaluation might also consist of conducting a year later a second needs assessment of both the department and community and determine whether needs are being better met. It can be done through additional surveys and interviews assessing reduced fear of crime and improved confidence in police. Are citizens making fewer complaints regarding police service? Are officers filing fewer grievances?

When evaluating, failures should be as important as successes—sometimes more important—because a department learns what doesn't work.

Dempsey (1995, pp. 60–61) lists the following areas that might be used to evaluate the effectiveness of community policing efforts: (1) A statistic review of reported crime rates in target area. (Certain types of crime seem to be good targets for community policing: domestic violence, residential and commercial burglary, vandalism [graffiti], street-level drug related crimes and gang activity.) (2) A comparative review of complaints filed against officers in the targeted communities. (3) A comparative review of commendations of officers from either citizens or supervisors. (4) A review of follow-up calls for service at the same address or to the same identified problem. (5) Survey tools should be developed to measure the perception of specific groups with regard to crime and police effectiveness.

Gnagey and Henson (1995, p. 25) describe a survey divided into five components: fear of crime, neighborhood disorder, police service evaluation, demographic information and open-ended response.

To assess fear of crime, the survey asked questions such as whether people feel crime has decreased, increased or remained the same; whether they have limited or changed their activities due to fear of crime; and whether their neighborhood is so dangerous that they have considered moving.

To assess neighborhood disorder, citizens were asked to indicate whether certain factors were a big problem, somewhat of a problem or no problem in their neighborhood. The factors included items such as abandoned/burned-out buildings, cars speeding/screeching tires, drug dealers operating openly, loud music from homes, parking/traffic problems, prostitutes/"johns" roaming the neighborhood, run-down buildings, stray/noisy animals, vandalism/graffiti, dilapidated streets/sidewalks, poor street lighting, public drinking, strangers trespassing, stripped/abandoned cars, unsupervised children and juvenile delinquency.

To assess police service, citizens were asked to rate the protection provided their neighborhood as excellent, good, fair or poor. The final question asked respondents whether they have any suggestions for improving police service.

Understanding Community Policing (p. 45) suggests that since one core component of community policing is community partnerships, an early measure of effectiveness could be the number and type of community partnerships formed. Other means of assessment include (pp. 46–47):

- The number and type of problems solved and the creativity and scope of the solutions.

- Increased levels of community participation in crime reduction and prevention efforts.

- Commitment of an increased level of community resources devoted to crime reduction efforts.

One aspect of evaluation sometimes overlooked is employee satisfaction. Moose et al. (2000, p. 44) contend: "As employees take on the roles of problem solving and working with the community, job satisfaction can be measured by an employee survey. The survey results indicate how well an organization is adapting to the new set of expectations that the transition to community policing brings." They (p. 45) further suggest: "With added responsibilities for police officers, job satisfaction becomes critical. If they are satisfied with their job, they perform better and are able to support their agency's mission. . . . Employee job satisfaction is not simply an indicator of success in community policing—it is a goal of community policing."

◆ GIVING COP IMPLEMENTATION A BOOST

To promote the community policing concept and recognize law enforcement executives who have strived to implement the COP philosophy, the American Association for the Advancement of Community-Oriented Policing (AAACOP or Triple A-Cop) was launched in May 2000. Composed of criminal justice theorists, academics and members of the policing community, Triple A-Cop is "a grassroots attempt to maintain community policing measures around the country" ("New Advocacy Group . . . ," 2000, p. 6). A major component of the group's effort is an awards ceremony named for the late Robert Trojanowicz, a pioneer in community policing, to honor individuals, police agencies and communities who have taken the concept to a higher level. Information on training courses, conferences and general COP information is available on-line at www.aaacop.org.

SUMMARY

The transition to community policing requires a change in mission statement, departmental organization, leadership style and the general approach to "fighting crime." A department's vision should include the essential elements of the community policing philosophy: problem solving, empowering everyone, forming community partnerships and being proactive—making preventing crime as important as enforcing the law. The vision is used to create a mission statement.

Once the vision and mission statement have been articulated, the next step is to conduct a needs assessment. A needs assessment should include not only the department but also the community of which it is a part. While conducting needs assessments, the department should pay attention to potential community leaders to enlist in the community policing initiative. It may be more important for COP-oriented police agencies to target the "critical mass" of individuals—the smallest number of citizens/organizations needed to support and sustain the community policing initiative—than to try to mobilize the community at large.

A strategic plan should include community partnerships and problem solving as well as any needed cultural and organizational changes in the department. It should also include a realistic timeline and ways to assess progress. It must also be tied to the department's budget. The most important consideration in selecting strategies to implement community policing is to ensure that the strategies fit the unique needs of the community.

Recruiting and selecting personnel is of great importance in the successful implementation of the community policing philosophy. "POST-21" is an add-on to an agency's existing application examination and selection process designed to identify applicants with traits and attitudes compatible with a community policing environment. Training is also critical for a successful transition to community policing. However, *don't* make training the spearhead of change. Among the most important areas to include in training are communication skills, problem-solving skills and leadership skills.

Managers should anticipate and prepare for resistance to the community policing philosophy and the changes that accompany the transition. They should also be aware of and try to avoid the common pitfalls in making the transition to community policing, including unrealistic expectations and focusing on short-term instead of long-term results; adopting a task force approach; resisting the move toward community empowerment; taking advantage of the position; and misrepresenting an inadequate program as legitimate to receive funding.

Impediments to COP implementation include organizational impediments (resistance from middle management, line officers and unions; confusion about what COP is; problems in line-level accountability; officers' concern that COP is "soft" on crime; and lack of COP training), community impediments (community resistance, community's concern that COP is "soft" on crime, civil service rules, pressure to demonstrate COP reduces crime and lack of support from local government) and transition impediments (balancing increased foot patrol activities while maintaining emergency response time).

When evaluating, failures should be as important as successes—sometimes more important—because a department learns what doesn't work.

DISCUSSION QUESTIONS

1. What do you consider the greatest obstacles to implementing community policing?
2. If you had to prioritize the changes needed to convert to community policing, what would your priorities be?
3. Find out what your police department's mission statement is. If it is not community policing focused, how might it be revised?
4. How would you determine whether community policing efforts are working?
5. Does your community have agencies and/or organizations that could become partners with the police department?
6. Why might citizens not want to become involved in community policing efforts?
7. Discuss the similarities between team policing and community policing and describe the most important lesson to be learned from team policing.
8. How would you go about assessing your community's needs regarding efforts to reduce crime and violence?
9. How would you enlist the support of the media? What resources are available in your community?
10. Are there conflicting groups within your "community"? Does one group have more political power than another?

INFOTRAC COLLEGE EDITION ASSIGNMENTS

- Use InfoTrac to help answer the discussion questions as appropriate.
- Find and outline two articles that discuss strategic planning. Do they suggest the same approach? If not, how do they differ?
- Research and take notes on critical mass or vision.

COMMUNITY PROJECTS

Conduct a community survey of business owners or campus or neighborhood residents. Ask about:

- Their fear of crime.
- Their opinion of police services in their community.

- What they think community policing means.
- Whether they believe their police or sheriff's department practices community policing.
- If they could decide, what would they direct the police to concentrate on?

Research the importance of mission statements to an organization. Collect some examples of mission statements. Ask employees of organizations if they know the mission statement of their organization. What are the implications of their knowing or not knowing their mission statement?

REFERENCES

Abshire, Richard and Paynter, Ronnie L. "Putting the 'Community' in Community Policing." *Law Enforcement Technology,* Vol. 27, No. 10, October 2000, pp. 50–58.

Benedict, Wm. Reed; Bower, Douglas J.; Brown, Ben; and Cunningham, Roger. "Small Town Surveys: Bridging the Gap between Police and the Community." *Journal of Contemporary Criminal Justice,* Vol. 15, No. 2, May 1999, pp. 144–145.

Capsambelis, Christopher R. "Selecting a New Breed of Officer: The Customer-Oriented Cop." *Community Policing Exchange,* Phase VI, #25, March/April 1999, p. 4.

Carter, David L. "A Response to Community Policing: Thriving Because It Works." *Police Quarterly,* Vol. 2, No. 1, March 1999, pp. 103–109.

Community Policing Consortium. The Police Organization in Transition (Monograph), 2000 http://www.communitypolicing.org/pforgtrans/index.html

Community Policing Pages. http://msnhomepages.talkcity.com/LibraryLawn/devere_woods/. Summer 2000 Edition, Vol. 6, No. 3.

Correia, Mark E. *Citizen Involvement: How Community Factors Affect Progressive Policing.* Washington, DC: Police Executive Research Forum, 2000.

Corsentino, Dan L. "A 10-Step Transformation Plan." *Community Policing Exchange,* Spring 1996, pp. 2, 8.

DeLong, Rhonda K. "Problem Solvers Wanted: How to Tailor Your Agency's Recruiting Approach." *Community Policing Exchange,* Phase VI, #25, March/April, 1999, p. 6.

Dempsey, Tom G. "Evaluating Community-Based Efforts." *Law and Order,* Vol. 43, No. 10, October 1995, pp. 54–55, 60–62.

DeParis, Richard J. "How Contemporary Police Agencies Can Adapt to the Community Policing Mission." *The Police Chief,* Vol. LXVII, No. 8, August 2000, pp. 108–114.

Duffee, David E.; Fluellen, Reginald; and Renauer, Brian C. "Community Variables in Community Policing." *Police Quarterly,* Vol. 2, No. 1, March 1999, pp. 5–35.

Edwards, Larry V. "Setting the Tone in Your Organization and in the Community." *Community Policing Exchange,* Phase VI, #23, November/December 1998, p. 5.

Friedmann, Robert R. "Community Policing: Some Conceptual and Practical Considerations." In *Home Affairs Review* (Hungarian), Vol. XXXIV, No. 6, pp. 114–123, 1996.

Gnagey, John and Henson, Ronald. "Community Surveys Help Determine Policing Strategies." *The Police Chief,* Vol. LXII, No. 3, March 1995, pp. 25–27.

Goldstein, Herman. *The New Policing: Confronting Complexity.* Washington, DC: National Institute of Justice Research in Brief, December 1993.

Harris, Wesley and Kolkman, Aaron. "Selecting Community Oriented Officers." *Law and Order,* Vol. 48, No. 4, April 2000, pp. 53–66.

Hoffmann, John. "How to Make Citizens Hate Community Policing." *Law and Order,* Vol. 48, No. 4, April 2000, pp. 53–56.

Johnson, Robert P. and Bromley, Max. "Surveying a University Population: Establishing the Foundation for a Community

Policing Initiative." *Journal of Contemporary Criminal Justice,* Vol. 15, No. 2, May 1999, pp. 133–143.

Koenig, Daniel R. "Community Policing, LAPD Style." *Law Enforcement News,* May 31, 1998, p. 8.

Kurz, David L. "Strategic Planning and Police-Community Partnership in a Small Town." *The Police Chief,* Vol. LXVII, No. 12, December 2000, pp. 28–36.

Lord, Vivian B. and Schoeps, Nancy. "Identifying Psychological Attributes of Community-Oriented, Problem-Solving Police Officers." *Police Quarterly,* Vol. 3, No. 2, June 2000, pp. 172–190.

Malinowski, Sean W.; Kalish, David J.; and Parks, Bernard C. "From *Dragnet* to the Internet: One Police Department Extends Its Reach." *The Police Chief,* Vol. LXVII, No. 9, September 2000, pp. 62–66.

Matthews, John. "Department-Wide Versus 'Task Force' Implementation." *Law and Order,* Vol. 43, No. 12, December 1995, pp. 34–37.

Mittleman, Pete. "Community Policing: Building Community Trust Thinking Outside of the Box." *The Police Chief,* Vol. LXVII, No. 3, March 2000, pp. 50–55.

Mook, Dennis and Dempsey, Tom. "University Partnership Educates Officers in Community Leadership." *The Police Chief,* Vol. LXVII, No. 8, August 2000, pp. 115–116.

Moore, Robert A. "Leadership and the 'Vision Thing.' " *Community Policing Exchange,* Phase VI, #23, November/December 1998, pp. 7–8.

Moose, Charles A.; Lin-Kelly, Wendy; Beedle, Steve; and Stipak, Brian. "Evaluating Community Policing with Employee Surveys." *The Police Chief,* Vol. LXVII, No. 3, March 2000, pp. 44–49.

Nagy, Richard A. "Improving the Quality of Life." *The Police Chief,* Vol. LXVII, No. 4, April 2000, pp. 33–44.

"New Advocacy Group to Boost Community Policing." *Law Enforcement News,* Vol. XXVI, Nos. 553, 554, May 15/30, 2000.

Paoline, Eugene A., III; Myers, Stephanie M.; and Worden, Robert E. "Police Culture, Individualism, and Community Policing: Evidence from Two Police Departments." *Justice Quarterly,* Vol. 17, No. 3, September 2000, pp. 575–605.

Pratt, C. E. "Five Steps to Community-Based Policing." *Law and Order,* Vol. 43, No. 10, October 1995, pp. 54–58.

Ramsey, Charles H. "Organizational Change: Preparing a Police Department for Community Policing in the 21st Century." *The Police Chief,* Vol. LXVII, No. 3, March 2000, pp. 16–25.

Rosen, Marie Simonetti. "A LEN Interview with Chief Dave Brown of Tempe, Arizona." *Law Enforcement News,* May 1994, pp. 8–11.

Sadd, Susan and Grinc, Randolph M. *Implementing Challenges in Community Policing: Innovative Neighborhood-Oriented Policing in Eight Cities.* Washington, DC: National Institute of Justice Research in Brief, February 1996.

Sherwood, Charles W. "Job Design, Community Policing, and Higher Education: A Tale of Two Cities." *Police Quarterly,* Vol. 3, No. 2, June 2000, pp. 191–212.

Smith, Steven K. and Hayeslip, David W. "Using City-Level Surveys to Better Understand Community Policing." *National Institute of Justice Journal,* October 1998, pp. 33–39.

Sparrow, Malcolm K. *Perspectives on Policing: Implementing Community Policing.* Washington, DC: U.S. Department of Justice, National Institute of Justice, November 1988.

Switzer, Merle. "In Search of Community-Oriented Policing." *The Police Chief,* Vol. LXVII, No. 3, March 2000, pp. 38–41.

350 Tested Strategies to Prevent Crime: A Resource for Municipal Agencies and Community Groups. Washington, DC: National Crime Prevention Council, 1995.

Understanding Community Policing. Washington, DC: Bureau of Justice Assistance, August 1994.

Walker, Samuel. "Does Anyone Remember Team Policing? Lessons of the Team Policing Experience for Community Policing." *American Journal of Police,* Vol. XII, No. 1, 1993, pp. 35–55.

Wittham, John. "Strategic Planning for Law Enforcement." *The Police Chief,* Vol. LXV, No. 3, March 1998, pp. 23–28.

Zhao, Jihong; Thurman, Qunit C.; and Lovrich, Nicholas P. "Community-Oriented Policing across the U.S.: Facilitators and Impediments to Implementation." *American Journal of Police,* Vol. XIV, No. 1, 1995, pp. 11–28.

RESOURCES

Community Policing Consortium	www.communitypolicing.org
COPS Office (Department of Justice)	www.usdoj.gov/cops/
Justice Information Center	www.ncjrs.org
National Center for Community Policing	www.ssc.msu.edu/~cj/cp/cptoc.html
Police Executive Research Forum	www.policeforum.org/
Upper Midwest Community Policing Institute	www.umcpi.org

Howard Rahtz. *Community Policing: A Handbook for Beat Cops and Supervisors.* Monsey, NY: Criminal Justice Press, 2001.

Building Relationships and Trust

With the basic background supplied in Section One, you are ready to look at the interaction occurring between the police and the publics they serve and protect. At the most basic level, police-community relations begin with one-on-one interaction between an officer and a citizen.

The section begins with a discussion of the interpersonal skills needed to interact effectively with average, mainstream adults (Chapter 6). Ensuing chapters discuss building bridges with individuals who differ from this norm in some respect. First, the challenge of multiculturalism is explored, including how to deal with members of racially, ethnically, religiously or socio-economically diverse cultures (Chapter 7). Next, interacting with other "special" populations is presented—people with disabilitites, including those who are visually or hearing impaired, mentally and emotionally disabled and those who have

epilepsy; and those who are elderly, including those who have Alzheimer's disease (Chapter 8); those who are young; and those who belong to gangs (Chapter 9). The following chapter discusses how to meet the needs of victims and witnesses (Chapter 10).

Although these special populations are discussed separately, overlap often exists. The more an individual differs from the "norm," the greater the challenge in establishing good relationships and trust. It must always be remembered that each member of the specific group discussed is first an individual.

The section concludes with a discussion on interaction with members of the media, the constitutional issues involved and how such interactions can help or hinder community policing implementation (Chapter 11).

CHAPTER 6

Basic Interpersonal Skills—
One-on-One

*What we are communicates far more eloquently
than anything we say or do. There are people we
trust because we know their character. Whether
they're eloquent or not, whether they have human-
relations techniques or not, we trust them and
work with them.*

    Stephen R. Covey

Do you know

How a person's world-view is largely created?

Why two people may see the same thing
    differently?

What the most basic rule of semantics is?

What police officers must recognize in
    themselves?

The difference between prejudice and
    discrimination?

What empathy is?

What networks are?

What the communication process consists of?

What individual characteristics are important in
    the communication process?

What can improve communication?

What are common barriers to effective
    communication?

Why police officers may have more barriers to
    communication than other professionals?

Why effective listening is often difficult?

What the primacy effect is?

What the four-minute barrier is?

What two human relations practices used in
    business might be adopted for improving
    police-community relations?

What networking is and how it functions?

Can you define these terms:

bias	kinesics	primacy effect
body language	networking	self-fulfilling prophecy
communication	networks	semantic environment
communication process	nonverbal communication	semantics
discrimination	perception	sensorium
empathy	phenomenological point of view	stereotyping
extensional world	preference	symbolic process
four-minute barrier	prejudice	verbal world
jargon		

INTRODUCTION

A woman executive at a shopping center discovered a minor theft of company property from her company car. The car had been parked outside a police office where several traffic officers took breaks between shifts. The office was not accessible to the public but had an identification sign on the locked door.

The woman knocked on the door and asked the sergeant who opened it who was responsible for watching the parking area. She also commented on the officers she could see sitting in the room and suggested they were not doing their jobs. The officers in the room stopped talking with each other and turned their attention to the conversation at the office door.

The sergeant and the woman never got around to discussing the missing item. Instead he responded to her comments with questions. "What do you mean by that?" "What are you trying to say?" She left to tell her supervisor, refusing to file a police report. She soon returned, however, and encountered another officer just outside the office. Their conversation, later characterized as "heated" by witnesses, centered on the woman's suggestion that the officers should do more to prevent theft in the parking lot. She implied they were lazy and shirked their responsibilities.

At this point the woman asked to file a police report, and the officer asked her to enter the police office with him to do so. They entered the office, but when the officer suggested they enter a private office away from the hubbub of the break area, she refused to do so. She later said the officer intimidated her by slamming drawers, moving quickly and ordering her into the room. She feared being alone with him.

The officer's perception of the incident was entirely different. He commented that the woman had a "chip on her shoulder" and an "attitude." She was demanding and impossible to deal with.

After refusing to enter the office to file the report, the woman sat down on a chair in the break area. She was told to either go into the other room and file the report or leave. When she refused to do either, she was escorted from the office and left outside the locked doors. The woman filed a complaint against the police department.

With better communication, this problem and thousands like it could be avoided. Effective communication with the public is vital to good police-community relations. In fact, at the heart of police-community relations are one-on-one interactions between officers and citizens.

The following discussion assumes that those involved in the interaction are adults with no serious physical or mental disabilities. Interactions involving individuals with disabilities are discussed in Chapter 8.

This chapter begins with a discussion of understanding yourself—a prerequisite for effective interpersonal relationships. This is followed by an explanation of understanding others and the nature of the interaction between police and citizens. Next the communication process is described, including nonverbal communication and body language, communication enhancers, communication barriers and active listening. Then the chapter discusses the primacy effect and the four-minute barrier. The chapter concludes with lessons learned from business.

◉ UNDERSTANDING YOURSELF

Officers who seek to build effective relationships with the citizens they serve first need to understand themselves and potential barriers to such relationships. They need to recognize their own level of self-esteem as well as the roles they play. Officers need to understand how their view of the world has been shaped and how it affects their interactions with others.

Your world-view is largely created by what you see and hear as you experience events.

Perception—What Is Seen

What is "seen" may not always be trusted as illustrated by the common phenomenon of optical illusions. One critical aspect of a person's world-view is individual *perception*. **Perception** is the process of becoming aware of something directly through the senses. Sight is one of the most important sources of perception. Two primary components of visual perception are the eye and the **sensorium,** that part of the brain that interprets what the eye takes in. The eye can handle stimuli of nearly five million bits per second, but the sensorium has limited abilities. Its resolving power is limited to about five hundred bits per second, so some stimuli fall by the wayside. The perception is in the "eyes" of the beholder.

The discrepancy between what the eye takes in (five million bits per second) and what the person actually processes (five hundred bits per second) accounts, in part, for why two witnesses can see the same thing differently.

Two witnesses' sensoriums process different portions of what the eye sees. Generally, the more objective a person is, the more their perception mirrors the perceptions of others. For example, if a group of people are given a ruler and asked to measure the size of a book, they would probably all come up with the same measurement. However, without a ruler, people would need to rely on their experiences, which may result in prejudices and stereotyping. Later in this chapter you will consider the problems prejudice and stereotyping present to police-community relations.

Perception—What Is Heard vs. What Is Said

In addition to what individuals see, the language they use also shapes their "reality." Individuals in the field of **semantics** research and study the meaning of language. According to Hayakawa (1949, pp. 21–22):

> Words—the way he uses them and the way he takes them when spoken by others—largely shape his beliefs, his prejudices, his ideals, his aspirations. They constitute the moral and intellectual atmosphere in which he lives—in short—his **semantic environment**. . . .
>
> It will be the basic assumption of this book [the classic, *Language in Thought and Action*] that widespread intraspecific co-operation through the use of language is the fundamental mechanism of human survival. A parallel assumption will be that when the use of language results, as it so often does, in the creation or aggravation of disagreements and conflicts, there is something wrong with the speaker, the listener, or both. Human "fitness to survive" means the ability to talk and write, and listen and read in ways that increase the chances for you and fellow-members of your species to survive together.

The following are some of Hayakawa's key assertions:

- The process by means of which human beings can arbitrarily make certain things *stand* for other things may be called the **symbolic process.** We are, as human beings, uniquely free to manufacture and manipulate and assign values to our symbols as we please (p. 25).

- Of all forms of symbolism, language is the most highly developed, most subtle, and most complicated. . . . Symbols and things symbolized are independent of each other; nevertheless, we all have a way of believing as if, and sometimes acting as if, there were necessary connections (p. 27).

- The symbol is *not* the thing symbolized. The four-legged animal that goes "moo" and gives milk is represented in English by three letters arranged to form the word *cow*. Other languages have very different words for the actual animal. The word is *not* the thing; the map is *not* the territory. There is a sense in which we all live in two worlds. First, we live in the world of happenings about us which we know at first hand. But this is an extremely small world. . . . Most of our knowledge, acquired from parents, friends, schools, newspapers, books, conversation, speeches and radio, is received *verbally*. Call this world that comes to us through words the **verbal world,** as opposed to our own experience, called the **extensional world.** Now this verbal world ought to stand in relation to the extensional world as a *map* does to the *territory* it is supposed to represent (pp. 21–32).

- Classification. What we call things and where we draw the line between one class of things and another depend upon the interests we have and the purposes of the classification. . . . Many of us, for example, cannot distinguish between pickerel, pike, salmon, smelts, perch, crappies, halibut, and mackerel; we say that they are "just fish, and I don't like fish." To a seafood connoisseur, however, these distinctions are real. . . . To a zoologist, even finer distinctions become of great importance. . . . When we name something, then, we are classifying. The individual object or event we are naming, of course, has no name and belongs to no class until we put it in one . . . (pp. 209–210).

There are few complexities about classifications at the level of dogs and cats, knives and forks, or cigarettes and candy, but when it comes to classifications at high levels of abstraction, for example, those describing conduct, social institutions, or philosophical and moral problems, serious difficulties occur. This can be a major source of conflict. When one person kills another, is it an act of murder, an act of temporary insanity, an act of homicide, an accident, or an act of heroism? As soon as the process of classification is completed, our attitudes and our conduct are to a considerable degree determined. We hang the murderer, we lock up the insane person, we free the victim of circumstances, and we pin a medal on the hero. Unfortunately, people are not always aware of the way in which they arrive at their classifications (pp. 211–212).

How do we prevent ourselves from getting into such intellectual blind alleys, or, if we find we are in one, how do we get out again? One way is to remember that practically all statements in ordinary conversation, debate and public controversy taking the form, "Business is business," "Boys will be boys," and so on, are *not* true. . . .

A simple technique for preventing classification from harming our thinking is the suggestion made by Korzybski to add "index numbers" to our terms, thus: Englishman$_1$, Englishman$_2$ . . .; cow$_1$, cow$_2$, cow$_3$ . . . The terms of the classification tell us what the individuals in that class have in common; **the index numbers remind us of the characteristics left out.** A rule can then be formulated as a general guide in all our thinking and reading: Cow$_1$ is *not* Cow$_2$, Politician$_1$ is *not* Politician$_2$, and so on. This rule, if remembered, prevents us from confusing levels of abstraction and forces us to consider the facts on those occasions when we might otherwise find ourselves leaping to conclusions that we may later have cause to regret (pp. 212–214).

The simplest and most basic rule of semantics is: Cow$_1$ is not Cow$_2$.

Pinizotto et al. (2000, p. 1) warn against officers forming what they call a "perceptual shorthand"—how officers perceive an incident's totality of circumstances to quickly assess the situation, "read" a suspect and decide on a course of action. To point out the potentially fatal consequences of perceptual shorthand, Pinizotto et al. present this true account:

On an extremely dark night, a uniformed patrol officer observed a minor traffic offense—only one headlight functioning on a vehicle. The officer initiated a traffic stop on an unlit portion of the rural roadway. The vehicle, a late model four-door sedan, pulled to the right and stopped. As the officer approached the vehicle, he noticed a bumper sticker supporting the local youth soccer league. When the officer reached the driver's door, he was shot once in the chest. As he fell to the ground, the car sped away. Unknown to the officer, the driver had stolen the vehicle earlier that evening and used it during a robbery. The driver later reported that he thought the officer was going to arrest him for those crimes. Fortunately, the officer had on a bullet-resistant vest and survived the deadly attack on his life.

This officer's perceptual shorthand involved some quick observations made about the driver and the vehicle: The driver was not speeding, driving erratically or acting suspiciously prior to the traffic stop; the vehicle appeared well cared for except for the burned-out headlight and displayed a sticker supporting a local soccer league, which, incidentally, the officer's child played in. These observations led the officer to assume the driver was a local soccer parent with whom the officer would probably have a friendly conversation. This assumption then influenced the officer's actions, including his decision not to notify the dispatcher and report the location of the stop; his failure to run the vehicle's license plates through the computer before approaching; and his advance toward the driver while psychologically, emotionally and tactically unguarded (p. 2).

Pinizotto et al. (pp. 3–4) emphasize that attention to safety-related training issues and an understanding of factors affecting officers' mental mind-set can help officers avoid the perceptual shorthand trap. They conclude (p. 6): "Officers must not become complacent when faced with everyday law enforcement duties. They must realize that they must treat each encounter as if their lives depended on their perceptions of reality because, as research has shown, they do."

Once aware of how perceptions are formed and the hazards they may pose, consider the natural tendency to have preferences and the danger it presents to effective police-community relations.

Preferences, Prejudice, Bias, Stereotyping and Discrimination

It is important to recognize that no one can be completely objective. Everyone, consciously or unconsciously, has certain preferences and prejudices.

It is critical to self-understanding to recognize preferences, prejudices and stereotypes.

A **preference** is selecting someone or something over another. You may, for example, prefer to interact with people of your own ethnic background, your own age or your own economic level.

A **prejudice** is a negative judgment not based on fact; it is an irrational, preconceived negative opinion. Prejudices are often associated with a dislike of a particular group, race or religion. Prejudices are often the result of the classifications discussed earlier. They represent *overgeneralizations*, a failure to consider individual characteristics.

Prejudices are also referred to as **bias,** a belief that inhibits objectivity. Taken to an extreme, a bias becomes hatred. It is important for law enforcement to understand bias and its extreme form—hate—in order to deal with the increase in bias and hate crimes. The manner in which police should deal with hate crimes is discussed Chapter 7. Prejudices or biases are the result of overgeneral classification or stereotyping.

Stereotyping assumes that all people within a specific group are the same; they lack individuality. Simply because a person is a member of a specific group, that person is thought to have certain characteristics. Common stereotypes associated with nationalities include the French being great lovers, the Italians being great cooks, the Scotch being thrifty and American Yankees being ingenious. Often the stereotype of Americans is very negative, as illustrated in the novel *The Ugly American.*

Many people stereotype police officers based on what they see on television—scenes showing cops in car chases and shootouts. Officers aren't shown standing on the street corner in late January directing traffic after an accident or being tended to at the medical center because they were bitten on the arm by a hooker who didn't want to be arrested.

Police officers may also stereotype those with whom they come in contact. In the traditional mode of policing, officers spend a considerable amount of time dealing with criminals and their victims. Some officers may begin to categorize certain types of individuals as perpetrators. Police officers focus so much attention on crime, they may develop a distorted view of who the "bad guys" are. Generalizing from a few to the many is a serious problem for many police in the case of immigrants.

An additional danger of stereotyping is that it may become a **self-fulfilling prophecy.** Psychologists tell us that if a person is labeled as being a certain way long enough, the person may come to actually be that way. For example, if you frequently tell a child he is a delinquent, that child may accept the label and actually become a delinquent.

It is a very natural tendency to stereotype people but one that can be fatal to effective police-community relations. Police officers must first recognize that those they deal with may have formed a stereotype of police officers. It is important for police officers to determine whether this is true and, if so, to determine whether it is a positive or negative image. Officers must also recognize their own prejudices and be certain they do not lead to discrimination on the job.

Prejudices may lead to **discrimination,** showing a preference in treating individuals or groups or failing to treat equals equally, especially illegally unequal treatment based on race, religion, sex or age. Some male traffic officers, for example, are known to issue warnings to females who violate traffic laws and to issue tickets to males for the same violation. It is often alleged that members of minority groups receive rougher treatment from police officers than a Caucasian would receive, as discussed in Chapter 7.

Prejudice is an attitude; discrimination is a behavior.

This difference between attitude and overt behavior was summed up by an English judge in his comments to nine youths convicted of race rioting: "Think what you like . . . But once you translate your dark thoughts into savage acts, the law will punish you, and protect your victim."

In the United States, the 1964 Civil Rights Act and the 1972 amendment to the act make it illegal for agencies with 15 or more employees to discriminate in education, housing and employment on the basis of race, religion, national origin or sex. It is critical that police officers understand their own prejudices, biases and stereotypes and that they avoid any form of discrimination.

◉ UNDERSTANDING OTHERS

Parker et al. (1989, p. 78) note: "To engage in professional work in many areas of life one needs to understand the behavior and motivation of individuals." Understanding others is particularly important in police work. Understanding others does not, however, mean that you sympathize with them or even that you agree with them. Parker et al. suggest: "Understanding involves sensing the view of others in attempting to grasp a feeling of what their world is like." It is synonymous with *empathy*.

Empathy *is understanding another person.*

Ciaramicoli (2000, p. 9) defines empathy as "the capacity to accurately perceive and respond to another person's thoughts and feelings. . . . Empathy is unquestionably the most important capacity for a successful personal and professional life." Ciaramicoli draws the following distinction between sympathy and empathy, which are often confused:

- **Sympathy** is an involuntary feeling—the passive experience of sharing another person's fear, grief, anger or joy.
- **Empathy** is an active process in which you try to learn all you can about another person rather than having only a superficial awareness.

Ciaramicoli suggests three steps to achieving empathy: (1) Ask open-ended questions. (2) Slow down. (3) Avoid snap judgments.

To empathize with someone is to see things from their perspective or, as the saying goes, to put yourself in another's shoes. The level of empathy can vary, falling along a continuum from low to high. Consider the following example of the levels of officer empathy when responding to an irate husband involved in a domestic dispute (Parker et al., p. 84):

> Husband: I know damn well she's whoring around, she's never around here when I come home. She's tired, she never prepares supper, doesn't give a crap about me.
>
> Low Empathy Officer: When does she come home at night?
>
> Moderate Empathy Officer: It really makes you angry that she seems to be fooling around with other men.
>
> High Empathy Officer: It makes you madder'n hell to think she's screwing around, but it also hurts a lot because the message is, "I don't care about you."

High empathy does not always require a response. Sometimes knowing when to just listen is important. Parker et al. (p. 85) stress: "Frequently, just listening attentively allows people to fully express their concerns, which may be extremely helpful in and of itself." Situations perceived as real are real in their consequences. One secret to effective communications is to attempt to see the world from the other person's perspective.

To empathize with others, you need to adopt the **phenomenological point of view,** which stresses that reality is different for each individual. This point of view is used by Noose (1992, p. 101) in his conceptualization of *networks*.

Networks *are the "complex pathways of human interaction that guide and direct an individual's perception, motivation and behavior."*

Such networks are vital to effective communication, including interviewing individuals. According to Noose: "Networks represent relationships, links between people, and between people and their beliefs. Without an understanding of these relationships, these networks, it is often quite difficult, and sometimes even impossible, to

City of Poughkeepsie (New York) policewoman explains part of a new community policing program to city residents at a meeting. Citizens are vital to implementing any new community policing strategy.

understand an event or the circumstances that led to it. The answers obtained may have very little in common with the questions asked." He asserts that all people act to create a personal reality that allows them to predict and control the world around them. Their associations with others and their own fundamental beliefs become part of this reality, with these networks determining how people act and how they will respond when questioned. Noose concludes: "Networks produce the context within which a statement from a complainant, victim, witness or suspect can be most clearly understood."

Among the most important networks are those that are social: family, neighbors and friends. Sometimes legal relationships help to form networks such as those between children and their parents or between spouses. In addition to these social networks, there are occupational and professional, political, cultural and religious networks. Any of these networks can affect how a person views reality as well as what they are willing to communicate about that reality. Noose (p. 102) points out: "Networks are critically important whenever perception is being questioned." He (p. 103) stresses: "Staying informed about the networks that operate within a community is vital for officers who hope to be effective interviewers."

Identifying the Nature of the Interaction

When making contact with individuals, it is important to know the purpose of the interaction. This will, in large part, determine the most effective tone to establish and image to project. Is the contact primarily social—an effort to create good public relations? Is the contact made primarily to seek information—about what? A person? A problem? An incident? Is the contact primarily persuasive—to get an individual to comply with a request? What role must you play? What roles are others playing?

Sometimes, of course, a contact may serve more than one purpose. It may begin as a social contact and turn into one that is persuasive or provides information. Without a clear purpose in mind, however, your communication may not be effective.

Once you consider with whom you are interacting (your audience) and why (your purpose), then focus on how the interaction generally occurs, that is, through communication.

◉ THE COMMUNICATION PROCESS

Communication is basically the transfer of information from one person to another. Fulton (2000, p. 130) stresses the importance of effective communication: "Communication at any level is an inexact art. But misunderstood communication can have grave consequences in the 'life and death' world of police work." Depending on the situation, the communication process involves four or five components.

The communication process *involves a sender, a message, a channel, a receiver and sometimes feedback.*

Communication involves transferring thoughts from one person's mind to another's. The people involved, how well the message parallels the sender's thoughts and the channel used will all affect the communication.

The sender *encodes* the message in words—spoken or written—and then transmits the message by telephone, fax, letter, in person or in some other way. The receiver *decodes* the message. The receiver may then provide the sender with some kind of feedback that indicates the message has been received. Many factors will influence the message.

Important individual characteristics in communication include age, education, gender, values, emotional involvement, self-esteem and language skills.

Imagine, by way of illustration, that people see the world through tinted glasses. The tint represents their particular world-view. If the sender of a message sees the world through yellow glasses and the receiver of the message sees the world through red glasses, the message received will be a mixture of the world-views of both and will result in a different color—orange. Sheehan (1996, p. 38) observes:

> It is a fact that most officers need training in advanced communication skills. While the concept of spending valuable training time to teach officers "how to talk" may seem unwarranted, consider how much of the job involves communicating, in direct personal conversation as well as over the radio, telephone, or computer. Clear communication is important with victims, witnesses, suspects, supervisors, residents and each other.

A recent Rutgers University study found law enforcement involves about 97 percent verbal interaction and only 3 percent physical interaction (Scott, 2000, p. 54). This finding underscores the importance of effective officer communication. According to Dr. George Thompson, an English-professor-turned-police-officer, the most dangerous weapon today's police officer carries is not the firearm but the "cocked tongue." He claims when we *react* to a situation, the situation controls us, but when we *respond*, we control the situation (Scott, p. 54). To help officers respond more effectively, Thompson developed a system of verbalization tactics called Verbal Judo. As Scott (p. 54) explains, the main theme of Verbal Judo is generating *voluntary compliance* through verbal persuasion and maintaining what Thompson calls "professional face." The three goals of Verbal Judo are officer safety, enhanced professionalism and reduced vicarious liability.

Not all communication is verbal. For officers to communicate effectively, they must also understand nonverbal communication.

Nonverbal Communication and Body Language

Nonverbal communication includes everything other than the actual words spoken in a message such as tone, pitch and pacing. Adams (1996, p. 46) stresses the importance of nonverbal cues: "In both business and personal dealings, it's your silent signals that often matter most." He cites statistics indicating a mere 7 percent of what's understood between two people derives from the spoken word, 38 percent from the tone of the voice, and a full 55 percent from nonverbal cues or "silent speech." For example, sometimes the tone in which something is said makes it obvious the speaker is being sarcastic. A nervous person may speak rapidly in a high-pitched voice. Nonverbal communication also includes a person's appearance—how well groomed an individual is and the type of clothing worn.

Body language refers to messages conveyed by how a person moves. To test the power of body language, consider what the following say about a person:

Walking—fast, slow, stomping

Posture—rigid, relaxed

Eye contact—direct, indirect, shifting

Gestures—nod, shrug, finger point

Physical spacing—close, distant

Nonverbal Communication and Body Language of Police Officers. The police communicate with the public most obviously through the uniform they wear, the way they wear it and the equipment they carry. Police uniforms resemble military uniforms. Frequently navy blue or black, they have accessories such as silver or gold badges, name plates, collar brass and patches. Police wear leather belts loaded with equipment: handgun, radio, handcuffs, nightstick, mace and ammunition. Through their uniforms, police officers convey many messages without ever speaking. Wearing a uniform may be called the ultimate in *power dressing*. Uniforms are authoritative and professional and have an impact on the public's behavior. Officers find that they can gain compliance and cooperation from most people very easily on request, even when people would prefer not to cooperate. The public is likely to ignore the same officer who makes the same request while wearing blue jeans and a T-shirt.

Other forms of body language are equally important. How officers stand, how they look at those to whom they are talking, whether they smile or frown—all convey a message. A warm smile is said to be the universal language of kindness. Even a handshake conveys messages. A limp handshake sends one message, a firm handshake another message. Touching, too, can be used to an officer's advantage or disadvantage.

The nonverbal message of the police officers at this pro-choice rally is clear: Don't cross this line.

Eye contact is a powerful nonverbal communication tool. According to Giuliano (1999, p. 104): "Eye contact is one of the most important skills a person can develop." Eye contact inspires trust and shows confidence, even if it's merely the illusion of confidence. It can buy you time if you're caught off guard and need to form a response. Eye contact quietly keeps control while deftly wielding power. Finally, Giuliano (p. 104) asserts, eye contact can effortlessly put others at ease and encourage them to open up.

Usually police officers want to convey the impression that they "know their way around." However, this may actually interfere with effective communication. For example, consider the person who asks directions about how to find a certain store in Boston. If the person is from Boston, the directions given are likely to be brief, with obvious landmarks omitted. If the person is from out of town, however, the directions are likely to be much more detailed. When interviewing a truthful witness, police officers may want to modify their body language and soften up their language, in a sense pretending to be from out of town. A relaxed manner may result in more in-depth communication and better understanding.

How others perceive officers is sometimes critical. Recall how officers may develop a perceptual shorthand based on messages received from offenders. Pinizotto and Davis (1999, p. 1) suggest this is a two-way street, and the way offenders perceive the police influences how they interact with officers. Furthermore, officers may be completely unaware of the nonverbal cues they send out. Consider the following account (adapted from Pinizotto and Davis, pp. 2–3):

An offender stated he had "planned to kill an officer" on the day he actually murdered one. The offender, a small-time drug dealer and major drug abuser, stated he had received a message from God telling him to kill an officer because the police were ruining his drug business. Under the influence of drugs and without a clear plan, the man went to a busy intersection near his home to find an officer to kill.

Once at the intersection, he saw a uniformed sergeant at a service station having a tire repaired on his marked patrol vehicle. The offender admitted approaching the sergeant with the intent to kill him but changed his mind, stating, "By looking at him, I could tell that he would be too difficult to overcome." When asked what aspects of the sergeant's appearance or demeanor made the offender believe he'd be unable to overcome the officer, the offender replied the sergeant wasn't particularly large in size or menacing in appearance but "just looked like he could handle himself."

The offender waited at the intersection for two hours until a traffic accident occurred. When a one-officer patrol vehicle responded to the scene, the offender needed only a short time to observe the officer before he "knew this was my victim." Having made that decision, the offender casually walked over to the officer and struck him with his fist. As the officer fell to the ground, the offender removed the officer's service weapon and shot him six times.

When asked what criteria he had used to evaluate the officer, the offender had difficulty putting his thought process into words. He could recall only that the officer appeared "overweight and looked easy." What the offender did not know was that the victim officer had refused to wear his department-issued soft body armor, had recently received a substandard performance evaluation and had been involved a year earlier in another incident where a subject had taken the officer's service weapon and was then shot and killed by the officer's partner. Apparently the victim officer had sent assorted nonverbal messages to a variety of individuals—officials, fellow officers, and offenders—before his death.

Reading the Nonverbal Messages and Body Language of Others. In addition to understanding nonverbal messages, many police officers develop an ability to interpret body language, also called **kinesics,** to such an extent that they can tell when a person is lying or about to become aggressive or flee. They learn to take control of situations by using a commanding tone of voice and authoritative body language.

Police officers, with time and experience, learn to read the nonverbal messages and body language of suspects, victims and witnesses. It is what some call a "sixth sense," and it alerts officers when something is not as it appears or when someone is suspicious, untruthful, afraid or hesitant. Officers will sometimes call it a gut feeling or a nagging suspicion. As many officers have discovered, acting on such inarticulable feelings can pay off.

Criminals are often apprehended because an officer thought they looked suspicious or because something did not feel right about a traffic stop or other contact. Many law enforcement officers develop an uncanny ability to spot stolen cars in traffic based on a driver's movements, actions and driving maneuvers. Officers also learn to read their own hunches. Acting on a hunch can save lives, however, as illustrated in the rescue of a driver by an alert, "tuned in" officer:

Officer James Northagen of the Silver Bay Police Department on Lake Superior was on his way to work on a late November night when he noticed tire tracks leading into a snowbank along the edge of the lake. He later said it looked like a vehicle had slipped into a ditch and then driven out. Northagen continued on his way to work, but he kept thinking about the tracks and decided to go back after he started his shift. More than an hour after he first saw the tracks, Officer Northagen looked over the snowbank and saw the wreckage of a pickup truck 60 feet below, in the icy cold water of Lake Superior. The lone occupant was conscious but pinned in the truck. It took an hour to rescue the man, whose head was just barely out of the water for the three hours he was trapped in his truck.

Police officers can tell story after story of nagging and intuitive feelings that they acted on, with similar results.

◇ COMMUNICATION ENHANCERS

Almost 30 years ago, the National Advisory Commission on Criminal Justice Standards and Goals: *Police* (1973, p. 407) emphasized the importance of interpersonal communication skills: "Every police agency should immediately develop and improve the interpersonal communications skills of all officers. These skills are essential to the productive exchange of information and opinion between the police, other elements of the criminal justice system, and the public; their use helps officers to perform their tasks more effectively."

According to Buchholz and Roth (1987, pp. 82–85), six behaviors can enhance communication.

Behavioral communication enhancers include describing, equality, openness, problem-orientation, positive intent and empathy.

These behavior modes are typical of individuals with a positive self-image.

Describing. "I see it like this." "I hear you saying. . . ." The message sender presents feelings or perceptions that do not judge others as wrong or needing to change.

Equality. "We're on the same team. We're in this together." People's differences are recognized and respected. "Differences in talent, ability, power, and status often exist," say Buchholz and Roth, "but the person who encourages communication seems to attach little importance to these distractors."

Openness. "What do you think? Who has an idea? You've got a good point there. You may be right!" Investigating options rather than steadfastly clinging to one solution greatly enhances communication. People work together toward solutions rather than choosing sides to debate the "best" solution. If people are open, they agree to disagree without being disagreeable.

Problem-orientation. "We're going to have to work this out. We're on the spot and need to come up with an answer." People are encouraged to share their perspectives on a problem. This is an important part of community policing.

Positive Intent. "Here's why I'm asking you to do this." Honest, open, candid, sincere behavior promotes communication. People react positively to situations they believe are represented accurately. People usually resent being used or subjected to hidden agendas.

Empathy. "I understand how you feel. I appreciate your concern." Empathy, as discussed previously, is synonymous with understanding others.

Other behaviors that can enhance communication, according to Buchholz and Roth, are: "leaning forward, smiling, nodding, having direct eye contact, sticking to the subject under discussion, and paying full attention."

◈ BARRIERS TO EFFECTIVE COMMUNICATION

Because effective communication is so critical to police-community relations, officers should be aware of barriers to effective communication. Buchholz and Roth (pp. 80–82) note six specific behaviors that tend to hinder communication.

Behavioral barriers to communication include judging, superiority, certainty, controlling, manipulation and indifference.

Note that these behavioral barriers to communication are the opposites of the communication enhances just discussed. Buchholz and Roth suggest: "These behavior modes are often engaged in innocently and unconsciously, certainly not deliberately by well-meaning people." Often these behavior modes are trademarks of individuals with low self-esteem.

Judging. The opposite of describing. "You're wrong." Judging seriously interferes with listening. Rather than focusing on the potential of what someone says, a judgmental person focuses on discrediting what is being said.

Superiority. The opposite of equality. An "I'm-more-important-than-you-are" attitude can seriously hinder communication. Central to this attitude is the feeling that what *I* have to say is ultimately much more important than what others say.

Certainty. The opposite of openness. "My mind's made up. Don't confuse me with the facts." People convinced of the truthfulness or accuracy of their information are generally unable to recognize the possibility of making a mistake.

Controlling. The opposite of problem-orientation. "Let me tell you how this should be done." Few people appreciate being told how to act or what to do. Of course, in certain situations, police officers *must* take control. When officers need effective personal interaction, however, such control is usually inappropriate and counterproductive.

Manipulation. The opposite of positive intent. "Gotcha." It is manipulative to communicate with hidden motives to get people to unknowingly agree or act in a certain way.

Indifference. The opposite of empathy. "What you think doesn't matter." An officer can convey indifference by the simple act of answering a call for service while talking to someone. To avoid misinterpretation, the officer must take care to explain the necessity of answering the call.

Police officers may have more barriers to communication because of the image they convey, their position of authority and the nature of their work.

According to Buchholz and Roth (p. 82), other behaviors that inhibit communication include "facial expressions such as frowning or raising eyebrows, shaking the head, yawning, sighing, leaning back, avoiding eye contact, gazing around the room, taking irrelevant notes, or changing the subject." Other factors may also hinder communication.

Other common communication barriers include prejudices and stereotypes, lack of time, use of jargon, lack of feedback and failure to listen.

Prejudices and stereotypes can greatly interfere with your ability to communicate. Preconceived ideas about a person's truthfulness or "worth" can result in strained relationships with individuals and little or no interchange of ideas. The very language used to refer to others can interfere with communication. For example, would you rather be called a *victim* or a *survivor*? A *cripple* or *person with a disability*?

Lack of time is another barrier to effective communication. Police officers and members of the public are busy. Often neither want to take the time to communicate fully and to establish high empathy. Bad timing can also interfere with communication. Police officers frequently are interrupted by calls for service and need to cut short conversations with others.

The use of **jargon,** the technical language of a profession, is another barrier to communication. Law enforcement has its own special terminology, for example, *alleged perpetrator, modus operandi* and *complainant.* Officers should avoid using such terms when talking with the public.

Lack of feedback can also reduce effective communication. *I know that you believe that you understand what you think I said, but I am not sure you realize that what you heard is not what I meant.*

A failure to *listen* is one of the most common and most serious barriers to effective communication. Our educational system concentrates on the communication skills of reading and writing. Some time is devoted to speaking, but little or no time is devoted to listening. It is simply assumed that everyone knows how to listen. Although most people believe themselves to be good listeners, Jenkins (1999, p. 59) notes: "Studies indicate that 75 percent of what we hear is heard incorrectly; and of the remaining 25 percent, we forget 75 percent within weeks. [One] study claims that the average listener has an immediate retention level of only 50 percent—and within 24 to 48 hours, the retention level drops to 25 percent."

Similar to the discrepancy between the rate at which the eye takes in stimuli compared to the rate at which the brain can process those visual stimuli, a significant difference exists between how rapidly most people talk and how quickly the human brain can process words. Unlike with vision, however, the brain's ability to process auditory cues far exceeds the rate at which such cues are delivered.

Effective listening is difficult because of the gap between how rapidly people talk (125 words per minute) and how rapidly the brain can process those words (500 words per minute). The difference between the speed of speech and the speed of thought creates a false sense of comprehension and promotes mental tangents.

To overcome this barrier, officers must work at becoming effective listeners, a process known as active listening.

ACTIVE LISTENING

Ryan (1999, p. 30) observes: "Each of us has a deep and innate desire to be listened to. It is a need so fundamental that when it is consistently denied in either adults or children, it can lead to mental illness. Conversely, when our desire to be heard and understood is fulfilled, we are energized, uplifted, more creative and significantly more productive."

When speakers realize officers listen to and evaluate what they say carefully, they generally make sure their output is factual and accurate and that their responses are appropriate under the circumstances.

Officers can use several techniques to improve listening effectiveness, including the following: actively work at listening, concentrate, look for the main points, listen between the lines, notice body language, keep your mind open and your emotions in check, avoid drawing conclusions, do not interrupt, offer encouragement and periodically clarify what's being said to you. Johnson (1996, p. 45) offers the following additional suggestions for being a good listener:

- Watch your body language. Open your arms to appear receptive and lean forward. Don't fold your arms across your chest and lean back in your chair.

- Nod at appropriate times. Look at the speaker. Do not glance at the clock on the wall, your watch, those reports you have been meaning to get to, or worse yet, the newspaper open on your desk.

- Make frequent use of conversation enablers such as, "Uh-huh," "Go on," "I see," etc. But do not fake attention.

- Minimize distractions. Have your calls held. Close the door to your office. Meet somewhere quiet to talk.

- Be aware of the tendency to formulate replies in your mind while the speaker is still talking. When in this process, you are not hearing what is being said.

The ability to listen and to assess the situation when communicating can help officers make the best first impression possible. First impressions are also heavily influenced by the primacy effect and the four-minute barrier.

◆ THE PRIMACY EFFECT AND THE FOUR-MINUTE BARRIER

The first few moments of a personal contact are critical to the impression you make on others.

The tendency to form impressions of people quickly is called the primacy **effect.**

You can test the primacy effect by asking yourself a few questions. Have you ever walked into a store, been approached by a salesperson, and known almost immediately that you would probably buy something—or would probably *not* buy anything? Have you ever been seated on an airplane next to a stranger and almost immediately wanted to talk to the person—or wanted to get a magazine and bury yourself in it? First impressions tend to set the tone for a positive or negative interaction. As Will Rogers so astutely put it, "You never get a second chance to make a first impression."

How long does it take for the primacy effect to occur? Usually in the first four minutes, according to Leonard and Natalie Zunin (n.d.), developers of the concept of the four-minute barrier.

The four-minute barrier *is the point in an initial meeting at which most people have formed a positive or negative opinion about the individual with whom they are communicating.*

If you can get past the first four minutes of an initial interaction with a person on a positive note, your relationship is likely to be positive.

◈ LESSONS FROM BUSINESS

Changes in technology and in our society have had a profound effect on business. Many businesses have changed their basic approach toward their employees as well as toward their customers. Businesses recognize the importance of service and of good customer relations.

Law enforcement might adopt two practices used successfully in business: networking and seeking customer satisfaction, that is, being service oriented.

Networking

Personal networks were discussed earlier in this chapter as connections individuals have with others in their lives. Consciously establishing such networks has become popular in the business world, with *networking* a popular buzzword.

Networking *is building and maintaining professional relationships for mutual benefit.*

Just as police officers need to communicate with the people in their jurisdiction, they also need to communicate with the institutions and agencies in the area including churches, schools and business associations such as the Lions, Rotary and Kiwanis; social service agencies; storefront organizations and shelters; hospitals, clinics and emergency care providers; city inspectors and licensors; courts and corrections personnel; politicians and members of advisory councils; and special-interest groups such as MADD. Networks including law enforcement agencies and human-services agencies can yield substantial benefits not only for the agencies involved but also for individuals who need help.

As suggested earlier, community policing creates a partnership between the police and groups of concerned individuals to address specific community problems. Those involved in the problem may also be part of its solution.

The Citizen as Customer—A Service Orientation

A *customer* is one who buys goods and services. Indeed, it is the citizens of a community who pay for the services provided by law enforcement. This dates back to the early days when citizens were expected to take their turn serving as watchmen and decided they would rather pay someone to do that job.

Police officers do not traditionally think of the members of their community as customers. In fact, one police fraternal organization had T-shirts printed up with the slogan "In my business, the customer is always wrong." Many officers think of criminals as their customers and the public as those who should just stay out of the way. Some officers consider the time they spend dealing with law-abiding citizens as wasted time or something that gets in the way of "real police work."

Law enforcement, like business, might benefit by emphasizing the value of customer service and the time-tested adage "The customer is always right." They must also keep in mind the unfortunate ripple effect of poor customer satisfaction: Customers who have bad experiences want to tell everyone about it, whereas customers who have positive experiences, perhaps because good service is expected and taken for granted, will maybe tell one or two people. In a very real sense, citizens are the customers of law enforcement agencies.

Leland and Bailey (1996, pp. 73–74) offer the following suggestions for treating citizens as consumers:

- Make customer service the most important part of your job.
- Fulfill your customers' basic needs. Go beyond giving your customers what they ask for by satisfying their needs for fairness, friendliness, understanding and empathy, control, options and alternatives, and information.
- Make direct eye contact with your customers.
- Give your customers easy access to you, e.g., a card with your phone number on it.
- Treat your co-workers as customers. Your co-workers are your internal customers and need special attention too.

Leland and Bailey (p. 74) also note that how you say something can make a big difference in customer satisfaction. For example:

Don't Say:	Do Say:
That's not my job.	This is who can help you.
I don't know.	I'll find out.
No.	What I can do is . . .
You want it by when?	I'll try my best.
I'm busy right now.	I'll be with you in just a moment.

In addition to external customer service, it is also important to consider your internal customers—for example, detectives, patrol, records and dispatch. Customer service is not just how the police work with the public; it is also how they help each other.

The organization must train the people who interact directly with customers, and then it must empower them. That is, it must give them the authority, responsibility and incentives to recognize, care about and attend to customer needs. Empowering the bottom of the organizational pyramid can be threatening, especially to middle-level managers, who may view such empowerment as an erosion of their own authority. Empowerment of all members of an organization is absolutely essential to good service. Employees close to the customer are the first to know about problems and are in the best position to determine what can be done to satisfy the customer.

Law enforcement agencies, like many successful businesses, would benefit from having an empowered workforce. It is vital to community policing to give patrol officers the authority and training necessary to make decisions and to reward them when they do so.

SUMMARY

A person's world-view is largely created by what they see and hear as they experience events. The discrepancy between what the eye takes in (five million bits per second) and what the person actually processes (five hundred bits per second) accounts, in part, for why two witnesses can see the same thing differently.

Perception is also affected by the words people use to communicate. The most basic rule of semantics is: Cow_1 is *not* Cow_2, that is, each item within a specific class also has individual characteristics.

Effective police-community relations depend on an understanding of oneself and of others. Critical to self-understanding is recognizing preferences, prejudices and stereotypes. Prejudice is an attitude; discrimination is a behavior. Empathy is understanding another person. Empathy depends, in part, upon determining the other person's networks, the "complex pathways of human interaction that guide and direct an individual's perception, motivation and behavior."

The quality of police-community relations depends largely on the communication process. The process involves a sender, a message, a channel, a receiver and sometimes feedback. Important individual characteristics in communication include age, education, gender, values, emotional involvement, self-esteem and language skills. Behavioral communication enhancers include describing, equality, openness, problem-orientation, positive intent and empathy. Conversely, behavioral barriers to communication include judging, superiority, certainty, controlling, manipulation and indifference. Police officers may have more barriers to communication because of the image they convey, their position of authority and the nature of their work. Other common communication barriers include prejudices and stereotypes, time, use of jargon, lack of feedback and failure to listen.

Effective listening is difficult because of the gap between how rapidly people talk (125 words per minute) and how rapidly the brain can process those words (500 words per minute). The difference between the speed of speech and the speed of thought creates a false sense of security and promotes mental tangents.

When seeking to improve human interactions, officers should keep in mind the tendency to form impressions of people quickly, that is, the primacy effect. The four-minute barrier is the point in an initial meeting at which most people have formed a positive or negative opinion about someone.

Law enforcement might benefit by adopting two practices used successfully in business: networking and seeking customer satisfaction, that is, being service oriented. Networking is building and maintaining professional relationships for mutual benefit.

DISCUSSION QUESTIONS

1. What are some of your strong preferences? Might they be called prejudices?

2. Do you prefer to communicate by speaking or writing?

3. Who is included in your network?

4. Do you have a hobby that has a specialized language (jargon)? What words might most people not understand?

5. Three umpires were discussing balls and strikes in baseball. The first said, "I call them like I see them." The second said, "I call them like they are." The third said, "They aren't anything 'til I call them." How does this relate to the study of semantics?

6. What role do euphemisms ("soft" words) play in communication?

7. Give examples illustrating the basic rule learned from semantics: Cow_1 is not Cow_2. Why is the rule important in police work?

8. How does empathy differ from sympathy? When is each appropriate?

9. Can you think of examples of when the four-minute barrier and the primacy effect operated in your life?

10. In what ways might the general public be perceived as "customers" of a police department? What implications does this have?

INFOTRAC COLLEGE EDITION ASSIGNMENTS

- Use InfoTrac to help answer the discussion questions as appropriate.
- Research at least one of the following subjects and write a brief (3–4 page) report of your findings: discrimination, jargon, listening, nonverbal communication, prejudices or stereotypes. Be prepared to share your report with the class.

COMMUNITY PROJECT

Use the yellow pages in your phone book to locate a community service provider. Contact a staff member and find out what networks they have established with other agencies and organizations within the community. Compare your agency with those of your classmates.

REFERENCES

Adams, Michael. "Every Move You Make." *Successful Meetings,* May 1996, pp. 46–50.

Buchholz, Steve and Roth, Thomas. *Creating the High-Performance Team.* New York: John Wiley & Sons, Inc., 1987.

Ciaramicoli, Arthur. "The Amazing Power of Empathy: It's in All of Us . . . How to Bring It Out." *Bottom Line: Personal,* September 15, 2000, p. 9.

Fulton, Roger. "On the Road to Good Communications." *Law Enforcement Technology,* Vol. 27, No. 9, September 2000, p. 130.

Giuliano, Peter. "Seven Benefits of Eye Contact." *Successful Meetings,* August 1999, p. 104.

Hayakawa, S. I. *Language in Thought and Action.* New York: Harcourt, Brace & World, Inc., 1949.

Jenkins, Tom. "Prick Up Your Ears." *Successful Meetings,* November 1999, pp. 59–62.

Johnson, Robert Roy. "Listening." *Law and Order,* Vol. 44, No. 2, February 1996, pp. 43–46.

Leland, Karen and Bailey, Keith. "Customer Service: Happy Holidays." *Successful Meetings,* December 1996, pp. 73–74.

National Advisory Commission on Criminal Justice Standards and Goals. *Task Force on Police.* Washington, DC: U.S. Government Printing Office, 1973.

Noose, Gregory A. "Basic Investigative Interviewing Skills: Networking an Interview." *Law and Order,* Vol. 40, No. 3, March 1992, pp. 101–107.

Parker, L. Craig, Jr.; Meier, Robert D.; and Monahan, Lynn Hunt. *Interpersonal Psychology for Criminal Justice.* St. Paul, MN: West Publishing Company, 1989.

Pinizotto, Anthony J. and Davis, Edward F. "Offenders' Perceptual Shorthand: What Messages Are Law Enforcement Officers Sending to Offenders?" *FBI Law Enforcement Bulletin,* Vol. 68, No. 6, June 1999, pp. 1–4.

Pinizotto, Anthony J.; Davis, Edward F.; and Miller, Charles E. "Officers' Perceptual Shorthand: What Messages Are Offenders Sending to Law Enforcement Officers?" *FBI Law Enforcement Bulletin,* Vol. 69, No. 7, July 2000, pp. 1–6.

Ryan, Anita. "Are You Listening?" *Talking Business,* March/April 1999, p. 30.

Scott, Brian. "Verbal Judo: Talk Your Way through Confrontations." *Police,* Vol. 24, No. 8, August 2000, pp. 54–56.

Sheehan, Kathy M. "Critical Police Communications." *Law and Order,* Vol. 44, No. 2, February 1996, pp. 37–41.

Zunin, Leonard and Zunin, Natalie. *Contact—The First Four Minutes.* No date.

CHAPTER 7

Finding Common Ground: Diversity and Community Policing

Police officers and their agencies can accomplish much by working in partnership with citizens to implement the American vision of diverse and tolerant communities that offer freedom, safety and dignity for all.

International Association of Chiefs of Police

Do you know

What ethnocentrism is?

What the three schools of thought are on what happens when more than one culture inhabits the same territory?

What types of diversity are found in the United States?

What one main barrier frequently associated with ethnic/racial diversity is?

What strategies might be used to communicate more effectively with those who do not speak English?

What racism refers to?

What racial profiling is?

How religious diversity affects community policing?

What the three basic socioeconomic classes are? What they are based on?

What the poverty syndrome is?

What has been the dominant culture in the United States?

What a bias or hate crime is?

Can you define these terms:

acculturation

assimilation

bias crime

cultural conflict

cultural pluralism

cultural window

culture

ethnicity

ethnocentrism

ghetto syndrome

hate crime

hyphenated American

poverty syndrome

race

racial profiling

racism

INTRODUCTION

Cherry (2000, p. 8) asserts: "As America has become more racially, religiously and ethnically diverse, the call for police departments to reflect and partner with these burgeoning groups has become more insistent." Dealing effectively with diversity is important to community policing because community outreach, communications, trust and activism are all necessary to community partnerships, and none of these can be achieved without accepting—indeed, embracing—diversity.

This chapter begins with an overview of multicultural diversity in the United States, including racial and ethnic diversity. This is followed by an examination of problems encountered with the language barrier and other obstacles to communication as well as legal issues pertaining to cultural diversity. Next racism is discussed, including a look at racial slurs and racial disparity, followed by racial profiling and strategies to overcome barriers based on racial or ethnic diversity. Religious diversity is then explored. Afterward, socioeconomic diversity is described, and a closer look is given to those in the lower socioeconomic class, the homeless and the privileged, including celebrities. An explanation of the majority versus the minority world-view is presented next, followed by a discussion of bias/hate crimes. The chapter concludes with a consideration of the challenges facing police in the 21st century as they strive to "serve and protect" an increasingly diverse society.

◈ MULTICULTURALISM: AN OVERVIEW OF CULTURAL DIVERSITY

The United States is a land of many cultures. **Culture** is defined as a collection of artifacts, tools, ways of living, values and language common to a group of people, all passed from one generation to the next. The specific items that make up a culture fall into two broad categories: material and nonmaterial. Material elements of one culture are readily borrowed or adopted by another culture if they are an obvious improvement. This is not the case, however, with the nonmaterial elements involved in "ways of living," such as religion, political beliefs, kinship roles, and values and laws, both moral and legal. Diversity is most obvious and sometimes most problematic when different "ways of living" coexist in the same community.

Chapter 6 discussed how language (an element of culture) shapes the way people view the world. The culture itself also provides a framework or world-view, a **cultural window** through which events are interpreted. Houston (1996, p. 124) suggests:

America has always been a country at war with itself. Our history is one of self-conflict. Perhaps our most profound wars have been our cultural wars—the ones fought for the soul of our nation. . . . Perhaps we are, at once, the most generous nation to have ever existed—and the most selfish. We are the most inclusive society that the world has ever known, and at the same time we have become the most exclusive in our attitudes towards others. We are a kaleidoscope of cultures.

Ethnocentrism *is the preference for one's own way of life over all others.*

People are naturally attracted to others who are similar to themselves. If we surround ourselves with others similar to us, we minimize uncertainty regarding how people will respond to us and maximize the likelihood we will be in agreement. Minimizing uncertainty motivates people because uncertainty is uncomfortable. Ethnocentricity and segregation are consequences of our desire to avoid uncertainty.

Several different cultures came to the "New World" and established the United States. In fact, everyone who was not a Native American or Mexican American was a boat person. The sociological literature on ethnic and racial diversity has three theories on the consequences of two or more cultures inhabiting the same geographic area: assimilation, cultural pluralism and cultural conflict. These are *not* mutually exclusive and may occur at the same time, creating problems for the transition to community policing.

Assimilation *theorists suggest that our society takes in or assimilates various cultures in what is commonly referred to as a "melting pot."*

Assimilation, also referred to as **acculturation,** was, indeed, what happened among the early colonists. Initially the colonists came from various countries with different religions. They settled in specific geographic areas and maintained their original culture, for example, the Pennsylvania Dutch.

The seemingly unlimited resources available and the mutual struggle for survival in the New World encouraged colonists to assimilate. Over time, the triple forces of continued immigration, urbanization and industrialization soon turned the United States into a "melting pot" with diverse cultures from the various colonies merging. The melting pot was accomplished relatively painlessly because of the many similarities among the colonists. They looked quite similar physically, they valued religion and "morality," most valued hard work and, perhaps most important, there was plenty of land for everyone. The "homogenization" of the United States was fairly well accomplished by the mid-1800s. The formerly distinct cultures blended into what became known as the American culture, a white, male-dominated, culture of European origin.

Unfortunately, the colonists excluded the Native Americans. Like animals, they were herded onto reservations. Native Americans have only recently begun to enter into the mainstream of American life. Some Native Americans no longer want to be assimilated—they seek to maintain their culture and heritage. The same is true of many African Americans. Consequently, cultural diversity will continue to exist in the United States. Assimilation does not always occur.

An alternative to assimilation is for diverse cultures to peacefully coexist.

Cultural pluralism *suggests many melting pots. Some groups are comfortable in one pot; other groups are comfortable in another.*

One example of cultural pluralism is the Native American. American Indians are a nation of over 450 recognized tribes and bands in this country, with populations ranging from less than 100 to more than 100,000. Prior to colonization of the United States, the Indian tribes had distinct territories, languages and cultures. Later, as the settlers took their lands, they joined together in self-defense. Today, Native Americans are often referred to as a single entity, although the individual tribes still maintain their unique identities.

Cultural pluralism is particularly noticeable when new immigrants arrive in the United States. Usually, instead of attempting to assimilate into the mainstream of the United States, immigrants seek out others from their homeland, resulting in China-towns, Little Italys, Little Havanas, Little Greeces and, most recently, Hmong and Somali communities. This has resulted in what is sometimes referred to as the **hyphen-ated American:** the Italian-American, the Polish-American, the Afro-American, the Asian-American and so forth.

Cultural pluralism rests on the assumption that diverse cultures can coexist and pros-per. The view that diversity strengthens a society is held by many. In Oakland, Califor-nia, for example, citizens consider the social studies textbooks antihistorical because they describe the United States as a "common culture," created by waves of immigrants. To see the story of the United States strictly as Europeans seeking a better way of life is to see only part of U.S. history. This is not the story of African Americans, Native Ameri-cans or Mexican Americans.

Nor is peaceful coexistence always the reality.

The **cultural conflict** *theory suggests that diverse cultures that share the same territory will compete with and attempt to exploit one another.*

Such cultural conflict was common between the early settlers and the Native Ameri-can tribes. Conflict was also common between the white immigrants and the more than six million slaves imported from Africa between 1619 and 1860. The hostile treatment of Japanese Americans during World War II was also rooted in cultural conflict. Following the attack on Pearl Harbor, many U.S. citizens saw Japanese Americans as a national threat. Over 110,000 Japanese, the great majority of whom were American-born citizens, were forced by the government to sell their homes and businesses and then placed in internment camps.

Cultural conflict can currently be seen in growing tensions between specific ethnic groups as they compete for the limited remaining resources available. In Minnesota, for example, only Native Americans are allowed to harvest wild rice or to spear fish. The Mille Lacs band of Chippewa has sued Minnesota, claiming treaty rights allow them to fish outside their reservation without state regulation. Native Americans are also lobbying to be allowed to take motorboats into the wilderness area to enhance their guide business.

A report from the U.S. Census Bureau ("Census Bureau . . . ," 1996, p. A14) sug-gests that the United States is experiencing "one of the most dramatic shifts in its racial and ethnic makeup since the slave trade transformed the racial composition of the South." This report predicts that non-Hispanic whites will account for only about half of the U.S. population by the middle of the next century (they currently comprise 82.3 percent of the total population). Hispanics will make up 24.5 percent, up from 11.5 percent. Asians will make up 8.2 percent, up from 4.0 percent. The African Ameri-can population will remain relatively stable at about 12 or 13 percent (U.S. Bureau of the Census, 1999). As former President Jimmy Carter notes: "We become not a melting pot but a beautiful mosaic. Different people, different beliefs, different yearnings, differ-ent hopes, different dreams."

Organizations working for women's rights, gray power and gay power make it clear that the United States is, indeed, a culturally pluralistic nation. Assimilation, cultural

Asian children gather on a sidewalk in San Francisco's Tenderloin district, home to many Asian refugee families.

pluralism and cultural conflicts coexist and are all realities in the United States, presenting a formidable challenge for those who must maintain the "public peace." Much of this cultural diversity can be categorized more specifically as racial or ethnic diversity.

◆ RACIAL AND ETHNIC DIVERSITY

Race and ethnicity are undeniably intertwined. And although the two terms are often used interchangeably, important basic differences exist. **Race** is based on science, biologically determined and refers to a group of people having the same ancestry, thereby possessing common genes for traits such as hair type/color, skin color, eye color, stature, bodily proportions, and so on. Most anthropologists contend there are only three primary races: Caucasoid, Negroid and Mongoloid.

The science of judging human character from facial features is called *physiognomy.* As Ambrose Bierce, journalist, aptly observed, it might better be defined as the art of determining the character of another by the resemblances and differences between the other person's face and our own, which is the standard of excellence. People tend to judge others who are different as somehow inferior, which leads to prejudices.

Ethnicity, on the other hand, is rooted more in sociology and geography and defines a group of people who share customs, language, religious beliefs and a common history based on national origin or the inhabiting of a specific geographical area. An ethnic group need not consist exclusively of people of the same race.

The United States is both racially and ethnically diverse.

In the United States, both racial and ethnic diversity present challenges to the implementation of community policing, specifically in the form of language barriers and other communication obstacles, the legality of certain cultural practices, racism and allegations of racial profiling.

The Language Barrier and Other Obstacles to Communication

In some parts of the country it is common for officers to deal with non-English speaking people or those who speak English as a second language. Try to imagine performing a carstop on a vehicle filled with people who do not understand anything you are saying and who you cannot understand. The language barrier can make just getting the job done safely very difficult, to say nothing of maintaining positive police-community relations.

The language barrier is a major problem in police interactions with some ethnic/racial groups.

Citizens who speak no English are protected by the same constitutional guarantees as anyone else. Any delays in the judicial process or in response to emergencies or any other problems arising from lack of communication put the officer, supervisor and entire department at risk of a lawsuit.

Ideally officers would be bilingual, speaking English and the language of the main ethnic minority in the area. An alternative is to learn the words and phrases used most frequently in policing in the other language. Tourists in foreign countries can usually communicate at an elementary level with the locals using a combination of words and gestures. If you were to learn one new word a day, in one year your working vocabulary would be 365 words. This vocabulary would be sufficient to understand most communications and to convey your own messages in most situations.

Officers could also benefit from a plasticized guide of the most common words and phrases along with their pronunciations. One such guide, *Speedy Spanish for Police Personnel,* includes words and phrases needed for, among other situations, routine traffic stops, D.U.I., burglary/theft reports, victim/witness interrogation, Miranda warning and waiver, domestic disputes, medical care and booking/body search.

Some departments have initiated their own specialized language and communication enhancement programs to extend community policing efforts. Hard (2000, p. 6) notes:

> Enlisting the help of several bilingual employees the [Corcoran,California] police department created the "Amigos de la Comunidad" program, a Spanish-language citizen police academy. Amigos de la Comunidad translates as "Friends of the Community." . . .
>
> Of the first 25 Amigos de la Comunidad graduates, six moved on to form a Spanish-language unit of the Corcoran Police Department's all-volunteer community patrol.

Until recently, Spanish was the primary language officers needed to learn. In the past few decades, however, refugee influxes from the former Soviet Union, Ethiopia, Poland, Romania and Asia have added to the challenge. Clement (1992, p. 26) describes a

.ysician's difficulty dealing with a Hmong patient and her interpreter who also spoke limited English. The doctor wanted to draw blood for a test. The interpreter, however, could not make the pronunciation distinction between "test" and "taste." Said Clement: "For a long time, we had to fight the myth that our doctor wanted to drink the blood. And when we asked for urine and stool specimens, they just laughed." Police officers could encounter a similar difficulty in a D.U.I. incident.

Strategies to help improve communication with non-English-speaking individuals include (1) learning the language or at least common words and phrases, (2) using a language guide, (3) having a list of local language teachers who could serve as interpreters and (4) subscribing to the Language Line.

In an effort to improve communications with non-English-speaking people, police could maintain a list of teachers of various foreign languages at local high schools, colleges and universities. Another option is to subscribe to AT&T's *Language Line*, a service providing immediate translation of more than 140 different languages, 24 hours a day, 365 days a year. The availability of cell phones in the field makes this service especially useful.

Cultural differences may exist regarding perceptions of what is safe. For example, in some Latin American countries, people frequently congregate, play and socialize in the streets, sometimes late into the evening, an indication of a safe neighborhood. For whites in this country, however, such gatherings may be considered disorderly and deserving of police intervention. Put these two groups in the same neighborhood, and the whites might be barricading themselves inside while the Latin Americans are out having a good time. Cultural differences such as these can create rifts between neighbors and involve the police, who may have difficulty communicating to one group or the other why they can or cannot engage in a particular activity.

It is important for police officers to be aware of other cultural differences that may hinder communication. For example, in some Asian cultures, only the oldest family member will deal with the police on behalf of the entire family. In the last few years many immigrants have come from Southeast Asia. Often victims of discrimination and crime, they tend to not seek police assistance or report crimes. Many, in fact, especially the elderly, fear the police. Compounding this communication problem is the fact that many immigrants from Asian and other Third World nations often mistrust U.S. banks and keep their money and other valuables at home. The cultural backgrounds of these people leave them extremely vulnerable to scams, burglaries and robberies, but even after they are victimized, they still hesitate to talk to the police.

Sometimes offenders within a particular culture take advantage of the cultural norms that dissuade crime victims from involving the law. An illustration of this is seen among the Hmong people of Southeast Asia. As Gustafson (1998, p. B1) reports: "The Asian Crips went on a 12-day rampage [in the spring of 1998], repeatedly raping at least seven young Hmong girls as part of a gang initiation. . . . Hmong gang members are well aware that rape victims are stigmatized in the Hmong community and reluctant to tell authorities what happened." Interacting effectively with culturally diverse victims is discussed in greater detail in Chapter 9.

Another example of a cultural communication barrier comes from the Native American Ojibwa culture, which considers direct eye contact a sign of disrespect or defiance.

Respect is shown by avoiding eye contact and saying very little, behaviors that in other cultures may signal lack of interest or even contempt. Police officers could easily misinterpret such a response.

Eye contact, in fact, varies greatly among different cultures. Most African Americans prefer indirect eye contact while listening and direct eye contact while speaking as a sign of attentiveness and respect. The opposite is true of most people of European descent, who prefer direct eye contact during listening and indirect eye contact during speaking as signs of attention and respect. To Hispanics, avoidance of direct eye contact is sometimes a sign of attentiveness and respect, but sustained direct eye contact may be interpreted as a challenge to authority.

Other cultural differences in nonverbal communication can result in misunderstanding. For example, hissing to gain attention is common for Hispanics, but to whites hissing is usually considered impolite and indicates hatred. A slap on the back in the white culture usually indicates friendliness; a slap on the back in Asian or Vietnamese cultures is usually insulting. The American "okay" sign—thumb and forefinger forming a circle, fingers pointing up—is considered an obscene gesture in Brazil and in Arab cultures. This same gesture means *money* in Japanese and *zero* or *worthless* in French. There is great potential for miscommunication between members of different groups.

Police officers should determine what racial/ethnic minorities reside in their jurisdiction and learn what cultural values they might misunderstand. In fact, what is legal in some cultures may be illegal in the United States.

Cultural Diversity and the Law

A few examples will show how legal problems might result from cultural diversity. A Southeast Asian family may be investigated for child abuse if health professionals note the skin lesions caused by traditional coin rubbing. The practice of "coining" involves rubbing warm oil and coins across the skin and often results in long, red bruises. Many Asians also believe in administering severe corporal punishment to children who misbehave.

Another cultural difference that causes problems is that the Hmongs have no age restriction on marriage. For example, a Hmong man who married a 12-year-old girl after paying her parents $2,000 was charged with third-degree criminal sexual conduct for having sexual relations with a minor because state law prohibited anyone under 16 to be married, even with parental consent.

Many of the cultural practices that conflict with U.S. laws are of a religious nature and will be discussed shortly. First, however, consider two associated aspects of racial and ethnic diversity that pose possibly the greatest challenges to successfully implementing community policing—racism and charges of racial profiling.

Racism

For the community policing philosophy to become a reality, racism, wherever it exists, must be recognized and dealt with.

Racism *is a belief that a human population having a distinct genetically transmitted characteristic is inferior. It also refers to discrimination or prejudice based on race.*

However, data from the human genome project indicate the concept of *race* is only skin deep and that no other human trait—intelligence, ambition, strength, athleticism or any of the more fundamental traits that make us human, such as walking upright or communicating symbolically through language—correlates with the genes responsible for appearance. Although expression of these genes manifests in superficial differences in appearance, allowing us to identify and categorize individuals as belong to a certain "race," without our skin we all look, and are, basically the same. Therefore, the racist idea that some groups (races) are somehow genetically superior to others has no scientific basis.

Racism in the United States has deep roots, particularly concerning the African American population, whose animosity toward the police establishment dates back to the slave patrols in the 18th century South. Recall from Chapter 1 how the white colonists' fear and perception of slaves as a dangerous threat led to the formation of special patrols whose sole purpose was to keep slaves "in their place," inferior and subservient to whites, laying the foundation for centuries of conflict between the police and African Americans. Scoville (2000, p. 17) adds: "Cops were the instruments by which Gov. George Wallace kept blacks from integrating into Alabama schools. They were the enforcers of Jim Crow laws, and arrested Rosa Parks for failing to surrender a bus seat to a white."

The issue of racism as it relates to community policing is multifaceted and extremely charged. Furthermore, racism flows in both directions between the police and the citizens within the communities they serve. Holmes (2000, p. 343) acknowledges: "Many minority citizens distrust the criminal justice system, just as many criminal justice agents distrust them. Nowhere is that tension more apparent than in the relation between minorities and the police."

Racial Slurs. One way racism manifests itself is through the use of racial epithets, which Mueck (2000, p. 29) declares have no place in law enforcement: "Even though it may not be against the law to use racial slurs, it is (and should be) against departmental policy and officer ethics." Noting the widespread use of racial slurs among officers, Mueck (p. 30) warns:

> Racial epithets of any kind taint a situation as racially based, giving a sense of unfair policing by the officer. As public servants, officers are expected to be neutral in their enforcement of the law. . . .
>
> Officers using racial epithets compromise the integrity of their occupations by allowing the suspicion that they do not enforce the law equally. . . .
>
> What an officer may fail to realize (or not care to realize) is that the use of such comments heightens racial tension . . . [leading] to poor community relations. This causes a mistrust of the police by members of minority communities, and automatically puts contacts with the police in a negative context by threatening community stability.

Some officers make the critical mistake of trying to achieve rapport by using terminology they hear members of a minority group using among themselves. According to Mueck (p. 31):

> One of the most explosive words in the English language, the "N" word (nigger), is used at times by African-Americans talking among themselves. But it is totally inappropriate when used by a member of any other race.

Every kind of hatred and dehumanizing event ever experienced by African-Americans through U.S. history is reflected in that word. When used by members of other races, the connotation is perceived strictly as racist, no matter what the intent of the speaker. When used by their own, however, it is accepted as simply a reference to other African-Americans.

Besides undermining general police-community relations, racial slurs may come back to haunt officers long after the words are actually spoken. In recounting the impact racial comments had on the jury during the O. J. Simpson trial, Mueck (p. 31) points out: "Using a racially charged word like the 'N' word may have grave consequences. Mark Fuhrman never thought that things he'd said years earlier would be used against him."

Racial Disparity. The connections between race, class and perceived police discrimination and misconduct have been the focus of much research. A study by Weitzer and Tuch (1999, p. 502) found:

> Consistent with prior research, race is the strongest predictor of attitudes toward the police and criminal justice agencies. Blacks are more likely than Whites to perceive racial disparities in policing and in the criminal justice system and to report personal experiences of discriminatory police treatment. A substantial proportion of Whites sees these institutions as operating in a colorblind fashion.

Their study also revealed (p. 502) that class, in addition to race, affects citizens' perceptions, with middle-class blacks sometimes more critical of the police and justice system than either lower-class blacks or middle-class whites. Furthermore, in some specific aspects of the research, higher-educated blacks were significantly more critical of criminal justice agencies than were higher-educated whites. Weitzer and Tuch (p. 502) offer the following reasons to support their findings:

> One possible explanation is that middle-class Blacks, more so than middle-class Whites or less advantaged Blacks, are acutely aware of race-based discrimination due to an expectation that class position should shield middle-class Blacks from mistreatment. . . . Another possible explanation is that better educated Blacks are more cognizant of racially charged mass-media events than are either less educated Blacks or better educated Whites.

They (p. 503) also note: "Irrespective of class position, Whites are more reluctant than Blacks to acknowledge racism in American society, whether in the police or in other institutions."

The effects of neighborhood class were also examined by Weitzer (1999, p. 843), who found: "Results of the present study suggest that class is important in shaping citizens' perceptions of police misconduct, but the crucial factor is not so much individuals' class as neighborhood class position." For example, middle-class Blacks may experience few problems with the police inside their residential neighborhoods, but if they travel outside their neighborhood, where their middle-class status is no longer visible to the police, they may experience more frequent police mistreatment, suspicion and conflict (Weitzer and Tuch, p. 503).

The race of the officer also affects the nature of citizen interactions. However, contrary to what many believe, minority officers do not necessarily treat minority citizens more favorably. Holmes (p. 343) explains: "The conflict theory of law stipulates that strategies of crime control regulate threats to the interests of dominant groups." He (p. 360) continues:

> Even though minorities remain underrepresented in the ranks of municipal police departments, their representation is increasing, and cities with relatively large minority populations generally have a relatively large number of minority police officers. Yet, police officers and more affluent citizens, irrespective of their racial/ethnic identity, may perceive a threat largely from minority underclass populations. For example, middle-class black police officers may maintain cordial relations with more affluent black citizens, but they, like white officers, may perceive proximate threats from more antagonistic lower class blacks in poorer neighborhoods perceiving them as representatives of an oppressive power structure.

The issue of racial disparity has created a snag in the fabric of police solidarity. A survey by the Police Foundation found race to be a divisive issue for American police, with black and nonblack (white and other minority) police officers in strong disagreement about the significance of a citizen's race in how they are treated by police. Weisburd et al. (2000) report: "Black and nonblack officers had significantly different views about the effect of a citizen's race and socioeconomic status on the likelihood of police abuse of authority and about the effect of community policing on the potential for abuse." In comparing black officers' views about police abuse with those of white and other minority officers, Weisburd et al. found:

> A small minority of white officers in the sample believed that police treat white citizens better than they treat black or other minority citizens in similar situations, while the majority of black police officers held this view. Similar differences existed between black and other officers' views on the likelihood of police using force against minorities and poor citizens. In addition, the survey found that black officers had a more positive view of community policing's ability to control the abuse of police authority. The magnitude of these race-based differences in opinion suggests a large gap between black police officers and other officers in the sample.

When asked whether police officers are more likely to use physical force against blacks and other minorities than against whites in similar situations, only 5.1 percent of white officers agreed that such unequal treatment occurs. However, 57.1 percent of the black officers surveyed thought officers were more likely to use physical force against blacks and other minorities than against whites in similar situations. Furthermore, the attitudes of "other minority" officers were more similar to those of white police officers than to those of black officers, with 12.4 percent of other minority officers agreeing with the statement concerning unequal treatment. Weisburd et al. conclude these findings "seem to corroborate the view that there is a racial divide between whites and blacks in American society—a divide so pronounced that even the apparently strong culture of policing does not transcend it."

Racial disparity is an unfortunate reality of the criminal justice system for both juveniles and adults. A report by the National Council on Crime and Delinquency (NCCD) states: "While 'Equal Justice Under Law' is the foundation of our legal system, and is carved on the front of the U.S. Supreme Court, the juvenile justice system is anything but equal. Throughout the system, minority youths—especially African American youths—receive different and harsher treatment" ("Race Disparity Seen . . .," 2000, p. 7). The same report (p. 6) notes: "Black youths are overrepresented at every decision point in the juvenile justice system, beginning with a police officer's decision about whether to arrest a youth, send him back to his parents, or simply give him a warning, and ending with the most severe outcome possible, prosecution as an adult and incarceration in an adult prison."

Data from the FBI, the Bureau of Justice Statistics and the Office of Juvenile Justice and Delinquency Prevention (OJJDP) indicate that minority youths face accumulating disadvantages as they move through the juvenile justice system. For example, even though blacks constitute only 15 percent of all youths under age 18, they make up 26 percent of juvenile arrestees, 31 percent of the cases referred to juvenile court, 46 percent of the cases that juvenile courts waive to adult court and 58 percent of the youths sent to adult prisons (p. 7).

Some argue that crime policy has become a substitute for public policy, with politicians inappropriately using the criminal justice system to deal with difficult economic, social and family problems. As the *Boston Globe* ("Increase in Black Inmates . . .," 1999, p. A3) reports: "Over the past five decades, the disparity between races has widened dramatically as minorities have replaced whites in the prison population."

A study on sentencing disparity by Spohn and Holleran (2000, p. 281) examined four offender characteristics—race/ethnicity, gender, age and employment status—and how they interact to affect sentencing decisions. Their study found:

> The four offender characteristics interact to produce harsher sentences for certain types of offenders. Young black and Hispanic males face greater odds of incarceration than middle-aged white males, and unemployed black and Hispanic males are substantially more likely to be sentenced to prison than employed white males. Thus, our results suggest that offenders with constellations of characteristics other than "young black male" pay a punishment penalty.

Whether or not the general public is aware of studies documenting the prevalence of racial disparity in the criminal justice system, such findings reflect the daily reality of citizens' experiences with police and explain why many minorities have lost the expectation of being treated fairly. Weitzer (p. 833) notes: "Although no one likes to be stopped by police, whites who have been stopped are more likely than blacks to see the stop as justifiable, whereas blacks tend to define it as illegitimate and to leave the encounter dissatisfied or angry." He tells of a young black man from a middle-class neighborhood who said he was "harassed" by an officer who followed his car (outside his neighborhood) for two miles and then stopped him:

> When asked to explain the stop, the officer replied, "You look suspicious. You were making too many turns." The young man was incredulous that "too many turns" could be deemed suspicious.
>
> Coupled with this resentment is a feeling that blacks must take special precautions in these situations, which whites have less cause to observe, such as keeping one's hands in plain view, avoiding sudden movements, and managing every impression carefully.

As an example, one black man explains how residents of his middle-class neighborhood instruct fellow blacks on proper etiquette during stops: "The police are kind of scared, or they're trigger-happy, and I tell young people, or people I know, whenever the police stop you, put your hands up high so they can see them, especially if you're black, because you don't want them to think that you are reaching for something" (Weitzer, p. 833).

The contention that police single out subjects based solely on the color of their skin frequently leads to allegations of racial profiling, a serious concern for any department engaged in such a practice and for the credibility of the police profession as a whole.

Racial Profiling

In some areas of the country, it seems motorists of certain racial or ethnic groups are being stopped more frequently by police, oftentimes, the drivers claim, for no apparent reason. Such an event may be called "DWB" ("Driving while Black"), "DWA" ("Driving while Asian"), or "DWM" ("Driving while Mexican"). Regardless of the acronym used, the event signals an unethical and illegal practice called racial profiling.

Matthews (1999, p. 38) defines **racial profiling** as the process of using certain racial characteristics, such as skin color, as indicators of criminal activity. Strandberg (1999, p. 62) adds that racial profiling is acting on personal bias, such as when an officer stops a car simply because the driver is of a certain race. Margolis et al. (2000, p. 18) note that racial profiling has been the subject of litigation, legislation and politics, stating: "The issue of racial profiling is one of the most important issues facing law enforcement today. Racial profiling is a national focal point of the wider concerns about race relations in law enforcement." Wexler (2000, p. 2) submits: "Issues like racial profiling are a manifestation of larger issues of effective communication, trust, respect, sensitivity and accountability."

In a recent Gallup Poll, a random sample of Americans responded to the following statement and question: "It has been reported that some police officers stop motorists of certain racial or ethnic groups because the officers believe that these groups are more likely than others to commit certain types of crimes. Do you believe that this practice, known as 'racial profiling,' is widespread?" Kurlander (2000, p. 148) reports:

> The poll . . . showed that six out of every 10 Americans, over the age of 18, believe the practice is widespread. Seventy-six percent of black Americans replied that they believe the practice to be commonplace, 56 percent of the whites polled agreed, and even more importantly, more than 80 percent of both races disapproved of the practice.

The International Association of Chiefs of Police (IACP) also disapproves, recommending zero tolerance for officers who commit racial profiling and the removal of such officers from positions of authority (Strandberg, p. 65). Cohen et al. (2000, p. 15) assert: "Racial profiling is inconsistent with the basic freedoms and rights afforded in our democracy. It erodes the foundation of trust between communities and public authorities. Worst of all, it inflames racial and ethnic strife and undermines America's progress toward color-blind justice."

Olson (2000, p. 2) concurs: "The stopping of any person solely because of the color of his skin is contrary to the law of our land, and intolerable."

Racial profiling is a form of discrimination and singles out people of racial or ethnic groups because of a belief that these groups are more likely than others to commit certain types of crimes. Race-based enforcement is illegal.

Profiling has been described as more of an art than an exact science. Scoville (p. 16) states: "While other types of profiling—such as the psychological profiling of serial killers and serial rapists practiced by the FBI—have been recognized and accepted as forensically viable, racial profiling stands alone as a vocational pariah. Its practice is often deemed tantamount to racism, and allegations of its use can stigmatize officers and whole departments."

However, Kurlander (p. 150) notes: "Profiles of common characteristics shared by the perpetrators of certain crimes have been used since the 1970s." Strandberg (p. 66) adds: "The catch-22 of it all is that race is part of the general description." And in questioning whether officers should be allowed to take appearance into account when "sizing up" a subject, Scoville (p. 23) asks: "What is law enforcement's mission? Do we want aggressive law enforcement when it comes to [crime]? Or are we expected to take a hands-off approach because of the possibility of offending sensibilities of certain racial groups?"

Addressing the Issue. Several recommendations have been proposed to help law enforcement address and overcome the problem of racial profiling. Wexler (p. 2) contends: "The issue of racial profiling is a challenge for many departments, but . . . it's [also] an important opportunity to reposition the department's relationship with the community it serves."

An example of such repositioning is found in Chicago ("Strengthening Relations between . . .," 2000, p. 1), where race relations improved after the police superintendent sponsored a daylong, closed-door meeting involving leaders from the city's minority community and police representatives from every rank in the department. To examine the practices and policies potentially responsible for the increasing tension between the police and members of some of Chicago's minority communities, the superintendent decided to go right to the source and "ask the customer" (p. 4):

> "I wanted a candid assessment of where we are with respect to police/community relations, and that's just what I got," [the superintendent] said. "In my 32 years as a police officer in this city, I never heard such honest, heartfelt, and forthright dialogue." . . .
>
> The community leaders freely expressed their concerns about the relationship between police and their communities. They also recognized the difficulties and complexities faced by police. In the end, their insights challenged the police to take a hard look at the way some department members interact with the community they serve.

Wexler (p. 2) concludes: "Rather than viewing the issue of racial profiling as simply a matter of prohibiting the practice and implementing adequate data collection systems, Chicago viewed this in the larger context of police-community relations."

Cohen et al. (p. 12) stress: "Profiling uses race as a proxy for criminal intent or culpability because police often lack specific information about specific individuals.

Modern information systems and strong police-community interaction that fosters the exchange of information will ensure that police make decisions based on facts and data instead of race."

They further contend: "What we need is the right kind of targeting, based on better information about lawbreakers and closer cooperation between the police and the community." To achieve this, Cohen et al. suggest replacing racial profiling with tools to help the police make better judgments, deploy resources more strategically and recruit citizens in reclaiming control of their neighborhoods. They also advocate focusing on "hot spots" and high-risk offenders.

Matthews (p. 38) asserts that officers get into trouble when they fail to look at the totality of the characteristics of profiling, choosing instead to consider only a few indicators and acting upon incomplete information. He (pp. 38–39) suggests:

> First, remember that profiling is simply a tool that may enable you to decide if you want to continue your observation of the individual or investigate further.
>
> Second, remember that profiling looks at the minute details of evidence or helps to provide the profiler with a comprehensive list of characteristics. Profiling must be evaluated in a systematic fashion that provides an overview and not an isolated environment where a few dominating factors (young, black, male) may outweigh others.
>
> Third, officers must have a legitimate and legal reason, *that they can properly articulate*, to stop and search a vehicle and its occupants.

Echoing the sentiment of the final suggestion, some advocate approaching every incident as if you will have to defend it in court, making sure the actions you take are based on observable, measurable behaviors and not a preconceived notion of a subject's criminal tendencies. Strandberg (p. 65) advises: "Almost any case can be perceived as racially motivated if there is a person of color involved, so it makes sense for law enforcement to go out of its way to explain the reasoning and procedures behind every stop, every detainment, every arrest."

The IACP Highway Safety Committee ("Policies Help Gain Public Trust," 2000, p. 24) stresses:

> From the standpoint of professional law enforcers, there are two overarching reasons why we must ensure that racial and ethnic profiling is not substituted for reasonable suspicion in traffic stops and other law enforcement activities. First and foremost, it is the right thing to do. The Constitution must always come first in law enforcement. The ends do not necessarily justify the means, and we cannot take shortcuts with civil liberties. Second, law enforcement needs the public's trust in order to be successful in our mission. This includes the trust of people of all races, ethnic groups, religions and political beliefs.

The Police Foundation's Institute for Integrity, Leadership, and Professionalism in Policing has developed computer software for collecting and analyzing data on police officer-citizen contacts, including traffic stop data. Their Risk Analysis Management System and Quality of Service Indicator produces detailed reports with the goal being to prevent racial profiling and other problems that widen racial divides in the criminal justice system. (See Resources for their Web site.)

But just how prevalent is the problem? How many incidents involve minority subjects, and what percentage of the total does this comprise? Zingraff et al. (2000, p. 1) state: "The research literature lacks a consensus on the issue of the extensiveness of discrimination in police stops, searches and arrests." To help present a more complete picture, many agencies now require the collection of additional racial data about drivers and passengers involved in traffic stops: "Civil rights groups and others have called for such data collection in order to determine whether police use 'racial profiles' in making traffic stops. As of midyear 1999, 32 state highway patrol agencies collected racial data on drivers who received traffic citations. . . . Twenty-three required officers to note the race of the driver, and nine required data for all of the vehicle's occupants" ("Many State Police Agencies . . .," 2000, p. 5).

A retired police lieutenant notes the paradox of this new requirement: " 'Tis ironic that in order to prove we're color-blind, we now have to keep stats of the race of the people we search so we can disprove allegations of bias" (Scoville, p. 18). Another police officer indicates a built-in flaw in the effort, citing officer discretion as a variable that can lead to reverse bias:

> I can tell you what it already has done in the two cities I am aware of (San Diego and San Jose) that are undertaking a study of the issue. They are making decisions based upon race, and not upon good policing. For instance, one officer I am aware of has decided to cite all white drivers he stops (instead of cutting them a break sometimes) so as to skew numbers higher for actual cites for whites (Scoville, p. 20).

Kurlander (p. 153) comments: "Whether agencies are forced to collect the data by legislation, litigation, or do so voluntarily, the fact remains that this is an issue that will not go away. Prudent law enforcement executives will take action to detect officers who are engaged in race-based enforcement and correct that behavior. Those that do not will be at risk for litigation."

Margolis et al. (pp. 22–23) offer several ways for agencies to minimize their risk of racial profiling charges, including hands-on instructive and corrective supervision, enforceable policies against discriminatory law enforcement, proper and ongoing officer training and aggressive action in handling allegations of racial profiling. They (p. 23) conclude: "If racial profiling exists in a department, it must be zealously, but fairly, abolished. If the problem does not exist, a department must stand firm." Weitzer and Tuch (p. 504) conclude:

> In terms of public policy, it is noteworthy than an overwhelming majority of the American public supports government intervention to ensure that minorities receive equal treatment by the criminal justice system. A recent poll found that 74 percent of Whites and 89 percent of Blacks agreed that it was the responsibility of the federal government "to make sure minorities have equality with Whites (even if it means you will have to pay more taxes) in treatment by the courts and police." Police departments have the responsibility to maintain the confidence of all members of the population and, thus, they should take steps to minimize actions (e.g., unwarranted stops, verbal abuse, and physical mistreatment) that contribute to citizens' perceptions of unequal racially based treatment.

Strategies to Overcome Barriers Based on Racial and Ethnic Diversity

Various strategies have been proposed to help agencies attack bias and overcome racial or ethnic barriers between the police and community. Some are very general, whereas others are quite specific.

One of the first steps to take is implementing a zero-tolerance policy for bias within police ranks and publicizing that philosophy. One police chief explains (Paynter, 2000b, p. 63): "With the advent and implementation of community policing, it's important that the police profession be viewed as the guardians of the Constitution and human and civil rights." Paynter (p. 66) asserts: "A police officer doesn't represent himself or herself, he/she represents every individual in the community. Biased attitudes among police officers violate every tenet of good policing, and tend to reinforce the isolation of the victims and the groups they represent."

Another strategy is to develop an outreach effort to diverse communities to reduce victimization by teaching them practical crime prevention techniques. A critical part of this effort involves training and education for both police and citizens, as well as the formation of key partnerships between law enforcement and community groups. According to the National Crime Prevention Council (1995, p. 143):

> The cornerstone of any relationship between the police and an ethnic community is trust, a bond that is not always simple to develop. In order for police to teach ethnic groups how to protect themselves from crime, communication and ethnic tradition barriers must be overcome through cultural and sensitivity training, patient instruction, and special information-sharing. Teaching ethnic populations about police procedures and services can assist in developing a good working relationship between law enforcement and non-American cultures.
>
> Police must often rely on the services of translators, interpreters, community liaisons, religious leaders, and other trusted members of an ethnic community to develop an effective crime prevention program for ethnic groups. Schools can also assist by including crime prevention techniques in classroom instruction and special ESL classes.

A third general strategy is to create formal programs and policies to support the assimilation and needs of recent immigrant groups. The National Crime Prevention Council (p. 27) lists key components of this strategy as the "recognition of recent immigrants' needs for information, services, and other support to help in their transition to life in American society; cooperation with community groups in surveying the needs of immigrant residents; policies and programs that ensure access to services needed by the immigrants; cultural awareness and language training for relevant local government employees; community-based transition assistance services to help educate new residents about communication and language skills, banking and managing family budgets, employment, conflict resolution, and crime reporting; victim and witness services in the language(s) of the immigrant community; and neighborhood-based services to help ensure access by residents in need."

A specific example of one community's outreach effort is Dallas's citizenship program, which targets Cambodian, Korean, Laotian, Thai and Vietnamese immigrants. Ward (2000, p. 7) explains:

During a five-week program, police employees who have been certified as "citizenship facilitators" teach American history and other appropriate lessons in the students' native languages. . . .

The main goal is to improve relations between police and the Asian community. For example, the classes give the police department an opportunity to educate the Asian community on crime issues and help motivate them to report crime, thus overriding a natural reluctance to interact with police personnel. And as the program helps the residents become citizens, it also is empowering them to make their neighborhoods safer—by making them citizens who are fully engaged and open to the idea of working with police.

Addressing and meeting the special needs of immigrant victims are presented in more detail in Chapter 9.

Before considering more issues surrounding cultural differences and the challenges posed to community policing, consider two other forms of diversity in the United States, religious diversity and socioeconomic diversity.

In addition to cultural diversity (including racial/ethnic diversity), the United States also has religious and socioeconomic diversity.

◉ RELIGIOUS DIVERSITY

Many of those who came to America did so to escape religious persecution. The colonists' desire for religious freedom is evident in our Bill of Rights. The First Amendment protects, among other freedoms, freedom of religion. The First Amendment was drafted and adopted to protect the segregated turfs of different religious communities in the early colonies: Congregationalism in New England, Quakerism in Pennsylvania and Catholicism in Maryland. Over the years, these distinctions have become much less important, with "Christians" becoming a sort of religious melting pot for people of quite similar religious beliefs. However, religious tension still exists between many Christians (the majority) and those of Jewish faith (the minority). Anti-Semitism is a problem in some communities and may result in hate crimes, as discussed shortly.

Many religions now exist in the United States, and religious diversity continues to increase, presenting unique challenges to community policing efforts aimed at enhancing citizens' levels of trust, communication and activism.

Cults may pose special challenges to community policing efforts because they zealously advocate beliefs that are unorthodox or counterculture, deviating significantly from what mainstream society considers normal or acceptable. Szubin et al. (2000, p. 16) observe:

There is a common tendency to view "cults" with a combination of mistrust and fear. Much of this hostility derives from widespread misconceptions about the nature of "cults," founded upon popular stereotypes and simple ignorance. While such misconceptions are unfortunate in the general populace, they may be dangerous when harbored by law enforcement officers charged with dealing with these groups and ensuring the safety of both "cult" members and the general public.

They (p. 17) further note: "Most scholars of religion avoid the word 'cult' altogether because it carries with it a set of negative connotations. . . . These scholars instead refer to cults as 'new religious movements' or 'NRMs.'"

It is important to recognize that most NRMs stay within the boundaries of the law and practice their religions peacefully. Some, however, such as the Aum Shinrikyo, which released deadly sarin nerve gas in a Tokyo subway, pose a serious threat to their communities. Others such as Heaven's Gate, whose members committed suicide believing they'd be "beamed up" to God's flying saucer, pose a threat to themselves. In some instances, members of the surrounding community may become so fearful or enraged by an NRM's presence as to attack its followers.

The perpetuation of myths, misconceptions and prejudices can spill over into law enforcement and compromise a department's efforts to build positive community relations. Szubin et al. (p. 23) assert: "Dealing with new religious movement leaders and their followers stands as one of the most sensitive and difficult tasks that face modern law enforcement agencies." As with other types of diversity, Szubin et al. (p. 18) contend: "To reach an accurate and effective understanding of NRMs, law enforcement officers must start from a clean slate without the prejudices that can hamper effective police work."

In recent years, devil worship or Satanism has come to the attention of some police departments. The First Amendment protects such practices. Police become concerned, however, when those engaged in Satanism desecrate churches, steal religious artifacts or sacrifice their neighbor's dog.

Sometimes the line between religious freedom and illegal activity is blurred. For example, in 1987 the city of Hialeah, Florida, adopted an animal-sacrifice prohibition after members of Santeria made plans to open a church there. This ancient African religion practices animal sacrifices at rites celebrating birth, marriage and death and also during ceremonies to cure the sick. In the ensuing case, *Church of the Lukumi Babalu Aye v. City of Hialeah*, opponents of the ban argued that the law was specifically aimed at animal slaughter for religious purposes. Noting no city interference with the sale of lobsters to be boiled alive or of live rats to be fed to pet snakes, they challenged the city had not made it a crime to kill animals but rather a crime to kill animals in a religious ceremony.

In Oregon a similar situation existed when a group lobbied for an exception to the general drug laws to make it legal for Native Americans to smoke peyote during their rituals. In this case, the Supreme Court ruled that such an exception need not be granted. Smoking peyote was illegal across the board; the Native Americans were not a special group that had been singled out.

◈ SOCIOECONOMIC DIVERSITY

Even the casual observer recognizes that social and economic class factors create diversity in the United States. Sociologists typically divide individuals within the United States into three basic classes.

The three basic socioeconomic classes, based primarily on income and education, are the lower, middle and upper classes. These basic classes may be further subdivided.

As noted in Chapter 3, the middle class is shrinking, and the gap between the rich and the poor has become wider, resulting in tension.

When considering the socioeconomic classes, do not forget the maxim that "Cow_1 is not Cow_2." Each person has unique, individual characteristics. Each socioeconomic class will also have members of all the diverse groups discussed in the previous section. Some groups, however, are more numerous in certain classes. As previously discussed, in their traditional role of crime fighter, the police interact most frequently with those from the lower socioeconomic class.

The Lower Socioeconomic Class

Poor people have more frequent contact with the criminal justice system because they are on the streets and highly visible. A poor person who drives an old car will get a repair ticket, whereas a wealthier person is more likely to drive a newer car not requiring repairs. In addition, the repair ticket issued to the poor person is likely to be a much greater hardship for that person than a similar ticket would be to someone in the middle or upper classes.

Certain races and ethnic groups are frequently equated with poverty and crime in an interaction described as the *poverty syndrome.*

The poverty syndrome *includes inadequate housing, inadequate education, inadequate jobs and a resentment of those who control the social system.*

One of the hazards associated with inadequate or substandard housing is the increased possibility of lead exposure, a serious threat to children's well-being. The Centers for Disease Control (CDC) (2000) report: "Lead poisoning is entirely preventable. However, nearly 1 million children living in the United States have lead levels in their blood that are high enough to cause irreversible damage to their health." The CDC also warns:

> Lead poisoning affects virtually every system in the body, and often occurs with no distinctive symptoms. Lead can damage a child's central nervous system, kidneys, and reproductive system and, at higher levels, can cause coma, convulsions, and death. Even low levels of lead are harmful and are associated with decreased intelligence, impaired neurobehavioral development, decreased stature and growth, and impaired hearing acuity.

According to the Natural Resources Defense Council (1997): "Young children of urban minority families are at greatest risk of lead poisoning." It is known that even low blood lead levels can impair cognitive and physical development. As exposure increases, the severity of symptoms increases as well. Consequently, lead exposure may be one of the most important, and least recognized, causes of school failure and learning disorders.

Often members of the lower socioeconomic class live in ghettos and must contend with another syndrome—the **ghetto syndrome**—a vicious circle of failure: poverty, poor education, joblessness, low motivation to work, welfare and poverty. Forty years ago ghettos were more commonly referred to as *slums.* At that time internationally known scholar, scientist, educator, author and former president of Harvard University, James B. Conant, wrote *Slums & Suburbs.* In this classic study of American education in the late fifties and early sixties, Conant (1961, p. 18) expressed a belief that mixing Negro (the socially accepted term in the 1950s and 1960s) children into purely white schools was not the solution to the problem of the inferior quality of the schools in the Negro slums: "I believe the evidence indicates that it is the socioeconomic situation, not the color of the children, which makes the Negro slum schools so difficult; the real issue is not racial integration but socioeconomic integration."

Conant (p. 3) noted that suburban schools spent $1,000 a year per student; the slum schools less than half that amount. Suburban schools were modern, spacious facilities with 70 staff per 1,000 pupils; slum schools were unattractive, dilapidated schools staffed by 40 or fewer professionals per 1,000 pupils. Conant (p. 2) cautioned: "I am convinced we are allowing social dynamite to accumulate in our large cities." He (p. 18) also sent a warning:

> What I should like to do is to create in the reader's mind a feeling of anxiety and concern. For without being an alarmist, I must say that when one considers the total situation that has been developing in the Negro city slums since World War II, one has reason to worry about the future. The building up of a mass of unemployed and frustrated Negro youth in congested areas of a city is a social phenomenon that may be compared to the piling up of inflammable material in an empty building in a city block. Potentialities for trouble—indeed possibilities of disaster—are surely there.

Not long after Conant wrote these words, riots occurred in the same slums. Much of the rioting erupted out of a sense of frustration at being denied the American Dream. Blacks trapped in the ghettos saw no way of getting out. Whites who attended schools in the suburbs seemed to have a fast track to college and a share of the Dream. In many areas, the situation has not changed much.

A major problem for many in the lower socioeconomic class is homelessness.

The Homeless

Police need to balance the needs of the homeless with protecting the public from interference with its rights. Because in many cases homelessness is a temporary condition, and people who are homeless one month may not be the following month, it is difficult to accurately measure the number of homeless on any given day. A recent estimate has found more than 700,000 people without a home on any given night, or about 2 million each year (National Law Center. . . , 1999).

Whatever the number, the police must interact with the population of homeless people sleeping on our nation's streets, including women and children, alcoholics and drug addicts, the retarded and the mentally ill. Carrying their worldly goods and camping everywhere from laundry rooms to train and bus stations, the homeless pose a challenge for the police who must look after their safety while attempting to minimize their public presence.

Data from the National Coalition on Homelessness (1999) indicates the homeless population includes veterans (approximately 40 percent of homeless men are veterans); mentally ill people (20–25 percent of the single adult homeless population suffers from some form of severe and persistent mental illness); physically disabled or chronically ill people who cannot work and have no means of support; elderly people who are on inadequate fixed incomes; men, women and families who have lost their source of income (families with children constitute about 40 percent of people who become homeless, and 20 percent of homeless people do have jobs but still can't escape homelessness); single parents, usually women without resources or skills, many of whom leave home because of domestic violence (as many as 50 percent of homeless women and children are fleeing abuse); runaway children, also commonly victims of abuse; immigrants, both legal and illegal; and traditional transients—those who prefer to live on the streets—sometimes called the "hard core homeless."

Many homeless are also alcoholics and drug abusers. National data reveal 38 percent of the homeless abuse alcohol and 26 percent abuse drugs (Klein, 2000, p. 42).

AP/Wide World Photos, Inc.

A homeless man, who would give his name only as John, walks his belongings through the flooded China Basin area of San Francisco. Homeless advocates say the city will push the homeless out of China Basin when they start construction on the new ballpark.

The needs of the homeless are as varied as the people who comprise the homeless population. Besides needing the obvious—a place to live and an income to support themselves—other needs include better nutrition, medical care, clothing, help in kicking an addiction and, especially for children, an education.

For some children, the mental and physical stress of being homeless spawns a host of other difficulties. According to the National Alliance for the Mentally Ill (NAMI), nearly 25 percent of homeless people in the United States are children, few of whom escape emotional, behavioral and academic problems. Furthermore, few receive help for such problems. In one study, more than a third (37 percent) of the homeless children had depression scores high enough to warrant a psychiatric evaluation, and 28 percent were in the borderline range for serious behavioral problems.

The homeless also face safety issues and are more often the victims of crime than the perpetrators. They may be robbed and assaulted and have no phone from which to call 911. According to Klein (p. 42), common problems of homeless people include:

- Lack of food—20 percent eat one meal a day or less, and 40 percent had gone one or more days in the previous month without anything to eat because they couldn't afford food.

- Health problems—26 percent have acute infectious conditions such as pneumonia or tuberculosis; 46 percent have chronic health conditions such as arthritis, diabetes or cancer; and 55 percent have no medical insurance.

- Victimization—38 percent have had money or possessions stolen directly from them, and 41 percent have had money or possessions stolen when they were not present.

Although being homeless in and of itself is not a crime, the activities of some homeless people do violate laws and local ordinances. Such activities include public drunkenness, public urination and defecation, loitering, trespassing, panhandling, littering, disorderly conduct, or more serious offenses such as vandalism, theft and assault. For example, Gazlay (1999, p. 34) explains, officers in the Fort Collins (Colorado) Police Department's District One Transient Team learned that some of the seemingly harmless drunks were actually hardcore criminals. Three transients were linked to a number of crimes in the area, including a wave of bike thefts in which the stolen goods were pawned or sold for cash and the proceeds used to purchase cocaine and alcohol.

Sampson and Scott (2000, p. 113) note even when the homeless obey the law, citizens feel that street-living and panhandling degrade a community's image. The average citizen is uncomfortable around and may feel threatened by those who are homeless. Whether motivated by guilt or fear, they want the homeless people "removed," and they look to the police for solutions to a problem that society has thus far been unable to resolve. In New York City, for example, the mayor called on the police to help clean up the city and sweep out the homeless, a practice not uncommon across the county. As Fabyankovic (2000, p. 113) states: "According to *Out of Sight—Out of Mind?* a report published by the National Law Center on Homelessness and Poverty, police in half of the 50 largest U.S. cities have engaged in sweeps in the past two years."

In those communities where sleeping on the streets is illegal, what begins as a social problem becomes a criminal justice problem, and the officer on the beat is expected to enforce the law. However, in some areas of the country the constitutionality of such notices is being contested in court. For example, in *Pottinger v. City of Miami* (1992), a U.S. District Court judge found the city's practice of conducting bum sweeps, making minor arrests of transients, and confiscating and destroying the property of the homeless was a violation of their constitutional rights. The central question in this case was whether the government can lock you up for being outside when you have no place to go.

Many have criticized laws that, in effect, criminalize homelessness, stating such legislation ignores the underlying reasons that people live on the streets and can even cause the problem to "spread." Fabyankovic (p. 115) contends: "Politicians are often more concerned with the so-called 'quality of life' issues than solving the homeless dilemmas. Ordinances that prohibit panhandling and sleeping in public places usually force many homeless people to become transient, moving from one jurisdiction to another rather than tackling a solution to the problem."

To address the challenges presented by homelessness, the police need to partner with many organizations, from detoxification facilities to children's shelters, from hospital crisis units to county social services. Police also need to move beyond the arrest-and-detain mentality and take on the role of educator and facilitator, making the homeless aware of available services and encouraging them to seek appropriate assistance. Fabyankovic (p. 113) notes: "As the national trend seems to hint toward criminalizing those who have no home, several cities have found productive approaches to deal with these concerns." An example of such an innovative effort is seen in Oregon (p. 113):

> Until recently, many Oregon police officers regularly swept encampments of homeless people after giving occupants a 24-hour notice. Now, through a collaboration with JOIN: A Center for Involvement and the Oregon Department of Transportation, two Portland officers and two JOIN outreach workers identify low profile encampment areas. The police allow the homeless to remain in these encampments while the outreach workers find them shelters, housing and services as a smooth transition.
>
> This project has improved relations between the city's police and its homeless residents, who now view the officers as helpful friends who are not harassing them. The plan is so successful that it is guaranteed funding in future years.

As with other diversity issues, sensitivity training for officers can be a valuable step toward improving relations with a community's homeless population. Taking a lesson from the Miami case, the Fort Lauderdale (Florida) Police Department has implemented a two-hour training session known as "Homelessness 101," in which every staff member explores the causes of homelessness and strategic responses to the problem. The assistant chief states: "We have a policy, we have a special report for homeless contacts, we have the training, and we encourage our officers, particularly in the downtown and along the River Walk, to make proactive contact with the homeless to assure ourselves that they're aware of the available social services" ("Ft. Lauderdale Learns . . . ," 2000, p. 1).

He (p. 14) also believes that educating officers about the causes of homelessness has effected a cultural change in the department and eliminated the narrow-minded notion that all homeless people are lazy bums who don't want to work and just cause problems for everyone else: "I learned myself about the issue of homelessness and learned how enforcement alone is not effective if you're going to have a long-term change with homeless people." Hibbert (2000, p. 47) adds that the Fort Lauderdale Homeless Outreach Program has taught officers to view the homeless as people who are in trouble instead of people who are trouble.

In Clearwater, Florida, an effort to deal with homelessness and quality-of-life issues led to a unique homeless shelter that includes a police substation. Getz (1999, p. 94) describes:

> It is not just a shelter. Virtually every area organization and agency working with the homeless has a presence at the shelter, dealing with everything from mental problems to substance abuse to job placement. Known as CHIP (Clearwater Homeless Intervention Project), it is an alliance of government, private and non-profit organizations with a shared vision of serving the homeless with compassion and dignity.
>
> It isn't all one-sided either. The homeless are expected to take responsibility for their actions and help themselves get back on their feet.

The Clearwater police chief advocates a balance between community policing—"the social work, the soft side of this business"—and traditional law enforcement, stating: "You must never lose sight of the law and order component" (Getz, p. 94). He also cautions others not to become overwhelmed or discouraged by the magnitude of the problem (p. 98): "Our goal is to reduce homelessness person by person. We've found that law enforcement can be a force for positive change when it comes to social issues. We give the homeless all the support we can. We don't pity them, we give them due rights and we attempt to instill a sense of responsibility."

Unfortunately, many departments do not provide the means, training or tools necessary for officers to successfully reach out to the community's homeless. In a recent survey of police, 30 percent of the respondents stated they had "no policies specifically relating to incidents involving street people and are not informed of available shelters and services. Some 96 percent mentioned they wanted a formal program or unit to address these unique needs" (Fabyankovic, p. 113).

However, in jurisdictions where police are educated and empowered to address the issue of homelessness, their intervention can benefit both the homeless and the neighborhood. This was the case in a community where a group of homeless men were hanging around a business district, worrying the local merchants. When the business owners complained to the police, the officer on that particular beat talked to those involved, and they worked out a solution. The homeless men swept the sidewalk and kept the area litter free in return for food and a place to sleep.

A New York City police officer, Fran Kimkowski, developed another innovative approach to the homeless problem for a particular group of homeless men in the Long Island City section of Queens, New York. Assigned to calm the fears of residents when the Salvation Army opened a shelter for homeless veterans in the neighborhood, Kimkowski wanted to show the residents that the homeless men could and would contribute to the community if given a chance. She organized V-Cops, a group of homeless veterans who volunteer to help prevent crime in the neighborhoods.

V-Cops use foot patrols to deter, detect and report crimes to the police. They patrol local banks, particularly when people cash social security and welfare checks. The V-Cops program has many other components, including crime prevention presentations to organizations, talks to high-school students and patrol of subways and "play streets" for neighborhood youths during the summer months. Furthermore, chemically dependent V-Cop members are required to participate in recovery programs for drug abuse or alcoholism. Consequently, beyond the obvious benefits to the community, the participating homeless veterans have an opportunity to make a contribution while regaining their self-esteem and getting their lives back on track.

The Privileged and Celebrities

At the opposite end of the socioeconomic scale are the privileged and celebrities. In the traditional role of crime fighter, the police seldom interact with the upper class, but when they must, problems can arise. Regarding community policing, however, the personal and financial resources of those in the upper socioeconomic level can be invaluable.

Imagine a community where most residents are better educated than the police, or where they earn six times more than police officers. In that community it may take a special effort to develop and maintain respect and confidence in the police department's credibility and expertise. It would also be important for the agency to minimize the cynical or negative attitudes officers may develop toward the privileged class. Officers may become bitter if powerful people misuse their political connections to obtain special privileges from the police or to circumvent the law.

An officer from Los Alamos, New Mexico, a highly educated population, commented that the police constantly deal with problems resulting from the differences between the officers and the educated community. Officers refer to citizens as "coneheads" in discussions among themselves, not helping matters. Likewise, citizens use the term "town clowns" to describe the police, a term that has remained with Los Alamos citizens for at least the past 40 years, despite the Los Alamos Police Department's having one of the best-educated departments in the state.

How can police departments address such situations? Perhaps the most effective way is for citizens to be involved in some area of the police department. Many departments have crime prevention programs, reserve officer organizations, citizen police academies and crime reward funds, all of which need citizen volunteers.

Some departments have educational incentive plans to pay the tuition of officers who go to college and give a salary increase to those who graduate. Educational achievement can be considered in the promotional process; officers with the most education should benefit. Officers should also receive regular inservice training to help maintain and update professional skills. Well-trained officers will have confidence in their own abilities, and that inspires confidence and respect in others.

Interacting with celebrities and other well-known citizens such as national politicians, especially if the interaction is a negative contact, can be very difficult for the police. Often media "hounds" will use a minor incident for publicity. On the other hand, they may try to exert undue influence on an officer by mentioning rich and powerful "close friends" who allegedly have the power to ruin the officer's career. In fact, the opposite is true. The powerful are more dependent on society and have more to lose. For example, a politician who is arrested for DWI may lose the next election, but a police officer can still take the next civil service test for promotion.

Problems occur when officers let themselves be intimidated and don't handle a case appropriately. Police need to recognize their own power and the limitations of the so-called powerful. Officers also need assurance from their department that they can do their job professionally and not be subject to reprimand because they take appropriate action against someone with powerful connections.

A population's socioeconomic profile can reveal much about the balance of power within a community. A community's power structure may also be regarded in the context of its members' world-view.

◈ THE MAJORITY VS. THE MINORITY WORLD-VIEW

Whenever cultural pluralism exists in a society, a majority and minorities will also exist. Which group one belongs to will greatly influence how one views the world.

The Majority World-View

The Minnesota Peace Officer Standards and Training (P.O.S.T.) Board has identified the several elements of the majority world-view. The majority view is that its philosophy and ideas are the most legitimate and valid. Minority viewpoints, while their expression may be tolerated, lack the force and power of the majority and, therefore, are less valid than and secondary to the majority viewpoint. The minority members have the option of leaving the society if they cannot abide by majority rule. Alternative viewpoints are often considered disruptive or disloyal. Finally, power, status and wealth are the result of hard work and/or genetics.

Traditionally the majority culture in the United States has been defined and controlled by a white, male, European world-view.

Given current population trends, however, the majority culture is rapidly changing, as noted earlier. Any group that does not fall within the majority world-view can be considered a minority.

The Minority World-View

The P.O.S.T. Board has identified the following elements as common to the minority world-view. Minorities must perform better to be accepted as average. Majority groups have the power and control major institutions. Minority groups lack power to control their own destiny. The minority views fairness as being more valid than power, status and wealth. The minority views success as being achievable by working through the rules set by the majority. Finally, the minority views the criminal justice system as biased against minorities.

Sometimes cultural conflicts between minority groups or between the majority and minority groups become so intense that they lead to bias crimes.

◈ BIAS OR HATE CRIMES

Many people feel threatened by simply coming in contact with those who are culturally different. No other nation is as culturally diverse as the United States, thrusting people of different customs, languages, lifestyles and beliefs together and hoping they can coexist peacefully in the same great melting pot. Unfortunately, this doesn't always happen, and severe tension can result between cultural groups when their members are poorly informed and suspicious of cultures and lifestyles outside their own. What people do not understand they tend to fear, and what they fear, they tend to hate.

The International Association of Chiefs of Police (IACP), in its publication *Responding to Hate Crimes: A Police Officer's Guide to Investigation and Prevention* (1999), answers the question, "What is a hate crime?"

A hate or bias crime *is a criminal offense committed against person, property or society that is motivated, in whole or in part, by an offender's bias against an individual's or group's race, religion, ethnic/national origin, gender, age, disability or sexual orientation.*

Levin (1999, p. 8) adds a more general definition recognizing the potential for victims to be targeted by mistake: "Generically, hate crime refers to those criminal acts committed because of someone's actual or perceived membership in a particular group."

Bias crimes include any act, or attempted act, to cause physical injury, emotional suffering or property damage through intimidation, harassment, racial or ethnic slurs and bigoted epithets, vandalism, force or the threat of force. The majority of hate crimes are against the person, including assault (the most common), harassment, menacing/reckless endangerment and robbery. Crimes against property include vandalism/criminal mischief (most common), arson/cross burning and burglary. According to Lieberman (2000, p. 3):

> In 1998, 7,775 bias-motivated criminal incidents were reported, a slight decline from the 8,049 crimes reported in 1997 (10,730 agencies participated in the [Hate Crime Statistics Act] reporting program in 1998, slightly lower than the 11,211 participating in 1997).
>
> Of the 7,775 total incidents, 4,321 (54 percent) were motivated by racial bias; 1,390 (18 percent) by religious bias; 1,260 (16 percent) by sexual-orientation bias; and 754 (10 percent) by ethnicity/national origin bias. Of the incidents motivated by religious bias, a little more than 77 percent were directed against Jews and Jewish institutions.

As noted by the U.S. Department of Justice's Community Relations Service, hate crimes are occurring with increasing frequency and more visibility and hostility in institutions of higher learning than in any other area ("College Campuses. . .," 2000, p. 11).

As discussed, cultural tension commonly occurs in this country due to an intolerance of racial and ethnic diversity. Although many would like to believe the intense racial hatred and slaughter of minorities is a relatively distant part of our nation's history and that we've come a long way from the "lynching era" of the late 1800s and early 1900s, recent accounts indicate otherwise (Petrosino, 1999, p. 22):

> On June 7, 1998, James Byrd, Jr., a Black man, was hitchhiking home following a relative's bridal shower when a truck pulled up. However, instead of receiving a lift home, Byrd was kidnapped, taken to a wooden area, beaten to unconsciousness, chained to the back of the truck, and then dragged for several miles. His head and right arm were torn from his body during the drag-

ging and were later found in a ditch along the road. His assailants were three White men with links to racist groups.

Homosexuals can also become targets of hate crime in what is sometimes called *gay-bashing*. Paynter (2000a, p. 52) describes one such incident:

> In October 1998, Aaron McKinney beat college student Matthew Shepard to death with a .357 Magnum pistol. But he didn't stop there. He and . . . Russell Henderson then tied Shepard to a rustic fence on the edge of town and left him there. Shepard's body wasn't found until 18 hours later by a bicyclist who nearly mistook it for a scarecrow.
>
> The reason behind this brutal murder—Shepard was gay and supposedly showed an interest in McKinney.

Neubauer (1999, p. 6) states: "The impact of hate crime on a community can be devastating; it can polarize citizens to divert their energy and attention away from other important issues. Unlike burglary or larceny, hate crimes perpetuated against one individual will affect the entire community." Senator Orrin Hatch concurs, adding: "As much as we condemn all crime, hate crime can be more sinister than non-hate crime. A crime committed not just to harm an individual, but out of the motive of sending the message of hatred to an entire community, is appropriately punished more harshly" ("Senate Moving to . . . ," 1999, p. 2).

Using a sample of students from a racially and ethnically diverse university in California, Vogel (2000, p. 1) found that hate motives are considered among the most serious motivations for crime among all respondents.

Several states have passed mandatory reporting laws that require police departments to keep statistics on the occurrence of bias and hate crimes. In 1990 the Federal Hate Crime Statistics Act was passed, mandating the justice department to secure data on crimes related to religion, race, sexual orientation or ethnicity. While the laws vary considerably, the most common elements include (1) enhanced penalties for common-law crimes against persons or property motivated by bias based on race, ethnicity, religion, gender or sexual orientation; (2) criminal penalties for vandalism of religious institutions; and (3) collection of data on bias crimes. Currently, 40 of the 50 states, the District of Columbia and the federal government have passed penalty-enhancement hate-crime laws (Anti-Defamation League, 1999).

Paynter (2000a, p. 53) asserts: "Law enforcement must be prepared to deal with hate incidents and hate crimes. Incidents can be simplified to anything that's hateful in nature, and crimes are defined as those incidents that are prosecutable under the law." The law, however, can also be a complicating factor in handling hate incidents, as Israel (1999, p. 97) explains: "A cornerstone of democracy is the First Amendment's protection of free speech. . . . Ironically, contemporary free speech protects groups such as Nazis, White and Black supremacists, pornographers, gangster rappers, TV violence, and gratuitous film profiteers; in short, these are agents of disorder, and have practically nothing of discourse value."

The First Amendment also protects people's right to peaceably assemble. However, police must not simply turn a blind eye to activities such as the distribution of hate literature or the holding of hate assemblies, no matter how "peaceful," within their community, because such hate incidents may be precursors to hate crimes. The IACP has defined a hate-crime continuum showing what can happen if a community ignores "minor" incidents, allowing them to grow into a major and potentially deadly situation: Hate literature can lead to hate tattoos, hate symbols and hate gatherings, which can lead to disturbing the peace, threats and vandalism, which may escalate into assault and other violations of civil rights, arson and even murder (Paynter, 2000a, pp. 52–53). In fact, an appropriate analogy is given in the likening of racism to carbon monoxide—it may be silent, you may not see or hear it, but uncontrolled, it can kill.

For this reason, officers *must* get out and talk with citizens to find out what's going on in their communities. Officers must address all hate-based events, whether major or minor. An IACP staffer (Paynter, 2000a, p. 53) contends: "If it's the police department's job to work closely with the community and make sure citizens feel safe, then it doesn't matter if it's a crime or an incident. Because if people are afraid, they're afraid, and you'd better tell them there's a way for them not to be afraid anymore." And as one police chief asserts (Paynter, 2000a, p. 58): "Hate crimes can be tackled through a combination of presence, partnership, prevention and outreach to the community. That's true community policing."

However, Nolan and Akiyama (1999, p. 114) caution officers and departments on going overboard in their outreach efforts and campaigns to call attention to the problem of hate crimes:

> Law enforcement officers have reported informally several reasons why they misidentify or choose not to identify hate crimes. Some police officers, for example, have attributed their lack of participation to burdensome, albeit well-intentioned, departmental policies which sensationalize hate crimes. The officers explain that when relatively minor crimes like simple assault or intimidation get labeled as hate crimes, the incidents can become so high-profile that they would have preferred not to have made such a distinction.

Nonetheless, police officers should recognize when crimes might be the result of bigotry and seek the causes for a particular incident. The IACP has compiled a list of key hate-crime indicators to help officers determine whether an incident was motivated by bias and therefore a hate crime (Paynter, 2000a, p. 56). Officers should consider the perceptions of the victim(s) and witnesses about the crime; the perpetrator's comments, gestures or written statements that reflect bias, including graffiti and other symbols; any differences between the perpetrator and the victim, whether actual or perceived by the perpetrator; and any similar incidents in the same location or neighborhood that show a pattern may exist.

They should also consider whether the victim was engaged in activities promoting his/her group or community; whether the incident coincided with a holiday or date of particular significance to the victim's group; any involvement by organized hate groups or their members; and the absence of any other motive such as economic gain.

It is recommended that officers dealing with victims of hate crimes acknowledge the prejudicial nature of the attack but not by telling the victim that it was indeed a hate crime (Paynter, 2000a, p. 56): "Simply empathize with him/her that dealing with an attack is a very difficult and painful thing. You do not want to suggest to the victim, 'Do you think this is a hate crime?' You want the victim to provide you with the kinds of information that will help an investigator make that determination."

Officers should supply victims with a contact person within the department so victims can stay informed on the status of the case. Officers should also be forthright with victims and communicate to them why certain actions are (or are not) being taken regarding their case (Paynter, 2000a, p. 58):

> Secondary victimization occurs if there's no communication between victims and the instruments of government. If I'm a victim and it's explained to me that we fully understand what happened, that we're working on it, that we're going to do community outreach, etc., but we're not going to prosecute it as a hate crime because we think we can more effectively prosecute it under a different statute, it goes a long way toward gaining a victim's trust.

Law enforcement can also forge partnerships with local businesses and institutions to better understand and tackle the issue of hate crimes (Paynter, 2000a, p. 61):

> In Provincetown, Massachusetts, the police department works with area hospitals to ensure that medical professionals identify potential hate crime victims seeking treatment. In its assessment of the community, the organizations involved found that homosexual victims often were reluctant to admit they'd been victimized, even in a hospital setting. The groups coalesced around what the community was dealing with in terms of assaults and gay-bashing incidents.

The National Crime Prevention Council lists various strategies for preventing the occurrence of bias crimes in a community, such as diversity and tolerance education in schools, ongoing police-cultural organization service partnerships, rapid response to reported incidents, media campaigns about community standards for tolerance, counseling for offenders involved in hate groups and community-based dispute mediation services.

Paynter (2000a, p. 61) notes that in tackling hate crimes, community policing is a vehicle to ensure victim support, community unity concerning these problems and the full prosecution of such crimes. He further asserts: "When law enforcement takes a leadership role, it plays a major part in getting citizens to stand up against hate incidents and hate crimes in their community." Creating a strong and unified voice condemning the proliferation of hate is what's needed to stamp out bias and keep it from jeopardizing public safety. One diversity trainer summarizes (Paynter, 2000a, p. 61): "If you're out there and you let these things happen, you might as well stop [policing]. If it escalates to the point where someone dies, people will say he did this, she did that, but WE did this because we did not say this behavior will not be tolerated."

FACING THE CHALLENGE

Keeping the peace, serving and protecting in a society as diverse as the United States presents an extreme challenge to police officers. To meet the challenge, police might consider the following guidelines:

- Each person is, first and foremost, an individual.
- Each group, whether racial, ethnic, religious or socioeconomic, consists of people who share certain values. Knowing what these values are can contribute greatly to effective police-community interactions.
- Each group can contribute to making the community safer.
- Communication skills are vital. Empathy, listening and overcoming language barriers are crucial to implementing the community policing philosophy.
- An awareness of personal prejudices and biases can guard against discrimination.
- An awareness of the language used to talk about different groups is extremely important.

The term *minorities*, for example, has subtle secondary, if not, caste status that implies the opposite of *majority*, frequently polite code for "white." *People of color* also places distance between those so designated and Caucasians. Officers should consider the terms they use and how they might be perceived by those who are being labeled. Of course, in an emergency when officers need to communicate with each other rapidly, a descriptive term such as *black* or *white* is appropriate and, indeed, necessary to rapid response. It is important for officers to know when to use certain terminology.

Police need multicultural training as one element of multicultural policing, which is only one element—though crucial—of community policing.

A Cultural Diversity Value Statement

The Aurora (Illinois) Police Department's cultural diversity value statement is a model of what departments might strive for (reprinted by permission):

As professional police officers, we commit to:

- The fair and impartial treatment of all individuals, placing the highest emphasis on respect for fundamental human rights.
- Nurturing and protecting the individual dignity and worth of all persons with whom we come into contact.
- Understanding the differences of all people.
- Zero tolerance for racially, sexual, gender or religious biased behavior.
- Maintaining a welcoming environment of inclusion through which communication is open to all people whose problems become our priorities to resolve.

SUMMARY

Ethnocentrism is the preference for one's own way of life over all others. Assimilation theorists suggest that our society takes in or assimilates various cultures in what is commonly referred to as a "melting pot." Cultural pluralism suggests many melting pots. Some groups are comfortable in one pot; other groups are comfortable in another. The

PROBLEM SOLVING IN ACTION

Homeless Alcoholics

The University of Wisconsin—Madison (UW—Madison) is one of the largest universities in the nation, with a total population of more than 60,000 students and staff. The area known as the "lower campus area" serves as the gateway to the university and sits at the edge of an energetic, pedestrian-dominated, downtown Madison business district.

During the 1960s and early 1970s, this area attracted many veterans seeking a forum in which to voice their opinions. While many vets were chemically dependent and homeless, the student population was very accepting of their behavior and lifestyle. Several factors continued to support a homeless lifestyle around the campus, but eventually some of the individuals became public nuisances and began to disrupt the university community. Police officers had to use caution in dealing with these people. Although some residents and business owners wanted and expected police intervention, others felt the homeless should be left alone, viewing any type of police action as harassment and a threat to the homeless people's welfare and safety.

This concern for safety and welfare was reinforced by the death of Theresa McGovern, an alcoholic who was occasionally homeless. She was the daughter of former U.S. Senator George McGovern, and she died on the streets of Madison during the winter of 1994–1995 after passing out in a snowbank and freezing to death.

In June 1995 the University Chancellor convened the Lower Campus Concerns Committee—consisting of representatives from the faculty, concerned students, the Dean of Students' office, city of Madison and University Police Departments, Dane County Board and local social service agencies—to study and develop recommendations to address safety issues in the lower campus area, including how to deal with the growing homeless population. One of the committee's first recommendations was for the university to establish its first community policing position, to be located in the lower campus area. I (officer Darden) filled that position in June 1996.

Scanning. People who are homeless and who suffer from alcoholism were responsible for several problems in the area, including sleeping inside and outside buildings, which blocked entry and exit; defecating and urinating in public places, often in public view; public consumption of alcohol; panhandling, which was sometimes aggressive; disruptive and disorderly conduct; thefts; drug usage; and littering. These people also caused problems for themselves through exposure to inclement weather, exposure to diseases, incapacitation due to alcohol abuse, improper nutrition and victimization due to a reduced ability to care for themselves.

Analysis. I discovered 11 people were responsible for 70–75 percent of the calls for service in the lower campus area. Of these 11,

cultural conflict theory suggests that diverse cultures that share the same territory will compete with and attempt to exploit one another.

The United States is both racially and ethnically diverse. The language barrier is a major problem in police interactions with some ethnic/racial groups. Strategies to help improve communication with non-English-speaking individuals include (1) learning the language or at least common words and phrases, (2) using a language guide, (3) having a two were from the Madison area and nine had moved to Madison.

Calls would start early in the morning, as employees and students encountered panhandlers or intoxicated people sleeping on the streets. The calls would taper off until midafternoon and then start again as panhandlers, intoxicated once more from the morning's profits, would become disruptive and disorderly. The busiest time for calls was the evening, when people would be found passed out either in or around campus buildings.

Members of the lower campus population were also contributing to the problem by giving money to the panhandlers, which they used to purchase more alcohol.

Response. My goal was to reduce the number of calls for police service required for these 11 people and to try to find a permanent solution for the problem. I also hoped to involve the community in the solution. The university funded an outreach worker to assist me.

I varied my schedule and made frequent contacts with the people involved, determining who needed which services and then sharing that information with an outreach worker and other agencies. I used enforcement whenever a person in the group violated the law, and I also requested court-ordered treatment for illness or disease when appropriate. I worked with the district attorney's office to get restrictions on any of the homeless who refused treatment and violated the law.

I urged community members not to give to panhandlers, and I used small-group meetings to educate citizens on alternative ways to help the homeless. I advised community members to report any illegal activity they witnessed and started a lower campus area crimewatch program to keep citizens involved in sharing responsibility for their safety and security.

Assessment. There was a significant decrease in calls for service in the area from November 1996 to June 1997 and only 12 calls for service involving the 11 people during that eight-month period.

Of the 11 targeted individuals, as of June 1997, three had left Madison, one had died of alcohol-related illness, two were in alcohol treatment facilities, one had gone to jail and was released, three found permanent housing, and one was in treatment for six months but relapsed. During the past year, another of the original 11 relapsed and died of alcohol-related illness.

From June 1997 to October 1998, calls for police service by employees and the general public in the lower campus area were down 70 percent from the same time period in 1995 and 1996. The lower campus has also experienced less theft and criminal damage and fewer burglaries.

[Adapted from Darden (1998, pp. 5–6).]

---

list of local language teachers who could serve as interpreters and (4) subscribing to the Language Line.

One challenge facing our increasingly diverse society is racism, a belief that a human population having a distinct genetically transmitted characteristic is inferior. It also refers to discrimination or prejudice based on race. The contention that racism exists among officers has led to allegations of racial profiling, a serious concern for any department engaged in such a practice and for the credibility of the police profession as a whole. Racial profiling is a form of discrimination and singles out people of racial or ethnic groups because of a belief that these groups are more likely than others to commit certain types of crimes. Race-based enforcement is illegal.

In addition to cultural diversity (including racial/ethnic diversity), the United States also has religious and socioeconomic diversity. Many religions now exist in the United States, and religious diversity continues to increase, presenting unique challenges to community policing efforts aimed at enhancing citizens' levels of trust, communication and activism. Socioeconomic diversity in the United States is seen in the distinction of three basic socioeconomic classes, based primarily on income and education: the lower, middle and upper classes. These basic classes may be further subdivided. Those in the lower class are often trapped by the poverty syndrome, which includes inadequate housing, inadequate education, inadequate jobs and a resentment of those who control the society.

Traditionally the majority culture in the United States has been defined and controlled by a white, male, European world-view. Sometimes cultural conflicts between minority groups or between the majority and minority groups become so intense that they lead to bias crimes.

A hate or bias crime is a criminal offense committed against a person, property or society that is motivated, in whole or in part, by an offender's bias against an individual's or group's race, religion, ethnic/national origin, gender, age, disability or sexual orientation.

DISCUSSION QUESTIONS

1. What is your ethnic background? What is the background of your classmates?

2. How diverse is your community?

3. Have you ever tried to communicate with someone who does not speak English? What was it like?

4. How would you define the American culture?

5. Do you believe your generation can achieve the American Dream?

6. Have there been any instances of hate crimes in your community? Your state? Does your state have mandatory reporting laws for hate crimes?

7. How do contemporary attitudes toward race differ from those of prior generations?

8. Would you favor eliminating the word *minority* when talking about diversity? If so, what term would you use instead?

9. Do you consider yourself "culturally literate"? Why or why not?

10. Have you encountered instances of ethnocentrism? Explain.

INFOTRAC COLLEGE EDITION ASSIGNMENTS

• Use InfoTrac to help in answering the discussion questions if applicable.

• Research and report on at least one of the following subjects: cultural conflict, hate crime, homelessness, racial profiling or racism.

COMMUNITY PROJECT

Visit a shopping mall or business district in the daytime and again after dark. How could CPTED be used to reduce crime or fear of crime? What suggestions would you make? Consider the following:

- Where are the public restrooms located? Are they isolated, dark or unlocked?
- Does the lighting in the parking lot provide a feeling of safety after dark?
- What crime problems do the shopkeepers experience? Are the police responsive to their needs?
- Look at the locations and conditions of public telephones and bus stops.
- Have the businesses hired security? Why? Do they feel it has helped?
- Is the area clean and well kept?
- Are there shrubs and trees? Do they block views of what is happening inside the store?
- Do stores have a back exit? Is it locked at all times?
- Where do employees park? Does it feel safe?

Visit some CPTED Web sites for other ideas to help with this evaluation.

REFERENCES

Anti-Defamation League. 1999 Hate Crime Laws, 1999. Found at www.adl.org/99hatecrime/

"Census Bureau Predicts Large-Scale Changes in U.S. Population's Makeup." (Minneapolis/ St. Paul) *Star Tribune,* March 14, 1996, p. A14.

Centers for Disease Control. "CDC's Lead Poisoning Prevention Program." October 27, 2000. http://www.cdc.gov/nceh/lead/factsheets

Cherry, Mike. "Cultural Diversity: Reaching Out to the Communities within the Community." *Community Policing Exchange,* Phase VII, #30, January/February 2000, p. 8.

Clement, Douglas. "Border Crossings: Refugees Travel Difficult Road to Health Care." *Minnesota Medicine,* March 1992, pp. 24–29.

Cohen, John D.; Lennon, Janet J.; and Wasserman, Robert. "Eliminating Racial Profiling—A 'Third Way.'" *Law Enforcement News,* Vol. XXVI, No. 530, March 31, 2000, pp. 12, 15.

"College Campuses Are Easy Targets for Acts of Hate." *NCJA Justice Bulletin,* Vol. 20, No. 6, June 2000, pp. 11–12.

Conant, James B. *Slums & Suburbs.* New York: McGraw-Hill, 1961.

Darden, Theodore. "University of Wisconsin— Madison Police Response to People Who Are Homeless and Suffer from Alcoholism." *Problem Solving Quarterly,* Fall 1998, pp. 5–6.

Fabyankovic, Janet. "Alternatives to Homeless Criminalization." *Law and Order,* Vol. 48, No. 8, August 2000, pp. 113–115.

"Ft. Lauderdale Learns a Lesson from Miami in Dealing with the Homeless." *Law Enforcement News,* Vol. XXVI, No. 530, March 31, 2000, pp. 1, 14.

Gazlay, Pete. "Community Oriented Policing Is Not Just for Specialists." *Police,* Vol. 23, No. 10, October 1999, pp. 32–36.

Getz, Ronald J. "A Positive Police Program for the Homeless." *Law and Order,* Vol. 47, No. 5, May 1999, pp. 93–98.

Gustafson, Paul. "Authorities Crack Down on Asian Gang Accused of Raping Hmong Girls." (Minneapolis/St. Paul) *Star Tribune,* June 7, 1998, pp. B1, B9.

Hard, Stefanie. " 'Amigos de la Comunidad' Makes New Friends in Corcoran." *Community Policing Exchange,* Phase VII, #30, January/February 2000, p. 6.

Hibbert, Alison D. "Homeless Outreach Program." *The Police Chief,* Vol. LXVII, No. 5, May 2000, pp. 44–47.

Holmes, Malcolm D. "Minority Threat and Police Brutality: Determinants of Civil Rights Criminal Complaints in U.S. Municipalities." *Criminology,* Vol. 38, No. 2, May 2000, pp. 343–367.

Houston, Paul. "For Whom the Bell Tolls." *Phi Delta Kappan,* October 1996, pp. 124–126.

"Increase in Black Inmates 'Staggering.'" From the *Boston Globe,* as reported in the (Minneapolis/St. Paul) *Star Tribune,* March 2, 1999, p. A3.

International Association of Chiefs of Police. *Responding to Hate Crimes: A Police Officer's Guide to Investigation and Prevention.* 1999.

Israel, Michael. "Hate Speech and the First Amendment." *Journal of Contemporary Criminal Justice,* Vol. 15, No. 1, February 1999, pp. 97–110.

Klein, Sid. "Dealing with the Homeless and Improving Quality of Life." *The Police Chief,* Vol. LXVII, No. 5, May 2000, pp. 34–43.

Kurlander, Neil. "Software to Track Traffic Stop Data." *Law Enforcement Technology,* Vol. 27, No. 7, July 2000, pp. 148–153.

Learning Objectives for Professional Peace Officer Education. St. Paul, MN: P.O.S.T. Board, July 1991.

Levin, Brian. "Hate Crimes: Worse by Definition." *Journal of Contemporary Criminal Justice,* Vol. 15, No. 1, February 1999, pp. 6–21.

Lieberman, Michael. "Responding to Hate Crimes." *Community Policing Exchange,* Phase VII, #30, January/February 2000, p. 3.

"Many State Police Agencies Requiring Racial Data Collection." *Criminal Justice Newsletter,* Vol. 30, No. 17, February 18, 2000, p. 5.

Margolis, Jeremy; Watts, Darren; and Johnston, Iain. "Proactive Defense Strategies Can Minimize Risk." *The Police Chief,* Vol. LXVII, No. 7, July 2000, pp. 18–23.

Matthews, John. "Racial Profiling: A Law Enforcement Nemesis." *Police,* Vol. 23, No. 11, November 1999, pp. 38–39.

Mueck, Robert P. "Racial Epithets by Police Officers." *Law and Order,* Vol. 48, No. 5, May 2000, pp. 28–32.

National Alliance for the Mentally Ill. © 1996–2000. www.nami.org

National Coalition on Homelessness. Various fact sheets, April 1999. nch@ari.net

National Law Center on Homelessness and Poverty. *Out of Sight—Out of Mind? A Report on Anti-Homeless Laws, Litigation and Alternatives in 50 United States Cities.* Washington, DC, 1999.

Natural Resources Defense Council. *Our Children at Risk: The 5 Worst Environmental Threats to Their Health.* November 1997. http://www.nrdc.org/health/kids

Neubauer, Ronald S. "Hate Crime in America— Summit No.5." *The Police Chief,* Vol. LXVI, No. 2, February 1999, p. 6.

Nolan, James J. and Akiyama, Yoshio. "An Analysis of Factors that Affect Law Enforcement Participation in Hate Crime Reporting." *Journal of Contemporary Criminal Justice,* Vol. 15, No. 1, February 1999, pp. 111–127.

Olson, Robert K. "From the President." *Subject to Debate,* Vol. 14, No. 9, September 2000, p. 2.

Paynter, Ronnie L. "Healing the Hate." *Law Enforcement Technology,* Vol. 27, No. 4, April 2000a, pp. 52–61.

Paynter, Ronnie L. "Protecting All the People." *Law Enforcement Technology,* Vol. 27, No. 4, April 2000b, pp. 62–66.

Petrosino, Carolyn. "Connecting the Past to the Future: Hate Crime in America." *Journal of Contemporary Criminal Justice,* Vol. 15, No. 1, February 1999, pp. 22–47.

"Policies Help Gain Public Trust: Guidance from the IACP Highway Safety Committee." *The Police Chief,* Vol. LXVII, No. 77, July 2000, pp. 24–29.

"Race Disparity Seen throughout Juvenile Justice System." *Criminal Justice Newsletter,* Vol. 30, No. 20, April 25, 2000, pp. 6–7.

Sampson, Rana and Scott, Michael S. *Tackling Crime and Other Public-Safety Problems: Case Studies in Problem-Solving.* Washington, DC: U.S. Department of Justice, Office of Community Oriented Policing Services, 2000.

Scoville, Dean. "A View Askew: A Sideways Look at Racial Profiling." *Police,* Vol. 24, No. 8, August 2000, pp. 16–23.

"Senate Moving to Expand Law on Prosecution of Hate Crimes." *Criminal Justice Newsletter,* Vol. 30, No. 6, March 16, 1999, pp. 2–3.

Spohn, Cassia and Holleran, David. "The Imprisonment Penalty Paid by Young, Unemployed Black and Hispanic Male Offenders." *Criminology,* Vol. 38, No. 1, February 2000, pp. 281–306.

Strandberg, Keith W. "Racial Profiling." *Law Enforcement Technology,* Vol. 26, No. 6, June 1999, pp. 62–66.

"Strengthening Relations between Police and Minority Communities: Ensuring Accountability for Effective Policing in Chicago's Diverse Neighborhoods." *Subject to Debate,* Vol. 14, No. 6, June 2000, pp. 1, 3–4.

Szubin, Adam; Jensen, Carl J.; and Gregg, Rod. "Interacting with 'Cults:' A Policing Model." *FBI Law Enforcement Bulletin,* Vol. 69, No. 9, September 2000, pp. 16–24.

350 Tested Strategies to Prevent Crime: A Resource for Municipal Agencies and Community Groups. Washington, DC: National Crime Prevention Council, 1995.

U.S. Bureau of the Census. "Resident Population of the United States: Estimates, by Sex, Race, and Hispanic Origin, with Median Age, 1999." www.census.gov

Vogel, Brenda L. "Perceptions of Hate: The Extent to which a Motive of 'Hate' Influences Attitudes of Violent Crimes." *Journal of Crime and Justice,* Vol. 23, No. 2, 2000, pp. 1–25.

Ward, Jennifer L. "Dallas Opens the Door to New Citizens to Flex Their Participatory Powers." *Community Policing Exchange,* Phase VII, #30, January/February 2000, p. 7.

Weisburd, David; Greenspan, Rosann; Hamilton, Edwin E.; Williams, Hubert; and Bryant, Kellie A. *Police Attitudes toward Abuse of Authority: Findings from a National Study.* Washington, DC: National Institute of Justice Research in Brief, May 2000.

Weitzer, Ronald. "Citizens' Perceptions of Police Misconduct: Race and Neighborhood Context." *Justice Quarterly,* Vol. 16, No. 4, December 1999, pp. 819–846.

Weitzer, Ronald and Tuch, Steven A. "Race, Class, and Perceptions of Discrimination by the Police." *Crime and Delinquency,* Vol. 45, No. 4, October 1999, pp. 494–507.

Wexler, Chuck. "From the Executive Director." *Subject to Debate,* Vol. 14, No. 6, June 2000, p. 2.

Zingraff, Matthew T.; Smith, William R.; and Tomaskovic-Devey, Donald. "North Carolina Highway Traffic and Patrol Study: 'Driving while Black.'" *The Criminologist,* Vol. 25, No. 3, May/June 2000, pp. 1, 3–4.

RESOURCES

American Association of Retired Persons (AARP), Criminal Justice Services, 601 E. Street, Washington, DC 20049; (800) 424-3410; www.aarp.org

American Indian Movement (AIM), 5050 43rd Ave. S., Minneapolis, MN 55417; (612) 721-3914.

Anti-Defamation League of B'nai-Brith, 823 United Nations Plaza, NY, NY 10017; (212) 490-2525.

Bureau of Indian Affairs (BIA), 1849 C Street NW, Washington, DC 20240; (301) 208-3711.

Centers for Disease Control and Prevention, 1600 Clifton Rd., Atlanta, GA 30333; (800) 311-3435; http://www.cdc.gov

Indian Human Development Services, 200 Independence Avenue SW, Washington, DC 20201; (301) 245-2760.

League of United Latin American Citizens (LULAC), 2000 L Street NW, Washington, DC 20036; (202) 833-6130.

Mexican American Legal Defense and Education Fund (MALDEF), San Francisco, CA 94102; (415) 543-5598.

Mexican Embassy, 1911 Pennsylvania Ave., NW, Washington, DC 20006; (202) 728-0694.

National Alliance for the Mentally Ill, Colonial Place Three, 2107 Wilson Blvd., Suite 300, Arlington, VA 22201-3042; Toll Free HelpLine 1-800-950-NAMI (6264); Front Desk (703) 524-7600; fax (703) 524-9094; TDD (703) 516-7227; www.nami.org

National Association for the Advancement of Colored People (NAACP), 1025 Vermont Ave. NW, Washington, DC 20005; (202) 638-2269.

National Association of Blacks in Criminal Justice (NABCJ), P.O. Box 66271, Washington, DC 20035; (215) 686-2961.

National Coalition for the Homeless; 1012 14th St. NW, #600, Washington, DC, 20005-3410; (202) 737-6444; FAX (202) 737-6445. e-mail: nch@ari.net

National Organization of Black Law Enforcement Executives (NOBLE), 4609 Pinecrest Office Park Drive, Suite F, Alexandria, VA 22312-1442; (703) 658-1529. e-mail: noble@noblenatl.org; website: www.noblenatl.org

National Rehabilitation Information Center, 1010 Wayne Ave., Suite 800, Silver Spring, MD 20910; (800) 346-2742. www.naric.com

National Urban League, 120 Wall Street, New York, NY 10005; (212) 558-5300. www.nul.org

State Department of Human Rights—locate in phone book.

The Police Foundation on the Internet: www.policefoundation.org

CHAPTER 8

Connecting with Persons with Disabilities and the Elderly

*Democracy is based on the conviction that there
are extraordinary possibilities in ordinary people.*
—Harry Emerson Fosdick

Do you know

What *the* most important guideline is for interacting with individuals with disabilities?

What disabilities police officers might frequently encounter?

How epilepsy can mimic intoxication or a drug high?

What the four civil criteria for detainment and commitment of mentally ill individuals are in most states?

What behaviors Alzheimer's sufferers have that may bring them into contact with the police?

How Alzheimer's disease can resemble intoxication?

How police departments can benefit from senior citizen volunteers?

Can you define these terms:

AARP	deinstitutionalization	personality disorders
ADA	disability	schizophrenia
Alzheimer's disease (AD)	epilepsy	seizure
Ameslan	graying of America	senility
catastrophic reaction	hearing impaired	TDD
crisis behavior	mental illness	TRIAD
deaf	mental retardation	

INTRODUCTION

The previous chapter described the various racial, ethnic, religious and socioeconomic subcultures found in the United States. These subcultures often overlap, making precise classifications difficult if not impossible. This chapter examines several other subcultures also existing in the United States—those with physical and mental disabilities and the elderly—populations that provide even more diversity and more challenge to community policing efforts. Consider an elderly Jewish woman from the upper class who is blind, has Alzheimer's disease and speaks only Yiddish. Or a homeless, mentally retarded Asian man who has just immigrated to the United States. Some might view such differences as too difficult for one society to handle, yet this very diversity should be considered a strength because each subculture adds richness to the mainstream culture of our country.

According to Fuller (2000, p. 84): "Many well-intentioned police officers have uncomfortable attitudes toward the disabled, often viewing them as individuals to be pitied or ignored. This attitude may originate from an uneasiness of being around people who are perceived to be 'different,' or simply from ignorance about disabilities in general."

This chapter begins with a discussion of physical and mental disabilities, facts about disability in the United States and general guidelines for dealing with those who are disabled. Next specific disabling conditions are described involving mobility; vision; and hearing; individuals with epilepsy; the mental disabilities, including mental illness and mental retardation; and suicidal individuals. This is followed by a look at crime prevention for the those with disabilities and the police response in handling individuals with disabilities who break the law.

The chapter next examines police interaction with the elderly, beginning with a discussion of the graying of America, followed by some of the attendant concerns: driving problems, Alzheimer's disease, senility, physical impairments and disabilities. Next crime prevention and community policing strategies are presented, as well as the use of older volunteers in law enforcement. The chapter concludes with a presentation of an exemplary program called TRIAD.

◉ UNDERSTANDING PHYSICAL AND MENTAL DISABILITIES

More than 50 million men, women and children in the United States have disabilities.

A police officer asks a woman to perform some field sobriety tests and she cannot do so even though she is not under the influence of any drug, including alcohol. Another person ignores the direct order of a police officer to step back on the sidewalk. Yet another person approaches an officer and attempts to ask directions, but his speech is so slurred he is unintelligible. These common occurrences for police officers can often be misinterpreted. In each of the preceding instances, the individual interacting with the officer has a disability: a problem with balance, a hearing impairment and a speech disability.

A **disability** is a physical or mental impairment that substantially limits one or more of a person's major life functions. According to a Census Brief (McNeil, 1997, p. 1):

"About 1 in 5 Americans have some kind of disability, and 1 in 10 have a severe disability. With the population aging and the likelihood of having a disability increasing with age, the growth in the number of people with disabilities can be expected to accelerate in the coming decades." The 1998 National Organization on Disability (NOD)/Harris Poll reports 54 million men, women and children in the United States have disabilities, making this population the nation's biggest "minority."

Greater recognition of this "minority" came on July 26, 1990, when then-President Bush signed into law the Americans with Disabilities Act **(ADA),** calling it "another Independence Day, one that is long overdue." Colbridge (2000b, p. 28) states: "For purposes of the ADA, disability means having a physical or mental impairment that substantially limits one or more major life activities, having a record of such an impairment, or being regarded as having such an impairment."

The ADA guarantees that persons with disabilities will have equal access to any public facilities available to persons without disabilities. Colbridge (2000a, p. 26) states the ADA also deals with broad issues concerning discrimination against those with disabilities in the areas of education, transportation, communications, recreation, institutionalization, health services and voting. The ADA does not, however, grant special liberty to individuals with disabilities in matters of law, nor does it dictate the police must take a "hands off" approach toward people with disabilities engaged in criminal conduct. As Litchford (2000, p. 15) notes: "The courts have held that the ADA does not prohibit officers from taking enforcement action, including the use of force, necessary to protect officer or public safety."

Because the ADA guarantees access to government services, it helps build partnerships for community policing. Under the ADA, all brochures and printed material must be available in braille or on audiotape if requested. To include people with disabilities in community partnerships, the police must be able to communicate with them and should conduct their meetings in barrier-free places.

Many people in our communities have made treatment of those with disabilities a priority and are available and willing to work with law enforcement agencies to ensure that people with disabilities are treated respectfully and protected from those who would victimize them. The outcome of increased awareness and service in this area will not only make police officers' jobs easier when they encounter people with disabilities, but will also help reduce their fear and vulnerability. The focus on those with disabilities will make the community a better and safer place for everyone and help to build police-community relations.

Facts about Disability in the United States

Combined data from the Bureau of the Census, the National Institutes of Health, the Centers for Disease Control, the National Center for Medical Rehabilitation Research and the Disability Statistics Center reveals the following facts about disability in the United States today:

• Disability is no respecter of age, sex or race. Even among children ages 6–14, about 1 in 8 has some type of disability.

• About 9 million people of all ages have disabilities so severe they require personal assistance to carry out everyday activities.

- More than one-third of all U.S. citizens age 65 and older have a severe disability.
- An estimated 2 million adults in the United States, particularly the elderly, have chronic impairment from dizziness or difficulty with balance.
- Nearly 1.2 million people are partially or completely paralyzed.
- Nearly 2.7 million people have speech impairments, and an estimated 6 to 8 million people in the United States have some form of language impairment.
- About 9.2 million people have developmental disabilities such as cerebral palsy or mental retardation.

General Guidelines for Dealing with Individuals with Disabilities

The most important guideline for interacting with people with disabilities is to treat them as people with the same needs and desires as any other citizen.

In addition, when interacting with most individuals with disabilities, be empathetic, do not shout, do not prejudge what they can or cannot do, and do not coddle them. They need to be challenged just like everyone else.

Disabilities police officers frequently encounter include mobility impairment, vision impairment, hearing impairment, impairment as a result of epilepsy, and mental or emotional impairment.

Now consider each of these disabilities and the recommended police response to each.

Mobility Impairments

An estimated 7.4 million Americans rely on devices to compensate for mobility impairments.

Included within this group are those who depend on wheelchairs (1.6 million people), walkers (1.8 million), canes (4.8 million) and other mobility aids. Many are accident victims. Many others have diseases such as muscular dystrophy or multiple sclerosis. Still others were born with birth defects. Never assume that a severely physically disabled person in a wheelchair is also mentally disabled.

The Police Response. When interacting with persons with disabilities, speak directly to them. Get at eye-level to converse with people in wheelchairs but don't lean on the chair. Don't shout or assume they need to be "taken care of." Most can negotiate routine obstacles, such as getting in and out of their cars, but be alert to physical conditions that might make access difficult for those with mobility impairments. If you think there is an insurmountable barrier, ask whether they would like assistance. And never presume someone wants to tell you how they became disabled. Also make certain handicapped parking spaces are provided and that nonhandicapped individuals who park in these places are either severely warned or ticketed.

Community relations programs that place mobile individuals, including business owners and police officers, in a wheelchair for a day are an excellent way to demonstrate the difficulties those with mobility impairments encounter.

Vision Impairments

More than 8 million U.S. citizens are visually impaired. Nearly 3 million are color blind; over 700,000 have cataracts; 1.1 million are legally blind; and nearly 200,000 are totally blind.

Sometimes people who are visually impaired are very noticeable because of their white canes or their service dogs. Other times, however, the disability is not readily apparent. Many people can see well enough to get around but not well enough to read signs. As a result, they may unknowingly break the law.

The Police Response. When interacting with a blind or severely visually impaired person, allow the person to feel your badge or arm patch to establish your identity and authority. This is especially important with children. Avoid the natural tendency to talk louder than usual to a visually impaired person unless, of course, they are also hearing impaired, a common combination.

Hearing Impairments

Twenty-eight million Americans are hearing impaired, two million of whom are deaf. 4.2 million use hearing aides.

The **hearing impaired,** commonly called *hard of hearing,* are those who have some residual hearing; that is, sounds may be audible but not clear. For them, words are not just softer, they are garbled. **Deaf** people have such extreme hearing loss they cannot understand spoken words. They may respond to loud noises but need visual communication clues.

Deaf people communicate differently depending on the age when they became deaf, the type of deafness and the person's language skills, intelligence, personality and education. Most deaf people cannot lip-read, and they may or may not use sign language. Be aware that sign language has its own grammar and syntax that might seem like baby talk and lead an officer to believe the person is mentally deficient. For example, "Come here home sleep."

Many deaf people prefer to communicate through sign language, the most common being **Ameslan** (American Sign Language). Consequently, interpreters may greatly assist police, just as language interpreters help them communicate with non-English-speaking people. *Interpreters* have special training and are registered. When using an interpreter to interact with a hearing impaired individual, provide good lighting. Speak clearly and directly to the deaf person, not the interpreter, and use a normal tone. Allow only one person to speak at a time, and remember the interpreter will be a few words behind the speaker.

Other people who can sign are considered *signers.* Because sensitive or confidential information may be involved, it is important to use certified signers. Their code of ethics requires that they keep all information strictly confidential and not interject personal opinions into the situation. Officers might consider taking "signing" classes so they can communicate more effectively with hearing impaired individuals.

Technology can greatly enhance interaction with those who are hearing impaired. Telecommunication devices for the deaf (**TDD**) consist of a receiver and a keyboard to transmit and receive written communication using the telephone. Civic groups such as the Lions or Rotary are often willing to purchase such equipment for a police department and the community's hearing impaired.

The Police Response. It is important to communicate respect, recognizing that deafness is not a defect but a cultural difference. The key in building trust with someone who is hard of hearing or deaf is to determine how that particular person communicates and use whatever combination of techniques works. To get the person's attention, gently tap their shoulder or wave. In deaf culture, it is common to touch people to get their attention, so they may try to touch you. Do not interpret this as hostility. Maintain eye contact, and use pantomime, body language and facial expressions. Also, know your state and local laws. In most states, when issuing the Miranda warning, you must use a certified interpreter. Finally, if you need it, ask for help.

Sometimes written communication is most effective. Write notes as you normally would, assuming the person can understand. However, using notes to communicate may not always be effective because to those who became deaf before learning to read, written English may be similar to a foreign language. Even those who can read often lose some capacity to use the written word. In fact, the average reading level is between third and fourth grade.

When interacting with the hearing impaired, consider the potential for other difficulties in their lives, such as violence, which is greater in deaf families, possibly because of the many daily frustrations. Also, recognize that handcuffing suspects with hearing impairments leaves them without a way to communicate. It is like gagging a hearing person.

Individuals with Epilepsy[1]

Two million Americans have epilepsy, although 80 percent of them show no symptoms because they use medication to control seizures.

Epilepsy is a disorder of the central nervous system. Known causes include head injuries, infectious diseases such as meningitis, encephalitis and brain abscesses. A person with epilepsy tends to have recurrent seizures. A **seizure** is a sudden, uncontrolled episode of excessive electrical activity in the brain. It may alter behavior, consciousness, movement, perception and/or sensation. Police officers need to be able to recognize seizures, administer the proper first aid and be responsive to the sensitivities and pride of people with epilepsy. Police officers' chances of encountering a seizure are probably greater than they may think.

---

[1]Adapted from *Epilepsy: A Positive ID* (1991), University of Minnesota Epilepsy Foundation, used by permission.

An epileptic seizure may be mistaken for a drug- or alcohol-induced stupor because the person may have incoherent speech, glassy-eyed staring and aimless wandering.

The Police Response. Police officers must not confuse the symptoms of an epileptic seizure with those of being high on drugs or alcohol. Table 8.1 summarizes the distinctions between an epileptic seizure and a drug reaction. Also, officers should be familiar with the medications people with epilepsy may take so they are not mistaken for illegal drugs.

If the person is conscious and having a seizure, it can last from thirty seconds to three minutes. The person may be confused or disoriented after the seizure. If possible, guide the person to a safe place to sit and let the seizure run its course. Keep the person calm and do not restrain him or her in any way. Determine the level of consciousness by asking the person's name, where he or she is and what day it is. Check for a medical-alert bracelet or tag.

If the person is unconscious and having a seizure, cushion the person's head. If he or she is wearing glasses, remove them. Loosen the collar and tie and clear the area of any hard objects the person may hit. Do not put anything in the person's mouth. After the seizure has subsided, turn the person on his or her side, allow the saliva to flow from the mouth and keep the airway open. Determine the person's level of consciousness and check for a medical-alert bracelet or tag.

Call an ambulance if the person has hit his or her head (a life-threatening situation requiring immediate action), if you suspect injury, if there is no medical-alert bracelet or tag, if the seizure lasts more than five minutes or if the seizures occur one after another.

Table 8.1   Epileptic Seizure or Drug/Alcohol Abuse

Complex Partial Seizure Symptoms	Drug/Alcohol Abuse Symptoms
• Chewing, lip-smacking motions	not likely
• Picking at clothes	not likely
• Should regain consciousness in 30 seconds to 3 minutes, except in the rare case of a complex partial status (when seizure continues)	a drunk/high person will not recover in 3 minutes or less
• No breath odor	a drunk will smell like alcohol
• Possibly wearing an epilepsy ID bracelet/tag	not likely
Symptoms Common to Both	
• Impaired consciousness	• Incoherent speech
• Glassy-eyed staring	• Aimless wandering

SOURCE: *Epilepsy: A Positive I.D.* Epilepsy Education, University of Minnesota, 1991. Reprinted by permission.

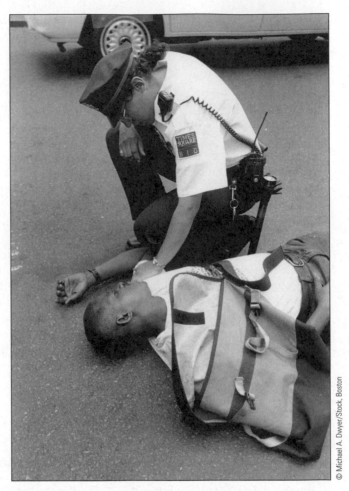

Police officers may be the first at the scene of an emergency and are trained to assist.

Mental Disabilities

More than 14 million people have mental disabilities.

Historically society institutionalized the people who were mentally ill or mentally retarded. In the mid-1960s, however, treatment in the community replaced institutionalization. **Deinstitutionalization** refers to the release of thousands of mentally ill individuals into society to be cared for by family or a special network of support services.

This was the result of several factors including development of medications to control mental illness; research showing that institutionalized people did not receive adequate treatment and could do better in the community; federal programs to build and operate mental health centers; and patients' rights litigation and state legislation.

Community-based mental health service rests on the premise that people have the right not to be isolated from the community simply because they are mentally ill. This premise works only if a support system for them exists. Unfortunately, the network of support services has developed slowly. As a result, thousands of mentally ill people are on the street, homeless, and hundreds more are living with families ill-equipped to provide necessary care and assistance. In both situations, the mentally ill persons are likely to have encounters with the local police, usually as a result of some bizarre behavior rather than committing a crime.

As Strandberg (2000, p. 90) notes: "States have closed mental health institutions across the country and pushed their patients out into the community, many times directly into the path of local law enforcement." He suggests: "Releasing the mentally ill has created a new problem for law enforcement that requires a new set of skills."

Louis (1997, p. 82) suggests: "A long-standing rift exists between law enforcement and those who provide public and private mental health treatment and resources. Issues of bed availability, jurisdiction, and accountability, cost considerations, and the whole issue surrounding behavior related to mental illness vs. criminal activity have all been a source of contention."

Mental Illness. *Five million people suffer from mental illness.* **Mental illness** is a severe disturbance that results in substantially diminished capacity to cope with the ordinary demands of life. According to the National Alliance for the Mentally Ill (NAMI): "Mental illnesses are physical brain disorders that profoundly disrupt a person's ability to think, feel, and relate to others and their environment." The Alliance also reports: "Mental illnesses are more common than cancer, diabetes, or heart disease." Furthermore: "On any given day, approximately 150,000 people with severe mental illness are homeless, living on the streets or in public shelters."

The problem is compounded by the fact that, as Strandberg (p. 94) explains: "The mental health care system can be a revolving door. . . . The medication used to treat these people makes them feel better and stabilizes them. Once they're doing better the hospital releases them. The problem is once they feel better, they stop taking their medication. Later, they have another psychotic episode where police are called to respond and the cycle begins anew."

Personality disorders are the most common form of mental illness encountered by police. Common symptoms include lack of self-control, inability to learn from experience, lack of good judgment and lack of moral or ethical values. People with personality disorders may provoke trouble, may think of themselves first, may be prodigious liars and may be adept at manipulating others.

The most chronic and disabling mental illness is **schizophrenia,** a deterioration in personality to the point where feelings, thoughts and behavior are not coherent. Common symptoms include social withdrawal; bizarre, meaningless, inappropriate behavior; prominent hallucinations; peculiar behavior such as collecting garbage or talking to oneself in public; rapid shifts in subject when speaking; confusion; and ambivalence.

Do not confuse mental illness with crisis behavior. **Crisis behavior** results when a person has a *temporary* breakdown in coping skills. Such people often fear they are going crazy and say things such as, "I must be losing my mind." Anyone can suffer from a crisis, and what may be a crisis for one person may not be for another person.

The mentally ill people police encounter frequently lack social support. They are difficult to manage and may have complications such as alcohol or drug abuse. Often people who feel threatened by the strange behavior of a mentally ill person may call the police to handle the problem. A common misconception is that schizophrenics, or anyone with a mental illness, are violent and belong behind bars, but according to NAMI:

> Individuals receiving treatment for schizophrenia are no more prone to violence than the general public. Unfortunately, almost one-third of all U.S. jails incarcerate people with severe mental illnesses who have no charges against them but are merely waiting for psychiatric evaluation or the availability of a psychiatric hospital bed. Today, roughly 159,000 people with severe mental illnesses are incarcerated in jails and prisons, mostly for crimes they committed because they were not being treated for their illness.

Officers become involved with the mentally ill because the police have the only 24-hour-a-day, seven-day-a-week, mobile emergency response capacity, as well as the authority to detain, arrest and use force when needed. When police are called to manage mentally ill persons, the behaviors they most frequently encounter are bizarre, unusual or strange conduct; confused thoughts or action; aggressive actions; destructive, assaultive or violent behavior; and attempted suicide.

One chief of police noted ("Congress Approves Grants. . . ," 2000, p. 3): "Our local police forces have become armed social workers. This is a mission that we are both ill-equipped and ill-trained to carry out. All too often, police officers confront the mentally ill equipped with little more than their verbal skills and the means to employ deadly force. The results are often disastrous."

Police in one city shot and killed a suspect who had just robbed a gas station. The suspect turned out to be a mentally disturbed female whom they had dealt with often over the past year. After robbing the gas station, she ordered the clerk to call 911 and stayed there until he did. The confrontation and subsequent shooting seemed orchestrated, forced by the woman who was depressed and suicidal. She claimed to have a gun, threatened to shoot the officers and advanced toward one with an object in her hand. The object turned out to be a comb. This tragic situation, where a suicidal person arranges to die at the hands of the police, is called suicide by cop.

Recognizing People with Mental Illness. Mentally ill persons can be difficult to identify. They can be intelligent, perceptive, articulate, employed and have strong family relationships. With the onset of a mental disorder, however, their ability to clearly think is impaired.

General symptoms of mental illness include behavior and mood inappropriate to the setting and inflexible or impulsive behavior. Specific indicators of mental illness include sudden lifestyle changes; major behavior changes; extreme anxiety, panic or fright; paranoia; delusions; hallucinations; depression; obsessions; unexplained loss of memory; confusion; and hypochondria.

Often people with mental illness take medication to counteract a chemical imbalance. These drugs, however, may cause side effects such as minor stiffness; a rigid shuffling gait; an at-rest hand jerk; acute muscle spasms; a constant, fine, fast tremor; blurry vision; rhythmic motion of the jaw or lips; tongue clucking; lip smacking; head tilting; or, in severe cases, facial distortion.

The Police Response to Mental Illness. To determine whether an individual may be mentally ill, note whether the person is using or threatening to use violence, threatening suicide or acting dangerously toward self or others. Has the person neglected personal care or bodily functions or self-inflicted physical damage? Has the person recently suffered a traumatic experience? Does the person have a history of mental illness, suffer from delusions or appear to be under the influence of alcohol or illegal drugs? If your assessment reveals that the person is likely to be mentally ill, your response should follow some suggested guidelines.

If possible, gather information about the mentally ill person before arriving on the scene. Obtain as much information as possible from witnesses, family members and friends. In the presence of a mentally ill person, avoid attracting attention. Also, remove as many distractions as possible, including bystanders and disruptive friends or family members.

Communication is essential; it lets you gain valuable information and establish rapport. Introduce yourself and explain the reason for your presence in a helping, caring tone. Be calm, avoid excitement and have a take-charge attitude. *Firm gentleness* is also effective. With a take-charge attitude and an insistence on your orders being followed, gently indicate that your only intention is to help. Do not excite, confuse or upset those who are mentally ill. Do not rush them or crowd their personal space. Do not use inflammatory language, lie to or deceive them. Do not dispute, debate or invalidate their claims or let them trick you into an argument.

Also be aware of the potential for violence and that your uniform, gun or handcuffs may frighten the person. If the subject is acting dangerously but not directly threatening himself or anyone else, give the person time to calm down. Violent outbursts are usually short. If the person is so violent that he or another person is likely to be harmed, use the least amount of force necessary to restrain the person. If restraint is needed, two or more officers should be present. Such a show of force could dissuade the person from resisting. If not, however, increased adrenaline and insensitivity to pain enable mentally ill people to resist a "normal" amount of restraint. Police should not always use handcuffs because they can injure the person. The ideal is a gurney with four-point restraints and body bands.

In handling calls involving mentally ill persons, officers often misinterpret civil criteria for detaining and committing those who are dangerous, which may lead to unnecessary, time-consuming delays in disposition.

The four civil criteria for detainment and commitment of mentally ill individuals in most states are (1) mental illness, (2) dangerous to self or others, (3) gravely disabled and (4) in need of (mental health) treatment.

These criteria are quite subjective. Usually mental illness and one other criterion must be present for an involuntary civil commitment. As mentioned earlier, however, commitment of mentally ill persons is no longer the preferred practice. Perkins et al. (1999, p. 296) note:

> Thirty years after the onset of deinstitutionalization, police handling of people with mental illnesses remains a major concern for both the police and the community. At the level of individual incident-handling, five sets of issues seem to be most problematic:

> • *Attitudes*—Many police officers and citizens continue to have misconceptions about, and irrational fears of, people with mental illness.

- *Training*—The extent of training provided to police officers is often inadequate. . . .
- *Policies*—Many police agencies do not have precise, clear, and well-understood policies and procedures to guide their officers in their responses to mental illness-related situations.
- *Communication*—Frequently, communication within police departments, as well as among the police, the medical community, and social service providers about the handling of people with mental illnesses is inadequate.
- *Systems*—Often, systems for obtaining involuntary commitment decisions are unnecessarily slow and cumbersome, as are processes for actual commitment after decisions are made.

Perkins et al. (p. 296) conclude:

> Improvements in any of these areas would likely lead to improved police handling of cases involving people with mental illness. Further progress might be possible if agencies utilize . . . community policing and problem-oriented policing approaches . . . [that] attempt to rectify chronic conditions, rather than merely respond better to repeated individual incidents . . . and try to engage more community resources in addressing the problem.

Crisis Intervention Teams. Ten years ago in Memphis, a Crisis Intervention Team (CIT) of specially trained officers was formed to respond around the clock to the some 4,000 calls each year involving "disturbed persons." Their primary objective was to minimize use of force without relinquishing public safety in potentially violent situations involving mentally disturbed people. Officers learned to use the Taser gun, a protective shield and Velcro leg wraps—vital equipment in interacting with a potentially dangerous mentally ill person. Understanding that mental illness is a disease rather than a crime made the crisis intervention approach a sensible alternative that often had a positive outcome for everyone involved. Indeed, as Wellborn (1999, p. 34) asserts: "A crisis intervention unit often removes the 'criminal' component of such encounters for officers and appears to be a clear win-win program for the police department, city, volunteers and community."

Crisis intervention teams, sometimes called crisis incident teams, are growing in popularity nationwide as departments implement community policing. According to Weiss and Dresser (2000, p. 133): "In the few seconds an officer has to act on a perceived threat, much can be set in motion: a sick person may be killed, a family shattered, police reputations ruined, government officials blamed, and cities held financially accountable." They (p. 133) explain: "CIT training identifies a person who needs mental health treatment. This works to prevent the person from ending up in jail on charges of 'disturbing the peace'—or dead." Noting wider applications of such training, Getz (1999, p. 51) adds:

> [CIT training courses are] not geared solely to the problems of mental illness and developmental disabilities. They also present approaches to high-risk situations where officers come in contact with suicidal individuals, substance abusers and

violent or stressed-out subjects. The basic knowledge will benefit every officer whether handling a domestic, a DUI or a confrontation with a citizen.

A CIT training course in St. Petersburg, Florida, partners the police department with the mental health professionals at the University of South Florida and takes a four-step approach to crisis intervention called CIAF—approaching the subject to *calm* him, *investigating* and *assessing* the situation, and finally, *facilitating* a solution. According to Getz (p. 54): "St. Petersburg, like a growing number of departments, understands that it is in the mental health business as first responder and as a proactive agency practicing community policing." Turnbaugh (1999, p. 53) adds: "This unique partnership of police, mental health providers and advocates is more than just training for the police. It is community policing at its best—an opportunity for police to enhance their image, gain public trust, show professionalism and demonstrate their sensitivity to community needs."

Weiss and Dresser (p. 136) describe how various CIT training programs recognize their "graduates." Some agencies issue pins to those completing CIT training, to identify them as being certified CIT officers. Some agencies issue laminated cards for officers to carry, providing the addresses of mental health facilities and services. Such cards also say: "Remain calm. Maintain eye contact. Lower voice volume. Be specific, concise. Be friendly, helpful. Build trust."

Another challenging and frequently misunderstood mental disability that police encounter is that of mental retardation, often, and incorrectly, equated with mental illness.

Mental Retardation.

An estimated 6 to 7 million people are mentally retarded, 90 percent of whom have mild retardation.

Mental retardation is the nation's fourth ranking disabling condition, affecting 3 percent of the U.S. population. **Mental retardation** means that normal intellectual development fails to occur. Unlike mental illness, mental retardation is permanent. It is diagnosed when three criteria exist: (1) significant subaverage general intellectual functioning (as measured by IQ tests), (2) resulting in, or associated with, defects or impairments in adaptive behavior, such as personal independence and social responsibility, (3) with onset by age 18.

The Police Response to Mental Retardation. The mentally retarded are usually aware of their condition and may be adept at concealing it. Thus, it may be more difficult to recognize mental retardation than mental illness. Communication problems, interaction problems, inability to perform tasks and personal history can help officers make this determination. The Arc (www.thearc.org) suggests: "There is often no one way of knowing if a person has mental retardation, but there are traits to look for in identifying an individual with this disability. . . . Look for clues in the person's communication, behavior and reaction to police contact."

More specifically, the Arc recommends police look for such *communication* clues as a limited vocabulary or speech impairment, difficulty understanding or answering questions or a short attention span. The *behavior* clues of a mentally retarded person may include acting inappropriately with peers or the opposite sex; being easily influenced by and eager to please others; becoming easily frustrated; and having difficulty with tasks such as reading, writing, telling time, making change, using the telephone or giving accurate directions. Clues to watch for during *police contact* include the person not wanting the disability to be noticed; not understanding rights or commands; acting overwhelmed or upset by the contact and trying to run away; having difficulty describing facts or details of the offense; saying what he or she thinks others want to hear; being the last to leave the scene and the first to get caught; and being confused about who is responsible for the crime and "confessing" even though innocent. The Arc also cautions:

> A person exhibiting these traits does not necessarily [have] mental retardation. If there is any question about someone having mental retardation, assume the person does and [follow some basic guidelines] to ensure that your contact and communication with the person is clear, especially if the person is read his or her Miranda rights.

When communicating with a mentally retarded person, or someone suspected of being retarded, speak directly to that person and keep sentences short. Use simple language, and speak slowly and clearly. Avoid asking questions rapidly or attempting to intimidate the person. Ask for concrete descriptions, colors, clothing and so on. Break complicated series of instructions or information into smaller parts. Whenever possible, use pictures, diagrams, symbols and actions to help convey meaning. Be firm, purposeful and very patient. Also be aware of the person's reluctance to discuss the matter and that they are likely to attempt to please. Treat adults as adults, and always give them the same respect you would give any person.

In addition to those who have mental illnesses or mental retardation, police officers may interact with people who have extreme emotional problems, including suicidal behavior.

Suicidal Behavior

In 1997 the total number of suicide deaths in the United States was 30,535.

Although the mentally ill may attempt to commit suicide, not all those who attempt suicide are mentally ill. Suicide is the eighth leading cause of death in the United States and the third leading cause of death among people age 15 to 24. In 1997 suicide outnumbered homicide 3 to 2. Firearms are the most common method for both men and women, accounting for 58 percent of all suicides.

For every "successful" suicide, an estimated eight to twenty-five attempts "fail." Although suicide itself is not a crime, in most states attempted suicide *is* a crime, allowing the state to take the person into custody for treatment. Persons who attempt suicide *must* receive professional counseling, not be placed in a holding or jail cell.

Danger signs of suicidal behavior include statements about hopelessness, helplessness and worthlessness; talk about suicide; and a preoccupation with death. Suicidal individuals may lose interest in things they care about, visit or call people as a way of saying good-bye, set their affairs in order or give away prized possessions.

The Police Response. To effectively deal with a suicidal person use a calm tone showing genuine concern. Insist in a nonthreatening manner that the person obtain mental health help. Talk about the finality of the act using the terms *suicide*, *death* and *kill your-self*. The belief that talking about suicide will prompt the person to follow through is a myth. The best way to help a suicidal person is to discuss the person's problems, the suicide plan and realistic alternatives. Suicide prevention guidelines include obtaining necessary personal data immediately, bringing the subject of suicide into the open, discussing the feelings of depression and how they are only temporary, removing the means, notifying and meeting with significant others, offering realistic hope, establishing a specific action plan and taking the person to receive medical attention.

After responding to the call and interacting with the suicidal person, officers must make a disposition. The two formal dispositions are arrest or civil commitment. Many informal dispositions are also available, such as releasing the person to family, friends or some other support network; referring the person to a mental health center for counseling; consulting with a mental health professional; and obtaining the person's agreement to seek voluntary examination.

Police officers are often the gatekeepers to the mental health system. Officers should be able to determine when someone needs referral to mental health professionals and should be familiar with the resources available, including the location of community mental health centers and hospitals that conduct mental health examinations, the services provided, hours of operation and staff to be contacted. They should also know the procedures to be followed at the facilities and what to do when the facilities are closed.

In addition to being victims of accidents or disease, disabled individuals are also frequently victims of crime.

Preventing Victimization of People with Disabilities

People with disabilities need the help of law enforcement to feel safe and to learn self-protection techniques. Criminals often prey on those with disabilities, viewing them as easy targets. Most veteran officers can tell stories about criminals who have cruelly taken advantage of disabled people. Unfortunately, however, most officers are unaware of how much they can do to reduce the vulnerability of the disabled, through participation in programs where police personnel teach people with disabilities how to protect themselves. Law enforcement can build positive relationships with the community by providing this vital assistance to some of our most vulnerable citizens.

The first steps a police department can take to better serve this segment of the community is to identify who they are, what types of disabilities they have, and where and under what circumstances officers are likely to encounter them. Next, specific crime prevention programs geared toward the disabled should be implemented and should cover topics such as community awareness, how to deal with strangers, shopping awareness, how to report crime and available resources. These programs should emphasize an awareness of how certain behaviors and circumstances may jeopardize one's personal safety. For instance, the disabled may, like many of us, develop predictable patterns of activity that make them vulnerable to victimization. As a specific example, retarded people, who frequently use public transportation, are often easily identified as vulnerable and, because of their dependency and often trusting nature, they are particularly prone to becoming victims (effective handling of victims with disabilities and their special needs is further discussed in Chapter 10).

Crime prevention programs should also incorporate most of the following tips in some way:

- Consider your limitations and decide what you will do if an assailant confronts you.
- Use direct deposit for government payments to you.
- Know your neighbors and decide who you could rely on in an emergency.
- Let family or friends know where you are going and what time you expect to return.
- Never let telephone callers know you are alone or disabled.
- When using public transportation, ride as near to the operator as possible.
- Travel with someone you know whenever possible.
- Be aware of body language. Transmit confidence and certainty.
- Carry enough money for telephone and emergency use, but never carry or display large amounts of cash.
- Be involved. Help your Neighborhood Watch with newsletters or telephone calls.

The basic premise is that almost everyone, even those with disabilities, can take responsibility for protecting themselves and their communities from crime once they are taught the correct responses to dangerous or suspicious circumstances. We all feel safer and *are* safer when we understand we have some power over what happens to us. Of course, differences in disabilities require different approaches to crime prevention, but what works for most people will usually work for people with disabilities too.

Some law enforcement departments have developed programs specifically for disabled people. In addition, some existing programs developed for the general population work well. Neighborhood Watch, for example, has a built-in component designed to enhance safety for the most vulnerable in the neighborhood. Block club members are encouraged to look after the elderly or disabled on their blocks, to be aware of suspicious activity around their residences, to check on them regularly and to assist them in participating in block activities.

Departments might also develop an ID for individuals with disabilities using a laminated card displaying the universal handicap logo for physically handicapped individuals and containing the person's name, address and phone number, as well as the name and phone number of an emergency contact or a doctor.

The Police Response—Handling Individuals with Disabilities Who Break the Law

It is natural to assume that disabled individuals are victims, not victimizers. However, this is not always true. Physically and mentally disabled people can also violate the law. Although people with severe physical or mental disabilities are highly unlikely to be among those who break the law, those with less limiting handicaps are certainly represented among lawbreakers, and most officers will encounter these offenders.

Of course, an individual's behavior will be limited by his or her physical or mental ability, and officers can expect a wide range in the severity of crimes committed by offenders with disabilities. However, the popular contention that mentally disabled people are unstable and therefore prone to more serious and violent offenses is unsupported by data: "The misconception that people with mental retardation usually commit serious crimes is unwarranted. . . . Research finds that people with mental retardation commit less serious crimes, such as misdemeanors and public disturbances" (Davis, 2000). Nonetheless, it is imperative to never become complacent and forget that disabled criminals can pose as much of a threat to safety as an able-bodied criminal can. It has happened where a mobility-impaired offender who seemed physically incapacitated and relatively harmless caught an officer off guard and was able to secure the officer's service weapon or perform another type of assault.

When disabled individuals violate the law, they should be treated as much like an able-bodied person as their disability will allow. This may involve the use of force, although officers are acutely aware that the public will usually react critically toward any type of force used by police against a physically or mentally disabled person. Knowing the law will help you feel confident when the use of force against a disabled offender is warranted.

When handling mentally retarded suspects, protecting the individual's rights is a concern. According to the Arc: "People with mental retardation often do not understand the Miranda warnings. In fact, many individuals with mental retardation often answer yes after they are read the Miranda warnings even when they do not understand their rights." Therefore, the Arc advises: "Although it's not an ADA requirement, when a person who is suspected of having mental retardation is questioned or interrogated about involvement in criminal activity, it's a good idea to have a guardian, lawyer or support person present to ensure that the individual's rights are protected." They recommend modifying the warnings using simple words. They also suggest videotaping interviews and interrogations to ensure questions are asked clearly and distinctly.

The ADA requires criminal justice agencies to accommodate disabled persons, and transporting arrestees with disabilities may be difficult logistically. Jail and detention facilities are also a concern. However, given the often nonviolent nature of their crimes, many disabled offenders serve their sentences and receive treatment in the community. These community-support programs are proving beneficial to both the offender and the community. Noting that this strategy addresses the criminal activity of mentally ill offenders, primarily crimes of theft, simple assault and drug use, the National Crime Prevention Council (1995, p. 26) states: "Community-based support and treatment systems for mentally ill offenders are a cost-effective crime prevention tool, leaving more space in jails and hospital facilities for those who require secure detention. The key component of this strategy is a community-based group willing to work with mentally ill offenders to ease their re-entry into the community and keep them safe and crime free."

A Final Note

Adapting law enforcement duties and services to accommodate the millions of disabled U.S. citizens will not only help accomplish law enforcement's objectives more efficiently and safely but will also help provide the services all citizens need and deserve. When that happens, excellent police-community relations are a likely by-product.

◈ UNDERSTANDING THE ELDERLY

In 1998 the number of persons in the United States age 65 or older exceeded 34 million.

Older, retired people are one of the fastest growing segments of our population. The U.S. Census Bureau estimates retired people will comprise more than 25 percent of the total population by 2025. During their careers, police officers have extensive contact with senior citizens. Police contact with older people rarely involves criminal activity; such contact usually arises from their vulnerability and the effects of the aging process.

Forst (2000, p. 125) suggests: "Police officers, like other professionals, may have difficulty understanding the needs of older citizens. This alienation is compounded by the fact that patrol officers are typically young and fit. . . . They may find it difficult to empathize with or relate to the physical and emotional challenges of the aged. Police organizations must be sensitized to aging issues in order that they may deliver the best possible service to the elderly."

Most gerontologists, those who study the elderly, do not focus solely on age to determine who is "old." Rather, they consider: (1) physical function—able to get around easily, physically active; (2) employment status—retired or engaged in some work, even part-time; (3) life activities—level of social activity; and (4) self-perception—view oneself as old. Some 55-year-olds seem as if they are 80 years old and vice versa. To determine whether someone is elderly, consider the preceding factors as well as chronological age.

The elderly tend to admire and respect authority, and they are often grateful for any help the police may offer. Older people are usually in contact with the police if they become victims of crime, are involved in an automobile accident or are stopped for a traffic violation. Some elderly people suffer from Alzheimer's disease, a progressive, irreversible disease of the brain that adversely affects behavior. Many elderly people have other serious medical problems for which they may require emergency medical assistance. Older people may also have one or more of the disabilities just discussed. In fact, more than half of the U.S. population over age 65 is disabled in some way (Fuller, p. 84).

The Graying of America

The **graying of America** is a metaphor reflecting the fact that our population is aging. The average American is living longer, the general population is becoming older, and the percentage of elderly in the general population is increasing. The Administration on Aging (AOA) (1999) reports:

> The older population—persons 65 years or older—numbered 34.4 million in 1998. They represented 12.7 percent of the U.S. population, about one in every eight Americans. The number of older Americans increased by 3.2 million or 10.1 percent since 1990. . . . Since 1900, the percentage of Americans 65+ has more than tripled (4.1 percent in 1900 to 12.7 percent in 1998), and the number has increased eleven times (from 3.1 million to 34.4 million). The older population itself is getting older. In 1998 the 65–74 age group (18.4 million) was eight times larger than in 1900, but the 75–84 group (12.0 million) was 16 times larger, and the 85+ group (4.0 million) was 33 times larger.

The AOA also notes a child born in 1997 could expect to live nearly three decades longer than one born in 1900.

The Elderly and Driving Problems

By 2020, 25 million people in the United States over age 75 will be eligible to drive, and many will. Some states require people over a specific age to retake their driving test, and more states are likely to follow as the number of elderly drivers increases. Some problems of the elderly that can affect driving include:

- Slower reaction time and loss of strength—the reduced ability to steer quickly, brake suddenly or accelerate rapidly results in more vehicle collisions and pedestrian accidents.
- Decreased visual acuity—results in difficulty reading road signs or judging speed and distance.
- Narrowed peripheral vision—results in more intersection accidents.
- Longer glare-recovery time—taking up to 50 percent longer for vision to readjust than for a younger person, night driving can become extremely dangerous. Headlight glare can be fatal.
- Memory impairments—confusion may cause wrong turns and lead them into unfamiliar, even dangerous, areas. Distracted by reading street signs to find their way back to familiar territory, elderly drivers may be oblivious to the other traffic or to pedestrians walking nearby.

Memory impairment may indicate the onset of disease; an especially devastating one is Alzheimer's.

Driving represents independence to young and old alike.

Alzheimer's Disease: A Police Problem, Too[2]

Imagine living in a world where every minute of your life is erased from memory as it passes. You can recall certain events from your childhood, school days, young adulthood, middle-age—but nothing from the past five years, five months or five minutes. You are unable to recall things you have known most of your life: your neighborhood, home, children, friends and spouse are all strange and foreign to you. This is the empty world of an Alzheimer's victim.

Alzheimer's disease (AD) is a progressive, irreversible and incurable brain disease affecting four million elderly Americans. Pronounced *Altz'-hi-merz*, it afflicts people of all social, economic and racial groups. AD afflicts about 10 percent of people over 65 and almost 50 percent of those over 85, affecting more women than men. One out of three families has a close relative with Alzheimer's.

The cause of Alzheimer's is unknown, and it is difficult to diagnose. The course of the disease averages eight years from when symptoms appear, but individuals have lived as long as twenty years with AD. Unfortunately, AD is always fatal and is the fourth leading cause of death in adults, causing 100,000 deaths per year. Although doctors cannot cure people with the disease, they can manage their symptoms.

Alzheimer's victims may look perfectly healthy and may be well dressed. They may also be very adept at concealing their disease. Because AD has no visible characteristics, officers should know the symptoms, the most classic of which is gradual loss of memory. Other symptoms include impaired judgment, disorientation, personality change, decline in ability to perform routine tasks, behavior change, difficulty in learning, loss of language skills and a decline in intellectual function.

Research has dispelled several *myths* associated with Alzheimer's. We now know that Alzheimer's disease is *not* a normal part of the aging process, nor is it contagious, caused by hardening of the arteries or lack of oxygen, or precipitated by alcoholism or malnutrition. It is neither a mental illness nor a form of insanity.

As the U.S. population ages, the number of people with AD will grow, along with the likelihood that police officers will encounter AD victims in the line of duty.

Behavior Patterns. A number of behavior patterns common to AD patients may bring them to the attention of police officers.

Alzheimer's victims may wander or become lost, engage in inappropriate sexual behavior, lose impulse control, shoplift, falsely accuse others, appear intoxicated, drive erratically and become victims of crime.

Any of these behaviors resulting from memory loss may cause the police to interact with an AD patient.

Wandering is common; an AD patient can become hopelessly lost, even when close to home and other familiar places. They may not remember where they have been, where they are going or where they live, even when driven past their homes. AD patients may make up a story rather than admit their confusion. They may be uncooperative or even hostile and combative.

---

[2]Condensed from *Victim, Not Criminal: The Alzheimer Sufferer* and the Alzheimer's Association Police Training materials. Reprinted by permission.

AD patients may fidget with their clothing, their buttons and zippers, usually without sexual intent. An AD victim who zips and unzips his pants or unbuttons her blouse in public may simply be fidgeting, but the actions may be misinterpreted as *inappropriate sexual behavior.*

AD patients may *lose impulse control* and do whatever occurs to them, for example, removing uncomfortable clothing or urinating or defecating when they feel the urge, wherever they may be.

AD victims may forget to pay for things, forget they have picked up merchandise or forget that they are even in a store. AD patients rarely *shoplift.* They simply forget that they have not paid for an item and sincerely believe they are being falsely accused.

AD patients forget their pocketbooks and wallets, how much money they had when entering a store or how much they have already spent. Unable to sort out the reality, they may *falsely accuse people* around them. AD patients may wrongly believe they have been victimized by friends and family, as well as strangers. They may report crimes that did not occur. In addition, neighbors may report that AD patients who live alone scream and yell at night. "Kidnap" or "adult abuse" reports may result from caregivers' attempts to limit an AD patient's behavior in public.

AD victims may *appear intoxicated* because many symptoms of the disease are identical to those of drunkenness. Both alcohol and AD diminish brain function—alcohol temporarily, AD permanently.

Many symptoms of intoxication and AD are identical: confusion and disorientation; problems with short-term memory, language, sight and coordination; combativeness and extreme reactions; and loss of contact with reality.

AD victims are often physically able to drive a car long after the time when their memory, judgment and problem-solving ability make it safe. Drivers who have Alzheimer's can *drive erratically;* "lose" their car and report it stolen; leave the scene of an accident because they actually forget it happened; and wander in the car because they are lost or have forgotten their destination. Sometimes drivers with AD are found several hundred miles from home.

People afflicted with AD may also become *victims of crime* because they are easy prey for con artists, robbers and muggers. Also, police may become aware of AD patients as a result of legal actions such as evictions, repossessions and termination of utility service due to the patients' forgetfulness or inability to make payments.

Is It Alzheimer's? AD patients forget; they forget that they have forgotten and will not be able to recall what they have forgotten. Consequently, it will not help to ask whether they have AD because they will forget they have the disease. However, the following signs can help determine whether a person has Alzheimer's:

- Identification bracelet or other item indicating memory impairment (usually the bracelet will *not* indicate Alzheimer's disease but will state memory impairment)
- Confusion—an inability to grasp even the simplest sight, sound or situation
- Blank or inappropriate facial expressions
- Inappropriate dress (heavy clothing on a hot day, or no shoes or coat in the winter)
- Forgetfulness, especially short-term memory loss

- Communication problems—difficulty remembering and understanding the meaning of words, keeping thoughts clear, speaking logically and following simple instructions

- Age (most are over age 65, but the youngest documented AD patient was 28 years old)

The Police Response. Although Alzheimer's disease is quite complicated, police officers can follow certain guidelines when they suspect or know they are dealing with an AD patient. The cardinal rule when dealing with an AD patient is to avoid the **catastrophic reaction,** which occurs when a situation overloads the AD patient's ability to think or act rationally and they revert to impulsive behavior. Behavior resulting from a catastrophic reaction can be relatively mild (such as sudden mood changes and restlessness) or can rapidly deteriorate into suspiciousness, stubbornness, inconsolable crying, anger and combativeness. During a catastrophic reaction, AD patients often lash out, verbally and/or physically, at people who try to help them.

When interacting with an AD patient, follow these guidelines: Look for an ID bracelet or other identification. Identify yourself and explain what you are or will be doing even if it is obvious. When possible talk one-on-one, away from crowds and noise. Avoid lectures or confrontation. Speak softly and slowly in a low-pitched voice. Loud speech could mistakenly indicate anger and lead to a catastrophic reaction. Keep communication simple. Maintain eye contact. Try to maintain a calm atmosphere. Any situation mildly stressful for the average citizen can be extremely difficult for the AD victim. AD patients will often mimic your mood. Do not overload the AD victim. If possible, avoid using handcuffs or other physical restraints because they are almost certain to cause a catastrophic reaction and eliminate any chance of a simple solution to the situation. However, because AD victims are unpredictable when frightened or upset, they may need to be restrained for their own safety and that of others.

The Helmsley Alzheimer's Alert program, started in 1991, provides information on missing patients to public safety agencies. When a person with AD is reported missing, the Alzheimer's Association sends an alert and identifying information to a fax service that transmits simultaneously to hundreds of locations, including police, hospital emergency rooms and shelters. When the patient is found, another fax is sent to inform the agencies that the search is over.

Senility

Senile dementia, organic brain syndrome (OBS), is another disabling condition often associated with aging. **Senility** is a disorientation or change in mental abilities and personality caused by generalized brain damage. Factors commonly associated with the onset of senility include head injuries, infection, drug reactions, toxic chemicals and other problems such as multiple sclerosis. Senility can also be caused by alcoholism, anemia, malnutrition, congestive heart failure, diabetes and chemical reactions. Common characteristics of OBS include memory loss, impaired judgment, disorientation, auditory or visual hallucinations, inappropriate behavior and emotional instability. When dealing with a senile person, officers should communicate slowly, not reacting to any delusions, and maintain a tolerant, calm manner.

Physical Impairments and Disabilities

In addition to the various mental impairments that may manifest during the aging process, older bodies also succumb to physical deterioration leading to mobility, visual and hearing impairments, as discussed at the beginning of the chapter. Elderly pedestrians with physical impairments such as arthritis can pose problems to motorists because they walk slowly. In some communities, elderly pedestrians are barely able to make it halfway across the street before the "Don't Walk" light begins flashing, and many times the light changes before they actually reach the other side.

Besides being the victims of disease and age-related disabilities, seniors can also be victims of crime or of elder abuse, as presented in Chapter 9. Departments, however, may implement a variety of crime prevention and community policing strategies to reduce elderly victimization.

Crime Prevention and Community Policing Strategies for the Elderly

The National Crime Prevention Council (p. 22) notes: "Elderly people can be particularly vulnerable to the crimes of burglars, purse snatchers, petty thieves, and con artists. They fear crime, especially violent crime, and that fear causes many to remain in their homes." Police department crime prevention programs aimed specifically at the elderly can help immensely, and the elderly are usually enthusiastic about participating in a department's special efforts. Such programs can remind seniors to have their social security checks deposited directly in their bank, to not carry much cash or other valuables on their person and to let go of a purse if it is grabbed. Too many senior citizens have tried to hold on to their purses and been dragged along, suffering broken bones and other injuries. The special challenge of handling elderly victims is explored in depth in Chapter 10.

To help the elderly avoid victimization, police might start a block or building watch, set up a daily telephone-contact program or enroll the elderly in Operation ID. These programs will help prevent crime and improve police-community relations among the elderly, as well as the rest of the community, by demonstrating the professional concern the police department has for its elderly citizens.

Police departments across the United States have developed many effective partnerships for older citizens. Such partnerships can easily be adapted to other communities and are successful because they can reduce victimization, reduce the fear of crime and improve police-community relations. Honolulu, for example, has a Senior Citizen Watch Program where organized senior citizen groups become the eyes and ears for the department.

In St. Louis, Missouri, the County Older Residents' Programs (CORP) Crime Prevention Program provides seniors the social and mental stimulation that helps keep them alert and alive. Program activities include an Opportunities Fair; crime prevention presentations and churches, social meetings and clubs; a cable-television show produced by retirees; telephone reassurance; and help with insurance forms and legal documents. CORP protects elderly residents and boosts the spirit of older, home-bound individuals (*350 Tested Strategies*, p. 23).

350 Tested Strategies (pp. 22–23) suggests the following components as successful crime prevention strategies for the elderly: a communication network to keep the elderly alert to potential crime; information and training on how to report crime; services to support elderly victims in dealing with the physical, emotional and financial impacts of crime; and access to products, training and other services to help prevent victimization. The council (p. 23) also notes the value in partnerships: "Key partners include the police, social services agencies, community groups, and religious groups. Volunteers can be used for escort or transportation services. . . . Working with the police and social service programs, grass-roots community groups such as Neighborhood Watch can greatly reduce the fear of crime among the elderly and help keep them safe."

Local law enforcement is also a vital element in the National Aging Services Network, a collaboration of federal, state and local agencies and services brought together under the Older Americans Act of 1965 and overseen by the Administration on Aging (AOA). The AOA works to heighten awareness among other federal agencies, organizations and the public about the valuable contributions older Americans make to the nation and alerts them to the needs of vulnerable older people. Figure 8.1 illustrates this network and helps officers identify resources available to address the needs and concerns of the elderly.

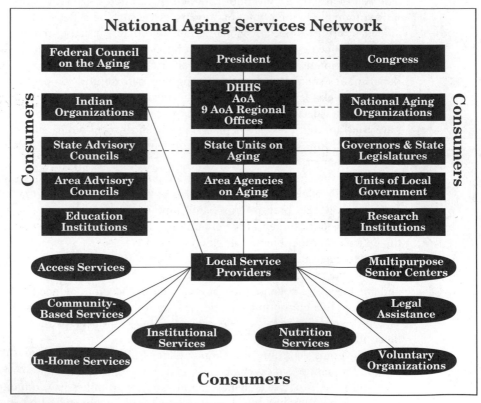

Figure 8.1 National Aging Services Network

SOURCE: AOA

Crime Trends and the Effect on the Elderly. The increasing age of the population in the United States suggests that the elderly will be victimized more often simply because they will be a large target population, some very vulnerable, some very wealthy. Also, the number of elderly people who commit crimes will probably increase, presenting a great challenge to the criminal justice system, particularly corrections, because the extensive medical and psychological care required for the long-term incarceration of the elderly will likely exceed the present capabilities of most corrections institutions.

Older Volunteers with Law Enforcement

Seniors make excellent volunteers. The AOA notes: "Older Americans represent a great reservoir of talent, experience, and knowledge which can and is being used to better their communities and the Nation." Older people tend to be dependable, experienced, stable, available, trainable, committed, skilled, conscientious and service oriented. In addition, older volunteers have fewer accidents, are more careful of equipment than younger volunteers, use good judgment, follow directions, like to avoid trouble, have good attendance records and tend to be team players.

Police departments across the country staff innovative programs with elderly citizens. Older volunteers are involved in neighborhood watch clubs, anonymous reporting and court watch programs and provide extensive benefits to both the police department and the community.

Benefits to a police department that uses senior volunteers may include improved service delivery, increased cost-effectiveness, relief of sworn personnel for other duties, improved public image, enhanced understanding of police functions, provision of new program opportunities, increased political support, restored community responsibility, reduced crime and increased property values.

In addition, volunteers may benefit from reduced fear of crime, use of their skills and expertise, the opportunity to help others, enrichment of their daily lives and a greater sense of belonging and worth. These benefits, compiled by the **AARP** (American Association of Retired Persons), are by no means exhaustive. Police-sponsored programs that use elderly volunteers have, however, raised some concerns.

Concerns about Using Seniors as Volunteers. One frequently expressed concern is that volunteers may do police officers' duties, thereby affecting future departmental hiring decisions. Other concerns are that volunteers need to be supervised while working in the department or that they may come in contact with sensitive or confidential material.

Volunteer programs can be tailored to address most objections. Volunteers rarely perform actual police functions. They frequently work in programs the department could not otherwise afford to provide such as fingerprinting children, distributing literature, maintaining equipment, entering computer data, organizing block groups, conducting department tours and translating. Volunteers do, however, need supervision and recognition, and volunteer programs need a coordinator to handle those tasks. In some cases a staff member can act as coordinator, or, when an extensive volunteer program is anticipated, a department may enlist a volunteer coordinator.

◈ TRIAD—A COORDINATED APPROACH

A joint resolution was adopted by the AARP, the International Association of Chiefs of Police (IACP) and the National Sheriffs' Association (NSA) to address criminal victimization of older people. The three organizations agreed to work together to design interjurisdictional approaches and partnerships to reduce victimization of older persons, assist those who have been victimized and generally enhance law enforcement services to older adults and the community.

This three-way partnership, called **TRIAD**, provides specific information such as crime prevention materials (brochures, program guides and audiovisual presentations on crime prevention and the elderly), policies, exemplary projects relating to the law enforcement response to the older community and successful projects involving the formation of senior advisory councils to advise departments on the needs of seniors. TRIAD also trains police about aging, communication techniques with elderly citizens, victimization of the elderly and management programs using older volunteers. TRIAD has been identified as a concrete example of community policing. Leadership is provided by an advisory group of older persons and those providing services to the elderly called Seniors and Law Enforcement Together (SALT). The organizational structure of SALT is illustrated in Figure 8.2.

SUMMARY

Fifty-four million U.S. citizens have disabilities. The most important guideline in interacting with people with disabilities is to treat them as individuals with the same needs and desires as any other citizen. Disabilities police officers frequently encounter include mobility impairment, vision impairment, hearing impairment, impairment as a result of epilepsy, and mental or emotional impairment.

Officers may need to interact with individuals who have epilepsy. An epileptic seizure may be mistaken for a drug- or alcohol-induced stupor because the person may exhibit incoherent speech, glassy-eyed staring and aimless wandering. Officers may also encounter mentally disabled individuals, some of whom may need institutionalization. The four civil criteria for detainment and commitment of mentally ill people are mental illness, dangerousness, being gravely disabled and being in need of (mental health) treatment.

Another population the police encounter daily is the elderly, people age 65 and older, whose numbers exceed 34 million in the United States. The elderly may be victims of Alzheimer's disease (AD), a progressive, irreversible brain disease affecting four million elderly Americans. Police contact with AD patients is likely because Alzheimer's victims may wander or become lost, engage in inappropriate sexual behavior, lose impulse control, shoplift, falsely accuse others, appear intoxicated, drive erratically and become victims of crime. Many of the symptoms of intoxication and Alzheimer's are identical: confusion and disorientation; problems with short-term memory, language, sight and coordination; combativeness; and in extreme reaction cases, loss of contact with reality.

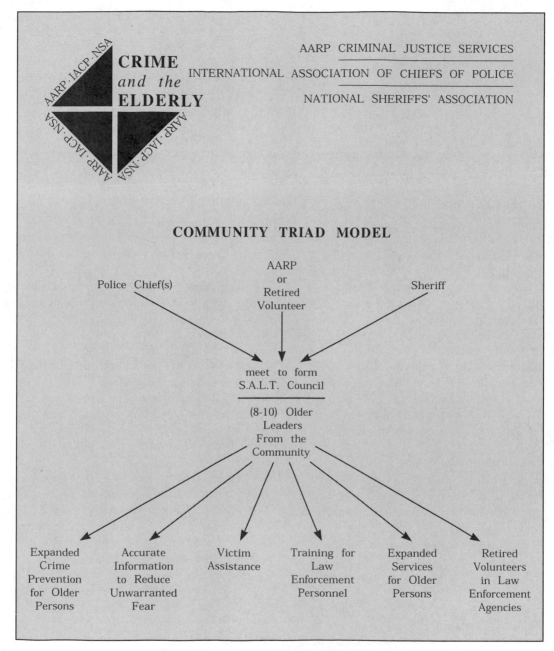

Figure 8.2 Community TRIAD Model - Organizational Structure of SALT

SOURCE: *Crime and the Elderly*, AARP Criminal Justice Services. Reprinted by permission.

The growing number of elderly citizens within a community presents a valuable resource to local law enforcement. Police departments across the country use elderly volunteers to staff innovative programs. Benefits to a police department that uses senior volunteers might include increased service delivery, increased cost-effectiveness, improved public image, relieving sworn personnel for other duties, provision of new program opportunities, increased political support, restored community responsibility, enhanced understanding of police functions, reduced crime and increased property values.

PROBLEM SOLVING IN ACTION

Mental Illness

St. Louis Officer Fran Krupp undertook several projects to address the often frustrating and time-consuming crime and disorder problems related to people with mental illness. In one case, by informing family members of the extremely high number of unfounded calls for service placed by an elderly relative, Krupp completely eliminated the calls. In another instance, she eliminated repeated shoplifting by a person with mental illness by locating an agency that would manage his disability income and ensure that he received medication to moderate the symptoms of his illness.

Case 1: Disturbance Calls
Scanning. In October 1993 officers Krupp and Lamczyk were called to 5876 Kennerly for burglars in a home. They met the caller, Mrs. R., in her late 80s and legally blind, who said people had broken into her basement and she could hear them talking while they did their laundry. The officers, however, found no signs of intruders.

Analysis. Krupp checked the CAD system and found records of 188 police calls to 5876 Kennerly in the past year. Over the past three years, police had been dispatched to the address almost 300 times for either "burglars in the building" or "disturbances." No reports had ever been completed on these calls, all designated as unfounded and requiring no further action.

Furthermore, the police department had spent an estimated 240 staff hours handling the previous calls.

Response. As an interim step, the supervisors agreed that every time a call was dispatched to this location, the precinct sergeant would call the complainant to determine whether the police were really needed. If not, the sergeant would call off the responding officers. The officers contacted a close relative of Mrs. R. and described the problem. The relative knew Mrs. R. called the police but was shocked to learn how often. The officers met with Mrs. R's family, who agreed to work with Mrs. R. to eliminate the unnecessary calls.

Assessment. Following up several weeks later, Krupp found that no calls had been dispatched to 5876 Kennerly. Concerned for Mrs. R's well-being, Krupp and Lamczyk went to the house to make sure she was all right. When they arrived, Mrs. R. greeted them at the door and told them her family had forbidden her to call the police without first checking with them. Over the next three months, only one call was dispatched to 5876 Kennerly.

Case 2: Shoplifting
Scanning. Officer Krupp was working secondary employment at a downtown mall when she arrested a 39-year-old man, Mr. G., who was caught stealing an alarm clock. After taking Mr.

G. to the security office, Krupp began filling out a summons release form. When Mr. G realized he was not going to be arrested, he started crying and begged Krupp to take him to jail, where he would be fed and given a place to sleep.

Analysis. Mr. G. explained that he stole almost daily, sold the goods on the street and used the money for food and transportation to the VA Hospital for outpatient care for mental illness. Mr. G. hears voices that tell him to do weird things. Several years before, he had been judged incompetent, and his disability checks were delivered to his mother who lived in Illinois. She had put him out of the house but continued to cash the checks. Realizing there was little she could do that evening, Krupp gave Mr. G. enough money for food and transportation to the hospital and told him to meet her at the mall the following day.

Response. The next day Krupp contacted a counselor from the Harbor Light Shelter and explained Mr. G's situation. When Mr. G. returned to the mall the following afternoon, Krupp arranged for them to go to the shelter together, where a counselor started the paperwork to reassign the payee for Mr. G's disability check. Harbor Light Shelter became the payee for Mr. G. and helped him recover from his illness, providing room and board as long as he needed it and supplying his medication through their pharmacy program.

Assessment. Several months passed, and Mr. G. had not been seen in at the mall.

(Adapted from Rana Sampson and Michael S. Scott. *Tackling Crime and Other Public-Safety Problems: Case Studies in Problem-Solving.* Washington, DC: U.S. Department of Justice, Office of Community Oriented Policing Services, 2000.)

DISCUSSION QUESTIONS

1. Do you support the deinstitutionalization movement of the late 1960s? Why or why not?

2. Have the local media covered any stories of people with mental disabilities coming into conflict with police officers? What was the outcome?

3. Are you aware of resources in your community available for the mentally ill? The physically handicapped?

4. Do you know anyone with a physical or mental disability? How do you feel about them?

5. Which type of disability do you feel would pose the greatest challenge for effective community policing? Why?

6. In what specific ways might individual officers improve their interactions with the elderly?

7. What problems might police officers encounter when working with nursing home staff?

8. Has the graying of America affected your community? If so, how?

9. Does your police department use elderly citizen volunteers? If so, how?

10. What do you think your main concerns will be when you are a "senior citizen?"

INFOTRAC COLLEGE EDITION ASSIGNMENTS

- Use InfoTrac to help answer the discussion questions as appropriate.
- Research how mental retardation affects the likelihood of criminal activity, conviction, incarceration and rehabilitation. What systemic changes, if any, would you recommend based on your research? Be prepared to share your findings with the class. OR
- Research what police services are available for the mentally ill. OR
- Research and discuss the deinstitutionalization of the mentally ill. How has it affected the mentally ill, and how has it changed police officers' jobs? Be prepared to share your findings with the class.

COMMUNITY PROJECTS

- What are the criteria for commitment in your state? How do they compare to other states—are they more or less restrictive?
- What resources does your community have for the elderly?

REFERENCES

Administration on Aging. "Profile of Older Americans, 1999." http://www.aoa.dhhs.gov/

The Arc. "Introduction to Mental Retardation." Publication #101–2. http://thearc.org/

Colbridge, Thomas D. "The Americans with Disabilities Act." *FBI Law Enforcement Bulletin,* Vol. 69, No. 9, September 2000a, pp. 26–31.

Colbridge, Thomas D. "Defining Disability under the Americans with Disabilities Act." *FBI Law Enforcement Bulletin,* Vol. 69, No. 10, October 2000b, pp. 28–32.

"Congress Approves Grants for Mental Health Courts." *Criminal Justice Newsletter,* Vol. 31, No. 2, October 24, 2000, pp. 2–3.

Davis, Leigh Ann. "People with Mental Retardation in the Criminal Justice System." 2000. http://thearc.org/

Disability Statistics Center. University of California, San Francisco. http://dsc.ucsf.edu

Epilepsy: A Positive ID. Minneapolis: Epilepsy Education, University of Minnesota, 1991.

Forst, Linda S. "Working with the Aged." *Law and Order,* Vol. 48, No. 10, October 2000, pp. 125–128.

Fuller, John. "Cultural Diversity? Don't Forget the Disabled!" *Law and Order,* Vol. 48, No. 11, November 2000, pp. 84–85.

Getz, Ronald J. "Reaching Out to the Mentally Ill." *Law and Order,* Vol. 47, No. 5, May 1999, pp. 51–54.

Litchford, Jody M. "ADA Decisions Provide Guidance for Enforcement Activities." *The Police Chief,* Vol. LXVII, No. 8, August 2000, pp. 15–17.

Louis, Richard, III. "Collaboration Builds Bridges: Police Work with Health Professionals to Assist the Mentally Ill." *Law and Order,* February 1997, pp. 82–83.

McNeil, John M. "Disabilities Affect One-Fifth of All Americans." *Census Brief.* U.S. Department of Commerce, Bureau of the Census, December 1997. (CENBR/97-5)

National Alliance for the Mentally Ill. © 1996–2000. www.nami.org

National Center for Medical Rehabilitation Research. *The Scope of Physical Disability in America—Populations Served.* No date. http://spot.pcc.edu/osd/disfacts.htm

National Institutes of Health. www.nih.gov

1998 NOD/Harris Poll. http://disability.nih.gov/news/presssurvey.htm

Perkins, Elizabeth B.; Cordner, Gary W.; and Scarborough, Kathryn E. "Police Handling of People with Mental Illness." In *Policing Perspectives: An Anthology,* by Larry K. Gaines and Gary W. Cordner. Los Angeles: Roxbury Publishing Company, 1999, pp. 289–297.

Sampson, Rana and Scott, Michael S. *Tackling Crime and Other Public-Safety Problems: Case Studies in Problem-Solving.* Washington, DC: U.S. Department of Justice, Office of Community Oriented Policing Services, 2000.

Strandberg, Keith. "De-Institutionalization." *Law Enforcement Technology,* Vol. 27, No. 10, October 2000, pp. 90–98.

350 Tested Strategies to Prevent Crime: A Resource for Municipal Agencies and Community Groups. Washington, DC: National Crime Prevention Council. 1995.

Turnbaugh, Donald G. "Crisis Intervention Teams: Curing Police Problems with the Mentally Ill." *The Police Chief,* Vol. LXVI, No. 2, February 1999, pp. 52–54.

U.S. Bureau of the Census. "Resident Population Estimates by Age and Sex, 1999." www.census.gov

Victim, Not Criminal: The Alzheimer Sufferer. Chicago: The Alzheimer's Disease and Related Disorders Association, Inc., 1987.

Weiss, Jim and Dresser, Mary. "Reaching Out to the Mentally Ill." *Law and Order,* Vol. 48, No. 6, June 2000, pp. 133–136.

Wellborn, Jeffrey. "New Orleans Finds a Successful Alternative when Dealing with the Mentally Ill." *Police,* Vol. 23, No. 10, October 1999, pp. 34–35.

RESOURCES

Administration on Aging, U.S. Department of Health and Human Services, 303 Independence Ave. SW, Washington, DC 20201; (202) 619-7501; fax (202) 260-1012. http://www.aoa.gov

Alzheimer's Disease and Related Disorders Association, Inc., 919 North Michigan Avenue, Suite 1100, Chicago, IL 60611-1676; (312) 335-8700, (800) 272-3900; fax: (312) 335-1110. http://www.alz.org

American Association of Retired Persons (AARP), 601 E. Street NW, Washington, DC 20049; (202) 434-2277; (800) 424-3410. www.aarp.org

American Psychiatric Association, 1400 K Street NW, Washington, DC 20005; (202) 682-6000; (888) 357-7924. www.psych.org

American Psychological Association, 750 First Street NW, Washington, DC 20002-4242; (202) 336-5500. www.apa.org

The Arc of the US - National Headquarters Office, 1010 Wayne Ave., Suite 650, Silver Spring, MD 20910; (301) 565-3842; fax (301) 565-5342. http://thearc.org

Centers for Disease Control and Prevention, 1600 Clifton Rd., Atlanta, GA 30333; (800) 311-3435. http://www.cdc.gov

Disability Statistics Center, 3333 California Street, Suite 340, San Francisco, CA 94118; Voice (415) 502-5210; TDD (415) 502-5205; fax (415) 502-5208. http://dsc.ucsf.edu

Epilepsy Education, University of Minnesota, 5775 Wayzata Boulevard, Suite 255, Minneapolis, MN 55416; (612) 525-4512

International Center for the Disabled (ICD), 340 East 24th Street, New York, NY 10010-4019; (212) 586-6000. www.icdrehab.org

Muscular Dystrophy Association, 3300 E. Sunrise Drive, Tucson, AZ 85718; (602) 529-2000; (800) 572-1717. www.mdausa.org

National Alliance for the Mentally Ill, (NAMI) Colonial Place Three, 2107 Wilson Blvd., Suite 300, Arlington, VA 22201-3042; Toll Free HelpLine (800-950) NAMI (6264); front desk (703) 524-7600; fax (703) 524-9094; TDD (703) 516-7227. www.nami.org

National Association for Hearing and Speech Action (NAHSA), 10801 Rockville Pike,

Rockville, MD 20852; (301) 897-8682; (800) 638-8255.

National Association of the Deaf, 814 Thayer Avenue, Silver Spring, MD 20910-4500; (301) 587-1788. www.nad.org

National Council on the Handicapped (NCH), Washington, DC 20591; (202) 267-3846; TDD (202) 267-3232.

National Council on Disability, 1331 F St. NW, Suite 1050, Washington, DC 20004-1107; Voice (202) 272-2004; fax (202) 272-2022; TTY (202) 272-2074. www.ncd.gov

National Easter Seal Society, 230 Monroe Street, Suite 1800, Chicago, IL 60602; (312) 726-6200; TDD (312) 726-4258: 800-221-6827. www.easter.seals.org

National Head Injury Foundation (NHIF), 1776 Massachusetts Ave. NW, Suite 100, Washington, DC 20036; (617) 879-7473; (202) 296-6443; 800-444-6443.

National Information Center for Handicapped Children and Youth (NICHCY), PO Box 1492, Washington, DC 20013; (202) 522-3332.

National Institute on Aging, Alzheimer's Disease Education and Referral Center, P.O. Box 8250, Silver Spring, MD 20907-8250; (800) 438-4380. http://www.alzheimers.org

National Institute of Mental Health (NIMH), Public Inquiries Branch, 6001 Executive Boulevard, Rm 8184, Bethesda, MD 20892-9663; (301) 443-4515. www.nimh.nih.gov

National Institute on Disability and Rehabilitation Research, National Rehabilitation Information Center, 400 Maryland Ave., SW, Washington, DC 20202-2572; (202) 205-8134; TTY (202) 205-9433. www.ed.gov

National Institutes of Health, Bethesda, MD 20892. www.nih.gov

National Mental Health Association, 1021 Prince Street, Alexandria, VA 22314; (703) 684-7722. www.nmha.org

National Society to Prevent Blindness (Formerly the National Society for the Prevention of Blindness), 500 E. Remington Road, Schaumburg, IL 60173; (708) 843-2020. www.preventblindness.org

Registry of Interpreters for the Deaf, Inc., 8630 Fenton St., Suite 324, Silver Spring, MD 20910; V/TTY (301) 608-0050; fax (301) 608-0508. www.rid.org

"Tips for Disability Awareness." National Easter Seal Society, 2023 Ogden Avenue, Chicago, IL 60612; (312) 253-8400; TDD (312) 243-8880.

United Cerebral Palsy Fund, 1522 K Street NW, Suite 1112, Washington, DC 20005; (800) 872-5827.

CHAPTER 9

Building Bridges with Youths and Gang Members

The moral test of government is how it treats those who are in the dawn of life, the children.
　　—Hubert H. Humphrey

Do you know

What three kinds of youths are combined into one "jurisdictional pot"?

How a welfare model and a justice model differ? Which is most often currently used?

What the *Big D*s of juvenile justice are?

What youths with special needs police officers should be familiar with?

What factors contribute to teen violence?

What needs are served by gangs?

How gang activity can be identified?

What can be an effective crime-fighting tool against gangs?

Why a community might be ambivalent toward gangs?

Can you define these terms:

attention deficit disorder

Big Ds of juvenile justice

crack children

decriminalization

deinstitutionalization

diversion

due process

EBD

fetal alcohol syndrome (FAS)

gang

graffiti

guardian *ad litem*

justice model

learning disability

moniker

"Norman Rockwell" family

one-pot jurisdictional approach

parens patriae

representing

status offenses

street gang

street justice

turf

welfare model

youth gang

INTRODUCTION

Added to the challenge of interacting with racial, ethnic, religious and socioeconomically diverse groups, as well as with people who are physically and mentally disabled and the elderly, officers also need to build bridges with a community's youths, including those belonging to gangs. Consider the challenges facing a black youth from the lower socioeconomic class who is also hearing impaired and involved with a gang.

This chapter begins with the purpose of understanding youths, including a definition of youths, a look at the importance of the preschool years and the turmoil many youths experience during adolescence. This is followed by an overview of juvenile justice in the United States and the challenges faced by youths with special needs. Distinctions are drawn between status offenders and youths who commit serious, often violent, crimes.

For some youths, violence becomes a way of life when they become members of a gang, the next population this chapter examines. The discussion begins with some definitions of gangs and how they developed in the United States. Next is an explanation of why some youths are attracted to and join gangs, descriptions of the various types of gangs, and a look at gang structure and membership, including gang member demographics. The gang subculture is then explored, followed by a discussion of the gang's outward trappings and how it achieves group identity. Next is a look at the prevalence and expansion of gangs in this country, as well as the activities gangs typically engage in. The police response to gangs is then presented, including the importance of intelligence gathering. The chapter concludes with a discussion of the gang's place within the community.

◆ UNDERSTANDING YOUTHS

In 1998 the number of youths age 17 and under in the United States was nearly 70 million.

A frequently overlooked segment of the population important to community policing implementation is youths. Snyder et al. report that in 1998, 69.9 million Americans—more than one in four—were under age 18, and a third of those (22.9 million) were age five or younger. The U.S. Census Bureau (1999) estimates more than one-fifth of the U.S. population is younger than 15. Because youths lack economic and political power, their problems and concerns may not receive the attention they deserve. But our nation's future depends on the values they form—they are the future decision makers of our country.

As you read this part of the chapter, do not become discouraged about the future of our youths. Most young people (95 percent according to FBI statistics) have not been in trouble with the law. Data from the Office of Juvenile Justice and Delinquency Prevention (OJJDP) shows that in 1998 law enforcement agencies made an estimated 2.6 million arrests of persons under the age of 18. Assuming no juveniles were arrested more than once and that the 2.6 million arrests corresponds to 2.6 million juveniles, this figure represents only 3.7 percent of the U.S. population under age 18. And almost certainly, some of these juveniles were arrested multiple times, pushing the actual percentage of youths who've been arrested even lower.

Youths in Austin, Texas, receive an antidrug message from a police officer.

The overwhelming majority of "good kids" should not be forgotten in community policing efforts. They can be valuable as volunteers and, if provided opportunities to become active in areas of interest to them, will most likely continue to be good citizens. This chapter, however, focuses on those youths with whom law enforcement most often interacts.

Youths Defined

Each state sets its own age defining youths, ranging from 16 to 19 years. The most common age for a person to legally become an adult is 18. Michigan, and perhaps other states, is moving toward lowering the age at which a person is considered an adult for prosecution purposes.

The Critical Preschool Years

Frequently the only contact police have with young people is with those who create problems or break the law. Consequently, police officers may stereotype youths, especially teenagers. Since the police do not interact with many preschool children, they are not considered a problem. Yet it is during the preschool years that many of our youths' problems begin.

The numbers show why America's children are an "endangered species." Millions are being raised by single mothers, many of whom received no medical care during pregnancy. Thousands are abused or neglected and have no supervision or have no home. In fact, the **"Norman Rockwell" family,** a term that used to describe most

American families—a working father, a housewife mother and two children of school age—now applies to only a small percentage of U.S. households.

Children enter school with ingrained habits, attitudes, psychomotor skills, cognitive abilities, social interaction patterns and health characteristics. Some five-year-olds entering school can count and say the alphabet; others cannot. Some can skip, throw a ball and build a block tower; others cannot. Some can play together, share and cooperate; others cannot. Some have strong bodies, good eating habits and healthy teeth; others do not. Some are enthusiastic, lively and eager to learn; others are not. Some know about music and books; others do not. Some know how it feels to be loved and accepted; others do not. In effect, what has happened to a child before entering school profoundly influences how well the child will do in school.

Adolescence

Adolescence is an extremely challenging time for all involved—the youths, their family and the community in which they live. As children grow into adults, passage through this evolutionary adolescent stage can be wrought with both internal and external conflict. It's a trial-and-error process. Juveniles want to feel important, express their opinions and make their own choices. However, their lack of experience from which to understand the consequences of their choices can sometimes lead to problems involving the police or another authority. Youths lack full appreciation of or respect for danger and are often unable to conceive of their own mortality. They may drive recklessly, experiment with drugs or engage in other risky or illegal behavior simply because they cannot envision a negative, or even fatal, outcome.

Juveniles desire to try things forbidden to them as younger children and to meet other people, especially those of the opposite sex. Anthropologists contend that every community has a place where youths gather to meet others. In one community, juveniles would congregate in a certain area on Friday and Saturday nights following high-school games. However, severe traffic congestion became a neighborhood concern, and the police cracked down on the gatherings. Reluctantly the youths dispersed and order was restored. The question then became: Where are the kids now? Before the crackdown, everyone knew. Afterward they didn't.

According to Johnson (1996, p. 1): "Some common problems between police and youths have been a lack of trust, little or no contact between line officers and youths except in negative contexts, high levels of anger and emotions, and racial and cultural differences. There is almost a natural adversarial relationship between police, who must control behaviors, and youths, who are anxious to experience new behaviors."

It is important that law enforcement officers, as first responders, identify possible causes of juvenile activity, behavior or dangerous conditions and forward this information to those involved in community policing efforts. Doyle (1996, p. 90) identifies "at-risk behaviors" including habitual truancy, incorrigibility, gang activity, criminal activity, vandalism, possession and use of weapons, drug abuse, alcoholism, promiscuity, tattooing or self-mutilating behaviors and suicide.

Before addressing the specific challenges youths present to law enforcement, consider how the juvenile justice system affects the way police officers interact with them.

A Brief Overview of Juvenile Justice in the United States

For police to effectively interact with their community's youths, officers should understand how the juvenile justice system and the adult system differ and the implications of such differences.

The basic assumption upon which the juvenile justice system rests is that of *parens patriae,* the government's right to take care of minors and others who cannot legally take care of themselves. The concept of *parens patriae* originated in thirteenth-century England, where common law established that the king was the "father of his country" and the guardian of all children. Children were considered wards of the state. The common-law notion of *parens patriae* is firmly entrenched in our system of juvenile justice.

During the early nineteenth century in the United States, prison reformers sought to keep wayward youths from being imprisoned with adult offenders by establishing a separate justice system exclusively for juveniles. Also during this time, rapid growth of the impoverished underclass and the apparently related increases in crime and disease became a concern to those in power, leading to the widespread perception that poverty bred criminality. In 1818 the term *juvenile delinquency* was first used and was equated with pauperism, that is, being poor. In 1825 delinquency was again associated with poverty when the New York House of Refuge was opened to house juvenile delinquents. Its charter defined juvenile delinquents as "youths convicted of criminal offenses or found in vagrancy."

In the second half of the nineteenth century, a group of reformers called the "child-savers" became active, establishing centers in urban areas to distribute food and clothing and to provide temporary shelter for homeless youths. However, this effort was not entirely altruistic because reformers admitted they were attempting to control a "potentially dangerous class." The link between delinquency and poverty was further strengthened by the first juvenile court act, passed in Illinois in 1899. This act regulated the treatment and control of dependent, neglected and delinquent children, again equating poor children and those in need of protection with children who committed crimes and treating them in essentially the same way.

Our juvenile justice system uses a **one-pot jurisdictional approach.** *Children who are abused or neglected, those who are status offenders and those who are truly criminal are all treated the same way.*

According to Springer (1986, p. 45): "All three kinds of children were thought to be the products or victims of bad family and social environments; consequently, it was thought, they should be subject, as wards of the court, to the same kind of solicitous, helpful care."

The philosophy of the first juvenile courts was to view children as basically good and in need of help—this approach is commonly referred to as the **welfare** *model.*

In the 1960s and early 1970s the national emphasis on civil rights greatly affected the juvenile justice system. The following milestone cases in juvenile justice continue to shape how law enforcement responds to youthful offenders:

- 1966—*Kent* v. *United States* established that if a juvenile court waives jurisdiction and transfers a case to adult court, it must follow the dictates of due process and fair treatment.

- 1967—*In re Gault* established that juveniles have the same constitutional rights as adults: notice of charges, right to counsel, right to cross-examine and to confront witnesses and privilege against self-incrimination.
- 1970—*In re Winship* established that in a juvenile court hearing, the youth must be proven guilty beyond a reasonable doubt, just as in adult criminal court. (The former standards were preponderance of evidence, clear and convincing proof and reasonable proof.)
- 1971—*McKeiver* v. *Pennsylvania* established that juveniles do *not* have the right to a jury trial in the juvenile court system.

The 1970s focused on the four Big Ds as described by Drowns and Hess (2000, p. 30).

The **Big Ds** *of juvenile justice are deinstitutionalization, diversion, due process and decriminalization.*

Deinstitutionalization, as the name implies, refers to efforts to release incarcerated youths through parole and community programs. **Diversion** means finding alternatives to placing juveniles into detention facilities. A major rationale underlying diversion was that not placing offenders into the justice system would avoid the danger assumed to be associated with criminal stigmatization and criminal association, thereby reducing the likelihood of subsequent crime by the offender. **Due process** suggests that the advances made in the rights of youths continued to be important considerations in the 1970s. **Decriminalization** refers to the efforts to make status offenses noncriminal actions.

Another important case involving juveniles is *Schall* v. *Martin* (1984), which established the state's right to place juveniles in preventive detention to protect both the youth and society.

A Change from the Welfare to the Justice Model. The 1980s again brought reform in the juvenile justice system: a change from the welfare model to a justice model.

A **justice model** *views youths as responsible for their actions. Under the justice model, the good of society takes precedence over society's responsibility to take care of its children, as in the welfare model.*

The justice model contends young law violators should not be considered by the juvenile courts as "sick" or victims of their environment. Juvenile judges are placed in an impossible situation when asked to diagnose the problem of a young offender, when often it is obvious that the youth does not *have* a problem—he or she *is* the problem.

This "get tough" attitude has been criticized by some, however, who suggest it means "let's get tough with minorities and the poor." This criticism might be addressed, in part, by dividing the juvenile justice system into two categories: civil and criminal. Included in the civil category would be children who are endangered, abused or neglected (victimization of children is discussed in Chapter 10); and youths who commit status offenses. The current juvenile justice system makes no such distinction. Consequently, police officers often use their discretion to make the distinction themselves.

Street justice occurs when police officers use their discretionary powers to simply talk to or warn youthful offenders, talk to the youth's parents, or make referrals to a social service agency. Street justice may also involve roughing an offender up rather than taking them into custody.

Youths with Special Needs and the Police

Police officers may have to deal with children who have very special needs.

Children with special needs include those who are emotionally/behaviorally disturbed, who have learning disabilities, who have an attention deficit disorder or who have behavior problems resulting from prenatal exposure to drugs, including alcohol, or to HIV.

Emotionally/Behaviorally Disturbed Children. One group of young people police will encounter are emotionally/behaviorally disturbed children, often referred to as **EBD.** Usually EBD youths exhibit one or more of the following behavioral patterns: severely aggressive or impulsive behavior; severely withdrawn or anxious behavior such as pervasive unhappiness, depression or wide mood swings; or severely disordered thought processes reflected in unusual behavior patterns, atypical communication styles and distorted interpersonal relationships.

Parents and teachers in some communities have expressed concerns that children labeled as EBD have fewer coping skills to deal with police contacts than other children and may be traumatized by such contacts. Suggestions that police not interview or contact such children unless an EBD specialist is present have, for the most part, not been implemented because it is usually impossible for the police to know who is EBD.

Police may assume that a large percentage of children who are suspects in crimes are EBD and that condition is one cause of their unlawful behavior. It is impossible, however, to arrange for an EBD specialist to be present at all police contacts because a majority of contacts are unplanned events that occur on the street.

Youths with Attention Deficit Disorder. Attention deficit disorder (ADD) is one of the most common disruptive behavior disorders in youths, with an estimated 5 to 10 percent of all children having it. Occurring four times more often in boys than girls, ADD is characterized by heightened motor activity (fidgeting and squirming), short attention span, distractibility, impulsiveness and lack of self-control. Children with ADD may do poorly in school and have low self-esteem. Although the condition often disappears by adulthood, by then former ADD children may have other behavior problems including drug abuse, alcoholism or personality disorders.

Youths with Learning Disabilities. An estimated five to ten million children in the United States have some form of **learning disability,** which the Association for Children with Learning Disabilities (ACLD) (p. 4) defines as "one or more significant deficits in the essential learning processes." Essential learning processes are those involved in understanding or using spoken or written language and do *not* include learning problems that result from visual, hearing or motor handicaps, mental retardation or emotional disturbance.

The ACLD (p. 3) identifies the most frequently displayed symptoms of learning disabilities as short attention span; poor memory; difficulty following directions; disorganization;

inadequate ability to discriminate between and among letters, numerals or sounds; poor reading ability; eye-hand coordination problems; and difficulties with sequencing. Such children are often discipline problems, are labeled "underachievers" and are at great risk of becoming dropouts.

Although learning disabilities are usually discussed in an educational context, the ACLD (p. 8) notes: "The consequences are rarely confined to school or work." Characteristics that may bring a learning disabled youth into conflict with the law include responding inappropriately to a situation, saying one thing and meaning another, forgetting easily, acting impulsively, needing immediate gratification and feeling overly frustrated, which results in disruptive behavior. Those who interact with such children need to be patient and communicate effectively. Youths with learning disabilities look like their peers. Inwardly, however, most are very frustrated, have experienced failure after failure and have extremely low self-esteem.

Youths Exposed to Drugs or HIV Prenatally. The term **crack children** is sometimes used to refer to children exposed to cocaine while in the womb. They may exhibit social, emotional and cognitive problems. Drug-damaged children may also have poor coordination, low tolerance levels and poor memory. Police officers should be aware of these symptoms and recognize that they reflect a condition over which the youth has limited or no control.

Another pressing problem is that of **fetal alcohol syndrome (FAS),** the leading known cause of mental retardation in the western world. FAS effects include impulsivity, inability to predict consequences or to use appropriate judgment in daily life, poor communication skills, high levels of activity and distractibility in small children and frustration and depression in adolescents.

Yet another group of at-risk children who present special problems to law enforcement are children prenatally exposed to HIV. Such children may have mental retardation, language delays, gross- and fine-motor skill deficits, and reduced flexibility and muscle strength.

Children with special needs are likely to be in contact with the police, and many may become status offenders. Others may become more serious offenders. Many youths with special needs are also likely to join gangs, as discussed shortly.

Status Offenders and the Law

An extremely important aspect of the juvenile justice system is its establishment of status offenses. **Status offenses** are actions by a juvenile that would not be considered criminal acts if done by an adult, for example, smoking cigarettes. In most states, status offenses include truancy, running away, curfew violations, smoking cigarettes, drinking alcoholic beverages and "incorrigibility."

The Police Response to Status Offenders. Between 80 and 90 percent of children under 18 commit some offense for which they could be arrested, yet only about 3 percent of them are. The reason: police discretion. The police response usually is based on two factors: the specific incident and the youthful offender's demeanor. If the incident is minor and the offender is respectful and appears contrite, the police will usually drop the matter. The older the offender, the more likely the police will be to take official action. Police also commonly release minor offenders with or without a warning and without making an official record or taking further action. These children, many of whom desperately need help of some kind, are not referred to the proper social agency in the community where such help is available.

Referral sources for juveniles vary from community to community. Among the services commonly available are child welfare and child protection services; community mental health centers; community recreation activities (often offered through local park and recreation departments); churches; crisis centers for high-risk/suicidal youths; detox services that take youths; drop-in centers or runaway shelters for youths; groups that work with special needs of adoptive parents and youths; human service councils (can provide brochures, information on food shelves, financial assistance, low-income housing); **guardian** *ad litem* programs (an individual appointed by the court to protect the best interests of a child—in some states this can only be an attorney); juvenile probation/court services; support groups (Alcoholics Anonymous, AlAnon, etc.); victim/witness services; YMCA or YWCA programs; and youth service bureaus that often run diversion programs.

The *National Juvenile Justice Action Plan* suggests that ideally a system of graduated sanctions be used to provide immediate intervention and treatment for delinquent juveniles (p. 3):

• Intermediate intervention (community restitution, day treatment centers, diversion programs and protective supervision projects) for first-time delinquent offenders and many nonviolent repeat offenders

• Intermediate sanctions (residential and nonresidential community-based programs, weekend detention, intensive supervision, probation, wilderness programs and boot camps) for many first-time serious and repeat offenders and some violent offenders

• Secure confinement (community confinement in small, secure treatment facilities or, where necessary, incarceration in training schools, camps and ranches) for offenders categorized as violent or repeat serious offenders

Again, community support is vital. If citizens have the NIMBY philosophy (not in my backyard), such efforts will be much more difficult.

Youths Who Commit Serious Crimes and the Law

The OJJDP (*Serious and Violent . . .* , 1998, p. 2) defines serious violent offenses as those involving homicide, rape, robbery, aggravated assault and kidnapping, noting: "Serious and violent juvenile (SVJ) offenders comprise a troubled and often dangerous population. Although their numbers are small, they are responsible for a disproportionate amount of crime."

Snyder (1999) reports the juvenile violent crime index arrest rate in 1998 was at its lowest level in 10 years—30 percent below the peak year of 1994. Bernard (1999, p. 337) asserts: "Current get-tough juvenile policy reforms are based on an assumption that juvenile crime has been increasing for some time. . . . The data show many conflicting trends, but [I] argue that the most consistent interpretation is that juvenile crime, with the exception of homicide, has declined by about one-third over the last twenty years."

Good news? Perhaps, but consider this: Fewer than half of all serious violent crimes by juveniles are reported to law enforcement. Data from the National Crime Victimization Survey (NCVS) reveal that in 1997 only 42 percent of all serious violent crimes by juveniles were reported to the police (Snyder and Sickmund, 1999, p. 63).

Furthermore, despite statistics indicating a drop in youth-perpetrated violent crime, juveniles are still involved in more than one-quarter of all serious violent victimizations. According to Snyder and Sickmund (p. 62), in 1997 juveniles under age 18 were involved in 27 percent of all serious violent victimizations, including 14 percent of sexual assaults, 30 percent of robberies and 27 percent of aggravated assaults. Juvenile homicides in 1997 were the lowest in a decade but still 21 percent above the average of the 1980s (p. 53).

Snyder and Sickmund also report that juveniles are twice as likely as adults to commit serious violent crimes in groups (p. 63) and that one-fifth (21 percent) of 16-year-olds who had been arrested were first arrested by the age of 12 (p. 60).

Factors contributing to teen violence are a shift in adolescent attitudes toward the value of life, a desensitization to violence and the ready availability of handguns.

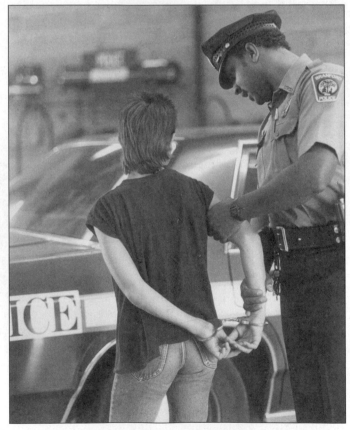

© Gale Zucker/Stock, Boston

This juvenile may learn a somber lesson from being taken into custody by police.

Regarding adolescent attitudes, Eitzen (1992, p. 584) notes: "Some young people act in antisocial ways because they have lost their dreams." He contends that families and the youths within those families are shaped by their economic situation and that our economy has changed dramatically. Eitzen uses the analogy of a boat and the traditional argument about the economy that "a rising tide lifts all boats." This was true from 1950 to 1973, when the average standard of living rose steadily. Since then, however, the "rising tide" analogy has not been accurate, for, as Eitzen notes: "Since 1973 the water level was not the same for all boats, some boats leaked severely, and some people had no boat at all."

The American Dream is fading for many. A home and a college education, things formerly taken for granted, are now out of reach for millions of Americans. In addition, says Eitzen (p. 587): "Children, so dependent on peer approval, often find the increasing gap in material differences between themselves and their peers intolerable. This may explain why some try to become 'somebody' by acting tough, joining a gang, rejecting authority, experimenting with drugs and sex, or running away from home."

More than any previous generation, today's youths are increasingly desensitized to violence. A three-year study by the University of California, Santa Barbara, concluded over 60 percent of all television programs contain violence (Ruben, 1998, p. 101). The American Psychological Association estimates that the average child witnesses 8,000 murders and 100,000 other violent acts on television before finishing elementary school (Martin, 1994, p. 38). Children are surrounded by games and media images glorifying deadly aggression, bloodshed and carnage. Yet, when the game or show is over, the players are still able to come back for more. Somehow kids are missing the message that real life doesn't work that way.

The availability of handguns also contributes to youth violence. In fact, as Snyder and Sickmund (p. 54) indicate, *all* of the increase in homicides by juveniles between the mid-1980s and mid-1990s was related to firearms. By 1994, 82 percent of homicides by juvenile offenders involved use of a firearm. Media coverage of school shootings around the country has raised public awareness of the problem, yet the tragedies continue:

> His father was in and out of prison. His mother, evicted from her home, sent him and his 8-year-old brother to live with an uncle in a dilapidated house. There, he did not even have his own bed and fell asleep in a place that neighbors say was filled with drugs and guns.
>
> And on Tuesday, the 6-year-old found one of those guns lying around in a bedroom, stuffed it into his pants pocket and went off to first grade, where he killed a classmate. . . . The boy put the gun in a desk after the shooting and simply walked away. Questioned by detectives, the boy said that . . . he had only been trying to scare the girl. The boy did not cry, and afterward he drew pictures ("Boy Who Shot Girl . . . ," 2000, pp. A1, A22).

Although society is not completely to blame for our wayward youths, the community must assume some responsibility and take an active role in working with police to deal effectively with the underlying causes of delinquency and crime, a recurrent theme throughout this text. (Specific programs aimed at youths are discussed in detail in Chapter 14.)

UNDERSTANDING GANGS AND GANG MEMBERS

An estimated 850,000 gang members are active in nearly 31,000 gangs nationwide.

Gangs have spread through our country like a plague and now exist in every community—rural, suburban and inner-city—in every metropolitan area. Some analogize the gang problem to a societal cancer, where street gangs prey upon the community like a malignant growth, eating away at its host until only a wasted shell remains. They use harassment, intimidation, extortion and fear to control their territory. Daily, countless news stories depict the tragedy of gang violence. The following document only the tip of the problem:

• A gang fight at a crowded park results in a seven-year-old girl being shot in the head while picnicking with her family.
• Shot gun blasts from a passing car, intended for a rival gang member, strike a child.
• A shoot-out between rival gangs kills a high school athlete as he jogged around the school track.

Gangs have been defined as "any ongoing organization, association, or group of three or more persons, whether formal or informal, having as one of its primary activities the commission of one or more of the criminal acts . . . , which has a common name or common identifying sign or symbol, whose members individually or collectively engage in or have engaged in a pattern of criminal gang activity" (California Penal Code Section 186.22[f]). A **gang** is an organized group of people existing for some time with a special interest in using violence to achieve status. Gangs are identified by a name, turf concerns, symbols, special dress and colors. A gang is recognized by both its own members and by others.

Esbensen et al. (2001, p. 105) discuss the varying definitions of what constitutes a gang, ranging from the least restrictive definition, which includes all youths who claim gang membership at some time, to the most restrictive definition, which includes only those youths who are current core gang members and who indicate that their gang has some degree of organizational structure and is involved in illegal activities. Esbensen et al. suggest that the definition used "greatly affects the perceived magnitude of the gang problem" (p. 124).

A **street gang** is a group of people whose allegiance is based on social needs and who engage in acts injurious to the public. Members of street gangs engage in an organized, continuous course of criminality, either individually or collectively, creating an atmosphere of fear and intimidation in a community. Most local law enforcement agencies prefer the term *street gang* because it includes juveniles and adults and designates the location of the gang and most of its criminal behavior. For criminal justice policy purposes, a **youth gang** is a subgroup of a street gang. It may refer to a juvenile clique within a gang.

Gangs, while not new to this country, are posing more of a challenge to law enforcement than ever before. McCorkle and Miethe (1998, p. 41) note: "The past decade has witnessed increasing concern about street gangs and their role in violent crime and drug trafficking. . . . A seasoned observer of the gang problem has asserted that contemporary street gangs are now 'more numerous, more prevalent, and more violent . . . than anytime in the country's history.'"

The Development of Gangs

Osman and Haskins (1996, pp. 1–3) trace the development of gangs to European settlement in the United States, when members from the poorer classes and from the same race or ethnic background tended to band together for protection, recreation or financial gain. In the 1820s Irish immigrants formed the first American criminal gangs in New York City. Called the Forty Thieves, these gangs engaged in murder, robbery and street muggings.

Early in the 1900s the U.S. economy worsened, the population grew rapidly, and the gap between rich and poor widened. Across the nation gangs appeared where poor, hopeless people lived. Throughout the middle of the twentieth century, gang violence fluctuated, increasing in the 1950s as gang members more often used guns, knives and homemade weapons, declining during the 1960s, and rising again in the 1970s. Since the 1980s guns have decided gang arguments quickly, but innocent bystanders are frequently killed in the crossfire. Despite all the social and economic advances made since the 1820s, many of the same conditions exist today and explain the continued existence of street gangs.

Why Youths Join Gangs

Gangs fulfill socialization and survival functions for youths in low-income, socially isolated ghetto or barrio communities and in transitional areas with newly settled populations.

A youth seeking protection, security, status, an identity and a sense of belonging can fulfill all of these needs through gang membership.

A gang member may receive a new identity by taking on a nickname, or **moniker,** which others in the gang world recognize. Monikers affirm a youth's commitment to gang life and may become their sole identity, the only way they see themselves and the only name they go by. They may no longer acknowledge their birth name, rejecting any previous identity or life outside the realm of the gang.

Gangs often take the place of family. According to Rowell (2000, p. 35): "The gang provides kids with basic human needs . . . including the need for security, love, friendship, acceptance, food, shelter, discipline, belonging, status, respect, identification, power and money." Zatz and Portillos (2000, p. 389) observe:

Historically, gangs have been important neighborhood institutions offering disenchanted, disadvantaged youth a means of coping with the isolation, alienation, and poverty they experience every day. . . .

The youths identify strongly with their neighborhoods, consider themselves to be integral parts of their barrios, and view their gangs as neighborhood institutions. They see themselves as protectors of their neighborhoods, at least against intrusion by rival gangs.

They (p. 396) further note how gangs were, and are, composed of brothers, sisters, cousins and neighbors, giving members a sense of community and a place where they belong: "Kicked out of school, assumed to be troublemakers, looking tough and feeling scared, these young people are well aware that their options in life are very much constrained by poverty, racial discrimination, cultural stereotyping, and inadequate education."

According to Osman and Haskins (p. 1): "Gangs are one of the results of poverty, discrimination and urban deterioration. Some experts believe that young people, undereducated and without access to good jobs, become frustrated with their lives and join gangs as an alternative to boredom, hopelessness and devastating poverty." An estimated 80 percent of gang members are illiterate. Finding it almost impossible to get a job, they may turn to gangs as a way to earn a living through drug trafficking, illegal weapons sales, robbery and theft, and as a way to earn respect. As gang expert Valdez (2000, p. 55) cautions: "Today, most street gangs base 'respect' on fear. The more you fear me the more you respect me. The traditional rules of not involving innocent women and children in gang warfare are gone. For lack of a better way to say it, the 'gang ethic' has changed."

Types of Gangs

Although gangs are often classified by racial or ethnic composition, it is usually more helpful to classify them by their behavior. Shelden et al. (2001, pp. 37–38) report that various studies by different researchers nationwide have identified several major types of gangs:

- *Hedonistic/social* gangs—only moderate drug use and offending; involved mainly in using drugs and having a good time; little involvement in crime, especially violent crime.

- *Party* gangs—commonly called "party crews"; relatively high use and sale of drugs, but only one major form of delinquency—vandalism; may contain both genders or may be one gender; many have no specific dress style, but some dress in stylized clothing worn by street gang members, such as baseball caps and oversize clothing; some have tattoos and use hand signs; their flexible turf is called the "party scene"; crews compete over who throws the biggest party, with alcohol, marijuana, nitrous oxide, sex and music critical party elements.

- *Instrumental* gangs—main criminal activity is property crimes (most use drugs and alcohol but seldom sell drugs).

- *Predatory* gangs—heavily involved in serious crimes (e.g., robberies and muggings) and the abuse of addictive drugs such as crack cocaine; may engage in selling drugs but not in organized fashion.

- *Scavenger* gangs—loosely organized groups described as "urban survivors"; prey on the weak in inner cities; engage in rather petty crimes but sometimes violence, often just for fun; members have no greater bond than their impulsiveness and the need to belong; have no goals and are low achievers; often illiterate, with poor school performance.

- *Serious delinquent* gangs—heavy involvement in both serious and minor crimes, but much lower involvement in drug use and drug sales than party gangs.

- *Territorial* gangs—associated with a specific area or *turf* and, as a result, get involved in conflicts with other gangs over their respective turfs.

- *Organized/corporate* gangs—heavy involvement in all kinds of crime; heavy use and sale of drugs; may resemble major corporations, with separate divisions handling sales, marketing, discipline, and so on; discipline is strict, and promotion is based on merit.

- *Drug* gangs—smaller than other gangs; much more cohesive; focused on the drug business; strong, centralized leadership, with market-defined roles.

Gang Structure and Membership Roles

Recall that "an organized group" is part of the definition of a gang. Gang organization and structure, whether formal or informal, includes members of varying commitment levels and gang experience. As with gang types, gang members may also be classified by their behavior. According to Shelden et al. (pp. 39–40), research has identified the following gang member types:

- *Regulars* or *hard-core* members—a small group (approximately 10 to 15 percent of the membership) who are the most influential and active members of the gang; they have few, if any, interests outside the gang. The hard-core members who hold leadership positions pose a threat to the community and the police because (1) they typically possess guns and other weapons, and (2) they tend to be aggressively antisocial and are encouraged to be so by the gang as long as their behavior does not violate gang rules or discipline.

- *Peripheral* members (or *associates*)—a larger group surrounding the hard-core members; have a strong attachment to the gang but participate less often than the regulars because they have other interests outside the gang; are not privy to the gang's inner activity and are relegated to follower roles; hard-core members are recruited from the peripheral membership.

- *Temporary* members—only marginally committed; join the gang at a later age than the regulars and peripherals; remain in the gang for only a short while.

- *Situational* members—join the gang only for certain activities (usually avoiding the more violent activities).

- *At risk* members—not really gang members but are *pregang* youths who have shown some interest by experimenting with certain gang attire and/or language (this may begin as early as the second grade).

- *Wannabes*—a term gangs themselves use to describe "recruits," who are usually in their preteen years and know and admire gang members; a notch above the "at-risk" youth, they are mentally ready to join a gang; may be called *Pee Wees*.

- *Veteranos/OGs* ("original gangsters")—usually men in their 20s or 30s (or even older) who still participate in gang activities; often hold the role of teacher and/or disciplinarian to younger gang members.

- *Auxiliary* members—those who hold limited responsibility; a common role for female members.

Females are used by gangs in a variety of ways, often because they arouse less suspicion than male adults. Females may serve as lookouts for crimes in progress, conceal stolen property or tools used to commit crimes, carry weapons for males who do not want to be caught with them, carry information in and out of prison, and provide sexual favors (they are often drug dependent and physically abused).

Gangs use children to commit shoplifting, burglaries, armed robberies and drug sales in schools. Their youthful appearance is an advantage because they often do not arouse suspicion. Furthermore, if they're caught, the criminal justice system deals more leniently with them than with adults.

Demographics—Profile of a Gang Member

The typical age range of gang members is 12 to 24, with an average age of about 17 or 18. Although younger members are becoming more common, it is the older membership that has increased the most. Gangs are overwhelmingly male organizations; the male-female ratio is approximately 9 to 1. However, the proportion of female gang members, while small, may be increasing.

The ethnic/racial makeup of gangs has also changed over the past few decades from predominantly white gangs to the majority of gangs now being African American, Hispanic and Asian. Some Native American gangs also exist in certain parts of the country. The racial makeup of gangs seems to correlate with the racial makeup of our society at or near the poverty level. A typical gang member is usually poor, a school dropout, unemployed and in trouble with the police.

The Gang Subculture

A gang member's lifestyle is narrow and limited primarily to the gang and its activities. Members develop fierce loyalty to their respective gang and become locked into the gang's lifestyle, values, attitudes and behavior, making it very difficult for a member to later break away from a gang.

Shelden et al. (p. 76) state: "An important part of the gang subculture . . . is the belief and value system . . . [which] includes honor, respect, pride (in oneself and in one's neighborhood), reputation, recognition, and self-esteem." They (p. 77) identify friendship, manliness and hedonism as other important values, noting that among gang members: "A sense of wildness and locura (craziness) are often admired as ideal characteristics."

Gang members are commonly antisocial, aggressive and hostile, rebelling against society and getting support from the gang for feelings of anger and frustration: "Gangs offer a distillation of the dark side of adolescent rebellion. . . . Their revolt is total; it confronts and confounds adult authority on every level—sex, work, power, love, education, language, dress, music, drugs, alcohol, crime, violence" (Shelden et al., p. 77).

Outward Trappings of the Gang—Achieving Group Identity

Like corporations, gangs use symbols or logos to identify themselves. In addition, a gang's choice of colors is important. The symbols and colors indicate whether the gang is an independent organization or a branch or affiliation of an established group. Common gang symbols include an all-seeing eye, a champagne glass, crossed pitchforks, a crown, five- and six-pointed stars, a pyramid, a ring of fire and variations of the "Playboy bunny." Other important symbols are tattoos; certain hair styles, including cutting gang designs in the hair; gold jewelry in gang symbols; and certain cars.

Hand signs show allegiance or opposition to another group. Most hand signs duplicate or modify the sign language used by those with hearing impairments. Occasionally, legitimate use of hand signs has jeopardized the users' safety. For example, two deaf women signing to each other on a street corner were shot and killed by gang members who thought they were members of a rival gang.

Representing, like hand signs, shows allegiance to a gang. It is a manner of dress that uses an imaginary line drawn vertically through the body. Anything to the left of the line represents "dress left" and vice versa. An example of right dress would be a hat cocked to the right side; right pants leg rolled up; a bandanna in gang colors tied around the right arm; one glove worn on the right hand; right-side pocket turned inside out and sometimes dyed gang colors; shoes or laces of the right shoe in gang colors; belt buckle worn loose on the right side; earrings worn in the right ear; and two fingernails on the right hand painted in gang colors.

Gangs establish **turf,** territorial boundaries, within which they operate and which they protect at all costs. A gang's turf is centered at its meeting place and spreads out through the community. The meeting place, which can be the backroom of a grocery store, the basement of a neighbor's home or a room in an abandoned building, provides a sanctuary when a gang member is in trouble, a refuge when home life is intolerable, a hideout from the police, a hiding place for weapons, a place to plot future gang activities, a retreat and a safe haven.

In the community, turf boundaries are well defined and often clearly specified among gangs in written pacts. Gangs also commonly define their boundaries and mark their turf by using **graffiti**—painted gang symbols on walls, buildings, bridges, bus stops and any other available public surface. Graffiti has very specific meanings to gangs and can be used to show opposition or contempt for rival gangs. By displaying another gang's symbols upside down, backward or crossed out, a gang delivers a serious insult to the rival. Any misrepresentation or destruction of a gang's graffiti may bring violent retribution against the offender. Likewise, if a gang crosses into another gang's territory, an event often marked by the defacement of the "home" gang's graffiti, it is understood that the response may be violent. Consequently, gangs seeking to acquire more turf may need to relocate to another community.

Prevalence and Expansion of Gangs

Gangs have been reported in all 50 states. According to a recent national survey, more than 80 percent of prosecutors in large cities acknowledge that gangs are a problem in their jurisdiction, that their numbers are growing and that levels of gang-related violence are increasing (McCorkle and Miethe, p. 41). A survey of U.S. law enforcement agencies found some type of youth gang problem existing in almost three-fourths of all cities with populations over 25,000 and in most suburban counties as well (OJJDP, *1996 National Youth Gang Survey,* 1999). Furthermore, in the largest U.S. cities, those with populations over 250,000, *all* of the responding police agencies reported gang problems.

An OJJDP Bulletin (1998) indicates youth gangs are especially widespread in certain cities with chronic gang problems. For example, Chicago is said to have around 132 gangs, with an estimated membership of 30,000 to 50,000 hard core members. Police in Los Angeles estimate the city ranks number one among all U.S. cities in terms of gang membership, with more than 58,000 gang members. Snyder and Sickmund (p. 78) contend the recent proliferation of gangs in smaller towns and rural areas across the country is *not* primarily the result of the physical migration of gang members from the larger cities:

> Some exceptionally well-organized gangs are thought to be engaged in interstate drug trafficking and to be deliberately expanding their reach through member relocation. But overall, migrating gang members are relatively few, and their

movements are attributable to normal residential relocation. Most law enforcement agencies regard their local gang problems as "home grown."

Petrone (2000) describes two conglomerate gangs, the People and the Folks, which originated in the Illinois penitentiary system and are now prevalent throughout the country. People consists mainly of the Vice Lords, Latin Kings and the Stones. They have the five-point star as their symbol and represent to the left. Folks consist primarily of the Disciples. They use a six-point star or a pitchfork and represent to the right.

The Internet may become a new avenue for gang expansion with gangs using the Web to reach new recruits and promote street gang alliance. Such technology may greatly enhance a gang's ability to expand its turf, while further complicating law enforcement efforts to keep track of gang members and their activities.

Gang Activities

Gangs have different characteristics based on the activities in which they engage. Some gangs are violent; others focus on crime commission with violence as a by-product. The same is true with a gang's relationship to drugs. Some focus on the drug business; others engage in business to meet their own drug needs. The OJJDP (1998) asserts: "Certain offenses are related to different racial/ethnic youth gangs. African-American gangs are relatively more involved in drug offenses; Hispanic gangs, in 'turf-related' violence; Asian and white gangs, in property crimes."

Indicators of gang activity include graffiti, drive-by shootings, intimidation assaults, murders and the open sale of drugs.

As mentioned, graffiti may appear on neighborhood buildings and walls to mark gang turf. Drive-by shootings, intimidation assaults and murders are also among the criminal activities of gangs. Residents of neighborhoods in which gangs flourish become filled with fear. Some citizens become virtual prisoners in their own homes, afraid of getting caught in the crossfire of a gang gun battle.

Some gangs sell drugs openly. Children as young as 11 or 12 are identified by the pagers they constantly carry as drug runners for gangs. The National Drug Intelligence Center reports more than 80 percent of the 1,250 significant gangs identified during a 1998 survey were involved in drug trafficking ("National Street Gang Survey," 1999, p. 21).

In a study comparison of gang and nongang criminal behavior (Huff, 1998, p. 4), gangs were found to differ most significantly in their commission rates of auto thefts and other types of thefts, intimidation and assault of victims and witnesses, drive-by shootings, carrying concealed weapons, possessing guns and/or knives in school, drug sales away from schools and drug thefts.

The Police Response

Typically, police chiefs in cities where gangs have recently arrived are slow to recognize the threat. If police chiefs deny a gang problem, despite mounting evidence, the gang problem often becomes unmanageable. On the other hand, if police publicly

Gang members at a national gang summit held in Kansas City in May 1993 displaying two fingers held together as a symbol of togetherness.

acknowledge the existence of gangs, this places the police administrator in a Catch-22. Publicly acknowledging gangs validates them and provides notoriety.

An important task in most police departments is gathering information or intelligence on gangs and their members.

Intelligence Gathering. Intelligence is knowing what gangs are out there, where they are, the names of the individual gang members and what gangs they belong to, where they have been seen and who they've been seen with.

A computerized Gang Intelligence System (GANGIS), including comprehensive gang profile data such as monikers and vehicle information, can be an effective crime-fighting tool.

National networks of gang intelligence databases can greatly enhance a department's effort to understand and respond to gang activities in their jurisdiction. Valdez (1999, p. 54) notes: "The Regional Information Sharing System (RISS) is a network between six regionalist intelligence databases . . . [and] has four components, one of which is a national gang database [RISS-GANGS]." RISS is a partnership among more than 4,500 federal, state and local law enforcement agencies. Another computer technology used for tracking gangs is the General Reporting, Evaluation and Tracking (GREAT) system—a combination hot sheet, mug book and file cabinet ("A G.R.E.A.T. Program . . . ," 1999). This system is not to be confused with the GREAT program used in schools to teach children about resisting gangs, discussed in Chapter 14. Over the past half century, the police response to gangs has included a variety of strategies, partnerships and programs, also presented in Chapter 14.

The Gang's Place within the Community

Despite a gang's desire for autonomy and rejection of outside authority, a relationship must still be maintained with the neighborhood and larger community. The OJJDP notes four factors that motivate gangs to make concerted efforts to establish ties with the community: (1) the gang's need for a "safe haven" and a place to exist; (2) the need for a recruitment pool from which to draw its membership; (3) the community's ability to provide important information such as details concerning other gang activity within the city; and (4) psychological reasons. Regarding this final factor, the OJJDP explains: "A bonding occurs between the gang and the community that builds a social adhesive that often takes a significant amount of time to completely dissolve."

These bonds may present a challenge to the dissipation and eradication of local gang activity and can hinder law enforcement's efforts to rally a community against the presence of such gangs.

According to the OJJDP: "Community ambivalence toward gangs exists because many of the gang members are children of residents, the gangs often provide protection for residents, residents identify with gangs because of their own or relatives' prior involvement, and the gang in some instances have become community institutions."

SUMMARY

A frequently overlooked segment of the population that is important to community policing implementation is youths. In 1998 the number of youths age 17 and under in the United States was nearly 70 million. Our juvenile justice system uses a one-pot jurisdictional approach, treating abused or neglected children, those who are status offenders and those who are truly criminal in the same way.

A justice model views youths as responsible for their own acts. Under the justice model, the good of society takes precedence over society's responsibility to take care of its children as in the welfare model. During the 1970s the handling of juveniles in the justice system focused on the Big Ds of deinstitutionalization, diversion, due process and decriminalization.

Children with special needs include those who are emotionally/behaviorally disturbed, have learning disabilities, have an attention deficit hyperactivity disorder or have behavior problems resulting from prenatal exposure to drugs, including alcohol, or to HIV.

Factors contributing to teen violence are a shift in adolescent attitudes toward the value of life, a desensitization to violence and the ready availability of handguns. For some youths, violence becomes a way of life when they join a gang. An estimated 850,000 gang members are active in nearly 31,000 gangs nationwide. A youth seeking protection, security, status, an identity and a sense of belonging can fulfill all of these needs through gang membership. Indicators of gang activity include graffiti, drive-by shootings, intimidation assaults, murders and the open sale of drugs.

A computerized Gang Intelligence System (GANGIS), including comprehensive gang profile data such as monikers and vehicle information, can be an effective crime-fighting tool. According to the OJJDP: "Community ambivalence toward gangs exists because many of the gang members are children of residents, the gangs often provide protection for residents, residents identify with gangs because of their own or relatives' prior involvement, and the gang in some instances have become community institutions."

PROBLEM SOLVING IN ACTION

Youths

In 1991 the Hamilton Wentworth (Ontario) Regional Police Community Service Traffic Safety Branch, concerned about traffic accidents involving school children, decided to evaluate its traffic safety program—"Elmer's Safety Rules." Delivered to first-graders, this 30-year-old program had an elephant mascot and consisted of seven traffic rules for children to follow.

Scanning. Police analyzed records of traffic collisions, focusing on children under age 16 who were pedestrians or cyclists. In 1990, 252 collisions involved the target group. Eighty percent involved children aged 6 to 8 and were "dart-out" collisions (children darting into traffic from between parked cars), a surprising result because one of Elmer's rules was not to play between parked cars.

Records from 1985 to 1989 were evaluated, with similar results. The number of collisions involving the target group averaged 250 annually over the five years studied. Again, almost 80 percent of accidents involving 6- to 8-year-olds were dart-out collisions.

Analysis. Officers determined that presenting Elmer's rules to first-graders didn't work. Realizing they needed to enlist the help of the community, the officers began calling people in related organizations, such as city traffic, public health, early education and parents' groups. After many calls and referrals, the officers invited people from a number of disciplines to take part in an advisory committee on traffic safety for children.

All the various groups were teaching traffic safety but using a different program, which led to a scattered and inconsistent approach. The advisory committee identified parents as the best teachers and formulated two clear goals. First, parents and caregivers must take an active role in providing traffic safety training to their children.

Second, a network of community organizations should assist parents, teaching the same message and reaching children whose parents might fail to educate them. The committee concluded community agencies must work together to address traffic safety issues, police officers are not the best safety educators, dart-out collisions are a major cause for concern, parents often fail to become involved in teaching traffic safety, and parents are an important part of any safety program.

The committee then studied existing programs and discovered a German program and book titled *Traffic Training: Parents Practice with Their Children* (English translation). They obtained permission to use the material in developing a similar program.

Response. The committee developed the Canadian version of this book—the KIDestrian book and education program—a series of simple, fun exercises that teach traffic safety, such as the idea of stopping at the curb or, in the book's terminology, developing "Kid Brakes." Other exercises teach crossing safely at mid-block and between parked cars.

Field tests were conducted to determine program effectiveness in communities where English is a second language, and revisions were made, after which a rough prototype of the book was produced and corporate sponsorships solicited. Canadian Tire's Child Protection Foundation offered $19,000 to produce a quality prototype of the book, available in both English and French. The estimated $25,000 needed to print 20,000 copies was generated through fundraising.

The KIDestrian Team was next developed to incorporate community input in making administrative decisions relating to the program. The team included police and community members. The national postal company offered to package and distribute the materials at no cost and to put KIDestrian advertising posters on all postal trucks.

The team sent letters and order forms to school principals, recreation centers and neighborhood associations, day care centers and home care providers, home-school organizations, parent associations, public health nurses, police officers and city traffic officials. In addition, the police video training branch produced a promotional video.

Assessment. Parents eagerly requested the books, as did community organizations. Since the team has not yet been able to measure the program's effect on reducing child traffic injuries, program assessment focused on whether the KIDestrian program reached its intended audiences and whether those audiences found it useful. Evaluation revealed that the KIDestrian program did indeed reach its intended audiences and that people found it useful.

As a result of the evaluations, the books have been redesigned, with new sections on rural and railroad-crossing safety. Elmer the safety elephant is still alive and well but now has help teaching traffic safety.

[Adapted from Kenneth Bond and Scott Rastin. "Police, Parents Team up to Teach Traffic Safety." *Problem-Solving Quarterly*, Spring/Summer 1995, p. 8.] *Reprinted by permission of the Police Executive Research Forum.*

PROBLEM SOLVING IN ACTION

Gangs

In Friendship Lane, a one-square-block area of Reno, Nevada, 95 percent of the residents are non-English-speaking Hispanics. Most work at low-income jobs, and many have extended families living in two-bedroom duplexes. Local gangs moved in by intimidating the residents. Reno police received numerous calls for service based on gang-related incidents, including drive-by shootings, loud parties, drinking in public and drugs.

Scanning. Officers gathered information from a number of sources including citizen meetings, calls for service, field interviews with gang members and officer observations.

A review of calls for service showed 255 calls from January to June 1995. Of these, 11 percent were gang related. Eleven percent of the total calls required a return visit by the officer; 9 per-cent involved crimes such as burglary, property destruction, auto theft and larceny; and 5 percent pertained to suspicious people and vehicles in the area.

The Reno Police Department Community Action Team (CAT) that works with local gangs had conducted several field interviews with gang members in the area. That information was reviewed for times, dates and circumstances of activity. Several officers on various shifts also drove through the area making independent observations.

The gang involved was a large Hispanic group, the Montellos (after a local street). According to the CAT's field interviews, no members lived in the area. The residents were easy prey for this gang, who threatened them if they called the police. Cultural and language barriers between residents and police resulted in many incidents going unreported and residents distrusting the police. The gang felt free to strip stolen vehicles, drink in public and use abandoned apartments to take drugs and store weapons used in drive-by shootings.

Analysis. Residents' growing concern about safety and an increase in drive-by shootings led to a series of community meetings that confirmed and added to the information gathered.

Officers asked residents what they thought the problems were and what they wanted the police to do. The residents listed several problems, but the number-one problem was the gang. Their graffiti was ruining the area's appearance, and residents were tired of the neighborhood's reputation as a gang-infested area. They also voiced serious concerns about their children's safety because the streets lacked lighting and gang members who drove their "low-rider" vehicles through the streets at high speeds would not see the children playing.

Information from residents, police and field interviews revealed two main factors that empowered the gang to act in this neighborhood: (1) poor communication between residents and police due to language and cultural barriers and intimidation of residents by gang members; and (2) environmental factors, such as poor lighting and streets well suited for fast driving.

Response. In the past the department had responded with a high level of visibility and enforcement. However, when the police directed their attention to other areas, the problem would resurface. Officers decided to build working relationships with community residents to gain their trust and support. They decided on several clean-up efforts to promote better police-community relations and improve the area's physical appearance.

The police contacted the media at the beginning of the response phase and did a walk-through of the neighborhood with them, explaining their approaches to eliminating the gang problem. Public awareness and support from the media stimulated businesses to assist in the project with donations.

The first step was a community clean-up day. The local disposal service donated three large dumpsters. Rakes, shovels and brooms were also donated, and a local tow company lent the community a truck. The abandoned cars were towed, the dumpsters were filled and removed, and the area was swept from one end to the other. Graffiti on the buildings was painted over, with businesses donating enough paint and equipment for all neighborhood duplexes to be painted.

The next phase of the project was lighting improvement. The local power company, with the city's cooperation, erected four large street lights in the darkest areas. A local hardware store donated 30 motion-detector lights, enough for each duplex. And a local construction company, doing the work at no charge, repaved the streets and added speed bumps to thwart speeding vehicles.

As a final step, police helped residents start a neighborhood watch group and plan regular monthly meetings to discuss crime issues. Police also developed a community advisory group that provided information on government services for residents.

Assessment. The residents were empowered to handle many problems themselves as they gained trust in the police department.

The calls for service were compared between the first six months of the year and the second six months, the project period. Although calls for service increased during the project period, this may be attributed to the residents' increased trust in the police department. Calls regarding gang activity, however, decreased by 100 percent, while calls regarding unwanted people in the area decreased by 50 percent. Additionally, family disturbance calls decreased 50 percent, an unexpected benefit of the community cohesion the project created.

The officers conducted a resident survey to assess the project's impact. They went with translators to every house in the community and questioned at least one member of each household. The survey had 10 questions in both English and Spanish. Because the residents'

number-one concern had been the gang problem, officers asked which activity completed seemed most successful at reducing the gang problem. Ninety percent said the improved lighting made the most difference, while others listed the neighborhood watch and the clean-up projects. In addition, officers asked residents to rate the department's performance in the neighborhood; all respondents gave the department the highest possible score. All the surveyed residents said they felt safer after the project.

[Adapted from Dave Bernardy. "Neighborhood Is Finally Free of Gang-Related Problems." *Problem-Solving Quarterly*, Spring/Summer 1995, pp. 1, 6–7.] *Reprinted by permission of the Police Executive Research Forum.*

DISCUSSION QUESTIONS

1. Do you feel the juvenile justice system should follow a welfare model or a justice model?

2. What examples of street justice have you witnessed? Do you think street justice is fair?

3. Do you feel status offenses should be decriminalized?

4. When you were a teenager, did you get into any trouble with the law?

5. At what age did you feel you should be considered an adult?

6. How does a street gang differ from a group such as a Boy Scout troop or a school club?

7. What do you think are the main reasons individuals join gangs?

8. How does a street gang member differ from other juvenile delinquents?

9. If you were to try to infiltrate a gang as an undercover agent, what factors would be important to you?

10. Do you think the gang problem will increase or decrease in the coming years? Why?

INFOTRAC COLLEGE EDITION ASSIGNMENTS

- Use InfoTrac to help answer the discussion questions as appropriate.
- Injunctions against gangs have been a highly successful strategy in some cities and states. Research the controversy surrounding the constitutionality of using injunctions in this way. Be prepared to share your findings with the class.
- The City of Boston, using community policing strategies, recently won an Innovations in American Government Award for its *Operation Cease Fire*. Research this much-replicated program and explain why it was considered innovative and how it affected gang violence and teenage deaths by handguns.

COMMUNITY PROJECTS

- Have youths committed any violent crimes in your community within the last few months?
- Are there gangs in your community? If so, do they cause problems for the police?
- Are there efforts in your community to combat the gang problem?

REFERENCES

Association for Children with Learning Disabilities. "Taking the First Step to Solving Learning Problems." Pittsburgh: Association for Children with Learning Disabilities (no date).

Bernard, Thomas J. "Juvenile Crime and the Transformation of Juvenile Justice: Is There a Juvenile Crime Wave?" *Justice Quarterly,* Vol. 16, No. 2, June 1999, pp. 337–356.

Bernardy, Dave. "Neighborhood Is Finally Free of Gang-Related Problems." *Problem-Solving Quarterly,* Spring/Summer 1995, pp. 1, 6–7.

Bond, Kenneth and Rastin, Scott. "Police, Parents Team up to Teach Traffic Safety." Problem-Solving Quarterly, Spring/Summer 1995, p. 8.

"Boy Who Shot Girl Lived in Squalor Amid Guns, Drugs." In *New York Times,* as reported by (Minneapolis/St. Paul) *Star Tribune,* March 2, 2000, pp. A1, A22.

Combating Violence and Delinquency: The National Juvenile Justice Action Plan. Washington, DC: Coordinating Council on Juvenile Justice and Delinquency Prevention, March 1996.

Doyle, Grey. "Juvenile Violence: Identifying the At-Risk Teenager." *Law and Order,* Vol. 44, No. 6, June 1996, pp. 90–92.

Drowns, Robert W. and Hess, Kären M. *Juvenile Justice,* 3rd ed. Belmont, CA: Wadsworth Publishing Company, 2000.

Eitzen, Stanley. "Problem Students: The Sociocultural Roots." *Phi Delta Kappan,* April 1992, pp. 584–590.

Esbensen, Finn-Aage; Winfree, L. Thomas, Jr.; He, Ni; and Taylor, Terrance J. "Youth Gangs and Definitional Issues: When Is a Gang a Gang, and Why Does It Matter?" *Crime & Delinquency,* Vol. 47, No. 1, January 2001, pp. 105–130.

"A G.R.E.A.T. Program: Stopping Gang Violence before It Starts." *Law and Order,* Vol. 47, No. 2, February 1999, pp. 73–74.

Huff, C. Ronald. *Comparing the Criminal Behavior of Youth Gangs and At Risk Youths.* National Institute of Justice Research in Brief, October 1998, p. 4. (NCJ-172851)

Johnson, Tim. "Community Policing: America's Best Chance to End Youth Violence."

Community Policing Exchange, January/ February 1996, p. 1.

Martin, Deirdre. "Teen Violence: Why It's on the Rise and How to Stem Its Tide." *Law Enforcement Technology,* Vol. 21, No. 1, January 1994, pp. 36–42.

McCorkle, Richard C. and Miethe, Terance D. "The Political and Organizational Response to Gangs: An Examination of a 'Moral Panic' in Nevada." *Justice Quarterly,* Vol. 15, No. 1, March 1998, pp. 41–64.

"National Street Gang Survey." *FBI Law Enforcement Bulletin,* Vol. 68, No. 7, July 1999, p. 21.

Office of Juvenile Justice and Delinquency Prevention. http://www.ojjdp.ncjrs.org

Office of Juvenile Justice and Delinquency Prevention. *1996 National Youth Gang Survey.* Washington, DC: Office of Juvenile Justice and Delinquency Prevention, 1999.

Office of Juvenile Justice and Delinquency Prevention. *Youth Gangs: An Overview.* Washington, DC: Office of Juvenile Justice and Delinquency Prevention, Juvenile Justice Bulletin, August 1998. http://ojjdp.ncjrs.org/ jjbulletin/9808/

Osman, Karen and Haskins, James. *Street Gangs Yesterday and Today, West Side Story Home Page.* 1996, pp. 1–5.

Petrone, Frank M. "People and Folks Street Gangs." *Law and Order,* Vol. 48, No. 12, December 2000, pp. 62–65.

Rowell, James D. "Kids' Needs and the Attraction of Gangs." *Police,* Vol. 24, No. 6, June 2000, p. 35.

Ruben, David. "What Makes a Child Violent?" *Parenting,* August 1998, pp. 96–102.

Serious and Violent Juvenile Offenders. Washington, DC: Office of Juvenile Justice and Delinquency Prevention, Juvenile Justice Bulletin, May 1998. (NCJ-170027)

Shelden, Randall G.; Tracy, Sharon K.; and Brown, William B. *Youth Gangs in American Society,* 2nd ed. Belmont, CA: Wadsworth, 2001.

Snyder, Howard. *Juvenile Arrests 1998.* Washington, DC: Office of Juvenile Justice and Delinquency Prevention, 1999. Internet citation: http://ojjdp.ncjrs.org/ojstatbb/qa256.html

Snyder, H.; Poole, R.; and Wan, Y. *"Easy Access to Juvenile Populations 1998."* http://www.ojjdp.ncjrs.org

Snyder, Howard N. and Sickmund, Melissa. *Juvenile Offenders and Victims: 1999 National Report.* Washington, DC: National Center for Juvenile Justice, September 1999. http://www.ncjrs.org/html/ojjdp/ nationalreport99/ (NCJ-178257).

Springer, Charles E. *Justice for Juveniles.* Washington, DC: U.S. Department of Justice, Office of Juvenile Justice and Delinquency Prevention, 1986.

U.S. Bureau of the Census. "Resident Population Estimates by Age and Sex, 1999." www.census.gov

Valdez, Al. "New Gang Trends?" *Police,* Vol. 24, No. 11, November 2000, pp. 66–67.

Valdez, Al. "Using Technology in the War against Gangs." *Police,* Vol. 23, No. 7, July 1999, pp. 52–54.

Zatz, Marjorie S. and Portillos, Edwardo L. "Voices from the Barrio: Chicano Gangs, Families, and Communities." *Criminology,* Vol. 38, No. 2, May 2000, pp. 369–401.

RESOURCES

Centers for Disease Control and Prevention, 1600 Clifton Rd., Atlanta, GA 30333; (800) 311–3435. http://www.cdc.gov

Learning Disabilities Assoc. of America, 4156 Library Road, Pittsburgh, PA 15234; (412) 341-1515. www.idanatl.org

Office of Juvenile Justice and Delinquency Prevention (OJJDP), 633 Indiana Avenue NW,

Washington, DC 20531; (202) 724-7782. www.ojjdp.ncjrs.org

"Together We Can Make a Difference." Pennsylvania Commission on Crime and Delinquency. www.pccd.state.pa.us

CHAPTER 10

Interacting with Victims and Witnesses

In the Nation's ongoing fight against crime, statistics tell only part of the story. More than a violation of the law, every crime is a violation of the rights, property, person, or trust of another human being. Thus, behind every tally of offenses ranging from misdemeanors to aggravated felonies are innocent victims—individuals and families who must be recognized in the administration of justice.

 —President George Bush, April 22, 1991
 Proclamation of National Crime Victims
 Rights Week

Do you know

How extensive victimization is?

How victims may be affected?

Who is most at risk of being victimized?

What major legislation regarding victims has been passed?

What national organizations exist to help victims?

What two types of programs have been established to help victims? What services are most commonly provided in each?

What rights victims have in most states?

What special populations have been targeted for additional needs if victimized?

How likely the elderly are to be crime victims?

What the usual police response should be in cases of elder abuse?

What a police officer's first concern is with an abused or neglected child?

How exposure to violence affects children?

Can you define these terms:

cognitive restructuring

culpability

elder abuse

granny bashing

granny dumping

post traumatic stress disorder
   (PTSD)

primary victim

second injury

secondary victim

victim compensation programs

victim impact statement (VIS)

victim statement of opinion
   (VSO)

victimology

victim/witness assistance
   programs

vulnerability

INTRODUCTION

If you haven't been there, you don't know the feelings of emptiness and fear and how it changes your life. I was in a state of shock. I walked around in a daze for weeks. I wasn't functioning. No one really understood how I felt.

—Sherry Price, rape victim.

Victimization is a much more extensive problem than people often realize. Strandberg (1997, p. 48) stresses:

> One of the most important things is for law enforcement to be sensitive to the needs of victims and witnesses. Witnesses are essential to the successful prosecution of any case, and working with witnesses to make them feel more comfortable and safe will certainly pay dividends. . . .
>
> Most experts feel that community policing is a major step in the right direction to curb implicit intimidation. When people know the police as members of their own community, they are much more willing to come forward.

This chapter begins by examining the extent of victimization and the distinction between primary and secondary victims. Next the results of being victimized are discussed, followed by a look at victim recovery and victimology. Victim assistance legislation, organizations and programs are then presented, as well as the victim's bill of rights. Next, the police response to victims is highlighted, followed by a look at special victim populations, including immigrants, people with disabilities, the elderly, youths and battered and sexually assaulted women. The chapter concludes with a discussion of the response of the criminal justice system to victims, a review of restorative justice and consideration of the direction of victims' rights and services in the 21st century. Although the material presented here focuses primarily on communicating with victims, most of it also applies to communicating with witnesses to crime.

◉ THE EXTENT OF VICTIMIZATION

According to Lurigio and Mechanic (2000, p. 22): "On the average, more than 40 million criminal victimizations and attempted victimizations take place each year in the

United States." The Bureau of Justice Statistics (BJS), through its annual National Crime Victimization Survey (NCVS), tracks victimization trends in the United States and reports (2000) U.S. residents age 12 and older experienced approximately 28.8 million crimes in 1999: 21.2 million (74 percent) were property crimes; 7.4 million (25 percent) were crimes of violence; and 0.2 million (1 percent) were personal thefts. The survey also revealed that in 1999, for every 1,000 persons age 12 or older, there occurred two rapes or sexual assaults, two assaults with serious injury and four robberies.

The good news, according to the BJS, is that from 1998 to 1999 the violent crime rate declined 10 percent, reaching the lowest level in NCVS history, and property crime declined 9 percent, continuing a more than 20-year decline.

The National Crime Victimization Survey estimates 28.8 million victimizations were committed against U.S. residents age 12 or older in 1999.

In addition to dealing with victims of crime, police officers also frequently deal with victims of accidents and natural disasters and should thus be trained to assist such victims. Officers may also encounter and be required to handle secondary victims.

◉ PRIMARY VS. SECONDARY VICTIMS

Two types of victims may result from natural disasters or violent crime. A **primary victim** is a person actually harmed by an incident. A **secondary victim** is one indirectly affected by the trauma. In a rape, for example, the woman is, obviously, the primary victim. Her husband

Police officers may also be victims. This police officer was riding on routine patrol in Canton, Massachusetts, when a drunk driver sped down the road and struck the horse and officer. The impact crushed the horse's rear leg. The severely injured horse was given a lethal injection.

may be a secondary victim who also suffers from the trauma. A secondary victim includes anyone who is close to the primary victim and can truly empathize with that victim.

It is vital for the criminal justice system to recognize and be sensitive to the difficulties faced by secondary victims—the friends and family members of crime victims.

RESULTS OF BEING VICTIMIZED

Lurigio and Mechanic (p. 26) observe: "Victimization can destroy people's basic trust of the world, challenge their assumptions about personal safety and security, and disrupt their abilities to function at work, school, and home." A study by Kilpatrick et al. (1998, p. 8) found:

> Crime victims experience a variety of losses relating to the crime. They may sustain physical or psychological injuries, with some victims requiring counseling. They may lose money or suffer property destruction, loss, or damage. Victims may lose time from work or school as a result of their injuries or as a consequence of time spent consulting with law enforcement or prosecutors, or attendance at court proceedings.

Officers are advised to counsel victims that lapses of concentration, memory losses, depression and physical ailments are normal reactions to being victimized. Furthermore, officers should be aware that the results of victimization vary depending on the specific crime committed and the individual who is victimized.

Protest against beating of illegal immigrants.

AP/Wide World Photos

Victims of crime may suffer physical injury, financial and property losses, emotional distress and psychological trauma. Some suffer from post traumatic stress disorder (PTSD), a persistent reexperiencing of a traumatic event through intrusive memories, dreams and a variety of anxiety-related symptoms.

PTSD, once referred to as battle fatigue or shell shock, used to apply only to war veterans. However, the medical community now recognizes it as a mental disorder that may afflict anyone who experiences trauma, such as physical or sexual abuse, the witnessing of violence and murder, or the suffering of any other type of victimization. As Heiskell (2000, p. 10) explains:

> PTSD is a syndrome that is a collection of symptoms. Individuals with PTSD may relive the distressing event again and again in dreams, thoughts or flashbacks. They are sometimes overly sensitive to loud noises. Emotional and psychological numbness, in which little interest is shown in old friends or important activities, may occur along with a feeling of being cut off from other people and friends.
>
> The emotional trauma may also leave individuals with PTSD tense and irritable. Individuals sometimes suffer from what is called hypervigilance, a condition in which there is a preoccupation with possible unknown threats. Some individuals demonstrate agitated behavior and outbursts of anger. They often have no sense of a future with no expectation of having a family or career. Difficulty concentrating and sleeping may grow to the point that it interferes with daily life.

Heiskell (p. 10) notes that people with PTSD may also experience a variety of physical and psychological problems, including chronic pain, substance abuse, phobias, panic attacks, anxiety, depression and suicide. Brogan (1999, p. 33) adds: "Other frequently observed accompanying symptoms [of PTSD] include . . . survival guilt, impulsive behavior and impairment in memory and concentration."

Police officers may also experience these symptoms, including PTSD, after responding to shooting incidents or other especially grisly crimes. In many cases, however, they either fail to recognize the symptoms or choose not to acknowledge them. Dumont (1999, p. 96) cautions:

> Many affected officers take the macho-superman approach, denying the existence of a problem and the need for treatment. Denial does not cure the symptoms or eliminate the associated problems. It can only exacerbate the problems and retard the recovery process. . . .
>
> It is extremely important that [officers] realize that the symptoms they may be experiencing are common and treatable. . . . Self medication with alcohol or drugs has no place in the recovery process and should be avoided at all costs.

Dumont (p. 97) notes that many police departments now employ a peer assistance program to help officers with PTSD: "Peer support is vital to the recovery process in that it allows the officer an opportunity to vent his/her feelings to someone who has 'been there, done that' and understands what they are experiencing."

The impact of victimization and the way individuals react to it is related to whether they report the incident to the police.

Nonreporting of Victimization

Victims and witnesses are a major source of common crime information known to law enforcement. Many victims feel it is their civic duty to report victimization and hope doing so will bring offenders to justice. Others report crimes simply because they want to recover their property or file an insurance claim. In the absence of such motivators, however, a large percentage of robberies, aggravated assaults, burglaries and rapes go unreported to the police. Victims may consider the matter private, feel ashamed, believe the police will be unable to do anything, expect the police to belittle the trauma or delay filing a report while discussing with family or friends what action to take.

Some victims and witnesses fear threats or retaliation from the offender(s). It is important for law enforcement to encourage the reporting of crime by reassuring victims and witnesses they will be protected against threats, intimidation or reprisals by the victimizers.

Victim and Witness Intimidation. Trauma to a victim or witness may continue after the criminal event through terrorization by the offender. In fact, many victims of violent crimes are warned by their attackers that going to the police will result in dire consequences for either the victims themselves or people they care about.

One reason gangs flourish is that they operate through intimidation, both inside and outside of court. Police must often deal with courtroom intimidation. Sometimes the court is packed with gang members who give threatening looks and suggestive signals to witnesses. Some departments counter this tactic by taking classes of police cadets into the courtroom. Confronted with this law enforcement presence, gang members usually give up and leave.

Further Victimization of Victims by the Criminal Justice System and Others

Victims may be emotionally hurt by the doctors, nurses and police officers they encounter immediately following their victimization, expecting more warmth and reassurance than these professionals can give. However, professionals who routinely deal with victims often assume businesslike attitudes as coping mechanisms, to protect themselves emotionally and allow them to function effectively in crises. When victims are treated badly by professionals who should assist them, including police officers, or interpret the necessary emotional detachment of such professionals as a personal rejection, victims receive what is commonly referred to as the **second injury.**

Lurigio and Mechanic (p. 25) observe: "Victims can be 'victimized' a second time by the unsympathetic reactions of police and attorneys, unnecessary trips to court, inadequate protection against offender intimidation and poor handling of property." This sentiment is echoed by Susan Herman, Director of the National Center for Victims of Crime (NCVC), who states: "In giving a statement to police, [victims] are sometimes made to feel like they are being interrogated" (Rosen, 1999, p. 8).

Many victims and their families think the criminal justice system treats defendants better than it treats them. In fact, the label "criminal justice" seems to place the emphasis on the rights of the accused criminal, rights that victims may perceive as inequities.

For example, when suspects are arrested, they must be informed of their rights; they are provided legal representation at the state's expense if they cannot afford their own lawyer; they are fed, clothed and given medical care while incarcerated; they may receive psychological counseling or treatment for substance abuse; they can be present at all criminal proceedings; they are entitled to confront their accuser(s) in court; and they may appeal to a higher court if found guilty.

To combat and eliminate the alienation many victims feel within the criminal justice system, Herman has suggested an innovative vision of justice—a new communal response to victims in addition to the established communal response to offenders: "We call this the search for parallel justice because we think it's trying to find a path for justice for victims, not just finding justice for offenders. This doesn't in any way say that we can't continue with the criminal justice system, with community justice and restorative justice efforts. Those are good as far as they go, but they don't go far enough in addressing the needs of victims." Herman (p. 9) concludes:

> I think it's always important to remember that only one out of three victims ever report crimes, and only 20 percent of those cases result in arrest. So if you think about what opportunities the crime system has to provide any relief or justice for victims, you're talking about a very small percentage of crime victims in this country. That's why we need to think about a system that helps all crime victims who are suffering trauma, suffering losses of money, property, jobs, mental health, academic achievement, all of that. We need to find a way to help them, and not rely on a criminal justice system that's not designed for them anyway.

Robinson (2000, p. 6) asserts: "The rights of crime victims must be high on our list of law enforcement priorities. Unless we teach our police officers and first responders the skills of compassion and show that sensitivity and sympathy are important tools in their arsenal for peace and safety, victims will continue to be victims."

◉ VICTIM RECOVERY

In general, officers should encourage crime victims to reestablish their normal routines as quickly as possible to help speed their recovery. However, a variety of factors affects how a victim recovers from a traumatic event, including the victim's age, sex, education, income and history of prior victimization. In general, younger victims cope better than older ones; women are more distressed by crime than men; victims with little formal education and low incomes are more traumatized than victims from higher socioeconomic and educational groups; and those who have been previously victimized typically adjust to the trauma more poorly.

The seriousness of the crime also affects victim recovery, with the severity of victim symptoms directly related to the degree of violence or injury. A victim's recovery is also affected by the victim's perception of the incident and their ability to cognitively restructure what happened. **Cognitive restructuring** is a coping mechanism where victims reinterpret the incident to minimize its adverse effects. For example, they may tell themselves, "It could have been worse" or may see the event as a test of character.

Sometimes, however, victims have difficulty recovering from a traumatic event because they succumb to self-blame or believe others hold them at fault for the victimization. The role victims play in their own victimization is a controversial concept addressed within the study of victimology.

◐ VICTIMOLOGY

During the 1940s scholars became interested in the relationship between criminals and their victims. Researchers in the 1940s and 1950s postulated that in a large percentage of cases, victims were partially responsible for their victimization. In *The Criminal and His Victim*, for example, von Hentig (1948) concludes that personality characteristics of some crime victims contributed to their victimization and that others became victims because of the community in which they lived.

Benjamin Mendelsohn coined the term *victimology* and proposed that this be a new field of study, not simply a branch of criminology. **Victimology,** the study of crime victims, includes the concepts of victims' vulnerability and culpability. **Vulnerability** suggests that certain groups of people are more susceptible to being victimized because of demographics rather than any unique, individual attributes.

Bureau of Justice statistics show that those most at risk of being victimized are young, black males with low incomes who live in urban areas.

In addition to vulnerability, victimology also examines culpability. **Culpability** refers to any action of the victim that may in some measure contribute to their victimization. For example, victims of auto theft may share responsibility for theft if they left the keys in the ignition and the car unlocked. The person who continues to live with a violent spouse may share responsibility for being repeatedly abused. The rape victim walking alone after dark in "sexy" or suggestive clothing may be "asking for it" when attacked.

The impact of victim vulnerability and culpability on crime has been described by Cohen and Felson's Routine Activities Theory (1979), which, as Buerger (1999, p. 151) explains:

> . . . proposes that crime occurs during the intersection, in time and space, of motivated offenders and suitable victims (or targets), under circumstances of absent or inadequate guardianship: a Crime Triangle similar to the fire triangle of fuel, heat and oxygen. Crime was presumed amenable to suppression if any of the three legs of the triangle [victim, suspect or location] was removed, or neutralized.

Culpability is controversial because "blaming the victim" shifts some responsibility from the criminal onto the injured party. Teresa Saldana, an actress who received nearly fatal stab wounds from a demented fan, explained this "blame-the-victim" syndrome following her attack in saying people told her she had no business walking alone and that actresses had to expect these things. Another victim likened the aftermath of a trauma to becoming a leper, noting how they were no longer invited to social events and were dropped by friends who were unable to relate, were afraid to bring up the subject, or who thought being supportive meant advising the victim to just snap out of it, get over it and move on.

Frequently society treats victims badly because people want to distance themselves from victims. Associating with victims makes people uncomfortable and may lead to an irrational fear that "If it can happen to them, then I'm vulnerable too." This may also partially explain why people do not want to get involved and, in fact, may not come to the aid of someone in distress. Often police officers and the entire criminal justice system add "insult to injury" rather than assisting victims.

ASSISTING VICTIMS

Society has made progress in assisting victims of crime. In 1981 then-President Ronald Reagan proclaimed National Victims of Crime Week, putting the full weight and influence of his office behind the victims' movement. In 1982 Reagan created a Task Force on Victims of Crime to undertake an extensive study on crime victimization. Since then, a variety of legislation, organizations and programs have been created to help victims receive the assistance they need.

Legislation

In 1982 Congress passed the Federal Victim and Witness Protection Act, recognizing that without the cooperation of victims, the criminal justice system would cease to function. This act established guidelines to ensure the fair treatment of victims and witnesses in the federal criminal justice system; criminal penalties to protect victims and witnesses from intimidation or retaliation, including provisions for civil restraining orders; and victim restitution. It also allowed the consideration of victims' situations in bail determinations. Perhaps most important, the act gave a voice to victims within the criminal justice system by allowing victim impact statements to be contained in presentence reports.

The Federal Victim and Witness Protection Act of 1982 (VWPA) established the victim impact statement (VIS) as a formal part of the presentence report.

The **victim impact statement (VIS)** is a written report describing in detail the full effect of a crime on the victim and is the principle means for communicating to the court the emotional impact and financial loss incurred. It helps ensure that restitution amounts are accurate and reflect the actual loss sustained. It may influence final sentences imposed by the court and may help victims recover psychologically.

Another important piece of legislation is the 1984 Victims of Crime Act (VOCA), which established an innovative funding mechanism that takes money away from convicted criminals to provide services to crime victims. The Crime Victims Fund, financed by federal criminals, is derived from criminal fines, penalties and bond forfeitures. The fund is administered by the Office for Victims of Crime (OVC), which plays a leadership role in the victims movement by supplying, reinforcing and encouraging the expansion of state compensation and assistance programs.

The Victims of Crime Act (VOCA), passed in 1984, established a fund making state grants available for victims' compensation, victim assistance programs and child abuse prevention and treatment.

The Crime Control Act of 1990 strengthened the Victim and Witness Act by mandating services and rights be accorded to all crime victims by employees of the federal criminal justice system engaged in detecting, investigating or prosecuting crime. These rights and protections were listed under Title V of the act that, in effect, created a Federal Crime Victims' Bill of Rights and codified the services to be made available.

The Seventy-Fourth Legislative session made a number of important changes to the Crime Victims' Compensation Act, including increasing the dollar amounts of certain benefits, adding new types of benefits available through the fund and expanding the definitions of those eligible for benefits under the act. A later congressional session created the provision of allowing the use of victim impact statements in sentencing convicted offenders in federal cases involving violent and sexual abuse crimes.

States usually compensate crime victims for medical expenses, rehabilitation, mental health counseling, replacement services and lost wages. Most states also compensate survivors of deceased victims for funeral expenses and loss of support. Few states compensate for property losses, and those that do often set strict limits on amounts and restrict eligibility to elderly victims.

Another alternative available to crime victims is to seek civil legal remedies, that is, to sue.

Organizations

Providing help to crime victims originated as a grassroots effort in the 1960s and 1970s to help battered women and victims of sexual assault. The first national organization to support victims' rights was the National Organization for Victim Assistance (NOVA), founded in 1976 in Fresno, California, by a small group of victim advocates. NOVA (1) helped formulate and pass the Victims of Crime Act, the Victim and Witness Protection Act, the Justice Assistance Act and bills of rights for victims; (2) provided crisis counseling, information, referral and assistance services to victims; and (3) provided local victim assistance programs with updated information on how best to serve their victim clients.

In 1986 NOVA established a Crisis Response Team (CRT) to assist communities that experienced disasters such as plane crashes, forest fires and shootings. CRT is a national network of trained volunteers who respond to a community's request for help. A team typically consists of a coordinator, mental health professional, law enforcement representative, medical specialist, member of the clergy and media liaison.

The Office for Victims of Crime (OVC) was established by the 1984 Victims of Crime Act (VOCA) to oversee diverse programs that benefit victims of crime. The OVC's mission is to enhance the nation's capacity to assist crime victims and to provide leadership in changing attitudes, policies and practices to promote justice and healing for all victims of crime. The OVC provides substantial funding to state victim assistance and compensation programs, the lifeline services that help victims to heal. The agency also supports trainings designed to educate criminal justice and allied professionals regarding the rights and needs of crime victims. The OVC is one of five bureaus and four offices with grant-making authority within the Office of Justice Programs, U.S. Department of Justice.

The National Victim Center, founded in 1985 and formerly called the Sunny von Bulow National Victim Advocacy Center, offers a broad range of programs including (1) training for personnel involved in rape crisis counseling, counseling survivors of homicide victims, child protection activities and assistance with domestic violence cases; (2) working for constitutional amendments creating "victims' bills of rights"; (3) providing information referral to individual crime victim service agencies; (4) maintaining a database on victims' rights; and (5) maintaining a database of the names and addresses of over 7,000 victim assistance agencies nationwide.

Organizations dedicated to helping victims include the National Organization for Victim Assistance (NOVA), founded in 1976; the Office for Victims of Crime (OVC), founded in 1984; and the National Victim Center, founded in 1985.

Other victim organizations have been formed including Mothers against Drunk Driving, Students against Drunk Driving, Parents of Murdered Children, the National Organization of Victim Assistance and Victims for Victims. In addition, victim compensation laws and victim advocacy and protection programs attempt to address what is widely perceived as the system's protection of the accused's rights to the victim's detriment.

One trend in victimization is for victims or secondary victims to become spokespersons and work for victims' rights and tougher sentencing. Examples include Fred Goldman, Denise Brown and Patty Wetterling.

Programs Implemented

Numerous programs have been implemented to help victims deal with the financial and emotional fallout of victimization.

The two main types of programs provided for victims are

- victim compensation programs *that help crime victims cope with crime-related expenses such as medical costs, mental health counseling, lost wages and funeral or burial costs.*
- victim/witness assistance programs *that provide services such as crisis support, peer support, referrals to counseling, advocacy within the justice system and, in some cases, emergency shelter.*

Crime victim compensation programs have been established in every state. Programs are based on identified needs of victims and witnesses. The most frequent services provided by victim/witness programs are summarized in Table 10.1.

In addition to the passage of legislation to provide funding and services for victims and the formation of victims' organizations and programs, progress has also been made in formalizing the rights of victims.

Table 10.1   Victim-Witness Program Services

Emergency Services	Claims Assistance
Medical care	Insurance claims aid
Shelter or food	Restitution assistance
Security repair	Compensation assistance
Financial assistance	Witness fee assistance
On-scene comfort	**Court-Related Services**
Counseling	Witness reception
24-hour hotline	Court orientation
Crisis intervention	Notification
Follow-up counseling	Witness alert
Mediation	Transportation
Advocacy and Support Services	Child care
Personal advocacy	Escort to court
Employer intervention	Victim impact reports
Landlord intervention	**Systemwide Services**
Property return	Public education
Intimidation protection	Legislative advocacy
Legal/paralegal counsel	Training
Referral	

SOURCE: Peter Finn and Beverly Lee. *Establishing and Expanding Victim Witness Assistance Programs.* Washington: National Institute of Justice, 1988. Reprinted by permission.

◆ VICTIMS' BILL OF RIGHTS

The struggle of individuals and groups to gain legal rights has occurred throughout history: civil rights, workers' rights, students' rights, women's rights, gay rights and prisoners' rights. This struggle was joined by victims' rights advocates in the late 1970s and 1980s.

In 1980 Wisconsin became the first state to enact a bill of rights for crime victims. Today every state has laws protecting victims' rights. Furthermore, victims' rights have been strengthened in 29 states by constitutional mandate. However, efforts to approve an amendment for victims' rights have been consistently unsuccessful: "The crime victims' rights Constitutional amendment advanced to the Senate floor but was withdrawn at the request of its sponsors when it became clear that it would fail if brought to a vote. . . . Opponents argued amending the Constitution was too drastic a step to take to ensure that such rights are honored" ("Constitutional Amendment Fails . . . ," 2000, p. 1).

Victims and witnesses have two basic rights: the right to obtain certain information from the criminal justice system and the right to be treated humanely by the system. Some victims' bills of rights laws also ensure the right to continued employment, provide medical or social support services and require the appointment of an ombudsman to protect the victim's rights throughout the trial process.

Most victims' bills of rights include both informational and participatory rights. They commonly require the victim to be informed about available financial aid and social services, as well as the whereabouts of the accused; advised of case status and scheduling; protected from harassment and intimidation; provided with separate waiting areas during the trial; and a speedy disposition of the case and return of property held as evidence.

Despite efforts to address the needs and rights of victims, some criticize states for their lack of promotion of victims' rights. Herman (Rosen, p. 8) contends:

> Even in states that have stronger protections, these rights are frequently not enforced. Victims don't know they have the rights; they're not given notice about them; and when they try to take advantage of these rights, they're often not permitted to by various criminal justice officials. In many states they have no enforcement mechanisms, so for some, these are hollow rights.

THE POLICE RESPONSE

The Office for Victims of Crime (2000) asserts: "The way people cope as victims of crime depends largely on their experiences immediately following the crime. As a law enforcement officer, you are usually the first official to approach victims. For this reason, you are in a unique position to help victims cope with the immediate trauma of the crime and to help restore their sense of security and control over their lives."

In addition to influencing how the department and its officers are perceived by the public, the way police interact with victims and witnesses can significantly affect the effectiveness of the entire justice system. By approaching victims appropriately, officers gain their trust and cooperation. Victims may then be more willing to provide detailed information about the crime to officers and later to investigators and prosecutors, which, in turn, will lead to the conviction of more criminals. A sensitive and effective police response also affects how they can develop informants, how many complaints are lodged against officers and/or the department and how far officers are able to advance in their careers. It is critical that officers interact effectively with victims and witnesses. Remember that you are there for the victim; the victim is not there for you.

Unfortunately, victims too often have to endure insensitive questioning, suspicion, indifference to their fear of retaliation or anxiety over testifying in court and lost wages due to time spent in court. In addition, property is often kept as evidence for a long time, and victims may feel "shut out" when police neglect to keep them informed on the status of their cases. According to Herman (Rosen, p. 8): "Over the last few years, we've seen a lot of creative problem-solving [by police]. I don't think, though, that we're seeing a lot of real, genuine partnering, particularly where victims are concerned."

Such partnering can be very valuable considering that police officers, during their careers, deal with many more victims than criminals. Still, most officers feel some frustration, even exasperation, with victims because their level of trauma, fear, anger or injury makes it difficult for them to be as cooperative as the officer needs them to be to obtain the maximum amount of information and evidence. This frustration does not go unnoticed by victims, who, as Herman notes: "Often feel that they are treated as a piece of evidence, [useful] only when they help prove the prosecution's case and when they help a police officer find the bad guy. . . . They often feel disrespected and ignored and that their interests and concerns are irrelevant" (Rosen, p. 9).

Victims, right after a traumatic incident, may be confused and in shock. Consequently, police must exercise patience when expecting these victims to submit to questioning and provide minute details of the crime and suspect. Many police departments are becoming more aware of the problem of officer insensitivity to victims and witnesses and are providing "consciousness-raising courses" to help officers understand and deal with victims empathetically.

The OVC (2000) contends officers can help victims by understanding the three major needs they have after a crime has been committed: the need to feel safe; the need to express their emotions; and the need to know "what comes next" after their victimization. The OVC publication *First Response to Victims of Crime* (2000) is a handbook for law enforcement officers with specific tips on how to approach and help a variety of victims, including elderly victims, victims of sexual assault, child victims, victims of domestic violence and survivors of homicide victims.

Occasionally a victim may have reason to lie about the events. They may fear being blamed for the event; they may fear retaliation if they "give up" the suspect; or they may themselves have been engaged in illegal conduct when the victimization occurred. Officers must be trained in how to coax truthful information from reluctant victims and witnesses.

Whether victims and witnesses are cooperative or not, officers must be able to conduct effective, yet sensitive interviews by calling upon the specific techniques and skills needed to obtain all available information from victims and witnesses while, at the same time, treating victims and witnesses respectfully and taking care of their immediate needs. The following interview skills will help gain the victim's cooperation:

- Take care of the victim's safety and medical needs first. Frightened people need to be assured they are safe and will be kept safe. Any injuries or pain must be attended to before they can be expected to provide meaningful information.

- Interview victims and witnesses individually so they will not alter their recollections to match each other's. Victims sometimes trust another victim's memory more than their own.

- Let the victim or witness know you need their help and that what they tell you is very important. They may fear retaliation or testifying in court.

- Provide victims with resources to help them deal with the problems that result from being a victim or, in some cases, a witness. They may need transportation, a place to stay, assistance in security for their house or business, the use of a telephone, a referral to counseling or an advocate to help them.

- Provide victims with a card listing the responding officer's name, the file or case number and key telephone numbers such as the local crisis center, criminal injuries compensation, the crime prevention unit, locksmiths, and a service that could help or refer the victim to other community services.

The 1999 IACP Summit on Victims of Crime identified a variety of strategies to help law enforcement officers honor victims rights and meet victim needs. These strategies and guiding principles were organized into six key need areas, identified by Robinson (p. 6) as:

- *Safety*—Protect victims from further victimization by perpetrators and the justice system, to the extent possible.
- *Access*—Allow victims to participate in the justice system process, to receive information about their case and to be notified of available services.
- *Information*—Provide clear, concise, user-friendly information, both verbal and written, about justice system processes, victim services and case developments, including changes in offender status.
- *Support*—Offer an equal, respectful and compassionate response to all victims. Encourage victims to tell their stories and listen to them carefully. Establish crisis and support services to help victims recover from trauma and advocacy services to assist victims in understanding and participating in justice processes. Focus on repairing the harm done by crime.
- *Continuity*—Provide consistent approaches and methods across all agencies and a "seamless continuum" of services and support through all stages of the justice process and victim recovery period.
- *Voice*—Empower victims to take part in case processing. Schedule investigative, court and postsentence proceedings to facilitate effective victim participation. Provide opportunities that enable victims to assist other victims and to serve the justice system. Engage victims in systemwide policy and protocol development.

Goven (2000, p. 17) notes the applicability of such strategies to community policing efforts: "Law enforcement plays a compelling and vital role in the treatment of victims of crime. . . . These hands-on strategies for innovation in police-based victim services provide an excellent opportunity for police to establish cross-disciplinary ties with victim assistance agencies and residents of their communities."

Police officers can also help victims by letting them know their rights, including the right to become active in the case processing and the right to prepare a victim impact statement (VIS). Tell victims what procedures and policies exist in their area. Some jurisdictions have a victim send a letter to the judge; some provide a VIS form sent by the police department, the prosecutor, a victim advocate or the probation department; in yet others victims talk directly to probation officers about the impact.

Some departments are using innovative approaches to reach out to victims and maintain lines of communication. For example, in some lower-income communities where few residents can afford telephone service, cellular phone links have been established to help crime victims reach the police. Cell phones have no lines to cut and can be preprogrammed with 911 and the general information number of the police department while locking out all other calling capability. An example of how communications are maintained with prior victims is seen in Jefferson County, Kentucky, where the Victim Information and Notification Everyday (VINE™) system automatically alerts victims with a telephone call when an inmate is released from custody. VINE could serve as a national model for using technology.

Acquiring information from witnesses presents its own challenges, particularly when the witnesses themselves may be sought by police. Boston has found an innovative approach to obtaining information about gang crimes—have a probation officer ride with a police officer. The probation officer can recognize most gang members on sight, many of whom are on probation and are violating that probation by being together. Furthermore, probation officers commonly have more leverage than do police officers in getting youths to talk because probation officers have the power to extend a youth's probation, revoke probation entirely and have the youth incarcerated, or cut a youth some slack in exchange for information about a crime.

◉ SPECIAL POPULATIONS

As discussed, interacting effectively with victims is a critical part of police officers' jobs that requires extreme skill and sensitivity. Some victims have additional medical and psychological needs that require officers to be quite sensitive. Officers should be aware of resources available for these "special" victims.

"Special" crime victims who require additional services include immigrants, people with disabilities, elderly victims of crime or abuse, abused children and battered or sexually assaulted women.

The first three categories of "special" crime victims were introduced in Chapters 7 and 8. Consider now how they, as victims, need to be treated by the police and the justice system as a whole.

Immigrant Victims

Perhaps the biggest challenge for police in dealing with immigrant victims, aside from the obvious language barriers, is the trust issue. Recall from Chapter 7 how immigrants commonly fear and distrust the police. Not only do such negative attitudes and perceptions make it difficult for officers to fully engage the cooperation of immigrant victims and witnesses in providing crime information; they also hamper efforts to dispatch the services and support such victims need, allow criminals to go free and significantly impair law enforcement's effectiveness by lowering the awareness that such victimization exists in the first place.

According to Davis and Erez (1998, p. 1), a National Institute of Justice survey of criminal justice professionals revealed: "Most (67 percent) . . . agreed that recent immigrants report crimes less frequently than other victims. Only 12 percent thought that recent immigrants were as likely or more likely to report crime." Furthermore: "Survey respondents said that domestic violence was the crime least reported. Sexual assault and gang violence were also thought more likely to go unreported."

Reasons for the underreporting (p. 3) included victims' fear of becoming involved with the authorities and possible embarrassment to the immigrants' families. Survey respondents believe one of the drawbacks of such underreporting is inadequate crime control based on inaccurate counts of crime in areas populated by recent immigrants (pp. 2–3). Respondents noted the allocation of funds for law enforcement resources is based partially on which areas show the highest levels of crime.

Despite the observed underreporting of crime by immigrant victims, Davis and Erez (p. 6) note some promising findings from the study:

> Although many criminal justice agencies had few or no programs and practices to help immigrant victims, in the course of conducting the national survey of criminal justice officials, researchers encountered many innovative ideas to accommodate immigrant victims, including incorporating leaders of immigrant communities into citizen advisory boards for police and prosecution agencies, enhancing ethnic diversity among the staff of criminal justice agencies, ensuring the availability of written material in languages other than English, sponsoring inservice training in the cultures of various ethnic groups, encouraging police officers to attend and speak at meetings of ethnic organizations in their communities and conducting special outreach from district attorneys' offices to victims belonging to particular ethnic groups.

Victims with Disabilities

According to Davis (2000): "Some researchers have found that people with disabilities are about twice as likely as others to be victimized." Sobsey et al. (1995) reviewed the available literature and concluded the best conservative estimate is that people with developmental disabilities are four to ten times more likely to be victims of crimes than are people without disabilities. The Disability Statistics Center (DSC) notes research suggesting the most frequent crimes against persons with disabilities were physical assault, sexual assault, robbery and economic crimes relating to benefit payments through third parties. Statistics also support a high probability of repeat victimization.

According to the DSC: "One recent study found that more than 70 percent of women with developmental disabilities are sexually assaulted in their lifetime, which represents a 50 percent higher rate than the rest of the population." Tyiska (1998, p. 2) reports: "Children with any kind of disability are more than twice as likely as nondisabled children to be physically abused and almost twice as likely to be sexually abused."

Tyiska (pp. 2–4) identifies several factors contributing to the heightened vulnerability of those with disabilities:

- Physical and social isolation—allows chronic abuse and victimization to go undetected and keeps the victim from reaching assistance.

- A reliance on others for care—while many caregivers provide ethical, honorable service to their disabled clients, some take advantage of their clients' vulnerabilities. Just as many pedophiles gravitate to youth-serving occupations, so do many other predators seek work as caregivers to people with disabilities. One survey revealed nearly half (48.1 percent) of the perpetrators of sexual abuse against people with disabilities had gained access to their victims through disability services.

- Limited physical accessibility—keeps victims from visiting criminal justice agencies, testifying about the victimization or attending victim assistance programs. Also prevents a disabled victim from escaping an abusive situation.

- Limited attitudinal accessibility—the ignorance or inability of some, including persons in criminal justice, the medical field and victim services, to open up to those with disabilities or to encourage them to report victimization; the failure to teach disabled persons how to proactively avoid victimization; an attitude among service providers, including police, that someone else more knowledgeable about disabilities should be responsible for handling referrals.

- Limited advocacy—despite progress by disability rights activists, advocacy on their own behalf remains limited. As with any other crime victim, a victim with a disability has difficulty gaining access to criminal justice decision-making processes without the tools required for full participation.

Tyiska (p. 14) contends: "While the United States is viewed as the world leader in civil and disability rights, crime victims with disabilities are largely invisible and their legal rights for service—and justice—go unaddressed." She (p. 2) provides the following example of how attitudinal accessibility, or lack of it, and limited advocacy can have severe, adverse impacts on disabled victims:

> In California, a woman was stabbed in the back during a robbery attempt. As a result of the assault, she became paraplegic. Unfortunately, neither the police nor hospital staff told her about victim assistance or independent living services. Because the assailant was never apprehended, the prosecutor-based victim assistance program did not provide her with services. In her anger and depression, she became suicidal. She survived a suicide attempt only because an alert nurse resuscitated her in time.

As with other categories of victims, the prevalence of crimes against persons with disabilities is underreported. Tyiska (pp. 2–3) explains:

> A crime may go unreported for many reasons: mobility or communication barriers, the social or physical isolation of the victim, a victim's normal feelings of shame and self-blame, ignorance of the justice system, or the perpetrator is a family member or primary caregiver. In crimes involving a victim with a disability, one or more of these factors may prevent the crime from ever being reported. When the crime is reported, the reporting agency often fails to note that the victim had a disability, especially if the crime is reported by someone other than the victim. Later, assumptions and prejudice about the reliability of victims with disabilities can deny them access to justice in the courts.

Tyiska (p. 4) offers an example of how media campaigns and outreach efforts can provide the lifeline abused individuals with disabilities need to end their victimization:

> A blind woman who was regularly beaten by her spouse received nothing but disdain from her family and few friends. She felt isolated and ashamed. After an appearance by the Executive Director of NOVA on a national television show, the woman called NOVA and asked for help—on the condition that she be allowed to maintain her anonymity.

Some victims who suffer from physical or mental impairments are made even more vulnerable because they are also elderly.

Elderly Victims

The elderly fear crime more than any other segment of our population. In some communities the elderly's fear of crime makes them prisoners in their own homes. However, data indicate the elderly population is not as likely as younger citizens to become victims of crime.

People age 65 and older have the lowest rate of victimization in the United States in both violent and property crimes.

Following a seven-year study, Klaus (2000) reports people 65 and older are substantially less likely than younger men and women to be violent crime victims. Most of the elderly victimization is nonviolent, with 92 percent consisting of property crimes. Klaus found an average of 2.5 million property crimes (household burglary, motor vehicle theft and household theft) against the elderly per year, 46,090 purse snatchings or pocket pickings, 165,330 nonlethal violent crimes (rape, robbery and assault) and 1,000 murders.

Elderly victims of violent crimes are often more drastically affected than younger victims. The elderly commonly live on a fixed, limited income, so financial losses can be especially devastating. In addition, the elderly are often physically vulnerable and frail. They can easily be injured during a victimization and take a long time to heal. Many elderly people have osteoporosis, and if they are pushed or beaten or if they fall, they may suffer broken bones and other serious injuries a younger person is not likely to sustain. In crimes such as purse snatchings and street robberies, the victims are often shoved down. Broken bones are common in this type of crime—more serious than the monetary loss. Furthermore, the elderly may also be less emotionally able to cope with victimization.

Compounding the challenge of handling elderly victims is the probability that older victims may have poor eyesight or memory, making them poor witnesses. Or they may fear retaliation or abandonment and thus refuse to cooperate with or report crime to authorities. Consider an example (Tyiska, p. 4):

> An elderly woman who was unable to walk was cared for at home by family members. Her grandson, a drug user, frequently stole money from her, especially after the third of each month, when her Social Security Disability Income check arrived. The woman would tuck her money under her to hide it from her grandson. Once, in a state of anger when he could not find her money, he flipped her over and she fell out of the bed onto the floor. She sustained several bruises but was not seen by a doctor. She did not report the abuse or the theft to the police out of fear that her family would no longer want to care for her.

The OVC (2000) notes:

> It is understandable why the elderly are the most fearful of crime. Elderly people, in fact, face a number of additional worries and fears when victimized. First, they may doubt their ability to meet the expectations of law enforcement and worry that officers will think they are incompetent. They may worry that a family member, upon learning of their victimization, will also think they are incompetent. Further, they may fear retaliation by the offender for reporting the crime. Finally, elderly people may experience feelings of guilt for "allowing"

themselves to be victimized. Depending on your approach as a first responder, you can do much to restore confidence in and maintain the dignity of the elderly victims you work with.

The OVC (2000) suggests the following tips for responding to elderly victims. Be attentive to whether victims are tired or not feeling well. Allow victims to collect their thoughts before your interview. Ask victims whether they would like you to contact a family member or friend. Ask victims if they are having any difficulty understanding you. Be sensitive to the possibility that they may have difficulty hearing or seeing, but do not assume such impairments. Ask victims if they have any special needs, such as eyeglasses or hearing aids. For hearing-impaired victims, choose a location free of distractions, interference and background noise.

The OVC further suggests that officers provide enhanced lighting if victims are required to read. Ensure that all print in written materials is both large enough and dark enough for victims to read. Ask questions one at a time, waiting for a response before proceeding to the next question. Avoid interrupting victims. Remember that elderly victims' recollections may surface slowly. Do not pressure them to recollect events or details; rather, ask them to contact you if they remember anything later. Provide victims written information that summarizes the important points you communicated verbally so they can refer to this information later. Be alert for signs of domestic violence or neglect, since studies indicate that 10 percent of the elderly are abused by their relatives. Protect the dignity of victims by including them in all decisionmaking conversations taking place in their presence.

Services a community might provide its older residents include transporting and escorting them to stores, clinics, hospitals and banks; establishing neighborhood block watch programs and neighborhood building patrols; installing video monitors in elevators and corridors of large apartment buildings; training youths to help elderly victims; establishing a special police unit to respond to senior burglaries, robberies, purse snatchings and assaults; installing new locks on doors and windows of elderly burglary victims; providing a 24-hour hotline and daily telephone reassurance; and making information and referral services readily available.

As the general population ages, law enforcement may likely encounter an increase in **granny bashing** or domestic violence against the elderly.

Elder Abuse. A television news program aired the story of a confused, helpless 82-year-old man who had been abandoned in his wheelchair at a dog racing track. He was shown sitting in a hospital bed clutching a teddy bear, wearing slippers and a sweatshirt that read "Proud to be an American," and holding a bag of diapers. Pinned to his sweatshirt was a typewritten note that said he was "John King, an Alzheimer's patient in need of care." All labels had been removed from his new clothing, and all identifying marks had been removed from his wheelchair.

Often those who care for the elderly are ill equipped to do so and lack resources themselves. Consequently, it is becoming more common for families faced with the rising medical costs of aging parents and the cost of raising their own children to abandon the elderly. Such abandonment, called **granny dumping,** is, however, only one form of elder abuse. **Elder abuse** encompasses physical and emotional abuse, financial exploitation and general neglect. And as Bettinger (2000, p. 86) notes, one out of every twenty-five Americans is the victim of abuse.

Most police agencies do not keep separate statistics on elder abuse. Agencies classify offenses by their traditional name (for example, assault, fraud or neglect) but not by age, so it is impossible to determine the full extent of the problem. Yet Strandberg (1999, p. 22) reports:

> Our oldest elders (80 and over) are abused and neglected at two to three times their proportion of the elderly population. Female elders are abused at a higher rate than males. Almost half of substantiated abused and neglected elderly were not physically able to care for themselves. In almost nine out of 10 incidents of domestic elder abuse and neglect the perpetrator is a family member. Adult children are responsible for almost half of all elder abuse and neglect.

The issue of elder abuse is extremely sensitive. In fact some officers still believe elder abuse cases are "family matters" in which police should not interfere. However, most states now have mandatory reporting laws regarding elderly abuse, so it is important that police officers recognize physical abuse of the elderly, as well as signs of extortion or fraud and other forms of elder abuse. Officers must also be sensitive to the fears and concerns of elderly victims. The arrest of their only caregiver could leave an elderly person in an even more precarious position than being abused. Furthermore, the victim of elder abuse may be extremely embarrassed by the treatment being given by "family."

It is in the best interests of the elderly and the caregiver if the police can help work out a solution. Improving the care of the elderly does, however, involve more than just police intervention. An effective response to elder abuse must incorporate the resources and expertise of many professional groups in addition to the police, such as social workers, mental health workers, victim services, elder protective services, home health agencies, hospital workers, transportation services, churches and shelters for the elderly.

The police response in cases of elder abuse should be one of concern and empathy for all involved. The solution should involve appropriate professional support services.

Another "special" population with increased vulnerability to crime is the victims at the other end of the age spectrum—youths.

Youth Victims

Like the elderly, youths may remained trapped in domestic violence because of their inability to protect themselves or to reach out to the appropriate agencies for help. Data from the National Center on Child Abuse Prevention Research ("Child Protective Services . . . ," 1999, p. 3) show that in 1998 an estimated 3.15 million children were reported to child protective service agencies as alleged victims of physical or sexual abuse or other maltreatment. According to the OVC (1999), children represent one-quarter of U.S. crime victims:

> Annually, an estimated 1 million violent crimes involving child victims are reported to the police, and another 1.1 million cases of child abuse are substantiated by child

protection agencies. As many as half a million children may be encountered by police during domestic violence arrests. Of the nation's 22.3 million adolescents aged 12 to 17, approximately 1.8 million reported having been victims of a serious sexual assault, 3.9 million report having been victims of a serious physical assault, and almost 9 million reported having witnessed serious violence during their lifetimes.

Sometimes the violence turns deadly. In 1997 the National Center for Health Statistics listed homicide as the fourth leading cause of death for children ages 1 through 4, third for youths ages 5 through 14, and second for persons ages 15 through 24.

The OVC (1999) notes children who are victims of or witnesses to violent crime are at an increased risk for delinquency, adult criminality, violent behavior, substance abuse, mental illness and suicide. In fact, children who have been abused or neglected are 53 percent more likely to be arrested as a juvenile.

Such statistics highlight what Widom (1995, p. 1) refers to as the "cycle of violence" or the "intergenerational transmission of violence." Says Widom: "The research clearly revealed that a childhood history of physical abuse predisposes the survivor to violence in later years, and that victims of neglect are more likely to engage in violent criminal behavior as well."

Often, the abuse is discovered accidentally by a teacher, babysitter or other service provider. Service providers legally required to report incidents of suspected child abuse and neglect include those working in child care, education, social services, hospital administration, healing arts, psychological treatment, psychiatric treatment, the clergy and law enforcement.

Some cases involve participation of and collaboration between several agencies. For example, child sexual abuse cases are often jointly investigated by a child protection service agency and the police department. To make a successful partnership, conduct joint training, interagency staff retreats and regular interagency meetings. Establish specialized units and maintain a policy of open communication.

Dealing with abused children, especially those who have been sexually abused, is a very sensitive type of case. The OVC (1999) asserts: "Police officers need to be trained to recognize the situations in which children may be victims. . . . Officers [also] need information on how to interview children." They suggest law enforcement agencies create special units or designate specialists to handle child victims:

> Professionals handling these cases should have reasonable case loads and access to victim assistance professionals who also have special training for working with child victims.
>
> Criminal justice agencies should provide a "child friendly," developmentally appropriate place to work with children. Many police departments and prosecutors' offices set aside a room designed to be comfortable and appropriate for interviewing or preparing children.

The OVC (2000) observes: "When children are victimized, their normal physiological and psychological adjustment to life is disrupted. . . . Child victims suffer not only physical and emotional traumas from their victimization. When their victimization is reported, children are forced to enter the stressful 'adult' world of the criminal justice

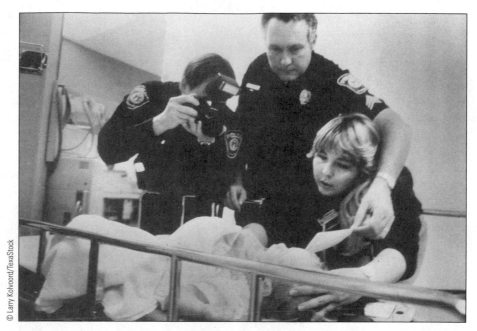

© Larry Kolvoord/TexaStock

Police officers and medical personnel gather evidence of child abuse in a hospital emergency room.

system." They contend: "As a law enforcement officer, you can play a key role in this process and lessen the likelihood of long-term trauma for child victims." The OVC (2000) recommends these tips for responding to child victims:

- Choose a secure, comfortable setting for interviewing child victims and take the time to establish trust and rapport:
  - Preschool children (ages 2–6) are most comfortable at home—assuming no abuse took place there. A parent or other adult the child trusts should be nearby.
  - For elementary school-age children (6–10), the presence of a parent is not usually recommended since children at this age can be reluctant to reveal information if they believe they or their parents could "get into trouble." However, a parent or other adult the child trusts should be close by, such as in the next room.
  - Preadolescents (ages 10–12 for girls and 12–14 for boys) are peer-oriented and often avoid parental scrutiny. For this reason, they may be more comfortable if a friend is nearby.
  - Since adolescents (generally, ages 13–17) may be fearful of betraying their peers, it may be necessary to interview them in a secure setting with no peers nearby.
- Realize that children tend to regress emotionally during times of stress, acting younger than their age. For example, 8-year-olds may suck their thumb.
- Use language appropriate to the victim's age. Avoid "baby talk."
- Assure children that they have not done anything wrong and they are not "in trouble."
- Be consistent with the terms you use and repeat important information often.

- Use care in discussing sexual matters with preadolescent and adolescent children, as their embarrassment and limited vocabulary can make conversation difficult for them. At the same time, do not assume that victims are as knowledgeable about sexual matters as their language or apparent sophistication might indicate.

- Maintain a nonjudgmental attitude and patiently answer all of the victim's questions.

- Because elementary school-age children are especially affected by praise, compliment them frequently on their behavior and thank them for their help.

- Remember the limited attention span of children and be alert to signs that victims are feeling tired, restless or cranky.

- Encourage preschool children to play, as it is a common mode of communication for them. You may find that as children play, they become more relaxed and thus more talkative.

- Limit the number of times victims must be interviewed. Bring together for interviews as many persons from appropriate public agencies as possible, including representatives from the prosecutor's office, child protective services and the medical/health care community.

- Include victims, when possible, in decisionmaking and problem-solving discussions.

- You can reduce victims' insecurity and anxiety by explaining the purpose of your interview and by preparing them, especially elementary school-age children, for what will happen next.

- Show compassion toward victims. Children's natural abilities to cope are aided immensely by caring adults.

- Although the immediate victim is the child, do not forget to comfort the nonoffending parents. Referrals regarding how they can cope, what they can expect, as well as how to talk to and with their child should be provided.

The OVC offers these general recommendations as a summary for law enforcement agencies in effectively handling youth victims:

- All officers should have at least basic training in recognizing and responding to children who are abused, neglected or exposed to violence.

- Agency heads should specially assign officers to handle cases involving child victims and witnesses, ensuring these officers receive indepth training in interviewing children, identifying injury, child development, and understanding the impact of victimization and witnessing violence on children.

- Law enforcement investigators should work in collaboration with medical and mental health providers, child protective service agencies and victim assistance providers.

- Police agencies should have written child abuse policies that provide sufficient guidance for making important decisions, such as whether to arrest a suspected perpetrator, whether to place a child in protective custody and how to deal with unusual or difficult situations.

Conditions that might lead a police officer to place a child in protective custody include maltreatment in the home, which could cause the child permanent physical or emotional damage; a child in immediate need of medical or psychiatric care but the parents refuse to obtain it; a child's age or physical or mental condition renders the child incapable of self-protection; the physical environment of the home poses an immediate threat to the child; the parents cannot or will not provide for the child's basic needs; the parents flee the jurisdiction or abandon the child.

The primary responsibility of police officers who deal with abused or neglected children is to protect the child, remove him or her from the home if necessary and collaborate with social service agencies to ensure that the child's needs are met.

Children Who Witness Violence. Just because a child suffers no physical trauma does not mean the child isn't profoundly affected by violence. Indeed, those who witness violence are also victimized for, to reiterate a previously mentioned fact, children who are victims of *or witnesses to* violent crime are at an increased risk for delinquency, adult criminality, violent behavior, substance abuse, mental illness and suicide. The OVC notes: "Children who witness violence often experience many of the same symptoms and lasting effects as children who are victims of violence themselves, including post traumatic stress disorder (PTSD)." Furthermore:

> Children who are exposed to domestic violence experience feelings of terror, isolation, guilt, helplessness, and grief. Many children exhibit psychosomatic complaints such as headaches, stomach problems, and other medical problems. Children can experience problems with depression, anxiety, embarrassment, and, if exposed to violence for an extended period of time, ambivalence. Children act out what they see.

Even when child witnesses do not suffer physical injury, the emotional consequences of viewing or hearing violent acts are severe and long lasting and may include many of the same symptoms experienced by children who are, themselves, victims of violence, including PTSD.

Children are particularly traumatized by witnessing sexual assaults and, not surprisingly, homicides. The OVC notes:

> Approximately 34 percent of rapes are estimated to occur in the victim's home where children are likely to be present to see or hear the sexual assault of their mothers or caretakers. . . . Children who are present during a sexual assault are at significant risk for developing post-traumatic stress disorder. Children may have recurrent and intrusive thoughts about the sexual assault and may reenact the event in repetitive play. Feeling a loss of control and an inability to protect their mothers may leave children feeling anxious, depressed, vulnerable, and angry. . . .
> Children witness many different types of homicide. They may witness the death of a sibling, parent, another relative, a friend, or a stranger. When a child witnesses the fatal abuse of a sibling or parent, it is highly probably that the child knows the perpetrator intimately as a parent or other family member.

For police to effectively handle children who witness violence and ensure such victims receive the necessary help and attention, partnerships and training are essential: "Since most law enforcement officers and prosecutors are not child development specialists, it becomes critical to do two things—to involve other professionals who can provide advice and assistance in dealing with children and to give police and prosecutors enough training to provide them a basic understanding of child development" (OVC). Of all the types of violent crime children may witness, perhaps the most common is that occurring within their own home—domestic violence.

Battered or Sexually Assaulted Women

Women, just as men, are vulnerable to victimization in a variety of offenses, including crimes against persons, but usually at a lower rate. The Bureau of Justice Statistics (BJS) notes that, for violent offenses, males are victimized at higher rates than females. In 1999 males were victimized at rates 22 percent higher than females. In fact, data from the *National Crime Victimization Survey* (BJS) indicates the victimization rate for males exceeds that for females in every category of violent crime . . . *except* one: rape/sexual assault. Females were raped or sexually assaulted at a rate about eight times that of males in 1999.

A significant difference also exists between male and female victims and their relationship to their victimizers—males are more likely to be victimized by a stranger, whereas females are more likely to be violently victimized by a friend, an acquaintance or an intimate. The BJS states: "Intimate violence is primarily a crime against women— in 1998, females were the victims in 72% of intimate murders and the victims of about 85% of nonlethal intimate violence."

Intimate violence, also called domestic violence, affects many U.S. households. The Family Violence Prevention Fund reports that one in every three American women has been a victim of domestic violence ("Partnership Combats . . . ," 2000, p. 173). A study based on data from the *National Crime Victimization Survey* and other sources found, in 1998 women were the victims in 876,340 incidents of reported violence, including rape, sexual assault, robbery, aggravated assault and simple assault, by former or current domestic partners. During the same year, men were victims of about 160,000 violent crimes by an intimate partner.

The BJS notes: "Women age 16–24 experienced the highest per capita rates of intimate violence (19.6 victimizations per 1,000 women). According to another report ("Women Still Bear . . . ," 2000, p. 11): "Women who are black, young, divorced or separated and living in rented housing in an urban area were associated with higher levels of [domestic] victimization."

Traditionally, police have not treated domestic violence as a crime except in extremely brutal cases. Police often considered domestic violence to be a "family matter." Wives had to press charges before the police could intervene. This requirement has been eliminated in most states. Now the police are authorized to make warrantless, probable-cause arrests and file complaints in domestic violence cases. No longer must the victim press charges, which, in effect, has shifted the burden of stopping the violence away from the victim. Domestic violence is now viewed as a serious crime.

According to the OVC (2000): "The three primary responsibilities of law enforcement in domestic violence cases are to (1) provide physical safety and security for victims, (2) assist victims by coordinating their referral to support services and (3) make arrests of domestic violence perpetrators as required by law." However, the OVC also notes restrictions on how effective the police response may be when handling these victims:

> Unlike most other victims of crime, victims of domestic violence do not usually suffer a "sudden and unpredictable" threat to their safety or lives. More often, domestic violence involves years of personal stress and trauma, as well as physical injury. Thus, in domestic violence cases—unlike in other crimes—your ability to help victims cope with and recover from their victimization may be limited.

The OVC (2000) provides the following tips for responding to victims of domestic violence:

- Because domestic violence cases present potential dangers, responding officers should arrive in pairs at the scene if possible. Introduce yourself and explain that you were called because of a possible injury. Ask permission to enter the residence to make sure everything is okay.

- Separate the parties involved in domestic violence before interviewing them, even if they are not violent or arguing when you arrive.

- Ask victims whether they would like you to contact a family member or friend.

- Even if no children are present at the scene, ask whether there are children in the family, and, if so, find out their whereabouts. Keep in mind that children sometimes hide or are hidden in these circumstances.

- Assure victims that the purpose of your intervention is to help address the problem, not to make the situation worse.

- Avoid judging victims or personally commenting on the situation. Abusive relationships continue for many reasons. Offering advice to the victim at the scene will not solve this complex problem.

- Remember that domestic violence can occur in same-sex relationships.

- Even when no domestic violence charges can be filed, encourage the parties to separate for a short period—at least overnight. If victims' safety at home can be assured, consider asking assailants to leave. Although law enforcement officers have traditionally asked victims to leave the home, this serves to disrupt their lives even further, especially when children are involved.

- Provide victims referral information on domestic violence shelters and battered women's programs. This should be done away from the offender.

Police should be familiar with referral sources that go beyond the immediate crisis, for example, job training and placement, low-cost housing, childcare needs, and drug or alcohol treatment programs. They should also be aware of the limitations of protective measures commonly employed in domestic violence cases. For example, according to Fagan (1996): "Reforms in the concept of restraining orders for battered women preceded reforms in arrest and criminal law. Beginning with the passage of the Pennsylvania Protection from Abuse Act in 1976, every State now provides for protection orders in cases of domestic violence." However, as research has shown: "There is little conclusive evidence of either deterrent or protective effects of legal sanctions or treatment interventions for domestic violence."

The Domestic Abuse Intervention Project is a national training project that includes seminars for law enforcement officers and trainers, prosecutors, legal advocates and police administrators. In addition to explaining the dynamics of domestic violence, the seminars teach state law and department policy regarding domestic violence; establishing probable cause in domestic violence cases; distinguishing between mutual assaults and self-defense; making the decision to arrest, mediate between or separate spouses; gathering evidence effectively and writing reports; enforcing civil protection orders; interviewing child witnesses; maintaining officer safety and awareness of liability issues; and understanding the psychological dynamics of battering in relationships.

Women who have been sexually assaulted also have unique needs. The OVC (2000) notes:

> In the investigation and prosecution of most sexual assault cases, the role of the victim is much more important than in other crimes since the victim is usually the sole witness to the crime. Unfortunately, sexual assault victims are sometimes reluctant to cooperate with law enforcement because they fear the perpetrator will return to retaliate.
>
> Only men and women who have suffered the trauma of sexual assault themselves can begin to understand the depth and complexity of the feelings experienced by sexual assault victims. Even so, your approach as a first responder to sexual assault victims can significantly affect whether the victims begin the road to recovery or suffer years of trauma and anguish.

According to the OVC (2000): "The three primary responsibilities of law enforcement in sexual assault cases are to (1) protect, interview, and support the victim; (2) investigate the crime and apprehend the perpetrator; and (3) collect and preserve evidence of the assault that will assist in the prosecution of the assailant." They suggest the following tips for responding to victims of sexual assault.

Be prepared for virtually any type of emotional reaction by victims. Be unconditionally supportive and permit victims to express their emotions, which may include crying, angry outbursts and screaming. Avoid interpreting a victim's calmness or composure as evidence that a sexual assault did not occur. The victim could be in shock. (False accusations of sexual assault are estimated to occur at the low rate of 2 percent—similar to the rate of false accusations for other violent crimes.) Approach victims calmly. Showing outrage at the crime may cause victims more trauma.

In addition, officers should ask victims whether they would like you to contact a family member or friend. Offer to contact a sexual assault crisis counselor. Ask victims if they would prefer a male or female counselor. Also, ask the victim if they would prefer talking with you or an officer of the opposite sex. Be careful not to appear overprotective or patronizing. Remember that it is normal for victims to want to forget, or to actually forget, details of the crime that are difficult for them to accept. Encourage victims to get medical attention, especially to check for possible internal injuries. A medical examination can also provide evidence for the apprehension and prosecution of the victim's assailant. Keep in mind, however, that victims may feel humiliated and embarrassed that their bodies were exposed during the sexual assault and must be exposed again during a medical exam. Explain what will take place forensically during the exam and why these procedures are important. Notify the hospital of the incoming victim/patient and request a private waiting room. Escort victims to the hospital. If no crisis intervention counselor is available, wait at the hospital until victims are released and escort them to their destination.

Finally, officers should be mindful of the personal, interpersonal and privacy concerns of victims. They may have a number of concerns, including the possibility of having been impregnated or contracting sexually transmitted diseases such as AIDS; the reactions of their spouse, mate or parents; media publicity that may reveal their experience to the public; and the reactions and criticism of neighbors and coworkers if they learn about the sexual assault. Interview victims with extreme sensitivity and avoid "Why" questions as they imply blame and put the victim on the defensive. Instead, ask "What"—"What happened next?" or "What did you do then?" Minimize the number of times victims must recount details of the crime to strangers. If possible, only one law enforcement officer should be assigned to the initial interview and subsequent investigation. Offer to answer any further questions victims may have and provide any further assistance they may need. Encourage victims to get counseling. Explain that your recommendation for counseling is based on having seen other victims benefit from it in the past. Explain that they may experience post traumatic stress symptoms in the next few months. Identify and refer them to support services for assistance.

◈ THE RESPONSE OF THE CRIMINAL JUSTICE SYSTEM

The entire criminal justice system should be sensitive to victims' needs. In most cases a sense of participation is more critical to victims' satisfaction with the criminal justice system than how severely the defendant is punished. Victims can participate in several ways:

- Plea bargaining—The majority of cases that remain in the criminal justice system are plea bargained. Victims should be allowed to participate or, at the least, be kept informed, as stipulated by the Federal Victim and Witness Protection Act of 1982.

- Victim involvement in sentencing—Almost all states allow some form of victim involvement in sentencing, the two most common being the VIS and the **victim statement of opinion (VSO)**. As discussed, the VIS lets victims describe the physical, emotional and financial injuries resulting from the crime. The VSO lets victims express their opinion on what sentence the defendant should receive.

- Court attendance—The Sixth Amendment to the Constitution establishes the defendant's right to be in the courtroom, but crime victims often have no such rights. Many victims are relegated to a hall or waiting room, which they may perceive as an insult.

- Probation and parole—Restitution is authorized or required in every state as a condition of probation. In almost half it is authorized as a condition of parole.

Recommendations

The National District Attorneys Association (n.d., p. 8) recommends that the following types of agencies be included in a victim/witness assistance referral network: community groups, daycare centers, domestic violence programs, food stamp distribution centers, job counseling and training programs, mental health care programs, physical health care programs, private sector allies, private and community emergency organizations, rape crisis centers, unemployment services, victim assistance or advocacy organizations, victim compensation boards, volunteer groups and welfare agencies.

Many criminal justice scholars and researchers are calling for an entirely new approach to "justice" in the United States—restorative justice.

◉ RESTORATIVE JUSTICE REVISITED

Recall that restorative justice seeks a balanced approach involving offenders, victims, local communities and government to alleviate crime and violence and obtain peaceful communities. Consider this hypothetical case:

> A youth breaks into a neighbor's house and attempts to steal a stereo system. When he is caught by the owner, the young man strikes the victim with a baseball bat, breaking his arm. Under the standard system, the youth probably would be charged with a felony and sentenced to ten years or less in jail. Under the restorative model, he might be committed to a youthful offender program in which prosecution would be suspended if he agreed to undergo a substance abuse evaluation, become assigned to a mentor, submit to drug tests, comply with a curfew, take classes to obtain a high-school-equivalency degree, perform community service, and possibly make victim restitution ("Restore Victim . . . ," 1995, p. 4).

◉ THE DIRECTION OF VICTIMS' RIGHTS AND SERVICES IN THE 21ST CENTURY

Today only a fraction of the nation's estimated 38 million crime victims receive much needed services such as emergency financial assistance, crisis and mental health counseling, shelter, and information and advocacy within the criminal and juvenile justice systems (Executive Summary, New Directions from the Field, p. vii, 1998).

New Directions from the Field: Victims' Rights and Services for the 21st Century is a comprehensive report and compilation of more than 250 recommendations targeted to nearly every profession that comes in contact with crime victims—from justice practitioners, to victim service, health care, mental health, legal, educational, faith, news media and business communities. The result of a collaborative effort of more than 1,000 individuals in a broad spectrum of occupations, *New Directions* encourages professionals who deal with crime victims to redouble their efforts to enhance the rights and services afforded to such victims. In listening to the voices of victims, their advocates and allied professionals who work with crime victims throughout the nation, five global challenges emerged for responding to victims of crime in the 21st century (p. viii):

• To enact and enforce consistent, fundamental rights for crime victims in federal, state, juvenile, military, and tribal justice systems, and administrative proceedings.

- To provide crime victims with access to comprehensive, quality services regardless of the nature of their victimization, age, race, religion, gender, ethnicity, sexual orientation, capability, or geographic location.

- To integrate crime victims' issues into all levels of the nation's educational system to ensure that justice and allied professionals and other service providers receive comprehensive training on victims' issues as part of their academic education and continuing training in the field.

- To support, improve, and replicate promising practices in victims' rights and services built upon sound research, advanced technology, and multidisciplinary partnerships.

- To ensure that the voices of crime victims play a central role in the nation's response to violence and those victimized by crime.

According to *New Directions* (p. xxi):

> In the last two decades, many promising practices in victim services have been developed across the nation. These innovative programs use a multidisciplinary or team approach to respond to the needs of diverse crime victims; maximize technology to deliver high-quality services to victims more quickly and effectively; and utilize community police, prosecutor, court, and corrections programs.

> Examples of "promising practices" that are transforming victim services include (pp. xxi–xxiii) children's advocacy centers; community criminal justice partnerships; crisis response teams; technologies to benefit crime victims (such as VINE); community police, prosecutors and court programs; initiatives of allied professionals (such as partnerships between criminal justice agencies, schools, the medical and mental health community, religious communities and the business community); comprehensive victim service centers; and specialized programs for diverse crime victims (including disabled victims and victims of gang violence).

SUMMARY

The National Crime Victimization Survey estimates 28.8 million victimizations were committed against U.S. residents age 12 or older in 1999. Victims of crime may suffer physical injury, financial and property losses, emotional distress and psychological trauma. Some suffer from post traumatic stress disorder (PTSD), a persistent re-experiencing of a traumatic event through intrusive memories and dreams and a variety of anxiety-related symptoms.

Victimology, the study of crime victims, includes the concepts of vulnerability and culpability. Bureau of Justice statistics show that those most at risk of being victimized are young, black males with low incomes living in urban areas.

Our society has made progress in helping crime victims by passing legislation, founding organizations and developing programs. The Federal Victim and Witness Protection Act of 1982 established the victim impact statement (VIS) as a formal part of the presentence report. The Victims of Crime Act (VOCA), passed in 1984, established a fund making state grants available for victims' compensation, victim assistance programs and child abuse prevention and treatment. Organizations dedicated to helping victims include the National

Organization for Victim Assistance (NOVA), founded in 1976; the Office for Victims of Crime (OVC), founded in 1984; and the National Victim Center, founded in 1985.

The two main types of programs provided for victims are (1) victim compensation programs that help crime victims cope with crime-related expenses such as medical costs, mental health counseling, lost wages and funeral or burial costs; and (2) victim/witness assistance programs that provide services such as crisis support, peer support, referrals to counseling, advocacy within the justice system and, in some cases, emergency shelter.

Most victims' bills of rights include both informational and participatory rights. They commonly require the victim to be informed about available financial aid and social services, as well as the whereabouts of the accused; advised of case status and scheduling; protected from harassment and intimidation; provided with separate waiting areas during the trial; and a speedy disposition of the case and return of property held as evidence.

"Special" crime victims who require additional services include immigrants, people with disabilities, elderly victims of crime or abuse, abused children and battered or sexually assaulted women. People age 65 and older have the lowest rate of victimization in the United States in both violent and property crimes. The police response in cases of elder abuse should be one of concern and empathy for all involved. The solution should involve appropriate professional support services.

The primary responsibility of police officers who deal with abused or neglected children is to protect the child, remove him or her from the home if necessary and collaborate with social service agencies to ensure that the child's needs are met. Even when child witnesses do not suffer physical injury, the emotional consequences of viewing or hearing violent acts are severe and long lasting and may include many of the same symptoms (including PTSD) experienced by children who are themselves victims of violence.

PROBLEM SOLVING IN ACTION

Domestic Violence

The crime of domestic violence is different from virtually every other type of crime in that it is preventable. However, in the past we associated cases of domestic violence with other crimes that involved "passion" as a motivating influence and, in so doing, dismissed them as unpredictable and therefore not preventable. We were looking at the problem with blinders on, missing telltale signs and information that we now understand and use as indicators of predictability and the basis for developing problem-oriented intervention and prevention strategies.

Examining the perpetrators of our domestic violence cases, their victims, the cyclical patterns of behavior associated with their violent relationships, and even the pattern of our own responses yielded an extraordinary amount of information. The following case illustrates the information available when you ask who, what, where, when and how questions to analyze a domestic violence problem and the potential for more effective response.

Who? This case involved an estranged husband, just released from county jail for violations of a restraining order; his wife; their two children; and the wife's male friend.

Notes: There was a pattern of escalating abuse and violence, and the main participants were known, having been principle parties in all previous cases.

What? This case involved domestic violence—a multiple homicide. The husband returned to the home he was forbidden to approach as a condition of a restraining order. The wife returned with the children and a friend to pick up belongings in anticipation of her husband's release and return. The husband and wife argued, the friend interceded, and the husband killed the friend, wife and then himself, all in front of the two children.

Notes: The crime type was the same as in previous cases involving this family—domestic violence. In this case however, the violence escalated to homicide. The involved parties were the same as previously, with the exception of the innocent friend.

Where? The crime took place at the "family" home, which had been the location for five previous police responses to complaints of domestic violence committed by the husband against the wife.

Notes: All previous cases involving this couple occurred at the home.

When? This case occurred several months ago. The "when" is the only component we can't fix with accuracy. However, whether domestic violence involves "simple" violence or homicide, we know that it is coming or may come at any time. Absent separation and treatment, the cycle of violence continues.

Notes: The husband had previously threatened to kill his wife should she ever try to leave him, and all of the previous cases occurred during a specific two-hour period on weekend evenings.

How? In this case, the husband used a handgun.

Notes: In previous cases he had struck his wife with his fists, but one case involved his brandishing a handgun, and he had previously threatened to shoot and kill her.

In the past, our responses to disturbance calls not involving actual domestic violence but that might have indicated a domestic violence problem were rarely put into police reports. Therefore, they could not be recovered as part of our domestic crime statistics and were never given a second look.

Minor domestic violence cases were often underinvestigated and underreported. In most cases, the substance of our responses and actions was captured on short form reports that sometimes lacked complete information. Appropriate enforcement (arrest) and follow-up actions were not routine or consistent. More serious domestic violence cases were usually appropriately investigated and documented, but our ability to support the victim ended with an arrest and/or providing standard victim information and assistance cards.

In summary, our response to domestic violence usually began with a minor "disturbance only" call that could have been associated with the cycle of domestic abuse. We would later respond to additional incidents at the same address involving abuse or violence between the same two people, and the circumstances would fit a predictable pattern. Finally, in all too many cases, we responded one final time—for a homicide. We arrested the suspect and did the most thorough form of investigation and reporting we knew how. The result, however, did absolutely nothing for the victim or the domestic violence problem in general. As in previous responses, we were, because of our limited perspective and response, much too late.

When Chief Michael Maehler committed our agency to institutionalizing and operationalizing the philosophy of community-oriented policing and a new focus on "Policing with Partners" to solve problems that afflict our community, we were led almost immediately to reassess the way we viewed the problem of domestic violence and our response to the problem.

Our efforts were guided by the newfound perspective that we had to (1) be more proactive in addressing the problem, (2) approach it with a keen understanding of the issues involved, (3) seek long-term solutions and (4) be able to bring more resources to bear on the problem than we currently had at our disposal. We realized that reducing the incidence of domestic violence would require the support and involvement of community partners.

The keys to our progress were our true belief that the problem's predictability provided opportunities for intervention and our partnership with the Support Network for Battered Women. The Network offered the support resource required to make eventual intervention strategies a reality.

Scanning. The problem of domestic violence must be as old as humankind itself and affects every jurisdiction in the world. We had lived with our problem for years, but despite rising media attention and public concern, our perspective remained quite traditional, marked only by the changing of our protocol on the subject in 1993.

Several things led us to examine the problem from a fresh perspective and to change our methods: (1) our notice of a pattern of multiple, repeat police responses to several homes where domestic violence recurred; (2) our notice that responses to actual domestic violence at these locations had been preceded by one or more responses to "disturbances" (noise, arguments, yelling, bothering, abuse not amounting to a crime, etc.) that should have indicated a potential for future domestic violence; (3) our chief's commitment to community-oriented policing; (4) city involvement in a countywide conference on domestic violence, the outgrowth of which was establishing a city task force on domestic violence; (5) the fielding of several complaints about our poor response to domestic violence calls; and (6) the start of our relationship with the Network, our primary local support agency for battered women.

Our relationship with the Network did more than anything else to give us a newfound awareness and sensitivity, which led us to determine that our problem with domestic violence was masked and growing, that real intervention and reductions in the crime were possible, and that

the problem deserved much more attention than we had previously given it.

Analysis. Investigative staff members responsible for addressing "persons" crimes noticed the problem with our response, as well as opportunities presented by our new relationship with the Network. They forged a formal relationship with the Network and developed problem-solving strategies.

Their study of our statistics showed that although documentation of actual domestic violence cases had remained quite static (35 cases per month), "disturbance" incidents that we might logically examine and connect to domestic relationships seemed to be escalating and were substantial in number. Investigators estimated their frequency at roughly twice that of actual domestic violence reports.

Interviews with our officers supported their sense that the weight and importance of domestic violence-related disturbance calls was substantial. Officers identified problem locations denoted by incidences of repeat responses and expressed their frustration at not having the time or resources to offer victims more than enforcement or referral information as a "solution."

Research conducted into what other agencies and individuals were doing and saying about the problem gave investigators valuable insights, alternative response methods and potential for real intervention and abatement. They focused specifically, and with gratitude, on work conducted by the San Diego Police Department and Ann O'Dell, who had years before effectively addressed the predictability of domestic violence-related homicides.

Meetings with the Network were held to share information and obtain their feedback about the problem and our response methods. We learned that victims and support agencies were unhappy with our response. Victims saw the police as more of an impediment and threat than a source for support and resolution. Furthermore, they found it hard to accept police officers as both report takers/enforcers and support providers.

The Network also pointed to problems with the way we made reports on domestic violence and asked that we do a better, more consistent job in this area. Finally, and most important, they expressed a strong desire to partner with us in developing problem-solving strategies designed to reduce the incidence of domestic violence.

Our analysis included consideration of the above-mentioned clues to predictability and the resulting belief that we could effectively predict future problems with domestic violence and then provide intervention services designed to prevent the likelihood of the actual occurrence.

Investigators thought we could do so by accurately documenting cases of domestic "disturbances," sound predictors of a domestic violence problem. This could be followed by intervening with potential victims identified in those reports as well as reports of domestic violence, then offering them appropriate support services.

To proceed from this analysis, we had to change response and reporting methods and also acquire additional personnel resources for adequate intervention and follow-up services.

Response. Investigators met with a variety of department personnel, members of the city task force and Network members to develop and choose a response plan. We set a goal and associated objectives constructed to incorporate the whole department in our response plan.

Goal: Reduce the incidence of domestic violence by providing intervention services to those documented as being victims of domestic violence and those predicted to be at risk of becoming domestic violence victims.

Objective 1: Enhance our reporting of domestic violence cases and create case documentation on other cases that could help predict the future incidence of domestic violence. Produce more complete, thorough and effective police investigations and fully document the considerable number of disturbance cases occurring that might predict domestic problems and future domestic violence incidents.

A range of alternatives was considered, including adding report forms, eliminating reporting forms and formats, increasing report review and changing data-recovery mechanisms. We ultimately decided to: (1) Adopt a new domestic violence protocol endorsed by the county chiefs of police. The protocol required more complete reporting, more severe and consistent enforcement, and the provision of better "up front" and follow-up support to victims. (2) Create a new report classification of "Domestic Disturbance" and require hard-copy documentation of such cases. Doing so would capture those disturbance cases that might predict a domestic problem and future violence. (3) Require review of disturbance cases by persons-crimes investigators. (4) Make statistics on the new disturbance category part of our monthly crime statistic reports.

Objective 2: Provide meaningful intervention services to victims of domestic violence or domestic disturbances as a follow-up to the original police responses and investigations. Doing so could effectively support victims to take actions to resolve their problems and reduce the likelihood of future violence.

Providing intervention services required personnel resources we didn't have at our disposal. We considered and rejected a plan to deliver such services through persons-crimes investigators—they were already taxed too heavily and felt provision of such services by people other than sworn officers would be better received. We also considered and rejected the use of nonsworn or volunteer members—budget, staffing and supervisory span of control were issues. True to our philosophy of "Police with Partners," we ultimately decided to create and implement a Victim Assistance Program (VAP) staffed within the Persons Crimes Unit by volunteers from the Network. VAP volunteers would receive copies of each domestic violence and disturbance case report made, review the cases, contact victims, offer victim-support services, provide investigators with feedback from victims and on police reports/actions and, as appropriate, serve as a liaison between investigators and victims regarding further investigations.

New protocols to implement new reporting requirements and the VAP program were issued following delivery of training.

Assessment. The problem of domestic violence will take years to abate. In our case, the success of this first response plan will take several years to measure. We will by then have amended the plan, perhaps once or twice, in response to analysis of its effects, shortcomings and successes, as well as changes in the problem itself.

However, we have already had some successes based on our stated goal and objectives. Notable successes are as follows:

- The quality and effect of our investigations are much improved. This assessment is based on feedback from both internal and external review of case work.

- Feedback from the Network, victims, citizens and our officers indicate that officers are showing more concern for victims of domestic violence and the problem itself.

- We are documenting an average of 66 domestic disturbance cases each month. These cases would previously have been buried, unnoticed or reflected only in statistics on the general category of "Disturbance Other" cases.

- The department and the Network are together issuing more emergency protective restraining orders and restraining orders than in the past.

We have contacted and offered services to an average of 50 victims of domestic violence or domestic disturbances each month through the VAP. While we average 97 cases of violence or disturbance each month and had set an objective of contacting a greater average number of victims (75+ percent), we have found this to be unattainable given the 20-hour-per-week volunteer allocation from the Network.

Analysis of this shortcoming prompted the department to partner with the Network in submitting a grant request to the COPS Office for funding that would allow the Network to provide the department with a full-time, paid VAP employee for one year.

Comparison of the four-month period prior to the start of the plan with the four-month period following showed (1) a decrease in the incidence of actual domestic violence cases by two per month but (2) an increase in arrests for domestic violence of almost 43 percent (21 vs. 30).

We have been quite satisfied with the results of our response plan to date. Resistance we expected from line personnel on reporting changes and from persons-crimes investigators who might have perceived the VAP as an intrusion have never materialized. Rather, all members have been impressed by and appreciative of the support provided by the VAP. Furthermore, our general ethic and response to the problem of domestic violence and its victims has been elevated by the influence of the VAP and our partnership with the Network. We look forward to the program and our response evolving in the future.

[Adapted from Larry C. Plummer. "'Predictability' of Domestic Violence Offers an Opportunity for Successful Problem Solving." *Problem-Solving Quarterly*, Fall/Winter 1996, pp. 9–12. Reprinted by permission of the Police Executive Research Forum.]

DISCUSSION QUESTIONS

1. Have you ever been victimized? How were you treated by those who "assisted" you?

2. How large a role do you believe culpability plays in victimization?

3. Do police and other professionals who assist victims treat those victims who are wealthy differently from those who are poor?

4. How do you balance professional detachment and the need for empathy?

5. Not everyone agrees that victim impact statements are appropriate, especially in capital cases. What role do you feel they should play in sentencing?

6. In what ways do police officers become victims?

7. What differences exist between assisting victims of crime and victims of accidents or natural disasters?

8. How could community policing affect crime reporting by immigrants?

9. How do fear of crime and the reality of becoming a crime victim relate? How do these differ among youths and the elderly?

10. Explain the important role of victims and witnesses in the criminal justice system.

INFOTRAC COLLEGE EDITION ASSIGNMENTS

- Use InfoTrac to help answer the discussion questions as appropriate.

- Although crime in the United States has fallen steadily in recent years, crime reporting is more sensational and more prevalent than ever. This kind of crime reporting contributes to an unrealistic level of fear of crime and, in many cases, revictimizes victims and their families. Research *crime and the press* for information on how crime reporting affects victims. Cite examples and discuss the probable reasons for such reporting.

- New community policing approaches to preventing domestic violence are often referred to as "Homicide Prevention." Research *domestic violence* prevention and decide whether this is an accurate title.

COMMUNITY PROJECT

- What victim services are available in your community? What services that are not currently available should be available?

REFERENCES

Bettinger, Keith. "Unlocking Family Secrets." *Law Enforcement Technology,* Vol. 27, No. 10, October 2000, pp. 80–88.

Brogan, George. "Post-Trauma Bereavement in Long Branch, New Jersey." *The Police Chief,* Vol. LXVI, No. 5, May 1999, pp. 31–34, 38.

Buerger, Michael E. "The Problems of Problem-Solving." In Larry K. Gaines and Gary W.

Cordner, *Policing Perspectives: An Anthology.* Los Angeles: Roxbury Publishing Company, 1999, pp. 150–169.

Bureau of Justice Statistics. *National Crime Victimization Survey 1999.* Washington, DC: U.S. Department of Justice, May 2000. www.ojp.usdoj.gov/bjs/cvictgen.htm (NCJ-181585)

"Child Protective Services Report Decline in Abuse Cases." *Criminal Justice Newsletter,* Vol. 30, No. 13, July 1, 1999, p. 3.

Cohen, L. and Felson, M. "Social Change and Crime Rate Trends: A Routine Activity Approach." *American Sociological Review,* Vol. 44, 1979, pp. 588–608.

"Constitutional Amendment Fails to Win Senate Approval." *Criminal Justice Newsletter,* Vol. 30, No. 21, May 16, 2000, pp. 1–2.

Davis, Leigh Ann. "People with Mental Retardation in the Criminal Justice System." 2000. http://thearc.org/

Davis, Robert C. and Erez, Edna. *Immigrant Populations as Victims: Toward a Multicultural Criminal Justice System.* Washington, DC: National Institute of Justice Research in Brief, May 1998. (NCJ-167571)

Dumont, Lloyd F. "Recognizing and Surviving Post Shooting Trauma." *Law and Order,* Vol. 47, No. 4, April 1999, pp. 93–98.

Fagan, Jeffrey. *The Criminalization of Domestic Violence: Promises and Limits.* Washington, DC: National Institute of Justice Research Report, January 1996.

Goven, Patricia. "Law Enforcement Takes Action for Victims: IACP Summit Recommendations Released." *The Police Chief,* Vol. LXVII, No. 6, June 2000, pp. 14–24.

Heiskell, Lawrence E. "Post-Traumatic Stress Disorder." *Police,* Vol. 24, No. 3, March 2000, p. 10.

Kilpatrick, Dean G.; Beatty, David; and Howley, Susan Smith. *The Rights of Crime Victims— Does Legal Protection Make a Difference?* Washington, DC: National Institution of Justice Research in Brief, December 1998. (NCJ-173839)

Klaus, Patsy A. *Crimes against Persons Age 65 or Older, 1992–97.* Washington, DC: Bureau of Justice Statistics, January 2000. (NCJ-176352)

Lurigio, Arthur J. and Mechanic, Mindy B. "The Importance of Being Responsive to Crime Victims." *Police,* Vol. 24, No. 10, October 2000, pp. 22–28.

National District Attorneys Association. *A Prosecutor's Guide to Victim Witness Assistance.* Alexandria, VA: National District Attorneys Association, n.d.

New Directions from the Field: Victims' Rights and Services for the 21st Century. Washington, DC: U.S. Department of Justice, Office for Victims of Crime, May 1998.

Office for Victims of Crime. *Breaking the Cycle of Violence: Recommendations to Improve the Criminal Justice Response to Child Victims and Witnesses.* Monograph. June 1999. http://www.ojp.usdoj/ovc/factshts/monograph. htm

Office for Victims of Crime. *First Response to Victims of Crime: A Handbook for Law Enforcement Officers.* Washington, DC: U.S. Department of Justice, May 2000. (NCJ-176971) www.ojp.usdoj.gov/ovc/infores/firstrep/ welcome.html

"Partnership Combats Domestic Violence." *Law and Order,* Vol. 48, No. 7, July 2000, p. 173.

Plummer, Larry C. "'Predictability' of Domestic Violence Offers an Opportunity for Successful Problem Solving." *Problem-Solving Quarterly,* Fall/Winter 1996, pp. 9–12.

Robinson, Michael D. "Seeking Justice for Victims of Crime." *The Police Chief,* Vol. LXVII, No. 9, September 2000, p. 6.

Rosen, Marie Simonetti. "A LEN Interview with Susan Herman, Director of the National Center for Victims of Crime." *Law Enforcement News,* Vol. XXV, No. 522, November 30, 1999, pp. 8–11.

Strandberg, Keith W. "Victim and Witness Intimidation." *Law Enforcement Technology,* Vol. 24, No. 2, February 1997, pp. 42–48.

Strandberg, Keith W. "Child and Elder Abuse." *Law Enforcement Technology,* Vol. 26, No. 6, June 1999, pp. 20–22.

Tyiska, Cheryl Guidry. *Working with Victims of Crime with Disabilities.* Washington, DC: U.S. Department of Justice, Office for Victims of Crime Bulletin, September 1998. (NCJ-172838)

Von Hentig. *The Criminal and His Victim.* 1948.

Widom, Cathy Spatz. *Victims of Childhood Sexual Abuse—Later Criminal Consequences.* Washington, DC: National Institute of Justice Research in Brief, March 1995.

"Women Still Bear the Brunt of Domestic Violence Victimization." *Law Enforcement News,* Vol. XXVI, No. 539, September 15, 2000, p. 11.

RESOURCES

Battered Women's Justice Project; (800) 903-0111.

Bureau of Indian Affairs, Indian Country Child Abuse Hotline (800) 633-5155.

Bureau of Justice Statistics Clearinghouse, National Criminal Justice References Services, P.O. Box 5000, Rockville, MD 20849-6000; phone: (800) 732-3277; e-mail: askncjrs@ncjrs.org.ojp.usdoj.gov/bjs/

Childhelp USA/Forrester National Child Abuse Hotline; (800) 422-4453; TDD (800) 222-4453.

Childhelp USA® National Child Abuse Hotline; phone 800-4-A-Child.

Family Violence Prevention Fund, 383 Rhode Island St., Suite #304, San Franciso, CA, 94103-5133; phone: (415) 252-8900; fax: (415) 252-8991; e-mail: fund@fvpf.org

Family Violence Prevention Fund/Health Resource Center; (800) 313-1310.

Justice Statistics Clearinghouse; (800) 732-3277.

Juvenile Justice Clearinghouse; P.O. Box 6000, Rockville, MD 20849-5000; phone (800) 638-8736; fax: (301)-519-5212; e-mail: askncjrs@ncjrs.org

Mothers Against Drunk Driving; (800) 438-6233; P.O. Box 541688, Dallas, TX 75354-1688; phone: (800) Get-MADD.

National Center for Missing and Exploited Children, 1835 K Street, NW, Suite 700, Washington, DC 20006; (202) 634-9821. Hotline: (800) 843-5678; TDD (800) 826-7653.

National Center for Victims of Crime 2111 Wilson Boulevard, Suite 300, Arlington, VA 22201; phone: (800) 394-2255; (703) 276-288, fax: (703) 276-2889.

National Children's Alliance 1319 F Street NW, Suite 1001, Washington, DC, 20044-11; phone: (202) 639-0597 or (800) 239-9950.

National Clearinghouse for Alcohol and Drug Information; (800) 729-6686; TDD (800) 487-4889; (800) 735-2258, Hearing Impaired.

National Clearinghouse on Child Abuse and Neglect; (800) 394-3366.

National Consumers League, 1701 K Street, NW, Suite 1201, Washington, DC 20006; phone: (202) 835-3323 or (800) 876-7060; fax: (202) 835-0747.

National Criminal Justice Reference Service; (800) 851-3420; TTY (800) 787-3224.

National Fraud Information Hotline; (800) 876-7060.

National Organization for Victim Assistance (NOVA), P.O. Box 11000, Washington, DC 20008; (202) 232-NOVA; (800) 879-6682.

National Resource Center on Domestic Violence 6500 Flank Drive, Suite 1300, Harrisburg, PA 17112-2778; phone: (800) 537-2238 or (717) 545-6400; fax: (717) 545-9456; TTY (800) 553-2508.

National Victims Resource Center, Box 6000, Rockville, MD 20850; (800) 627-6872.

Office for Victims of Crime Resource Center; (800) 627-6872.

Parents of Murdered Children; (888) 818-7662

Rape, Abuse and Incest National Network; (800) 656-4673.

Resource Center on Domestic Violence, Child Protection, and Custody P.O. Box 8970, Reno, NV 89507; phone: (800) 527-3223. http://www.nclnet.org

CHAPTER 11

Forming Partnerships with the Media

Police work is very much an "us-and-them" kind of thing. They are the beleaguered minority who are out there protecting the citizens from themselves, and the citizens are not smart enough to appreciate them. And the newsies are out there lying in wait, and the moment they screw up, we're there to jump their throats and tell the world.

—Kevin Diaz

Do you know

What the common goal of the police and the media is?

Why the police-media relationship can be called symbiotic?

What amendment protects "freedom of the press"?

What amendment guides the police in their relationship with the media?

What are legitimate reasons for not giving information to the press?

What "off the record" really means?

How to enhance the safety of members of the media during explosive situations?

Whether conflict between the police and the press must be dysfunctional?

Whether it is ever appropriate or justifiable to lie to the media?

Why reporters may foul up stories? What implications this has for law enforcement?

How officers can improve relations with the media?

Why partnerships with the media are critical to the successful implementation of community policing?

Can you define these terms:

news media echo effect

Pager Information Network (PIN)

perp walks

public information officers (PIOs)

symbiotic

INTRODUCTION

The National Crime Prevention Council (350 *Tested Strategies* . . . , 1995, p. 2) states: "Media organizations are among the most visible and influential institutions in American communities." But Westfeldt and Wicker (1998, p. xi) note that the media are not always welcomed with open arms by the criminal justice system, including law enforcement:

> Given its size, power and cost, given the number of Americans who run it and who are caught up by it, the criminal justice system should be the target of constant monitoring by the press.
>
> It is not.
>
> More often than not, the press—defined as newspapers and broadcast news operations—actually is absent from the courtroom. . . .
>
> Millions of men, women and children move through the criminal justice system for the most part unobserved by the free American press, the public's supposed watchdog over all agencies of government. Unless he or she is a national figure, like O. J. Simpson, or someone accused of a crime that outrages the community, like the young British *au pair* in Massachusetts, his or her day in court probably will be unknown to the public because it will be unobserved by the press.

The media can be a powerful ally or a formidable opponent in implementing the community policing philosophy. Positive publicity can enhance both the image and the efforts of a department. Conversely, negative publicity can be extremely damaging, as evidenced by the "Rodney King Affair" aired internationally by CNN. Therefore, police agencies can and should make every effort to build positive working partnerships with the media.

The police and members of the media share the common goal of serving the public.

In addition to sharing a common goal, they also rely heavily on each other.

This chapter begins with a discussion of the mutual reliance of the police and the media and the inherent conflict between the guarantees of the First Amendment and the Sixth Amendment. This is followed by an examination of victims' privacy rights. Next is a discussion of the conflict between the media and the police, including the sources and the potential benefits of such conflict. General policies and protocols for media relations are presented, as well as recommendations on how to be professional when interviewed, whether police should ever lie to the media, the role of public information officers and how departments commonly address photographing and videotaping at crime scenes. The chapter concludes with suggestions for improving media relations and how police can adopt specific strategies for developing positive relationships with the media.

◈ MUTUAL RELIANCE OF THE POLICE AND THE MEDIA

Police departments and individual officers need the press. The press can shape public opinion, and most police agencies are concerned about their public image. Administrators know that crime and police activities are covered by the media regardless of whether the police provide reporters with information. Most police departments understand that the level of police cooperation will ultimately affect how the public views the police.

Garner (1995, p. 41) explains this mutual dependency: "The news business needs law enforcement as its largest single source of news that readers, viewers, and listeners want to know about. Law enforcement, meanwhile, needs the access to the public that the press can provide; to recognize good work by the frontline troops, enlist the citizenry's aid in solving a tough case or get the community's help with an important new police program or project." Garner further observes (p. 44): "Considering the many mutual benefits to be gained from getting along, cooperation is a win-win proposition for both sides."

The police and the media share a symbiotic *relationship; they are mutually dependent upon each other.*

To understand the relationship between the police and the media, officers should be aware of what rights the media have, what their mission is and why law enforcement does not always appear in a positive light in the media.

◉ THE FIRST AMENDMENT AND FREEDOM OF THE PRESS

The First Amendment to the U.S. Constitution states: "Congress shall make no law . . . abridging the freedom of speech or of the press." According to Rosenthal (1996a, p. 19): "The free flow of information is one of the cornerstones of our society. If the public asks (or if the media asks on behalf of the public) then law enforcement is legally required to respond and generally encouraged to do so (DOJ guidelines)."

The First Amendment to the U.S. Constitution guarantees the public's right to know, that is, freedom of the press.

According to the Freedom Forum (2000): "Freedom of the press was *specifically* mentioned in the First Amendment because James Madison and other supporters of the Bill of Rights felt it was necessary to the health of a democratic society. . . . [They] believed a free press [could] counter government's tendency to misuse power and to restrict the free flow of information." In fact, our society deems the public's right to know so important that the media operate without censorship but are subject to legal action if they publish untruths.

Police beat reporters are often eager and aggressive in carrying out their duty to inform the public. Anxious to do well and to be the first with information, they gather and publicize police and crime news as much as they can. The police beat is a visibility beat, considered a prestigious assignment by many newspapers and television stations and is, therefore, sought by the experienced, aggressive reporters.

Coverage of crime events also draws increased viewership and readership, prompting many news organizations to give "top billing" to such stories. In fact, many media markets are unofficially guided by the axiom, "If it bleeds, it leads." While keeping the public informed about situations affecting their personal and community's safety is an important and valuable service, the priority and emphasis placed on these stories often confuse the public about the true extent of crime and inflate the general level of fear people feel regarding their chances of personal victimization.

The Media and the Public's Fear of Crime

The public's rising fear of crime, despite reports the crime rate is decreasing, has led to much scrutiny of the media and their practices. Consider this common criticism: "The national news media—too often motivated primarily by profit and either bored by process or convinced that viewers and readers are—focus only on sensational crime cases in which the famous or infamous are accused of or victimized by some violent or bizarre misdeed" (Westfeldt and Wicker, p. vii).

A one-day survey of 102 local television news shows in 52 metropolitan areas revealed the amount of air time given to crime-related stories was 26.9 percent, with disaster news topics a distant second (12.2 percent) and health and government stories receiving 10.1 percent and 8.7 percent of air time, respectively (Rocky Mountain Media Watch, 1998, p. 6). News topics related to economics (8.5 percent of air time), education (3.6 percent), children (2.3 percent) and peace (0.5 percent) received significantly less air time. Paul Klite, executive director of the respected television watchdog, contends: "Night after night, audiences are terrified and titillated, aroused and manipulated, but not informed. Like an unbalanced diet which gradually can lead to serious illness, the local TV news threatens the health of our community." According to Westfeldt and Wicker (pp. 1–2):

> Americans tend to believe that crime is more prevalent than it actually is. . . . Inadequate, often sensational, sometimes misleading press reporting—both in print and on television—bears much responsibility for these frequently irrational public attitudes. . . . Crime in America . . . is not out of control. Its incidence remains too high, certainly, and no doubt many crimes are never reported. But available evidence shows that reported crime rates are *declining*. . . .
>
> Nevertheless, the fear of crime persists everywhere in the nation. So does sensational press coverage of violence and criminality—scare headlines in the newspapers and blaring reports on the nightly news programs.

In fact, the Rocky Mountain Media Watch found that 74 of the 102 stations surveyed had at least one murder-related story, with some prominently featuring particularly brutal or bizarre murders even if they occurred outside the station's local viewing area.

The local media are not alone in fueling the public's fear of crime. The Center for Media and Public Affairs reports that although the national murder rate dropped 20 percent from 1990 to April 1998, the number of murder stories on *network* newscasts rose by approximately 600 percent, from a total of 80 on NBC, ABC and CBS in 1990 to 486 in 1997, not including the many broadcasts of or about the O. J. Simpson trial ("It's Murder," 1998).

The recent media focus on violence in schools has also drawn widespread criticism. Lawrence (2000, p. 1) notes: "Hundreds of newspaper and television stories have been done on incidents of school violence, in spite of the fact that school violence has not been increasing, and the fact that the number of youth killed or injured per day by other means far outnumbers those killed or injured at school." John Stossel, correspondent for

ABC's *20/20*, criticized the media for perpetuating the distorted perception of crime and violence in schools through its extensive coverage of the Columbine High School shooting tragedy on April 20, 1999:

> Lightning kills more people. Bathtubs kill more kids. But the media's obsessed with school shootings. We make it seem like this is likely to happen in your town soon. . . . All the media hysteria has encouraged people who run schools to do crazy things, like spending thousands of dollars on endless security cameras, on police who guard the doors. . . . Some schools run SWAT team drills. The result? Though school violence is down, the kids are more scared. . . . We're terrorizing kids.

Surette (1998, p. 68) notes the paradox that the relative infrequency of violent crime in our society actually increases its newsworthiness and the amount of media coverage it receives, turning rare crime events into common crime images. This distortion and skewed crime reporting is identified by media critics as one reason the majority of people believe the country is not making progress in the war on crime (Beil, 1998). Westfeldt and Wicker (p. 2) argue that such skewed reporting is *the* main reason people fear crime: "It is primarily the media's sheer emphasis on crime and violence—almost invariably 'the lead' on local television newscasts, for example—that is most responsible for alarming the public."

Some researchers, however, contend the media are not alone in propagating the public panic and that, in many instances, the community policing effort is compromised by politicians and criminal justice professionals themselves. Welch et al. (1998, p. 220) assert: "Though crime news exists as a product manufactured by the media, it is shaped significantly by state managers [e.g., criminal justice practitioners] who contribute to its distinct ideological qualities."

According to these researchers, political leaders and law enforcement officials use the media to serve propaganda functions in the state's ideological machinery and to promote their "law-and-order" crime control agendas. They influence public perception of crime by filtering or screening the information provided to the media and, therefore, share responsibility with the media for the misleading depictions of crime and crime policy. Welch et al. (p. 223) contend: "The media, together with state managers, reproduce an image of public disorder that is based overwhelmingly on street crime, especially offenses committed by low-income individuals. . . . In publishing messages about certain forms of crime news, the media warn the public about some of the threats to their safety (e.g., street offenses) but neglect other social harms (e.g., white-collar and corporate offenses) because of ideological constraints." Welch et al. (p. 237) further report:

> Our research clarifies the roles of the media and the state in the social construction of distorted images of crime. . . . We find that several state managers repeatedly invoked crime-control mantras blending elements of political "tough-talk" and "crimespeak" with simplistic views of crime causation [for example, three state governors are quoted as saying basically the same thing in their governor's messages: "We're sending a message: If you commit the crime, you will do the time."] These remarks are ideologically self-serving because they reinforce the popular perception that the problem of crime is the sole domain of the criminal justice apparatus; thus other forms of state intervention (e.g., public health services) are excluded.

Such remarks also undermine the efforts of community policing by diminishing the importance of and need for partnerships between law enforcement and the community to effectively address crime.

In addition to heavily influencing the public's perception of crime, the media also play a significant role in how the public views the criminal justice system, including law enforcement.

The Media and the Police Image

The public's image of the police is shaped largely by what they see on television, and most of what they see is fictional. Noting the popularity of entertainment crime and police programs, Maguire et al. (1999, p. 171) state: "Americans are more likely to encounter television police rather than real police."

But how do the media portray the real police? A study of national, big city and small town television newscasts (Maguire et al., p. 185) revealed:

All levels of newscasts in the sample aired more positive than negative stories about the police, [although] there was a difference in degree. [The national and small-town newscasts] were much more likely [than the big city newscasts] to present stories sending out a favorable police image.

A second finding, one that is consistent with other media images of the police, is that television news tends to portray the police as crime fighters. Once again, however, there was not an even pattern: National (84%) and big city (72%) newscasts were more likely to highlight the crime fighting role than was the case for small town (63%) newscasts.

Maguire et al. (pp. 185–188) conclude that the depiction of the police on television news influences how viewers judge the effectiveness and integrity of the local police:

These . . . findings suggest a difference between big city and small town television news coverage of police and policing. For example, [big city newscasts were] more likely to depict the police negatively than [were small town newscasts]. Interestingly, survey data show that only 52% of urban residents have "a great deal" or "quite a lot" of confidence in their local police, whereas the comparable figure for small city residents is 65%. . . .

Another difference between [the big city and small town] newscasts is that the latter presented proportionately more reports that highlighted the community service function of the police. This [may be] due to the fact that there is less crime to report on . . . [or] may be . . . because small town television stations are interested in portraying their communities as safe and enjoyable places in which to live, conduct business, and visit.

The Media's Impact on the Criminal Justice System

Acknowledging the power of the media to shape public perception, some have also speculated that the media, through their coverage of isolated, high-profile cases, can influence the operations of the criminal justice system and even the disposition of individual cases. Much like a pebble thrown into a pond, the impact of a highly publicized case has a rippling effect that spreads throughout the judicial system and affects the entire process. Surette (1999, p. 601) calls this the **news media echo effect:**

> In high-profile trials, media attention affects the actions of attorneys, witnesses, judges, jurors, and the audience involved with the publicized case. High-profile trials also influence the everyday practices of law enforcement and adjudication, and affect the outcomes of numerous low-profile cases.

Under such an echo effect, defendants in a similar crime category as one recently publicized may be treated differently within the criminal justice system from the way they would have had such a high-profile case not preceded theirs. To examine the echo effect, Surette analyzed the processing of nearly 3,500 criminal cases over a ten-year period, including five years before and five years after a highly publicized case involving the sexual abuse of toddlers at a private day-care facility. He (p. 628) reports: "This study offers an empirically supported example of an echo effect in criminal justice generated by the news media. The analysis showed marked increases in filings of cases involving child victimization following the publicized case, a short-term increase in the length of sentences in cases adjudicated guilty, and a possible increase in the number of not guilty pleas."

Although research on the existence and magnitude of echo effects is scant, Surette (pp. 628–629) states: "Echo effects are a media-induced reconstruction of reality concerning the importance of a set of cases. . . . In the contemporary infotainment, hyper-media atmosphere, echo effects are likely to be ever-present."

The media have been aided in their quest for newsworthy information through the passage of some legislation, including the Freedom of Information Act. This act, however, is a double-edged sword, also protecting certain information.

Freedom of Information Act

Rosenthal (1996a, p. 18) describes the *Freedom of Information Act (FOIA),* which governs what police can and cannot disclose: "The Freedom of Information Act establishes a presumption that records in the possession of agencies and departments of the executive branch of the U.S. Government are accessible to the people . . . the 'need to know' standard has been replaced by a 'right to know' doctrine. The government now has to justify the need for secrecy." Rosenthal cites the following exceptions when the free flow of information can and should be restricted:

• When anyone's safety could be jeopardized
• When the integrity of an investigation and/or subsequent prosecution could be jeopardized
• When a confidential source would be revealed
• When limited internal personnel matters are involved
• When release of such information jeopardizes the privacy rights of sex crime victims, juveniles or mentally ill persons

Every state has a public records law that specifies what information a law enforcement agency must release, what information must not be released and what is discretionary.

Such laws are enacted to protect the rights of citizens under suspicion of breaking the law, as guaranteed by the Sixth Amendment.

◆ THE SIXTH AMENDMENT, SUSPECTS' RIGHTS AND CRIMINAL INVESTIGATIONS

The Sixth Amendment of our Constitution establishes that "in all criminal prosecutions, the accused shall enjoy the right to a speedy and public trial, by an impartial jury of the state and district wherein the crime shall have been committed."

The Sixth Amendment guarantees suspects the right to a fair trial and protects defendants' rights.

In addition to ensuring these rights, police officers are also responsible for investigating the crimes suspects are accused of committing. Law enforcement officers sometimes view reporters as an impediment to fulfilling their duties. Law enforcement officers often try to protect information they deem imperative to keep out of the media and may, therefore, be at odds with reporters. Such conflicts arise when police try to prevent public disclosure of information that may tip off a criminal of impending arrest, make prosecution of a particular crime impossible or compromise privacy rights or safety of a victim or witness. Reporters are anxious to do well on their assignments while officers try to avoid weakening their case and reprimands for being too open with the press. The parties' conflicting interests may result in antagonism.

◆ VICTIM PRIVACY RIGHTS

As mentioned, the FOIA protects the privacy rights of some people such as sex crime victims. However, amidst the shock and confusion that often occur immediately after a crime event, victims may easily be caught off guard by aggressive media personnel and may unwittingly put themselves or the investigation at risk by agreeing to an interview. To help victims and witnesses protect their own rights, as well as safeguard the criminal investigation, some departments have begun distributing media relations advisory cards. The Fairfax County (Virginia) Police Department (FCPD) is one such agency, as Rosenthal (2000d, p. 21) notes:

> For several years, supervisors in the FCPD public information office and victim services section have tried to find some way of assisting victims and witnesses who've been involved in serious incidents that draw media attention. The goal has always been to ensure the public's right to know, while also protecting the rights of privacy and safety of victims and witnesses.
>
> An additional concern was law enforcement's legitimate need to temporarily withhold information when its release might jeopardize the successful conclusion of an investigation. . . .
>
> An incident involving the attempted forcible sodomization of a [5-year-old] boy . . . spurred FCPD to draft a victim/witness media information card. A reporter covering the story for a television station broadcast an interview with the boy's distraught mother—and even broadcast video of the little boy.

In response, the FCPD, led by the public information office director, Warren Carmichael, created a brief media advisory the size of a business card for officers to distribute to victims and witnesses of certain serious or sensitive cases. The card, available in English, Spanish, Korean, Vietnamese and Farsi, reads:

> *News media may wish to interview you regarding this incident. You have the right to grant or refuse interviews. If you choose to give an interview, please call one of the numbers on the reverse side. You will be given advice important to protecting your rights and the investigation, but there is no legal requirement to contact police prior to an interview.*

The back of the card gives the phone number for the public information office and the victim services section. Rosenthal (2000d, pp. 21–22) also reports:

> In a further effort to balance the rights of all concerned, FCPD has developed guidelines for distribution of the cards. These state, in part:
>
> "These information cards are intended for distribution only in connection with serious or high profile cases, such as homicides, robberies, sex offenses and certain fatal accidents. The *cards should only be presented in conjunction with the other victim services information normally provided.* Any discussion about media interviews should . . . always [emphasize] that the decision to speak with the media is solely the individual's. *Advising against interviews should be done only in cases where there are legitimate personal safety issues and/or extremely sensitive investigative issues*" (Italics are FCPD's).

Such cards, however, have caused concern among some journalists who contend the advisories will interfere with news gathering:

> Members of the Society of Professional Journalists [SPJ], a group that includes a broad range of media professionals, said the practice could have an impact on whether immigrants and those who do not know their rights decide to speak with reporters.
>
> "People who are told by police, 'Call us first before you talk to a reporter,' are going to listen and not talk," said . . . a member of the society's District of Columbia chapter ("The Right to Remain . . . ," 2000, p. 1).

The president of the SPJ contends: "Accurate and timely information on crimes is important to any community. That means victims should not be deterred from talking to reporters." A *Washington Post* editorial clearly expresses a firm opposition to the advisory cards: " . . . precisely because police departments should not be the sole source of information, they should not be in the business of putting a damper on the willingness of people to share with fellow citizens valuable news about crime." But the FCPD and many other law enforcement agencies disagree (Rosenthal, 2000d, p. 22). Carmichael argues: "We advise criminals of their rights. Why is it so out of line for us to advise victims and witnesses of their rights?"

Not surprisingly, these opposing perspectives generate substantial conflict between the media and the police, which can contaminate an agency's efforts to fulfill its community policing mission.

◇ CONFLICT BETWEEN THE MEDIA AND THE POLICE

The press and the police are two powerful forces in our society that depend on one another but are often hostile toward and mistrust each other. At the outset of one workshop that brought law enforcement and media personnel together to air grievances, discuss issues of common concern and generally get to know one another better so that the two groups could work more effectively together, participants were asked to list three adjectives they thought best described "the other side." Rosenthal (2000b, p. 22) reports:

> The responses were very telling. While there were a few positives, the majority of the adjectives from both sides were negative.
>
> Law enforcement described the media as "demanding," "unethical," "uncaring," "biased," "arrogant," and "negative." The media participants described their police peers as "evasive," "uncooperative," "non-trusting," "self-important," "indifferent," and "withholding."

Another question posed to conference participants was: "What is the most important thing you think the 'other side' doesn't understand about you and your work that you want them to learn from this conference?" Again, Rosenthal (2000c, p. 21) observes: "The written responses from each side were enlightening."

A major theme among media participants was their need to get information from law enforcement in a timely manner to keep the public informed. Some of their comments:

> "The public has the right to know. . . . The media are vital to keeping the public informed about what law enforcement does on its behalf. . . . Media is the connection between police and public. . . . We have deadlines. We wish they'd [police] respect them and try to help. . . . Sometimes we are under a major time crunch. . . . We're not trying to be difficult; that information, even a little, can help us in breaking news situations" (Rosenthal, 2000c, p. 21).

Police participants, of course, had their own slant on the issue of timely information release:

> "There are times during an ongoing investigation that divulging information would jeopardize the case. We're not simply being evasive. . . . We can't publicly disclose all info or give opinions on issues. . . . Laws and guidelines that we must abide by prohibit us all too often from commenting on certain subjects, but the 'other side' [of the case] can and do, thus giving a very slanted view. . . . We are busy investigating, helping people, [and are] too busy to talk. . . . Police often do not know all of the story within the first minutes of the investigation. . . . We do not always have time for them [media]. . . . They need to learn patience with the gathering of information. . . . We are more concerned about doing our job than giving them a story" (Rosenthal, 2000c, pp. 21–22).

This last comment perhaps strikes the greatest nerve between the police and the media, for part of the community policing job *is* communicating with the public through the media, and the media are often in a position to help police reach vital sources of information about crime within the community. Nonetheless, conflict continues because significantly different perspectives exist between the police and the media concerning what the priorities should be for officers in "doing their jobs."

Sources of Conflict

While conflict between the media and the police may arise from a variety of sources, perhaps the most basic are competing objectives, contradictory approaches to dangerous situations and stereotyping.

Competing Objectives. A fundamental source of conflict is the competing objectives of the press and the police. The First Amendment guarantee of freedom of the press is often incompatible with the Sixth Amendment guarantee of the right to a fair trial and protection of the defendant's rights. This leads to a basic conflict between the public's right to know and the individual's right to privacy and a fair trial.

Police may need to withhold information from the media until next of kin are notified, in the interest of public safety or to protect the integrity of an investigation.

To do their job, members of the media need information from the police. Press people say they have problems obtaining information they are entitled to because the police refuse to provide it. In some cases, reporters believe they have been singled out by the police for "punishment" in response to a negative story about the police. Reporters tell of police who restrict information, refuse requests for interviews, disregard reporters' deadlines, hang up the telephone on reporters, provide inaccurate information, play dumb or even blackball a particular reporter in retaliation for a story they did not like.

Indeed, some police agencies or officers who have had negative experiences with the media or believe they have been tricked into releasing information do react by becoming uncooperative, not giving information to which the press is entitled, playing favorites among reporters and even lying. However, this behavior only aggravates an already difficult relationship.

Motivated by a desire to protect their case and the privacy of those involved, police complain that the press is critical and biased against the police, that reporting is often inaccurate, that reporters lack sensitivity, especially toward victims, and that the press releases sensitive material and betrays the trust of officers.

One point of contention concerns "off the record" comments some public officials are inclined to make to reporters. Many have been unpleasantly surprised to be quoted in the next edition of the newspaper. Officers must learn to say only that which they can accept attribution for and are prepared to read or hear reported in the media.

To speak to a reporter "off the record" does not guarantee the information will not be reported. It may, in fact, make it more likely to be reported.

In some cases, reporters promise to keep information "off the record" when they have no authority to do so. And while many media professionals do respect "off the record," they may misquote, which can cause significant problems and additional conflict.

Sometimes the media distort information received from the police department for a political purpose. For example, Houston had two newspapers—the *Houston Chronicle* and the *Houston Post*. The editors of the *Post* disliked the mayor and took every opportunity to twist police department information into damaging prose. In one instance, *Post* reporters had counted the number of dead body investigations listed in the Homicide Division log book to compare with published UCR statistics. Noting discrepancies, the *Post* eagerly printed "news" of the department's cover up and tampering with statistics. The department, in turn, issued a report explaining why the dead body log differed from the UCR data (some deaths were determined to be from natural causes, suicides, etc.). The *Post*, however, refused to acknowledge the explanation and continued to repeat the accusations even after the discrepancies were justified. The department then restricted *Post* reporters' freedom to roam around, limiting their access to the Public Information Office. The *Post* eventually went out of business.

As discussed, the way the public views crime and the police depends in large part on what the media report. Although many police officers are keenly aware of the conflict between themselves and the media, they often do not understand how the need to withhold information contributes to the conflict and the resulting negative coverage or what they and their department can do to alleviate the problem. Officers must remember, however, that the media consist of businesses in fierce competition with each other for readers, listeners and viewers. What officers may consider sensationalism, reporters might consider the competitive edge.

Contradictory Approaches to Dangerous Situations. Another source of conflict between law enforcement and the media is the danger members of the media may expose themselves to in getting a story and the police's obligation to protect them. As

CHP (California Highway Patrol) Officer Fred Bowes promotes the agency's crackdown on drunk drivers in front of a wrecked car. Enlisting community support often depends on the media's cooperation.

© Bob Clay/Jeroboam, Inc.

with that of the general public, the safety of the media at crime scenes or riots or poten- tially dangerous situations is important. While most reporters and photographers will not cross yellow police tape lines, many are willing to risk a degree of personal safety to get close to the action.

If a situation is unfolding and the police and the media are both on the scene, officers should not tell journalists to stay away—a red flag to most reporters. Instead, officers, bet- ter trained at reading dangerous situations, should urge reporters and photographers to leave an area if they deem it unsafe and tell them why, not just shout, "Get out of here!"

A television news director whose crew was attacked during a riot talked with police after the incident. The officers said they knew their first responsibility was to secure the area and calm things down, but they also felt responsible for the safety of the media, and it angered them that the media were "stupid" enough to be in the middle of the riot. The crew was told to leave and was doing so when attacked. But despite their alleged dislike of the media, the officers didn't want to see the media crew hurt.

To avoid similar scenarios, police should meet with local media representatives to discuss rules of safety so they might, together, develop a general policy. This should be done *before* an incident arises. It might boil down to deciding the media have the right to make decisions about their own well-being but that officers will issue warnings to try to ensure the safety of news crews.

To help ensure the safety of media personnel at explosive situations, police should meet with media representatives to explain the safety rules before an incident arises.

The issue of media crew safety, and whether the police are responsible for that safety, remains a big issue.

Stereotyping. Chapter 6 discussed the need for police to avoid stereotypes. Stereotyp- ing is a dangerous habit and can greatly impede good working relationships between law enforcement and members of the media. While it happens to both the police and the media, by each other as well as by the general public, it is important for officers and reporters to see each other as individuals. Both work under the U.S. Constitution and, thus, need to open the lines of effective communication and work together for the pub- lic good.

Understanding differences in personality can help build effective relationships between individual police officers and individual media personnel and greatly reduce the barriers between the two professions. There can and must be a *trust factor* for this to be effective. For example, a radio newscaster who has the trust of the police department can be given confidential information, knowing that he or she will not release it until given the go-ahead. This one-on-one relationship can be of value to law enforcement and to the media.

Dissolving stereotypic views of each other is a significant step toward changing a dys- functional conflict between the police and the media into a healthy, beneficial conflict.

Benefits of Conflict

Conflict between the police and the media is necessary because each must remain objective and able to constructively criticize the other when needed. In fact, Brooks

(1999, p. 22) notes: "The news media have a distinct role in a democracy to oversee the actions of the traditional three branches of government and thereby prevent abuses of power by those branches."

Conflict need not be dysfunctional. In fact, healthy conflict between the media and the police is necessary and beneficial.

Conflict can stimulate people to grow and change. It can diffuse defensiveness if those in conflict recognize that their roles are, by definition, conflicting yet complementary. Better understanding of each other may lead to a cooperative effort to serve the public.

Most large law enforcement agencies recognize that a cooperative relationship with the media is to their benefit. Many have developed media policies that set forth for officers exactly what may and may not be released to the press, how information will be released and by whom.

◆ GENERAL POLICIES AND PROTOCOL FOR MEDIA RELATIONS

Most agencies have developed written policies governing release of information to the press. These policies recognize the right of reporters to gather information and often direct officers to cooperate with the media. Woodall (1998, p. 72) asserts:

> A complete media Standard Operating Procedure will establish authority, delegate responsibility and define the rules to be followed when dealing with reporters and photographers from newspapers, radio and television. A solid media SOP will be a valuable asset, particularly when the agency must confront a high-visibility case and intense media coverage.

Officers who encounter and release information to the media are expected to display the highest level of professionalism, for not only will their message be relayed to the public but so will their image and, by reflection, the image of their department. Consequently, many agencies have specific policies and protocol to guide officers during media interviews.

Being Professional When Interviewed

It has been said, "You don't argue with people who buy ink by the barrel." This may be helpful to keep in mind when preparing for an interview with a news reporter. In addition to knowing and following your agency's media guidelines, Garner (1995, p. 51) offers several tips for surviving an interview. Find out what you are to be interviewed about and gather the facts you will need to respond to anticipated questions. Realize it is all right to be a bit nervous, but remain courteous and in control of your emotions. Look, sound and act like the professional you are. Get to the point; do not wander or waste words. Always tell the truth—and nothing but. And finally, if you do not know the answer, say so. If you cannot give the answer, say so and explain why.

Avoid using "no comment," and instead provide a truthful explanation of why you can't respond, for as the director of media relations for one police department contends: "'No comment' implies that there is a story there that you are not telling" (Strandberg, 2000, p. 93).

To allay concerns over being misquoted, ask the reporter to provide a transcript of your quotes. Strandberg (p. 93) notes: "In most cases, the media will not allow its sources to review the complete story before it is printed or aired, but many times they will provide quotes." Other suggestions for getting your message across during an interview include (Garner, 1996, pp. 50–51, 111):

Choose your words carefully. Steer clear of off-color terms or derogatory remarks—it is precisely that kind of statement that is most likely to get on the air or into print.

Do not play favorites and stay on the record. Telling secrets to the press—going "off the record"—is extremely risky. Also beware of live electronics and assume every camera or microphone in your presence is live.

Be clear and offer to clarify anything that remains unclear. Clarify convoluted questions by requesting the interviewer to explain exactly what it is that is being asked. Defeat the interrupter by speaking over them if necessary. Correct the misinterpreter by addressing any incorrect information immediately.

Finally, maintain good eye contact and do not hesitate to smile if appropriate.

Rosenthal (1996b, p. 89) offers the following recommendations for handling "hostile" reporters:

First, commit your department to openness and fairness with the media. Whatever you do, don't lose your head. Talk with the reporter face-to-face and try to set the record straight. If the reporter persists, and continues the attack, respond right away with all your clout. Bring out your "big gun": the chief or sheriff should seek an immediate meeting with the reporter's publisher or general manager. . . . Your goal is to present the facts, counter the unfair reporting, get a correction and prevent future abuse. A publisher or general manager may well hear you, where an overly aggressive reporter has not.

Garner (1996, p. 43) suggests when handling bad news, don't lie, ever; don't hide from the press or refuse to see reporters—this raises suspicions; don't dribble out bad news; don't alter press policies to make them more restrictive during bad news; and don't lose your cool.

The press knows that bad relations between the media and the police can result in limited access to police information. Cooperation and mutual trust benefit both the press and the police.

Lying to the Media

Lying to the press is always a bad idea. So is making promises that you cannot keep or misleading reporters. Such actions usually haunt the individual officer or the agency in the form of negative press or lack of media cooperation when the police need help. It is better to honor commitments to the media and be straightforward when information is to be released.

Agencies and officers who make a practice of deceiving the media are at great risk of losing public confidence, for as Brooks (p. 24) notes: "The decision to lie to the media remains, in effect, a decision to lie to the general public." Rosenthal (2000a, p. 17) adds: "For law enforcement to have effective public relations, it must build bridges of cooperation with the media. Three essential pillars of those bridges are mutual trust, mutual credibility, and mutual respect." However: "There are those extraordinary circumstances under which police may be justified in lying to the media." The following incident illustrates such a justification (details from Rosenthal, 2000a, pp. 17–18):

In the summer of 2000, Jimmy Gordon and his wife, Shirley, were going through a divorce, and he was taking it badly. One day while Shirley was at the home of friends, the Clarks, Jimmy got desperate and went looking for her, with a double-barreled 12-gauge shotgun and a handful of shells.

At the Clarks, Jimmy forced his way into the house and demanded to see his wife. The Clarks managed to escape with one of their children, but four other children, ranging in age from 6 to 23, remained inside as hostages. Shirley Gordon was also in the house, hiding in a basement storage space. The Clarks called the police, and the tactical unit, including a negotiator, responded. So did the media.

Unaware that she was hiding in the basement, Jimmy demanded to the police to talk to his wife. The Clarks told the police Shirley was still in the house, which elevated the tension surrounding the event because Jimmy had told the negotiator earlier that he planned to kill his wife and himself.

In the meantime, all three local TV stations and a radio news station were interrupting normal programming with live broadcasts from the scene. In fact, Jimmy told police he, too, was watching reports of the event on the TV inside the house. Reporters were kept informed by Public Information Officer Sergeant Bruce Elrod, who had worked hard over the years to earn the trust and respect of the media. But they were pressing PIO Elrod for details. What was Jimmy Gordon demanding, and how did the police plan to handle the situation? Elrod found himself in a precarious position. He knew he could stall reporters for awhile but that, eventually, whatever he told the media would also reach Jimmy. So Elrod, after consulting with the tactical unit commander, made the tough decision to lie to the media.

He told them Jimmy Gordon's demand was that he be allowed to talk to his wife (true); that she was not in the house (false); that the police didn't know where she was (false); and that authorities were looking for her (false). The message got through—negotiators and the news reports convinced Jimmy that his wife was nowhere to be found and that he was at a dead end. He began releasing his hostages, walked out of the house and surrendered, with no one getting hurt.

As soon as Jimmy was in handcuffs, the first thing Elrod did was go back to the media and admit he'd been lying to them all afternoon. He stressed he'd never deceived the press during his four years as PIO, but that in this case, where Shirley Gordon's life, as well as those of the hostages, was at stake, he had no other option than to lie and that he hoped the media would understand.

Afterward, a news director for one of the local stations agreed Elrod's decision was "perfectly justifiable in order to ensure the woman's safety. She was in clear danger. Lying does not come naturally to Elrod. I don't think there were any [negative] repercussions or hard feelings on the part of the media."

Brooks (p. 24) asserts: "Law enforcement officials contemplating intentionally deceiving the media should ask . . . if the official would be willing to publicly explain why the deception was used, and if they are willing to accept any consequences of the public disclosure."

"If some morally overriding reason, such as public safety, obliges an official to lie, then it also requires an explanation or apology for the deception later, after the crisis has passed" *(Brooks, p. 24).*

The nature of police business often requires the delicate handling and release (or retention) of information, and it is frequently difficult and time-consuming, particularly for larger agencies, to keep all officers equally informed about which details of a case may be provided to the media. Consequently, many agencies now employ public information officers.

Public Information Officers

Some police departments feel comfortable allowing any member to talk to the media and provide information. Former Minneapolis Chief of Police, Tony Bouza, did not have press officers during his administration: "Every member of the department serves as a spokesperson. Reporters are free to call any member of the department and ask them any questions they want. And you will get an answer, regardless of the rank of the officer you speak to." Bouza was fond of saying that the Minneapolis Police Department had 714 public information officers. Journalists, however, often complain that although any officer could speak on behalf of the police department, the police usually release far less information than such an open policy permits.

Some departments discourage individual officers from talking to reporters and instead designate **public information officers (PIOs)** to disseminate all information to the media. PIOs are officers trained in public relations who try to consistently provide accurate information while controlling leaks of confidential or inaccurate details and managing controversial or negative situations to the department's benefit.

The PIO has a significant amount of responsibility. When PIOs properly carry out their responsibilities, they can improve police-media relations. Following are some tips from award-winning PIOs (Rosenthal, 1999, pp. 21–22):

> "You're a conduit to project the image of your agency. You try to give the public a fair representation of what's going on within the agency. You do that by highlighting some of the unique achievements of your personnel."
>
> "My work ethic as a PIO is service. It goes hand in hand with what law enforcement does. We're there to serve the community. As PIO, I'm serving the public. But I'm also serving the agency, and the media."
>
> "Being a PIO is a profession. The PIO is just as visible as the chief or sheriff, and has to be able to professionally represent the agency."

"When there are minor errors of fact I don't ask for a correction, but I contact the reporter and give the correct information, make sure they understand, then ask that in succeeding stories they use the correct information. If a correction is required, I always put the request in writing to get it on the record, and I send it to the editor as well as the reporter. I make the request right away, by fax, right to the newsroom, and ask that they contact me that day to help them get it right."

"I make sure that all media personnel have my pager number, and encourage them to use it. When I get a page I immediately return the call, and they appreciate it. It's valuable in building relationships and they've never abused the privilege."

While talking with reporters is one thing, allowing the media to photograph or shoot video at crime scenes is something quite different because there are important Fourth Amendment constraints for police to consider. As a result, many departments have policies in place regarding the use of cameras at crime scenes.

Policies Regarding Photographing and Videotaping at Crime Scenes

They say a picture is worth a thousand words. Crawford (2000, p. 26) recounts:

> The American public recently awoke to the news that INS agents had ended a standoff with the relatives of young Elian Gonzales by forcibly entering the relatives' Miami home under the authority of a federal search warrant and seizing the boy. Within hours of the operation, poignant pictures of the seizure appeared on televisions and front pages of newspapers across the country. Probably the most memorable photograph is one depicting a terrified young Elian, cowering in the arms of a man, as an armed INS agent reaches for him.

According to Crawford (p. 26): "Americans have grown accustomed to detailed news coverage of law enforcement activities. The public's seemingly unquenchable interest in viewing the exploits of law enforcement officers has spawned the ever increasing media coverage of such events." Indeed, the popularity of television shows where camera crews ride along with officers as they patrol the community and respond to calls is evidence of the public's fascination with such activities. Crawford (p. 27) also notes, however: "When the media is present to document law enforcement activities inside most private premises, they are there at the invitation of the officers. It is this invitation . . . that has given rise to a number of civil suits against law enforcement officers."

In *Wilson v. Layne* (1999), the U.S. Supreme Court confronted the issue of whether a media presence, at law enforcement's invitation, to document police activities conducted on private premises violated privacy rights protected by the Fourth Amendment. In this case, the police and accompanying journalists were seeking a fugitive but went to the wrong address, that of the fugitive's parents. Early one morning, Charles and Geraldine Wilson awoke to the sounds of someone forcibly entering their home. Moments later they encountered not only several armed police officers but also a photographer taking pictures and a reporter taking notes. When the officers learned of their mistake, they left, but the entire incident had been captured on film by the media. And although the photographs taken that day were never published, the Wilsons filed suit against the officers who had invited the media into their home.

The Court found that, although the officers had entered the residence under the lawful authority of a warrant, the media were not present for any purpose reasonably related to the execution of the warrant and, thus, the officers exceeded the authority of the warrant by inviting the media to take part. Furthermore, the Court ruled that, while law enforcement does possess a legitimate objective in publicizing its efforts to combat crime and minimize the likelihood of both police abuse and physical resistance of subjects, those objectives were not sufficient to outweigh the "right of residential privacy at the core of the Fourth Amendment." Zeichner (1999, p. 24) concludes: "This ruling by the U.S. Supreme Court, which was unanimous, should sharply curb a common practice in which newsmen accompany officers into private homes to obtain dramatic shots of law enforcement in action."

Perp walks, another once-common police practice where suspects were paraded before the hungry eyes of the media, have also fallen on shaky legal ground. Brandon (1999, p. 99) states:

> It's a recurring scene for news reporters, photographers, and camera crews; a handcuffed figure, often wearing a jail uniform, is escorted through a crowd of news media people by a group of law enforcement officers. Reporters shout questions as the cameras roll. . . .
>
> There is seldom a legitimate reason to move the suspect through an area of public access where the media is located. It is simply done for the publicity provided by the news media.
>
> Journalists and law enforcement officers don't agree about a lot of things, but they both benefit from "perp walk." The media get the pictures they need for the evening news and the morning's paper. Officers get a chance to take a public bow for their work.

However, this nearly century-old tradition may not see much action in the 21st century. As with the media ride-alongs, courts have begun ruling that perp walks violate a suspect's right to privacy. Many jurisdictions have suspended the practice of perp walks, while others await rulings by the appellate courts ("Putting the Hobbles . . . ," 1999, p. 10).

Police departments vary in whether they allow news cameras in or around crime scenes. Prohibiting cameras may give the impression that the police have something to hide. However, people not involved in an investigation must *not* be allowed to contaminate the crime scene.

Another problem with allowing cameras at crime or accident scenes is viewed not from the police perspective but from that of the victim or complainant, who might not want themselves, their family members or their home to be on someone's video, documentary or TV series. However, nobody has a right to expect privacy in a public place.

Police officers should also be aware of the news system called "file video" or "file photos," where pictures are kept indefinitely and can be reused at anytime. For example, in one case a photographer arranged to go with a squad on a high-risk entry into a crack house. The police department let the reporter come along to get some video of how they are working to curb drug traffic in the city. The reporter did the story, and the police were pleased with the resulting public image. Two years later, one officer involved in the high-risk entry unit faced an indictment by a federal grand jury for police brutality. The reporter mentioned to his boss that they had video of this officer breaking into the home of some poor black citizens on the north side. The editors decided that was just what they needed for the story, and the video the police had at one time encouraged the media to take was used against the officer.

◉ IMPROVING RELATIONS WITH THE MEDIA

Rosenthal (1996c, p. 19) suggests: "With law enforcement suffering a number of body blows to its image in the last couple of years, the profession cannot afford to take media relations lightly or pass up any opportunity to improve its public image." An important first step to improve relations with the media is to be aware of three basic reasons why reporters may foul up a story.

Reporters may bungle a story due to ignorance, oversimplification or time constraints.

Reporters, particularly rookies or those new to the police beat, may be ignorant of law enforcement procedures and of Sixth Amendment requirements. Journalists must often fashion a complicated investigation or series of events into a paragraph-long news story or a 15- to 20-second story at the top of the hour. Furthermore, they commonly work under severe deadline pressure. Rosenthal (1996b, p. 18) stresses: "Reporters live and die by deadlines. Deadlines are critically important to the media and therefore do demand an awareness and sensitivity on the part of law enforcement, if the two professions are to have a mutually effective relationship." Officers who are aware of these common problems can more effectively deal with reporters.

To improve police-media relations, inform the press of your department's policies and procedures regarding the media and crime scenes; simplify your information, avoiding police jargon and technical terminology; and respect reporters' deadlines by releasing information in a timely manner so the press has a chance to fully understand the situation.

Training is another way to improve relationships and enhance the media's understanding of what police work involves. The Lakewood (Colorado) Police Department, for example, invited the local newspaper and broadcast reporters to enroll in a citizens' police academy. The reporters were given laser guns and acted out different scenarios to demonstrate the difficult decisions police must make. Inviting members of the media to ride in squad cars is also an effective way to enhance the media's understanding of policing. (Recall, however, such invitations should not extend into citizens' private premises.) Conversely, police officers could benefit from learning more about the media and their mission and responsibilities. Officers must remember that reporting is a highly competitive *business.*

A good rapport with the media can also help the police department accomplish its mission, for improved media relations leads to improving community relations. As stated earlier, the media are often the primary link between the law and the citizenry. To reach the community, the victims of crime and possible witnesses, the police must first reach the media.

The media can also be of assistance in public education programs. For example, an agency in California wanted to increase the accuracy of citizens' reports of suspicious and criminal activities. They enlisted the aid of the local newspaper to run a public announcement about what to include in suspect and vehicle descriptions.

In Chicago, the police use the media in their crime prevention efforts. The Federal Communications Commission (FCC) requires all media to set aside airtime or publication space for community projects. This is another excellent avenue for law enforcement agencies to convey educational messages to the residents of their communities.

Other media possibilities include talk shows, in which an agency spokesperson can discuss a controversy or a trend. Sometimes the editor of a local newspaper or publication will permit an organization a regular column. Letters to the editors may be written in response to other letters sent in to the editorial page.

Rosenthal (1997, p. 12) believes: "Good media relations is the best investment police administrators can make. There are good days and very bad days in police work. If you build up the trust and good will of the media during the good times they'll tend to be on your side when things turn tough." Wexler (1997, pp. 2–3) offers the following suggestions for working effectively with the media:

- As media police guru Jerry Nachman has advised, more police chiefs will lose their jobs due to the barrel of a camera lens than the barrel of a gun. So Nachman advises, get to know editors and reporters during non-stressful times. Take them to lunch and tell them what you and your department are doing. Ask them what types of stories they are interested in doing and how you and your staff can provide the information they need when they need it.

- Don't overlook the editorial boards and op-ed page editors of newspapers or television. Again, develop a relationship with them and let them in on the "big picture" of your department's goals and plans.

- Be careful about giving exclusive interviews to national correspondents while you bypass local reports. National correspondents will leave town and local reporters will feel like second-class citizens. These are the reporters who can help make you or break you in the local news.

The National Crime Prevention Council (350 *Tested Strategies* . . . , p. 2) adds these recommendations:

- Involve owners and senior management of prominent local media organizations in prevention task forces and other initiatives.

- Ensure that media representatives are on guest lists for community events, prevention workshops, parades and other activities.

- Work with media representatives to help shape policies about violence in programming and to use the media to encourage positive responses to crime problems.

- Consider the media as both a partner and a resource.

When the relationship between the police and media is improved, effective and valuable partnerships can be forged for the benefit of the entire community, as well as the individual agencies involved.

◈ STRATEGIES FOR DEVELOPING PARTNERSHIPS WITH THE MEDIA

Recall from Chapter 1 the definition of community policing: a philosophy that emphasizes working proactively with citizens to reduce fear, solve crime-related problems and prevent crime. It is a collaborative effort founded on close, mutually beneficial ties between the police and the people. There is no more effective or efficient way for law enforcement to forge a relationship with the community than to partner with the media. The National Crime Prevention Council (*350 Tested Strategies* . . . , p. 31) observes: "Community leaders, key elected officials, church leaders, school board and Parent Teacher Association members, philanthropists, and local celebrities often maintain contact with media sources." The council suggests these people could be brought together through a police-media partnership to sponsor or support crime prevention activities in the community.

Such partnerships with the media are not entirely new. For example, the McGruff "Take a Bite Out of Crime" national media campaign and other crime prevention public service announcements have existed for decades. (Using the media in crime prevention efforts is discussed again in Chapter 12). However, local efforts to enjoin the media in the police effort to prevent crime have been lacking. The National Crime Prevention Council (*350 Tested Strategies* . . . , p. 30) advocates the strategy of using the local media as an ally in the police effort to focus attention on community-based crime prevention projects and organizations:

> By highlighting such efforts, the media reinforces the community's standard in opposition to all types of crime and helps build crime prevention awareness among the public.
>
> Key tasks of this strategy include recognizing the power of the media as the public's source of information on a variety of topics; identifying media contacts; and establishing cooperation between community programs and media resources. The media should be asked to publicize community events and promote public education on crime prevention through articles, public service announcements, radio shows, news programs, and cable television shows.

Sparks and Staszak (2000, p. 22) suggest: "Because the media covers issues of public interest, prudent managers should realize the importance of proactively using the media as a tool to get their department's message out to the community."

Young (1997, p. 20) states: "Many departments have ignored an existing, and in most cases, readily available resource that could reach out to the community with minimal effort from line officers. . . . This potentially powerful, but often untapped, resource is the public access programming component of the cable television industry." She (pp. 21–22) adds: "As the most visible arm of municipal government, the police department can work with the cable company to provide a wealth of public service programming."

Some police departments have formed successful unions with this valuable medium. Keith (1998, p. 5) describes one such partnership:

> In August 1985, the Oxnard [California] Police Department created a television program to air on the cable company's local access channel. The program,

StreetBeat, offers residents the chance to learn more about their police department, find out about crime trends in their neighborhoods, and learn crime prevention techniques that could help them avoid becoming a victim. The program is extremely well-received and is the cable channel's most watched program. Estimates from the cable company put the number of viewers at between 5,000 to 8,000 each week. . . .

From 1985 to 1991, *StreetBeat* enjoyed a loyal following. Then in the summer of 1991, a young woman was raped at gunpoint on a public beach in Oxnard. . . . The department decided to host a 90-minute edition of *StreetBeat* focusing on the incident . . . [which] aired on a Monday night and was a huge success, with dozens of people calling in during the program to talk about the rape incident. . . .

The beach neighborhood responded in another positive way. Calls reporting suspicious activity in the area increased. Officers patrolling the area saw a corresponding decrease in crime. . . . In fact, for the three months following the televised meeting, crime dropped nearly 90 percent in the neighborhood!

Keith (p. 5) notes the Oxnard cable program costs nothing for the police department to produce because the cable company covers all the production costs. Furthermore, the program generates a profit, with the advertising revenues split between the cable company and the department: "The department's share, well over $20,000 a year, funds crime prevention efforts."

Other departments have also caught on to the effectiveness of televised law enforcement programs. According to Klein and Getz (1999, p. 237):

The Clearwater (FL) Police Department discovered that crime does pay—on TV. Not only has the program—Blueline CPD—been a ratings success, but it's proved to be one of the most effective ways for the department to market itself, its programs and its officers. . . .

Blueline CPD capitalizes on the latest technology to produce a format they call "Interactive TV" . . . where the audience can interact in real time with the top law enforcement executive as he responds to callers who pose questions, make comments and—yes—sometimes complain about what they consider problems that have not been resolved by the department.

Klein and Getz (p. 237) explain how Blueline CPD uses the computerized crime-mapping capability of the Geographic Information System (GIS): "As residents view Blueline, maps depicting crime in the neighborhood where they live are highlighted on a Chroma Key screen like the ones TV weathermen employ. It's the ultimate technique to show people graphically where crime is happening in their own backyard." They (p. 242) conclude: "In an era where law enforcement is expected to be proactive, oriented toward quality customer service, and expected to play a greater role in fulfilling social services through community policing, a show like Blueline CPD fulfills a vital role."

Another example of how technology can enhance police-media partnerships is seen in New York. Press information officers from the Albany Police Department, the New York State Police and other area law enforcement agencies as well as representatives from the media formed the Capital District Law Enforcement/Media Group. This group, representing 80 different agencies as well as print and electronic media, met bimonthly to discuss areas of mutual concern. One problem the group tackled was the need to get information to all the media rapidly. Most media personnel believed the practice of PIOs calling down through a media list was inequitable and also required a great deal of the PIOs' time. The group found a mutually acceptable solution to the problem: a **Pager Information Network (PIN).** The PIO can make one phone call from anywhere—the department, home, cellular telephone or pay phone—and simultaneously notify all the media enrolled in the network.

Pagers can display full text messages and also have printing capability. They can been used to advise drivers of major traffic obstructions on highways and hazardous road conditions, to warn citizens of shams and cons, to announce newsworthy criminal events or arrests and to announce press conferences. The system is kept secure through the use of passwords and identification codes.

The National Crime Prevention Council (*350 Tested Strategies* . . . , p. 31) described another successful police-media partnership:

> In Memphis, Tennessee, the mayor, citizens, businesses, and community groups recently raised $1 million in donations for the police department through "Operation Drive Out Crime," which engaged local television and radio stations and the local newspaper as cosponsors.
>
> The campaign relied on local television and radio news . . . for publicity. . . . [The] radio station also [ran] daily advertisements, highlighted the project during shows, and ran weekly interviews with sponsors and police officers. The newspaper carried stories and contributed advertising. In addition, it included contribution envelopes in two different Sunday editions of the paper. Effective local publicity led to national publicity, and donations have poured in from across the state and around the country.

In Cleveland the mayor obtained sponsorship of a local television and radio station to publicize the city's gun exchange, violence reduction and crime prevention initiatives: "The television station not only helped to announce these very successful initiatives, it also operated the telephone banks for donations" (*350 Tested Strategies*, p. 31).

Law enforcement officials in San Antonio, Texas, invited prominent local media figures to participate in a city crime prevention commission. By involving the media in the panel's deliberations and programs, the department "created a partnership that has generated positive media coverage, as well as provided free broadcast equipment and facilities for public service announcements and other programming" (*350 Tested Strategies*, p. 2).

The Utah Council for Crime Prevention also invited local media personnel to serve on the council's board, a collaboration resulting in "locally produced television documentaries and public service announcements, as well as other activities raising public awareness of crime prevention throughout the state" (*350 Tested Strategies*, p. 2).

While these collaborations, and many others throughout the country, have generated a plethora of benefits for their respective communities, the strategy of developing partnerships with the media is not without obstacles. According to the National Crime Prevention Council (*350 Tested Strategies* . . . , p. 31): "Community groups may find it difficult to see local media as partners in crime prevention. Media of all types have frequently been characterized as part of the problem communities have with violence." Furthermore (p. 2): "Media personnel are typically busy and may be reluctant to commit to or to take part in new projects or time-consuming activities. Additionally, concerns about the media's independence may keep editors and reporters from taking part in [crime prevention] coalition efforts in an official capacity."

Despite these potential obstacles, police departments should take every opportunity to forge creative, supportive, respectful partnerships with the media.

Remember: As police departments adopt the community policing philosophy and implement its strategies, public support is vital. The media can play an important role in obtaining that support—or in losing it.

SUMMARY

One important group with which the police interact is the media. The police and the media, sharing the common goal of serving the public, have a symbiotic relationship; they are mutually dependent upon each other. However, the media are guided by the First Amendment to the U.S. Constitution, which guarantees the public's right to know, that is, freedom of the press, while the police are guided by the Sixth Amendment, which guarantees the right to a fair trial and protects the defendant's rights. The differing objectives of these amendments may lead to conflict between the media and the police.

Police may need to withhold information from the media until next of kin are notified, in the interest of public safety or to protect the integrity of an investigation. When police do give information to the press, they should be aware that to ask to speak "off the record" does not guarantee that the information will not be reported. It may, in fact, make it more likely to be reported.

Another source of conflict between the press and the police is the danger members of the press may place themselves in when trying to obtain a story. To help ensure the safety of media personnel at explosive situations, police should meet with media representatives to explain the safety rules *before* an incident arises. Conflict between the police and the media need not be dysfunctional. In fact, healthy conflict between the media and the police is necessary and beneficial.

Lying to the press is always a bad idea, and it is better to be straightforward when disseminating information. However, there are occasional extraordinary circumstances where an exception to this rule exists. If some morally overriding reason, such as public safety, obliges an official to lie, then it also requires an explanation or apology for the deception later, after the crisis has passed.

A step toward improved media relations is to recognize why reporters may foul up a story. Reporters may bungle a story because of ignorance, oversimplification or time constraints. To improve police-media relations, inform the press of your department's policies and procedures regarding the media and crime scenes; simplify your information, avoiding police jargon and technical terminology; and respect reporters' deadlines by releasing information in a timely manner so the press has a chance to fully understand the situation.

Developing partnerships with the media is critical to the successful implementation of community policing because, as police departments adopt the community policing philosophy and implement its strategies, public support is vital. The media can play an important role in obtaining that support—or in losing it.

DISCUSSION QUESTIONS

1. Why should the police never lie to the press?
2. Does your police department have a press information officer?
3. How fairly do you feel the media in your community report crime and violence?
4. How fairly do you feel national media (radio, television, magazines, newspapers) cover crime and violence?
5. What might make good topics for PIOs during crime prevention week?
6. Have you ever conducted a news conference or issued a press release? If so, what went well? What was difficult?
7. Why is it important to remember that journalism is a for-profit business?
8. Do you feel the media are sometimes insensitive to victims and could also be part of the second injury of victimization? If so, can you give examples?
9. What media are available in your community to inform the public of police department operations?
10. Which media do you feel have the most impact on the public?

INFOTRAC COLLEGE EDITION ASSIGNMENTS

- Use InfoTrac to help answer the discussion questions when appropriate.
- Find and outline the article by Jane Kirtley, "When Rights Collide."
- Driven by TV ratings or newspaper sales, media news coverage has become almost completely crime reporting. Insensitivity toward victims, close-up photos of carnage, revelation of sensitive case facts or of suspects and often just plain poor taste have many Americans fed up with the media. Reporters have accompanied officers on arrest warrant services, ridden along with officers and photographed police work in-progress. Research crime reporting in more depth than you did in the last chapter ("police and the press") and discuss the pros and cons of the current sensational atmosphere around crime and the media.

COMMUNITY PROJECTS

- Examine a weeks' worth of local media crime reporting (newspaper and television). How often do crime stories lead? Do they appear sensationalized? Are crime stories overrepresented?
- If possible, interview a local crime reporter and a police department representative about crime reporting in your city. How does the reporting relate to the level of crime?

REFERENCES

Beil, Laura. "Study Finds News Doesn't Reflect True Face of Nation's Homicides." *Dallas Morning News,* October 12, 1998.

Brandon, Craig. " 'Perp Walks' Questioned." *Law and Order,* Vol. 47, No. 9, September 1999, pp. 99–102.

Brooks, Michael E. "The Ethics of Intentionally Deceiving the Media." *FBI Law Enforcement Bulletin,* Vol. 68, No. 5, May 1999, pp. 22–26.

Crawford, Kimberly A. "Media Ride-Alongs: Fourth Amendment Constraints." *FBI Law Enforcement Bulletin,* Vol. 69, No. 7, July 2000, pp. 26–31.

Freedom Forum Online. http://www. freedomforum.org/press/resources/ resources.asp

Garner, Gerald W. "Meeting the Press." *Law and Order,* Vol. 43, No. 12, December 1995, pp. 41–44.

Garner, Gerald W. "The Interview Game." *Police,* Vol. 20, No. 8, August 1996, pp. 49–51.

"It's Murder." *USA Today,* April 20, 1998.

Keith, David. "Cable Television: A Medium Too Important to Ignore." *Community Policing Exchange,* July/August 1998, p. 5.

Klein, Sid and Getz, Ronald. "Blueline CPD: Interactive TV Fights Crime." *Law and Order,* Vol. 47, No. 10, October 1999, pp. 237–242.

Lawrence, Richard. "School Violence, the Media, and the ACJS." *ACJS Today,* Vol. XX, Issue 2, May/June 2000, pp. 1, 4–6.

Maguire, Brendan; Sandage, Diane; and Weatherby, Georgie Ann. "Television News Coverage of the Police: An Exploratory Study from a Small Town Locale." *Journal of Contemporary Criminal Justice,* Vol. 15, No. 2, May 1999, pp. 171–190.

"Putting the Hobbles on Perp Walks?" *Law Enforcement News,* Vol. XXV, No. 509, April 15, 1999, pp. 1, 10.

"The Right to Remain Silent Takes on a New Meaning." *Law Enforcement News,* Vol. XXVI, Nos. 537, 538, July/August 2000, p. 1.

Rocky Mountain Media Watch. *Not in the Public Interest: Local TV News in America.* Denver, CO: 1998.

Rosenthal, Rick. "Media Brutality." *Law and Order,* Vol. 44, No. 7, July 1996a, pp. 85–90.

Rosenthal, Rick. "Media Deadlines." *Law and Order,* Vol. 44, No. 12, December 1996b, pp. 18–19.

Rosenthal, Rick. "The Public Information Officer." *Law and Order,* Vol. 44, No. 8, August 1996c, pp. 19–20.

Rosenthal, Rick. "The IACP's PIO Section." *Law and Order,* Vol. 45, No. 2, February 1997, pp. 12–13.

Rosenthal, Rick. "Tips from Award-Winning PIOs." *Law and Order,* Vol. 47, No. 7, July 1999, pp. 21–22.

Rosenthal, Rick. "Don't Ever Lie to the Media, But . . . ." *Law and Order,* Vol. 48, No. 9, September 2000a, pp. 17–18.

Rosenthal, Rick. "Meeting with 'The Enemy.' " *Law and Order,* Vol. 48, No. 7, July 2000b, pp. 22–24.

Rosenthal, Rick. "Messages from the Front Lines." *Law and Order,* Vol. 48, No. 8, August 2000c, pp. 21–22.

Rosenthal, Rick. "Victims, Witnesses and the Media." *Law and Order,* Vol. 48, No. 3, March 2000d, pp. 21–22.

Sparks, Ancil B. and Staszak, Dennis D. "Fine Tuning Your News Briefing." *FBI Law Enforcement Bulletin,* Vol. 69, No. 12, December 2000, pp. 22–24.

Stossel, John. *20/20,* October 22, 1999 episode. Canton, MI: ABC News Transcripts, 1999.

Strandberg, Keith W. "Back to Basics: Media Relations 101." *Law Enforcement Technology,* Vol. 27, No. 8, August 2000, pp. 90–94.

Surette, Ray. *Media, Crime, and Criminal Justice: Images and Realities,* 2nd ed. Pacific Grove, CA: Brooks/Cole, 1998.

Surette, Ray. "Media Echoes: Systemic Effects of News Coverage." *Justice Quarterly,* Vol. 16, No. 3, September 1999, pp. 601–631.

350 Tested Strategies to Prevent Crime: A Resource for Municipal Agencies and Community Groups. Washington, DC: National Crime Prevention Council, 1995.

Welch, Michael; Fenwick, Melissa; and Roberts, Meredith. "State Managers, Intellectuals, and the Media: A Content Analysis of Ideology in Experts' Quotes in Feature Newspaper Articles on Crime." *Justice Quarterly,* Vol. 15, No. 2, June 1998, pp. 219–241.

Westfeldt, Wallace and Wicker, Tom. *Indictment: The News Media and the Criminal Justice System.* Nashville, TN: The First Amendment Center, 1998.

Wexler, Chuck. "Rules for Reformers." *Subject to Debate,* February/March 1997, pp. 2, 4.

Woodall, Elliott. "Why Have a Written Media Relations Policy?" *The Police Chief,* Vol. LXV, No. 6, June 1998, pp. 72–73.

Young, Theresa. "Public Access: Reaching the Community through Cable TV." *FBI Law Enforcement Bulletin,* Vol. 66, No. 6, June 1997, pp. 20–26.

Zeichner, Irving B. "Inside Justice." *Law and Order,* Vol. 47, No. 8, August 1999, p. 24.

RESOURCES

Parrish Institute for Law Enforcement and Media, 34 Huntington Drive, Fredericksburg, VA 22405; (540) 368-8168. e-mail: pparrish@fbiacademy.edu

Radio Television News Director's Association, 1000 Connecticut Avenue NW, Suite 615, Washington, DC 20036; (202) 659-6510.

SECTION THREE

Community Policing in the Field: Coordinated Efforts

Thomas C. Frazier (2000), former director of the Office of "Community-Oriented Policing Services, states: "Community oriented policing is a proactive, solution-based, community-driven, four-tiered approach to policing that occurs when a law enforcement agency and law-abiding citizens work together to (1) prevent crime, (2) arrest offenders, (3) solve on-going problems and (4) improve the overall quality of life."

As explained in the previous section, communities consist of individuals, organizations, businesses, agencies, the media, citizen groups, schools, churches and police departments. Effective interactions with the members of ethnic and cultural minorities, the disabled, the elderly, the young, crime victims and witnesses and the media are critical to developing projects and programs to meet a community's needs.

This section begins by describing early experiments in crime prevention and community polic-

ing strategies (Chapter 12). Among the most pressing problems in the United States is violence: domestic violence, gun violence, workplace and school violence. Strategies to reduce or prevent violence in these settings is the focus of Chapter 13. Next, strategies to help youths become contributing members of society and to avoid gang involvement are discussed, as well as how to effectively approach the gang problem (Chapter 14). Chapter 15 discusses community policing efforts to address the interrelated problems of drugs and crime. The section concludes with a look at what research reveals about the effectiveness of various strategies, including where efforts might be focused in the future (Chapter 16).

Reference: Frazier, Thomas C. "A Definition of Community Policing." Washington, DC: Office of Community Oriented Policing Services, April 25, 2000. www.usdoj.gov/cops/

CHAPTER 12

Early Experiments in Crime Prevention and the Evolution of Community Policing Strategies

Don't be afraid to take a big step if one is indicated.
You can't cross a chasm in two small jumps.

> David Lloyd George, former prime minister
> of England

Do you know

What the most commonly implemented crime prevention programs have traditionally been?

What types of special crime watches have been used?

What organizations have concentrated their efforts on community crime prevention?

How volunteers are used in crime prevention?

What traditional programs for youths have promoted positive police-community relations and enhanced crime prevention efforts?

What a police-school liaison program is? What its dual goals are?

What the most common strategies used in community policing have traditionally been?

What was demonstrated in studies of community policing in Flint? Newark? Oakland? San Diego? Houston? Boston? Baltimore County?

What was demonstrated in studies of community crime prevention programs in Seattle, Portland and Hartford?

What the CPTED Commercial Demonstration Project in Portland found?

What components of the criminal justice system can help reduce the crime problem?

What court-based approaches have proven effective?

What corrections-based approaches have proven effective?

How successful the McGruff national campaign was?

How successful crime prevention newsletters are?

What are characteristics of several exemplary police-community strategies?

What impediments might hinder implementing community policing?

Can you define these terms:

CPTED	Guardian Angels	PSAs
cross-sectional analysis	PAL	qualitative evaluations
DARE	panel analysis	reciprocity
empirical study	police-school liaison program	statistically significant

INTRODUCTION

Community involvement with and assistance in accomplishing the mission of law enforcement is becoming widely accepted. The change toward community involvement is illustrated in a change in the Portland Police Department's mission statement. The old mission statement proclaimed:

> The Bureau of Police is responsible for the preservation of the public peace, protection of the rights of persons and property, the prevention of crime, and the enforcement of all Federal laws, Oregon state statutes and city ordinances within the boundaries of the City of Portland.

The new mission, in contrast, is:

> To work with all citizens to preserve life, maintain human rights, protect property and promote individual responsibility and community commitment.

The change from traditional policing to community involvement does require many chiefs of police and their officers to take risks. Are the results of the shift toward community policing worth the risks? This chapter reviews experiments conducted across the country to answer this question.

Although this chapter may appear somewhat dated, it is a necessary addition to document efforts during the past four decades to improve crime prevention strategies and to involve citizens in such efforts. Many lessons were learned from the experiments of this time period.

The chapter begins with a look at traditional approaches to crime prevention and other effective initiatives, including traditional programs for youths. Next is a description of empirical studies in crime prevention conducted in the 1970s and 1980s, followed by a discussion of how community policing efforts may be enhanced through partnerships with the other elements of the criminal justice system—namely, the courts and corrections. Use of the media in crime prevention is discussed as well as lessons learned from previous decades. The chapter concludes with a discussion of qualitative evaluations and salient program features, impediments to community policing and the important distinction of programs versus community policing.

◉ TRADITIONAL APPROACHES TO CRIME PREVENTION

When crime prevention became popular in the late 1960s and early 1970s, many communities undertook similar types of programs. These programs have continued into the 21st century.

Among the most commonly implemented crime prevention programs have been street lighting projects, property marking projects, security survey projects, citizen patrol projects and crime reporting, neighborhood watch or block projects.

Claims of success should be carefully examined. Critics often say that the evaluations are flawed. Indeed, research within communities is extremely difficult because:

- Measuring what *did not happen* is nearly impossible.
- Crime is usually underreported.
- A reduction in reported crime could be the result of the crime prevention program or because the responsible criminal or criminals left town, went to jail on some other charge, died and so on.
- Crime can be influenced by everything from seasonal and weather changes, school truancy rates and the flu, to road construction or even a change in a bus stop location. A drop in the crime rate does not necessarily mean a crime prevention program is working.

In addition, many of these programs are evaluated by people who have no training or experience in appropriate research methods; consequently, they sometimes produce flawed results.

Some also argue that crime is not prevented by programs like Neighborhood Watch but instead is displaced to neighborhoods where the residents are not as likely to report suspicious activity to the police. Even if this is true, such programs do raise community awareness and have a "chilling effect" on criminals who are inhibited by those who watch and call the police.

Use of crime data to evaluate crime prevention projects poses special problems. Crime data, obviously, are limited to *reported* crimes. Practitioners are aware of the *dark side of crime,* that is, the huge amount of crime that is *unreported.* When projects are instituted to enlist the community in preventing crime, the citizens' heightened awareness and involvement often results in an *increase in reported crime,* but this does *not* necessarily mean that crime itself has actually increased.

As you read this chapter, consider the difficulties in evaluating crime prevention projects or, indeed, any project involving many diverse individuals and problems.

Street Lighting Projects

Since ancient times, lighting has been one means to deter and detect crime. Street lighting projects aimed at crime prevention through environmental design (CPTED) are important elements in a community's crime suppression efforts. Most street lighting projects seek to not only improve the likelihood of deterring and detecting crime but also to improve the safety of law-abiding citizens. Available research indicates that street lighting does *not* decrease the incidence of crime in participating target areas but that it is useful to reduce citizens' fear of crime and increase their feelings of security.

Property Identification Projects

Often referred to as "Operation Identification" or "O-I" projects, property identification is aimed at deterring burglary and at returning property that is stolen when deterrence fails. Most property identification projects provide citizens with instructions, a marking tool and a unique number to be applied to all valuable items within a household. Stickers are provided to homeowners to display on windows and doors warning possible burglars that the residents have marked their valuables and they are on record with the police. In addition to its deterrent effect, the property identification program also helps police track the source of stolen goods and return stolen property to its rightful owners.

It is sometimes difficult to get people to participate in the program. In addition, although the burglary rate may drop for those enrolled in the program, it may not drop citywide. There is no evidence available to suggest a difference in the number of apprehended or convicted burglars in communities that do or do not participate in the program.

Crime Prevention Security Surveys

Crime prevention security surveys are also usually an integral part of projects that focus on the environmental design of facilities and on "target hardening" as a means to deter or prevent crime. As noted by Crowe (1992, p. 22A):

> CPTED [Crime Prevention Through Environmental Design] is based on the theory that the proper design and effective use of the built environment can lead to a reduction in the incidence and fear of crime and an improvement in the quality of life. Years of experiments and field applications have demonstrated that CPTED works in all environments—that is, it applies to commercial, residential, transportation, recreational and institutional environments.
>
> It has worked on scales as small as a single room and as large as an entire community. [emphasis added]

Surveys used to determine the effectiveness of the existing "environmental design" are usually conducted by police officers specially trained in this area. They do comprehensive on-site inspection of homes, apartments and businesses. Of particular interest are doors, windows, locks, lighting and shrubbery that might be used to a burglar's advantage. The officer offers specific suggestions on how a location might be made more secure.

Citizen Patrol Projects

Many variations of citizen patrol exist in the United States. Some are directed at a specific problem such as crack houses and the sale of drugs in a neighborhood. Others are aimed at general crime prevention and enhanced citizen safety. Citizen patrols may operate throughout a community or may be located within a specific building or complex of buildings such as tenement houses.

The most successful patrols are affiliated with a larger community or neighborhood organization, sustain a working relationship with law enforcement and are flexible enough to engage in noncrime prevention activities when patrolling is patently unnecessary.

One hazard of citizen patrols is the possibility of vigilantism which has a long, often proud, history in the United States and, indeed, in the history of law enforcement and criminal justice. Now this hazard is quite serious because of the increase of readily available handguns in our country.

Probably the best known citizen patrol is the **Guardian Angels,** a group of private citizens who seek to deter crime and to provide a positive role model for young children. Greenberg (1991, p. 42) notes: "The Angels wear bright red berets and T-shirts imprinted with a flapping wing and badge insignia. They carry a pad, pen, whistle and—sometimes—handcuffs. Although they carry no weapons, they do attempt to arrest felony suspects and hold them for the police."

A modern expansion of the Angels is their all-volunteer Internet Safety organization. Membership in this group unites more than 1,000 users from 32 countries who "police the Internet" through what they call "Cyberspace Neighborhood Watch." Calling themselves CyberAngels, they focus on protecting children from online abuse by fighting child porn and advising online victims of hate mail.

Citizen Crime Reporting, Neighborhood or Block Programs

Citizen crime reporting programs (CCRP) help to organize neighborhoods as "mutual aid societies" and as the "eyes and ears" of the police. Thousands of Neighborhood Watch programs exist in the United States, and many describe them as the backbone of the nation's community crime prevention effort. Typically local residents hold meetings of such programs in their homes or apartments. During the meetings, neighbors get to know each other and what is normal activity for their neighborhood. They receive educational information about crime prevention from the local police department and are told how to contact the police if they see something suspicious. Signs are posted throughout the neighborhood warning possible offenders of the program. Often the programs provide safe houses for children to use if they encounter danger on their way to or from school.

Some programs work to enhance citizens' reporting capability. Whistlestop programs, for example, provide citizens with whistles which they can blow if they are threatened or see something requiring police intervention. Anyone hearing the whistle is to immediately call the police. Whistlestop programs are the modern-day version of the "hue and cry." Other programs have implemented special hotlines whereby citizens can call a specific number with crime information and perhaps receive a monetary reward.

Table 12.1 illustrates the types of activities engaged in by Neighborhood Watch programs and the relative popularity of each. Very few of the programs concentrate on only the "neighborhood watch." Project Operation Identification and home security surveys are by far the most common activities of Neighborhood Watch programs. Street lighting programs, crime tip hotlines and physical environmental concerns are also quite common.

Table 12.1   Activities Engaged in by Neighborhood Watch Programs (Based on Program Survey Responses)

Activity	Number	Percent
Neighborhood Watch Only	49	8.9
Crime Prevention Specific		
Project Operation Identification	425	80.6
Home security surveys	357	67.9
Street lighting improvement	183	34.7
Block parenting	144	27.3
Organized surveillance	66	12.0
Traffic alteration	37	7.0
Emergency telephones	24	4.6
Project Whistle Stop	18	3.4
Specialized informal surveillance	18	3.4
Escort service	12	2.3
Hired guards	11	2.1
Environmental design	7	1.3
Lock provision/installation	4	0.7
Self-defense/rape prevention	3	0.5
Crime Related		
Crime tip hotline	197	37.5
Victim witness assistance	101	19.2
Court watch	17	3.2
Telephone chain	7	1.3
Child fingerprinting	2	0.4
Community Oriented		
Physical environmental concerns	201	38.1
Insurance premium deduction survey	20	3.6
Quality of life	9	1.6
Medical emergency	4	0.7

SOURCE: James Garofalo and Maureen McLeod. *Improving the Use and Effectiveness of Neighborhood Watch Programs.* U.S. Department of Justice, National Institute of Justice Research in Action Series, April 1988, p. 2.

Special Crime Watch Programs

In addition to the traditional types of crime watch programs commonly implemented throughout the country, some communities have developed more specialized types of crime watch programs.

Specialized crime watch programs include mobile crime watch, youth crime watch, business crime watch, realtor watch and carrier alert.

Honolulu's mobile crime watch enlists the aid of motorists who have CBs, car phones or cell phones. Volunteers attend a short orientation that trains them to observe and report suspicious activity. Participants also receive Mobile Watch decals for their vehicles. They are advised to call 911 if they hear screaming, gunshots, breaking glass or loud explosive noises or if they see someone breaking into a house or car, a car driven dangerously or erratically, a person on the ground apparently unconscious, anyone brandishing a gun or knife, or an individual staggering or threatening others.

They are also trained to recognize and report other unusual behaviors such as children appearing lost; anyone being forced into a vehicle; cars cruising erratically and repetitively near schools, parks and playgrounds; a person running and carrying something valuable; parked, occupied vehicles at unusual hours near potential robbery sites; heavier than normal traffic in and out of a house or commercial establishment; someone going door-to-door or passing through backyards; and persons loitering around schools, parks or secluded areas or in the neighborhood.

Pace (1991, p. 266) describes three other specialized watch programs implemented by the Miami-Dade Metro Police Department. *Youth Crime Watch:* Elementary and secondary students are trained in crime prevention and in observing and reporting incidents in their schools. *Business Crime Watch:* A general meeting of all businesses is held to conduct crime prevention and crime watch training. *Realtor Watch:* Realtors throughout the county are trained to "crime watch" during their working hours in the neighborhoods and commercial areas in which they are selling.

Another specialized type of crime watch is the *Carrier Alert* program, initiated by the U.S. Postal Service. Mail carriers are asked to become aware of elderly citizens or citizens with special needs on their routes, to look out for them and to report any lack of activity or suspicious activity at their homes to the police.

Most successful community-based programs that focus on crime prevention or safety issues have a close partnership with law enforcement. The community and law enforcement have vital components to offer the other, making cooperation between the two highly desirable. It is difficult to imagine, for instance, an effective community-based Crime Watch program without input or cooperation from the local police agency. Crime Watch programs are built on the premise of mutual aid—citizens and police working together.

◆ OTHER EFFORTS TO ENHANCE CRIME PREVENTION

Continuing the community crime prevention momentum generated during the 1960s and 1970s, new programs were initiated during the 1980s and 1990s to encourage citizens to play an active role in reducing crime in their own neighborhoods. These initiatives have included National Night Out; the creation of organizations focused on crime prevention, such as Crime Stoppers and MADD; and the expanded use of volunteers.

National Night Out

National Night Out (NNO) is a program that originated in 1984 in Tempe, Arizona. Held annually on the first Tuesday of August, this nationwide program encourages residents to turn on their porch lights, go outside and meet their neighbors. Neighborhood Watch programs are encouraged to plan a party or event during National Night Out.

Since 1984, when 2.5 million people in 23 states gathered for the first NNO, the event has grown significantly. In 1999 an estimated 32 million people in nearly 9,500 communities located in all 50 states and a large number of U.S. territories, Canadian cities and U.S. military bases around the world gathered with police officers and administrators to celebrate the event with block parties, safety fairs, youth events, cookouts and parades. According to Sharp (1999, p. 43) a 1998 survey of NNO participants revealed that 96% of the responding law enforcement officers reported that NNO enhanced their agencies' community policing programs; 75% of residents reported that because of NNO, they felt much more comfortable contacting their police or sheriff's departments; and 64% of the residents reported feeling safer in their communities as a result of NNO.

Organizations Focused on Crime Prevention

Among the most visible organizations focused on crime are citizen crime prevention associations, Crime Stoppers and MADD.

Citizen Crime Prevention Associations. Among the many activities undertaken by citizen crime prevention associations are paying for crime tips; funding for police-crime prevention programs; supporting police canine programs; raising community awareness through crime prevention seminars, newsletters, cable TV shows and booths; providing teddy bears for kids; raising money through sources such as business contributions, membership fees, charitable gambling and sales of alarms, mace and "Call Police" signs (usually sold as a service to a community, not to raise any substantial money); and funding specific programs such as rewards to community members who call the hotline with crime information.

Crime Stoppers. Crime Stoppers is a nonprofit program involving citizens, the media and the police. Local programs offer anonymity and cash rewards to people who furnish to police information that leads to the arrest and indictment of felony offenders. Each program is governed by a local board of directors made up of citizens from a cross-section of the community, the businesses of the community and law enforcement. The reward money comes from tax-deductible donations and grants from local businesses, foundations and individuals.

When a crime-related call is received by Crime Stoppers, it is logged in with the date, time and a summary of the information given by the caller. Callers are given code numbers to be used on all subsequent calls by the same person regarding that particular case. Each week, one unsolved crime is selected for special treatment by the media. Over 850 programs throughout the United States, Canada, Australia, England and West Africa are members of Crime Stoppers International.

Mothers Against Drunk Driving (MADD). Mothers Against Drunk Driving (MADD) is a nonprofit, grassroots organization with over 400 chapters nationwide. Its membership is open to anyone: victims, concerned citizens, law enforcement, safety workers and health professionals. As noted in their literature: "The mission of Mothers Against Drunk Driving is to stop drunk driving and to support victims of this violent crime."

MADD was founded in California in 1980 after Candy Lightner's 13-year-old daughter was killed by a hit-and-run driver. The driver had been out of jail on bail for only two days for another hit-and-run drunk driving crash. He had three previous drunk driving arrests and two convictions. But he was allowed to plea-bargain to vehicular manslaughter. His two-year prison sentence was spent not in prison but in a work camp and later a halfway house.

MADD differentiates between accidents and crashes:

> Those injured and killed in drunk driving collisions are not "accident victims." The crash caused by an impaired driver is a violent crime. Drunk driving involves two choices: to drink AND to drive. The thousands of deaths and injuries caused each year by impaired driving can be prevented . . . they are not "accidental" ("Help Keep Families Together," n.d., p. 2).

MADD seeks to raise public awareness through community programs such as Operation Prom/Graduation, their Poster/Essay Contest, their "Tie One on for Safety" Project Red Ribbon campaign and a Designated Driver program. Their national newsletter, *MADD in Action*, is sent to members and supporters. MADD also promotes legislation to strengthen existing laws and adopt new ones. In addition, MADD provides victim services. Annual candlelight vigils are held nationwide to allow victims to share their grief with others who have suffered loss due to drunk driving.

Using Volunteers

Many police departments make extensive use of volunteers.

Volunteers may serve as reserve officers, auxiliary patrol, community service officers or on an as-needed basis.

Reserve officers, auxiliary patrol or community service officers (CSOs) usually wear uniforms and badges but are unarmed. However, in some departments, reserve officers are armed and receive the same training as sworn officers. They are trained to perform specific functions that assist the uniformed patrol officers. They may be used to patrol watching for suspicious activity, to direct traffic, to conduct interviews with victims of and witnesses to crimes and to provide crime prevention education at neighborhood watch meetings, civic groups, churches and schools.

CSOs may work with youths to prevent delinquency, refer citizen complaints to the appropriate agency and investigate minor thefts. They are usually heavily involved in public relations activities as well. Some CSOs are paid, but much less than police officers.

Many departments ask professionals such as physicians, teachers and ministers to volunteer their services, sometimes as expert witnesses.

Often volunteers perform office functions in police departments, such as conducting tours or answering telephone messages. They might also provide assistance to police at crime prevention programs and Neighborhood Watch meetings. Many departments use the AARP volunteer program, capitalizing on the experience and free time of the elderly citizens of the community.

Volunteers provide a communication link between the citizens and the police department. They can help establish the credibility of the department's public relations and educational efforts. Volunteers provide additional sources of information and perspectives. Hogan (1995, p. 8) reports on the results of a survey of 1,000 law enforcement agencies, in which respondents indicated the following benefits of using volunteers: stability, reliability and dependability of workers (57 percent); experience and knowledge (52 percent); wisdom, maturity and leadership (47 percent).

Using volunteers may, however, cause certain problems. In fact, some police officers feel volunteers are "more trouble than they are worth." Among the reasons commonly given for not using volunteers are that people who are "joiners" or have time and/or money often lack sensitivity to minorities; some citizens seek profit and gain for themselves and develop programs that are mere window dressing; some citizens lack qualifications and training; since volunteers receive no pay, they cannot be docked or penalized for poor performance; citizens lack awareness of the criminal justice system in general and specific agencies in particular; and the use of volunteers by some departments has led to the failure of the local communities and politicians to take responsibility for solving the larger social problem and/or the refusal to hire adequate numbers of personnel or pay better wages.

In addition, some police unions have reacted negatively to volunteers, sometimes viewed as competitors for police jobs. Reserve officers, in particular, tend to cause patrol officers to feel their jobs are threatened by those willing to do police jobs for free or at least at greatly reduced pay. Officers should know that programs using volunteers are those that could not otherwise exist due to lack of personnel and funding.

◉ TRADITIONAL PROGRAMS FOR YOUTHS

Youths have traditionally been included in police-community relations efforts and crime prevention initiatives in several ways.

Common programs aimed at youths include the McGruff "Take a Bite out of Crime" campaign, police athletic leagues (PALs), Officer Friendly, police explorers, police-school liaison programs and the DARE program.

Other efforts have included school safety programs, bicycle safety programs and programs to fingerprint young children. In different localities, police have developed variations of many of these programs. (Chapter 14 is devoted entirely to projects and programs aimed at youths and gangs.)

The McGruff "Take a Bite out of Crime" Program

The traditional McGruff as a crime prevention spokesperson program, for example, has expanded in some areas to include McGruff Houses, which are safe havens for young children. Another expansion is the McGruff crime dog robot developed by Robotronics. Operated by remote control, the robot winks, blinks, moves his hands and arms, tips and turns his head and has a two-way wireless voice system allowing the operator to talk and listen. The McGruff media campaign is discussed in greater detail later in this chapter.

Police Athletic Leagues

Police departments have also expanded upon the PAL program. The National Police Athletic League (**PAL**), now over 50 years old, was developed to provide opportunities for youths to interact with police officers in gyms or ballparks instead of in a juvenile detention hall.

The Portland (Oregon) Police Department has adapted the PAL program to deal with escalating gang violence and street sale of drugs. As Austin and Braaten (1991,

A young girl holds the hand of a McGruff crime dog robot during an anti-drug rally at the Texas State Capitol building.

© Larry Kolvoord/TexaStock

p. 36) note, the goals of the Portland-area PAL are to reduce the incidence of juvenile crime, substance abuse and gang violence; provide positive alternative activities for boys and girls; guide boys and girls to make responsible decisions in life; and foster better understanding between youths and the police.

To accomplish their goals, the department has undertaken several activities, including a week-long Sport Quickness Day Camp for 600 at-risk youths that keeps them productively occupied for eight hours a day in boxing, wrestling, football, soccer, martial arts, basketball, racquetball, track and field, volleyball and speed and quickness training. The department also organizes events in which officers can participate with PAL youths, including a one-day fishing excursion, trips to Seattle Sea Hawks football games and scholarships to summer camps.

Officer Friendly

Officer Friendly programs are designed for elementary-school children and generally include a police officer who goes into classes to discuss good citizenship, responsibility and general safety. The program uses coloring books and a special activity book that teachers can use with their regular social studies curriculum.

Police Explorers

The traditional police explorers program, an advanced unit of the Boy Scouts of America, also serves many communities. Explorers are typically trained in various aspects of police work such as fingerprinting, identification techniques, first aid and firearms safety. The minimum age for most programs is 15. Explorers usually have a three- to six-month

Explorers. A Dallas police officer meets with his explorer troop in the city's Little Asia district. This East Dallas Community and Refugee Affairs Center was named "Best Inner-City Crime Reduction Project in U.S." by the Police Foundation, Washington, DC.

probation with full membership contingent on completing training and meeting proficiency standards as well as acceptable personal conduct.

Explorer programs have two purposes: (1) positive community relations and (2) early recruitment for police departments. Some departments, in fact, make even greater use of their explorer programs. The Chandler (Arizona) Police Department, for example, used two 18-year-old explorers in a sting operation involving a bar and liquor store's employees who sold alcohol to minors.

Many programs for juveniles involve the schools, which have historically been charged with instilling discipline in the students who attend.

Police-School Liaison Programs

In 1958 Flint, Michigan, developed a highly publicized delinquency prevention program involving joint efforts of school authorities, parents, businesses, social agencies, the juvenile court and the police department. Known as a school-liaison program, it became widely replicated across the country.

A police-school liaison program *places an officer in a school to work with school authorities, parents and students to prevent crime and antisocial behavior and to improve police-youth relationships.*

The goals of most police-school liaison programs are to reduce crime incidents involving school-age youths, to suppress by enforcement of the law any illegal threats that endanger the children's educational environment and to improve the attitudes of school-age youths and the police toward one another.

According to Drowns and Hess (2000, p. 275): "The techniques used by school liaison officers involve counseling children and their parents, referring them to social agencies to treat the root problems, referring them to drug and alcohol abuse agencies and being in daily contact in the school to check the progress of behavior. Often school liaison officers deal with pre-delinquent and early delinquent youths with whom law enforcement would not have been involved under traditional programs."

Police-school liaison officers do not get involved in school politics or in enforcing school regulations. The school administrators are involved in these matters.

The joint goals of most police-school liaison programs are to prevent juvenile delinquency and to improve police-youth relations.

The police-school liaison programs can also do much to promote better relations among the police, school administrators and teachers. A number of organizations can focus attention on school-police relations and provide supportive programs both on the community and national levels, for example, the International Association of Chiefs of Police, the National Association of Secondary School Principals and the National Association of School Boards.

Drug use is often a target of police educational programs. Frequently, officers work with schools to develop and promote programs aimed at preventing drug and alcohol abuse, one of the most popular of which is DARE.

The DARE Program

The Drug Abuse Resistance Education (**DARE**) program was developed jointly by the Los Angeles Police Department and the Los Angeles Unified School District. This controversial program is aimed at elementary-age school children and seeks to teach them to "say no to drugs," to resist peer pressure and to find alternatives to drug use. The program uses a "self-esteem repair" approach consisting of 17 classroom sessions taught by experienced police officers.

The City of Ridgecrest, California, initiated a DARE program and wanted a public relations program to help promote it. Ridgecrest used cards similar to baseball cards, each featuring numerous officers in different settings.

DARE is not without its critics, however. It has met with a great deal of opposition in some communities, and the design of some of the research done on DARE is questionable. In addition, much of the research fails to support any long-term, positive results of the program. One study by the University of Kentucky found:

> While DARE produced some initial changes in the attitudes held by children about drug use, the effects were not long-lasting. The findings are nearly identical to those of a 1996 study that followed the progress of some 2,000 students five years after participating in the DARE program. . . .
>
> According to the findings, . . . DARE had no significant effect on either the students' use of drugs, cigarettes and alcohol or their expectancies about the substances. . . . [And] consistent with the findings of earlier research, the study said there appear to be "no reliable short-term, long-term, early adolescent or young adult positive outcomes associated with receiving DARE intervention" ("DARE Chief Raps . . . ," 1999, p. 1).

The founder and president of DARE America concedes the program is not a "magic bullet" but believes it's a valuable part of the big picture and is confident it helps reduce drug use. Nonetheless, many police departments who have used the DARE program for years are discontinuing its use—and this appears to be a growing trend. Perhaps the reason is that not enough emphasis is placed on what to say "yes" to.

During the 1980s many of these early strategies and programs were adopted by departments moving toward community policing. Also during this time, many departments began experimenting with a variety of community policing strategies. As evidenced by numerous studies, some strategies were successful; others were not.

EMPIRICAL STUDIES OF COMMUNITY POLICING

An **empirical study** is based on observation or practical experience. Greene and Taylor (1991, pp. 206–221) describe studies of community policing in major cities throughout the country, including Flint, Newark, Oakland, San Diego, Houston, Boston and Baltimore.

The most common strategies traditionally used in community policing were foot patrol, newsletters and community organizing.

Flint, Michigan

The classic *Neighborhood Foot Patrol Program* of Flint, Michigan, was conducted from January 1979 to January 1982. It focused on 14 experimental neighborhoods to which 22 police officers and 3 supervisors were assigned. The officers were given great discretion in what they could do while on foot patrol, but communication with citizens was a primary objective.

The Flint Neighborhood Foot Patrol Program appeared to decrease crime, increase general citizen satisfaction with the foot patrol program, reduce citizens' fear of crime and create a positive perception of the foot patrol officers.

Mastrofski (1992) explains that the Flint study tried to document what police did on foot patrol and how that differed from motorized patrol. He (p. 24) notes:

Looking at the department's daily report forms, the researchers found that foot officers reported many more self-initiated activities—such as home and business visits and security checks—than police in cars. Officers on foot averaged much higher levels of productivity across most of the standard performance measures: arrests, investigations, stopping of suspicious persons, parking citations, and value of recovered property. The only category in which motor patrol officers clearly outproduced their foot patrol counterparts was in providing miscellaneous services to citizens.

According to citizen surveys (Trojanowicz, 1986, pp. 165–167), 64 percent were satisfied with the project and 68 percent felt safer. When asked to compare foot patrol and motorized patrol officers, citizens rated the foot patrol officers higher by large margins on four of the six areas: preventing crime, encouraging citizen self-protection, working with juveniles and following up on complaints. Motorized patrol officers were rated superior only in responding to complaints. In addition, in the foot patrol neighborhoods crime rates were down markedly, and calls for service were down more than 40 percent.

No statistical tests were done, however, and results across the 14 neighborhoods varied greatly. Therefore, the results should be interpreted with caution. In addition, problems were encountered in the Flint Foot Patrol Program. For example, because the program was loosely structured, some officers were not accountable, and their job performance was poor. Nonetheless, according to Skolnick and Bayley (1986, p. 216):

Foot patrol . . . appears from our observations and other studies to generate four meritorious effects. (1) Since there is a concerned human presence on the street, foot patrol is more adaptable to street happenings, and thus may prevent crime before it begins. (2) Foot patrol officers may make arrests, but they are also around to give warnings either directly or indirectly, merely through their presence. (3) Properly carried out, foot patrol generates goodwill in the neighborhood, which has the derivative consequence of making other crime prevention tactics more effective. This effectiveness in turn tends to raise citizen morale and reduce their fear of crime. (4) Foot patrol seems to raise officer morale.

Newark 1

The original Newark Foot Patrol Experiment was done between 1978 and 1979 and addressed the issues of untended property and untended behavior. This experiment used 12 patrol beats. Eight of the beats, identified as using foot patrol, were divided into pairs, matched by the number of residential and nonresidential units in each. One beat in each pair dropped foot patrol. An additional four beats that had not previously used foot patrol added foot patrol officers. As in the Flint experiment, officers had great flexibility in their job responsibilities while on foot patrol.

In the first Newark Foot Patrol Experiment, residents reported positive results, while business owners reported negative results.

In areas where foot patrol was added, residents reported a decrease in the severity of crime and evaluated police performance more positively. Business owners, however, believed that street disorder and publicly visible crime increased and reported that the neighborhood had become worse. Pate (1986, p. 155) summarizes the results of the first experiment:

> The *addition* of intensive foot patrol coverage to relatively short (8–16 block) commercial/residential strips during five evenings per week over a one-year period can have considerable effects on the perceptions of residents concerning disorder problems, crime problems, the likelihood of crime, safety, and police service. Such additional patrol, however, appears to have no significant effect on victimization, recorded crime, or the likelihood of reporting a crime.
>
> The *elimination* of foot patrol after years of maintenance, however, appears to produce few notable negative effects. Similarly, the *retention* of foot patrol does not prove to have notable beneficial effects.

Newark 2

A second foot patrol experiment was conducted in Newark in 1983 and 1984. This experiment used three neighborhoods and a control group (which received no "treatment").

The second Newark Foot Patrol Experiment included a coordinated foot patrol, a cleanup campaign and distribution of a newsletter. Only the coordinated foot patrol was perceived to reduce perception of property crime and improve assessments of the police.

The cleanup effort and newsletter programs did not affect any of the outcome measures studied. In addition, the cleanup effort and newsletter programs did not reduce crime rates. Nonetheless, the Police Foundation (1981, p. 118) notes: "If vulnerable and weak people feel safe as a result of specific police activity and if that feeling improves the quality of their life, that is terribly important."

Oakland

In 1983 Oakland assigned 28 officers to foot patrol in Oakland's central business district. In addition, a Report Incidents Directly program was established whereby local businesspeople could talk directly to the patrol officers about any matters that concerned them. Mounted patrol and small vehicle patrols were also used.

The Oakland program, using foot patrol, mounted patrol, small vehicle patrol and a Report Incidents Directly program, resulted in a substantial drop in the rate of crime against individuals and their property.

The crime rate dropped in the Oakland treatment area more than citywide declines, but again, no statistical tests were reported for this experiment.

San Diego

San Diego conducted a community profile project from 1973 to 1974 designed to improve police-community interactions. Twenty-four patrol officers and three supervisors were given 60 hours of community-orientation training. The performance of these officers was compared with 24 other patrol officers who did not receive the training.

The San Diego Community Profile Project provided patrol officers with extensive community-orientation training. These officers became more service oriented, increased their nonlaw enforcement contacts with citizens and had a more positive attitude toward police-community relations.

The project did not consider the effect of community profiling on crime or on citizens' fear of crime.

Houston

Like the second Newark experiment, Houston conducted a fear-reduction experiment between 1983 and 1984, testing five strategies: a victim recontact program following victimization, a community newsletter, a citizen contact patrol program, a police storefront office and a program aimed to organize the community's interest in crime prevention.

The victim recontact program and the newsletter of the Houston Fear Reduction Project did not have positive results. The citizen contact patrol and the police storefront office did, however, result in decreases in perceptions of social disorder, fear of personal victimization and the level of personal and property crime.

The victim recontact program, in fact, backfired, with Hispanics and Asians experiencing an increase in fear. Contact was primarily with white homeowners rather than minority renters. As Skogan and Wycoff (1986, pp. 182–183) note, the police storefront officers developed several programs, including monthly meetings, school programs, a fingerprinting program, a blood pressure program, a ride-along program, a park program and an anticrime newsletter. A comparison of these results to those achieved in the Newark experiment is made on pp. 350–351.

Boston

In 1983 Boston changed from predominantly two-officer motorized patrol to foot patrol and shifted the responsibilities of the foot patrol and motorized one-officer patrol to less serious crimes and noncrime service calls. The experiment studied 105 beats to determine whether high, medium, low, unstaffed or no change in foot patrol affected calls for service by priority.

The Boston Foot Patrol Project found no statistically significant relationship between changes in the level of foot patrol provided and number of calls for service or the seriousness of the calls.

Violent crimes were not affected by increased or decreased foot patrol staffing. After the department shifted to foot patrol, the number of street robberies dropped, but the number of commercial robberies rose.

Baltimore County

The Baltimore Citizen Oriented Police Enforcement (COPE) Project, started in 1981, focused on the reduction of citizens' fear of crime. This problem-oriented project focused on solving the community problems of fear and disorder that lead to crime. According to Taft (1986, p. 10): " 'Citizen Oriented Police Enforcement' officers would engage in intensive patrol, develop close contacts with citizens, conduct 'fear surveys' (door-to-door canvassing to identify concerns) and use any means within their power to quell fear."

Baltimore County's COPE Project reduced fear of crime by 10 percent and crime itself by 12 percent in target neighborhoods. It also reduced calls for service, increased citizen awareness of and satisfaction with the police, and improved police officer attitudes.

A study conducted in 1985 indicated that the COPE Project "passed its first statistical test with flying colors" (Taft, p. 20). The results of the study are summarized in Figure 12.1.

Summary and Implications of the Experiments

Greene and Taylor (p. 215) note that "there is not much consistency in findings across studies." Regarding *fear of crime*, Newark 1 observed a reduction; Newark 2 observed a reduction in the **panel analysis** (where the data were analyzed by individuals responding). It did not show a reduction in the **cross-sectional analysis** (where the data were analyzed by area rather than by individuals responding). The Houston study had the opposite results: a reduction in fear in the cross-sectional analysis but not in the panel analysis. In the Flint study, citizen perceptions of the seriousness of crime problems increased. In Baltimore County it declined slightly. The San Diego, Oakland and Boston programs did not consider fear of crime. Greene and Taylor (p. 216) conclude: "Based on the problems associated with the evaluation of each of these programs, there is at present no consistent evidence that foot patrol reduces fear of crime."

Greene and Taylor also note inconsistent findings regarding crime rates. The Oakland study was the only one to demonstrate a reduction, but no statistical treatment was done. Again they (p. 216) conclude: "Clearly, these studies do not point to decreases in crime or disorder as a consequence of community policing or foot patrol."

Greene and Taylor discuss several problems with the research designs of the eight studies of community policing and suggest ways to improve the designs. This is *not* the view taken by Wycoff (1991, p. 103), however, who states that the fear-reduction studies conducted in Houston and Newark: "provide evidence of the efficacy of what the authors referred to as 'community-oriented' policing strategies for reducing citizen fear, improving citizens' attitudes toward their neighborhoods and toward the police and reducing crime."

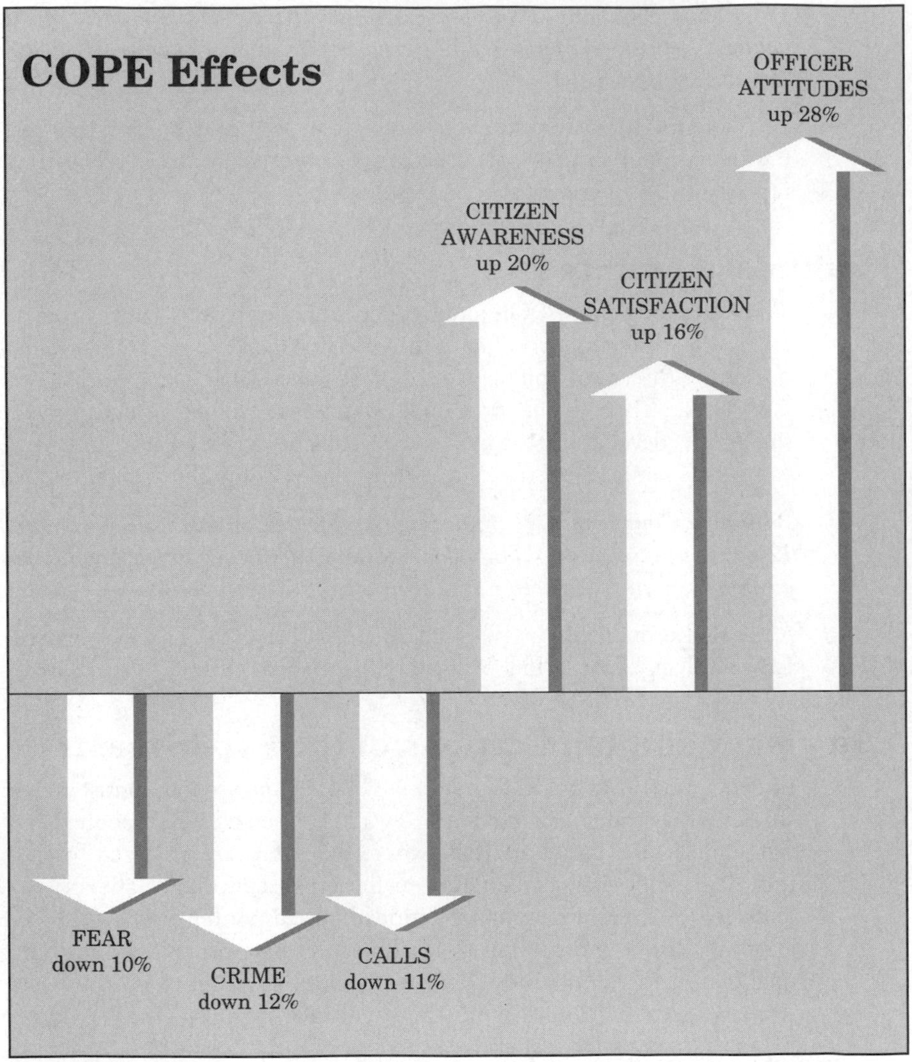

COPE Effects

OFFICER
ATTITUDES
up 28%

CITIZEN
AWARENESS
up 20%

CITIZEN
SATISFACTION
up 16%

FEAR
down 10%

CRIME
down 12%

CALLS
down 11%

Figure 12.1   COPE Effects

SOURCE: Philip B. Taft, Jr. *Fighting Fear: The Baltimore County COPE Project.*© Washington, DC: The Police Executive Research Forum, 1986, p. 20. Reprinted with permission of PERF.

Fear Reduction Strategies Experiments Compared

Wycoff (pp. 107–108) summarizes the seven strategies tested in the Newark and Houston experiments as follows:

Newsletters (Houston and Newark). These were tested with and without crime statistics. They were police produced and provided residents of the test area with information about crime prevention steps they could take, the police department, and police programs in their area.

Victim Recontact (Houston). Patrol officers made telephone contact with victims to inform them of the status of their case, inquire whether they needed assistance, offer to send crime prevention information, and ask whether victims could provide additional information.

Police Community Station (Houston). A neighborhood storefront operation was conducted by patrol officers. The station provided a variety of services for the area.

Citizen Contact Patrol (Houston). Officers concentrated their patrol time within the target area where they made door-to-door contacts, introducing themselves to residents and businesspeople, and asking whether there were any neighborhood problems citizens wished brought to the attention of the police.

Community Organizing (Houston). Officers from the Community Services Division worked to organize block meetings attended by area patrol officers. They organized a neighborhood committee that met monthly with the district captain and developed special projects ("safe" houses for children, identifying property, and a clean-up campaign) for the area.

Signs of Crime (Newark). This program focused on social disorder and conducted "random intensified enforcement and order maintenance operations" (e.g., foot patrol to enforce laws and maintain order on sidewalks and street corners; radar checks; bus checks to enforce ordinances and order; enforcement of disorderly conduct laws to move groups off the street corners, road checks for DWI, improper licenses, stolen vehicles). Addressing physical deterioration involved an intensification of city services and the use of juvenile offenders to conduct clean-up work in the target areas.

Coordinated Community Policing (Newark). This was the "kitchen sink" project that included a neighborhood community police center, a directed police-citizen contact program, a neighborhood police newsletter, intensified law enforcement and order maintenance, and a neighborhood clean-up.

Two types of samples were used: (1) cross-sectional analysis that gave data for each area and (2) panel respondents who gave data for individuals. The results of the testing are summarized in Tables 12.2 and 12.3. The checks in the tables indicate that the results were **statistically significant** at the .05 level. This measurement means that the results would occur by chance only five times in one hundred. This level is most frequently used in such studies. A statistically significant finding at the .01 level means the results would occur by chance only one time in one hundred.

The programs were least effective reducing concerns about property crime and most effective reducing perceived social disorder. According to the data provided by individuals, the Newark Coordinated Community Policing study met the greatest number of goals.

◈ OTHER CRIME PREVENTION PROGRAM STUDIES IN THE 1980S

Several communities conducted crime prevention studies in the 1980s. Studies in Seattle, Portland and Hartford focused on citizen efforts to prevent residential crime; the study in Portland also focused on preventing crime in and around commercial

Table 12.2 Effects of Fear Reduction Programs (Cross-Sectional Results) (Area Results)

Programs	Reduce Perceived Area Physical Deterioration	Reduce Perceived Area Social Disorder	Reduce Fear of Personal Victimization	Reduce Worry about Property Crime	Reduce Perceived Area Personal Crime	Reduce Perceived Area Property Crime	Improve Evaluation of Police	Increase Satisfaction with Area
Houston Newsletters with and without Statistics	n.a.	n.a.						
Newark Newsletters with and without Statistics	n.a.	n.a.						
Houston Victim Recontact Program	n.a.	n.a.						
Houston Police Community Station	n.a.	✔	✔		✔	✔		
Houston Citizen Contact Patrol	n.a.	✔	✔		✔	✔		✔
Houston Community Organizing Response Team	n.a.	✔					✔	
Newark "Signs of Crime" Program		✔		✔				
Newark Coordinated Community Policing		✔			✔	✔	✔	

✔ = Desired goal achieved; significant at .05 level

n.a. = Not applicable

SOURCE: A. M. Pate, W. G. Skogan, M. A. Wycoff and L. W. Sherman. *Reducing the "Signs of Crime: The Newark Experience."* Washington, DC: The Police Foundation, 1986©. Reprinted by permission.

Table 12.3 Effects of Fear Reduction Programs (Panel Results) (Individual Results)

Programs	Reduce Perceived Area Physical Deterioration	Reduce Perceived Area Social Disorder	Reduce Fear of Personal Victimization	Reduce Worry about Property Crime	Reduce Perceived Area Personal Crime	Reduce Perceived Area Property Crime	Improve Evaluation of Police	Increase Satisfaction with Area
Houston Newsletters with and without Statistics	n.a.	n.a.						
Newark Newsletters with and without Statistics	n.a.	n.a.						
Houston Victim Recontact Program	n.a.	n.a.						
Houston Police Community Station	n.a.		✔		✔			
Houston Citizen Contact Patrol	n.a.	✔					✔	✔
Houston Community Organizing Response Team	n.a.	✔	✔	✔	✔	✔	✔	✔
Newark "Signs of Crime" Program		✔	✔	✔				
Newark Coordinated Community Policing		✔	✔		✔	✔	✔	✔

✔ = Desired goal achieved; significant at .05 level

n.a. = Not applicable

SOURCE: A. M. Pate, W. G. Skogan, M. A. Wycoff and L. W. Sherman. *Reducing the "Signs of Crime: The Newark Experience."* Washington, DC: The Police Foundation, 1986, p. 28©. Reprinted by permission.

establishments. Two studies examined the media and crime prevention: the McGruff national media campaign and the effectiveness of anticrime newsletters.

According to Heinzelmann (1986, p. 7): "In general, the results of these evaluations are favorable, indicating that community crime prevention programs can serve to reduce crime and fear, and at the same time improve the quality of life and the economic viability of urban neighborhoods and commercial settings."

The Seattle Program

The Citywide Crime Prevention Program (CCPP) of Seattle, described by Lindsay and McGillis (1986, pp. 46–67), focused on residential burglaries and included three primary police services: property identification, home security checks and organizing neighborhood block watch programs.

The Seattle Citywide Crime Prevention Program used property identification, home security checks and neighborhood block watches to significantly reduce the residential burglary rate as well as the number of burglary-in-progress calls.

Fleissner et al. (1992, p. 9) note:

When citizens and police in South Seattle banded together to fight crime, quarterly crime statistics showed dramatic improvements in the quality of life. Citizen activity spread in the city's other three police precincts; now community policing is a going concern throughout Seattle—a citywide success.

According to Lindsay and McGillis (p. 65), not only did the burglary rate drop significantly, "burglary-in-progress calls as a proportion of all burglary calls to police increased significantly in treated areas, and their quality was relatively high as measured by presentation of suspect information and the occurrence of subsequent arrests."

The Portland Program

Portland also instituted a burglary prevention program, described by Schneider (1986, pp. 68–86), which included providing citizens with information about locks, alarms, outside lighting around entrances, removal or trimming of hedges and precautions to take while on vacation. The program also encouraged citizens to mark property with identification numbers. Door-to-door canvassing and a heavy emphasis on neighborhood rather than individual protection were important components of the program.

The Portland antiburglary program succeeded in reducing the burglary rate for those who participated.

As Schneider (p. 84) notes: "In the high crime areas of Portland more than 20% of the homes could expect to be burglarized at least once a year. This was reduced to about 8% for participating households in those areas." Schneider (p. 85) also points out a class bias in this study: "Those attending meetings, engraving their property, and displaying the decals tended to be in the higher socioeconomic groups."

The Hartford Experiment

The Hartford Experiment, described by Fowler and Mangione (1986, pp. 87–108), used a three-pronged approach to reduce crime and the fear of crime: changing the physical environment, changing the delivery of police services and organizing the citizens to improve their neighborhoods. This experiment centered on the interdependence of citizens, the police and the environment. As Fowler and Mangione (p. 89) note: "The approach focuses on the interaction between human behavior and the (physically) built environment. It was hypothesized that the proper design and effective use of the built environment can lead to a reduction in crime and fear."

The program was based on four previous research efforts. First was that of Jacobs (1961), which found that neighborhoods that were relatively crime free had a mix of commercial and residential properties, resulting in many people on the streets and a great opportunity for police surveillance. In addition, a community with such mixed use property tended to have residents who cared about the neighborhood and watched out for each other.

Angel (1968) described similar findings in his concept of "critical density," which states that if quite a few people are present on the most frequently used streets, they will serve as deterrents to burglary. In addition, Newman's classic work (1972) suggests that crime can be reduced by redesigning buildings to increase the number of doorways and other spaces that could be easily observed. Finally, Repetto (1974), like Newman, found that opportunities for surveillance could reduce crime and, like Jacobs, that neighborhood cohesiveness could have the same result.

Based on this research, the Hartford Experiment focused on Asylum Hill, a residential area a few blocks from the central business district of Hartford that was rapidly deteriorating. It was found that due to the high rate of vehicle traffic, residents did not use their yards and felt no ties to the neighborhood. The physical design of the neighborhood was changed to restrict through traffic and visually define the boundaries of the neighborhood. Cul-de-sacs were built at a few critical intersections, and some streets were made one way.

A second change in the neighborhood involved patrol officer assignments. Instead of rotating assignments within a centralized department, Hartford began using a decentralized team of officers assigned permanently to the Asylum Hill area.

Finally, the Hartford Experiment helped organize the neighborhood, including the establishment of block watch programs, recreational programs for youths and improvements for a large neighborhood park.

As a result of these changes: "Residents used their neighborhood more, walked more often both during the day and evening hours, used the nearby park more often, and spent more days per week outside in front of their homes" (Fowler and Mangione, p. 96).

The Hartford Experiment restructured the neighborhood's physical environment, changed the way patrol officers were assigned and organized the neighborhood in an effort to reduce crime and the fear of crime.

Fowler and Mangione (p. 106) caution: "A crime control program such as this must be custom fit to a particular set of circumstances. What one would want to derive from the Hartford project is not a program design, but rather an approach to problem analysis and strategies to affect them."

◆ THE PORTLAND COMMERCIAL DEMONSTRATION PROJECT

The Crime Prevention through Environmental Design (CPTED) Commercial Demonstration Project implemented in Portland from 1974 to 1979, described by Lavrakas and Kushmuk (1986, pp. 202–227), also built upon the research of Jacobs (1961) and Newman (1972) and the concept of "defensible space."

The CPTED Project incorporated four major strategies: motivation reinforcement, activity support, surveillance and access control, as described in Figure 12.2. The CPTED project developed seven specific strategies (Lavrakas and Kushmuk, pp. 206–207): (1) creation of a "Safe Streets for People" component, (2) creation of a Residential Activity Center and miniplazas along Union Avenue Corridor (UAC), (3) general promotion of UAC, (4) improved transportation both into and out of UAC, (5) security services provided by a UAC security advisor, (6) increased law enforcement support throughout UAC and (7) development of a "Cash Off the Streets" program. The first two strategies of the CPTED Project involved redesigning some streets, improving roads, adding street lighting and generally making the area more attractive.

The Portland CPTED Commercial Demonstration Project found that the most successful strategies were security services, organization and support of the business community and the street lighting program.

According to Lavrakas and Kushmuk (p. 223): "Of moderate success were the economic development activities. Large-scale and comprehensive improvements in the physical environment (with the exception of the redesign of Union Avenue itself), promotional events, and residential social cohesion were judged to have achieved, at best, low levels of success." (See Figure 12.3.)

Lavrakas and Kushmuk (pp. 223–224) suggest three important lessons learned from this project. First, it is essential to have a realistic time frame and strong political support. Second, the more groups involved, the more complicated and difficult the project will become. And third, changes in the social environment of a community are much more difficult to make than those in the physical environment.

◆ COMMUNITY POLICING AND THE CRIMINAL JUSTICE SYSTEM

The criminal justice system includes law enforcement, the courts and corrections. What happens in each component of the criminal justice system directly affects the other two components, and many of the trends that affect the criminal justice system as a whole directly affect the type of programs police departments should implement to improve

MOTIVATION REINFORCEMENT

Design and Construction: Design, build, and/or repair buildings sites to enhance security and improve quality.

Owner/Management Action: Encourage owners and managements to implement safeguards to make businesses and commerical property less vulnerable to crime.

Territorial Identity: Differentiate private areas from public spaces to discourage trespass by potential offenders.

Neighborhood Image: Develop positive image of the commercial area to encourage user and investor confidence and increase the economic vitality of the area.

ACTIVITY SUPPORT

Land Use: Establish policies to prevent ill-advised land and buildings uses that have negative impact.

User Protection: Implement safeguards to make shoppers less vulnerable to crime.

Social Interaction: Encourage interaction among businessmen, users, and residents of commercial neighborhoods to foster social cohesion and control.

Police/Community Relations: Improve police/community relations to involve citizens in cooperative efforts with police to prevent and report crime.

Community Awareness: Create community crime prevention awareness to aid in combating crime in commercial areas.

SURVEILLANCE

Surveillance Through Physical Design: Improve opportunities for surveillance by physical design mechanisms that serve to increase the risk of detection for offenders, enable evasive actions by potential victims, and facilitate intervention by police.

Mechanical Surveillance Devices: Provide businesses with security devices to detect and signal illegal entry attempts.

Private Security Services: Determine necessary and appropriate services to enhance commercial security.

Police Services: Improve police services in order to efficiently and effectively respond to crime problems and to enhance citizen cooperation in reporting crimes.

ACCESS CONTROL

Access Control: Provide secure barriers to prevent unauthorized access to building grounds, buildings, and/or restricted building interior areas.

Figure 12.2   Commercial Environment Objectives of CPTED

NOTE: The four key hypotheses are not mutually exclusive. Surveillance objectives also serve to control access; activity support involves surveillance; and motivation reinforcement provides support for the other three hypotheses.

SOURCE: H. Kaplan, K. O'Kane, P. J. Lavrakas and S. Hoover. *CPTED Final Report on Commercial Demonstration in Portland, Oregon.* Arlington: Westinghouse Electric Corporation, 1978©. Reprinted by permission.

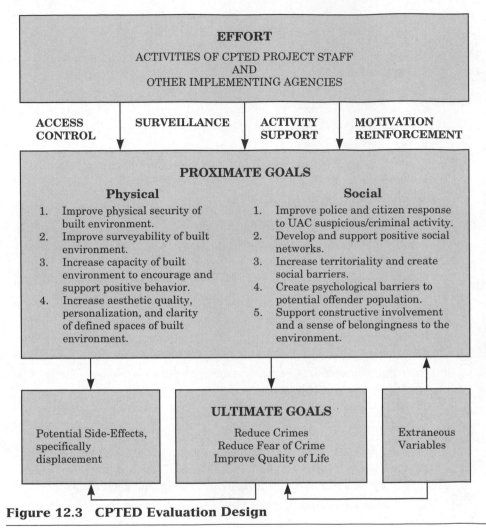

EFFORT

ACTIVITIES OF CPTED PROJECT STAFF
AND
OTHER IMPLEMENTING AGENCIES

| ACCESS CONTROL | SURVEILLANCE | ACTIVITY SUPPORT | MOTIVATION REINFORCEMENT |

PROXIMATE GOALS

Physical	**Social**
1. Improve physical security of built environment.	1. Improve police and citizen response to UAC suspicious/criminal activity.
2. Improve surveyability of built environment.	2. Develop and support positive social networks.
3. Increase capacity of built environment to encourage and support positive behavior.	3. Increase territoriality and create social barriers.
4. Increase aesthetic quality, personalization, and clarity of defined spaces of built environment.	4. Create psychological barriers to potential offender population.
	5. Support constructive involvement and a sense of belongingness to the environment.

| Potential Side-Effects, specifically displacement | **ULTIMATE GOALS**

Reduce Crimes
Reduce Fear of Crime
Improve Quality of Life | Extraneous Variables |

Figure 12.3   CPTED Evaluation Design

SOURCE: P. J. Lavrakas, J. Normoyle and J. Wagener. *CPTED Commercial Demonstration Evaluation Report.* Evanston: Westinghouse Electric Corporation, 1978©. Reprinted by permission.

community relations. Consequently, partnerships between the various entities within the criminal justice system are vital to achieving the community policing mission.

A coordinated effort among law enforcement, courts and corrections is required to effectively deal with the crime problem and to elicit the support of the community in doing so.

Effective efforts are those that partner various community institutions to address issues of housing, unemployment, illiteracy, lack of recreational opportunities for youths and other social problems.

Community Policing and the Courts

The way courts address the accused has a direct impact on the crime problem and on community policing efforts. The National Symposium identified two model court programs: the Albany (New York) Community Dispute Resolution Centers and the Madison (Wisconsin) Deferred Prosecution/First Offenders Unit.

Model court programs also involving the police include community dispute resolution centers and a deferred prosecution/first offenders unit.

Community Dispute Resolution Centers (Albany New York). The 32 dispute resolution centers were independent, community-based, nonprofit organizations contracted by the Unified Court System of the State of New York, Albany, to (1) provide dispute resolution resources for local communities, (2) prevent escalation of disputes, (3) relieve the courts of matters not requiring judicial intervention and (4) teach individuals to resolve their problems through mediation.

Police officers, probation officers, judges, district attorneys and legal aid offices could refer cases to a local dispute resolution center, or individuals could be self-referred. The mediation, conciliation or arbitration services were provided free. Mediation rather than law enforcement or court intervention was effective.

The Deferred Prosecution/First Offenders Unit (Madison, Wisconsin). This program sought to prevent offenders' further involvements in crime by deferring prosecution on the condition that they satisfactorily complete appropriate treatment and rehabilitation programs. The program recognized the hazards of labeling individuals and the potential of treatment for first offenders who accept responsibility for their actions.

An offender's suitability for the program was based on several criteria: the nature of the offense, prior criminal record, admission of guilt, attitude, whether the offender was dangerous to self or community, likelihood of repeating the crime and whether the offender would benefit from the treatment process.

The program used a large network of social service agencies and public and private organizations. Because a "substantial portion" of program participants were shoplifters, the staff conducted a one-day Saturday workshop on retail theft. Another integral part of the program was voluntary community service, not as a means of punishment, but as a way to repay the community for the crime committed and to change the offender's behavior patterns. The program conserved police, prosecutorial, judicial and correctional resources. In addition, offenders' lives were minimally disrupted because they could continue to pursue their occupations and fulfill family obligations.

Community Policing and Corrections

Community-based corrections gained popularity in the 1990s but is still resisted by many neighborhoods. Sometimes referred to as *intermediate sanctions*, community corrections may take many forms including halfway houses, prerelease centers, transition centers, work furlough and community work centers, community treatment centers, restitution centers and a host of other innovative approaches to involving the community in efforts to reintegrate offenders into the community *without* danger to the citizens.

Residents may live either part time or full time at such centers, depending on the other conditions set forth by the court. Evans (1996, pp. 124–125) notes: "Community corrections is effective and efficient when it works in partnership with local communities and other agencies interested in safer communities and justice."

Community corrections can be viewed as a part of the broader justice system and represents a growing interest in what many are referring to as *community justice*. According to Evans (p. 125), community corrections can more effectively accomplish its goals and enhance public safety by fostering partnerships with law enforcement and the community at large by encouraging citizens to join in the challenge of creating safer communities and by recognizing the importance of positive relationships between the community and the offender.

The National Symposium identified one model corrections program, the Volunteers in Parole program of the State Bar of California in San Francisco.

The model corrections program Volunteers in Parole provided a support system for young parolees and eased their transition from incarceration to productive citizenship.

This program was designed to ease the caseload of parole officers, many of whom had caseloads of up to 150 parolees. As Sulton (1990, p. 93) notes:

Many of the individuals supervised are youthful offenders without family, friends, permanent housing, employment, or other resources. These teenagers and young adults are uneducated and illiterate, unmarried parents of small children, struggling with drug or alcohol dependency, stigmatized by lengthy criminal records, suspicious, fearful, and uncertain. They frequently commit new crimes or violate the conditions of their parole because adequate support systems are unavailable.

The program, modeled after the Big Brothers and Big Sisters programs, paired youthful parolees, ages 15 to 23, with attorneys who volunteer their time. Attorneys are used because, as Sulton (pp. 93–94) notes, they: "(1) understand the legal system; (2) are familiar with community resources and have referral skills; (3) are experienced in dealing with bureaucracies; (4) are not intimidated by the sophistication of parolees; and (5) have an office where they can conveniently meet with parolees and privately discuss their concerns." In addition, attorneys have undergone a licensing procedure that should ensure they are of good moral character and will be able to answer the numerous questions parolees may have about the criminal justice system, governmental agencies, leases, contracts and other legal issues.

In addition to matching parolees with attorneys, the program conducts street law classes and informal lectures for the youthful parolees. Although no studies have been conducted on the effectiveness of the program, given the high cost of incarceration, according to Sulton (p. 96): "Should only a small number of the matches result in a reduction of the number of youth being returned to detention facilities or prisons, the State of California probably saved millions of dollars by investing in this program."

Strategies Recommended by the National Crime Prevention Council

The National Crime Prevention Council (*350 Tested Strategies*, 1995) has suggested several strategies the criminal justice system, particularly courts and corrections, might use to prevent crime—most of which focus on juveniles.

Boot Camps (pp. 246–247). Boot camps focus on physical conditioning, leadership and counseling in a military-type setting, diverting juvenile offenders from more expensive long-term detention while building life skills to help youths avoid criminal behavior when they return to the community. The council notes that juvenile justice system partnerships with correctional agencies, military resources and community-based programs increase the likelihood that discipline imparted during the program will continue through reintegration into the community. Support from local and state legislators is also important.

Restitution by Juvenile Offenders (pp. 245–246). Restitution programs usually originate as a sentencing option imposed on nonviolent offenders. Court-ordered community service programs require juvenile offenders to work at jobs in public agencies or community organizations and contribute a portion of their stipend as payment for damages caused. Many restitution programs have expanded to include training in job skills, life skills and values. Some include academic enrichment and tutoring. Such programs are usually operated by juvenile courts. Key partnerships include public agencies, community organizations and private firms that make jobs available to youthful offenders. A potential obstacle is that community members may feel such programs are "soft" on youths.

In-School Probation (pp. 249–250). In-school probation allows nonviolent offenders to remain connected to the educational setting, helps ensure discipline and improves compliance with behavioral standards through intensive supervision provided by a probation officer placed in the school. This officer helps address behavior standards, assists with academic difficulties and addresses absenteeism issues and discipline problems. Key partnerships include teachers, parents, substance abuse treatment, counseling and other services youths and their families need. A potential obstacle is that school staff and community leaders may feel students on probation should be expelled or put on long-term suspension to prevent them from disrupting the learning environment.

Diversion from Incarceration (pp. 250–251). Diverting juvenile offenders into intensive monitoring and support programs in community settings provides communities with a less costly and more effective strategy for reducing recidivism. According to the council, juvenile diversion programs include an array of community-based services to support youthful offenders, prevent reoffending through supervision and promote academic and employment success. Successful programs require small caseloads for staff so they have time to develop partnerships with the youth, family members, counselors and others assisting the youth. Again a potential obstacle is that community members may feel such a strategy is inadequate punishment and may put the public at risk of additional victimization.

Combine Corrections with Treatment (pp. 243–244). Juvenile offenders who are incarcerated should also be provided with treatment, opportunities for achievement and aftercare focused on reintegration into the community. The council (p. 243) notes: "Programs that incorporate community reintegration emphasize partnerships with local employment programs; community-based, residential treatment facilities; and family support services—to increase the likelihood that the treatment's effects will last beyond the detention term." The most likely obstacle to this strategy is the cost.

In addition to partnering with the courts and corrections, collaborative efforts with the media (as discussed in Chapter 11) may enhance community policing strategies aimed at crime prevention.

◈ USING THE MEDIA IN CRIME PREVENTION EFFORTS

Two different approaches to using the media have also been extensively studied: the "McGruff" media campaign and the use of police-community anticrime newsletters.

The "McGruff" National Media Campaign

McGruff, the crime dog, is to law enforcement what Smokey the Bear is to the National Forest Service. A press release from the National Crime Prevention Council describes the creation of McGruff and the campaign:

> The concept of a national public education campaign to teach Americans that they could prevent crime (and how to do so) was first conceived in 1978. The Department of Justice supported the plan, as did distinguished civic leaders and such organizations as the AFL-CIO, the International Association of Chiefs of Police, and the National Sheriffs' Association. The Advertising Council, Inc. agreed to support the campaign. Research and program development advisory groups helped formulate a strategy. . . . The first McGruff public service ads were developed in 1979 and premiered in February 1980. . . .
>
> The campaign's objectives were clear: (1) to change unwarranted feelings and attitudes about crime and the criminal justice system, (2) to generate an individual sense of responsibility for crime prevention, (3) to initiate individual action toward preventing crime, (4) to mobilize additional resources for crime prevention efforts and (5) to enhance existing crime prevention programs and projects conducted by national, state and local organizations.

This campaign, also known as the "Take a Bite Out of Crime" campaign, was aimed at promoting citizen involvement in crime prevention activities through public service announcements (**PSAs**). As O'Keefe (1986, p. 259) notes: "Most said they thought the ads were effective in conveying the message, that they liked the McGruff character and that they felt the information in the ads was worth passing on to other people." In addition, people indicated they felt more confident about their own ability to protect themselves from crime. Most important, almost one-fourth of the people took preventive action after exposure to the PSA, particularly to improve their own household security and work with neighbors in cooperative efforts—the two main themes of the McGruff promotions.

The public favorably received the "McGruff" format and content, and the campaign had a sizeable impact on what people know and do about crime prevention.

Police-Community Anticrime Newsletters

Lavrakas (1986, pp. 269–291) reviewed the results of three studies on a relatively new crime prevention strategy at the time, the police-community anticrime newsletter. Included in the review were *ALERT*, the Evanston (Illinois) Police Department newsletter; the *Community Policing Exchange* newsletter of the Houston Police Department; and *ACT I*, the newsletter of the Newark Police Department.

One important finding of these three studies was that although readers were much more aware of crime, at a statistically significant level, their fear of crime did *not* increase. According to Lavrakas (p. 286): "In each of the cities, results indicated that residents were overwhelmingly positive in their assessments of the newsletters, especially the versions that included crime statistics. Not only was exposure greater to the version with crime statistics, but it was rated as significantly more interesting and more informative."

Studies of three police-community anticrime newsletters found them to be highly effective, especially if crime statistics were included.

Lavrakas (pp. 289–290) concluded that the three tests "suggest that such newsletters merit consideration elsewhere as one strategy in the arsenal in the fight against crime."

◉ LESSONS LEARNED

Yin (1986, pp. 294–308) analyzed 11 research studies of community policing/crime prevention and suggests that they "point to the desirability of joint police-citizen initiatives in successful community crime prevention efforts" (p. 304). Table 12.4 summarizes the research studies Yin analyzed and the results of each.

A key finding, according to Yin, is that any crime prevention strategy, taken singly, is likely to be ineffective. A second finding points to the importance of improving the police-community relationship. Yin (p. 306) suggests that the results of these studies provide a general pattern and a major lesson about crime prevention: "Successful crime prevention efforts require joint activities by the residents and police and the presumed improvement of relationships between these groups."

Skolnick and Bayley (p. 212) describe this as police-community **reciprocity:** "Police-community reciprocity means that police must genuinely feel, and genuinely communicate a feeling, that the public they are serving has something to contribute to the enterprise of policing." Both parties can benefit from working together.

In addition to these relatively formal evaluations, other less quantitative evaluations have been conducted.

◉ QUALITATIVE EVALUATIONS AND SALIENT PROGRAM FEATURES

Qualitative evaluations are more descriptive and less statistical. One large-scale qualitative evaluation, undertaken by the National Symposium on Community Institutions and Inner-City Crime Project, sought to identify model programs for reduction of inner-city

Table 12.4 Summary of Eleven Evaluation Studies

Description of Intervention	Study Author(s)	Intervention Sites and Period	Type of Crime Addressed	Type of Outcomes Examined	Nature of Outcomes	Analytic Criteria Used in Test Outcomes
Hartford Project: physical redesign, police redeployment and community organizing	Fowler & Mangione	Hartford, Connecticut, 1973–1979	residential	informal social control; burglary and robbery victimization rates; fear of crime	crime reduction when whole intervention in place	statistical significance
Crime Newsletters: distribution of community newsletters in target neighborhoods	Lavrakas	Evanston, Illinois, 1981 Houston, Texas, 1983 Newark, New Jersey, 1983	residential	awareness of newsletter; perceived crime problem; fear of crime	positive changes at one of three sites	statistical significance
Portland Project: physical redesign, police assistance and business organizing	Lavrakas & Kushmuk	Portland, Oregon, 1974–1980	commercial	reported burglaries; fear of crime; quality of life	burglary reduction	statistical significance
Seattle Community Crime Prevention Program: block watch, security inspections and property engraving	Lindsay & McGillis	Seattle, Washington, 1974–1975	residential	burglary victimization rate	burglary reduction	statistical significance
McGruff National Media Campaign: information used in mass media and in pamphlets	O'Keefe	Nationwide campaign, 1979	residential	awareness of announcements; reported learning; reported preventive actions	reported learning and actions increase	data in supplemental report
Newark Foot Patrol: foot patrols from 4 P.M. to midnight	Pate	Newark, New Jersey, 1973–1979	residential	reported crime victimization rates; perceived crime, safety and satisfaction with police	no crime reduction; changed perceptions	statistical significance
Urban Crime Prevention Program: block watches and related neighborhood meetings	Rosenbaum, et al.	Chicago, Illinois, 1983–1984	residential	victimization rates; perceived crime; fear of crime; perceived efficacy; social disorder; physical deterioration	crime reduction at only one of four sites; increases at others	statistical significance
Portland Anti-Burglary Program: street lighting, property engraving and community education	Schneider	Portland, Oregon, 1973–1974	residential	reported burglaries; victimization rates	burglary reduction	statistical significance
Commercial Security Field Test: security surveys undertaken by business proprietors	Tien & Cahn	Denver, Colorado, 1981 Long Beach, California, 1981 St. Louis, Missouri, 1981	residential	burglary victimization rates; fear of crime	burglary reduction at one of three sites	statistical significance
Neighborhood Foot Patrol: foot patrol and community organizing	Trojanowicz	Flint, Michigan, 1979–1982	residential	reported crime; satisfaction with police	crime reduction; increase in satisfaction	descriptive data only
Storefront Police Office: location of storefront office, staffed by police, in local neighborhood	Wycoff & Skogan	Houston, Texas, 1983–1984	residential	fear of crime; perceived crime, safety; and satisfaction with police	fear reduction; improved perceptions	statistical significance

SOURCE: "Community Crime Prevention, A Synthesis of Eleven Evaluations." In *Community Crime Prevention: Does It Work?* edited by Dennis P. Rosenbaum. Beverly Hills: Sage Publications, 1986, pp. 297–299.© Reprinted by permission.

crime. According to Sulton (p. 8) almost 3,500 national organizations, criminal justice scholars and federal, state and local government agencies were asked to recommend outstanding local programs. This resulted in the identification of approximately 1,300 programs. Each was sent a request for detailed information, and 350 (27 percent) responded. From these, 18 were selected for site visits.

Sulton (p. 10) notes that although each program was unique, they shared some common characteristics.

Eighteen model programs shared the following characteristics. The program:

- *Focused on causes of crime.*
- *Built on community strengths.*
- *Incorporated natural support systems.*
- *Had an identifiable group of clients.*
- *Targeted those who were less affluent.*
- *Had clearly stated goals and well-defined procedures.*
- *Had sufficient resources.*
- *Had a strong leader.*

Sulton (p. 10) observes that many of the problems focus on specific social problems of inner-city residents "identified as correlates with, if not causes of, inner-city crime, such as emotional or family instability, lack of education, absence of vocational skills, unemployment, drug and alcohol abuse, juvenile gangs and sexual abuse and exploitation." The programs have a clear focus, a clear audience and a clear idea of how to proceed.

On a much smaller scale, but equally instructive, is the Newport News Police Department's reliance on data to identify a problem and to evaluate their solution (adapted from Guyot, 1992, p. 321):

Local hunters and other gun owners held target practice at an excavation pit. Officer Hendrickson found that between April and September one year, the department had been called 45 times to chase away shooters and that the problem had existed for at least 15 years. Most of the calls had come from a couple whose nearby home was bullet-riddled and who thought the police were doing a good job because each time they chased away the shooters.

Officer Hendrickson interviewed shooters and learned that most were soldiers from nearby Ft. Eustis; many others were sent to the pit by gun shop owners. The officer also determined the pit was close enough to a highway to make any firearms discharge there illegal. Deciding to use education backed by legal sanctions, he first photographed the damage and other evidence, which he used to persuade a judge to give anyone convicted once of illegal shooting a suspended sentence and a small fine; a second offense would result in confiscation of the weapon and a jail sentence. The officer obtained from the property owners permission to arrest on their property and the same from the C & O Railroad for shooters crossing the tracks to reach the pit. He also wrote a pamphlet defining the problem and the department's intended enforcement action, and distributed it to the military base and all area gun shops. Finally, he had "no parking—tow zone" signs erected on the shoulder where most shooters parked.

The results were simple. Officers issued 35 summonses to shooters in September, 15 in October, and the last on November 12. The pit soon became so overgrown that it was uninviting for target practice.

Success in the preceding incident and others might indicate that community policing and problem-solving policing would be readily accepted by law enforcement officials and the communities they serve. Such acceptance is not, however, always the case because of several impediments.

◈ IMPEDIMENTS TO COMMUNITY POLICING

Recall from Chapter 5 the challenges facing implementation of community policing as described by Sadd and Grinc (1996, pp. 1–2):

- Resistance by police officers
- Difficulty involving other agencies and organizing the community
- Reluctance of average citizens to participate, either because of fear or cynicism

Resistance to change is common, especially in a tradition-oriented profession such as law enforcement. Sadd and Grinc (p. 8) suggest: "Community policing is a fight for 'hearts and minds' of patrol officers and the public . . . involving a shift in the culture of policing." Skolnick and Bayley (pp. 225–226) describe six impediments to implementing innovative community-oriented policing.

Impediments to implementing innovative community-oriented policing include:

- *The powerful pull of tradition.*
- *Substantial segments of the public do not want the police to change.*
- *Unions will continue to be skeptical of innovation.*
- *Innovation may prove costly.*
- *Lack of vision on the part of police executives.*
- *Police departments' inability to evaluate their own effectiveness.*

A challenge noted by Sadd and Grinc is that projects were usually established as special units that some saw as elite: "The perception of elitism is ironic because community policing is meant to close the gap between patrol and special units and to empower and value the rank-and-file patrol officer as the most important agent for police work."

Another substantial impediment is how to respond to calls for service. A potential conflict exists between responding to calls for service and community policing efforts because calls for service use much of the time needed for problem identification and resolution efforts. The unpredictability of calls for service presents management problems for agencies wanting to implement community policing strategies. Departments must set their priorities and determine how to balance calls for service (reactive) with a problem-oriented approach (proactive). As stressed throughout this text, the one-on-one interaction between police officers and the citizens they serve is critical.

Cost vs. Benefit

Some simple services that police departments might provide for the community cost little and require limited personnel. For example, relatively inexpensive efforts to enhance community safety through crime prevention might include conducting monthly meetings, meeting with school administrators, conducting fingerprinting programs and blood pressure programs, participating in athletic contests, publishing newsletters and providing ride-alongs. Other services, however, may be relatively expensive and require many officers.

Whatever the cost to implement, community policing appears to offer a realistic approach to reducing violence, crime and the drug problem. The remaining chapters discuss several approaches to community policing and problem solving to address these issues.

◈ A FINAL NOTE: THE IMPORTANT DISTINCTION BETWEEN PROGRAMS AND COMMUNITY POLICING

It must be stressed that programs identified throughout this chapter are *not* community policing, although community policing may incorporate the use of these and other strategies. Too many police officials think that because they have a Neighborhood Watch Program or a ride-along program, they are doing community policing. In fact, some police chiefs and sheriffs state with pride that they are deeply involved in community policing because they have a DARE program. Community policing is an overriding *philosophy* that affects every aspect of police operations; it is not a single program or even a hundred programs. Such programs, particularly in isolation, are more community relations or even public relations, not community policing.

SUMMARY

Crime prevention became popular in the late 1960s and early 1970s, with many communities taking an active role. Among the most commonly implemented crime prevention programs have been street lighting projects, property marking projects, security survey projects, citizen patrol projects and crime reporting, neighborhood watch or block projects. Specialized crime watch programs include mobile crime watch, youth crime watch, business crime watch, realtor watch and carrier alert.

Continuing the community crime prevention momentum generated during the 1960s and 1970s, new programs and organizations were initiated during the 1980s and 1990s to encourage citizens to play an active role in reducing crime in their own neighborhoods. Among the most visible organizations focused on crime are citizen crime prevention associations, Crime Stoppers and MADD. Many police departments also expanded their use of volunteers, who may serve as reserve officers, auxiliary patrol, community service officers or on an as-needed basis.

Youths, who had traditionally been included in police-community relations efforts and crime prevention initiatives, were also addressed through programs including the

McGruff "Take a Bite out of Crime" campaign, police athletic leagues (PALs), Officer Friendly, police explorers, police-school liaison programs and the DARE program. Many programs for juveniles involve the schools, which historically have been charged with instilling discipline in their students. For example, police-school liaison programs place an officer into a school to work with school authorities, parents and students, to prevent crime and antisocial behavior and to improve police-youth relationships. The joint goals of most police-school liaison programs are to prevent juvenile delinquency and to improve police-youth relations.

The most common components of community policing experiments have been foot patrol, newsletters and community organizing. Several empirical studies in the 1980s assessed the effectiveness of community policing efforts. The Flint Neighborhood Foot Patrol Program appeared to produce a decrease in crime, an increase in general citizen satisfaction with the foot patrol program, a decline in the public's fear of crime and a positive perception of the foot patrol officers.

In the first Newark Foot Patrol Experiment, residents reported positive results, while business owners reported negative results. The second Newark Foot Patrol Experiment used coordinated foot patrol, a cleanup campaign and distribution of a newsletter. Only the coordinated foot patrol reduced the perception of property crime and improved assessments of the police.

The Oakland program, using foot patrol, mounted patrol, small vehicle patrol and a Report Incidents Directly program, resulted in a substantial drop in the rate of crime against persons and their property. The San Diego Community Profile Project provided patrol officers with extensive community orientation training. These officers became more service oriented, increased their nonlaw enforcement contacts with citizens and had a more positive attitude toward police-community relations.

The Houston Fear Reduction Project did not achieve desired results from the victim recontact program or the newsletter. Citizen contact patrol and the police storefront operation did, however, result in decreases in the public's perception of social disorder, fear of personal victimization and the level of personal and property crime.

The Boston Foot Patrol Project found no statistically significant relationship between changes in the level of foot patrol provided and number of calls for service or the seriousness of the calls. Baltimore County's COPE Project reduced fear of crime by 10 percent and crime itself by 12 percent in target neighborhoods. It also reduced calls for service, increased citizen awareness of and satisfaction with the police, and improved police officer attitudes.

Other studies have reviewed the effectiveness of community crime prevention efforts. The Seattle Citywide Crime Prevention Program, using property identification, home security checks and neighborhood block watches, significantly reduced the residential burglary rate as well as the number of burglary-in-progress calls. The Portland antiburglary program also succeeded in reducing the burglary rate for the participants. The Hartford Experiment restructured the physical environment, changed how patrol officers were assigned and organized the neighborhood in an effort to reduce crime and the fear of crime.

The Portland CPTED Commercial Demonstration Project found that the most successful strategies were security services, organization and support of the business community and the street lighting program.

The criminal justice system includes law enforcement, the courts and corrections. What happens in each component of the criminal justice system directly affects the other two components. Consequently, a coordinated effort among law enforcement, courts and corrections is required to effectively deal with the crime problem and to elicit the support of the community in doing so. Model court programs include a community dispute resolution center and a deferred prosecution/first offenders unit. The model corrections program Volunteers in Parole provides a support system for young parolees and eases their transition from incarceration to productive citizenship.

The effectiveness of the media in assisting crime prevention efforts is another evaluation focus. The public has favorably received the "McGruff" format and content. The "McGruff" campaign has had a sizeable impact on what the public knows and does about crime prevention. Studies of three police-community anticrime newsletters found them to be highly effective, especially if they included crime statistics.

Some general conclusions can be drawn from the preceding studies, including the finding that successful crime prevention efforts require joint activities by the residents and police and the presumed improvement of relationships between these groups.

Eighteen model programs identified by the National Symposium on Community Institutions and Inner-City Crime Project shared the following characteristics: The programs (1) were focused on causes of crime, (2) built on community strengths, (3) incorporated natural support systems, (4) had an identifiable group of clients, (5) targeted those who were less affluent, (6) had clearly stated goals and well-defined procedures, (7) had sufficient resources and (8) had a strong leader.

The implementation of community policing must be weighed against several impediments including the powerful pull of tradition, substantial segments of the public who do not want the police to change, the skepticism of unions with regard to innovation, the cost of innovation, lack of vision on the part of police executives and the incapacity of police departments to evaluate their own effectiveness.

DISCUSSION QUESTIONS

1. Why is it difficult to conduct research on the effectiveness of community policing?

2. Which studies do you think have the most value for policing in the next few years? Which studies have the most promise?

3. Why would a police department want to reduce fear of crime rather than crime itself?

4. Which of the fear reduction strategies do you believe holds the most promise?

5. What do you think are the most reasonable aspects of the Crime Prevention Through Environmental Design (CPTED) approach?

6. If you believe in the CPTED approach and see individuals ignoring its potential to reduce crime, do you think that if they are victimized the concept of culpability should be considered?

7. Has your police department conducted any research on community policing or crime prevention efforts? If so, what were the results?

8. Does your police department have its own McGruff? If so, how does the department use him?

9. What do you think are the most important questions regarding police-community relations that should be researched in the next few years?

10. How much of a police department's budget should be devoted to research? Which areas should be of highest priority?

INFOTRAC COLLEGE EDITION ASSIGNMENTS

- Use InfoTrac to help answer the discussion questions as appropriate.
- Research and outline at least one of the following subjects: citizen crime reporting, DARE, National Night Out, Police Athletic Leagues.

COMMUNITY PROJECTS

- What changes have been made in your police department in the last five years?
- What police-community relations programs does your police department participate in?
- Does your department permit ride-alongs? If so, who can participate?

REFERENCES

Angel, S. *Discouraging Crime through City Planning.* Berkeley: University of California Press, 1968.

Austin, Dave and Braaten, Jane. "Turning Lives Around: Portland Youth Find a New PAL." *The Police Chief,* May 1991, pp. 36–38.

Crowe, Timothy D. "The Secure Store: A Clean, Well-Lighted Place." *Security Management,* March 1992, pp. 22A–24A.

"DARE Chief Raps 'Bogus Research' as New Study Questions Anti-Drug Program's Long-Term Impact." *Law Enforcement News,* Vol. XXV, No. 518, September 30, 1999, pp. 1, 10.

Drowns, Robert W. and Hess, Kären M. *Juvenile Justice,* 3rd ed. Belmont, CA: Wadsworth Publishing Company, 2000.

Evans, Donald G. "Defining Community Corrections." *Corrections Today,* October 1996, pp. 124–145.

Fleissner, Dan; Fedan, Nicholas; and Klinger, David. "Community Policing in Seattle: A Model Partnership between Citizens and Police." *National Institute of Justice Journal,* August 1992, pp. 9–18.

Fowler, Floyd J., Jr. and Mangione, Thomas W. "A Three-Pronged Effort to Reduce Crime and Fear of Crime: The Hartford Experiment." In *Community Crime Prevention: Does It Work?* edited by Dennis P. Rosenbaum, pp. 87–108. Beverly Hills: Sage Publications, 1986.

Greenberg, Martin Alan. "Volunteer Police: The People's Choice for Safer Communities." *The Police Chief,* May 1991, pp. 42–44.

Greene, Jack R. and Taylor, Ralph B. "Community-Based Policing and Foot Patrol: Issues of Theory and Evaluation." In *Community Policing: Rhetoric or Reality,* edited by Jack R. Greene and Stephen D.

Mastrofski, pp. 195–223. New York: Praeger Publishers, 1991.

Guyot, Dorothy. "Problem-Oriented Policing Shines in the Stats." In *Source Book: Community-Oriented Policing: An Alternative Strategy,* edited by Bernard L. Garmire, pp. 317–321. Washington: ICMA, May 1992.

Heinzelmann, Fred. "Foreword." *Community Crime Prevention: Does It Work?* edited by Dennis P. Rosenbaum, pp. 7–8. Newbury Park: Sage Publications, 1986.

"Help Keep Families Together." Irving, TX: MADD, no date.

Jacobs, J. *The Death and Life of Great American Cities.* New York: Vintage, 1961.

Lavrakas, Paul J. "Evaluating Police-Community Anticrime Newsletters: The Evanston, Houston, and Newark Field Studies." In *Community Crime Prevention: Does It Work?* edited by Dennis P. Rosenbaum, pp. 269–291. Beverly Hills: Sage Publications, 1986.

Lavrakas, Paul J. and Kushmuk, James W. "Evaluating Crime Prevention through Environmental Design: The Portland Commercial Demonstration Project." In *Community Crime Prevention: Does It Work?* edited by Dennis P. Rosenbaum, pp. 202–227. Beverly Hills: Sage Publications, 1986.

Lindsay, Betsy and McGillis, Daniel. "Citywide Community Crime Prevention: An Assessment of the Seattle Program." In *Community Crime Prevention: Does It Work?* edited by Dennis P. Rosenbaum, pp. 46–67. Beverly Hills: Sage Publications, 1986.

Mastrofski, Stephen D. "What Does Community Policing Mean for Daily Police Work?" *National Institute of Justice Journal,* August 1992, pp. 23–27.

Newman, O. *Defensible Space: Crime Prevention through Urban Design.* New York: Macmillan, 1972.

O'Keefe, Garrett J. "The 'McGruff' National Media Campaign: Its Public Impact and Future Implications." In *Community Crime Prevention: Does It Work?* edited by Dennis P. Rosenbaum, pp. 252–268. Beverly Hills: Sage Publications, 1986.

Pace, Denny F. "Community Policing Defined." *Law and Order,* August 1992, pp. 46, 56–58.

Pate, Anthony M. "Experimenting with Foot Patrol: The Newark Experience." In *Community Crime Prevention: Does It Work?* edited by Dennis P. Rosenbaum, pp. 137–156. Beverly Hills: Sage Publications, 1986.

Police Foundation. *The Newark Foot Patrol Experiment.* Washington, DC: The Police Foundation, 1981.

Repetto, T. A. *Residential Crime.* Cambridge: Ballinger, 1974.

Sadd, Susan and Grinc, Randolph M. *Implementation Challenges in Community Policing.* Washington, DC: National Institute of Justice Research in Brief, February 1996.

Schneider, Anne L. "Neighborhood-Based Antiburglary Strategies: An Analysis of Public and Private Benefits from the Portland Program." In *Community Crime Prevention: Does It Work?* edited by Dennis P. Rosenbaum, pp. 68–86. Beverly Hills: Sage Publications, 1986.

Sharp, Arthur G. "A Porch Light that Keeps Shining Brighter." *Law and Order,* Vol. 47, No. 4, April 1999, pp. 42–46.

Skogan, Wesley G. and Wycoff, Mary Ann. "Storefront Police Offices: The Houston Field Test." In *Community Crime Prevention: Does It Work?* edited by Dennis P. Rosenbaum, pp. 179–199. Beverly Hills: Sage Publications, 1986.

Skolnick, Jerome H. and Bayley, David H. *The New Blue Line: Innovation in Six American Cities.* New York: The Free Press, 1986.

Sulton, Anne Thomas. *Inner-City Crime Control: Can Community Institutions Contribute?* Washington, DC: The Police Foundation, 1990.

Taft, Philip B., Jr. *Fighting Fear: The Baltimore County C.O.P.E. Project.* Washington, DC: Police Executive Research Forum, 1986.

350 Tested Strategies to Prevent Crime: A Resource for Municipal Agencies and Community Groups. Washington, DC: National Crime Prevention Council, 1995.

Trojanowicz, Robert C. "Evaluating a Neighborhood Foot Patrol Program: The Flint, Michigan, Project." In *Community Crime Prevention: Does It Work?* edited by Dennis P. Rosenbaum, pp. 157–178. Beverly Hills: Sage Publications, 1986.

Wycoff, Mary Ann. "The Benefits of Community Policing: Evidence and Conjecture." In *Community Policing: Rhetoric or Reality,* edited by Jack R. Greene and Stephen D. Mastrofski, pp. 103–120. New York: Praeger Publishers, 1991.

Yin, Robert K. "Community Crime Prevention: A Synthesis of Eleven Evaluations." In *Community Crime Prevention: Does It Work?* edited by Dennis P. Rosenbaum, pp. 294–308. Beverly Hills: Sage Publications, 1986.

RESOURCES

Many organizations offer expertise in building partnerships and provide a variety of publications, training and services that can strengthen local efforts. A sampling follows.*

Bureau of Justice Assistance Clearinghouse, Box 6000, Rockville, MD 20850; (800) 688-4252.

Center for Community Change, 1000 Wisconsin Ave. NW, Washington, DC 20007; (202) 342-0519.

Citizens Committee for New York City, 305 7th Ave., 15th Floor, New York, NY 10001; (212) 989-0909.

Community Policing Consortium, 1726 M St. NW, Suite 801, Washington, DC 20006; (202) 833-3305 or (800) 833-3085.

National Center for Community Policing, School of Criminal Justice, Michigan State University, East Lansing, MI 48824; (517) 355-2322.

National Crime Prevention Council, 1700 K St. NW, 2d Floor, Washington, DC 20006-3817; (202) 466-6272.

National Training and Information Center, 810 North Milwaukee Ave., Chicago, IL 60622-4103; (312) 243-3035.

Police Executive Research Forum, 2300 M St. NW, Suite 910, Washington, DC 20006; (202) 466-7820.

*Every interested organization has a Web page on the Internet, including several federal agencies. A search using the words *community policing* or *crime prevention* will yield a tremendous amount of current information.

CHAPTER 13

Understanding and Preventing Violence

We are a violent nation. We are the most violent and self-destructive nation on the face of the earth.

　　U.S. Senate Judiciary Report

Violence is one of the most pressing social problems and important public health issues in American society.

　　National Crime Prevention Council
　　(NCPC)

Do you know

What causes violence?

Why identifying the causes of violence is important?

What is required for effective violence prevention tactics?

What three strategies are suggested for general violence prevention?

What the three phases in the gun violence continuum are?

What strategy for each phase is suggested by the National Crime Prevention Council?

Who the OJJDP has identified as potential partners in efforts to combat gun violence?

How partner abuse differs from violent crime?

What predisposing factor to domestic assault was identified by the Memphis police and medical community?

What cultural diversity issue must be addressed when forming partnerships to prevent domestic abuse?

What three risks face children in violent homes?

What the CD-CP Model emphasizes?

How many people are victims of violent crime at work each year?

What common motivations behind workplace violence are?

Can you define these terms:

macrosocial	negative emotionality	psychosocial
microsocial	process mapping	straw purchasers

INTRODUCTION

According to the National Crime Victimization Survey (NCVS) ("Violent Crime Rate Falls," 2000, p. 12), approximately 28.8 million violent crimes were experienced by U.S. citizens age 12 or older during 1999. Although violent victimization rates fell 34 percent from 50 to 33 victimizations per 1,000 persons age 12 or older between 1993 and 1999, reducing violence is still an extremely important challenge for community policing efforts.

Violence occurs on our streets as road rage, in our schools and workplaces as shooting sprees and behind closed doors as domestic abuse. It permeates and weakens our social fabric. Eskridge (1999, p. 4) contends: "For young black males today, the odds of being killed on the streets of America are greater than they were for soldiers on the battlefield during the war in Vietnam."

This chapter begins with a discussion of the causes of violence and general guidelines on its prevention. This is followed by an examination of gun violence, which is often manifested in other types of violence as well. Next domestic violence is examined, including spousal abuse and child abuse. The chapter concludes with a brief look at violence in the workplace. School violence is discussed in the next chapter.

CAUSES OF VIOLENCE

The causes of violence are as difficult to pinpoint as the causes of crime. Many suggest that the ready availability and lethal nature of guns, especially handguns, is a major factor. But in the colonial days every household had guns—survival depended on it. Yet children did not shoot each other in their one-room schoolhouses. Nonetheless, the gun factor must be considered and, in fact, is the first specific type of violence this chapter examines because it is such a major problem.

Another major cause of violence is desensitization to violence. Oliver and McLaughlin (1998, p. 51) note: "The recent trend to embrace, glamorize, exploit and capitalize on violent imagery, particularly through print media and advertising, may serve to normalize and perpetuate the culture." They pose the question: "What happens when 'normal' is the problem?" and suggest the focus should shift to the other side of the crime scene tape where onlookers might consist of unemployed and homeless people, pregnant teenagers and truant children. In other words, social and economic conditions also give rise to violence.

Causes of violence may include ready availability of guns, drugs and alcohol; a desensitization to violence; disintegration of the family and community; social and economic deprivation; and increased numbers of children growing up in violent families.

Eskridge (p. 5) suggests other causes underlying violence including cultural values that glorify violence, the oppositional culture of the street with its own code of behavior and an increasing sense of frustration and futility harbored by residents of the inner cities regarding what they see as a double standard of justice. In addition, a growing number of individuals with behavior-influencing abnormalities are able to function in a seemingly normal fashion within the community, for example, Jeffrey Dahmer.

In Table 13.1 Roth (1994, p. 7) presents risk factors for violent behavior in a matrix illustrating the complexity of social and individual factors that may cause violence. Notice the presence of weapons in both the **macrosocial** (big picture) and **microsocial** (smaller picture) situations. The macrosocial environment includes the amount of social capital available as discussed in previous chapters as well as existing diversity, including

Table 13.1   Matrix for Organizing Risk Factors for Violent Behavior

Units of Observation and Explanation	Proximity to Violent Events and Their Consequences		
	Predisposing	Situational	Activating
SOCIAL Macrosocial	–Concentration of poverty –Opportunity structures –Decline of social capital –Oppositional cultures –Sex role socialization	–Physical structures –Routine activities –Access: weapons, emergency medical services	–Catalytic social event
Microsocial	–Community organizations –Illegal markets –Gangs –Family disorganization –Pre-existing structures	–Proximity of responsible monitors –Participants' social relationships –Bystanders' activities –Temporary communication impairments –Weapons: carrying, displaying	–Participants' communication exchange
INDIVIDUAL Psychosocial	–Temperament –Learned social responses –Perceptions of rewards/ penalties for violence –Violent deviant sexual preferences –Social, communication skills –Self-identification in social hierarchy	–Accumulated emotion –Alcohol/drug consumption –Sexual arousal –Premeditation	–Impulse –Opportunity recognition
Biological	–Neurobehavioral* traits –Genetically mediated traits –Chronic use of psychoactive substances or exposure to neurotoxins	–Transient neurobehavioral* states –Acute effects of psycho- active substances	–Sensory signal processing errors

*Includes neuroanatomical, neurophysiological, neurochemical, and neuroendocrine. "Traits" describe capacity as determined by status at birth, trauma, and aging processes such as puberty. "States" describe temporary conditions associated with emotions, external stressors, etc.
Adapted from Albert J. Reiss, Jr. and Jeffrey A. Roth, eds. *Understanding and Preventing Violence*, Washington, DC: National Academy Press, 1993, p. 297.
SOURCE: Jeffrey A. Roth. *Understanding and Preventing Violence*. Washington, DC: National Institute of Justice Research in Brief, p. 7.

economic diversity. The microsocial environment focuses on smaller units such as the family. **Psychosocial** factors refer to individual psychological characteristics such as temperament and self-identity.

A problem-solving approach to preventing violence must attempt to identify the underlying causes of specific violent situations that threaten a community before solutions can be devised.

PREVENTING VIOLENCE

A panel consisting of the National Institute of Justice, the National Science Foundation and the Centers for Disease Control and Prevention reviewed existing knowledge about violence and concluded (Roth, p. 1): "Although findings of research and program evaluations suggest promising directions for violence prevention strategies—

Developing effective prevention tactics will require long-term collaborations between criminal justice and juvenile justice practitioners, other social service agencies, and evaluation researchers. It also requires involvement of the entire community of which these agencies are a part."

The panel recommends: "Long-term prevention should include strategies directed toward children and their caregivers; interventions undertaken at the social and community level; and biomedical strategies in such areas as substance abuse by pregnant women. More immediate effects may be obtainable by intervening in situations where violent events cluster, such as illegal drug markets, certain places where alcohol and firearms are readily available, and physical locations conducive to crime." The panel concludes:

> Because evaluations are not yet conclusive enough to warrant a commitment to any single strategy, violence control policy should proceed through a problem-solving strategy in which many tactics are tested, evaluated, and refined. This approach requires sustained, integrated efforts by criminal justice, social service, and community-based organizations.

The effort should also include citizens within the community.

One NCPC publication, *350 Tested Strategies to Prevent Crime* (1995), contains specific strategies that have worked in specific communities. They may or may not work in other communities, as each community is unique. "The hallmark of community policing is that the response can be tailored to local wants and needs" ("Community Policing and Domestic Violence," p. 2). Nonetheless, the strategies present a convenient starting place.

Strategies for general violence prevention include public dialogue and community mediation, corporate support for antiviolence projects and addressing violence as a public health problem.

One strategy suggested for general violence prevention is *public dialogue and community mediation (350 Tested Strategies* pp. 240–241). Community-based public dia-

Community members, with police assistance, publicly express their determination to end violent crime in their neighborhood.

logues help identify neighborhood issues and resolve disputes among groups before they escalate into violence. Community groups, the courts, police and other city agencies refer cases to community-based mediators and help to identify neighborhood issues requiring resolution. Volunteer mediators and discussion leaders help disputants identify issues, accept responsibility for individual behavior without threats and identify ways to resolve the conflict. Formal hearings may be held to discuss some complaints, giving structure and credibility to the mediation process. Other disputes may be settled informally using discussion leaders working through community organizers.

Key partnerships in the public dialogue and community mediation strategy include schools, police, probation agencies, area courts and community organizations. Youths are vital partners in mediating school-related disputes. In addition community newspapers and grassroots word-of-mouth networks help publicize the community dialogue and mediation services. The Community Board Program in San Francisco, which uses community activism to resolve conflict among groups, has used this strategy. A potential obstacle to the service is that it may be difficult to finance. This obstacle might be overcome by another strategy suggested by the National Crime Prevention Council, corporate sponsorship.

Corporate support for antiviolence projects (350 Tested Strategies, pp. 268–269) encourages corporations to contribute to or implement antiviolence campaigns using their products, services and resources. The council notes: "Corporate America's resources and high profile provide a prominent platform from which to advocate nonviolence." On their own and in partnership with local, state and national organizations, corporations can promote antiviolence messages and products. For example, two of the nation's largest toy store chains, Kay-Bee and Toys R Us, decided in late 1994 to stop selling toy guns. Allstate Insurance Company served as a major corporate sponsor for a 5K "Race against Violence: America's #1 Challenge." The proceeds from registrations for the race, held in 10 major cities, went to local boys and girls clubs and the National Citizens' Crime Prevention Campaign (NCCPC). Another year the proceeds from the race went to Big Brothers and Big Sisters and the NCCPC. A potential obstacle to this strategy is that overreliance on corporate support can leave a program vulnerable to corporate managers' decisions.

A third strategy suggested by the National Crime Prevention Council is to *address violence as a public health problem* (350 *Tested Strategies*, pp. 248–249). A successful public health campaign against violence requires violence prevention curricula, community partnerships, public awareness involving the mass media and clinical education and training. Coalitions focus on identifying and addressing neighborhood-level risk factors for violence. Community groups, the clergy, business leaders, schools and parents can all contribute to a network of services. In addition, physicians, nurses and other health care providers are trained in violence prevention techniques, including counseling and teaching patients anger management.

The Boston City Department of Health and Hospitals initiated the Boston Violence Prevention Project in 1982 to prevent youth violence. It began in high-school classrooms with lessons presenting violence statistics and addressing ways to avert violence and expanded into a comprehensive effort to reach the entire community. This nationally known program also incorporates education and training for youth-serving agencies and has trained thousands of people and hundreds of agencies. The program also spurred development of the "Friends for Life, Friends Don't Let Friends Fight" media campaign and "Increase the Peace" weeks.

A potential obstacle to this strategy is that citizens may view violence as an intractable problem. This obstacle needs to be addressed for the strategy to be successful. Dr. Mark Rosen, director of the National Center for Injury Prevention and Control at the Centers for Disease Control and Prevention, suggests that it takes more than a village to raise a child—it takes an "intact" village (Oliver and McLaughlin, p. 51).

Potter and Krider (2000) describe a course developed by the Centers for Disease Control and Prevention: "Teaching about Violence Prevention: A Bridge between Public Health and Criminal Justice Education." The course overviews the public health approach to the prevention of violence and related injuries and compares it to the traditional approach taken by criminal justice. If courses such as this proliferate, they will better prepare future law enforcement officers and public health officials to effectively apply community policing strategies aimed at preventing violence.

Chapter 3 discussed the concept of community and its social capital. Some researchers suggest that communities with limited social capital will be a harder "sell" for community policing efforts. Others suggest that communities consisting largely of minority members will be a harder "sell." However, a study released in 1999 by the National Institute of Justice (NIJ) suggests differently ("We're Not Gonna Take it," 1999, p. 1). This study, "Attitudes toward Crime, Police, and the Law: Individual and Neighborhood Differences," examined racial and ethnic differences in attitudes toward social deviance in 343 urban communities in Chicago. It found significantly lower levels of tolerance for antisocial behavior among black and Latino residents than among white residents.

NIJ Director Jeremy Travis says: "The data support a framework for community policing that is both tough on crime, but even tougher on police departments with regard to building stronger relationships within the community." Travis (p. 10) suggests: "Law enforcement could use the constructive forces already present in the community to help develop strong local support for the legitimacy and need for police activities." In addition, Travis notes:

> In the context of community policing there is a second bottom line after reducing crime — community support. It is a great asset for law enforcement to recognize that there will be strong support in disadvantaged communities, not necessarily because residents like police tactics, but because there is strong support for social norms.

Many violence prevention programs are aimed at a specific type of violence, including gun violence, which often manifests itself in other specific types of violence that can be addressed through community policing strategies.

◈ GUN VIOLENCE

According to the FBI's Uniform Crime Reports (www.fbi.gov/ucr/), approximately 7 out of every 10 murders in the United States in 1999 involved a firearm, with handguns accounting for 51 percent of the murder total for which weapon data were submitted. Murphy (2000, p. 9) reports: "In 1998 a total of 30,708 persons died from firearm injuries in the United States. This number was 5.3 percent lower than the 32,436 deaths in 1997. . . . Despite the decrease, in 1998 children under 20 years still accounted for 12.3 percent of all firearm deaths."

The final issue of *Law Enforcement News* for 1999 has a two-page photo display titled "Shooting Gallery: A Graphic Roundup of the Mass Murders and Spree Shootings that Colored 1999 Blood Red." Targets included people in churches, schools, apartments, hotels, offices and community centers. Ages of the shooters ranged from 15 to 38. Weapons included a 9mm. pistol, 9 mm. semiautomatic rifle, semiauto pistol, pump-action shotgun, sawed-off shotgun, 45-cal. pistol and a 38-cal. revolver. Of the 14 shooters described, 6 died of self-inflicted gunshots at the scene. And these were just incidents that captured national headlines. In communities throughout the country, gun violence threatens the safety of citizens. Former Attorney General Janet Reno (1999, p. iii) asserts:

> Gun-related violence, in particular, represents a major threat to the health and safety of all Americans. Every day in America, 93 people die from gunshot wounds, and approximately 240 sustain gunshot injuries. In addition to the human suffering caused by these injuries and fatalities, gunshot wounds cost approximately $40 billion in medical care, public service, and work-loss costs each year.

Sheppard (1999, p. 1) adds: "The impact of gun violence is even more pronounced on juveniles and young adults. For persons between the ages of 15 and 24, the homicide rate of 15.2 per 100,000 U.S. residents is higher than the combined total homicide rate of 11 industrialized nations." Data from the FBI show that in 1999, the age group incurring the greatest number of firearms deaths was the 20- to 24-year-old group (1,812 deaths), followed by the 25–29 group (1,384) and the 17–19 group (1,068).

Gun violence may be considered as a three-phase continuum: (1) the illegal acquisition of firearms, (2) the illegal possession and carrying of firearms and (3) the illegal, improper or careless use of firearms.

Effective gun control strategies focus on one, two or all three of these points of intervention. *Promising Strategies to Reduce Gun Violence* (1999) describes 60 strategies and programs that can serve as models for communities to consider. These strategies and programs focus on three points of intervention: (1) interrupting sources of illegal guns, (2) determining illegal possession and carrying of guns and (3) responding to illegal gun use.

Strategies to Interrupt Sources of Illegal Guns

These strategies include law enforcement initiatives that disrupt the illegal flow of firearms by using intelligence gathered through crime gun tracing and regulatory inspections or undercover operations involving suspected illegal gun dealers. Comprehensive crime gun tracing facilitates both the reconstruction of the sales history of firearms associated with crime and the identification of patterns of illegal gun trafficking. Similarly, focusing criminal and regulatory enforcement on suspect dealers allows law enforcement to efficiently focus limited resources. Suspect dealers include those at the greatest risk of selling firearms to **straw purchasers,** that is purchasers fronting for people linked to illegal gun trafficking.

Initiated in 1994, the Boston Gun Project includes gun trafficking interdiction as one component in their broad strategy to stop gun violence in Boston. Partners in the project include the Bureau of Alcohol, Tobacco and Firearms (ATF), the Boston Police Department (BPD), the Suffolk County District Attorney's Office and the U.S. Attorney's Office. A seasoned violent crime coordinator was assigned by ATF to pursue federal firearm arrests. Six ATF agents were also assigned to collaborate with ballistics and crime laboratories at BPD to trace recovered handguns and match them to other crimes.

The ATF established the National Tracing Center (NTC) as the sole agency responsible for tracing firearms used in crimes and recovered at crime scenes. In addition, Project LEAD is the ATF's automated data system that tracks illegal firearms. It provides investigative leads by analyzing crime gun trace data and multiple sales information to identify indicators of illegal firearm trafficking.

Based on the ATF tracing data set, the working group established priorities for disrupting the illegal gun market. First the group prioritized investigating every trace that showed a gun with a time-to-crime of less than 30 months. Priority was also given to certain types of guns popular with youths, for example, semiautomatic handguns; those with restored obliterated serial numbers; those found in high-risk neighborhoods; and those associated with gang members or territories. Priority was also given to swift federal prosecution for gun trafficking.

The project was evaluated by the Kennedy School of Government at Harvard University and found to be successful. Based on this demonstrated success, ATF launched the Youth Crime Gun Interdiction Initiative in 17 demonstration cities in 1996.

The National Crime Prevention Council suggests that regulations and ordinances on gun licensing may interrupt sources of illegal guns.

As the NCPC notes, municipal ordinances may affect the first two phases of gun violence simultaneously. Interrupting the sale of illegal firearms also reduces the number of people possessing and carrying guns illegally.

Strategies to Deter Illegal Gun Possession and Carrying

Strategies to deter illegal gun possession and carrying include municipal gun ordinances, weapons hotlines, directed police patrols, focusing on hot spots where disproportionate amounts of crime and violence occur and focusing on individuals most likely to possess and carry firearms illegally, including gang members and probationers.

A 1992 report by the Violence Policy Center showed that the United States had more licensed gun dealerships than it had gas stations—280,000. In response the Bureau of Alcohol, Tobacco and Firearms (ATF) implemented stiffer licensing requirements and raised the licensing fee from $30 to $200. Applicants were now to be fingerprinted and to undergo more extensive background checks aimed at weeding out unscrupulous dealers. The new requirements resulted in a 19 percent drop in the number of licensed gun dealers in three years.

This same strategy can be implemented locally if stakeholders work together to get legislation passed. For example, the East Bay Gun Violence Prevention Project was initiated by the East Bay Public Safety Corridor Partnership, a regional coordinating body formed to reduce crime and violence in response to an alarming level of gun violence among cities in the East Bay Corridor. As the OJJDP (p. 91) notes: "In 1994, faced with the presence of more than 400 gun dealers in Alameda County and 700 in Contra Costa County, the Corridor cities of Oakland, Richmond, and San Pablo began working to pass municipal ordinances to better regulate gun sales and eliminate residential gun dealers, that is, dealers who sell guns out of their homes or cars." Ordinances aimed at reducing gun violence included banning the manufacture and sale of "junk guns," requiring trigger locks at the point of sale, restricting the number of licensed gun dealers and the areas in which they can operate and placing a gross receipts tax on merchandise sold by gun dealers.

The NCPC suggests that gun interdictions may be an effective deterrent to illegal gun possessing and carrying.

Gun interdictions, as described by the NCPC (pp. 279–280) are a law-enforcement-led strategy whereby local police direct intensive patrols to specific geographic areas with high rates of gun-related incidents of violence. Proactive patrols focus on traffic stops and other mechanisms to detect illegal or illegally concealed weapons and seize them. The council stresses that community support for the interdiction strategy is vital because searches and seizures can raise controversy. Community input should be sought in identifying the targeted areas, thereby reducing the chance of charges of racial disparity should the hot spot be inhabited by members of a minority group. A potential obstacle in gun interdiction is the violation of civil liberty laws. Officer training in constitutional searches and seizures is imperative.

Gun interdictions also affect the third phase of the gun violence continuum.

Strategies to Respond to Illegal Gun Use

Strategies to respond to illegal gun use include identification, prosecution and aggressive punishment of those who commit multiple violent crimes, are armed drug traffickers or have used a firearm in a crime; intensive education; and strict monitoring of offenders.

The OJJDP (p. 141) describes programs developed by the courts to deter gun use with swift, sure and severe penalties. It is anticipated that increasing the likelihood of imprisonment and lengthening its duration will deter those who engage in gun violence.

The NCPC suggests that local gun courts that deal exclusively with gun law violations reinforce community standards against violence and ensure swift punishment of violators.

The country's first adult gun court was established in the Providence (Rhode Island) Superior Court in 1994 by a statute creating a separate gun court calendar with concurrent jurisdiction with all other superior court calendars. Within four months of its implementation, the backlog of gun-related cases was reduced by two-thirds. All cases are tried within 60 days, and most carry mandatory prison terms, including ten years to life for a third offense. The mayor obtained support from the National Rifle Association (NRA) and from local advocates of gun control—a tricky combination. The NRA has spent $10,000 on billboards placed around the city announcing: "Gun Court Is Now in Session" (*350 Tested Strategies*, p. 262).

Comprehensive Gun Violence Reduction Strategies

Comprehensive gun reduction involves partnerships through which the community, law enforcement, prosecutors, courts and social services agencies:

• Identify where gun violence occurs and who is perpetrating it.

• Develop a comprehensive vision and plan, grounded in an understanding of the risk factors associated with gun violence.

• Create strategies to convince those who illegally possess, carry and use guns that they can survive in their neighborhoods without being armed (Sheppard, p. 2).

Partners in gun violence reduction identified by the OJJDP include the U.S. attorney, chief of police, sheriff, federal law enforcement agencies (FBI, ATF, DEA), district attorney, state attorney general, mayor/city manager, probation and parole officers, juvenile corrections officials, judges, public defenders, school superintendents, social services officials, leaders in the faith community and business leaders.

The OJJDP (p. 11) suggests a somewhat more detailed outline for developing a comprehensive strategy. The steps they suggest are to (1) establish appropriate stakeholder partnerships, (2) identify and measure the problem, (3) set measurable goals and objectives, (4) identify appropriate programs and strategies, (5) implement the comprehensive plan, (6) evaluate the plan and (7) revise the plan on the basis of the evaluation. The OJJDP (p. 17) identifies several characteristics of communities who have successfully implemented gun control strategies:

• The community recognizes its gun violence problems.

• Law enforcement and other key institutional administrators are enlisted as key partners.

- The collaborative has access to resources.
- The collaborative develops a comprehensive vision and plan.
- The collaborative mobilizes and sustains gun violence reduction activities.
- The collaborative develops a leadership structure.

Other entities becoming involved in the gun violence issue are those in the medical field and health services because, as the OJJDP (p. 169) notes: "Gun violence is not only a criminal justice problem but also a public health problem." This broadening of scope is described by Blendon et al. (1996, p. 22):

> Traditionally, gun control debates have involved professionals from the field of law, the police, and others concerned with the criminal justice system. However, in the past decade a number of physicians and public health professionals have entered the debate over gun control. For example, in a 1994 JAMA commentary, firearm violence was called "a public health emergency," and recommendations were made for stiffer gun control measures.

The Centers for Disease Control (CDC) now keep statistics on gun-related injuries and deaths.

The public health approach to reducing violence includes (1) emphasizing the prevention of violence, (2) making science integral to identifying effective policies and programs and (3) integrating the efforts of diverse organizations, communities and disciplines.

To be comprehensive, gun violence prevention strategies must also include educational efforts to change attitudes toward guns and violence and to promote gun safety, particularly among young people.

Education Initiatives and Alternative Prevention Strategies

A 1997 Police Foundation survey found 192 million privately owned firearms in the United States, enough to provide every adult American with one gun. On any given day in this country, 3 million adults carry a gun, either on their person (1 million) or in their vehicle (2 million). Furthermore, according to the Center to Prevent Handgun Violence (www.handguncontrol.org), 43 percent of American homes with children have guns. Many contend they need to keep a gun "for protection." That belief, however, too often proves tragic when the weapon meant to keep the family safe is accidentally, or intentionally, used to take a family member's life.

The *New York Times* ("Personal Health," 1997) reports firearms are one of the deadliest consumer products on the American market, second only to motor vehicles and accounting for 40,000 deaths each year. In addition to accidental deaths, child access to firearms results in some of the more than 8,000 nonfatal gun injuries reported every year in this country.

The prevalence of guns in our society demands an educational response. Education to prevent gun violence can take many forms, including promoting safe storage and other strategies to reduce access to firearms by children, youths and other unauthorized people; teaching safe behavior around firearms; and programs to prevent or reduce youth violence.

Reducing Access to Firearms. The Center to Prevent Handgun Violence reports more than 2.5 million kids currently live in homes where firearms are stored unlocked and loaded or with ammunition nearby. Common Sense about Kids and Guns (www.kidsandguns.org), a nonprofit group of gun owners and nonowners committed to protecting America's children from gun deaths and injuries, notes 48 percent of gun-owning households with children do not regularly make sure that guns are equipped with child safety or other trigger locks. Furthermore, although nearly 80 percent of Americans think it is important to reduce children's access to guns, approximately two-thirds of students in grades 6–12 say they have ready access to guns and could obtain a firearm within 24 hours. Common Sense also states:

- Though overall firearm deaths for children and teens were down 10% in 1998, non-homicide firearm deaths (i.e., accidents/suicides) declined only 4% from 1997 to 1998.
- For kids under 15, nonhomicide firearm deaths actually *increased* 4%.
- Among 5–9 year olds, accidental firearm deaths *increased* 21%.
- In 1998, one child or teen was killed in a firearm-related accident or suicide every 5.5 hours.

Such data highlight the critical importance of teaching gun owners safe storage practices and other strategies to prevent unauthorized firearm access in the effort to reduce gun violence, both intentional and accidental.

Child Access Prevention (CAP) laws, or "safe storage" laws, require adults to either store loaded guns in a place reasonably inaccessible to children or to use a safety device to lock the gun if they choose to leave the weapon accessible. If a child obtains an improperly stored, loaded gun, the adult owner is criminally liable. Currently, only 17 states have enacted CAP laws.

The primary goal of CAP laws is to prevent accidental injury by firearms. The Center for the Prevention of Handgun Violence states: "Research demonstrates that in the 12 states which had passed CAP laws by 1997, accidental deaths of children from firearms decreased 23% in the two years after the laws went into effect."

CAP laws also help reduce juvenile suicide by keeping guns out of the reach of children. For youths, particularly adolescents, rapid and intense fluctuations in mood are fairly common. However, a child going through a particularly difficult time emotionally may, with easy access to a firearm, turn a temporary situation into a permanent mistake. According to Common Sense, among 10–14 year olds, there was a 21 percent *increase* in the number of firearm suicides in 1998. From 1994 to 1999, 6,827 children age 19 and under committed suicide with a firearm.

Teaching Gun-Safe Behavior. When adults fail to keep firearms securely locked away or to teach others in the house, especially children, proper gun safety techniques, they place their entire family and anyone who may be in or near their house at tremendous risk. One police officer, despite educating her two young sons about gun safety and how to handle firearms, lost her older boy to an accidental shooting. He had gone next door to play with a neighbor, who had found a gun in one of the bedrooms and, while playing with it, accidentally shot his friend in the face. His mother, like many parents, had never considered asking the parents of her childrens' playmates if they kept guns in their house.

While the ultimate responsibility for teaching kids gun-safe behavior lies with parents, many adults themselves need coaching in this area. Common Sense reports 70 percent of Americans feel that more needs to be done to educate parents about how to keep their children safe from guns and on proper storage methods. Statistics indicate that the firearms used in most accidental deaths, injuries and suicides are obtained not on the street but from familiar surroundings—the homes of family or friends. According to Common Sense, in 72 percent of unintentional deaths and injuries, suicide and suicide attempts with a firearm of 0–19 year-olds, the firearm was stored in the residence of the victim, a relative or a friend.

In addition to teaching gun-safe behavior, adults must teach youths appropriate behavior in managing anger and conflict, that is, without violence and the use of a firearm.

Programs to Prevent or Reduce Youth Violence. Conflict mediation is becoming more common in public education curricula across the country, although such efforts have existed for more than a decade. In 1989 the Center to Prevent Handgun Violence started the Straight Talk about Risks (STAR) pilot curriculum. The program was developed through collaboration of teachers, counselors, parents, police and child development specialists. The curriculum, in both English and Spanish for grades kindergarten through twelve, teaches students to peacefully resolve conflict, manage anger and dangerous situations, and cope with negative peer pressure. A formal, in-depth evaluation of the program's long-term effect is under way.

Prevention of gun violence may greatly affect the other types of violence discussed next in this chapter: domestic violence and workplace violence.

DOMESTIC VIOLENCE

"If ever a problem demanded a community policing approach, it is the complex and serious challenge of domestic abuse. As our sophistication about the dynamics of human behavior grows, it becomes ever clearer that family violence is a key to the expanding cycle of violence that puts all of us at risk" ("Community Policing and Domestic Violence," www.policing.com). In the words of the late Robert Trojanowicz, a community policing pioneer: "We must remember that until we are all safe, no one is truly safe."

Building trust with the victims of domestic violence was discussed in Chapter 9. Those who have been victimized by spousal abuse, stalking, child abuse or elder abuse can sometimes be of great assistance in community efforts to prevent such victimization. This part of the chapter focuses on strategies to reduce or prevent domestic violence. As in other areas, collaboration is the key to success. McFadden (1998, p. 8) stresses:

> Collaboration among criminal justice agencies is an essential part of addressing crimes of domestic violence. Successful intervention efforts begin when the primary players—law enforcement leaders, prosecutors, judges, probation officers,

court clerks and administrators—identify each agency's legal and operational responsibilities, and their relationship to each other, then reach agreements that govern how the agencies will operate together to meet these responsibilities.

In addition to collaboration among criminal justice agencies, all other stakeholders in the community need to be involved in identifying problems and working toward solutions.

Partner Abuse and Stalking

According to statistics compiled by the National Institute of Justice, one out of four women in the United States say they've been victims of domestic violence or stalking by a husband, partner or date at some point in their lives ("Did You Know That . . . ?" 2000, p. 16). Also of importance is a 1998 Department of Justice report on the National Violence against Women Survey that found 36 percent of domestic violence victims were men (Baker and Piland-Baker, 2000, p. 129).

Important Research Finding. Research conducted by Moffitt et al. (2000) found that partner abuse and general crime shared the common characteristic of a trait called negative emotionality. "**Negative emotionality** is a generalized propensity for experiencing aversive affective states, including anger, anxiety, suspiciousness, and irritability. People with chronically high levels of negative emotionality are emotionally brittle; they live in a world darkened by a rapid, excessive response to minor stressors, a sense that others are malicious, and a propensity to react to even slight provocation with rage" (Moffitt et al., p. 222). Negative emotionality is a shared risk factor for both partner abuse and crime. The researchers found a significant difference between those who abuse their partners and those who commit violent crimes—a difference in constraint. Constraint is equated with self-control. According to the researchers it is about heeding societal prohibitions against expressing impulses.

Constraint trait is related to only a person's criminal behavior, not to abuse of a partner.

"In other words, the same individual who attacks someone *impulsively* in a bar, at a sports event, or during a robbery may use violence *strategically* to control his or her partner in the privacy of home" (p. 223) [emphasis added]. The fact that partner violence is "strategic, planful, and willful" (p. 24) has important implications for individuals working on strategies to prevent domestic violence.

Legislation to Prevent Stalking and Domestic Violence. Chapter 8 discussed legislation to prevent stalking and domestic violence, but one law, the Violence against Women Act (VAWA), merits review. As Robinson (1998, p. i) notes, this act "represents a giant step forward in our country's response to violence against women, including domestic violence and stalking. This legislation has transformed the criminal justice system's efforts to address this serious problem, making it a systemwide institutional priority."

In October 2000 Congress voted to reauthorize VAWA, restoring authorization for VAWA programs for five years, with more than $3 billion in funding ("Congress Votes . . . ," 2000, p. 1). The Violence against Women Act of 2000 also reauthorizes, at $65 million per year, grants to state and local governments to implement mandatory arrest policies, or policies that encourage arrests, of perpetrators of domestic violence. In addition, it renews programs for enforcement of domestic violence laws in rural areas and on college campuses, programs for battered women's shelters and the National Domestic Violence Hotline. Further, it expands the victims eligible for various VAWA services to include women abused by their boyfriends and battered immigrant women. It also provides assistance to programs targeting dating violence and gives more money to Native American domestic violence victims.

Problem Solving and Domestic Violence: A Case Study (Brookoff et al., 1999, pp. 113–150). In 1995 the Tennessee legislature enacted a new domestic violence law encouraging arrests and mandating the filing of reports and development of domestic violence databases. A group of Memphis police officers and doctors met to discuss their mutual frustrations about their lack of progress with victims and perpetrators of domestic assault: "Repeat 911 calls were mounting, emergency room visits for battering were skyrocketing and the batterers kept on battering" (p. 113).

In response to the new law, the police asked medical personnel to accompany them on domestic violence calls to see whether a "caregiver approach," using a nonthreatening, private and caring manner, could help identify ways to improve victims' treatment and identify prevention opportunities. After patrol officers had responded and stabilized the scene, a survey team entered the home and interviewed the officers about the circumstances of the call and their decision whether to arrest. If the incident fit the legal criteria for domestic violence, victims, assailants and adult family members in the house when the police arrived were also asked to participate in the survey. In addition, medical personnel were able to help assess batterers and their victims.

One predisposing factor to domestic assault the Memphis police and health care workers identified was intoxication with alcohol or drugs.

In nearly every case, the survey team delineated risk factors for future assault that could be reduced by treatment. They also identified young children apparently traumatized by witnessing the assault and in need of help (p. 133). Brookoff et al. (p. 134) report: "The deficiency in the care of families affected by domestic violence was not a lack of caring resources, but rather the lack of an organized approach to initiating and delivering care." Social and psychological barriers stand between domestic violence participants and the help they need. Interviewing participants brought many of these barriers to light.

Some victims cited economic dependence. Others had an exaggerated dependence on their batterers. Some reported their assailants had forced them into criminal activity or drug abuse as a leverage should they try to find a job or leave the relationship. The most common barrier found by the team was an assailant's drug abuse. Two-thirds had used cocaine and alcohol the day of the assault—a mixture likely to incite violent behavior. As part of their problem-solving efforts, the team collected specimens for toxicological testing from domestic assailants. Efforts were made to help them get treatment.

As is often the case when problem-solving is used to address a community problem, tracking of calls revealed that police had been called to the home on a previous domestic violence call in 85 percent of the cases. In 50 percent of domestic homicide cases, police had responded more than five times to domestic violence calls at the home in the previous two years. And, as is frequently the case in problem solving, additional problems are brought to light. In the case of the Memphis collaboration, officers and health care providers alike came to realize the devastating effect domestic abuse had on children who witnessed it. Such children far outnumber the direct victims of domestic assault. And if these children witness repeated episodes of family violence, they may come to believe it is normal and acceptable.

The team videotaped some of the cases, and a team doctor wrote an article based on one case called "The Faces of the Children." In it he wrote (Brookoff et al., p. 141):

> I remember one case where we were leaving a home and found a three-year-old boy who had just seen his mother badly beaten. The boy was sitting in the corner and holding the family's kitten by the throat and punching it.
>
> One of the police officers called out to the mother, "Your boy is about to kill your cat."
>
> "Oh don't worry about that," she called back. "He always does things like that when he sees the way his daddy beats me."

Because of what they had seen on domestic calls, a group of police officers and physicians approached the Tennessee legislature and asked for legislation making beating a woman in front of her children a felony, raising the behavior from simple assault to aggravated assault and the risk of prison. Other states, such as Florida, have passed such laws. However, when the idea was brought to a senate committee, it was rejected as being "too expensive." One senator asked if they were trying to put a third of the male population of Tennessee in state prison.

When forming partnerships to prevent domestic violence, the issue of cultural diversity between male-dominated police organizations and female-dominated grassroots advocate groups must be addressed.

Corporate Partnership to Combat Domestic Violence. The Lakewood (Colorado) Police Department and Motorola joined forces to apply sophisticated law enforcement and business principles to develop new strategies for managing domestic violence cases. The partnership uses **process mapping,** a program Motorola developed as part of its quality management process. An alternative to traditional top-down methods of internal analysis, process mapping takes a horizontal view of a system and involves personnel at all levels. It uses a series of flowcharts or maps to visually depict how information, materials and activities flow in an organization and how work is handed off from one unit or department to another. It also identifies how processes work currently and what changes should be made to attain a more ideal process flow.

The process-mapping program not only identifies areas for improvement but also facilitates communication between the city, police department and community. Lakewood Mayor Steve Burkholder said of the partnership: "At a time when the concept of community policing has the attention and financial support of both the public and private sectors, the partnership demonstrates what can be accomplished in the spirit of collaboration. Together, Motorola and the Lakewood Police Department are having a dramatic impact on our understanding and approach to the crime of domestic violence" (Partington, 2000, p. 173).

The department has also developed a domestic violence registry, which provides responding officers with a profile of the address on a laptop including whether weapons have been involved in prior incidents and whether back-up would be advisable (Youngs, 2000, p. 3).

A Domestic Violence Reduction Unit. In 1992 the Portland Police Bureau identified a need to provide additional services to families. In keeping with the community policing philosophy, the agency turned to the community to help define the new programs. They consulted over 100 community leaders and groups. To design the administrative framework for their Domestic Violence Reduction Unit (DVRU), the bureau looked for models other agencies had designed. It also held discussions with the district attorney and judges as well as leaders in the battered women's movement. It was agreed that officers would not only vigorously enforce the laws but that they would also become advocates for victims. It was also agreed that they would need increased cooperation between the police and other public safety agencies to enhance reporting and enforcement.

The unit's activities are not confined to working with individual cases. It is also a source of training for other officers and for community education outside the Portland Police Bureau. In addition, the officers have provided training to over 20 other police agencies in the country. According to Butzer et al. ("The Role of Police . . . ," p. 9):

> The Domestic Violence Reduction Unit in the Portland Police Bureau demonstrates how acting on the values of community policing can result in the integration of fresh perspectives and new approaches into police work. Perhaps more importantly, it illustrates how implementing community policing strategies can result in a closer alignment between the police agency and the community. The community policing perspective required a conscious effort to consult with different groups within the community, and to incorporate those groups into the process of creating the DVRU, its priorities and strategies. In a democratic society such consultation with the community helps tie the police agency into the society, and helps the agency to adapt to societal changes. Community policing can make a difference, but it takes more than rhetoric: it takes real action as illustrated by the creation and implementation of the Domestic Violence Reduction Unit.

National League of Cities Community Policing Award 1998. The National League of Cities selected the City of Cheektowaga, New York, for their community policing and violence against women project. "Transitions" is a collaborative effort among the police department, a local women's shelter and the National Conference, an organization founded to combat prejudice and discrimination. The project's purpose is to develop the organizational culture, values and attitudes to ensure an effective and appropriate response to the community's domestic violence needs. The project uses nontraditional training methods, including theatrical vignettes and open-forum discussions on sensitive issues as innovative approaches to change negative attitudes ("NCL's Community Policing Project," p. 6).

S*T*O*P Violence against Women. The Department of Justice's S*T*O*P Violence against Women grant program provides money directly to states and Native American tribes as a step in helping to restructure the criminal justice system's response to crimes of violence against women. The acronym stands for services, training, officers and prosecution, the vital components in a comprehensive program for victims of domestic violence and its perpetrators. This program requires collaboration between victim advocates, prosecutors and police. Funding can provide improvements such as:

• Crisis centers and battered women's shelters serving tens of thousands of victims a year.

• Hundreds of new prosecutors for specialized domestic violence or sexual assault units.

• Hundreds of volunteer coordinators to help run domestic violence hotlines ("The Violence against Women Act: . . . ," p. 5).

An evaluation by the Urban Institute ("Study Finds STOP . . . ," 1999, pp. 6–7) reported the program has had a "major impact" on the experience of female victims of violence in the criminal justice system. According to the study, after receiving STOP funds, the ability of agencies to meet most of the needs of domestic violence victims rose from 2 to 61 percent, and their ability to meet most of the needs of sexual assault victims rose from 4 to 46 percent and from 3 to 26 percent for stalking victims.

The study found that victims felt safer, better supported by the community and were treated more uniformly and with more sensitivity. The study also found that grant recipient jobs were made easier because of greater collaboration among different divisions in the criminal justice system.

Court Programs to Assist Victims of Domestic Violence (*350 Tested Strategies,* p. 263). Court-based domestic violence programs help victims understand court proceedings, exercise their right to prosecute their abuser and obtain referrals to services outside the court system, enhance victims' ability to make informed decisions, reducing the likelihood of additional victimization. Training for court personnel focuses on understanding victims' financial, emotional and medical needs and informing victims of their legal rights, such as obtaining a protective order or pursuing their abuser. Court programs also seek to increase cooperation among courts, police, prosecutors and community advocates for victims.

In 1977 the city of Quincy, Massachusetts, designed Emerge, a pretrial probation and drug treatment program for offenders, and developed procedures for informing victims about the services available to help them cope with the physical and emotional trauma of abuse. Since its inception, many more women have pursued abuse claims through the courts. Potential obstacles to this strategy include the court resisting providing services to victims because of potential costs or the belief that court personnel are not trained to provide such services.

Treatment for Male Batterers (*350 Tested Strategies,* p. 264). Mandated treatment programs for male batters reduce the incidence of additional physical abuse of spouses. Long-term counseling programs for batterers now mandated in some localities train batterers (90 percent of whom are men) to take full responsibility for their behavior, adopt new ways of communicating with their partner and children, understand the effects of abuse on their partner and the children, and identify and change attitudes that lead to abusive behavior.

Such programs rely on partnerships with police and court officials to locate men needing treatment referrals. A potential obstacle to this strategy is that many spouses, police officers and court personnel do not believe that counseling for batterers reduces the likelihood that battering will continue. Further, most batterers strongly resist admitting to their abusive behavior, reducing the chances of progress through treatment.

However, local criminal justice officials who believe it is effective rely upon the Emerge project previously described. Evaluations of the program indicate that 70 percent of male clients will repeat battering behavior, as opposed to nearly 100 percent who receive no treatment.

The Corporate Sector Response to Domestic Violence. Research conducted by Isaac (1998, p.76) found that most executives and managers in the corporate sector have given little or no thought to the impact of partner abuse on the health and safety of their employees. Potential barriers to understanding and helping employees who are victims of partner abuse include lack of awareness, denial, embarrassment, privacy and confidentiality concerns, victim blaming, expectations of self-identification by abused women, fear of advocating for change and concern that outreach to abused women may alienate male employees, damage the company image or be too expensive.

A survey of employee assistance professionals (EAPs) found that a large majority of EAP providers had been faced with cases of partner abuse, including restraining order violations and stalking in the workplace. General policies on "workplace violence" exist, but few specifically address domestic violence. Among larger corporations, EAP staff use a range of practices to assist employees affected by abuse, including use of leaves of absence, medical leaves and short-term disability. The affect of domestic violence on the workplace is discussed shortly.

An International Partnership to Reduce Domestic Violence. Cronin (2000) describes Project Harmony, a nonprofit organization in Waitsfield, Vermont, which has partnered with the Russian region of Karelia in the northwest region of Russia to implement the Domestic Violence Community Partnership Program (DVCPP). The concept for this program was rooted in community programs implemented in central Massachusetts in 1994. The Greater Gardner Health Study identified domestic violence as the number-one health problem for women in Gardner. As a result, the Gardner police chief formed an alliance with several community resources, including Battered Women's Resources, Inc., Heywood Hospital, the Gardner Court Probation Office, the Gardner Public Schools and other resources and organizations in the region. This alliance implemented a multidisciplinary approach to combat the problem of domestic violence.

The results of the two-year program showed that a full community response to domestic violence really makes a difference. The success of this program led to Project Harmony's proposal to create community-coalition-based training in Russia and Ukraine.

During the fact-finding mission to set up the program, the same theme was encountered: "Domestic violence against women and children was a very serious problem that is considered very private and not openly discussed. Severe economic conditions, alcoholism and homelessness had exacerbated the problem" (p. 44).

Seminars and training were conducted. Trainers went into communities to make presentations to staff working at each location handling domestic violence. Personal witnessing and role-playing by presenters proved to be most effective: "The role-play and witness presentations were very powerful, effective tools. They showed in a nonjudgmental manner how America has come to grips with the problem of domestic violence" (p. 46). The minister of internal affairs, who is in charge of the local police, has committed to implementing domestic violence training in the police academy as well as a Teenage Domestic Violence Gender Respect Program in the schools. In addition, American restraining order documents are being translated into Russian, with the intent of bringing about change in Russian laws to protect victims.

One participant commented: "I have never been able to speak to police until this program. . . . I did not believe that anything could really be done about this problem (of domestic violence) when we first began this training" (p. 46). Cronin (p. 46) contends: "This program has produced concrete results and proved to be a rewarding experience for everyone involved, and its work continues."

The problem of partner abuse often also involves child abuse, whether it be the trauma a child experiences witnessing such abuse or actually being physically abused as well.

Child Abuse

The cycle of violence was discussed in Chapter 9. According to the Council against Domestic Abuse (Ziegler, 2000, p. 65): "It is estimated that one-half of the men who beat their partners also abuse their children." Published studies report a 30 to 60 percent overlap between violence against children and violence against women in the same families. Although they use different methods and different sample sizes and examine different populations, they consistently report a significant level of co-occurrence ("In Harm's Way . . . ," p. 1). Figure 13.1 illustrates this overlap.

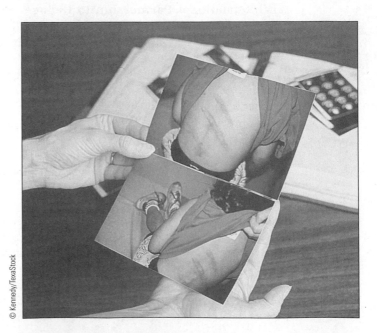

Photographs of a child abuse victim beaten with a broomstick by his father.

© Kennedy/TexaStock

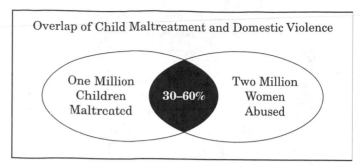

Figure 13.1 Overlap of Child Maltreatment and Domestic Violence

SOURCE: "In Harm's Way: Domestic Violence and Child Maltreatment." http://www.calib. com/nccanch/pubs/otherpubs/harmsway.htm

Children in violent homes face three risks: (1) the risk of observing traumatic events, (2) the risk of being abused themselves and (3) the risk of being neglected.

In addition, Garbarino (1999) notes, youths likely to engage in violent behavior may have been exposed to violence at home or in the community. Wolfe et al. (1998, p. 25) compared 102 children in violent families drawn from shelters and 96 children from nonviolent families drawn from the community. They found that children from violent families had a rate of behavior and social competency problems 2.5 times higher than those from nonviolent families.

Important Research Finding. A study by the University of North Carolina at Chapel Hill, "Paths across Generations: Academic Competence and Aggressive Behavior in Young Mothers and Their Children," found no conclusive evidence that an intergenerational "cycle of violence" exists ("Intergenerational Cycle of Violence May Not Exist," 1999, pp. 12–13). This 17-year study monitored violent females from childhood to motherhood and then monitored offspring of the mothers through second grade. The researchers concluded that violence and aggression are not predestined from one generation to another as commonly believed. Rather, there are "windows of change," providing hope for mothers determined not to let their children become violent or aggressive.

Training Professionals to Recognize Child Victims. The National Crime Prevention Council (*350 Tested Strategies,* pp. 239–240) suggests a strategy to train professionals to recognize child victims. Hospital personnel, lawyers, justice system officials and psychiatrists should receive training to enable them to recognize child victims of violence and abuse, understand their special needs and act as their advocates. Law and medical schools can provide trainers. Professional associations can also cooperate in creating training programs and fostering cooperation among their members who staff key agencies.

A potential obstacle is that professionals such as lawyers and physicians may be reluctant to admit their inability to recognize and assist child victims. The American Academy of Pediatrics and the Center to Prevent Handgun Violence sponsor educational and training materials for pediatric health care professionals through the Stop Firearm Injury program. The program provides doctors and others with brochures, posters, reading lists and other information to help them recognize child victims of gun violence and refer them and their families to other service providers as needed. Thousands of physicians have received and used the materials.

The Child Development-Community Policing (CD-CP) Model. This pilot initiative emphasizes the importance of developing collaborative relationships between law enforcement and mental health communities to ensure that youths exposed to violence have access to a wide array of services offered in their communities.

The CD-CP Model emphasizes cross-training of criminal justice and mental health professionals to develop collaborative problem-solving techniques that go beyond the reach of either "system" acting alone.

Ennis (1999, p. 55) notes that the distinction between law enforcement and child protection agencies are beginning to blur with police spending more time in noninvestigative activities and child protection workers spending more time as investigators. Their spheres of influence have come to overlap in many areas, and both have shifted emphasis from reactive to proactive responses whenever possible.

The CD-CP program began in New Haven, Connecticut, and has been facilitated by resources of and researchers at the Yale University Child Study Center. Specifically, the CD-CP Model's training and collaboration principles include ("Young People Exposed to Violence," 1999, p. 16):

• Child development fellowships for police supervisors, which provide supervisory officers with the necessary expertise to lead a team of community-based officers in activities and services related to children and families, and create opportunities to interact with the child mental health professionals with whom they will collaborate in the future.

• Police fellowships for clinicians, which provide clinicians the opportunity to observe and learn directly from law enforcement officers about the responsibilities of community-based policing, while also building collaborative relationships with law enforcement officials.

• Seminars on child development, human functioning and policing strategies are offered for clinicians, community police officers and related justice practitioners that incorporate case scenarios to apply principles of child development to the daily work of policing.

• Consultation services that give law enforcement the ability to make referrals and obtain immediate clinical guidance if necessary.

• Program conferencing, where CD-CP police officers and clinicians meet weekly to discuss difficult and perplexing cases.

Because the initiative is fairly new, it has not yet been empirically evaluated, but steps have been taken to ensure that the data collection necessary to support a rigorous evaluation of the effort is in place.

Forming a Multidisciplinary Team to Investigate Child Abuse. A booklet by this name has been developed by the U.S. Department of Justice. The need for such a team is graphically illustrated in the introduction to the booklet (Ells, 1998, p. i):

Two months before her seventh birthday in 1995, Elisa Izquierdo was killed. Over a period of months, she had been physically and emotionally abused, repeatedly violated with a toothbrush and a hairbrush, and finally beaten to death by her mother. Elisa's mother told police that before she smashed Elisa's head against a cement wall, she made Elisa eat her own feces and used her head to mop the floor. The police told reporters that there was no part of the 6-year-old's body that had not been cut or bruised. Thirty marks initially thought to be cigarette burns turned out to be the imprints of a stone in someone's ring.

An investigation after her death revealed that Elisa had been the subject of at least eight reports of abuse and that several government agencies had investigated the reports. Nonetheless, Elisa Izquierdo was left with her abuser and eventual killer.

Unfortunately, this failure to respond to reports of child abuse in a timely and appropriate manner has happened many times—and is continuing to happen— in probably every state in the country, and almost always for the same reason . . . there has been an appalling lack of communication and coordination among the agencies investigating reports of possible abuse.

A key to avoiding such tragedies is the formation of a multidisciplinary team (MDT) representing the government agencies and private practitioners responsible for investigating crimes against children and protecting and treating children in the community. Ells (pp. 2–3) suggests that keys to forming a successful MDT are committed members who have the support of their agencies, an initial meeting during which each member's role and experience in investigating child abuse and neglect are respectfully heard, development of a mission statement and creation of a team protocol specifying the responsibilities of the members and procedures to follow.

Ells (p. 3) also outlines keys to the successful operation of an MDT: confidentiality policies, conflict resolution practices to ensure core issues are aired and resolved satisfactorily and periodic self-analysis and outside evaluation as to how effectively they are performing.

Promising Service Developments for Children. Schechter and Edleson (2000) describe several "extremely promising projects" that have emerged in the past 10 years. Based on common characteristics found in these projects, the Center on Crime, Communities and Culture for the Open Society Institute makes four recommendations for communities and governmental bodies to help children experiencing domestic violence (pp. 12–14):

(1) Every community should conduct an audit of its current response systems and develop an infrastructure of protections and a range of services for children and families experiencing violence. (2) Local, state and federal legislative and administrative bodies; private organizations; and foundations should create funding and policy mandates to support an infrastructure of community services for children exposed to family and community violence. (3) Professional organizations and training institutions should immediately establish guidelines for educational training, licensing and certification standards, continuing education and practice for those working with families exposed to violence. (4) Government agencies,

private foundations, and service providers should collaborate on research efforts that enhance our understanding of children experiencing domestic violence and shed light on the impact of interventions with these families.

WORKPLACE VIOLENCE

Jones (1997, p. 18) suggests: "All social problems will find their way into the workplace. . . . Is it any surprise that violence has found its way into the workplace?" He states that murder is now the number-two cause of death in the workplace and the number-one cause of death to women in the workplace. Slahor (1998, p. 34) also notes: "The violence that prevails in American culture has indeed walked through our workplace thresholds."

Annually more than 2 million people become victims of violent crime at work according to the U.S. Bureau of Justice Statistics.

Every work day, nearly 8,000 Americans are violently attacked or threatened with a violent attack at work or while working outside the office ("Violent Crime Strikes . . . ," 1998, p. 1). "Workplace violence is the most important security threat to America's largest corporations according to the sixth-annual survey of Fortune 1000 security executives conducted by Pinkerton's Inc." ("Employee-Related Security . . . ," 1999, p. 6). However Podolak (2000, p. 152) cautions: "Workplace violence joins phenomena such as road rage and hate crimes that are exploited to attract readers, expand political empires, or advance careers." He notes that the term *workplace violence* "is nothing more

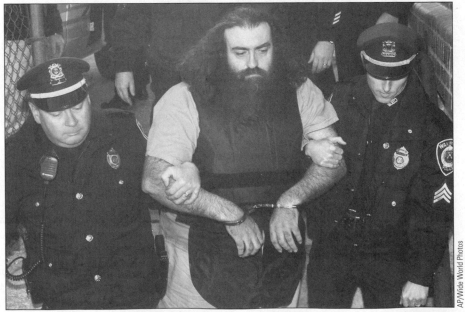

Michael McDermott, 42, of Haverhill, Mass., an employee at Edgewater Technology, was arrested as a suspect in an office shooting at Edgewater Technology that left seven co-workers dead in December 2000.

than a catch-all phrase referring to criminal misbehavior committed against people who have jobs. Those dealing with this problem should formulate a clear definition of what constitutes workplace violence."

Most study results and experts identify the driving forces behind the increase in workplace violence as being (1) an economic system that fails to support full employment (downsizing), (2) a legal system that fails to protect citizens and releases criminals from prison early due to overcrowding, (3) a cultural system that glamorizes violence in the media and (4) the universal availability of weapons.

Common motivations behind violent behavior in the workplace include robbery, loss of a job, anger from feelings of mistreatment, substance abuse and mental problems.

According to Harwood (1998, p. 32), the typical perpetrator is a 25- to 50-year-old white male who tends to be a loner, has a history of violence and conflict with others and may exhibit signs of depression. This profile fits Michael McDermott, a shooting suspect who, in December 2000, supposedly upset by an IRS request to garnish his wages, killed seven co-workers in Wakefield, Massachusetts. McDermott is white, age 42 and had an angry outburst in the accounting department the week before over the prospect of losing some of his wages. McDermott gave up to police without a struggle.

Partington (p. 6) describes warning signs including unusual fascination with weapons, a display of unwarranted anger, irrational beliefs and ideas, feelings of victimization, talk of hurting self and others, substance abuse, inability to take criticism, constant complaining, attendance and productivity problems and past threats or acts of intimidation.

Albert Einstein said that "thought is father of the action," referring to the sequence of thoughts known as personal fantasies. In fantasies people console and entertain themselves, plan and even rehearse possible actions. According to Depue and Depue (1999, p. 66) those concerned with security can watch for external signs of abnormal fantasies, which may be "precursors to destructive behavior." Doing so may stop these "crimes in process before they become reality." They (p. 68) note: "Fantasies may become obsessions, building until the person is driven to fulfill them regardless of the consequences."

Workplace Violence and Domestic Violence

Albrecht (1996, p. 47) cautions: "Domestic violence is no longer confined to the home. More than ever, household troubles are creeping into the workplace." Sometimes it's harassing phone calls to an employee or an angry spouse bursting into the workplace threatening violence or actually assaulting the partner. It may include homicide. According to May (2000, p. 42), it may also include physical assaults that affect an individual's ability to perform job functions. He notes: "Domestic violence costs hundreds of millions of dollars in health-care costs, mostly paid by employer benefits."

Corporations are increasingly raising the profile of battered women and encouraging individuals, businesses and communities to take action to prevent domestic violence ("Corporate Outreach Programs . . . .," 1998, p. 3). The article gives as an example Bell Atlantic Mobile, which works with domestic violence and law enforcement agencies distributing preprogrammed 911 wireless phones to victims so they can quickly get help if threatened. As part of its "Wireless at Work" program, the company sets up "HopeLine" voice-mail boxes at domestic violence shelters so victims can talk to prospective employers and landlords privately without fearing interference from an abusive partner. Other companies with outreach program for domestic violence victims include Liz Claiborne, Marshalls, Polaroid, the Body Shop and the Limited.

Workplace Violence and Hospital Emergency Rooms

The National Crime Prevention Council (350 *Tested Strategies*, p. 186) suggests that one strategy communities might consider to reduce the violence often experienced in hospital emergency rooms by violent patients and visitors is to train the staff in violence prevention. A survey of 103 hospitals in Los Angeles and other urban areas of California found that nearly 60 percent of hospital staff had been injured by visitors or patients. The NCPC suggests that hospital administrators develop partnerships with physicians, nurses and staff to understand past events and devise training strategies and security policies to prevent further incidents. Administrators should also seek assistance from the police or other crime prevention and security specialists who can assess security issues.

A potential obstacle to this strategy is that staff training and physical changes in hospital facilities can be expensive. Partnerships with law enforcement might reduce the training expenses.

Preventing Workplace Violence

Most security experts dealing with preventing workplace violence recommend forming a team. Braverman (1999, p. 41) suggests the workplace violence team be composed of stakeholders representing a range of functions, including health and safety, legal, human resources, labor relations/employee relations, employee assistance, union and operations. Ideally the team would also include professionals from outside the workplace such as law enforcement representatives, health care professionals and the like. The team should consider not only physical measures to increase the security of employees but also developing clear, fair procedures for terminations and layoffs. Other policies aimed at preventing workplace violence might include zero tolerance for harassment, pre-employment screening, substance abuse screening, no weapons on the property and the right to search personal property (Partington, p. 6).

SUMMARY

Causes of violence may include ready availability of guns, drugs and alcohol; a desensitization to violence; disintegration of the family and community; social and economic deprivation; and increased numbers of children growing up in violent families. A problem-solving approach to preventing violence must attempt to identify the underlying causes of specific violent situations that threaten a community before solutions can be devised.

Developing effective prevention tactics will require long-term collaborations between criminal justice and juvenile justice practitioners, other social service agencies and evaluation researchers. Strategies for general violence prevention include public dialogue and community mediation, corporate support for antiviolence projects and addressing violence as a public health problem.

Gun violence may be considered as a three-phase continuum: (1) the illegal acquisition of firearms, (2) the illegal possession and carrying of firearms and (3) the illegal, improper or careless use of firearms. The National Crime Prevention Council suggests that regulations and ordinances on gun licensing may interrupt sources of illegal guns. The NCPC suggests that gun interdictions may be an effective deterrent to illegal gun possessing and carrying. It also suggests that local gun courts that deal exclusively with gun law violations reinforce community standards against violence and ensure swift punishment of violators.

Partners in gun violence reduction identified by the OJJDP include the U.S. attorney, chief of police, sheriff, federal law enforcement agencies (FBI, ATF, DEA), district attorney, state attorney general, mayor/city manager, probation and parole officers, juvenile corrections officials, judges, public defenders, school superintendents, social services officials, leaders in the faith community and business leaders.

Domestic violence is another type of problem in most communities. It is encouraging that constraint trait is related to only a person's criminal behavior, not to abuse of a partner. Therefore most domestic abuse is seen as acting consciously rather than impulsively, making treatment efforts more likely to be successful. One predisposing factor to domestic assault the Memphis police and health care workers identified was intoxication with alcohol or drugs. When forming partnerships to prevent domestic violence, the issue of cultural diversity between male-dominated police organizations and female-dominated grassroots advocate groups must be addressed.

Children in violent homes face three risks: (1) the risk of observing traumatic events, (2) the risk of being abused themselves and (3) the risk of being neglected. The CD-CP Model emphasizes cross-training of criminal justice and mental health professionals to develop collaborative problem-solving techniques that go beyond the reach of either "system" acting alone.

Yet another type of violence challenging communities is workplace violence. Annually more than 2 million people become victims of violent crime at work according to the U.S. Bureau of Justice Statistics. Common motivations behind violent behavior in the workplace include robbery, loss of a job, anger from feelings of mistreatment, substance abuse and mental problems.

DISCUSSION QUESTIONS

1. Explain why some experts recommend a problem-solving approach to violence prevention.
2. What is the public health model of violence prevention?
3. Why do gun interdiction strategies frequently lead to charges that the police have targeted the minority community, and what can be done to allay such concerns?
4. What risks exist for children who live in homes where domestic violence occurs?
5. Corporations are suggested in this chapter as partners in violence prevention. Why would corporations have any interest in prevention or their ability to affect it?

6. Since violent crime is declining, why is there any need to be concerned about or to plan for prevention?

7. Name some likely types of people who might pose a risk of violence in a workplace.

8. What is the likelihood of repeated spousal battering behavior by men who have not gone through a treatment program?

9. How can the cultural diversity difference between male-dominated police organizations and female-dominated advocate groups be addressed?

10. Explain the difference researchers found between those who are violent to their partners and those who commit violent crimes against others.

INFOTRAC COLLEGE EDITION ASSIGNMENTS

- Use InfoTrac to help answer the discussion questions as appropriate.

- Research gun violence statistics in the United States, and compare what you find to that of other industrialized nations. How can the differences be explained? Be prepared to share your findings with the class.

- Research either family violence or workplace violence. Write a brief (3–4 page) report on the topic of your choice, and be prepared to share the key points with the class.

COMMUNITY PROJECT

Working in a group, design a crime/violence prevention plan for your educational institution or a place of business. Include likely partners/stakeholders, an overview of any previous crimes or violent incidents and identification of challenges and strategies to address them. Also include a critical incident response plan. Where could you find information about designing such a plan? (Prior crime history, maps of facility, current prevention plan, hours of operation and accessibility, the policy on employee dismissals, how student/employee complaints are handled and the like.)

REFERENCES

Albrecht, Steven. "The Public Challenge of Private Problems." *Security Management,* Vol. 46, No. 5, May 1996, pp. 47–50.

Baker, Thomas E. and Piland-Baker, Jane. "Domestic Violence: The 'Enigma Call.'" *Law and Order,* Vol. 48, No. 10, October 2000, pp. 129–138.

Blendon, Robert J.; Young, John T.; Hemenway, David. "The American Public and the Gun Control Debate." *Journal of the American Medical Association,* Vol. 275, No. 22, June 12, 1996, pp. 1719–1722.

Braverman, Mark. "Seven Steps to Preventing Workplace Violence." *Access Control & Security Systems,* June 1999, pp. 41–42, 47.

Brookoff, Daniel; Crews, Walter; Cook, Charles S.; and Thompson, Terry. "Responding to Domestic Violence: A Collaboration between the Police and the Medical Community." In *Problem-Oriented Policing,* Vol. 2. Edited by

Corina Sole Brito and Tracy Allan. Washington, DC. Police Executive Research Forum, 1999, pp. 113–148.

Butzer, David; Bronfman, Lois Martin; and Stipak, Brian. "The Role of Police in Combating Domestic Violence in the United States: A Case Study of Domestic Violence Reduction Unit, Portland Police Bureau." www.ncjrs.org/policing/role161.htm

Center to Prevent Handgun Violence. www.handguncontrol.org

Common Sense about Kids and Guns. Washington, DC. www.kidsandguns.org

"Community Policing and Domestic Violence." www.policing.com/articl/cpanddv.html

"Congress Votes to Reauthorize Violence against Women Act." *Criminal Justice Newsletter,* Vol. 31, No. 2, October 24, 2000, pp. 1–2.

"Corporate Outreach Programs Target Domestic Abuse, Workplace Violence." *Workplace Violence Report,* 1998, p. 3.

Cronin, Edward F. "Project Harmony Domestic Violence Community Partnership Program." *The Police Chief,* Vol. LXVII, No. 1, January 2000, pp. 41–46.

Depue, Roger L. and Depue, Joanne M. "To Dream, Perchance to Kill." *Security Management,* Vol. 43, No. 6, June 1999, pp. 66–72.

"Did You Know That . . . ?" *Security Management,* Vol. 44, No. 10, October 2000.

Ells, Mark. *Forming a Multidisciplinary Team to Investigate Child Abuse.* Washington, DC: U.S. Department of Justice, November 1998. (NCJ-170020)

"Employee-Related Security Concerns Top List of Business Threats." *Access Controls & Security Systems,* May 1999, p. 6.

Ennis, Charles. "Child Protection Teamwork." *Law and Order,* Vol. 47, No. 4, April 1999, pp. 55–58.

Eskridge, Chris W. *Criminal Justice: Concepts and Issues—An Anthology,* 3rd ed. Los Angeles: Roxbury Publishing Company, 1999.

Federal Bureau of Investigation. *Uniform Crime Reports, 1999.* www.fbi.gov/ucr.htm

Garbarino, James. *Lost Boys: Why Our Sons Turn Violent and How We Can Save Them.* New York: The Free Press, 1999.

Harwood, Emily. "Going to Work on Workplace Violence." *Access Control & Security Systems,* June 1998, pp. 1, 31–33.

"In Harm's Way: Domestic Violence and Child Maltreatment." http://www.calib.com/nccanch/pubs/otherpubs/harmsway.htm

"Intergenerational Cycle of Violence May Not Exist." *NCJA Justice Bulletin,* Vol. 19, No. 1, January 1999, pp. 12–13.

Isaac, Nancy E. "Corporate Sector Response to Domestic Violence." In *Legal Interventions in Family Violence: Research Findings and Policy Implications.* Washington, DC: National Institute of Justice, July 1998. (NCJ-171666)

Jones, Al. "Violence in the Workplace." *Business and Facility Concepts,* May 1997, pp. 18–23.

May, Johnny. "Workplace Violence: A Tragedy in the Making." *Access Control & Security Systems,* October 2000, pp. 42–43.

McFadden, Marilyn. "The Little Group that Couldn't." *Community Links,* Spring 1998, p. 8.

Moffitt, Terrie E.; Krueger, Robert F.; Caspi, Avshalom; and Fagan, Jeff. "Partner Abuse and General Crime: How Are They the Same? How Are They Different?" *Criminology,* Vol. 38, No. 1, 2000, pp. 199–232.

Murphy, Sherry L. *Deaths: Final Data for 1998.* U.S. Department of Health and Human Services, Centers for Disease Control and Prevention, National Vital Statistics Report, Vol. 48, No. 11, July 24, 2000. www.cdc.gov/nchs

"NLC's Community Policing Project." http://www.nlc.org/CPAward.htm

Oliver, Jerry and McLaughlin, Colleen R. "Focusing on the Other Side of the Crime Scene Tape: What Happens When 'Normal' Is the Problem?" *The Police Chief,* Vol. LXV, No. 11, November 1998, pp. 50–53.

Partington, George. "Partnership Combats Domestic Violence." *Law and Order,* Vol. 48, No. 7, July 2000, p. 173.

"Personal Health." *New York Times,* May 21, 1997.

Podolak, Andrew G. "Is Workplace Violence in Need of Refocusing?" *Security Management,* Vol. 44, No. 6, June 2000, pp. 151–152.

Potter, Roberto Hugh and Krider, Jeanne E. "Teaching about Violence Prevention: A Bridge between Public Health and Criminal Justice Educators." *Journal of Criminal Justice Education,* Vol. 11, No. 2, Fall 2000, pp. 339–351.

Promising Strategies to Reduce Gun Violence. Washington, DC: OJJDP Report, 1999.

Reno, Janet. "Foreword." *Promising Strategies to Reduce Gun Violence.* Washington, DC: OJJDP Report, 1999, p. iii.

Robinson, Laurie. "Preface." *Stalking and Domestic Violence: The Third Annual Report to Congress under the Violence against Women Act.* Washington, DC: Office of Justice Programs, July 1998, p. i.

Roth, Jeffrey A. *Understanding and Preventing Violence.* Washington, DC: National Institute of Justice Research in Brief, February 1994.

Schechter, Susan and Edleson, Jeffrey L. *Domestic Violence and Children: Creating a Public Response.* Open Society Institute's Center on Crime, Communities and Culture, 2000.

Sheppard, David. *Strategies to Reduce Gun Violence.* Washington, DC: OJJDP Fact Sheet, February 1999, #93.

Slahor, Stephenie. "No Workplace Is Immune." *Access Control & Security Systems,* June 1998, pp. 34–35.

"Study Finds STOP Program Has Had a Significant Impact on Services to Victims of Violence." *NCJA Justice Bulletin,* Vol. 19, No. 10, October 1999, pp. 6–7.

350 Tested Strategies to Prevent Crime: A Resource for Municipal Agencies and Community Groups. Washington, DC: National Crime Prevention Council, 1995.

"The Violence against Women Act: Breaking the Cycle of Violence." http://www.ojp.usdoj.gov/vawol/laws/cycle.htm

"Violent Crime Rate Falls." *Law Enforcement Technology,* Vol. 27, No. 10, October 2000, p. 12.

"Violent Crime Strikes 2 Million People in the American Workplace Each Year." *Workplace Violence Report,* Business Publishers, Inc., 1998.

"We're Not Gonna Take It." *Law Enforcement News,* Vol. XXV, No. 517, September 15, 1999.

Wolfe, David A.; Jaffe, Peter; Wilson, Susan Kaye; and Zak, Lydia. "Impact of Domestic Violence on Children's Behavior." In *Legal Interventions in Family Violence: Research Findings and Policy Implications,* Washington, DC: National Institute of Justice, July 1998. (NCJ-17166)

"Young People Exposed to Violence More Likely to Experience Stress Disorder." *NCJA Justice Bulletin,* Vol. 19, No. 7, July 1999, pp. 14–17.

Youngs, Al. "Colorado P.D. Gets Tough on Domestic Violence." *Subject to Debate,* Vol. 14, No. 11, November 2000, pp. 1, 3–5.

Ziegler, Stephen J. "Battered Women: Why Do They Stay?" *Police,* Vol. 24, No. 10, October 2000, pp. 64–66.

RESOURCES

Center to Prevent Handgun Violence. www.cphv.org

Domestic Violence Directory of Professional Services from the Center on Crime, Communities and Culture. http://www.soros.org/crime/new-at-cccc.html

Handgun Control. www.handguncontrol.org

National Domestic Violence Hotline; (800) 799-SAFE (7233).

National Resource Center on Domestic Violence; (800) 537-2238.

Physicians for Social Responsibility. www.psr.org/violence.htm

Resource Center on Domestic Violence: Child Protection/Custody; (800) 527-3223.

CHAPTER 14

Focus on Youths

If society wishes greater protection from juvenile crime, more attention has to be paid to the costly process of promoting moral order and of preventing crime.

    Lamar Empey, criminologist (1978)

Children are likely to live up to what you believe of them.

    Lady Bird Johnson

Do you know

What important group is often overlooked when implementing the community policing philosophy?

How negative attitudes toward the police can be changed?

What the youth development strategy involves?

What the developmental asset approach to children involves?

What youth-focused community policing involves?

What many consider to be the cornerstone of the community?

How schools should be viewed?

Why it is important to build students' sense of community in school?

At minimum, what links the school should have with the community?

What the school safety pyramid rests on and what its components are?

What most violent students do before they commit acts of violence?

What common characteristics of workplace and school violence are?

What is bullying more accurately termed?

What the "tell or tattle" dilemma is?

What two highly successful programs to build safe schools are?

What the seven prongs in effective school security are?

Whether zero tolerance is an effective deterrent to nonconforming behavior?

What the top security strategy at all grade levels was in 2000?

What strategies have been used to address the gang problem? Which has been found to be most effective?

What OJJDP initiatives are available to help communities address the gang problem?

What the G.R.E.A.T. program is?

What strategies are currently being used to address the gang problem?

What additional strategies the National Crime Prevention Council recommends?

Can you define these terms:

bullying	psychopath	sociopath
developmental assets	pulling levers	zero tolerance
peer child abuse		

INTRODUCTION

The vast majority of today's youths are "good kids" who may occasionally get into trouble. If community policing is to succeed, it is imperative that this important segment of the community not be forgotten. If youths can come to feel a part of their community and their school early on, many future problems might be eliminated. Unfortunately, the violence so prevalent within our society has found its way into our schools, as the bloody school shootings in the past few years have dramatically shown. In addition, many youths turn to gangs for the support and feelings of self-worth they cannot find at home or school.

This chapter begins with a discussion of the importance of involving youths in community policing and some strategies for building positive relationships between law enforcement and youths as well as some strategies aimed at engaging them in community policing efforts. Then the importance of involving parents in community policing efforts to prevent youth delinquency and violence is discussed. Next the role of the school in promoting healthy growth and development is described, followed by the problem of violence in our schools. This is followed by a discussion of the importance of early intervention. The chapter concludes with the challenges presented by gangs in the school and in the community.

◈ YOUTHS AND COMMUNITY POLICING

Williams (1999, p. 150) notes that much research has been done on citizen perceptions and satisfaction with community policing but that an important segment of citizens has been overlooked and left out of this process—children and teenagers.

Children and teenagers are an important segment of the community often overlooked when implementing the community policing philosophy.

Williams used focus group interviewing to collect information about the perceptions and attitudes of East Athens, Georgia, citizens ages 6 to 18. The questions concerned issues of (1) community problems, (2) trust or satisfaction with police services, (3) knowledge of the ideals of community policing and (4) empowerment.

From these focus groups, four themes emerged (p. 160). The first theme was *infrequent, impersonal and negative interactions with police.* Negative experiences that participants, their family members or friends had with the police were a key factor in all focus group discussions. One youth said: "One day we were walking to the store at about nine o'clock that night and the police stopped us. And when they got out of the car, we took off running. They stopped us for no reason. I wasn't fixing to stay around and get locked up, so I took off running." This general perception reinforces the contention that personal contact with police is a more significant factor than demographic variables.

A second theme was *lack of knowledge of or familiarity with police or community policing*. Except for one male child and one female teenager, all participants were reluctant to establish any rapport with community policing officers. When asked specifically about the community policing concept, few participants understood it. Nor did they understand the idea of partnerships.

A third theme was *a perception of lack of respect for the East Athens community and its inhabitants by police officers*. This perception surfaced in four complaints: slow response time, lack of timely intervention, alleged officer harassment and the perception that officers did not care about the community.

The fourth theme was *community passivity as opposed to community apathy*. Participants generally expressed little interest in helping officers solve community problems, often because of their fear of violent retribution: "I may know what happened, but I ain't giving away no names. . . .'cause I ain't got nothing to do with it . . . 'cause the person could come back and get you . . . they did my sister like that." Williams (p. 168) concludes:

> Passivity can undermine any community policing initiative. This study sheds light on the underpinnings of community passivity among East Athens teenagers and children. Their interactions with police tended to be infrequent, impersonal and negative. Consequently, they were not personally familiar with police officers and vice versa. This combination seems to explain their lack of respect toward all police. When combined with the real and ever present fear of nonrandom violence or retribution from within the neighborhood, it might be rational for children and teenagers to be passive toward officers assigned to community policing.

Although the study focused on just one small area of one community, it brings out the importance of considering youths as an important part of community policing efforts. It also draws attention to the sometimes negative perceptions of police held by youths, often because of having only negative contacts with them.

Another study by Jones-Brown (2000, p. 209) of 125 high-school African American males regarding attitudes toward police found: "A majority of the males report experiencing the police as a repressive rather than facilitative agent in their own lives and in the lives of their friends and relatives."

To counteract negative perceptions of police held by children and youths, many departments have programs aimed at fostering positive relations with them.

◉ BUILDING PERSONAL RELATIONSHIPS

Departments across the country have developed programs to allow youngsters and police officers to get to know and understand each other better. The Denver Police Department, for example, has a program called "Brown Baggin' with the Blues" in which children have lunch with police officers.

The Kops 'n' Kids program, endorsed by the International Association of Chiefs of Police (IACP), brings together children and officers to have fun rather than to deliver antidrug or anticrime speeches. Officers come with their motorcycles and their K-9s for demonstrations; they share lunch; they form running clubs; they do whatever helps present police as positive role models and build trust with the children.

The Greeley (Colorado) Police Department has a similar program, "Adopt-an-Officer," in which police officers volunteer to be "adopted" by fourth- and fifth-grade students. They share meals, write letters, exchange cards and visit the police station. The LaGrange Park (Illinois) Police Department's Adopt-a-Cop Program calls on each participating elementary grade-school level to "adopt" an officer who serves as their liaison for the entire school year (McCollum, 2000).

The Las Vegas Metropolitan Police Department's "Shop with a Cop" is designed to make the Christmas season happy for abused, neglected and disadvantaged children. Sporting badges rather than beards and driving squad cars rather than sleighs, these police officers are still like Santa to dozens of underprivileged Las Vegas youngsters. Over 100 officers each take an underprivileged child on a shopping spree at the local K-Mart. Each child has $75 to spend, the money contributed by local businesses.

◉ CONNECTING YOUTHS AND THE COMMUNITY

The first issue of *Community Links*, a publication of the Community Policing Consortium, stressed the importance of connecting youths and communities. As Diehm (1997) notes: "While the efforts of each jurisdiction are unique, there is an increasing focus on building neighborhoods through a process of reconnecting youths, families and communities." Central to that process is the "youth development approach."

The Youth Development Approach

The youth development approach was designed by the U.S. Department of Health and Human Services over two decades ago.

The youth development strategy suggests that communities first explore what they want for young people, rather than what behaviors they would like to prevent among youths. More important, it involves young people in rebuilding communities.

The focus is on the positive rather than the negative. It is focused on the great majority of "good kids" rather than the minority who are delinquents, violent or gang members. "By identifying what they want for young people, they can then develop a plan to provide the range of services and opportunities necessary to enable young people to move through adolescence to healthy, productive adulthood."

By involving young people in developing services and opportunities, communities can draw on youths' unique talents and perspectives, building on their strengths and giving them a sense of community and of hope for the future.

The Developmental Asset Approach

Gersh (2000, p. SS15) describes "The Asset Approach: Giving Kids What They Need to Succeed" developed by the Search Institute, Minneapolis. The Search Institute promotes establishing 40 ideals, experiences and qualities—**developmental assets**—that "help young people make wise decisions, choose positive paths, and grow up competent, caring and responsible." These 40 developmental assets are grouped into eight categories.

The developmental asset approach promotes (1) support, (2) empowerment, (3) boundaries and expectations, (4) constructive use of time, (5) commitment to learning, (6) positive values, (7) social competence and (8) positive identity to help youngsters succeed in school and in life.

Gersh suggests that parents, guardians, grandparents, teachers, coaches, friends, youth workers, employers, volunteers and others can all help children in the community to build these assets. He notes: "A survey of 100,000 youths in grades 6–12 found that the more assets a young person possesses, the less likely they are to engage in problem alcohol use, illicit drug use, sexual activity and violence. In addition, increasing numbers of assets correlate with increased success in school, value of diversity, maintenance of good health and delay of gratification."

Youth-Focused Community Policing

Youth-Focused Community Policing (YFCP) is a collaborative effort of the Office of Juvenile Justice and Delinquency Prevention (OJJDP), the Office of Community Oriented Policing Services and the Community Relations Service (Connelly, 1999, pp. 1, 8).

Youth-Focused Community Policing is a U.S. Department of Justice initiative instrumental in establishing law enforcement/community partnerships to focus on prevention, intervention and enforcement.

YFCP emphasizes locally driven responses to locally based problems and has been implemented in eight communities: Boston, Chicago, Houston, Los Angeles, Kansas City (KS), Mount Bayou (MS), Oakland and Rio Grande (TX).

A Partnership to Prevent Juvenile Delinquency

An alliance in Livermore, California, has Horizons Family Counseling operating out of the police department. The program began in 1973 when the city received a grant for a juvenile delinquency program. When it was learned that the activities funded by the program were not having any effect on youthful offenders, the state Office of Criminal Justice Planning asked the Livermore Police Department to oversee the program. The focus of the program became high-risk youths who were running away, truant or beyond parental control, with Horizons brought in to provide counseling.

As Soto (2000, p. 8) notes: "Horizons understood from the start that the whole family needed to be involved in the counseling to have any effect on a youth's internal environment." Police became concerned that counselors were giving up too early on families who resisted coming in for counseling. Their frustration led to creating a diversion program where first-time youthful offenders arrested for minor offenses may have the arrest erased if the family attends three family therapy sessions. This incentive created the chance to consider the arrest within the context of family dynamics.

This diversion program made police and Horizons more interdependent than ever and set the stage for the partnership's next evolution. In 1995 the police department and

Horizons shared quarters in a new facility. Horizons has a separate public entrance, but inner doors permit regular interface with law enforcement. According to the Livermore police chief: "Horizons is a tremendous asset. Other departments have to travel miles to get services. Horizons fits perfectly within the community policing mold of reaching out, helping parents, working with kids and supporting alternatives in enforcement" (Soto, p. 8).

Involving Youths in Violence Prevention

The National Crime Prevention Council (*350 Tested Strategies*, 1995, pp. 255–256) recommends that youths be involved in planning and carrying out strategies to prevent violence in their communities. Youths can contribute a valuable perspective on community problems as they build skills that will help them make positive contributions to their neighborhoods.

The council (p. 256) suggests that youths may play many roles: "They join task forces of planning coalitions, volunteer in community-based prevention projects, mediate conflicts in schools and the community, perform in prevention-focused programs for younger children, counsel peers, and organize neighborhood antidrug and anticrime events. Many successful programs involve at-risk and other teens." Partnerships should include youths at all levels of activity, with their roles considered as important as that of adults.

A potential obstacle is the attitude of some adult policymakers and leaders that youths are the source of the community's violence problems rather than part of the solution. Forums where youths can present their views can help overcome this bias.

This strategy was applied in Teens on Target, a peer education program established by Youth Alive in partnership with Oakland, California's Unified School District and Pediatric Spinal Injury Service. Established after two high-school students were shot by peers, the program trains high-risk students to advocate violence prevention by educating and mentoring their peers and younger children on gun violence, drugs and family conflict. The youths arrange trips to local hospital emergency rooms to give their peers a first-hand look at violence's impact on victims.

◈ THE IMPORTANCE OF PARENTAL INVOLVEMENT

Findings released by the Office of Juvenile Justice and Delinquency Prevention (OJJDP) suggest that violent acts of delinquency are less likely to be committed by youths who have adult supervision after school than by those who are unsupervised one or more days a week. Even more important than actual adult supervision is whether parents even know where their children are after school. In addition, as noted by Eskridge (1999, p. 68): "There is widespread agreement that strong parental attachments to consistently disciplined children in watchful and supportive communities are the best vaccine against street crime and violence."

The family is viewed by many as the cornerstone of the community.

A report by the Bipartisan Working Group on Youth Violence ("Youth Violence Task Force . . . ," 2000, p. 4) says: "Parents are in the best position to teach children that hostility is not a means of problem-solving, and that actions have consequences."

Adams (2000, p. SS21) also stresses: "Community involvement starts with parents. . . . Students whose families are involved in their growth both inside and outside of school are more likely to experience school success and less likely to become involved in antisocial activities."

The Thousand Oaks (California) Police Department offers a program called the "Parent Project." This program, described by Tumbleson (1999), is specifically designed to help parents change destructive adolescent behavior. Parents learn and practice specific prevention and intervention strategies for behaviors such as truancy, alcohol and other drug use, gangs, practice of the occult, running away, violence and suicide. Parents are referred to the program by police officers, juvenile detectives, diversion programs, the juvenile probation department, school officials and the court system. The program lasts 10 to 16 weeks and includes two phases. Phase I, "Laying the Foundation for Change," consists of six activity-based instructional units where parents learn identification, prevention and intervention techniques. Phase II, "Changing Behavior and Rebuilding Family Relationships," consists of 10 topic-focused parent support group sessions designed to give parents practical and emotional support as they begin the process of change in their homes. Since its inception, the department has trained more than 80 parents.

The Reno (Nevada) Police Department has also stressed the importance of families in their "Kid's Korner" program, which focuses on forging new ties with families living on the fringe of the city in the city's temporary housing—weekly hotels. Described as a "knock and talk" program by the Bureau of Justice Statistics, the bureau says: " 'Kid's Korner,' with its emphasis on building positive relationships between law enforcement officers and the residents they serve, is an example of community policing at its finest" ("Cops Fight Crime . . . ," 2000, p. 10).

The National Crime Prevention Council (*350 Tested Strategies,* p. 261) suggests as a strategy family therapy to address conflict and delinquency. It notes that counseling from a trained therapist helps families manage conflict and address antisocial or delinquent behavior: "Treatment emphasizes positive family interactions and clear standards for behavior." Another strategy suggested by the council (pp. 272–273) is to hold parents accountable for their children's behavior. Numerous localities have enacted ordinances to implement this strategy:

> In thirty-three states, local judges can require parents to pay restitution for crimes committed by their children. City councils have designed late-night curfew, truancy, graffiti, gang enforcement and gun ordinances that impose penalties and possible arrest for parents whose children repeatedly violate the ordinances' behavior standards. In effect, the ordinances constitute a system of graduated sanctions against the parent and the youth.

◈ SCHOOLS AND THE COMMUNITY

"America was founded on the promise of opportunity. Every child in our nation deserves the chance to live the American dream, and education is the pathway to that dream and to a fulfilling and productive life. We must not allow fears engendered by bullying, gangs, weapons and substance abuse to disrupt children's journey toward a better tomorrow" (Bilchik, 1998, p. 1).

An officer explains bike safety to elementary school children. Bicycling clinics promote safety and build trust between children and police.

A school should be viewed as a community, not as an institution.

The Child Development Project (CDP) is a comprehensive, whole-school improvement program developed by the Developmental Studies Center in Oakland, California. This project fosters children's cognitive, ethical and social growth by providing all students with engaging, challenging learning opportunities and creating a strong sense of community among students, teachers and parents. The CDP (Schaps and Lewis, 1999, p. 216) defines "sense of community" as "the student's experience of being a valued, influential member of a group committed to everyone's growth and welfare."

Research suggests that students' academic motivation, commitment to democratic values and resistance to problem behaviors all depend on their experience of the school as a community.

CDP research suggests that increases in children's sense of community are linked to their later development of intrinsic academic motivation, concern for others, democratic values, skill and inclination to resolve conflicts equitably, intrinsic prosocial motivation, enjoyment of helping others learn, inclusive attitudes toward outgroups and positive interpersonal behavior in class. Schaps and Lewis (p. 215) contend: "In a caring school community, students can experience a developmentally appropriate version of the just and caring society we hope they will create a generation hence."

In addition to building a sense of community within the school, schools should also partner with the community of which they are a part. A 1998 report from the U.S. Department of Education and Justice, *Early Warning, Timely Response: A Guide to Safe Schools,* stresses that schools should develop links to the community.

At minimum schools need to link with parents and with local law enforcement departments to teach students about the dangers of crime.

According to the report, students whose families are involved in their growth both inside and outside of school are more likely to experience school success and less likely to become involved in antisocial activities. Adams (p. SS21) suggests that school staff, students and families should be involved in the development, discussion and implementation of fair rules. In addition, law enforcement can be brought into the school to get to know students and through select police/school programs can help students become mentors, peacekeepers and problem solvers.

School Teams

Some schools have developed school teams to watch for signs of trouble and to step in to prevent problems. Butte County's Safe Schools teams are one example. These teams are a partnership of the Chico (California) Police Department, which assigns a full-time youth services officer to each school in the program; the Butte County Probation Department, which redefined its caseloads to correspond to specific schools; and the Chico Unified School District, which provides office space and equipment and integrates its referral services with those of the police and probation department. As noted by Harberts (2000, p. 6): "Having probation and police officers on campus has resulted in swift and appropriate intervention with juveniles who attend the schools or frequent the campus. Because of the improved coordination among the agencies involved, matters that once took 30 days moving through the system now take 30 minutes."

The officers monitor the behavior of all students but focus on those on probation. They conduct safety checks, perform searches and enforce curfew and attendance policies. The team also makes a point of supporting youths working hard to "stay on track" by attending sporting events, graduations and other activities in which youths are taking part.

Another way the team is proactive is in forging relationships with gang members, their peers and others "in the know." Students alert team members when they think something is "going down." Harberts concludes: "Many teenagers, it should be remembered, are impulsive by nature. In order to impact behaviors, swift intervention must closely follow a negative choice. But we must also respect the fact that the behavior we are seeing might be more a family problem and less a criminal problem. We can keep it that way if we intervene successfully, and soon enough."

The School Safety Pyramid

The School Safety Pyramid, illustrated in Figure 14.1, was developed by the Center for the Prevention of School Violence. It shows the importance of the community concept in school safety. Paynter (1999, p. 34) suggests: "The community sits at the pyramid's base because the school environment often mirrors what's happening in the community. Community problems can disrupt the school environment and contribute to crime and violence in that environment."

The school safety pyramid rests on the community and has as its components school resource officers, law-related education, conflict management and peer mediation, S.A.V.E. (Students against Violence in Education), teen/student court, and physical design and technology.

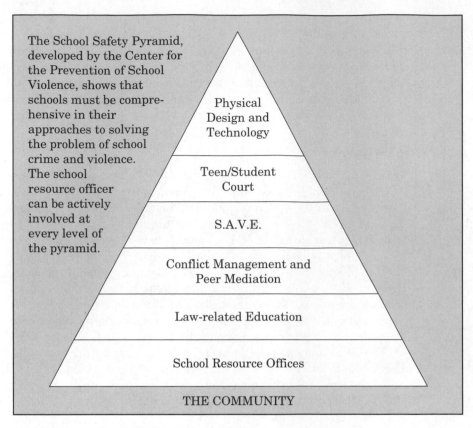

The School Safety Pyramid, developed by the Center for the Prevention of School Violence, shows that schools must be comprehensive in their approaches to solving the problem of school crime and violence. The school resource officer can be actively involved at every level of the pyramid.

Physical Design and Technology

Teen/Student Court

S.A.V.E.

Conflict Management and Peer Mediation

Law-related Education

School Resource Offices

THE COMMUNITY

Figure 14.1   The School Safety Pyramid

SOURCE: Ronnie L. Paynter. "Policing the Schools." *Law Enforcement Technology*, Vol. 26, No. 10, October 1999, p. 35. Reprinted by permission of the Center for the Prevention of School Violence.

School resource officers (SROs) are the next level, functioning as an integral connection between the school and the community. Lavarello (2000, p. 6) notes: "The fact remains that school-based policing programs are now one of the, if not THE, fastest growing areas of law enforcement." Says Paynter (pp. 34–35): "The SRO is probably the best example of a community-oriented policing effort that exists today." In a teaching capacity, an SRO can educate students about their legal rights and responsibilities. They can also assist in efforts to teach conflict management and peer mediation skills. Having a S.A.V.E. (Students against Violence in Education) group can help build respect between students and SROs.

In addition to strategies aimed at keeping schools safe, schools also need to be aware of the potential for school violence and take steps to deal with it should it occur.

◎ SCHOOL VIOLENCE

Pearl, Mississippi; West Paducah, Kentucky; Jonesboro, Arkansas; Fayetteville, Tennessee; Springfield, Oregon; Richmond, Virginia; Littleton, Colorado; Conyers, Georgia; Santee, California—these are schools that come to mind when school violence is mentioned. And they were shocking instances of violence in our country's schools. But they are just the tip of the iceberg. Hall (2000, p. 6) reports that an estimated 100,000 to 250,000 guns are carried to schools every day in this country, and since 1992 there have been 250 deaths at public schools.

Arnette and Walsleben (1998, p. 7) report on a survey conducted by the Centers for Disease Control and Prevention that found nearly 12 percent of the polled students in grades 9 through 12 carried a weapon on school property during the 30 days preceding the survey, and 7.3 percent were threatened or injured with a weapon on school property during the 12 months preceding the survey.

Common Traits among School "Shooters"

Holmes and Holmes (1999) identified the following as part of a school shooter profile: white male, disenfranchised, outgroup membership; interested in the Internet and computer games and abandonment of former friends. Marlin and Vogt (1999, p. 169) describe the following common traits among youths involved in school shootings: "An orientation towards violent shows, videos and music; a feeling of inferiority or being picked on, with a grudge against some student or teacher; an easy access to weapons; suicidal tendencies and above-average intelligence; the presence of ample warning signs, either in writing or talking about killing others."

Other "early warning signs" of impending violent behavior include being a victim of violence, feelings of being picked on and persecuted, low school interest and poor academic performance, uncontrolled anger, intimidating and bullying behaviors, a history of discipline problems, drug and alcohol use and affiliation with gangs (*Early Warning, Timely Response*, pp. 8–10). This same publication (p. 11) describes signs of *imminent* violent behavior: serious physical fighting with peers or family members, severe destruction of property, severe rage for seemingly minor reasons, detailed threats of lethal violence, possession and/or use of firearms and other weapons, other self-injurious behaviors or threats of suicide.

Most violent students "leak" their feelings and intentions in the weeks and months before committing the violent act. Such messages should never be ignored.

A study by the FBI's National Center for the Analysis of Violent Crime (NCAVA), *The School Shooter: A Threat Assessment Perspective*, reports: "Children who commit violent acts in school typically do not have a moment at which they 'snap' from nonviolence into violence, but rather evolve gradually toward violence, with signposts along the way." The report stresses: "The task for law enforcement agencies and school officials is to learn how to interpret the 'leakage,' and accurately assess whether a particular student poses a real threat to others or is merely 'having a bad day or blowing off steam.' "

The aftermath of the shooting spree at Columbine High School in Littleton, Colorado in April of 1999 when two young male students armed with four guns and multiple bombs lured students and teachers out into a schoolyard by pulling the fire alarm. The killing spree left 12 students and 1 teacher dead and 23 students wounded. The killers committed suicide at the scene.

Kanable (1999, p. 68) explains violent children by dividing them into two categories: sociopaths and psychopaths. A **sociopath** is usually a bully—outgoing and manipulative, instigating fights. The sociopath is a type of violent leader. A **psychopath,** in contrast, tends to be a loner like the "Trench Coat Mafia" kids. Psychopaths tend to be socially inept.

School violence shares many characteristics with workplace violence and is, in fact, a form of workplace violence for school staff. Nicoletti et al. (1999, p. 78) report that: "Violence in the workplace has existed much longer than its more insidious twin."

Common characteristics in workplace and school violence include the profiles of the perpetrators, the targets, the means and the pathways to violence.

Nicoletti et al. note: "The perpetrators are frequently described as 'loners' with poor social skills, who are often obsessed with violence and weapons. . . . The targets of choice . . . include authority figures, women who have rejected them and peers who are in conflict with them. . . . The shared motives of the killers is revenge. Perpetrators often bring an arsenal of weapons and will kill anyone who stands in their way."

Bullying

Bullying—name calling, fistfights, purposeful ostracism, extortion, character assassination, repeated physical attacks and sexual harassment—has been a common behavior in schools since they first opened their doors. According to Hamit (2000, p. 89): "Bullying has always been one of the less pleasant features of growing up, usually excused as part of social maturation." Its occurrence is often taken lightly, referred to as "Kids will be kids." However, Arnette and Walsleben (p. 3) suggest: "Today, bullying is rightfully being recognized for what it is: an abusive behavior that often leads to greater and prolonged violent behavior."

Bullying is more accurately termed **peer child abuse.**

Marlin and Vogt (p. 169) caution: "Some kids who have been bullied romanticize a gun as being an equalizer. 'I am not insane. I am angry,' said a note from Luke Woodham. 'I killed because people like me are mistreated every day.' " Arnette and Walsleben (p. 3) suggest the following strategies to mediate bullying: rules against bullying that are publicized, posted school wide, and accompanied by consistent sanctions; student and adult mentors who assist victims and bullies to build self-esteem and to foster mutual understanding of and appreciation for differences in others; a buddy system that pairs students with a particular friend or older buddy with whom they share class schedule information and plans for the school day and on whom they can depend for help; peer mediation programs and teen courts that train students to mediate problems among themselves; and close monitoring of cafeterias, playgrounds and "hot spots" where bullying is likely to occur away from direct adult supervision.

The "tell or tattle" dilemma occurs when a student hesitates to tell anyone that he or she is being bullied because it is seen as tattling—something they have been taught not to do.

A Johnson Institute program gives teachers step-by-step guidelines on how to teach students the difference between telling and tattling. Children and teenagers alike need to learn that it is not "tattling" to go to a teacher or counselor if they hear someone talking about "killing" as opposed to making a vague threat about getting back at someone. They should also immediately tell a teacher or counselor if a peer points out that he has access to a gun and a plan to get it.

Dr. Dan Olweus, University of Bergen in Norway, has developed a program to prevent bullying that is used throughout the world. A basic tenet is intervention by teachers when they see bullying behavior. Olweus recommends seven strategies: (1) adult supervision at recess, (2) strict enforcement of clear rules for student behavior, (3) consistent, nonphysical punishment of students who misbehave, (4) assistance to bullying victims that helps them to assert themselves, (5) parental encouragement that students develop and maintain friendships, (6) clear and positive communication between parents and school officials and (7) clear and swift reaction to persistent physical or verbal bullying. Schools that implemented the program found a 40 to 50 percent reduction rate in bullying behavior within the first two years ("Protecting Kids . . . ," 2000, p. 7).

Creating Safe Schools

Argon and Anderson (2000, p. C6) note: "Media attention to random schoolyard violence has toned down considerably lately, suggesting that we as a society are becoming either numb to the problem or tired of hearing about it. But no one suggests that the problem is going away." "School violence is not just a school problem, it's a community problem. The entire community needs to get involved in these issues to make schools safer for everyone" (Paynter, 2000, p. 72). This sentiment is echoed by Cody (1998, p. 31): "Coordinated school efforts can help. But the solution does not just rest in the schools. Together we must develop solutions that are community-wide and coordinated, that include schools, families, courts, law enforcement community agencies, representatives of the faith community, business, and the broader community."

Grassie (2000, p. 89) suggests: "The best defense against all forms of school threats and risks is a fully integrated school security program that carefully and effectively blends a wide variety of proven risk reduction strategies into a flexible, responsive school security program."

Two highly successful programs to build safe schools are **Student Crime Stoppers** *and* **PeaceBuilders®**.

Student Crime Stoppers, like the adult program, offers youths tools to stand up against crime and violence with reprisal or peer pressure through an anonymous TIPS line to get the information to those who can stop the crime or violence. Those with information about solving crimes on school property or at school events can qualify for cash awards up to $100.00.

PeaceBuilders® is a long-term, community-based, violence reduction or prevention program designed to help create an environment that reduces violence and establishes more peaceful ways of behaving, living and working in families, schools, organizations and communities. Schools may send up to four people to attend a two-and-one-half-day training session to become site trainers. These site trainers then provide four-hour Peace-Builders® Staff Implementation Workshops at their schools or in their own district. Up to 60 people may attend this workshop.

Safe schools depend not only on programs such as those just described but also on a comprehensive approach to safety.

A seven-pronged approach is needed for effective school security: (1) school/law enforcement/community partnerships, (2) education about violence, (3) problem-solving training, (4) mediation and anger-management training, (5) clear policies on accepted behavior with consequences for nonconformity, (6) security procedures and technology and (7) crisis planning.

School/Law Enforcement/Community Partnerships. The International Association of Chiefs of Police has published a *Guide for Preventing and Responding to School Violence*, which includes as one topic developing partnerships with schools. One of the oldest and most commonly used partnerships is assigning police officers to schools—the school resource officer (SRO). In addition, the U.S. Department of Education has published *Early Warning, Timely Response: A Guide to Safe Schools*, which has been distributed to every school in the country.

Bilchik (2000, p. 57) stresses: "To foster safety in schools, the entire community must get involved. Some of the most promising prevention and intervention strategies involve administrators, teachers, families, students, law enforcement officers, juvenile justice practitioners and community members, working together to establish a crisis response plan as well as a long-term strategy to form positive relationships with all children and families."

Schuiteman (2000, p. 77) reports on the initial evaluation of 57 Department of Criminal Justice Services (DCJS) grants supporting 63 SROs in 44 localities. The initial evaluation findings are that: "SROs report success in reducing violence, preventing conflict and improving school security."

Mattson (2000) describes the Phoenix "Wake Up" program, which resulted from the Phoenix Police Department's meeting with the community, school and business leaders to approach the problem of youth crime and violence. Together they identified the two biggest problems facing the area's youths as limited money and lack of things to do. Another problem was a lack of positive role models. Their solution: "Wake Up!" formally known as the Community Efforts to Abate Street Violence. The program placed Wake Up! clubs in the schools and had police officers teach students to make better choices in their lives. The clubs also taught positive life lessons such as communication, teamwork, self-confidence, leadership and respect. All seventh- and eighth-grade students were invited to join the clubs, which meet for an hour each week at school. About once a month, each club had a community service project, making them feel a part of the community and encouraging them to make it better.

After one year data were obtained from over 242 individuals from a pool of over 1,500 participants. School referrals were given to 144 nonclub students and 25 club students (whose referrals were for less serious offenses such as gum chewing). The incidence of truancy for club members was half that of the general population. Six students were arrested during the year, none of whom were club members. In the Wake Up! school, the crimes-against-person rate was 40 percent lower than that at the control school. The crimes-against-property rate in the club school was 70 percent lower than that at the control school. Testing of academic achievement also showed positive results. In the basic battery sections, the control school showed no change; the club school showed a 0.4 grade-level increase. On reading, the control school showed a 0.3 grade-level increase; the club school a 1.0 grade-level increase.

The Miami "Do the Right Thing" program, described by Makholm (2000), recognizes and rewards young people for good deeds. This program reinforces socially desirable behavior among youths, demonstrates that good kids are newsworthy and enhances the relationship between underprivileged youths, police officers, police departments and area businesses.

Education about Violence. Among the strategies suggested by the National Crime Prevention Council (*350 Tested Strategies*) are to teach teens to prevent dating violence (p. 265), teach juveniles the consequences of violence (pp. 247–248), teach children about gun safety (p. 270) and implement a comprehensive curriculum (pp. 238–239). The council notes that many school systems have successfully relied on counselors, nurses and other specialists to supplement teachers' efforts to teach nonviolence. Participation of these other professionals gives students a sense of a supportive network of adults available to help them resolve problems nonviolently.

Problem-Solving Training. Kenney (1998) describes the School Safety Program, a research project sponsored by the National Institute of Justice (NIJ) incorporated into a social studies class curriculum in a high school in Charlotte, North Carolina. At the project's center is a problem-solving curriculum developed by teachers and research staff, integrated into social studies classes required of all 11th grade students.

When students looked at school problems, they found fighting and disorder in the lunchroom to be the biggest problem. When they analyzed the problem, they found that nearly the entire school population of 1,000 to 1,500 was released for lunch at the same time, and there were only two serving lines, which were split between one serving salad and the other an entrée such as pizza or hamburgers. Lines were long, and students with classes farthest from the cafeteria would arrive late and cut into line, causing fights. The students proposed several solutions, including an open campus, which was rejected by the administration. They finally agreed together to open additional serving lines and decrease the ratio of salads to other entrées. The plan succeeded, and the lunchroom fighting ceased.

Among the conclusions the researchers reached were that (1) a problem-solving approach to school issues demonstrates that those who have the most to gain—students—should be full partners in identifying, explaining and developing responses to problems; (2) the most significant problems in schools are not necessarily issues popularly considered to be important—little things do matter; (3) students are interested in a safer, more orderly school environment; and (4) the School Safety Program should be replicated in different school settings in different areas of the country.

Mediation and Anger Management Training. Among the strategies suggested by the National Crime Prevention Council (pp. 257–258) is training school-age youths to mediate conflicts: "School-based programs in conflict mediation give youth participants the communications, decision making, and anger management skills they need to remain resilient against violence in their community." When a dispute occurs on school grounds, the involved parties seek out a teacher or the program's adult coordinator. The coordinator assigns peer mediators to intervene and attempt to resolve the dispute peacefully through the parties' mutual agreement and commitment to a contract with set standards for conduct. Such mediation may substitute for detention or suspension of youths involved in fights, verbal threats or intimidation of others on school grounds.

Potential obstacles to this strategy include lack of funds for staff to train students and faculty and coordinate mediator assignments. In addition, convincing students that violence can be prevented can be difficult. New York's Resolving Conflict Creatively Program, cosponsored by the city's public schools and Educators for Social Responsibility, has successfully implemented this strategy. Seventy percent of teachers involved in this nationally recognized program say it has resulted in less name-calling, less classroom violence and more cooperation and understanding among students.

Clear Policies on Accepted Behavior with Consequences for Nonconformity. Skiba and Peterson (1999, p. 374) report on the discipline issues from those considered most serious to least serious issues in their schools—issues for which clear policies should be established: tardiness, (40 percent) absenteeism/class cutting, physical conflicts among students, student tobacco use, verbal abuse of teachers, student drug use, vandalism of school property, student alcohol use, robbery or theft, gangs, racial tensions, possession of weapons, physical abuse of teachers and sale of drugs on school grounds (2 percent).

Consequences for unacceptable behavior vary from detention to suspension to expulsion. Many schools have adopted **zero tolerance** toward possession of guns, drugs or alcohol in schools, that is, no matter what the underlying circumstances, a student bringing a weapon, drugs or alcohol to school will be suspended or expelled. Skiba and Peterson (p. 373) explain that "zero tolerance"—punishing all offenses severely, no matter how minor—grew out of state and federal drug enforcement policies in the 1980s. By the early 1990s zero tolerance policies were being adopted by school boards across the country. According to *School Security Roundtable 2000* (p. SS12), the second most common strategy used for school security at the elementary, middle- and high-school level was a zero tolerance policy. One of the central components of zero tolerance is school expulsion. They (p. 382) contend: "Zero tolerance strategies have begun to turn our schools into supplemental law enforcement agencies, but they have demonstrated little return despite a decade of hype."

"Virtually no data suggest that zero tolerance policies reduce school violence" (Skiba and Peterson, p. 376). Such policies result in sometimes unreasonable suspensions and expulsions.

Hyman and Snook (2000, p. 491) assert: "Many believe that safe and orderly schools require automatic punishments based on zero tolerance policies. The routine and unquestioning acceptance of these policies is not only undermining and distorting students' understanding and belief in constitutional rights; there is also the simple fact that such policies do not work." They suggest: "In contrast to toxic schools, schools that encourage participatory democracy are characterized by a climate in which students and staff members understand the need to respect one another's rights."

Curwin and Mendler (1999, p. 119) suggest: "Schools should have zero tolerance for any policy that treats all students the same." They (p. 120) believe eliminating zero tolerance policies will be difficult because the concept is simple to understand, sounds tough and gives the impression of high standards for behavior. They cite as an example a young boy who was suspended from school for violating the three-cut policy by missing his family living class. Investigation revealed he waited outside his apartment to intercept his crack cocaine-addicted mother's government check (which she would cash and use to buy drugs). He took the check to the bank where the manager gave him cash, which he put into envelopes: one to pay the rent, another for food, another utilities and so on. By the time he got the bills paid, he was late for school. Was suspension really warranted?

Hamit (p. 90) also describes unfortunate results of zero tolerance policies:

> Zero tolerance for drugs in schools has led to incidents where female students have been expelled or suspended for giving Motrin for menstrual cramps. This is hardly crack cocaine, and if the women involved were of age, it would be perfectly legal. Zero tolerance for weapons has led to incidents where a child has been expelled for bringing to school a kitchen knife intended only to cut a chicken sandwich.

In addition, as an OJJDP report ("Adult Supervision . . . ," 1999, pp. 6–7) notes: "Although suspensions and expulsions may be justified from the school authorities' point of view, common sense would indicate that simply releasing large numbers of adolescents out into the community, unsupervised during school hours, is likely to raise the number of delinquent acts committed."

Security Procedures and Technology. "U.S. public schools are not designed as fortresses," says Bridges (2000, p. 22). "However, by using basic crime prevention techniques and precautionary measures, communities can help create safer schools." A U.S. Department of Education survey of public schools (Grassie, p. 89) reports that 96% required visitors to sign in before entering the school building, 80% had a closed campus policy that prohibited most students from leaving the campus for lunch, 53% controlled access to their school buildings, 24% controlled access to their school grounds, 19% conducted drug sweeps, 4% of public elementary schools required students to wear uniforms during the school year, 4% performed random metal detector checks on students and 1% used metal detectors daily.

A National School Board Association survey of 720 school districts throughout the United States found that 39 percent of urban school districts use metal detectors, 75 percent use locker searches and 65 percent use security personnel (Welsh et al., 2000, p. 243). Some schools require students to use backpacks and book carriers made of clear material to allow visibility of their contents.

The National Crime Prevention Council (350 *Tested Strategies*, p. 277) suggests that school organization and policy can be used to address violence. The council notes that schools can combat juvenile crime through staffing, communications about school policies and cooperative planning involving parents, administrators, teachers and students. It suggests that reviews of school organization and policy are especially important in schools with low student achievement scores, high dropout rates, poor attendance, minimal parental involvement, considerable crime and violence and high teacher turnover.

Crisis Planning. Another aspect of proactively making schools safer includes having a contingency plan should a crisis occur, including violence by insiders or outsiders. The plan should be carefully thought out based on the unique characteristics of the specific school. It should be made known to and practiced by staff and students.

Hoang (2000, p. 107) suggests three "Ps" when dealing with school violence: prevention, planning and practice. Hoang suggests that a key element in planning is a tactical survey whose results should be contained in a tactical survey packet. Among the elements to be included are a general area road map, a neighborhood area road map, an aerial photograph, a floor plan of the school, blueprints/schematics, a property diagram and exterior photographs.

Schmitt (2000, p. 139) reports: "Some plans are simple, some so complex they require a notebook to hold them, but most stressed that, if word reaches the classrooms that a shooter is loose in the building, teachers should turn out their lights, lock their doors (if possible) and have their students hide while waiting for the SWAT team that will rescue them. This is the current norm."

Schmitt questions the wisdom of this approach, saying a simpler response plan would be more effective: "Get out of the building. NOW." This plan is based on the teaching of Frega and Heinrich (Geneva, Illinois, PD): "(1) Leave the kill zone. If you can't, then (2) find a safe room. If there isn't one, then, as a last resort, (3) Lock down." Maps of the buildings and likely escape routes should be known.

Whichever combination of strategies is selected to promote safe schools and communities, early intervention with at-risk children and youths is important.

◇ EARLY INTERVENTION

Pedersen (2000, p. 66) notes: "Changing the paths of at-risk youth requires early intervention." This is reinforced by the statement of the Bipartisan Working Group on Youth Violence ("Youth Violence Task Force . . . ," p. 4): "Despite the range of issues, there were several recurring themes that spanned the breadth of the discussion. The first theme is that prevention and early intervention programs are essential to reducing youth violence."

The top security strategy for elementary, middle and high school in 2000 was intervention programs for troubled children (School Security Roundtable 2000, p. SS12).

One such program is Huntington Park's J.A.R. (Juveniles at Risk) Program, which combines the concepts of juvenile referral, parenting, "Scared Straight" approach, community services, counseling and schools (Luna et al., 2000). Targeted are at-risk youths: gang members, taggers, habitual truants and recalcitrant juveniles. Arrested juveniles are referred to the program, which includes mandatory completion of a number of community service hours. Mandatory participation of the family includes mothers, fathers and siblings. The program has six components:

- Pre-Intake—each juvenile and his/her parent(s) reports to the police department for an interview with the project coordinator.
- Intake Night—guest speakers graphically describe the harsh realities of confinement in the county and state prisons. The cadre of police officers is introduced and their roles explained.
- Day "Zero" Saturday—each youth is inspected, given a uniform and searched for weapons and contraband.
- Bootcamp—(weeks 1–5) emphasis on self-discipline, respect, integrity, leadership and teamwork. The majority of participants are strong-willed and energetic. Staff tries to re-direct this energy towards becoming productive and responsible individuals.
- Weeks 6–16—training focuses on education. Military recruiters speak to participants. Participants also participate in graffiti removal, trash clean-up and other community involvement projects.
- Graduation Day—a new direction and chance at success characterizes graduation day.

Another program, which received one of the 1999 Community Policing Awards sponsored by the IACP and ITT Industries Night Vision, is the Beaufort (South Carolina) Police Department's Mentoring Program, which gives at-risk elementary students, primarily from single-parent families in the inner city, one-on-one-time with an officer (Kanable, 2000, p. 36).

Programs aimed at keeping students from abusing drugs are also important. *Making the Grade: A Guide to School Drug Prevention Programs* reviewed 49 programs and found that only 10 had been rigorously evaluated, and of those 10 only a few showed favorable results and were expensive. Probably the most evaluated program is D.A.R.E., but most long-term studies of the program do not support its effectiveness.

Rosenbaum's (1999) program, *Safety First*, stresses a reality-based approach to drug education. She (p. 1) notes that: "Despite expenditures of more than $2.1 billion on prevention this year, government surveys indicate that many teenagers experiment with drugs." She believes the reason is that drug education is flawed in assuming that drug use is the same as drug abuse. Many programs use the terms interchangeably, but teenagers know there is a difference. The "gateway" theory, a drug education mainstay, argues that using marijuana leads to using "harder" drugs, but there is no evidence of this. Again, teenagers believe they are being told "untruths." Says Rosenbaum (p. 9): "The consistent mis-characterization of marijuana may be the Achilles Heel of conventional approaches to drug education because these false messages are inconsistent with students' *actual* observations and experience."

The "Safety-First," reality-based alternative rests on three assumptions: (1) Teenagers can make responsible decisions if given honest, science-based drug education. (2) Total abstinence may not be a realistic alternative for all teenagers. (3) Use of mind-altering substances does not necessarily constitute abuse.

Rosenbaum (p. 14) concludes: "Reality-based drug education will equip students with information they trust, the basis for making responsible decisions."

Early intervention is also important in keeping at-risk youths from joining gangs—another significant challenge to community policing efforts.

◈ THE CHALLENGE OF GANGS IN AND OUT OF SCHOOL

As McCorkle and Miethe (1998, p. 41) note: "The past decade has witnessed increasing concern about street gangs and their role in violent crime and drug trafficking. According to a recent national survey, more than 80 percent of prosecutors in large cities now acknowledge that gangs are a problem in their jurisdiction, that their numbers are growing, and that levels of gang-related violence are increasing."

Valdez (2000, p. 32) notes: "Street gangs and the associated crime has impacted the police, the courts, corrections and most importantly the quality of life for many Americans." The *1998 National Street Gang Survey* with 373 law enforcement agencies responding identified more than 13,700 gangs with more than 750,000 gang members, a 56 percent increase in the number of gangs from 1996. Gang involvement is increasing perhaps because existing programs don't make up for the dismal lives many high-risk youths live. This survey also found that more than 80 percent of the 1,250 significant gangs identified were involved in drug trafficking.

Evolution of Strategies for Dealing with the Gang Problem

The Office of Juvenile Justice and Delinquency Prevention (OJJDP) reports a distinct difference in the approach used in the 1950s and 1960s compared to that used in more recent years. In the 1950s and 1960s law enforcement used a social services approach toward gangs. During more recent years the focus has been on suppression. Neither approach is clearly superior. Some communities have adopted a comprehensive approach combining social services intervention and suppression strategies.

According to the OJJDP, law enforcement has used five strategies to address the gang problem: suppression, social intervention, social opportunities, community mobilization and organizational development or change.

Suppression includes tactics such as prevention, arrest, imprisonment, supervision and surveillance. *Social intervention* includes crisis intervention, treatment for youths and their families, outreach and referral to social services. *Social opportunities* include providing basic or remedial education, training, work incentives and jobs for gang members. *Community mobilization* includes improved communication and joint policy and program development among justice, community-based and grassroots organizations. Finally, *organizational development* or *change* includes special police units and special youth agency crisis programs.

Community mobilization was found to be the most effective strategy to address the gang problem (OJJDP).

Providing gang members with basic social opportunities is also important in combating the gang problem. Sociologists, social workers, law enforcement personnel and citizens from battered communities have suggested strategies such as creating jobs for young people; developing programs in the arts, sports and so on; making sure young people receive a good education; preventing children from joining gangs in the first place by providing other challenging opportunities; creating alternative living situations for children who cannot stay at home; providing counseling services for families and young people; and inducing society as a whole to look at problems of poverty and discrimination (Osman and Haskins, 1996, p. 5).

Assistance from the OJJDP

Marble (2000, p. 39) describes how the OJJDP can help communities with the gang problem: "OJJDP has developed a comprehensive, coordinated response to youth gang problems. The response encompasses a wide range of programs and projects, including research, prevention, intervention, suppression and information sharing."

OJJDP initiatives to help communities address the gang problem include the Comprehensive Gang Model, the National Youth Gang Center, the Rural Gang Initiative and Gang Prevention through Targeted Outreach.

The *Comprehensive Gang Model* includes five strategies: mobilizing communities, providing youth opportunities, suppressing gang violence, providing social interventions and street outreach, and facilitating organizational change and development. The *National Youth Gang Center*, in Tallahassee, Florida, is a "one-stop shop" for information about gangs and effective responses to them.

The *Rural Gang Initiative* funds adaptation of the Comprehensive Gang Model at four rural sites and funds evaluation, training and technical assistance for these efforts. Finally, the *Gang Prevention through Targeted Outreach* enables local boys and girls clubs to prevent youths from entering gangs, intervene with gang members early in their involvement and divert youths from gang life into more constructive activities. In addition, the OJJDP provides publications, funding opportunities, training and technical assistance.

The G.R.E.A.T. Program

One nationally used program with some proven success is the G.R.E.A.T. Program ("A G.R.E.A.T. Program . . .," 1999, pp. 73–78).

The Gang Resistance Education and Training (G.R.E.A.T.) Program is aimed at stopping gang violence.

The G.R.E.A.T. Program is a proactive approach to deter violence before it begins. The program builds a foundation focused on teaching children the life skills they need to avoid violence and gang membership. A study supported by the NIJ documented the benefits of the program in a cross-sectional evaluation. The study showed that students who graduated from the G.R.E.A.T. course showed lower levels of delinquency, impulsive behavior, risk-taking behavior and approval of violence. The study also found that students demonstrated higher levels of self-esteem, parental attachment, commitment to positive peers, antigang attitudes, perceived educational opportunities and positive school environments ("A G.R.E.A.T. Program," p. 74).

Other Strategies to Prevent Gangs and Gang Violence

Current strategies to address the gang problem include behavior codes, graffiti removal programs, drug-free zones (DFZs) around schools, conflict prevention strategies, pulling levers, obtaining civil injunctions and community involvement.

Behavior codes should be established and firmly, consistently enforced. These codes may include dress codes and bans on showing gang colors or using hand signals. On the positive side, schools should promote and reward friendliness and cooperation.

Graffiti removal programs should be put in place that call for the prompt removal of graffiti anywhere it appears. Graffiti is not only unattractive, it also enables gang members to advertise their turf and authority. In some instances photographs of the graffiti may aid certain police investigations. School officials should give to the police remaining paint cans and paint brushes that might be used as evidence. As an alternative to graffiti, students might be encouraged to design and paint murals in locations where graffiti is most likely to occur.

Drug-free zones (DFZs) around schools is another commonly used strategy. This may include rewiring any pay phones so that only outgoing calls can be made.

Conflict prevention strategies are also important to address the problem of gangs. Teachers should be trained to recognize and deal with gang members in nonconfrontational ways. Staff should identify all known gang members and try to build self-esteem and promote academic success for all students, including gang members.

Pulling levers refers to a multiagency law enforcement team imposing all available sanctions (pulling levers) on gang members who violate established standards for behavior. This strategy was used in Boston with a small group of youths with extensive involvement in the justice system who accounted for a majority of youth homicides. Their two-pronged pulling levers program was initiated by a multiagency law enforcement team convening a series of meetings with the chronic gang offenders where law enforcement communicated new standards for behavior. Violence will no longer be tolerated. When the standards were violated, the multiagency law enforcement team responded by impos-

A teen participant in a neighborhood cleanup project prepares to paint over gang-related graffiti on a bench in an inner-city park.

ing all available sanctions. Since Boston implemented the strategy in 1996, youth homicides have fallen by two-thirds (*Promising Strategies to Reduce Gun Violence*, 1999, p. 96).

Another way to address the gang problem is through *civil injunctions*. This strategy was used by the Redondo Beach (California) Police Department in an award-winning experiment. The department got an injunction against the gang members who had essentially taken over a city park. The department sued them and won. The injunction resulted from a partnership between the community and the police department and exemplifies an innovative, proactive approach to ensuring public safety. The injunction restricted the following actions:

• Possessing, or remaining in the company of anyone with dangerous weapons, including clubs, bats, knives, screwdrivers, BB guns and so on.

• Entering private property of another without prior written permission of the owner.

• Intimidating, provoking, threatening, confronting, challenging or carrying out any acts of retaliation.

• A gang member under 18 years of age cannot be in a public place after 8:00 P.M. unless going to a legitimate business, meeting or an entertainment activity.

• Gang members cannot associate or congregate in groups of three or more in the park or within 10 yards of the outside fence surrounding the park.

The constitutionality of such an approach needs to be considered by any community wishing to implement this innovative strategy.

Community involvement is also needed to effectively reduce and prevent gang activity. Parents and the general public should be made aware of gangs operating in the community, as well as of popular heavy metal and punk bands that may be having a negative influence on youths. They should be encouraged to apply pressure to television and radio stations and to book stores and video stores to ban material that promotes use of alcohol, drugs, promiscuity, devil worship or violence. This may raise constitutionality or censorship issues, but as long as it is private citizens who apply the pressure, it should not present a problem.

Although problem-oriented policing is an important component of the community policing philosophy, Klein (1998, p. 57) cautions that problem-oriented policing may actually increase gang members' sense of importance: "Many intervention efforts, such as the 'small wins' of the problem-oriented approach, increase the bonds of cohesiveness among members and make the gang more attractive to gang-prone youths in the community." Klein (p. 81) suggests:

> In the long run, gangs are not the problem. Rather, gang-generating communities are the problem. In the arena of gang control, problem-oriented policing holds less promise than the strong version of community policing. Although it is very difficult to bring about a strong version of community policing, the community must be empowered to prevent gang membership.

Other Strategies Recommended by the National Crime Prevention Council

The National Crime Prevention Council recommends using state laws and ordinances to combat gangs, using multiagency gang interdiction teams, preventing gangs through community intervention with high-risk youths, providing positive alternatives to gang activity and setting up information networks on gang activity.

State Laws and Ordinances to Combat Gangs (pp. 269–270). This strategy seeks to create laws and ordinances that equip police and prosecutors with effective tools against gang-related crime. Laws that have been passed include classifying buildings in which gang activity occurs as a public nuisance that should be abated, increasing penalties for drive-by shootings, making repeated vandalism a felony, prohibiting sale of graffiti implements to minors and providing special penalties for coercive behavior by gang members. Key partnerships in this strategy include legislators, state and local law enforcement officials, judges, prosecutors, probation officers, school personnel and parents. A potential obstacle is the cost of enforcing the laws.

Multiagency Gang Interdiction Teams (p. 242). A multiagency team can provide a support system to rehabilitate gang members, helping them avoid gang activity. According to the council: "Teams led by law enforcement and representing multiple agencies include school personnel, residents, youth diversion counselors, staff of the district attorney's office, probation department personnel and, in some cities, university research staff who provide support for crime analysis." A potential obstacle to this strategy is agency "turf" issues and institutional biases against certain prevention or enforcement strategies, which may impede cooperation.

Community Intervention with High-Risk Youths (pp. 278–279). Programs using this strategy combine service coordination, partnerships between police and the community, suppression of gang activity through coordinated enforcement and prosecution, neighborhood mobilization and job training for youths. Key partnerships include police agencies, educators, job-training resources, parents and community groups. A potential obstacle is reluctance of residents to become involved in such a project out of fear of gangs.

A review of nearly 100 studies of gangs summarizes what is known about youth gangs and offers suggestions about how to design prevention programs. *Preventing Adolescent Gang Involvement* (Esbensen, 2000) reports that most gang members were already committing crimes before joining a gang, but youths' delinquency rates increase dramatically after joining a gang. The report recommends that, because of this, gang prevention campaigns should not be limited to programs that target existing gangs trying to shut them down. Gang prevention efforts should include programs aimed at the entire population of adolescents. In fact, gang-suppression programs targeting youths who are already involved with gangs "have shown little promise," and some have had the unintended result of "increasing gang cohesion."

Providing Positive Alternatives to Gang Activity (pp. 24–25). Strategies to deter gang membership include education, counseling and alternative activities such as recreation and job training. Key partnerships include community groups providing services and community members who can identify the services most needed by youths involved in gangs: local schools, youth programs, recreation centers, religious groups, citizen patrols and police. Again, a potential obstacle is fear of gang activity making some individuals and groups reluctant to get involved.

Setting Up Information Networks on Gang Activity (pp. 241–242). The council suggests that shared information include photos, arrest records, intelligence on on-going investigations and resource lists of services to which gang-involved youths can be referred. Sharing of information might be by newsletters, on-line networks and fax links. A potential obstacle in using this strategy is concern about legal restrictions on sharing confidential juvenile records.

Using Technology to Address the Gang Problem

Valdez (1999, p. 52) suggests: "Managing information on gangs has become easier through use of the latest technology." He (p. 54) describes the Regional Information Sharing System (RISS), a national network linking six regional intelligence databases, which has more than 4,500 local, state and federal law enforcement agencies as members. Connected in an Intranet system, access to any one database can prompt a search of the entire system with access through phone, fax, mail, e-mail or riss.net. One component of this information system is a national gang database: RISS-GANGS. This nationally accessible site contains a crime-specific database used to track information on gang members. The system also stores images. Such a system allows departments to quickly access information, search databases and retrieve specific information.

Task Forces

Another collaborative approach to addressing the gang problem is to form a task force, either regionally or statewide. Lesce (2000) describes how New Mexico established such a task force to coordinate information regarding gangs statewide. To date 48 law enforcement agencies are involved. The task force is funded by a federal grant derived from drug money administered by the Bureau of Justice Assistance and allocated for drug enforcement. Exchanging information helps identify habitual offenders and has allowed the district attorney's office to identify, arrest and prosecute senior gang members. It has also enabled identifying and classifying the various types of gangs in the state.

Although most individuals involved in programs for youths see gangs as a negative influence, there may be a positive side to gangs on which to build relationships leading to a rechanneling of gang members' energies.

A Hopeful Finding

Recall that Zatz and Portillos (2000, p. 389) reported: "Historically, gangs have been important neighborhood institutions offering disenchanted, disadvantaged youths a means of coping with the isolation, alienation, and poverty they experience every day." They (p. 396) believe: "The gang was, and is, composed of brothers, sisters, cousins, and neighbors. The gang gives them a sense of community, a place where they belong. Kicked out of school, assumed to be troublemakers, looking tough and feeling scared, these young people are well aware that their options in life are very much constrained by poverty, racial discrimination, cultural stereotyping, and inadequate education."

Zatz and Portillos (p. 389) also note: "Regardless of what other neighborhood residents may think of them, the youths identify strongly with their neighborhoods, consider themselves to be integral parts of their barrios, and view their gangs as neighborhood institutions. They see themselves as protectors of their neighborhoods, at least against intrusion by rival gangs." This would imply that, at least for Hispanic gang members, a sense of community might be there to build on.

SUMMARY

Children and teenagers are an important segment of the community often overlooked when implementing the community policing philosophy. To counteract negative perceptions of police held by children and youths, many departments have programs aimed at fostering positive relations with them. The youth development strategy suggests that communities first explore what they want for young people, rather than what behaviors they would like to prevent among youths. More important, it involves young people in rebuilding communities.

The developmental asset approach promotes (1) support, (2) empowerment, (3) boundaries and expectations, (4) constructive use of time, (5) commitment to learning, (6) positive values, (7) social competence and (8) positive identity to help youngsters succeed in school and in life. Youth-Focused Community Policing is a U.S. Department of Justice initiative instrumental in establishing law enforcement partnerships to focus on prevention, intervention and enforcement.

The family is viewed by many as the cornerstone of the community and should be included in community policing efforts focused on youths. Likewise, a school should be viewed as a community, not as an institution. Research suggests that students' academic motivation, commitment to democratic values and resistance to problem behaviors all depend on their experience of the school as a community. At a minimum, schools need to link with parents and with local law enforcement departments to teach students about the dangers of crime.

The school safety pyramid rests on the community and has as its components school resource officers, law-related education, conflict management and peer mediation, S.A.V.E. (Students against Violence in Education), teen/student court, and physical design and technology. A threat against school safety that has gained national attention is school shootings. Common characteristics in workplace and school violence include the profiles of the perpetrators, the targets, the means and the pathways to violence. A precursor to school violence is bullying. Bullying is more accurately termed *peer child abuse*. The "tell or tattle" dilemma occurs when a student hesitates to tell anyone that he or she is being bullied because it is seen as tattling—something they have been taught not to do.

Two highly successful programs to build safe schools are Student Crime Stoppers and PeaceBuilders®. In addition, a seven-pronged approach is needed for effective school security: (1) school/law enforcement/community partnerships, (2) education about violence, (3) problem-solving training, (4) mediation and anger-management training, (5) clear policies on accepted behavior with consequences for noncomformity, (6) security procedures and technology and (7) crisis planning.

One of the most popular strategies to promote safe schools is a zero tolerance policy against violence, guns and drugs in school. However, virtually no data suggest that zero tolerance policies reduce school violence. Such policies result in sometimes unreasonable suspensions and expulsions. The top security strategy for elementary, middle and high schools in 2000 was intervention programs for troubled children.

According to the OJJDP, law enforcement has used five strategies to address the gang problem: suppression, social intervention, social opportunities, community mobilization and organizational development or change. Community mobilization was found to be the most effective strategy to address the gang problem.

OJJDP initiatives to help communities address the gang problem include the Comprehensive Gang Model, the National Youth Gang Center, the Rural Gang Initiative and Gang Prevention through Targeted Outreach. The Gang Resistance Education and Training (G.R.E.A.T.) Program is aimed at stopping gang violence. Current strategies to address the gang problem include behavior codes, graffiti removal programs, drug-free zones (DFZs) around schools, conflict prevention strategies, pulling levers, obtaining civil injunctions and community involvement.

The National Crime Prevention Council recommends using state laws and ordinances to combat gangs, using multiagency gang interdiction teams, preventing gangs through community intervention with high-risk youths, providing positive alternatives to gang activity and setting up information networks on gang activity.

DISCUSSION QUESTIONS

1. Which of the programs for youths do you feel are the most effective?
2. Why do school administrators not consider drugs a security or crime problem?
3. What major differences in philosophy often exist between school administrators and police?
4. On which age group do you think police-school programs should focus? Why?
5. Was violence a problem in the high school you attended? If yes, what was the major problem?
6. Which of the strategies to combat gang activity in schools do you think seem most workable? What about gang activity in the community?
7. What are the advantages and disadvantages of expelling disruptive gang members from school?
8. Is zero tolerance for violence, drugs and weapons in school a workable policy? Why or why not?
9. Were gangs present in your high school? How did you know? If they were, did they present a threat?
10. How did you feel about the police when you were a child? Did that attitude change as you grew older? Why or why not and, if so, how?

INFOTRAC COLLEGE EDITION ASSIGNMENTS

- Use InfoTrac to help answer the discussion questions as appropriate.
- Research either bullying or school violence. Outline your findings and be prepared to share them with the class.

COMMUNITY PROJECTS

- What programs for youths are available in your community? Your school system?
- What strategies does your community use to address the gang problem?

REFERENCES

Adams, Carey. "Community Involvement: A Partnership between Schools and the Community." *School Security Roundtable Supplement,* October 2000, p. SS21.

"Adult Supervision Seen as Key to Preventing Youth Violence." *Criminal Justice Newsletter,* Vol. 30, No. 10, May 17, 1999, pp. 6–7.

Argon, Joe and Anderson, Larry. "School Security by the Numbers." *School Security 2000: A Special Supplement to Access Control & Security Systems Integration,* May 2000, pp. C-6 to C-12.

Arnette, June L. and Walsleben, Majorie C. *Combating Fear and Restoring Safety in*

Schools. Washington, DC: OJJDP Juvenile Justice Bulletin, April 1998.

Bilchik, Shay. "Collaboration among Federal Agencies Equals School Safety." *Corrections Today,* Vol. 62, No. 1, February 2000, pp. 56–58.

Bilchik, Shay. "From the Administrator." In *Combating Fear and Restoring Safety in Schools.* Washington, DC: OJJDP Juvenile Justice Bulletin, April 1998.

Bridges, Dennis. "Safeguarding Our Schools." *FBI Law Enforcement Bulletin,* Vol. 68, No. 9, September 2000, pp. 22–25.

Cody, Wilmer. "Conclusion." In *Early Warning, Timely Response: A Guide to Safe Schools.* Washington, DC: U.S. Department of Education, August 1998.

Connelly, Helen. "Youth-Focused Community Policing: Establishing Partnerships for Addressing Juvenile Crime and Victimization." *Community Policing Exchange,* Phase VI, #24, January/February 1999, pp. 1, 8.

"Cops Fight Crime by Investing in Kids." *Law Enforcement News,* Vol. XXVI, No. 539, September 15, 2000, p. 10.

Curwin, Richard L. and Mendler, Allen N. "Zero Tolerance for Zero Tolerance." *Phi Delta Kappan,* October 1999, pp. 119–120.

Diehm, Cynthia. "Reconnecting Youths and Communities." *Community Links: Progress through Partnerships,* Vol. 1, No. 1, January 1997.

Early Warning, Timely Response: A Guide to Safe Schools. Washington, DC: U.S. Department of Education, April 1998.

Esbensen, Finn-Aage. *Preventing Adolescent Gang Involvement.* Washington, DC: Juvenile Justice Clearinghouse, 2000. (NCJ-182210)

Eskridge, Chris W. *Criminal Justice: Concepts and Issues—An Anthology,* 3rd ed. Los Angeles: Roxbury Publishing Company, 1999.

Gersh, David. "Asset Approach Helps Children Succeed." *School Security Roundup Supplement,* October 2000, p. SS15.

Grassie, Richard P. "Indulging Contemporary Risks: Road Rage and School Violence." *Security Technology & Design,* January 2000, pp. 88–90.

"A G.R.E.A.T. Program: Stopping Gang Violence before It Starts." *Law and Order,* Vol. 47, No. 2, February 1999, pp. 73–74.

Guide for Preventing and Responding to School Violence. www.theiacp.org

Hall, Dennis. "School Safety Panel Message: Hike the Profile of Officers." *Police,* Vol. 24, No. 1, January 2000, p. 6.

Hamit, Francis. "The Problem with Kids Today." *Security Technology & Design,* Vol. 10, No. 4, April 2000, pp. 89–90.

Harberts, Helen. "School Team Watches for Signs of Trouble, Steps in to Prevent Problems." *Community Policing Exchange,* Phase VII, #32, September/October 2000, p. 6.

Hoang, Francis Q. "Preplanning for School Violence." *Law and Order,* Vol. 38, No. 12, December 2000, pp. 107–109.

Holmes, Ronald M. and Holmes, Stephen T. "School Shootings: A Country's Concern." *Law and Order,* Vol. 47, No. 6, June 1999, pp. 109–113.

Hyman, Irwin A. and Snook, Pamela A. "Dangerous Schools and What You Can Do about Them." *Phi Delta Kappan,* March 2000, pp. 489–501.

Jones-Brown, Delores D. "Debunking the Myth of Officer Friendly." *Journal of Contemporary Criminal Justice,* Vol. 16, No. 2, May 2000, pp. 209–229.

Kanable, Rebecca. "Community Policing at Its Best: Award Winners Share Ideas Worth Replicating." *Law Enforcement Technology,* Vol. 27, No. 10, October 2000, pp. 34–40.

Kanable, Rebecca. "Patrolling the Schools." *Law Enforcement Technology,* Vol. 26, No. 9, September 1999, pp. 68–73.

Kenney, Dennis. *Crime in the Schools: A Problem-Solving Approach.* National Institute of Justice Research Preview. Washington, DC: U.S. Department of Justice, August 1998.

Klein, Malcolm. "The Problem of Street Gangs and Problem-Oriented Policing." In *Problem-Oriented Policing: Crime-Specific Problems, Critical Issues and Making POP Work,* edited by Tara O'Connor Shelley and Anne C. Grant. pp. 57–88. Washington, DC: Police Executive Research Forum, 1998.

Lavarello, Curtis. "School Based Policing: Specialized Training Will Ease Liability." *The Law Enforcement Trainer,* Vol. 15, No. 6, November/December 2000, pp. 6–8.

Lesce, Tony. "New Mexico Gang Task Force: Coping with a Growing Problem." *Law and Order,* Vol. 38, No. 10, October 2000, pp. 211–214.

Luna, Antonio; Hernandez, George; Winn, Rae; and Etienne, Stephen. "Juveniles at Risk Program." *Law and Order,* Vol. 48, No. 7, July 2000, pp. 93–96.

Makholm, John A. " 'Do the Right Thing: A Prescription for the Future.' " *Police,* Vol. 24, No. 12, December 2000, pp. 30–32.

Making the Grade: A Guide to School Drug Prevention Programs. Washington, DC: Drug Strategies, 1999.

Marble, Lynn. "The Youth Gang Problem: Fed Resources Are There to Assist." *Police,* Vol. 24, No. 6, June 2000, pp. 38–41.

Marlin, Gene P. and Vogt, Barbara. "Violence in the Schools." *The Police Chief,* Vol. LXVI, No. 4, April 1999, pp. 169–171.

Mattson, Sean A. "Phoenix Police's 'Wake Up!' Program Proves Effective Crime Prevention Tool." *The Police Chief,* Vol. LXVII, No. 11, November 2000, pp. 78–80.

McCollum, Daniel. "Adopt-a-Cop Program: An Opportunity to Interact with Schools." *Law and Order,* Vol. 48, No. 7, July 2000, p. 130.

McCorkle, Richard C. and Miethe, Terance D. "The Political and Organizational Response to Gangs: An Examination of a 'Moral Panic' in Nevada." *Justice Quarterly,* Vol. 15, No. 1, March 1998, pp. 42–64.

Nicoletti, John; Zinna, Kelly; and Spencer-Thomas, Sally. "The Dynamics of 'Schoolplace' Violence." *The Police Chief,* Vol. LXVI, No. 10, October 1999, pp. 74–92.

1998 National Street Gang Survey. FBI Law Enforcement Bulletin, Vol. 68, No. 7, July 1999, p. 21. Available on the National Drug Intelligence Center home page at www.usdoj.gov/ndic

Osman, Karen and Haskins, James. *Street Gangs Yesterday and Today, West Side Story Home Page,* 1996, pp. 1–5.

Paynter, Ronnie L. "Back-to-School Security." *Law Enforcement Technology,* Vol. 27, No. 9, September 2000, pp. 72–79.

Paynter, Ronnie L. "Policing the Schools: Community Policing Can Get the Whole Village Involved in Combatting School Violence." *Law Enforcement Technology,* Vol. 26, No. 10, October 1999, pp. 34–40.

Pederson, Dorothy. "Big Crimes, Little Culprits." *Law Enforcement Technology,* Vol. 27, No. 10, October 2000, pp. 66–78.

Promising Strategies to Reduce Gun Violence. Washington, DC: OJJDP, February 1999.

"Protecting Kids from the Internet and More." *Law Enforcement News,* Vol. XXVI, No. 541, October 15, 2000, p. 7.

Rosenbaum, Marsha. *Safety First: A Reality-Based Approach to Teens, Drugs, and Drug Education.* New York: The Lindesmith Center, 1999.

Schaps, Eric and Lewis, Catherine. "Perils on an Essential Journey: Building School Community." *Phi Delta Kappan,* November 1999, pp. 215–218.

Schmitt, Sheila. "Unlocking the Lockdown Mentality: Officers Teach Alternatives in School-Shooting Situations." *Law and Order,* Vol. 48, No. 6, June 2000, pp. 139–144.

School Security Roundtable 2000. Special Supplement to *Access Control & Security Systems Integration,* October 2000.

School Shooter: A Threat Assessment Perspective. Washington, DC: Federal Bureau of Investigation, 2000. www.fbi.gov

Schuiteman, John G. "Early Returns Positive for Virginia's Model SRO Program." *The Police Chief,* Vol. LXVII, No. 11, November 2000, pp. 74–77.

Skiba, Russ and Peterson, Reece. "The Dark Side of Zero Tolerance: Can Punishment Lead to Safe Schools?" *Phi Delta Kappan,* January 1999, pp. 372–382.

Soto, Ileana. "An Alliance Based on Interface and Interdependence." *Community Policing Exchange,* Phase VII, #32, September/October 2000, p. 8.

350 Tested Strategies to Prevent Crime: A Resource for Municipal Agencies and Community Groups. Washington, DC: National Crime Prevention Council, 1995.

Tumbleson, Ed. "Connecting with the Cornerstone of the Community: Family." *Community Policing Exchange,* Phase VI, No. 24, January/February 1999, pp. 3–4.

Valdez, Al. "Trying to Work Gangs? It's All About History, Infrastructure, and, Today, Even the Internet." *Police,* Vol. 24, No. 6, June 2000, pp. 32–37.

Valdez, Al. "Using Technology in the War against Gangs." *Police,* Vol. 23, No. 7, July 1999, pp. 52–54.

Welsh, Wayne N.; Stokes, Robert; and Greene, Jack R. "A Macro-Level Model of School Disorder." *Journal of Research in Crime and Delinquency,* Vol. 37, No. 3, August 2000, pp. 253–283.

Williams, Brian N. "Perceptions of Children and Teenagers on Community Policing: Implications for Law Enforcement Leadership, Training, and Citizen Evaluations." *Police Quarterly,* Vol. 2, No. 2, June 1999, pp. 150–173.

"Youth Violence Task Force Says Early Intervention Is Key." *Criminal Justice Newsletter,* Vol. 30, No. 18, March 2000, pp. 4–5.

Zatz, Majorie S. and Portillos, Edwardo L. "Voices from the Barrio: Chicano/a Gangs, Families, and Communities." *Criminology,* Vol. 38, No. 2, 2000, pp. 369–402.

RESOURCES

Center for the Prevention of School Violence. www.ncsu.edu/cpsv/

Department of Education: Keeping Schools and Communities Safe. www.uncg.edu/edu/ericcass/violence/index.htm

A Guide to Safe Schools, U.S. Department of Education. www.ed.gov/offices/OSERS/OSEP/earlywrn.html

Juvenile Offenders and Victims: 1999 National Report. www.ojjdp.ncjrs.org

National PTA Violence Prevention Kit. www.pta.org/events/violpre/index.htm

National School Safety Center. www.nsscl.org

PAVNET (partnership against violence network). www.pavnet.org

PeaceBuilders.® http://www.peacebuilders.com.

Student Crime Stoppers. http://www.studentcrimestoppers.com

White House Conference on School Safety. www.whitehouse.gov/WH/New/safety/

Working against Violence Everywhere. www.waveamerica.com/schools/schooldefaultOLD.htm

CHAPTER 15

Community Policing, Crime and Drugs

In the last analysis, the most promising and so the most important method of dealing with crime is by preventing it—by ameliorating the conditions of life that drive people to commit crime and that undermine the restraining rules and institutions erected by society against anti-social conduct.

President's Commission on Law Enforcement and Administration of Justice, 1967

Do you know

What synergism is and how it relates to crime prevention efforts?

What role crime prevention plays in community policing?

What three federal initiatives can assist communities in implementing community policing?

What the Weed and Seed program does?

What the three primary components of CPTED are?

On what five principles CPTED is based?

How CPTED directly supports community policing?

What the risk factor prevention paradigm is?

What strategies have been implemented to prevent/reduce crime and disorder?

What the two primary messages of most auto theft programs are?

What the key to reducing drug abuse is?

What the first initiative to reduce drug-related crime and violence proposed by the National Drug Control Strategy is?

What strategies have been implemented to combat the drug problem in neighborhoods?

How the conservative and liberal crime control strategies differ?

Can you define these terms:

infrastructure   risk factor   synergism

protective factor   risk factor prevention paradigm target hardening

INTRODUCTION

Whose job is it to prevent crime? Many Americans, including many police, believe crime prevention is solely the responsibility of law enforcement. Many of the programs already discussed seek to prevent crime, including many of those aimed at youths. When crime surges in a community, the usual public response is to demand the hiring of more officers. Citizens often believe that a visible police presence will deter and reduce crime, even though most studies indicate this is not the case. For example, the classic study, *Kansas City Preventive Patrol Experiment*, found overwhelming evidence that decreasing or increasing routine preventive patrol within the range tested had no effect on crime, citizen fear of crime, community attitudes toward the police on the delivery of police services, police response time or traffic accidents. In 1975 the FBI's *Uniform Crime Reports* noted:

> Criminal justice professionals readily and repeatedly admit that, in the absence of citizen assistance, neither more manpower, nor improved technology, nor additional money will enable law enforcement to shoulder the monumental burden of combating crime in America.

In commenting on the "remarkable decline in the rate of crime," Neubauer (1999, p. 8) suggests: "No factor has been more crucial to the reduction in crime levels than the partnership between law enforcement agencies and the communities they serve." Other reasons for the decline in the crime rate are suggested in a new study "To Establish Justice, To Insure Domestic Tranquility." This report suggests that economic good times, not get tough criminal justice policies, are the primary reason for the "dizzying drop in the nation's crime rate over the past seven years" ("Good News, Bad News . . . ," 2000, p. 1).

Whatever factors one attributes the decreasing crime rate to, the broad nature of policing in the 1990s highlighted the critical contributions citizens, community agencies and organizations can make to combat crime. For communities to thrive, citizens need to have a sense of neighborhood and to work together as a team. The resulting synergism can accomplish much more than isolated individual efforts.

Synergism *occurs when individuals channel their energies toward a common purpose and accomplish together what they could not accomplish alone.*

The technical definition of *synergism* is "the simultaneous actions of separate entities which together have greater total effect than the sum of their individual efforts." A precision marching band and a national basketball championship team are examples of synergism. Although there may be some outstanding solos and a few spectacular individual "dunks," it is the total team effort that produces the results.

The police and the citizens they serve must realize that their combined efforts *are* greater than the sum of their individual efforts on behalf of the community. When police take a problem-solving approach to crime and include the community, what they are doing often falls under "crime prevention."

Crime prevention is a large part, in fact a cornerstone, of community policing.

Community policing and crime prevention are, however, distinct entities.

This chapter begins with a discussion of the national focus on community policing and crime prevention and the assistance offered by COPS, the Community Policing Consortium and the Weed and Seed program. This is followed by descriptions of CPTED and the risk factor prevention paradigm. Next the discussion turns to tested strategies for preventing/reducing crime and disorder including programs aimed at preventing auto theft and deterring prostitution. This is followed by examples of partnerships to prevent crime. Then the focus shifts to the link between crime and drugs, the "war on drugs" and the National Drug Control Strategy. This is followed by strategies for dealing with the drug problem and a discussion of collaborative efforts to do so. The chapter concludes by examining the relationship between crime, drugs and the American dream.

◆ NATIONAL EMPHASIS ON COMMUNITY POLICING AND CRIME PREVENTION

Three federal initiatives to assist communities in implementing community policing are the COPS Office, the Community Policing Consortium and the Weed and Seed program.

The Office of Community Oriented Policing Services (COPS)

The Violent Crime Control and Law Enforcement Act of 1994 authorized $8.8 billion over six years for grants to local police agencies to add 100,000 officers and promote community policing. To implement this law, Attorney General Janet Reno created the Office of Community Oriented Policing Services (COPS) in the Department of Justice.

The COPS Office has been given a five-year extension into the 21st century. Weiss and Dresser (1999, p. 26) describe what the COPS office was designed to do:

- Increase the number of community policing officers on the beat by 100,000
- Promote the implementation of department-wide community policing in law enforcement agencies across the country
- Help develop an infrastructure to institutionalize and sustain community policing after federal funding has ended
- Demonstrate and evaluate the viability of agencies practicing community policing to significantly improve the quality of life by reducing the levels of violence, crime and disorder in communities

The Community Policing Consortium

Another organization that might provide assistance is the Community Policing Consortium, a partnership of five police organizations: the International Association of Chiefs of Police (IACP), the National Organization of Black Law Enforcement Executives (NOBLE), the National Sheriffs' Association (NSA), the Police Executive Research Forum (PERF) and the Police Foundation (PF). The consortium is funded and administered by COPS within the Department of Justice. They provide training throughout the United States, especially to agencies that receive COPS grants. The training materials emphasize community policing from a local perspective, community partnerships, problem solving, strategic planning and assessment. Their quick-read periodicals, *The Community Policing Exchange, Sheriff Times* and the *Information Access Guide*, relate real-life experiences of community policing practitioners across the country.

The Weed and Seed Program

A third federal initiative is the Weed and Seed program. Launched in 1991 with three sites, it has since grown to include 200 sites nationwide. The program strategically links concentrated, enhanced law enforcement efforts to identify, arrest and prosecute violent offenders, drug traffickers and other criminals operating in the target areas and community policing (weeding) with human services—including after-school, weekend and summer youth activities; adult literacy classes; and parental counseling—and neighborhood revitalization efforts to prevent and deter further crime (seeding).

The Weed and Seed program seeks to identify, arrest and prosecute offenders (weed) while simultaneously working with citizens to improve quality of life (seed).

The National Institute of Justice (NIJ) conducted a national evaluation of the program by selecting eight sites representing different aspects of Weed and Seed ("Weed and Seed Evaluation," 1999, p. 7). The evaluation found:

- Preexisting community features—such as the strength of the social and institutional **infrastructure** (an established network of community-based organizations and community leaders), the severity of crime problems, geographical advantages favoring economic development, and transience of the community population—may make the program easier or more difficult to operate effectively.

- The mix of weeding and seeding activities and the sequencing of these components—including early seeding, sustained weeding, high-level task forces combined with community policing and an active prosecutorial role—represent important factors in gaining community support for the program.

- Greater success occurred when sites concentrated their program resources on smaller population groups, especially if they could also channel other public funds and leverage private funds.

- Active, constructive leadership of key individuals represented a less tangible ingredient in the more successful programs.

- Implementation strategies that relied on bottom-up, participatory decision-making approaches, especially when combined with efforts to build capacity and partnership among local organizations, proved the most effective.

According to Geller (1998, p. 154): "Weed and Seed has been an intriguing metaphor waiting to happen more than halfway. The program has, indeed, helped some communities thin their gardens of people (and conditions) contributing to crime, disorder, and fear. It is the seeding that has been dubious." Geller poses several thought-provoking questions: "What if communities, with a helping hand from the police, really could incubate what anthropologist Jane Goodall calls the 'roots and shoots'—people and institutions that make for a vibrant, ecologically sound social garden? What if we could grow gardens with fewer weeds and more immunity to the weeds that do appear? What if we could convert most weeds into acceptable if not productive residents of the garden?" It is hoped the Weed and Seed program might help communities answer these questions affirmatively.

An approach to combating crime and disorder that also focuses on the environment but in a much more literal sense, is the Crime Prevention through Environmental Design (CPTED) approach being used in many community policing efforts.

◈ CRIME PREVENTION THROUGH ENVIRONMENTAL DESIGN (CPTED)

Crime Prevention through Environmental Design (CPTED) was introduced in Chapter 12. It has been a strategy for dealing with crime for decades and has had some proven successes.

Crime Prevention through Environmental Design has three major components: target hardening, changes to the physical environment and community building.

Target hardening refers to making potential objectives of criminals more difficult to obtain. The three main devices used for target hardening are improved locks, alarm systems and security cameras. Most people do not object to locks and alarm systems properly used, but some have "Big Brother" concerns about surveillance cameras. Gorovici (2000, p. 36) notes: "Most of us have become accustomed to video monitoring in banks, at ATMs, in convenience stores, in large parking areas and other locations. In recent years, video monitoring has expanded into other public areas—city centers, schools, transportation hubs, housing projects—and the evidence so far suggests this crime-fighting tool has tremendous potential. In the U.S. today, there are more than one million cameras in use for security monitoring."

What can be done to make such surveillance acceptable to the majority of citizens? Gorovici (p. 38) says: "Create partnerships. From the beginning, strive to form a wide coalition of partnership that includes law enforcement, government bodies, neighborhood groups, businesses, retail associations and individual citizens. The more wide-ranging the partnership, the more sources of funding, expertise and potential support."

Changes in the physical environment very often include lighting. Increasing lighting has been a means of increasing security for centuries. Phillips (p. 10) contends: "Although there is a strong indication that increased lighting decreases the fear of crime, there is no statistically significant evidence that street lighting affects the actual level of crime." Other changes usually involve removing items that give potential offenders the ability to hide, for example dense vegetation, high shrubs, walls and fences.

Community building, the third element of CPTED, can have the greatest impact on how individuals perceive the livability of their neighborhood. Community building seeks to increase residents' sense of ownership of the neighborhood and of who does and does not belong there. Community building techniques can include social events such as fairs or neighborhood beautification projects.

Files (1999, p. 42) outlines the five principles underlying CPTED.

Five principles underlying CPTED are territoriality, natural surveillance, access control, activity support and maintenance of the environment.

Territoriality establishes ownership and sends a clear message of who and who does not belong there. *Natural surveillance* allows potential victims a clear view of surroundings and inhibits crime. *Access control* delineates boundaries and where people do and do not belong. *Activity support* involves programming activities that promote proper site use and discourages nonlegitimate use. *Maintenance of the environment* provides both physical maintenance and continuing education of the public, increasing awareness of surroundings.

Fleissner and Heinzelmann (1996) conclude: "CPTED and community policing emphasize a problem-solving approach to crime prevention as well as close cooperation between police and residents in reducing both crime and fear of crime."

By emphasizing the systematic analysis of crime in a particular location, CPTED directly supports community policing by providing crime prevention strategies tailored to solve specific problems.

◉ THE RISK FACTOR PREVENTION PARADIGM

The risk factor prevention paradigm *seeks to identify key risk factors for offending and then implement prevention methods designed to counteract them.*

According to Farrington (2000, p. 3): "By definition, a **risk factor** predicts an increased probability of later offending." The paradigm also includes a **protective factor**—which is not as easily defined. Some believe a protective factor is just the opposite end of the scale from a risk factor. Others believe this may not be true. In some instances a variable might be a protective factor but not a risk factor. For example, if high income predicts a low risk of delinquency, while medium and low income predict a fairly constant average risk, income could be regarded as a protective factor but not a risk factor (pp. 8–9). This is important because when conducting research, it is necessary to investigate risk and protective factors in a way that allows them to be independent.

The risk factor prevention paradigm is highly relevant to community policing efforts as Farrington (p. 1) explains: "This paradigm has fostered linkages between explanation and prevention, between fundamental and applied research, and between scholars, practitioners, and policy makers."

Risk factors were a consideration in the last chapter when at-risk youths were identified for early intervention. These same risk factors are relevant in considering strategies to prevent/reduce crime and disorder.

◇ TESTED STRATEGIES FOR PREVENTING/REDUCING CRIME AND DISORDER

The National Crime Prevention Council's *350 Tested Strategies to Prevent Crime* (1995) contains numerous strategies communities might adopt or adapt to fit their unique situations.

Strategies to prevent/reduce crime and disorder include beautification projects, business anticrime groups, local government-community crime prevention coalitions, community coalitions, cooperation with grassroots organizations, working with landlords and residents in public housing, using advances in technology and celebrating community successes.

Beautification Projects (pp. 4–15)

Neighborhood and business district improvements such as cleaning up trash, landscaping and planting flowers can serve as a focus for community organizing and help residents take pride in their neighborhoods. Key partnerships include police departments, public works staff, the business community and residents.

Business Anticrime Groups (pp. 16–17)

Business Watch groups can deter, detect and report crime in business and commercial districts. They can participate in Operation Identification. This strategy helps reduce many kinds of crimes in and around businesses, including shoplifting, theft, burglaries, drug dealing and vandalism. Police can provide education and training on robbery and burglary prevention as well as other forms of self-protection. A potential obstacle is that business owners may not feel they can significantly reduce crime by such efforts.

Local Government-Community Crime Prevention Coalitions (pp. 35–36)

A comprehensive local crime prevention plan developed through a coalition of community groups, local government agencies and other sectors has a good chance of success. This strategy can protect against all types of crimes. Key components include support of key political leaders and law enforcement officials, a commitment to a process open to all sectors of the community, a vision shared by all participants, specific goals and objectives and evaluation. A potential obstacle is that community members may hesitate to participate, fearing their input would not be valued.

This strategy was implemented by the mayors of the seven largest cities in Texas, who formed Mayors United on Safety, Crime and Law Enforcement (MUSCLE). With the support of the Bureau of Justice Assistance, the seven cities initiated local government-grassroots crime prevention planning projects. Of the plan's 56 objectives, 55 were implemented within two years, including the following: obtaining a $10 million increase in funding for youth recreation programs, establishing a late-night curfew for teenagers, initiating a locally developed gang prevention effort highlighted by a public education campaign, establishing youth leadership development programs at area schools, implementing school-based conflict resolution programs, expanding community policing, establishing a business crime commission, garnering corporate support for mentoring programs and coordinating a week-long focus on prayer for violence prevention by area religious leaders. Since the plan was implemented, youth victimization by crime during curfew hours has declined significantly, and overall crime has dropped each year (p. 36).

Community Coalitions (pp. 21–22, 37)

According to the NCPC: "Mobilizing community coalitions for neighborhood revitalization through resident partnership with government will reduce crime and drug trafficking and improve the quality of life." Key partnerships include residents, parent groups, block watches, businesses, schools, and civic and service organizations. The strategy involves (1) a grassroots approach to local citizen empowerment, (2) citizen identification of priority issues for action, (3) a partnership among residents and community organizations and local government and (4) development of strategies that residents and government officials can use to achieve their specific goals. Activities include rallies and marches, youth recreation programs, parent-teen workshops, citizen crime patrols, media involvement and intensive application of city services in targeted neighborhoods (p. 37).

Key components can include "drug-free school zones, drug abuse prevention curricula in schools, parent education and counseling groups, after-school programs and activities for youths, drug-free home and apartment lease clauses, identification of and action against drug "hot spots," allocation of community resources for rehabilitating drug abusers, youth employment and training programs, neighborhood beautification and revitalization and community rallies against drugs (p. 21).

Cooperation with Grassroots Organizations (pp. 117–118)

The NCPC contends: "When law enforcement supports the community-building efforts of an existing organization, the community benefits from a stronger network built on citizen concern and law enforcement expertise." One such grassroots organization found in many communities is Mothers Against Drunk Driving (MADD). Other groups might include the Parent Teacher Association (PTA) and local civic groups. In one instance, residents of a Waterloo, Iowa, neighborhood enlisted the support of police to close down bars that had been selling alcohol to minors. They transformed one abandoned bar into a recreation center for area youths.

Working with Landlords and Residents of Public Housing (p. 379)

The NCPC describes 18 specific approaches to work with landlords and/or residents of public housing to deter crime and disorder (and drug dealing, discussed later in the chapter): access control, cleanup projects, closed circuit television, crime prevention and awareness training, drug abuse prevention, enforcement of trespass law, enhanced outdoor lighting, eviction, fencing, partnerships with law enforcement, pay phone restrictions, police-in-residence programs, resident initiative groups, security headquarters, tenant screening, undercover street-level drug purchases, voluntary resident patrols and youth leadership development.

Using Advances in Technology (p. 40)

Advances in technology, including cellular phones, fax machines, e-mail and video cameras, can be used effectively in crime prevention efforts. Whisenant and Panther (2000, p. 8) describe how the Arlington County (Virginia) Police Department uses Crimereports.com, a Web-based service that allows police departments to send crime alerts, reports, statistics, pictures and other notices to members of the community via e-mail. A similar service used in the Seminole County (Florida) Sheriff's Office is described by Olson and Robinson (2000, pp. 1–2): eLert is an electronic alert subscriber list that sends information via e-mail to subscribers about sex offenders, sexual predators or registered felons who have moved into the neighborhood. It offers crime alerts about traveling criminals, people with active warrants or others about whom the sheriff's office believes the public should be aware. Another technology police departments are using is a miniature video camera capable of filming participants in a drug transaction and recording their voices without their ever being aware of what is occurring (Meyers, 2000a, p. 3).

Celebrating Community Successes (pp. 47–48)

An inexpensive and often overlooked strategy is to celebrate community successes. According to the NCPC: "Celebrating a community's accomplishments in planning and implementing anticrime projects and revitalization or redevelopment activities builds community pride and supports the sustainability of communities of all types." Key partnerships include neighborhood services agencies, which should work with community groups to identify opportunities to note accomplishments of individuals and local projects. The media should be involved, and businesses may agree to underwrite the costs of events and awards.

Strategies Aimed at Preventing Auto Theft

Many police departments furnish citizens with information on how to prevent auto theft. Information may be provided in the form of pamphlets, newspaper stories, PSAs on television or speeches made to civic organizations.

The two main messages of anticar theft programs are to not leave the keys in the car ignition and to lock the car.

These messages are conveyed in a variety of ways from stickers to put on dashboards to posters warning that leaving keys in the ignition is a violation of the law if the car is parked on public property. In addition, leaving one's keys in the ignition is an invitation to theft, could become a contributing cause of some innocent person's injury or death and could raise the owner's insurance rates.

New York City has developed a voluntary antiauto theft program that enlists the aid of motorists. The Combat Auto Theft (CAT) program allows the police to stop any car marked with a special decal between 1 A.M. and 5 A.M. Car owners sign a consent form affirming that they do not normally drive between 1 A.M. and 5 A.M., the peak auto theft hours. Those who participate in the program waive their rights to search and seizure protection.

A Strategy to Deter Prostitution

The Des Moines Police Department encourages citizens to send "Dear John" letters to registered owners of vehicles involved in prostitution. Citizens are told they can obtain the owner's name, address, make, year and color of a vehicle by taking its license number to the Iowa Department of Transportation. The information is free. Citizens are also given a sample letter (see Figure 15.1) they can send to the registered owner. In addition, citizens are instructed to send copies of the letter to the county attorney and to the vice squad. The Sunset Park, New York, neighborhood used this strategy, which resulted in more than 700 arrests and longer jail terms for prostitution (350 *Tested Strategies*, p. 118).

Many of these strategies have been used in community policing partnerships throughout the country.

PARTNERSHIPS IN ACTION AGAINST CRIME AND DISORDER

Partnerships across the country are working on reducing crime and disorder, some focusing on one specific area, others taking more comprehensive approaches.

Norfolk, Virginia, cut homicides by more than 10 percent and has reduced overall crime rates citywide by 26 percent and in some neighborhoods by as much as 40 percent. A good share of the credit goes to Police Assisted Community Enforcement (PACE), a crime prevention initiative that works neighborhood by neighborhood in conjunction with teams of social, health and family services agencies (the Family Assistance Services Team, or FAST) and public works and environmental agencies (Neighborhood Environmental Assistance Teams, or NEAT) to cut through red tape and help residents reclaim their neighborhoods (NCPC).

The Minnesota Crime Prevention Association enlisted the support of families, public officials and 45 statewide and local organizations, including schools and churches, to wage a campaign against youth violence. Actions ranged from encouraging children and parents to turn off violent television shows to providing classroom training in violence prevention (NCPC).

In Trenton, New Jersey, a partnership of schools, parents, city leaders and others led to a Safe Haven program in which the schools in the neighborhood became multipurpose centers after school hours for youth activities including sports, crafts and tutoring. Children have flocked to the centers as a positive alternative to being at home alone after school or being at risk on the streets (NCPC).

Crime near a college campus in Columbus, Ohio, became an opportunity for a partnership formed by the City of Columbus, the State of Ohio, Ohio State University, the Franklin County Sheriff and the Columbus Police. The Community Crime Patrol puts two-person, radio-equipped teams of observers into the neighborhoods near the campus during potential high-crime hours. A number of these paid, part-time observers are college students interested in careers in law enforcement (NCPC).

In Danville, Virginia, a partnership approach to working with public housing residents resulted in a 53 percent reduction in calls about fights, a 50 percent reduction in domestic violence calls and a 9 percent reduction in disturbance calls. The Virginia

Date: _____

_____

_____

_____

_____

Mr. and/or Mrs. _____ :

Your _____ was seen picking up a
               (DESCRIPTION OF VEHICLE)

prostitute in the vicinity of _____ in
                              (AREA)

Des Moines on _____ , at approximately_____ .
                   (DATE)   (TIME)

We hope you realize that by participating in such behavior you risk criminal prosecution, as well as exposing yourself — and possibly your family — to public humiliation and a host of diseases including the deadly AIDS virus.

Prostitution is unacceptable and it will not be tolerated any more in our neighborhood. A detailed description of your vehicle, complete with the license number, has been circulated to area residents.

                                  Sincerely,

                                  North Side Neighbors

cc: James Smith
    Polk County Attorney

    Vice Squad
    Des Moines Police Department

Figure 15.1   Sample "Dear John" Letter

SOURCE: Des Moines Police. *Drugs: A Municipal Approach, A Community Handbook*, p. 15. Reprinted by permission.

Crime Prevention Association worked with the Danville Housing Authority to bring public housing residents, local law enforcement, social services and other public agencies together into an effective, problem-solving group. Residents were at the heart of the group, identifying problems that were causing high rates of aggravated assault in the community and working to provide remedies such as positive alternatives for youths, social services and counseling for adults and children. Residents developed a code of conduct for the community, spelling out expectations for the behavior of those who live there (NCPC).

Boston's Neighborhood Justice Network, in partnership with the Council of Elders, the Jewish Memorial Hospital, the Boston Police Department, the Department of Public Health and the Commission on Affairs of the Elderly, created a program to help reduce violence and other crimes against older people. It provides basic personal and home crime prevention education, assistance in dealing with city agencies, training in nonconfrontational tactics to avert street crime and other helpful services that reduce both victimization and fear among the city's older residents (NCPC).

The Fort Meyers (Florida) Police Department has implemented a very successful Weed and Seed program, experiencing a 41 percent increase in drug arrests in 1999 (Winton, 2000, p. 12). The seeding component of the program has also flourished with social service organizations providing residents with specialized programs that reached more than 42,000 families and children in 1999.

Maryland began a "Hot Spots Communities" initiatives in 35 sites statewide. The effort identifies high-crime areas and seeks to systematically help neighborhoods reduce crime. As Wooten and Schulten (2000, p. 7) note: "At the core of the initiative are probation and police teams that follow the Community Probation-Community Police Team (CP-CPT) process." This process, sometimes called Operation Spotlight, develops high-performance teams from agencies that traditionally have never worked closely together. It is based on three premises: (1) the problems of high-risk offenders are too numerous and complex for probation and police officers; (2) well-trained teams are more effective than individuals acting alone; and (3) knowledge is power. One team in South Cumberland reduced its crime rate by 21 percent, compared to the countywide drop in crime of only 4 percent.

Forst (1998, p. 143) describes what she considers the "ultimate community policing project"—police and citizens working together to protect the environment. She suggests police designate a liaison to maintain relations with environmental groups within the community and that they establish an environmental crimes unit. They might also facilitate a clean-up effort. Environmental awareness training might address issues such as pesticides, water quality, air pollution, the ozone layer, global warming and solid waste. Forst (p. 146) notes: "An environmental initiative will require a minimal investment from the police organization but will yield substantial rewards and the less tangible 'better quality of life.' "

These are just a few of a wide range of programs designed by community groups that are changing the quality of life in small towns and large cities, in neighborhoods and housing complexes, in schools and on playgrounds. These groups have proved that there is strength in numbers and that partnerships can provide the community basis for correcting the problems and conditions that can lead to crime. They achieved success because they developed the skills to work together effectively.

◈ CRIME AND DRUGS

The National Drug Control Strategy (1998, p. 36) says: "The correlation between drugs and crime is well established. Drug users are involved in approximately three to five times the number of crimes as arrestees who do not use drugs. Approximately three-fourths of prison inmates and over half of those in jails or on probation are substance abusers, yet only 10 to 20 percent of prison inmates participate in treatment while incarcerated."

This document (p. 17) also notes: "The increase in drug offenders accounts for nearly three-quarters of the growth in the federal prison population between 1985 and 1995 while the number of inmates in state prisons for drug-law violations increased by 478 percent over the same period."

The NCPC (p. 283) states: "Drug use breeds crime. Individuals on drugs often commit violent acts or steal in order to support their habit. Dealers fight territorial wars, for drug markets, that often result in deaths." The council (p. 21) also notes: "Drug abuse is a known factor in many types of crime, including shoplifting, burglary, robbery, squatting in abandoned buildings, assault, child and spouse abuse, suicide and murder."

◈ THE "WAR ON DRUGS"

In 1914 the Harrison Act made buying, selling or using certain drugs illegal. McNamara (2000, p. 8) believes that since then we have had one drug war after another. He says the current war began in 1972 when President Nixon coined the phrase. That year the federal budget for the drug war was roughly $101 million. In 2000 the budget was $17.8 billion. To explain how drastic this increase is, McNamara says: "In 1972, the average monthly Social Security check was $177. If those benefits had increased at the same rate the drug war spending had increased, the average Social Security check today would be $30,444 a month. The average weekly salary of $144 would be $19,000 a week, and if you had a mortgage of $408 a month in 1972 and it had increased at the same rate, your mortgage today would be over $60,000 a month."

Even with all this money, many people believe we are losing the war. Oliver (2000, p. 9), for example, says: "Our nation's premier drug-war strategy of more police, more interdiction, and more incarceration is failing. . . . Our rigid anti-drug strategy and our punitive prohibition efforts are failing."

Another negative aspect of the current war on drugs is noted by Welch et al. (1998), who point out the "volume of evidence documenting that the war on drugs disproportionately affects people of color and the impoverished."

◈ THE NATIONAL DRUG CONTROL STRATEGY (NDCS)

The National Drug Control Strategy (pp. 3–4) suggests that we not use this analogy: "The metaphor of a 'war on drugs' is misleading. Although wars are expected to end, drug control is a continuous challenge. . . . Cancer is a more appropriate metaphor for the nation's drug problem. Dealing with cancer is a long-term proposition. It requires the mobilization of support mechanisms—medical, educational, and societal—to check the spread of the disease and improve the prognosis. The symptoms of the illness must be managed while the root cause is attacked."

The key to reducing drug abuse is prevention coupled with treatment.

Oliver (p. 9) concurs saying: "Former Secretary of State George Schultz said recently that any real and lasting change that occurs in a democratic society is done through education and persuasion and not through coercion and force. Perhaps it's time to heed his sage advice and search for alternative approaches to our current drug-control strategies that will be more effective, fair, and humane in reducing drug usage and drug dependency; that will emphasize treatment, prevention, and education; and that will rely on our social and health systems more than on our criminal justice systems."

This is how the NDCS is approaching the drug problem. The ten-year plan has six sections, the first three of which present background information on the problem and set forth strategic goals and objectives. The fourth section presents a "comprehensive approach" and begins with youth-oriented prevention initiatives. Several such initiatives were the focus of Chapter 14. The next set of initiatives is addressed to reducing drug-related crime and violence.

The first initiative to reduce drug-related crime and violence is community policing.

The NDCS (p. 35) acknowledges: "Our police forces continue to be the first line of defense against criminals. Men and women in uniform exhibit supreme dedication and face risks on a daily basis while confronting violent crime, much of it induced by drugs." The document then suggests: "The more we can link law enforcement with local residents in positive ways that create trusting relationships, the more secure our communities will be. . . . The strength of the COPS program is its emphasis on long-term, innovative approaches to community-based problems. This program reinforces efforts that are already reducing the incidence of drug-related crime in America."

◈ STRATEGIES FOR DEALING WITH THE DRUG PROBLEM

Dealing with the drug problem requires the collaborative efforts of the police, public housing authorities, other agencies and, most important, the residents themselves.

Strategies to deal with the drug problem include improving the physical environment, removing offenders, reducing the demand for drugs, improving intelligence and empowering residents.

Although residents living in private dwellings can do much to reduce or prevent crime, efforts that have the most effect are usually aimed specifically at public housing in inner-city neighborhoods.

Improving the Physical Environment. Improving indoor and exterior lighting has been successfully used in some projects. Clean-up efforts in trash-strewn lots, which provide easy hiding places for drugs, have also been successful. Some housing projects have developed identification cards for their residents so that outsiders can be readily observed. Others have limited access by limiting the number of entrances and exits.

Removing Offenders. Increased efforts at *enforcing laws* against dealing drugs and *increasing prosecution* are also deterrents to drug dealers. Sometimes the housing authority makes an apartment available to the local police department in which to set up an office. This visible police presence can be a strong deterrent. It can also provide residents with a feeling of security as well as concrete evidence that the city is working on the problem.

Some housing agencies, residents and police departments have worked to create drug-free zones (DFZs) similar to those used around schools. Patrol efforts are concentrated in DFZs, and arrests for drug dealing carry increased penalties. Other cities, such as Fort Lauderdale, Tampa and Louisville, have targeted small geographic areas.

Asset seizures of drug dealers are also frequently used by police. Police departments use federal or state forfeiture laws that allow them to seize property and assets of drug dealers, including drugs, cars, boats, airplanes, mobile homes, land and cash—a type of financial death sentence. Asset seizures not only punish the offenders but also send a strong message to the youths of the community who may be quite impressed with the material possessions that drug dealers flaunt. Domash (1997, p. 69) says: "Used correctly, this legal tool can be a potential windfall for law enforcement agencies while knocking the wind out of criminal pursuits."

Police may also use *lease enforcement*. Beginning in April 1989, the Department of Housing and Urban Development (HUD) has required that leases include an explicit provision permitting eviction if any member of a household engages in drug-related criminal activity.

Finally police have found that, simply *making drug dealing inconvenient* may be an effective deterrent. San Diego police, for example, discovered that drug dealers were using public phones on certain street corners. The police worked with the phone company to fix the phones so that they could be used only for outgoing calls, thereby stopping outsiders from calling in orders for drugs.

Reducing the Demand. Another approach to the drug problem is to focus on those who use drugs. Some police departments have used *sting operations* during which undercover police agents sell drugs and then arrest those who buy them. These operations have sometimes been criticized as unethical or even an illegal form of entrapment. Police must exercise extreme care if they use such operations as a strategy to reduce the drug problem.

Educating users may be a more fruitful and perhaps more ethical approach to the drug problem. School programs can help youths resist peer pressure to experiment with drugs. *Providing diversions or alternatives* to finding acceptance or excitement through drug use may also help. Providing community recreational programs, improving ballfields and parks, installing a basketball court or sponsoring athletic contests are all important additions to a community in its fight against drugs.

Providing treatment and rehabilitation for drug users is sometimes also an effective strategy. Often residents are not aware of the existence of such treatment facilities. In many communities, however, such facilities do not exist.

Improving Intelligence. If police can enlist citizens to provide information about drug dealing to the police, much can be accomplished. Most residents in public housing know where drug deals are made. Many also believe, however, that the police either do not care or are actually corrupt because they arrest few dealers. When dealers are arrested, they are often back on the street within hours. Residents should be educated about the difficulties of prosecuting drug dealers and the need for evidence.

Some departments conduct *community surveys* in low-income neighborhoods to learn about how residents view the drug problem. Some departments have established *tip lines* where residents can provide information anonymously.

Improved reporting can be accomplished in a number of ways. Police can also improve the information they receive about problems in other ways. Intelligence can be increased by unusual procedures. Police have been known to interview arrestees to obtain inside information on how certain criminal activities are conducted. In other agencies, arrestees have been interviewed in jail with a jail debriefing form. This kind of information is useful as police continue to document the link between drugs and criminal activity.

Housing personnel are often the closest to drug problems in public housing. These housing personnel can be trained to identify drugs or drug dealing behaviors, and cooperate with police in following up on complaints.

Intelligence information can also be improved by facilitating the communication between narcotics investigators and patrol officers. For example, in Atlanta, a narcotics supervisor recognized that patrol and narcotics had historically used a different radio frequency and were unable to communicate. The problem was quickly corrected.

Empowering Residents. Many police agencies have focused on the broader needs of residents of low-income housing. In Tulsa, for example, officers believed that limited job opportunities were a problem for youths living in public housing. The officers now steer youths into Job Corps, a training and job service program that is an alternative to the traditional high school. Residents can also be empowered in other ways, for example by forming associations or holding rallies.

◈ COLLABORATIVE EFFORTS TO COMBAT THE DRUG PROBLEM

Just as one of the underlying causes of violence in this country is believed to be the ready availability of guns, another cause commonly acknowledged is the ready availability of drugs. Scoville (2000, p. 8) graphically notes: "Stopping the flow of drugs in this country is a lot like having bailing duty on the Titanic." Nonetheless, communities across the country are rallying to stop that flow.

In Minneapolis, Minnesota, police and property owners are using black and gold "No trespassing" signs in inner-city neighborhoods. The signs are part of a new program intended to improve residents' security and deter street-level drug dealing by telling officers that they can enter the properties to question loiterers without a call from the property owner. This expands the power of the police greatly and removes from landlords the sometimes threatening responsibility of signing a citizen's arrest form before the police can act.

Children from an eastside Detroit neighborhood march against crack houses in their neighborhood.

In another area of the city, a group called HOPE (Homes on Portland Enterprise) marched with their children near known crack houses, carrying signs and demanding that the dealers leave the neighborhood. Lacking money and no political clout, these citizens are determined to live in a safe neighborhood.

The city of St. Paul also enlisted the aid of residents to forge an alliance to fight drug dealers. The program, called FORCE (Focusing Our Resources on Community Empowerment), centered on getting longtime residents to permit narcotics officers to use their homes to monitor drug sales in the neighborhood. The FORCE team worked with a network of block club leaders to target drug dealers and to force the removal of, or improvements to, ramshackle drug houses. Ramsey County provided child protection services for youths found in drug houses.

Another grassroots effort has taken place in Price, Utah, a community of 10,000 people. The family services, school district, police and mental health professionals have established a volunteer interagency committee known as SODAA (Stop Our Drug and Alcohol Abuse). This committee coordinates prevention and education programs and strives to eliminate duplication of efforts. The committee developed and promoted a Substance Abuse Awareness Sabbath. They developed a five-page informational fact sheet, which they then distributed to the 44 churches in town. They asked each church to distribute a copy to every adult member and to spend part of their Sabbath on substance abuse awareness. The local newspaper also dedicated an entire page to the campaign, recognizing every church that participated.

Another very successful crime prevention program was developed in Wilson, North Carolina. Their program, "Operation Broken Window," was rooted in the broken window philosophy discussed earlier. The 500 block in Wilson was their "broken window," an open-air drug market widely known as a place where drugs could be easily bought. Undercover police operations had been unsuccessful in reducing the problem. The Wilson Police Department turned to problem-oriented policing as a possible solution. The department formulated a four-pronged attack: undercover operations, increased uniform police presence with more officers and a satellite police station in the target area, two K-9 units assigned to drug interdiction at the local bus station and attention to social and environmental conditions. They identified conditions that facilitated drug sales in the target area; cut grass; removed trash; and installed, repaired or replaced street lights. They inspected buildings for code violations and notified owners to correct the problems. They also boarded up abandoned buildings frequented by drug users. Operation Broken Window was a success. The drug dealers left, and crime rates went down.

In Honolulu a Weed and Seed program has been implemented in which the problem they most wanted to eliminate was drug dealing, which was occurring on the streets in broad daylight. Branson (2000, p. 83) describes how the Housing and Community Development Corporation of Hawaii made available a two-bedroom unit to house a center, a safe haven where sports and recreation equipment, as well as donated computers, were available for people to use under supervision. To assist drug users and pushers arrested in the Weed part of the program, the state encouraged minor offenders to participate in drug treatment while on probation. As part of the seeding, adults tutor children in their homework and school subjects after school. A Head Start Early Childhood Center class also has begun.

In Rialto, California, a successful Operation Clean Sweep was conducted. The department used the SARA model to identify the problem. Their first step was to develop a target list of drug hot spots and dealers. Meetings were held with patrol officers, detectives and Neighborhood Watch groups, which provided valuable, up-to-the-minute insight into activity on the street. Meyers (2000b, p. 23) contends: "The community's involvement via these methods proved critically important. Neighborhood residents often know even more information than the best beat officers do; they can provide important intelligence."

This project used small video cameras to tape record dozens of transactions made by undercover officers in unmarked patrol cars. The drug dealers "sauntered away" after completing their deals, not realizing the drugs they had sold would be taken to the crime lab for evidentiary analysis. The project also involved establishing liaisons with the district attorney and other agencies. Knowing the project would need a multiagency effort to "sweep" those involved in the 89 separate video-taped hand-to-hand narcotics buys, an arrest plan was made including 15 other agencies. For three days these agencies as well as the California Highway Patrol helped serve arrest warrants. According to Meyers (p. 24):

> Operation Clean Sweep resulted in the arrest and prosecution of more than 100 felons. . . . The department recovered significant amounts of drugs, weapons, cash, and stolen property and also discovered a clandestine methamphetamine laboratory. Based on the evidence obtained during the roundup, the department obtained 12 additional search warrants, with the follow-up investigations yielding even more contraband. Several offenders—including a serial rapist who recently had been released from prison—face three-strike enhancements and long prison sentences.

The National Crime Prevention Council provides three additional examples of community efforts to combat the drug problem.

Helping Parents Get Drug Treatment in Ohio. A congregation was the focus of efforts to reach addicted parents and their children. Tutoring for children, courtesy of the local college, courses on black history taught by church members and recreational activities helped raise the spirits and self-esteem of the children. The addicted parents were counseled and supported by church members both during and after treatment. The majority of the parents are now holding steady jobs and reaching out to help others.

Enforcing Local Codes to Reduce Drugs in Oakland, California. Residents allied themselves with police, utility workers, housing and other code inspectors, and sanitation crews to help rid the neighborhood of drug activity. They worked to aggressively enforce a variety of laws and codes against drugs, ranging from noise abatement to building codes to health standards.

Discouraging Drug Dealers in Cleveland, Ohio. A community-based organization helped police remove drug pushers operating on a vacant lot. City officials then pitched in to help the nonprofit group build affordable, owner-occupied homes on the site. Meanwhile, the group used a series of strategies including vigils and rallies to help discourage drug dealers from operating on the neighborhood's main thoroughfare. They also enlisted the support of businesses and residents to tidy up the area and keep it clean.

⬥ COMPREHENSIVE, COORDINATED COMMUNITY APPROACHES

The Des Moines Police Department has a *Community Involvement Handbook*, developed jointly by the police department, the United Way and over 35 neighborhood groups. The handbook serves as a source of information as well as a guide for action. It is intended to help neighborhood groups become active and start making a difference. Called the "municipal approach," the program has four "prongs": community involvement, enforcement, prevention/education and treatment. Portions of the handbook have been translated into Spanish, Vietnamese, Cambodian and Laotian. The handbook covers topics such as when to call the police; improving street lighting and residential security lighting; removing trash and litter; cutting down shrubbery; working with landlords and businesses in the area; boarding up abandoned houses; forming neighborhood associations; conducting neighborhood block walks, rallies and marches; occupying parks and streets; and writing newsletters.

The handbook contains an extensive list of suspicious activity and common indicators of residential drug trafficking that could be of much help to communities seeking to tackle this problem. (See Figure 15.2.) This practical guide might serve as a model for other police departments that wish to involve the community in the fight not only against drugs but also against crime and violence.

Groups that can benefit from a partnership with law enforcement include home/ school organizations such as parent-teacher associations; neighborhood associations;

1. A high volume of foot and/or vehicle traffic to and from a residence at late or unsual hours.

2. Periodic visitors who stay at the residence for very brief periods of time.

3. Alterations of property by the tenants, including the following:

   a. Covering windows and patio doors with materials other than curtains or drapes;

   b. Barricading windows or doors;

   c. Placing dead bolt locks on interior doors; and

   d. Disconnecting fire alams.

4. Consistent payment of rent and security deposits with U.S. currency, especially small denominations of cash. (Large amounts of 20 dollar bills are commonly seized from drug dealers.)

5. The presence of drug paraphernalia in or around the residence, including, but not limited to, glass pipes, syringes, propane torches, paper or tinfoil bundles, folded shiny-slick paper (snow seals), large quantities of plastic baggies, scales, money wrappers and small glass vials.

6. The presence of unusual odors coming from the interior of the residence, especially the odor of pungent chemical substances and/or burning materials.

7. The presence of firearms, other than sporting firearms, including fully automatic weapons, assault weapons, sawed off shotguns, machine pistols, handguns and related ammunition and holsters.

8. The presence of tenant's possessions and furnishings which are inconsistent with the known income level of the tenant. This would include, but is not limited to, the following:

   a. New and/or expensive vehicles;

   b. Expensive jewelry and clothing; and

   c. Expensive household furnishings, stereo systems and other large entertainment systems.

9. Tenants who are overly nervous and apprehensive about the landlord visiting the residence.

Any of the indicators, by itself, may not be reason to suspect drug trafficking. However, when combined with other indicators, they may be reason to suspect drug trafficking. If you suspect drug trafficking in your neighborhood, please contact the police department at 555–5555.

Figure 15.2   Suspicious Activity and Common Indicators of Residential Drug Trafficking

SOURCE: Des Moines Police. *Drugs: A Municipal Approach, A Community Handbook*, p. 26. Reprinted by permission.

tenants' groups; fraternal, social and veterans' groups; community service clubs (such as Lions, Kiwanis, JayCees, Rotary); religiously affiliated groups; and associations of home-owners, merchants or taxpayers.

Schmitt (1995, pp. 52–56) describes the Resident Officer Program of Elgin, Illinois (ROPE). ROPE officers live and work in a specific neighborhood, dealing with problems affecting only their neighborhood and residents. According to Schmitt (p. 56): "The most important thing an officer can do in their neighborhood, however, seems merely to be a reliable presence in the area."

Whiteside (1997, p. 3) suggests an eight-step process for initiating community action to solve problems of crime, disorder and fear of crime: (1) information gathering, (2) community analysis—history, past conflicts, current politics and problems, (3) relevant group identification—police, citizens, elected civic officials, the business community, other agencies, the media, (4) identification of leaders, (5) bring leaders of relevant groups together, (6) identify areas of agreement and disagreement and discuss them, (7) implementation and (8) quality control and continuous development and updating. This requires meaningful feedback from the relevant groups, testing of new ideas, evaluation and individual and group introspection.

The National Crime Prevention Council (*Working as Partners*, 1994, pp. 3–6) recommends the following: acknowledge the reality of fear of crime, agree on a strategy (or strategies) to address the problems, secure broad-based participation, train members of the partnership, secure resources, implement the strategies in a sound environment, evaluate the result and celebrate successes. The National Crime Prevention Council (p. 6) concludes: "Crime prevention that is problem-focused, based in communities and neighborhoods, fueled by the energies of the people who live and work there, helped by outside resources and can be supported by all levels of government is a model that has consistently produced positive results."

The City of Richmond, Texas (Richmond Police Department, p. 4), was awarded the 1998 IACP/ITT Community Policing Award for its projects and initiatives in community policing. They developed 10 geographical beats and assigned an officer to each beat. Each of these officers then recruited 10 block captains, resulting in 100 block captains. They conducted numerous neighborhood meetings and developed action plans resulting in improvement of the quality of life for residents. They also initiated a bicycle patrol, conducted numerous Citizen's Police Academies and developed an Apartment Managers Council to reduce crime in apartment complexes. They formed a "Lunch Bunch" program, where officers eat lunch with area school children, conducted a "Children's Safety Fair" with area businesses and promoted the annual National Night Out. They organized a Thanksgiving Dinner Program for underprivileged families and started a "Santa behind the Badge" program to help underprivileged families have toys for their children at Christmas. They collaborated with federal, state and local law enforcement agencies to investigate, arrest and prosecute drug suspects and with the U.S. Attorney General's Office to implement a Weed and Seed initiative in partnership with the Shalom Zone group. And the list goes on.

As their Web site notes: "The implementation of community policing . . . has transformed our agency from a reactive 'Law and Order' philosophy to a proactive 'Community Policing' philosophy which is inclusive of a traditional policing role, while at the same time expands to bring more focus on collaboration, problem solving and partnership building with various community groups to improve the quality of life for the citizens of Richmond."

Members of the Philadelphia, PA, Anti-Drug Network who live in neighborhoods threatened by the trade in illegal drugs gather and then march through their neighborhoods to let both the drug dealers and the police know of their opposition to the drug trade.

In 1999 the first James Q. Wilson Award for Excellence in Community Policing was presented to the Santa Rosa Police Department (California Attorney General's Office). This award is named in honor of James Q. Wilson, coauthor of the classic "Broken Windows" article, which was instrumental in launching community policing efforts throughout the country. The department engages in problem solving and has formed several committees, including a Downtown Partnership, a multicultural advisory board and a task force comprised of city representatives from various departments to address the concerns and issues of crime-ridden neighborhoods. There is a high level of agency collaboration with other public and private organizations/agencies to address and resolve public safety and disorder issues. Through community policing, this department has built broad-based community support among business owners, community leaders, taxpayers and voters, civic officials, other government agencies, nonprofit groups and average citizens.

Before leaving the subject of community policing, crime and drugs, it is appropriate to revisit a previous discussion of the American Dream.

CRIME, DRUGS AND THE AMERICAN DREAM

Messner and Rosenfeld (2001, p. ix) draw a very distinct correlation between crime and the American Dream: "The American Dream contributes to crime directly by encouraging people to employ illegal means to achieve goals that are culturally approved. It also exerts an indirect effect on crime through its interconnections with the institutional balance of power in society." They suggest that:

> Conservative crime control policies are draped explicitly in the metaphors of war. We have declared war on crime and on drugs, which are presumed to promote crime. Criminals, according to this view, have taken the streets, blocks, and sometimes entire neighborhoods from law-abiding citizens. The function of crime control policy is to recapture the streets from criminals to make them safe for the rest of us (p. 92). . . .
>
> In contrast to conservative crackdowns on criminals, the liberal approach to crime control emphasizes correctional policies and broader social reforms intended to expand opportunities for those "locked out" of the American Dream (p. 96).

The conservative camp traditionally wages war on crime and drugs; the liberal camp wages war on poverty and on inequality of opportunity.

Messner and Rosenfeld (p. 101) suggest that what is needed is crime reduction through social reorganization: "Crime reductions would follow from policies and social changes that vitalize families, schools, and the political system, thereby enhancing the 'drawing power' of the distinctive goals associated with institutions and strengthening their capacity to exercise social control."

This echoes the statements by the National Crime Prevention Council and in the panel papers from the NIJ Research Forum *What Can the Federal Government Do to Decrease Crime and Revitalize Communities?* The NCPC (350 *Tested Strategies*, p. 223) has a large section devoted to economic development because, as they state: "Economic underdevelopment is both a cause and a symptom of crime. Crime is an important factor in businesses' decisions to take flight from the places where it occurs, thereby worsening the economic problems that underlie an area's deterioration." Finally, the panel papers from the NIJ Research forum (1998, p. 14) conclude: "Our real crime reduction and community revitalization challenges involve finding ways to reduce poverty, the number of high-poverty communities, family disintegration, and the number of young people entering criminal careers. . . . Federal agencies with mandates to reduce crime and rebuild communities need to focus more attention on asset building, reshaping school suspension policies, and designing programs and policies to engage fathers as positive economic and social agents in families."

SUMMARY

Synergism occurs when individuals channel their energies toward a common purpose and accomplish together what they could not accomplish alone. It can greatly enhance community policing efforts to prevent/reduce crime and disorder. Crime prevention is a large part, and in fact a cornerstone, of community policing.

Three federal initiatives to assist communities in implementing community policing are the Community Oriented Policing Services (COPS) Office, the Community Policing Consortium and the Weed and Seed program. The Weed and Seed program seeks to identify, arrest and prosecute offenders (weed) while simultaneously working with citizens to improve quality of life (seed).

One frequently used strategy is CPTED—Crime Prevention through Environmental Design. CPTED has three major components: target hardening, changes to the physical environment and community building. Five principles underlying CPTED are territoriality, natural surveillance, access control, activity support and maintenance of the environment. By emphasizing the systematic analysis of crime in a particular location, CPTED directly supports community policing by providing crime prevention strategies tailored to solve specific problems.

The risk factor prevention paradigm seeks to identify key risk factors for offending and then implement prevention methods designed to counteract them. It is useful in identifying strategies that might be effective for a specific community. Strategies to prevent/reduce crime and disorder include beautification projects, business anticrime groups, local government-community crime prevention coalitions, community coalitions, cooperation with grassroots organizations, working with landlords and residents of public housing, using advances in technology and celebrating community successes. The two main messages of anticar theft programs are (1) do not leave the keys in the ignition and (2) lock the car.

The key to reducing drug abuse is prevention coupled with treatment. The first initiative to reduce drug-related crime and violence is community policing. Strategies to deal with the drug problem include improving the physical environment, removing offenders, reducing the demand for drugs, improving intelligence and empowering residents.

Crime, drugs and the American Dream are related, and, in fact, crime and the drug problem may be the result of the American Dream for many people. How to approach crime prevention/reduction is often political. The conservative camp traditionally wages "war" on crime and drugs; the liberal camp wages "war" on poverty and on inequality of opportunity.

DISCUSSION QUESTIONS

1. What examples of synergy have you been a part of or witnessed?

2. What crime prevention programs are in your community? Have you participated in any of them?

3. Which of the programs discussed in this chapter seem most exemplary to you? Why?

4. What steps might be taken to repair a community's "broken windows" and protect against having them broken again?

5. What do you see as the relationship between crime, drugs and the American Dream?

6. Explain how "lease enforcement" reduces criminal activity in public housing.

7. Name and explain the five principles underlying CPTED.

8. Since taxes pay for police to combat crime, why should citizens get involved?

9. To what do you attribute the dramatic decline in crime: community policing, the economy, the dramatic rise in the prison population, the increased number of police officers or some other reason?

10. How has technology helped prevent crime?

INFOTRAC COLLEGE EDITION ASSIGNMENTS

- Use InfoTrac to help answer the discussion questions as appropriate.
- One of the most effective and least expensive security initiatives is to design and build safety from crime and fear of crime into a structure. Research CPTED and discuss how the following can affect crime and/or fear of crime: smell and sound, parking garages, maintenance, color, mix of activities, restrooms, signage, vehicle/pedestrian conflicts, loitering and "hanging out."

COMMUNITY PROJECTS

- Do you have any "broken windows" in your community? If so, how would you characterize them? What might be done to mend them?
- Conduct a survey of a portion of your institution's campus and determine whether any of the CPTED principles might make that portion of campus safer.

REFERENCES

Branson, Helen Kitchen. "Weed and Seed in Honolulu: The Key Is Community Input." *Law and Order,* Vol. 24, No. 12, September 2000, pp. 82–86.

California Attorney General's Office. Statewide Community Oriented Policing Clearing House: Success Models—The James Q. Wilson Award for Excellence in Community Policing. http://caag.state.ca.us/cvpc/Models.html

Domash, Shelly Feuer. "The Assets of Asset Forfeiture." *Police,* Vol. 21, No. 10, October 1997, pp. 69–72.

Farrington, David P. "Explaining and Preventing Crime: The Globalization of Knowledge—The American Society of Criminology 1999 Presidential Address." *Criminology,* Vol. 38, No. 1, February 2000, pp. 1–24.

Federal Bureau of Investigation. *Uniform Crime Reports.* Washington, DC: U.S. Department of Justice, September 1975.

Files, L. Burke. "Crime Fighting by Design." *Police,* Vol. 23, No. 10, October 1999, pp. 52–56.

Fleissner, Dan and Heinzelmann, Fred. *Crime Prevention through Environmental Design and Community Policing.* Washington, DC: National Institute of Justice Research in Action, August 1996.

Forst, Linda. "Protecting Our Environment: The Ultimate Community Policing Project." *Law and Order,* Vol. 46, No. 10, October 1998, pp. 143–146.

Geller, William A. "As a Blade of Grass Cuts through Stone: Helping Rebuild Urban Neighborhoods through Unconventional Police-Community Partnerships." *Crime & Delinquency,* Vol. 44, No. 1, January 1998, pp. 154–177.

"Good News, Bad News: An Update of Landmark 1969 Violence Report." *Law Enforcement News,* Vol. XXVI, Nos. 525, 526, January 15/31 2000, pp. 1,10.

Gorovici, Eli. "10 Recommendations for Responsible Implementation of CCTA in the Fight to Reduce Crime." *Security Technology & Design,* January 2000, pp. 36–40.

McNamara, Joseph D. "The Hidden Cost of the Drug War: Police Integrity Pays the Price." *Law Enforcement News,* Vol. XXVI, Nos. 525, 526, January 15/31, 2000, pp. 8–9.

Messner, Steven F. and Rosenfeld, Richard. *Crime and the American Dream,* 3rd ed. Belmont, CA: Wadsworth Thomson Learning, 2001.

Meyers, Michael. "Creative Use of Technology and Partnerships Shuts Down Drug Dealers." *Community Policing Exchange,* Phase VII, #31, Spring 2000a, p. 3.

Meyers, Michael. "Operation Clean Sweep: Curbing Street-Level Drug Trafficking." *FBI Law Enforcement Bulletin,* Vol. 69, No. 5, May 2000b, pp. 22–24.

The National Drug Control Strategy, 1998. A Ten Year Plan. Washington, DC: Office of National Drug Control Policy, 1998.

Neubauer, Ronald S. "Community Partnership— The Key to Maintaining Safe Communities." *The Police Chief,* Vol. LXVI, No. 5, May 1999, p. 6.

Oliver, Jerry. "The Drug War Is Exacting a Terrible Price." *Law Enforcement News,* Vol. XXVI, No. 541, October 15, 2000, p. 9.

Olson, Steve and Robinson, Pete. "Technology Brings Policing to Higher Level—and Closer to Community Level." *Community Policing Exchange,* Phase VII, #31, Spring 2000, pp. 1–2.

Phillips, Eric. *Crime Prevention through Environmental Design in the Bancroft Neighborhood.* http://freenet.msp.mn.us/org/npcr/reports/npcr1034/npcr1034.html

Richmond Police Dept. Community Policing Award. www.richmondtxpolice.com/award.htm

Schmitt, Sheila. "ROPE: The Resident Officer Program of Elgin." *Law and Order,* Vol. 43, No. 5, May 1995, pp. 52–58.

Scoville, Dean. "The War on Drugs: Where Are We?" *Police,* Vol. 24, No. 12, December 2000, p. 8.

350 Tested Strategies to Prevent Crime: A Resource for Municipal Agencies and Community Groups. Washington, DC: National Crime Prevention Council, 1995.

"Weed and Seed Evaluation." *FBI Law Enforcement Bulletin,* Vol. 68, No. 12, December 1999, p. 7.

Weiss, Jim and Dresser, Mary. "COPS: The Policing Revolution at Work in the Real World." *Police,* Vol. 23, No. 8, August 1999, pp. 26–31.

Welch, Michael; Wolff, Russell; and Bryan, Nicole. "Decontextualizing the War on Drugs: A Content Analysis of NIJ Publications and Their Neglect of Race and Class." *Justice Quarterly,* Vol. 15, No. 4, December 1998, pp. 719–742.

What Can the Federal Government Do to Decrease Crime and Revitalize Communities? Washington, DC: NIJ Research Forum, 1998.

Whisenant, Greg and Panther, Tom. "For All Eyes to See: Community in the Know on Neighborhood Crime." *Community Policing Exchange,* Phase VII, #31, Spring 2000, p. 8.

Whiteside, William B. "Initiating Action." *Community Links,* January 1997, p. 4.

Winton, Kara. "Fort Myers, Florida: A Case Study in Successful Community Policing." *The Law Enforcement Trainer,* Vol. 15, No. 2, March/April 2000, pp. 10–12, 32–33.

Wooten, Harold B. and Schulten, Sue. "Community Teams Take a Case-by-Case Approach." *Community Policing Exchange,* Phase VII, #32, September/October 2000, pp. 1,8.

Working as Partners with Community Groups. Washington, DC: BJA Community Partnerships Bulletin, September 1994.

RESOURCES

Many organizations offer expertise in building partnerships and provide a variety of publications, training and services that can strengthen local efforts. A sampling follows.

Bureau of Justice Assistance Clearinghouse, Box 6000, Rockville, MD 20850; (800) 688-4252.

Center for Community Change, 1000 Wisconsin Ave. NW, Washington, DC 20007; (202) 342-0519.

Citizens Committee for New York City, 305 7th Ave., 15th Floor, New York, NY 10001; (212) 989-0909.

Community Policing Consortium, 1726 M St. NW, Suite 801, Washington, DC 20006; (202) 833-3305 or (800) 833-3085.

National Center for Community Policing, School of Criminal Justice, Michigan State University, East Lansing, MI 48824; (517) 355-2322.

National Crime Prevention Council, 1700 K St. NW, 2nd Floor, Washington, DC 20006-3817; (202) 466-6272.

National Training and Information Center, 810 North Milwaukee Ave., Chicago, IL 60622-4103; (312) 243-3035.

Police Executive Research Forum, 2300 M St. NW, Suite 910, Washington, DC 20006; (202) 466-7820.

CHAPTER 16

What Research Tells Us and a Look to the Future

The best way to predict the future is to create it.
  Peter Drucker

Do you know

What is at the heart of experimental design?

What issues are raised by experiments in criminal justice?

Whether the American Society of Criminology supports experiments in criminal justice?

What assistance is available to departments wishing to conduct experiments?

What percentage of distributed surveys is required to validate an evaluation?

What features characterize the structure of successful community-oriented police departments?

What patterns of community policing exist in the United States?

Whether the citizen complaints generated by community policing and traditional policing differ?

What effect community policing is having on crime statistics?

What other types of statistics might be more helpful?

Whether community policing helps build stronger communities?

Whether the COPS program has been successful?

What strategies research shows do work? Do not work? Hold promise?

What role research should play in community policing?

What four trends may affect implementing community policing?

What two views of the future Bucqueroux provides?

Can you define these terms:

administrative density

coercive isomorphism

experimental design

horizontal differentiation

implant hypothesis

isomorphism

mimetic isomorphism

normative isomorphism

random assignment

refraction

two-wave survey

INTRODUCTION

"By now the term 'community policing' is pretty much old hat. The concept, however, is still going strong and the flow of federal monies continues to feed a flurry of new ideas and programs" (Morrison, 1998). How can departments determine which of these ideas and programs are effective? Why is research important, and what pitfalls might be encountered? What has been learned that will affect community policing efforts in the future?

This chapter begins with a discussion of why research is important, what experimental research involves and some legal and ethical problems to consider. This is followed by an examination of a commonly used "research" tool, the survey. Next a description of what limited research tells us about the structure of successful community-oriented policing departments and what patterns of community policing can be found around the country. Then the chapter discusses crime statistics and what they can and cannot tell us about the success of community policing. After that the question of whether community policing helps build stronger communities is addressed, followed by an evaluation conducted on the COPS Office. Next is a summary of what research has found to work, not to work and to hold promise. The discussion of research concludes with a look at the role of scholarly research in guiding community policing implementation and what other factors might be influential. The discussion then turns to four trends that will affect community policing. It concludes with two possible futures for law enforcement.

◉ THE IMPORTANCE OF RESEARCH

Oakley contends: "Choosing social policy interventions on the basis of well-designed experimental tests is a prerequisite of a democratic and equitable society" (2000, p. 326). Feder et al. (2000, p. 398) concur: "Experiments offer us the most clear and unmistakable evidence on the effectiveness of an intervention."

Experimental Design

At the heart of experimental design *is the* random assignment *of individuals to experimental and control conditions.*

Boruch et al. (2000, p. 351) define random assignment as "dependence on a random number table or machine-generated random number that indicates the particular treatment group to which an individual or entity will be assigned." Whether a person is a member of the treatment group or the control (no treatment) group is purely a matter of chance. Boruch et al. (p. 339) note that in an experiment assessing the effectiveness of arrest on domestic violence, it is possible that the majority of people assigned to the arrest group could be primarily African American and the nonarrest group primarily Caucasians, which is "likely to offend political as well as ethical sensibilities." To eliminate this problem, the randomization might be within blocks, that is a pair consisting of one African American and one Caucasian: "Within pairs, an individual is selected with a .5 chance to be put into the treatment group; the second becomes a member of the control group."

Although support for experiments is strong, Cordray (2000, p. 401) cautions: "Randomized field experiments can provide trustworthy evidence about the effects of interventions. But investigators have limited control over important features of the field experiment (e.g., program implementation, receipt of intended and unintended services, retention of participants in the study). Unchecked, these factors can limit the technical adequacy and utility of the study."

Experiments in criminal justice are not without critics. Feder et al. (p. 398) suggest: "Randomized experiments engender suspicion, making it difficult for the researcher to conduct the research." In addition, experiments in criminal justice have raised important issues.

Experiments in criminal justice raise ethical issues as well as privacy issues.

The ethical issue centers around denying those in the control group "treatment." This was tested in 1997 when the American Society of Criminology (ASC) executive board was convinced to take a stand on the desirability and ethicality of randomized experiments in evaluation research. As Short, Jr. et al. (2000, p. 296) explain, the ASC received a letter from Professor Feder of Florida Atlantic University for a friend-of-the-court brief in support of her NIJ-funded evaluation of a court-mandated counseling program for domestic offenders in Broward County. Her experiment called for a randomly assigned group of men in an experimental group to be placed on one-year probation and participation in a 26-week batterer counseling program and a control group of men who received only the one-year probation. The Broward County prosecutor's office sought an injunction against Dr. Feder's experiment on legal and ethical grounds: "(a) judicial misuse of discretion (a legal issue) and (b) that it was unethical to deny treatment based on chance (random assignment)."

The ASC conducted an e-mail poll, which resulted in "virtually unanimous" support for Dr. Feder's request.

The ASC concluded: "The principle is that random assignment to treatment options is the best scientific method for determining the effectiveness of options." (Short, Jr. et al., p. 296).

Support for experimental research is also attested to by the formation of the Academy of Experimental Criminology (AEC) in 2000, with Lawrence Sherman as its first president (Feder and Boruch, 2000, p. 291). Feder and Boruch (p. 292) state: "There is little disagreement that experiments provide a superior method for assessing the effectiveness of a given intervention. However, although the number of experiments in criminal justice has grown in recent years, experiments continue to be underutilized."

Dunford (2000, p. 433) suggests: "Because of the difficulties associated with employing experimental group–control group research designs, researchers continue to conduct nonexperimental evaluations of interventions of all kinds, producing findings that are impossible to accurately interpret." He also cautions: "The results are quite likely to lead to mistaken conclusions—conclusions that may have serious consequences."

Assistance in experiments in criminal justice is available through the NIJ's Locally Initiated Research Partnerships in Policing.

In this initiative, partners share responsibility throughout the entire project, jointly selecting an area of interest to the department (locally initiated) and collaborating on the

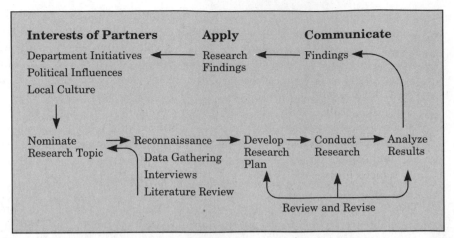

Figure 16.1   The Action Research Model

SOURCE: Tom McEwen. "NIJ's Locally Initiated Research Partnerships in Policing: Factors that Add up to Success." *National Institute of Justice Journal*, Issue 238, January 1999, p. 7.

research design, implementation and interpretation of findings. Started in 1995, the NIJ partnership program currently has 41 projects. Usually the partnerships involve a local police department or other law enforcement agency and a local university. Often graduate students are used and can receive credit for research projects. McEwen (1999, p. 2) notes: "The new approach complements the basic premise of community policing: working as partners achieves more than working alone."

At the heart of the partnerships is the Action Research Model, illustrated in Figure 16.1. The cyclical, multistep process starts with nomination of a research topic, continues with development and implementation of the research design and ends with communicating and applying the findings.

Surveys

One commonly used method to evaluate the effectiveness of a strategy is the survey—either in person, mailed or phoned. Sometimes a **two-wave survey** is used, the first wave consisting of a pretest before a strategy is implemented and the second wave a posttest after the strategy has been implemented for a given amount of time.

Other times surveys are used to determine what citizens feel a neighborhood's main problems are or how effective residents feel the police in their neighborhood are.

To validate an evaluation conducted by survey, 60 percent of distributed surveys must be returned.

Travis III et al. (2000) conducted research on the impact of citizen surveys by police on public attitudes. Their results indicate that such surveys may lead to lower ratings of citizen satisfaction with the police. They (p. 100) suggest two possible reasons for this result. First, citizens may be generally uncomfortable in the presence of the police and be suspicious of an unsolicited police contact. Another possibility is that they may question the professionalism of the police, that is, think the police aren't sure of what they are doing. It might be comparable to going to a physician and having the physician ask, "What's wrong with you and what should I do to help?"

Travis III et al. suggest that this negativism might be alleviated by phoning those to be surveyed in advance to alert them of the upcoming interview and telling them of the purpose. They (p. 101) also suggest: "A wiser strategy might be to use less intrusive techniques such as mailed or telephone surveys." They conclude: "Although there is some commentary that door-to-door surveys of citizens by the police can improve police-citizen relations, it now appears that such surveys are at least equally likely to damage those relations."

Departments wishing to use surveys might benefit from the Bureau of Justice Assistance's free report, "A Police Guide to Surveying Citizens."

◆ RESEARCH FINDINGS ON COMMUNITY POLICING DEPARTMENTS

Recent research has shed light on the structure of successful community-oriented police departments, on patterns of community policing currently found in the United States and on the difference in citizen complaints between community policing departments and traditional police departments.

The Structure of Successful Community Policing Departments

Anthony (2000) reports on research comparing the structural dimensions of community-oriented police departments to traditional departments. The research suggests that community-oriented police departments exhibit **isomorphism,** that is, they have similar structural characteristics.

Community-oriented police departments differ in structure from traditional police departments in that their organization is less complex, their decision making less centralized and their administration less dense.

A sample of 20 community-oriented police departments was compared to a control group of 10 traditional police departments. Data obtained from the 28 surveys returned showed that community-oriented police departments had less complex organizations based on three variables: (1) commissioned specialization is lower, (2) civilian specialization is lower and (3) horizontal differentiation is lower. **Horizontal differentiation** refers to the degree to which an organization's tasks are broken into functionally distinct units. In short, community-oriented police departments have reduced the level of hierarchy.

Community-oriented police departments are also less centralized based on six variables: (1) lower vertical differentiation (decentralized decision making), (2) reduced span of control of the chief executive, (3) reduced span of control of the patrol first-line supervisors, (4) lower commissioned supervisor to patrol officer ratio, (5) participation of first-level police officers in developing the strategic plan and (6) participation of first-level police officers on committees.

The third major difference in structure is in **administrative density,** that is, the ratio of all employees to supervisory personnel. Community-oriented police departments have increased the ratio of employees to supervisors.

Patterns of Community Policing in the United States

Maguire and Mastrofski (2000, p. 4) explore the dimensionality of the community policing movement using four national data sets collected between 1993 and 1997. They first review the literature on this area, summarizing the key dimensions of community policing identified by various researchers. For example, Skolnick and Bayley (1988) identified four dimensions: community-based crime prevention, reorientation of patrol activities, increased police accountability and decentralization of command. Bayley (1994) identified four dimensions: consultation, adaptation, mobilization and problem solving. Bratton (1996) identified the three p's: partnership, problem solving and prevention. Rohe et al. (1996) also identified three dimensions: shared responsibility, prevention and increased officer discretion. Roth and Johnson (1997) identified four dimensions: problem solving, community partnership building, preventive interventions and organizational change. Finally, Cordner (1997) identified four dimensions: philosophical, strategic, tactical and organizational.

Common patterns found in community policing in the United States include crime prevention, problem solving, partnerships, shared responsibility and decentralization.

Maguire and Mastrofski, like Anthony, also found isomorphism occurring across the country, that is, departments tending to become similar in structure. They (pp. 10–11) identify three types of isomorphism: mimetic, coercive and normative. **Mimetic isomorphism** occurs when an organization copies or imitates another. **Coercive isomorphism** occurs when organizations adopt something due to pressure either from the state or other organizations, with probably the greatest source of coercive isomorphism being the U.S. Justice Department, which controls billions of dollars in funding. **Normative isomorphism** results from professionalism, with influences coming from such organizations as the Police Executive Research Forum and the IACP.

In addition to isomorphism, however, Maguire and Mastrofski (p. 9) also found **refraction,** which they explain: "is the term used to describe how light rays and energy waves are deflected from their straight paths when they pass from one medium to another (such as through a prism). The variety of forms of community policing found throughout the country are the result of the United States having more autonomous police agencies than any other country in the world." They (p. 11) contend: "With thousands of police executives throughout the United States making very different and often conflicting decisions, the net effect will be a refractive community policing movement."

In short, refraction results in fragmented implementation nationwide while isomorphism results in a one-size-fits-all approach to community policing. Maguire and Mastrofsi (p. 15) suggest:

> The early stages of a reform movement like community policing might be characterized as refractive, with local agencies adopting its various aspects or portions as dictated by local contingencies. Later, as the movement becomes more

institutionalized, the diffusion process might be characterized as isomorphic, with agencies jumping on the bandwagon based on institutional concerns for legitimacy rather than other, more technical concerns.

Citizen Complaints

Hickman et al. (2000) investigated whether community policing generates greater numbers and different types of citizen complaints than traditional policing. They followed graduates of a 1995 Philadelphia Police Academy class, the first to produce officers hired and trained under the Community-Oriented Policing Services Accelerated Hiring, Education, and Deployment (COPS AHEAD) program. After 3.5 years, they obtained the official complaint records from the Philadelphia Police Department for officers in the experimental and the control group. Their results failed to support the hypothesis that community policing would result in a higher number of complaints.

Community policing and traditional policing officers generated a similar proportion of complaints, similar types of complaints and a similar number of complaints.

Their research raised an interesting question—what does the record on zero tolerance show? Commissioner William Bratton attributes the decrease in crime in New York City to the adoption of zero tolerance (for disorder and criminal activity) and the use of the COMPSTAT program. However, many scholars argue that although zero tolerance may satisfy short-term interest in law and order, this approach may return the police and the community to a relationship of conflict.

COMMUNITY POLICING AND CRIME STATISTICS

The effectiveness of community policing is often measured using crime rates for a given jurisdiction. Dropping crime rates would indicate success. As discussed earlier, many attribute our nationally decreasing crime rate to the implementation of community policing throughout the country. Others, however, suggest that is just one factor. Other factors include the robust economy, a graying population and fewer teenagers. Rogers (1998, p. 43) suggests: "There is a direct correlation between the number of officers on the street and the decline in crime." The COPS office has added thousands of officers, but whether these officers are implementing community policing strategies is not as clear.

Morrison questions using local crime statistics to support community policing efforts, asking whether community policing might simply be displacing crime. This might be used to advantage, identifying hot spots, implementing a potentially effective community policing strategy and seeing whether the hot spot moves.

McDevitt and Cardarelli (1999, p. 1) state: "Far too many law enforcement agencies rely on traditional indicators generated solely within the agency—the number of arrests, changes in numbers of calls for service, the number of incident reports filed—as the only measures for gauging effectiveness.

Crime statistics are seldom sufficient to understand the extent and character of a particular strategy's impact. Most research on community policing strategies shows only modest and statistically insignificant effects on crime rates, drug abuse and trafficking and fear of crime.

McDevitt and Cardarelli contend that if departments want more effective approaches to evaluating community policing efforts, they must incorporate community-wide information in the process. It is especially important to use data collected and maintained by public and private agencies other than law enforcement agencies.

To evaluate the effectiveness of specific community policing strategies, police departments should consider data from the health care system (especially emergency rooms), schools, housing and licensing departments and community surveys.

To evaluate the effectiveness of family violence prevention programs, the number of abused women referred by medical personnel to shelters may be a more reliable indicator of program success or lack thereof than the number of domestic violence arrests. Strategies aimed at youths might use data on truancy, suspensions and expulsions as one means of measuring effectiveness.

Several researchers have suggested that law enforcement not concentrate on crime statistics but rather focus on whether community policing efforts are able to build stronger communities—a major goal of the philosophy.

◈ COMMUNITY POLICING AND STRONG COMMUNITIES

Kerley and Benson (2000) conducted such a study using data from a comprehensive community policing study conducted in Oakland, California, and Birmingham, Alabama, from 1987 to 1989.

Research findings (p. 46) indicate that community policing strategies do not have strong effects on community processes.

Kerley and Benson (p. 64) discuss the **implant hypothesis,** which asks whether collective citizen action by a small group of neighborhood residents, for example, Neighborhood Watch groups, can make a difference in the attitudes and behaviors of local residents. They suggest that the implant hypotheses might be proven true if community policing efforts meet two criteria: (1) stimulation of community processes be made the main goal and outcome measure of community policing programs and (2) police seek to more actively involve community residents in the strategies. They reason that crime rates and fear should be secondary goals and outcome measures:

> The reasoning for this is straightforward. If stimulation of community processes is the intervening variable between community policing programs and reductions in crime rates and fear, it would follow that it should be the primary goal and outcome measure of community policing programs. Unfortunately, given the current state of crime-centered politics and evaluation, this has not been the case.

Such a shift in focus might also be considered when evaluating the success of the COPS program.

◈ EVALUATION OF THE COPS OFFICE

Cameron (2000, p. 54) calls the COPS program a "political football" and notes: "Research shows promoted figures are fabrications." He cites statements by Senator Biden such as: "The COPS program has delivered on its goal of 100,000 new police officers under budget and ahead of schedule." This was not borne out by an independent study of the program's first four years.

The Urban Institute, a Washington, DC-based policy research group, undertook a study reported in *The COPS Program after 4 Years—National Evaluation*. Article titles suggest that the evaluation is primarily positive: "Urban Institute Declares COPS Program a Partial Success" (2000, p. 3) and "COPS Program Evaluation Shows Promising Results" (2000, p. 1).

The COPS Program has been a partial success, increasing policing levels due to COPS grants to between 69,000 and 84,600, well short of the 100,000 target. COPS funding has gone to the high-crime areas that need it most and, overall, has "energized" the national community policing effort.

It is difficult to estimate the actual additional number of officers on the street because some leave while others are added, comparable to an open house event. The number of people at the open house at any one time will be significantly fewer than the total number of people coming through. The researchers found that the COPS program "provided fuel, but not the launch pad, for the nationwide proliferation of community policing tactics between 1995 and 1998" ("Urban Institute Declares . . . ," p. 3).

The report notes a high participation level by high-crime jurisdictions, with 50 percent of all COPS awards going to 10 percent of police agencies with the highest number of murders in the years studied ("Urban Institute Evaluation . . . ," 2000, pp. 9–10).

◈ WHAT WORKS, WHAT DOESN'T AND WHAT'S PROMISING

Sherman et al. (1998) reviewed more than 500 prevention program evaluations meeting minimum scientific standards and conclude that there is minimally adequate evidence to establish a provisional list of what works, what doesn't and what's promising as of late 1996.

What Works

Sherman (1999, p. 143) summarizes the key findings on what works.

What works: increased directed patrols in street-corner hot spots of crime, proactive arrests of serious repeat offenders, proactive drunk driving arrests and arrests of employed suspects for domestic assault.

Sherman et al. list other strategies that work:

• For infants: Frequent home visits by nurses and other professionals.
• For preschoolers: Classes with weekly home visits by preschool teachers.

- For delinquent and at-risk preadolescents: Family therapy and parent training.
- For schools:
  - Organizational development for innovation.
  - Communication and reinforcement of clear, consistent norms.
  - Teaching of social competency skills.
  - Coaching of high-risk youth in "thinking skills."

- For older male ex-offenders: Vocational training.
- For rental housing with drug dealing: Nuisance abatement action on landlords.
- For high-risk repeat offenders: Monitoring by specialized police units or incarceration.
- For convicted offenders: Rehabilitation programs with risk-focused treatments.
- For drug-using offenders in prison: Therapeutic community treatment programs.

The Urban Institute's evaluation of the COPS program also found some statistically significant effective strategies among grant awardees.

What also works: joint crime prevention projects with local businesses, citizen surveys to obtain information about residents' views on crime problems, incorporating probation officers into problem-solving policing initiatives, late-night recreation programs to give youths an alternative to gangs and criminal activities, new rules designed to increase officers' time on the beat and give them more discretion and employee evaluation measures to give credit for community policing work by officers.

What Doesn't Work

According to Sherman's summary of key findings, several strategies, some very popular, do not work.

What doesn't work: neighborhood block watch, arrests of some juveniles for minor offenses, arrests of unemployed suspects for domestic assault, drug market arrests and community policing with no clear crime-risk factor focus.

The list of what doesn't work is extensive: gun "buyback programs, community mobilization against crime in high-crime poverty areas, police counseling visits to homes of couples days after domestic violence incidents, counseling and peer counseling of students in schools, Drug Abuse Resistance Education (D.A.R.E.), drug prevention classes focused on fear and other emotional appeals (including self-esteem), summer jobs or subsidized work programs for at-risk youths, short-term nonresidential training programs for at-risk youths, diversion from court to job training as a condition of case dismissal, increased arrests or raids on drug market locations, storefront police offices, police newsletters with local crime information, correctional boot camps using traditional military basic training and "Scared Straight" programs whereby minor juvenile offenders visit adult prisons. Also found to be ineffective were shock probation, shock parole and split sentences adding jail time to probation or parole; home detention with electronic monitoring; intensive supervision on parole or probation; rehabilitation programs using vague, unstructured counseling; and residential programs for juvenile offenders using challenging experiences in rural settings.

What's Promising

Sherman's summary of what is promising includes seven strategies.

What's promising: police traffic enforcement patrols against illegally carried handguns, community policing with community participation in priority setting, community policing focused on improving police legitimacy, zero tolerance of disorder (if legitimacy issues can be addressed), problem-oriented policing generally, adding extra police to cities (regardless of assignments) and warrants for arrest of suspect except when police respond to domestic violence.

Again, Sherman et al.'s research revealed an extensive list of promising practices including proactive drunk driving arrests with breath testing (may reduce accident deaths), community policing with meetings to set priorities (may reduce perceptions of crime), police showing greater respect to arrested offenders (may reduce repeat offending), polite field interrogations of suspicious persons (may reduce street crime) and higher number of police officers in cities (may reduce crime generally).

Also seen as promising were gang monitoring by community workers and probation and police officers, community-based mentoring by Big Brothers/Big Sisters of America (may prevent drug abuse), community-based aftershool recreation programs (may reduce local juvenile crime) and battered women's shelters (may help some women reduce repeated domestic violence).

Other promising strategies were "schools within schools" that group students into smaller units (may prevent crime), training or coaching in "thinking" skills for high-risk youths (may prevent crime), building school capacity through organizational development (may prevent substance abuse), improved classroom management and instructional techniques (may reduce alcohol use), Job Corps residential training programs for at-risk youths (may reduce felonies) and prison-based vocational education programs for adult inmates (in federal prisons).

Still other promising strategies cited include moving urban public housing residents to suburban homes (may reduce risk factors for crime), enterprise zones (may reduce area unemployment, a risk factor for crime), two clerks in already-robbed convenience stores, redesigned layout of retail stores (may reduce shoplifting), improved training and management of bar and tavern staff (may reduce violence, DUI), metal detectors (may reduce skyjacking, weapon carrying in school), street closures, barricades and rerouting (may reduce violence, burglary) and "target hardening" (may reduce vandalism of parking meters and crime involving phones).

The last six promising strategies are "problem-solving" analysis unique to the crime situation at each location, proactive arrests for carrying concealed weapons (may reduce gun crime), drug courts (may reduce repeat offending), drug treatment in jails followed by urine testing in the community, intensive supervision and aftercare of juvenile offenders (both minor and serious) and fines for criminal acts.

Sherman (p. 143) suggests areas in which research is lacking: "Gang prevention, for example, is a matter about which we could not find a single impact evaluation of police practices. Police curfews and truancy programs lack rigorous tests. Police recreation activities with juveniles, such as Police Athletic Leagues, also remain unevaluated."

As departments and those interested in community policing consider specific strategies, they should take heed of what Laycock (2000, p. 3) stresses: "You need to know

© 1992 Star Tribune, Minneapolis/St. Paul, Bruce Bisping

In many jurisdictions bike patrols are being used extensively. A bicycle unit provides high visibility, accessibility and increased mobility. The effectiveness of bicycle patrol as compared to foot and vehicle patrol should be rigorously evaluated.

what works where and why. This question is central to the present agenda. In my view, nothing works everywhere, but something will work in every jurisdiction. That is why the where and why are important. You need to know the principles that determine what works and that will enable you to replicate successful initiatives in your own jurisdiction."

A LOOK TOWARD THE FUTURE

Despite the call for more experiments and research in criminal justice, Bayley (1998, p. 5) says: "Unhappily for my scholarly self-esteem, I am beginning to suspect that the future of American policing will not be shaped by research or strategic planning. The role, function, and strategies of police are more likely to reflect the impact of forces that are unseen by either scholars or police practitioners." Bayley believes the future of American policing will be shaped "most profoundly" by four factors.

The future of American policing may be shaped by privatization; restructuring of government; group violence stemming from the inequities of race, class and ethnicity; and growth in the destructiveness of criminal violence, especially with regard to terrorism and organized crime.

The third trend is part of the two views of the future of community policing presented by Bucqueroux (2000, pp. 1, 3–4, 9). She suggests that in the future, in a perfect world, community policing would be the cornerstone for a new community criminal justice system, part of the "new paradigm" of community-oriented government: "It didn't take long for average citizens to see that 'locking up the bad guys' was not always the best answer. Politicians who once ran on 'three strikes and you'ie out' now embrace collaborative, community-based solutions."

However, many departments have accepted the rhetoric of community policing, but not the philosophy itself. And then Ecstasy hit hard among middle-class youths and affluent, suburban parents demanded that the police do something other than locking up their children. Some chiefs even blamed community policing for being too soft on crime. The police response in affluent neighborhoods was different from what they employed in urban hot spots: sweeps, crackdowns, battering rams and overhead helicopters. The new surge of arrests led to another massive overcrowding of prisons.

African American activists, long angry that penalties for crack cocaine (for which blacks were more likely to be arrested) were much harsher than those for the powdered form of cocaine preferred by the white middle class, became even angrier as they saw the disparity in the way Ecstasy users in urban and suburban neighborhoods were treated. Rumors began to fly about an impending race war, surging through the Internet around the country. Many of the "new breed" of officers left the department as departments reverted to the military mode to be ready for any uprisings. Bucqueroux (p. 4) says: "Two-track policing—different for rich and poor, urban and suburban, white and everyone else—became an increasingly stark reality."

Bucqueroux envisions two possible futures for law enforcement: one where the community policing philosophy pervades the criminal justice system or one where two-track policing exists.

She (pp. 4, 9) urges: "The choice between these two futures is rapidly upon us. As new problems emerge, a series of small and large decisions will make the difference between a future where police embrace an inclusive and collaborative model or succumb to the illusory promise of solving crime and disorder problems through aggressive military-style repression." She concludes:

> The future we will inherit should not be decided by a coin flip between these two simplistic visions. Real solutions demand real changes. Those who know the checklist of changes that community policing demands must not only tell the community what it takes for meaningful reform, but they must find the courage to challenge the prevailing wisdom inside and outside the department when it is clear that the emperor is naked. The choice of whether or not community policing will be allowed to fulfill its potential will dictate the future, and the choice is ours to make.

SUMMARY

At the heart of experimental design is the random assignment of individuals to experimental and control conditions. Experiments in criminal justice raise ethical issues as well as privacy issues. The ASC concluded: "The principle is that random assignment to treatment options is the best scientific method for determining the effectiveness of options." Assistance in experiments in criminal justice is available through the NIJ's Locally Initiated Research Partnerships in Policing. Surveys are commonly used by police departments. To validate an evaluation conducted by survey, 60 percent of distributed surveys must be returned.

Research has found that community-oriented police departments differ in structure from traditional police departments in that their organization is less complex, their decision making less centralized and their administration less dense. Common patterns found in community policing in the United States include crime prevention, problem solving, partnerships, shared responsibility and decentralization. It has also been found that community policing and traditional policing officers generated a similar proportion of complaints, similar types of complaints and a similar number of complaints.

Crime statistics are seldom sufficient to understand the extent and character of a particular strategy's impact. Most research on community policing strategies shows only modest and statistically insignificant effects on crime rates, drug abuse and trafficking and fear of crime. Research findings indicate that community policing strategies do not have strong effects on community processes.

The COPS program has been a partial success, increasing policing levels due to COPS grants to between 69,000 and 84,600, well short of the 100,000 target. COPS funding has gone to the high-crime areas that need it most and, overall, has "energized" the national community policing effort.

A study of over 500 research efforts identified what works, doesn't work and holds promise. What works: increased directed patrols in street-corner hot spots of crime, proactive arrests of serious repeat offenders, proactive drunk driving arrests and arrests of employed suspects for domestic assault. What also works: joint crime prevention projects with local businesses, citizen surveys to obtain information about residents' views on crime problems, incorporating probation officers into problem-solving policing initiatives, late-night recreation programs to give youths an alternative to gangs and criminal activities, new rules designed to increase officers' time on the beat and give them more discretion and employee evaluation measures to give credit for community policing work by officers.

What doesn't work: neighborhood block watch, arrests of some juveniles for minor offenses, arrests of unemployed suspects for domestic assault, drug market arrests and community policing with no clear crime-risk factor focus.

What's promising: police traffic enforcement patrols against illegally carried handguns, community policing with community participation in priority setting, community policing focused on improving police legitimacy, zero tolerance of disorder (if legitimacy issues can be addressed), problem-oriented policing generally, adding extra police to cities (regardless of assignments) and warrants for arrest of suspect except when police respond to domestic violence.

The future of American policing may be shaped by privatization; restructuring of government; group violence stemming from the inequities of race, class and ethnicity; and growth in the destructiveness of criminal violence, especially with regard to terrorism and organized crime.

Bucqueroux envisions two possible futures for law enforcement: one where the community policing philosophy pervades the criminal justice system or one where two-track policing exists.

DISCUSSION QUESTIONS

1. What future predictions does Bucqueroux make for community policing?
2. What percentage of returned surveys is required for validation and why?
3. Researchers have identified many strategies that work to decrease crime. Name and discuss three of these strategies.
4. What is the implant hypothesis? Describe it in detail.
5. Why do crime and arrest statistics fall short of explaining the success or failure of a particular strategy? What other kinds of data should also be looked at?
6. Discuss the importance of research in criminal justice.
7. Some police agencies conduct citizen surveys to gauge public attitudes toward the police. Discuss the impact different methods of conducting surveys can have on the results.
8. How does the availability of funding affect patterns of community policing within police departments?
9. What organizational and structural differences exist between traditional police departments and those that are engaged in community policing?
10. What is a two-wave survey, and when might it be appropriate to use it?

INFOTRAC COLLEGE EDITION ASSIGNMENTS

- Use InfoTrac to help answer the discussion questions as appropriate.
- Crime researchers in Canada have formed the Network for Research on Crime and Justice, which allows researchers to network and share knowledge, avoid duplication of effort and build on existing findings. Their *Research in Brief* page on their Web site includes results from the U.S. Department of Justice research on the continued decline of serious crime levels in 1999. Discuss the measures used in this research and the sources of the data. Also explain what *NCVS* and *UCR* mean.

COMMUNITY PROJECT

Design and conduct a survey (campus, neighborhood or law enforcement agency). Surveys can be conducted on a wide range of topics, including fear of crime, crime reporting, police attitudes, community attitudes, victimization surveys and so on. Some ready-made surveys may be available from the Office of Community Oriented Policing Services and other community policing or crime prevention Web sites.

REFERENCES

Anthony, Stavros S. "The Structure of Successful Community-Oriented Police Departments." *The Police Chief,* Vol. LXVII, No. 11, November 2000, pp. 69–73.

Bayley, David H. *Police for the Future.* New York: Oxford, 1994.

Bayley, David H. *Policing in America: Assessment and Prospects. Ideas in American Policing,* Washington, DC: The Police Foundation, February 1998.

Boruch, Robert F.; Victor, Timothy; and Cecil, Joe S. "Resolving Ethical and Legal Problems in Randomized Experiments." *Crime & Delinquency,* Vol. 46, No. 3, July 2000, pp. 330–353.

Bratton, W. J. "New Strategies for Combating Crime in New York." *Fordham Urban Law Journal,* Spring 1996, pp. 23, 781–795.

Bucqueroux, Bonnie. "Two Views of the Future of Community Policing." *Subject to Debate,* Vol. 14, No. 9, 2000, pp. 3–4, 9.

Cameron, Bruce. "COPS: A Political Football." *Law and Order,* Vol. 48, No. 10, October 2000, pp. 54–55.

The COPS Program after 4 Years—National Evaluation. www.urban.org

"COPS Program Evaluation Shows Promising Results." *NCJA Justice Bulletin,* Vol. 20, No. 9, September 2000, pp. 1, 8.

Cordner, G. W. "Community Policing: Elements and Effects." In *Critical Issues in Policing: Contemporary Readings,* 3rd ed. edited by R. G. Dunham and G. P. Alpert. pp. 451–468. Prospect Heights, IL: Waveland, 1997.

Cordray, David S. "Enhancing the Scope of Experimental Inquiry in Intervention Studies." *Crime & Delinquency,* Vol. 46, No. 3, July 2000, pp. 401–424.

Dunford, Franklyn W. "Determining Program Success: The Importance of Employing Experimental Research Designs." *Crime & Delinquency,* Vol. 46, No. 3, July 2000, pp. 425–434.

Feder, Lynette and Boruch, Robert F. "The Need for Experiments in Criminal Justice Settings." *Crime & Delinquency,* Vol. 46, No. 3, July 2000, pp. 291–294.

Feder, Lynette; Jolin, Annette; and Feyerherm, William. "Lessons from Two Randomized Experiments in Criminal Justice Settings." *Crime & Delinquency,* Vol. 46, No. 3, July 2000, pp. 380–400.

Hickman, Matthew J.; Piquero, Alex R.; and Greene, Jack R. "Does Community Policing Generate Greater Numbers and Different Types of Citizen Complaints than Traditional Policing?" *Police Quarterly,* Vol. 3, No. 1, March 2000, pp. 70–84.

Kerley, Kent R. and Benson, Michael L. "Does Community-Oriented Policing Help Build Stronger Communities?" *Police Quarterly,* Vol. 3, No. 1, March 2000, pp. 46–69.

Laycock, Gloria. "Becoming More Assertive about Good Research." *Subject to Debate,* Vol. 14, No. 7, July 2000, pp. 1, 3–4.

Maguire, Edward R. and Mastrofski, Stephen D. "Patterns of Community Policing in the United States." *Police Quarterly,* Vol. 3, No. 1, March 2000, pp. 4–45.

McDevitt, Jack and Cardarelli, Albert P. *Community Policing Exchange.* Phase VII, #29, November/December 1999, pp. 1–2.

McEwen, Tom. "NIJ Locally Initiated Research Partnerships in Policing." *National Institute of Justice Journal,* Issue 238, January 1999, pp. 2–10.

Morrison, Richard D. "Measuring Performance: What Effect Is Community Policing Having on Crime Statistics?" *Law Enforcement Technology,* Vol. 10, No. 10, October 1998, pp. 26–28.

Oakley, Ann. "A Historical Perspective on the Use of Randomized Trials in Social Science Settings." *Crime & Delinquency,* Vol. 46, No. 3, July 2000, pp. 315–329.

"A Police Guide to Surveying Citizens." Bureau of Justice Assistance. www.ncjrs.org

Rogers, Donna. "Community Policing and the Crime Rate." *Law Enforcement Technology,* Vol. 25, No. 10, October 1998, pp. 42–44.

Rohe, W. M.; Adams, R. E.; Arcury, T. A.; Memory, J.; and Klopovic, J. *Community Oriented Policing: The North Carolina Experience.* Chapel Hill, NC: The Center for Urban and Regional Studies, 1996.

Roth, J. A. and Johnson, C. C. *COPS Context and Community Policing.* Presentation at the American Society of Criminology, San Diego, CA, November 1997.

Sherman, Lawrence W. "Policing for Crime Prevention." In *Criminal Justice: Concepts and Issues: An Anthology,* 3rd ed. edited by Chris W. Eskridge. pp. 131–148. Los Angeles: Roxbury Publishing Company, 1999.

Sherman, Lawrence W.; Gottfredson, Denise C.; MacKenzie, Doris L.; Eck, John; Reuter, Peter; and Bushway, Shawn D. *Preventing Crime: What Works, What Doesn't, What's Promising.* National Institute of Justice Research in Brief, July 1998.

Short, James F., Jr.; Zahn, Margaret A.; and Farrington, David P. "Experimental Research in Criminal Justice Settings: Is there a Role for Scholarly Societies?" *Crime &*

Delinquency, Vol. 46, No. 3, July 2000, pp. 295–298.

Skolnick J. H. and Bayley, D. H. "Theme and Variation in Community Policing." In *Crime and Justice: A Review of Research,* Vol. 10, edited by M. Tonry and N. Morris. Chicago: University of Chicago Press, 1988.

Travis, Lawrence F., III; Novak, Kenneth J.; Winston, Craig N.; and Hurley, David C. "Cops at the Door: The Impact of Citizen Surveys by Police on Public Attitudes." *Police Quarterly,* Vol. 3, No. 1, March 2000, pp. 85–104.

"Urban Institute Declares COPS Program a Partial Success." *Criminal Justice Newsletter,* Vol. 31, No. 1, September 15, 2000, pp. 3–4.

"Urban Institute Evaluation of the COPS Office." *Subject to Debate,* Vol. 14, No. 9, September 2000, pp. 9–10.

Epilogue

Traditionally, the driving forces of change in police work have been legislative and judicial mandates. Though no Miranda-like decisions are coercing change today, a fundamental shift in the way officers do their jobs is taking place in departments across our country. Why is this happening? Profound changes in our world have occurred and are forcing police departments to adapt. These changes are forever shifting the way American institutions respond to the external environment. Those most profound trends are:

- **Public expectations.** We have more educated Americans than at any time in our history. As a result, they know how governmental systems work and that the "squeaky wheel gets the grease." Consequently, there is an ever-increasing demand by Americans to have a say in the way all levels of government operate.

- **Worker expectations.** Pyramidal-shaped organizations cannot rely on traditional order-giving tactics to enhance worker productivity and effectiveness. In public and private sectors, today's workers are demanding to have a say in the decisions that will affect them.

- **Technology.** Technological advances give line personnel an array of information previously unavailable to line workers. Consequently, they are capable of making some work decisions once restricted to supervisors and managers. Hence, technological advances have increased the importance of line workers.

- **Commitment to the value of diversity.** The most effective partnerships will be those that capitalize on the diversity within the community and within the police department.

- **Strategic alliances/partnerships.** From NAFTA to the Saturn automobile, government and private industry are increasingly reliant on developing synergies created by strategic partnerships. Likewise, the partnership component of community policing is emulating this trend that is occurring on a much broader scale.

This text has presented an enormous amount of information about community policing organized into chapters which may tend to lose sight of the big picture. To bring closure to the topic, Commander Michael Nila, formerly with the Aurora (Illinois) Police Department, has graciously provided a commentary on two basic requirements to successfully implement community policing: making diversity an integral part of the effort and engaging the community.

◈ DIVERSITY—AN INTEGRAL PART OF COMMUNITY POLICING

As policing in America changes from "traditional" to "community policing," the critical challenge is to change the relationship between the police and the community. Namely, communities at risk—our poor, our youth, our elderly and our minority communities. The "us v. them" mentality that exists between the police and the community often prevents officers from willingly engaging citizens in the neighborhoods we spend the greatest amount of our time policing.

In any typical urban setting, the police very often have an adversarial relationship with citizens whose background, culture, economic condition and race are very different from their own. Too often, the police see citizens in at-risk neighborhoods as "the enemy" while the community views the police as an "invading army." Rarely, until the community policing movement took root, did the police proactively and sincerely cultivate positive relationships and truly commit to resolving problems in at-risk neighborhoods.

Progressive police agencies today recognize that embracing a community policing philosophy means making a commitment to improving police/community relationships and changing the police culture, often the greatest barrier to true police-community partnerships. The growing commitment to diversity is exemplified by the increasing number of police agencies who include "diversity" in their official organizational values such as in Aurora, Illinois:

> We value diversity, and commit to nurturing a welcoming environment of inclusion, in which we recognize the unique skills, knowledge, abilities and backgrounds of all people as our strength.

Diversity is a term often misunderstood by police officers who consider diversity initiatives intrusive, unnecessary, often accusatory and an opportunity for "finger pointing." Through aggressive diversity discussions and training, coupled with a strong diversity/harassment policy, and most important, a commitment from top management to a "managing diversity" concept—police departments are changing the internal culture and their external relationships.

In the past, inclusion of diversity in the workforce reflected legal requirements, moral imperatives or social responsibility. As is clearly evident, today all organizations are in the throes of the explosion of a diverse workforce; and it is the police in any community who have the most contacts with a wider range of diverse people than any other profession.

Today, community policing makes managing diversity critical to success and, simply, is good management! Managing diversity is a philosophy developed by Dr. Roosevelt Thomas who established the American Institute for Managing Diversity at Moorehouse College in Atlanta, Georgia. Recognizing that the changing face of America, driven by rapidly growing minority and immigrant populations, would lead to increasingly diverse organizations, Dr. Thomas moved beyond affirmative action and quota systems. He developed a philosophy of diversity that focuses not only on understanding and respecting differences, but goes further by creating an environment where *all people* can contribute to their maximum potential. As described by one diversity student, "Managing diversity is about getting 100 percent out of 100 percent of our people."

All organizations must realize that diversity does not stop at ethnicity and gender. Instead, diversity must include developing understanding, acceptance and respect of all differences including lifestyle, sexual preference, geographic origin, style of dress, hobbies, habits, interests, physical differences, and so on. Diversity is about developing an environment of inclusion where those who are different from the mainstream are made valuable contributors to any organization's success.

While managing diversity is critical to organizational success and maximizing productivity, the concept holds true for communities as well. Only when the police and the community both understand and respect each other can true collaboration take place. Maximizing any community's "human capital" requires everyone's involvement and commitment.

Changing the police culture, changing the police perception of the community and the community's feelings toward the police is a difficult, challenging undertaking. If the culture does not support the desired behavior change, the culture must be addressed. While difficult, this can be achieved if the commitment is made.

One success story in diversity initiatives is the Reno (Nevada) Police Department, which began community policing in 1987 under Chief of Police Robert Bradshaw. Chief Bradshaw boldly reorganized the department under a community policing philosophy. He also recognized that community policing and cultural diversity could not be separated. With equal emphasis, Bradshaw directed massive community policing and cultural diversity training for all personnel. The result—in Reno today, police officers view diversity as a way of life that's critical to community policing, as exemplified by one Reno sergeant who stated: "The driving motivation to diversity is community policing—developing all community resources as partnerships through understanding."

While focusing on the internal culture is important to changing police officers' behaviors, so too is developing proactive initiatives that change citizens' perceptions of the police and one another. In Aurora, Illinois, community policing officers have developed a number of outreach strategies to overcome barriers with the minority community such as:

• A Spanish Citizens Police Academy that targets Hispanic community members and teaches police topics while providing information that facilitates community involvement and assimilation.

• Diversity training conducted for citizen groups that patrol and take proactive steps to address crime and disorder problems in the neighborhoods. This prevents the tendency to "pick on" the minority element in the community simply because they are the neighborhood "newcomers."

• Police-sponsored neighborhood festivals and community events that bring minority neighborhoods together with mainstream neighborhoods in celebrating the community's diversity.

Effectively managing diversity programs that work to change the culture and behaviors of all those within the organization must include the following components:

• An internal audit to assess organizational health as related to diversity issues such as employee relations, perceptions of employees to minorities, inappropriate jokes and cartoons, and so on.

- A strict harassment/diversity policy that is adhered to.
- Nonconfrontational introductory training (4–8 hours), which should be a soft sell to diversity, emphasizing the need for agency-wide commitment.
- Advanced training (ongoing training in 4-hour block) that addresses specific racial issues in the community, historical issues, gay/lesbian issues and sexual harassment concerns.
- Specialized needs training that focuses on the needs of specialized units such as Field Training Officers, Gang Officers, Community Policing and Recruiting. Each of these specialized areas has a unique role to fill that heavily affects minority relations and internal cultural issues.
- Establishing an organizational commitment to diversity through developing a core set of organizational values that reflect a diversity commitment and living that commitment through every decision and action.

Organizational change begins with a vision articulated throughout the organization which, over time, begins to change an organization's very heart, soul and culture. In developing a foundation for organizational success and a vision for the next century, progressive police leaders will include effective diversity programs that target internal behaviors and attitudes and external relationships with all segments of the community. *The key to community policing lies in the strength of our diversity commitment and our ability to successfully engage our communities.*

COMMUNITY POLICING AND COMMUNITY ENGAGEMENT*

The two core components of community policing are community partnerships and problem solving. A community policing philosophy demands that the police develop partnerships with all components of our communities to facilitate community problem solving. Police officers do not generally resist problem solving—however, it is difficult to overcome the unwillingness of officers to engage the community. Community partnerships demand that the police actively engage the community if problem-solving efforts are to be effective.

If we were to analyze why community engagement is difficult, we would focus on barriers that prevent police/community partnerships. These barriers include:

1. The police culture is one that promotes an "us v. them" mentality, which by its very nature inhibits building trust and positive relationships with our citizens.
2. The police have accepted the responsibility for crime in our communities and have become the crime "experts" and openly resist efforts by the citizens to assist with the crime issues.
3. The police rarely make any efforts to understand the very people with whom they spend the majority of their time policing. The profile of the average officer is very

*Presented at the 1995 IACP Conference by Commander Michael J. Nila, Aurora (Illinois) Police Department.

different than the profile of the citizens who make up the neighborhoods demanding continuous police services. The two profiles illustrate a clash of cultures, values, expectations and accepted behaviors, which results in an unwillingness and inability to partner with our citizens. It is human nature to resist what we are unfamiliar with: the unknown makes us uncomfortable, and what makes us uncomfortable, we tend to avoid.

4. Our citizens often perceive the police negatively, and the police have an equally negative perception of the citizens whose problems we are asking them to solve through partnerships.

5. Community organization and mobilization attempts by the police often lead to frustration due to citizens' apparent unwillingness to get involved and to work with the police. Police view the reluctance to "get involved" as apathy and quickly lose interest. The common refrain becomes, "If they don't care, why should we?" Police officers must have patience and be persistent in building of trust and confidence in our citizens.

6. Police often fail to realize how much the police need the community, and the community has a narrow view of the police role in their communities.

7. The reality of policing is that the police cannot resolve crime and community issues alone. The police simply do not have enough presence, resources or skills to address the challenges our communities are facing today. Partnering with the community and enhancing citizen involvement ultimately increases our numbers, resources and skills, making policing safer and easier.

We often hear police chiefs state that the police are "empowering the community," when in fact, it is the reverse. Sir Robert Peel, in his nine principles of modern policing, addresses that fact stating that the police receive their authority from the public; and he succinctly addresses the partnership issue with this principle:

> To maintain at all times a relationship with the public that gives reality to the historic tradition that the police are the public and the public are the police; the police being the only members of the public that are paid to give full-time attention to the duties that are incumbent on every citizen in the interest of the community welfare and existence.

Most of Peel's principles of modern policing actually address the importance of community support and participation if the police are to be effective.

Community engagement means that the police must begin:

- Talking to, listening to and collaborating with citizens;
- Valuing sharing information with citizens;
- Valuing all people and all groups in the community;
- Replacing an "us vs. them" mentality with "we";
- Replacing "we do it for" with "we do it together";
- Reorganizing policing as a service, and citizens and the community as our customers;
- Allowing the community to identify problems and solutions;

- Bringing the community into the department to help define mission, vision, values and priorities; and
- Developing and working with civilian advisory councils.

When we think of "community," we must think of all the community stakeholders and the many communities and neighborhoods within the larger community. Community policing has a strong neighborhood focus where beat officers work to instill a strong sense of shared "community" and responsibility for one another. It means providing customized policing services to all neighborhoods.

The goal is to recapture a sense of "community" which appears to be lost in today's communities. Neighborhoods are no longer caretakers for their fellow neighbors. In fact, we are becoming a "nation of strangers" where neighbors don't know or interact with neighbors and the community as a whole.

If we are to regain a sense of "community," then we must instill a sense of "community" in our neighborhoods—we accomplish this by developing a sense that citizens can affect what is occurring in their lives and neighborhoods.

The community partnership process involves the police, government and the community collaborating, not when a problem arises, but as a way of conducting daily business. In community policing communities, the collaboration is continuous, ongoing and leads to constant communication and an environment of trust. The greater the extent of collaboration, the more effective partnerships will become. The goal of community policing is to enlarge the area of community collaboration. If community collaboration is to be successful, the following conditions must exist: (1) a common need, purpose and/or vision, (2) recognized leadership to guide the process, (3) a perception that personal involvement can make a difference and (4) information available about how to realistically change the existing conditions.

Citizens in community policing communities are more likely to willingly, enthusiastically support the police and engage in active partnerships activities such as:

- Participate in Neighborhood Watch Groups;
- Participate in Business Watch Groups;
- Attend Citizen Police Academies;
- Serve in citizen patrols coordinated by the police;
- Serve on citizen advisory councils at the neighborhood and community-wide level;
- Work with the police to identify and resolve community or neighborhood problems;
- Help to develop policing philosophies and strategies including mission, vision, values and priorities; and
- Organize and work with teen and youth organizations.

For community policing to be successful, the police must overcome barriers to partnerships. We must work to actively engage all aspects of our communities and aggressively pursue a sense of "community" in our neighborhoods. Only by policing "with" the community can we effectively solve community problems.

Glossary

Number in parentheses indicates the chapter in which the term is introduced.

AARP   American Association of Retired Persons. (8)

acculturation   A society takes in or assimilates other cultures. Also called *assimilation*. (7)

ADA   The Americans with Disabilities Act of 1990. (8)

administrative density   The ratio of all employees to supervisory personnel. (16)

Alzheimer's disease (AD)   A progressive, irreversible and incurable brain disease with no known cause and affecting four million elderly Americans. The classic symptom is loss of memory. (8)

Ameslan   Stands for American Sign Language, the preferred communication mode for the majority of deaf individuals. (8)

assimilation   A society takes in or assimilates various other cultures to become a "melting pot." Also called *acculturation*. (7)

attention deficit disorder   A common disruptive behavior disorder of children characterized by heightened motor activity (fidgeting and squirming), short attention span, distractibility, impulsiveness and lack of self-control. (9)

bias   A prejudice that inhibits objectivity. Bias can evolve into hate. (6)

bias crime   A criminal offense committed against a person, property or society that is motivated, in whole or in part, by an offender's bias against an individual's or group's race, religion, ethnic/national origin, gender, age, disability or sexual orientation. Also called *hate crime*. (7)

bifurcated society   The widening of the gap between those with wealth (the "haves") and those living in poverty (the "have nots"), with a shrinking middle class. (3)

Big Ds of juvenile justice   Refers to deinstitutionalization, diversion, due process and decriminalization. (9)

body language   Messages conveyed by how a person looks, moves and gestures. (6)

broken window phenomenon   Suggests that if it appears no one cares about the community, as indicated by broken windows not being repaired, disorder and crime will thrive. (3)

bullying   Name calling, fistfights, purposeful ostracism, extortion, character assassination, repeated physical attacks and sexual harassment. Also called *peer child abuse*. (14)

catastrophic reaction   Impulsive behavior that results when a situation overloads an individual's mental ability to think or act rationally. Associated with Alzheimer's disease. (8)

change management   The development of an overall strategy to review the present state of an organization, envision the future state of the organization and devise a means of moving from one to the other. (5)

coercive isomorphism   Occurs when organizations adopt something due to pressure either from the state or other organizations. (16)

cognitive restructuring   A coping mechanism where victims reinterpret an incident to minimize its adverse effects. (10)

communication   The transfer of information and understanding from one person to another. (6)

communication process   Involves a sender, a message, a channel, a receiver and sometimes feedback. (6)

community   The specific geographic area served by a police department or law enforcement agency and the individuals, organizations and agencies within that area. (3)

community policing   A philosophy or orientation that emphasizes working proactively with citizens to reduce fear, solve crime-related problems and prevent crime. (1)

community relations   Efforts to interact and communicate with the community—team policing, community resource officers, school liaison officers. See also *public relations*. (1)

community wellness   Emphasizes a proactive police-community partnership to prevent crime. (4)

CPTED   Crime Prevention through Environmental Design—altering the physical environment to enhance safety, reduce the incidence and fear of crime, and improve the quality of life. (12)

crack children   Children who were exposed to cocaine while in the womb. (9)

creativity   A process of breaking old connections and making useful new connections. Often synonymous with innovation. (4)

crime-specific planning   Uses the principles of problem solving to focus on identified crime problems. (4)

crisis behavior   Results when a person has a *temporary* breakdown in coping skills. It is not the same as mental illness. (8)

critical mass   The smallest number of citizens/organizations needed to support and sustain the community policing initiative. (5)

cross-sectional analysis   A research method whereby data are analyzed by area rather than by individuals responding. (12)

culpability   Any action of a victim that may in some measure contribute to the victimization. (10)

cultural conflict   A theory that suggests that diverse cultures sharing the same territory will compete with and attempt to exploit one another. (7)

cultural pluralism   A theory that suggests there are many melting pots. Some groups are comfortable in one pot; other groups are comfortable in another. (7)

cultural window   A framework or world-view through which cultural events are interpreted. (7)

culture   A collection of artifacts, tools, ways of living, values and language common to a group of people, all passed from one generation to the next. (7)

DARE   Drug Abuse Resistance Education, a program aimed at elementary-age school children, seeking to teach them to "say no to drugs." (12)

deaf   Persons having extreme hearing loss; they cannot understand spoken words. (8)

decentralization   An operating principle that encourages flattening of the organization and places decision-making authority and autonomy at the level where information is plentiful, usually at the level of the patrol officer. (2)

decriminalization   Refers to the efforts to make status offenses noncriminal actions. (9)

deinstitutionalization   Refers to the release of thousands of mentally ill individuals into society to be cared for by family or a special network of support services. (8) Also refers to efforts to release incarcerated youths through parole and community programs. (9)

demographics   The characteristics of a human population or community. (3)

developmental assets   Forty ideals, experiences and qualities established by the Search Institute to "help young people make wise decisions, choose positive paths, and grow up competent, caring and responsible." (14)

directed imbalance   An imbalance created in anticipation of a proposed change in orientation. (5)

disability   A physical or mental impairment that substantially limits one or more of a person's major life functions. (8)

discretion   Freedom to make choices among possible courses of action or inaction, for example, to arrest or not arrest. (2)

discrimination   Showing a preference or prejudice in treating individuals or groups; failing to treat equals equally. Discrimination is a behavior based on an attitude or prejudice. (6)

diversion   Turning youths away from the criminal justice system, rerouting them to another agency or program. (3) Finding alternatives to placing juvenile status offenders and delinquents in detention facilities. (9)

DOC model   Dilemmas-Options-Consequences. Challenges officers to carefully consider their decisions and the short- and long-term consequences of those decisions, with the goal of fusing problem solving and morality. (4)

due process   The rights guaranteed by the Fifth Amendment: notice of a hearing, full information regarding the charges made, the opportunity to present evidence in self-defense before an impartial judge or jury and to be presumed innocent until proven guilty by legally obtained evidence. (9)

EBD   Emotionally/behaviorally disturbed. (9)

effectiveness   Producing the desired result or goal. Doing the right things. (4)

efficiency   Minimizing waste, expense or unnecessary effort. Results in a high ratio of output to input. Doing things right. (4)

elder abuse   Includes physical and emotional abuse, financial exploitation and general neglect of the elderly. (10)

empathy   Truly understanding another person. (6)

empirical study   Research based on observation or practical experience. (12)

empowered   Granting authority and decision making to lower level officers. (2)

epilepsy   A disorder of the central nervous system that may cause recurrent seizures. (8)

ethnicity   Rooted more in sociology and geography, and defines a group of people who share customs, language, religious beliefs and a common history based on national origin or the inhabiting of a specific geographical area. An ethnic group need not consist exclusively of individuals of the same race. (7)

ethnocentrism   The preference for one's own way of life over all others. (7)

experimental design   Research method involving the random assignment of individuals to experimental (treatment) and control (no treatment) conditions. (16)

experimental imbalance   Creates an atmosphere of trial and error and of risk taking. Encourages officers at all levels to be creative and seek innovative ways to approach community problems. (5)

extensional world   The world that comes to us through experience, as opposed to the verbal world. (6)

fetal alcohol syndrome (FAS)   The leading known cause of mental retardation in the western world; effects include impulsivity, inability to predict consequences or to use appropriate judgment in daily life, poor communication skills, high levels of activity and distractibility in small children and frustration and depression in adolescents. (9)

flat organization   Typical pyramid organization charts have the top pushed down and the sides expanded at the base. In a police department, it means fewer lieutenants and captains, fewer staff departments, fewer staff assistants, more sergeants and more patrol officers. (2)

formal power structure   Includes divisions of society with wealth and political influence: federal, state and local agencies and governments, commissions and regulatory agencies. (3)

four-minute barrier   The point in an initial meeting at which most people have formed a positive or negative opinion about the individual with whom they are communicating. (6)

frankpledge system   The Norman system requiring all freemen to swear loyalty to the king's law and to take responsibility for maintaining the local peace. (1)

gang   An organized group of people existing for some time with a special interest in using violence to achieve status. See also *street gang* and *youth gang*. (9)

geographic profiling   A crime mapping technique that takes the locations of past crimes and, using a complex mathematical algorithm, calculates probabilities of a suspect's residence. (4)

ghetto   An area of a city usually inhabited by individuals of the same race or ethnic background who live in poverty and apparent social disorganization. (3)

ghetto syndrome   A vicious circle of failure: poverty, poor education, joblessness, low motivation to work, welfare and poverty. (7)

graffiti   Painting or writing on buildings, walls, bridges, bus stops and other available public surfaces. Used by gangs to mark their turf. (9)

granny bashing   Domestic violence against the elderly. (10)

granny dumping   Abandoning the elderly. (10)

graying of America   A metaphor reflecting the fact that the U.S. population is aging. (8)

guardian ad litem   An individual appointed by the court to protect the best interests of a child in the juvenile justice process. In some states this can only be an attorney. (9)

Guardian Angels   Private citizen patrols who seek to deter crime and to provide a positive role model for young children. (12)

hate crime   A criminal offense committed against a person, property or society that is motivated, in whole or in part, by an offender's bias against an individual's or group's race, religion, ethnic/national origin, gender, age, disability or sexual orientation. Also called *bias crime*. (7)

hearing impaired   Those who have some residual hearing, that is, sounds may be audible but not clear. Words are not just softer, they are garbled. Also called *hard of hearing*. (8)

heterogeneous   Involving things (including people) that are unlike, dissimilar, different. The opposite of *homogeneous*. (3)

homogeneous Involving things (including people) that are basically similar, alike. The opposite of *heterogeneous*. (3)

horizontal differentiation Refers to the degree to which an organization's tasks are broken into functionally distinct units. (16)

hot spots Locations where most crimes occur. (4)

hue and cry The summoning of all citizens within earshot to join in pursuing and capturing a wrongdoer. (1)

human relations Efforts to relate to and understand other individuals or groups. (1)

hyphenated American Tendency to include ethnic background in a person's nationality—for example, Italian-American, Polish-American—illustrating America's tendency to pluralism or a multicultural approach. (7)

implant hypothesis Asks whether collective citizen action by a small group of neighborhood residents, for example, Neighborhood Watch groups, can make a difference in the attitudes and behaviors of local residents. May be proven true if community policing efforts (1) make stimulation of community processes the main goal and outcome measure of community policing programs and (2) lead police to more actively involve community residents in the strategies. (16)

incident An isolated event that requires a police response; the primary work unit in the professional model. (4)

incivilities Occur when social control mechanisms have eroded and include unmowed lawns, piles of accumulated trash, graffiti, public drunkenness, fighting, prostitution, abandoned buildings and broken windows. (3)

informal power structure Includes religious groups, wealthy subgroups, ethnic groups, political groups and public interest groups. (3)

infrastructure An established network of community-based organizations and community leaders. (15)

innovation A new way of doing something, often synonymous with creativity. (4)

isomorphism Similar in structural characteristics. Isomorphism results in a one-size-fits-all approach to community policing, in contrast to refraction. (16)

jargon The technical language of a profession. (6)

justice model Views lawbreakers as responsible for their own actions. In comparison to the medical or welfare model. (3, 9)

killer phrases Judgmental, critical statements that serve as put-downs and stifle creativity. (4)

kinesics The study of body movement or body language. (6)

learning disability One or more significant deficits in the essential learning processes. (9)

macrosocial Referring to the big picture. The macrosocial environment includes the amount of social capital available as well as existing diversity, including economic diversity. (13)

magnet address An address that is easy for people to give and, consequently, is often mistakenly associated with reported crimes. (4)

magnet phenomenon Occurs when a phone number or address is associated with a crime simply because it was a convenient number or address to use. (4)

magnet telephone One that is available when no other telephones are; consequently, it is often mistakenly associated with reported crimes. (4)

mediation The intervention of a third party into an interpersonal dispute, where the third party helps disputants reach a resolution. Often termed "ADR" or Alternative Dispute Resolution. (4)

medical model Sees those who break the law as victims of society, not responsible for their own actions. Sometimes called the welfare model. In comparison to the justice model. (3)

mental illness A severe mental disturbance that results in substantially diminished capacity to cope with the ordinary demands of life. (8)

mental locks Ways of thinking that prevent creativity. (4)

mental retardation Normal intellectual development fails to occur. Criteria for diagnosis include significant subaverage general intellectual functioning resulting in, or associated with, defects or impairments in adaptive behavior, such as personal independence and social responsibility, with onset by age 18. Unlike mental illness, mental retardation is permanent. (8)

microsocial Referring to the smaller picture. The microsocial environment focuses on smaller units such as the family. (13)

mimetic isomorphism Occurs when an organization copies or imitates another. (16)

mission statement A written declaration of purpose. (2)

moniker A nickname, often of a gang member. (9)

negative contacts   Unpleasant interactions between the police and the public. They may or may not relate to criminal activity. (2)

negative emotionality   A generalized propensity for experiencing aversive affective states, including anger, anxiety, suspiciousness and irritability; emotional brittleness causing a rapid, excessive response to minor stressors, a sense that others are malicious and a propensity to react to even slight provocation with rage. Negative emotionality is a shared risk factor for both partner abuse and crime. (13)

networking   Building and maintaining professional relationships for mutual interest. (6)

networks   The complex pathways of human interaction that guide and direct an individual's perception, motivation and behavior. (6)

news media echo effect   The theory that the media have the power, through their coverage of isolated, high-profile cases, to influence the operations of the criminal justice system and even the disposition of individual cases. (11)

NIMBY syndrome   "Not in *my* backyard." It is fine to have a half-way house—across town, not in my backyard. (3)

911 policing   Incident-driven, reactive policing. (2)

nonverbal communication   Includes everything other than the actual words spoken in a message, such as tone, pitch and pacing. (6)

"Norman Rockwell" family   A working father, a housewife mother and two children of school age—only a small percentage of U.S. households today. (9)

normative isomorphism   Results from professionalism, with influences coming from other organizations involved in the same profession. (16)

one-pot jurisdictional approach   Treating children who are abused or neglected, those who are status offenders and those who are truly criminal all the same. (9)

Pager Information Network (PIN)   A system to simultaneously notify all the media. (11)

PAL   Police Athletic League, developed to provide opportunities for youths to interact with police officers in gyms or ballparks instead of in a juvenile detention hall. (12)

panel analysis   A research method where data are analyzed by individuals responding rather than by area. (12)

paradigm   A model or a way of viewing a specific aspect of life such as politics, medicine, education and the criminal justice system. (1)

paradigm shift   A new way of thinking about a specific subject. (1)

paradox   A seemingly contradictory statement that may, nonetheless, be true; for example, the less one has, the less one has to lose. (2)

parens patriae   Refers to the government's right and responsibility to take care of minors and others who cannot legally take care of themselves. (9)

participatory leadership   A management style in which each individual has a voice in decisions, but top management still has the ultimate decision-making authority. (2)

patronage system   Politicians rewarded those who voted for them with jobs or special privileges. Prevalent during the political era. Also called the *spoils system*. (1)

peer child abuse   Another term for bullying—name calling, fistfights, purposeful ostracism, extortion, character assassination, repeated physical attacks and sexual harassment. (14)

perception   The process of becoming aware of something directly through the senses. (6)

perp walks   The police practice of parading suspects before the media, often simply for the publicity provided by news media coverage. (11)

personality disorders   The most common form of mental illness encountered by police. Inflexible and maladaptive personality traits that significantly impair social and occupational functioning, such as lack of self-control, inability to learn from past experience, lack of good judgment and lack of moral or ethical values. (8)

phenomenological point of view   Stresses the fact that reality is different for each individual. (6)

plea bargaining   A practice in which prosecutors charge a defendant with a less serious crime in exchange for a guilty plea, thus eliminating the time and expense of a trial. (3)

police culture   The informal values, beliefs and expectations passed on to newcomers in the department; may be at odds with the formal rules, regulations, procedures and role authority of managers. (2)

police-school liaison program   Places an officer in a school to work with school authorities, parents and students to prevent crime and antisocial behavior and to improve police-youth relationships. (12)

post traumatic stress disorder (PTSD) A persistent reexperiencing of a traumatic event through intrusive memories, dreams and a variety of anxiety-related symptoms. (10)

poverty syndrome Includes inadequate housing, inadequate education, inadequate jobs and a resentment of those who control the social system. (7)

preference Selecting someone or something over another. (6)

prejudice A negative judgment not based on fact; an irrational, preconceived negative opinion. An attitude that may result in discriminatory behavior. Also called *bias*. (6)

primacy effect The tendency to form impressions of people quickly. (6)

primary victim A person actually harmed by an incident. (10)

privatization Using private security officers or agencies to provide services typically considered to be law enforcement functions. (3)

proactive Anticipating problems and seeking solutions to those problems, as in community policing. The opposite of *reactive*. (1)

problem-oriented policing (POP) A department-wide strategy aimed at solving persistent community problems by grouping incidents to identify problems and then determine possible underlying causes. (4)

problem-solving approach Involves proactively identifying problems and making decisions about how best to deal with them. (4)

process mapping A method of internal analysis that takes a horizontal view of a system, in contrast to the traditional vertical view. It involves personnel at all levels and uses flowcharts to visually depict how information, materials and activities flow in an organization; how work is handed off from one unit or department to another; and how processes work currently and what changes should be made to attain a more ideal process flow. (13)

professional model Emphasized crime control by preventive automobile patrol coupled with rapid response to calls. The predominant policing model used during the reform era (1970s and 1980s). (1)

progressive era Emphasized preventive automobile patrol and rapid response to calls for service. Also called the *reform era*. (1)

protective factor Predicts a decreased probability of later offending. Often considered to exist at the opposite end of the scale from risk factors but not always necessarily so. (15)

PSAs Public service announcements. (12)

psychopath A category of violent individuals who tend to be socially inept loners, like the "Trench Coat Mafia" kids. In contrast to a sociopath. (14)

psychosocial Factors that refer to individual psychological characteristics such as temperament and self-identity. (13)

public information officers (PIOs) Officer trained in public relations and assigned to disseminate information to the media, thereby providing accurate, consistent information while controlling leaks of confidential or inaccurate information and managing controversial or negative situations to the department's benefit. (11)

public relations Efforts to enhance the police image. (1)

pulling levers Refers to a multiagency law enforcement team imposing all available sanctions on gang members who violate established standards for behavior. (14)

qualitative evaluations Assessments that are more descriptive and less statistical. The opposite of quantitative evaluation. (12)

race Based on science, biologically determined and refers to a group of people having the same ancestry, thereby possessing common genes for traits such as hair type/color, skin color, eye color, stature, bodily proportions and so on. Most anthropologists contend there are only three primary races: Caucasoid, Negroid and Mongoloid. (7)

racial profiling A form of discrimination that singles out people of racial or ethnic groups because of a belief that these groups are more likely than others to commit certain types of crimes. Race-based enforcement is illegal. (7)

racism A belief that a human population having a distinct genetically transmitted characteristic is inferior. It also refers to discrimination or prejudice based on race. (7)

random assignment Dependence on a random number table or machine-generated random number that indicates the particular group to which an individual or entity will be assigned. Whether a person is a member of the treatment group or the control (no treatment) group is purely by chance. (16)

reactive Responding after the fact; responding to calls for service. The opposite of *proactive*. (1)

recidivism Repeat offending. (3)

reciprocity A cooperative interchange. Each party in the effort has something to offer and also something to gain from the relationship. (12)

reform era Emphasized preventive automobile patrol and rapid response to calls for service. Also called the *progressive era*. (1)

refraction The bending and deflection of light rays and energy waves from a straight path as they pass from one medium to another (such as through a prism). The term is used to explain the fragmented implementation of community policing in the United States due to the abundance of autonomous police agencies and the thousands of police executives throughout the country making very different and often conflicting decisions. In contrast to isomorphism. (16)

representing A manner of dress to show allegiance or opposition to a gang. Uses an imaginary line drawn vertically through the body. (9)

restorative justice Advocates a balanced approach to sentencing that involves offenders, victims, local communities and government to alleviate crime and violence and obtain peaceful communities. (3)

risk factor Predicts an increased probability of later offending. In contrast to a protective factor. (15)

risk factor prevention paradigm Seeks to identify key risk factors for offending and then implement prevention methods designed to counteract them. (15)

schizophrenia A deterioration in one's personality to the point where feelings, thoughts and behavior are not coherent. (8)

second injury Occurs to victims when they are treated badly by professionals who should be helping them, including police officers and the entire criminal justice system. (10)

secondary victim A person indirectly affected by a trauma. (10)

seizure A sudden, uncontrolled episode of excessive electrical activity in the brain. It may alter behavior, consciousness, movement, perception and/or sensation. Does not always involve a stiffening or jerking of the body. (8)

selective enforcement The use of police discretion, deciding to concentrate on specific crimes such as drug dealing and to downplay other crimes such as white-collar crime. (2)

self-fulfilling prophecy The belief in self-talk or what others say about you that causes it to come true. (6)

semantic environment The way words are used and the way they are interpreted shape beliefs, prejudices, ideals and aspirations. They constitute the moral and intellectual atmosphere in which a person lives. (6)

semantics The study of the meanings of words. (6)

senility A disorientation or change in mental abilities and personality caused by generalized brain damage; a disabling condition associated with aging. Also called *senile dementia* or *organic brain syndrome* (OBS). (8)

sensorium The part of the brain that interprets what the eye takes in. (6)

social capital Refers to the strength of a community's social fabric and includes the elements of *trustworthiness* (citizens' trust of each other and their public institutions) and *obligations* (expectation that service to each other will be reciprocated). Two levels of social capital are local (found among family members and citizens and their immediate, informal groups) and public (found in networks tying individuals to broader community institutions such as schools, civic organizations, churches and various levels of government, including the police). (3)

social contract A legal theory that suggests that for everyone to receive justice, each person must relinquish some individual freedom. (3)

sociopath A category of violent individuals usually characterized as bullies—outgoing and manipulative, instigating fights. The sociopath is a type of violent leader. In contrast to a psychopath. (14)

spoils system Politicians rewarded those who voted for them with jobs or special privileges. Prevalent during the political era. Also called the *patronage system*. (1)

statistically significant A predetermined level at which the results of a study would not occur by chance. The most common level is .05, meaning the results would occur by chance no more than five times in one hundred. (12)

status offenses Actions by a juvenile that would not be crimes if committed by an adult, for example, truancy or smoking cigarettes. (9)

stereotyping Assuming all people within a specific group are the same, lacking individuality. (6)

strategic planning Long-term, large-scale, futuristic planning. (5)

straw purchasers Weapons buyers fronting for people linked to illegal gun trafficking. (13)

street gang A group of people whose allegiance is based on social needs and who engage in acts injurious to the public. The preferred term of most local law enforcement agencies. (9)

street justice Occurs when police officers use their discretionary powers to simply talk to or warn youthful offenders, talk to their parents or make referrals to a social service agency. May also involve roughing an offenders, talk to their parents or make referrals to a social services agency. Street justace may also involve roughing an offender up rather than taking them into custody. (9)

symbiotic A relationship in which those involved mutually depend upon each other for existence and survival. (11)

symbolic process The process by which people can arbitrarily make certain things stand for other things. (6)

syndrome of crime A group of signs, causes and symptoms that occur together to foster specific crimes. (3)

synergism Occurs when individuals channel their energies toward a common purpose and accomplish what they could not accomplish alone. (15)

systems thinking A conceptual framework that recognizes the contribution of each component to a system (i.e., everything affects everything else). Thinking in terms of the whole rather than the individual parts. (5)

target hardening Refers to making potential objectives of criminals more difficult to obtain through the use of improved locks, alarm systems and security cameras. (15)

TDD Telecommunication device for those who are deaf. (8)

"thin blue line" The distancing of the police from the public they serve. (1)

tipping point That point at which an ordinary, stable phenomenon can turn into a crisis. (3)

tithing A group of 10 families. (1)

tithing system The Anglo-Saxon principle establishing the principle of collective responsibility for maintaining local law and order. (1)

Total Quality Management (TQM) A management system that tries to ensure that an organization consistently meets and exceeds customer requirements. (2)

transition management Overseeing, controlling and leading the change from an organization's present state to its future state. (5)

TRIAD A three-way partnership between the AARP, the International Association of Chiefs of Police (IACP) and the National Sheriffs' Association (NSA) to address criminal victimization of older people. (8)

turf Territory occupied by a gang, often marked by graffiti. (9)

two-wave survey Study method where the first wave consists of a pretest before a strategy is implemented and the second wave consists of a posttest after the strategy has been implemented for a given amount of time. (16)

verbal world The world that comes to us through words, as opposed to the extensional world. (6)

victim compensation programs Programs that help crime victims cope with crime-related expenses such as medical costs, mental health counseling, lost wages and funeral or burial costs. (10)

victim impact statement (VIS) A written report describing in detail the full effect of a crime on the victim and the principle means for communicating to the court the emotional impact and financial loss incurred. May influence the sentence passed by the judge. (10)

victim statement of opinion (VSO) Victim's opinion of what an offender's sentence should be. (10)

victimology The study of crime victims; includes the concepts of vulnerability and culpability. (10)

victim/witness assistance programs Provide services such as crisis support, peer support, referrals to counseling, advocacy within the justice system and, in some cases, emergency shelter. (10)

vision Intelligent foresight; starts with a mental image that gradually evolves from abstract musings to a concrete series of mission statements, goals and objectives. (5)

vulnerability Suggests that certain groups of people are more susceptible to being victimized because of demographics rather than any unique individual attributes they can control. (10)

welfare model View that children are basically good and in need of help. In comparison to the medical model. (9)

youth gang A subgroup of a street gang; may refer to a juvenile clique within a gang. (9)

zero tolerance A policy of punishing all offenses severely, no matter how minor the offense. (14)

LIST OF ACRONYMS

AAACOP American Association for the Advancement of Community-Oriented Policing

AARP American Association of Retired Persons

ACLD Association for Children with Learning Disabilities

AD Alzheimer's disease

ADA Americans with Disabilities Act

ADD attention deficit disorder

AEC Academy of Experimental Criminology

AIM American Indian Movement

AOA Administration on Aging

ASC American Society of Criminology

ATF Alcohol, Tobacco and Firearms, Bureau of

BIA Bureau of Indian Affairs

BJS Bureau of Justice Statistics

CAD computer-aided dispatch

CAP Child Access Prevention (laws)

CAT Combat Auto Theft

CCPP Citywide Crime Prevention Program

CCRP Citizen Crime Reporting Program

CDC Centers for Disease Control

CD-CP Child Development-Community Policing

CDP Child Development Project

CIT crisis intervention team

COP community-oriented policing

COPE Community/Citizen-Oriented Police Enforcement

COPPS community-oriented policing and problem solving

COPS Community Oriented Policing Services (Office of)

CPA citizen police academy

CPC Community Policing Consortium

CP-CPT Community Probation-Community Police Team

CPTED Crime Prevention through Environmental Design

CRB civilian review board

CRT crisis response team

CSO community service officer

DARE Drug Abuse Resistance Education

DCJS Department of Criminal Justice Services

DFSZ drug-free school zone

DFZ drug-free zone

DOC Dilemmas-Options-Consequences

DOJ Department of Justice

DSC Disabilities Statistics Center

DVCPP Domestic Violence Community Partnership Program

DVRU Domestic Violence Reduction Unit

DWB driving while black

EAP employee assistance professional

EBD emotionally/behaviorally disturbed

FAS fetal alcohol syndrome

FAST Family Assistance Services Team

FCC Federal Communications Commission

FORCE Focusing Our Resources on Community Empowerment

GANGIS Gang Intelligence System

GIS Geographic Information System

GREAT Gang Resistance Education and Training

GREAT General Reporting, Evaluation and Tracking (of gangs)

HIV human immunodeficiency virus

HMO health maintenance organization

HOPE Homes on Portland Enterprise

HUD Housing and Urban Development (Department of)

IACA International Association of Crime Analysts

IACP International Association of Chiefs of Police

IBN interest based negotiation

JAR Juveniles at Risk

JCA juvenile correctional agency

KISS keep it straight and simple

LEAA Law Enforcement Administration Assistance

LEEP Law Enforcement Education Program

MADD Mothers Against Drunk Driving

MDT multidisciplinary team

NAACP National Association for the Advancement of Colored People

NABCJ National Association of Blacks in Criminal Justice

NAD National Association for the Deaf

NAMI National Alliance for the Mentally Ill

NCCD National Council on Crime and Delinquency

NCCPC National Citizens Crime Prevention Campaign

NCH National Council on the Handicapped

NCPC National Crime Prevention Council

NCVC National Crime Victimization Survey

NDCS National Drug Control Strategy

NEAT Neighborhood Environmental Assistance Team

NIJ National Institute of Justice

NIMBY not in my backyard

NNO National Night Out

NOBLE National Organization of Black Law Enforcement Executives

NOD National Organization on Disability

NOVA National Organization for Victim Assistance

NRM new religious movement

NSA National Sheriffs' Association

OBS organic brain syndrome

OG original gangster

OI Operation Identification

OJJDP Office of Juvenile Justice and Delinquency Prevention

OJP Office of Justice Programs

OVC Office for Victims of Crime

PACE Police Assisted Community Enforcement

PAL police athletic league

PAT Process Action Team

PERF Police Executive Research Forum

PIN Pager Information Network

POP problem-oriented policing

POST Peace Officer Standards and Training

POST Police Officer Screening Test

PSA public service announcement

PSLC Private Sector Liaison Committee (of the IACP)

PTA Parent Teacher Association

PTSD post traumatic stress disorder

RMS records management system

RISS Regional Information Sharing System

SALT Seniors and Law Enforcement Together

SARA scanning, analysis, response, assessment

SAVE Students against Violence in Education

SODAA Stop Our Drug and Alcohol Abuse

SPJ Society of Professional Journalists

SRO school resource officer

STAR Straight Talk about Risks

SVJ serious and violent juvenile

SWAT Special Weapons and Tactics (team)

TDD telecommunications device for the deaf

TQM Total Quality Management

TRO temporary restraining order

UCR Uniform Crime Reports (FBI)

VAP Victim Assistance Program

VAWA Violence against Women Act

VICAP Violent Criminal Apprehension Program (FBI)

VINE Victim Information and Notification Every Day

VIS victim impact statement

VOCA Victims of Crime Act

VSO victim statement of opinion

YFCP youth-focused community policing

AUTHOR INDEX

PHOTO CREDITS

Chapter 1. 5: © David R. Frazier/Photolibrary, Inc. **10:** © Charles Harbutt/Actuality, Inc. **17:** © David Rae Morris/Impact Visuals

Chapter 2. 27: © Beringer-Dratch/The Image Works **38:** © Bob Daemmrich/The Image Works

Chapter 3. 59: © Hazel Hankin/Stock, Boston **62:** © Spencer Grant/Stock, Boston

Chapter 4. 108: © Roy Stevens, Helena Frost Associates

Chapter 6. 150: © Kathy McLaughlan/ The Image Works **153:** © Debra DiPeso/ Actuality, Inc.

Chapter 7. 168: © Nita Winter/The Image Works **185:** AP/Wide World Photos, Inc.

Chapter 8. 210: © Michael A. Dwyer/Stock, Boston **221:** © David R. Frazier/Photolibrary, Inc.

Chapter 9. 237: © Larry Kolvoord/The Image Works **244:** © Gale Zucker/Stock, Boston **253:** © 1993 Star Tribune, Minneapolis/St. Paul, Mike Zerby

Chapter 10. 263: © Jim Mahoney/The Image Works **283:** © Larry Kolvoord/TexaStock **264:** AP/Wide World Photos

Chapter 11. 311: © Bob Clay/Jeroboam, Inc.

Chapter 12. 340: © Larry Kolvoord/TexaStock **341:** © Paul Conklin

Chapter 13. 375: Courtesy of Commander Michael J. Nila, Aurora, (Illinois) Police Department **390:** © Kennedy/TexaStock **394:** AP/Wide World Photos

Chapter 14. 408: © CLEO/Jeroboam, Inc. **412:** AP/Wide World Photos **423:** © Larry Kolvoord/TexaStock

Chapter 15. 448: © Jim West/Impact Visuals **453:** © David H. Wells/The Image Works

Chapter 16. 470: © 1992 Star Tribune, Minneapolis/St. Paul, Bruce Bisping